HAEGE'S
HOMESTYLE
ARTICLES

The Detroit News, 1995-99

Glenn Haege

Edited by Kathy Stief
Cover Photo by Edward R. Noble
Back Cover Photo by Ewald Stief

MASTER HANDYMAN PRESS, INC.

HAEGE'S
HOMESTYLE
ARTICLES
The Detroit News, 1995-99

Glenn Haege

Edited by Kathy Stief

Published by:
Master Handyman Press, Inc.
Post Office Box 1498
Royal Oak, MI 48068-1498 USA

First Printing February 2001

Printed in the United States of America

Library of Congress Card Number: 00-192833
Haege, Glenn
        Collected Detroit News Homestyle Magazine Handyman articles.
        Bibliography: h.

ISBN 1-880615-64-9

To my Detroit News Editors:
Kelly Kolhagen, Linda Page,
Rita Holt and Judy Diebolt

In memory of the best
dad a son ever had.
Robert Haege, 1925 - 2000

Acknowledgments

Over the years I have written many articles for magazines and newspapers. There was always one special newspaper for which I wanted to write a column. Finally Marty Fischhoff, Assistant Managing Editor - Features, at the Detroit News, decided to give the kid a chance and my first column for the Saturday HOMESTYLE appeared on April Fools Day, 1995.

I am very proud to be associated with HOMESTYLE because I believe it could be the measure against which every other newspaper magazine in the home genre is judged. If you haven't discovered it yet, click onto detnews.com, go to the Homestyle Section and review some of the back issues.

Each issue contains a wide selection of unique offerings: Design Editor Marge Colburn does the heavy lifting with a big feature article. Marney Rich Keenan writes from the heart and gives the magazine its soul. The gardening gals, Janet Macunovich and Nancy Szerlag, each give their advice on how to make things grow. Lawrence B. Johnson keeps readers up to speed on the latest in high tech toys, while the newspaper's mysterious "Gadget Guy" reviews tools. Then there's me and the book reviews.

The local cast is supported by the best of the syndicated home oriented writers: Martha Stewart, Mary Engelbreit, Carol Endler Sterbenz, Ellen James Martin, Dr. Michael Fox on pets, and my home improvement friends, C. Dwight Barnett and Tim Carter.

Combine them all together with great graphics and you get a fascinating weekly read.

I wish I could claim all the credit for my columns, but I call on hundreds of experts in the home improvement field. In addition, Kathy and Ewald Stief, my editor and publisher at Master Handyman Press, do much of the digging and fine-tuning. Kelly Boike and her mother, Barbara Anderson, double and triple-check all the phone numbers. Rob David, my marketing director, proofreads almost every article. Gordon Sommer uploads the articles, creates the indexes and maintains communications with the web heads at the News (he also formatted this entire book and worked with Doug Beauvais at Data Reproduction to create the reality).

Then the stories go to the HOMESTYLE Editor and the real checking, editing, improving gets done. While I have been writing for the paper the HOMESTYLE has had four editors: Kelley Kolhagen, Linda Page, Rita Holt and Judy Diebolt. They are the reason the magazine just keeps getting better and better. Each improved the section while displaying the patience of job whipping my and the other columnists' words into shape. In this they have been very ably supported by Sandy Silfven, wine connoisseur, lighthearted spirit and copy editor. Over the years, the Detroit News photojournalists, design editors and the miracle men and women of the web site crew have all done their bit to make me look good.

As always, I have enjoyed the whole hearted support of my radio show producer, Dave "King Pin" Riger, my engineer, Brian "Award-Winning" Belesky, V.P. and GM Rich Homberg and the entire staff of my home radio station, WXYT-1270 Detroit, CBS/Infinity Broadcasting as well as all the folks at my syndicator, Westwood One.

Special thanks to Chris and Mary Ehlin for the use of their house as a backdrop in my cover photo and to Paul Reiz of the Detroit Newspaper Agency for use of the historic Detroit News bag from his personal newspaper memorabilia collection. Ed Noble shot the photo but he couldn't have done it without your help.

Last of all are the most important people on my list: My wife, Barbara, who puts up with me, my grown-up-and-gone-away kids, Eric and his wife Julie, and Heather and her husband Ray, granddaughter, Emily, my mom, Marion, and the love of her life, my dad, Robert Haege, who passed away this year.

Dad made every round of golf a learning experience about the game of life. By example, he taught me what it means to truly be a gentle man. I can only hope that I offer my kids half as good an example.

Glenn Haege
Royal Oak, Michigan

Table of Contents

Chapter 5 1999   403

Table of Subjects

INTERIOR

GENERAL

Introduction

This book came about for three reasons:

    1: Most books on home improvement, including my own, are deadly dull. As home improvement writers we do everything we can to be entertaining, but our first job is to be informative not fun. No matter how you slice it, reading two or three chapters on air conditioning, roofing or waterproofing can be a mind-numbing experience.

    Newspaper articles are a whole different ball game. The writer not only has to be informative, he or she has to captivate and entertain. Editors have no mercy if you fail to motivate the reader to come back, you're out of there.

    Taken collectively this book contains a huge amount of information about the home improvement industry, but the entire book is filled with 750 - 800 word snippets of information. Each stands alone and is designed to inform and entertain.

    2: As the host of the longest running, long format how to radio show in the United States, I talk to more people about home improvement each week than anyone else in America.

Since the program is a talk show you could say that I have the longest running audience led "How To" class in the country. My newspaper articles are the "class notes" for the radio show. On the air my average caller question and answer is 2 1/2-minutes. That does not give me a lot of time for depth. The newspaper column lets me flesh out problems and give in-depth explanations.

3: One of my most frequent compliments is: "I save all your articles." Recently I had lunch with one of the premium builders in the country. He told me that he has them filed by category. Even more impressive: my mother-in-law, Jeanette, saves all my articles. When a guy's mother-in-law saves his clippings, he has to be doing something right.

Confirming their usefulness, the archive of my articles on the Detroit News' web site, detnews.com, gets a lot of hits every month from people who need this type of information.

I have also included a listing of my most requested phone numbers and their web sites, special reports made for Detroit News readers and a very comprehensive subject index so that you can pin point the information you need. Kelly and her mother called every company I wrote about and updated the articles to include the most current phone listing. Toll-free numbers are used wherever possible.

For general information, read the articles sequentially. You'll soon get caught up in the flow of the seasons. Many home improvement writers create their work a month or more in advance. My staff and I wait for the last possible moment so our articles can contain solutions to current problems. If it's winter and a big snow is on the way, my article will probably be on the latest in ice melters and snow removal. If basements are flooded all over town, we'll write about basement clean up. By reading the articles week by week you get the flavor of what was happening to our part of the country.

If you want to read about broad topic areas, use the Table of Subjects. For the answer to a specific problem, use the index at the back of the book. Start with the most recent articles and work your way back. You will find that many of the first articles are the most informative, but the most recent stories give cutting edge information on the state of the industry.

Enjoy the read.

WARNING - DISCLAIMER

This book is designed to provide information for the home handy man and woman. It is sold with the understanding that the publisher and author are not engaged in rendering legal, contractor, architectural, or other professional services. If expert assistance is required, the services of competent professionals should be sought.

Every effort has been made to make this text as complete and accurate as possible, and to assure proper credit is given to various contributors and manufacturers, etc.. However, there may be mistakes, both typographical and in content. Therefore, this text should be used only as a general guide and not as the ultimate source of information. Furthermore this book contains information only up to the printing date.

The purpose of this book is to educate and entertain. The author and Master Handyman Press shall have neither liability nor responsibility to any person or entity with respect to any loss or damage caused directly or indirectly by the information contained in this book.

WARNING - DISCLAIMER

Trademark Acknowledgments

Trademarked names, rather than confusion inducing, generic names, are used throughout this book so that readers can ask distributors, retailers, and contractors, about products that interest them. Rather than list the names and entities that own each trademark or insert a trademark symbol with each mention of the trademarked name, the publisher states that it is using the names only for editorial purposes and to the benefit of the trademark owner with no intent of infringing upon that trademark.

Trademark Acknowledgments

Chapter 1

1995 Articles reprinted from The Detroit News HOMESTYLE

It's time for spring repairs: The first step is to take a hike

by America's Master Handyman, Glenn Haege

Spring has sprung. It's time to be out and about.

Here are some ideas on how to get the old homestead up to snuff after a dreary winter.

Start with the inspection. This is not something you should put off. Do it right now, before the spring rains come.

■ Manage by walking around outside.

Walk around the house three times. The first time, be as far away from the house as possible and check out the roof for shingles and eaves. Damaged shingles can cause water damage.

The second time around the house, look at the windows and walls.

The third time, look at the ground. The bitter freezes we had this year caused huge chuckholes on the roads; it probably did the same thing to the ground around your house. The driveways on many homes have heaved and will send torrents of water washing against the house.

Fill in any puddles around the foundation, called bird bathing, immediately, and get driveways or walks mud-jacked if they will direct water toward the house.

If you discover shingle or ground problems, take action immediately. This inspection process is so important that I will devote an entire column to it next week.

■ Window washing.

The outside windows have a winter's worth of grime on them. Making them sparkle doesn't have to be a hassle.

For outside windows use this sample procedure: Add 4 ounces of vinegar and 1 teaspoon TSP (Trisodium phosphate is available at any hardware store) to one gallon of water. Sponge on the water, then squeegee off. Wipe up water drips with a cotton towel.

The inside of your house has different dirt, so you need a different cleaning solution.

Mix 4 ounces of ammonia and 1 teaspoon of TSP to a gallon of water. Lay a big Turkish towel on the windowsill before you clean. Sponge on the water, then squeegee off.

You will now not only be able to see through them, your windows will sparkle like diamonds.

■ Clean the deck.

Here's an easy way to deep clean the deck. Mix an organic cleaner, like Simple Green or Clear Magic 50/50 with water. Pour the solution into a garden pump-type sprayer. Then deep clean your deck 8 to 10 square feet at a time.

The procedure is simple. Soak down an 8-to 10-square-foot section with the cleaning solution. Scrub with a stiff push broom until suds appear. Then hose off.

This technique often makes the deck look so good you may not have to reseal or stain.

■ **Get outdoor power equipment ready for the mowin' and growin' season.**
Check all electrical cords for nicks, breaks or brittleness. Replace all suspect wires. Replace the sparkplugs on small engines, check the muffler. If it is badly corroded, replace it. Make certain that all safety equipment is in good shape.

If you didn't do it last fall, the lawn mower needs to have the gas drained, oil changed and blade sharpened.

If you don't have a spare lawn mower blade, splurge and buy one. Resharpen blades often. The sharper the blade, the more beautiful the lawn.

■ **Go downstairs and put your furnace on vacation.**
Your furnace had a heck of a workout this year. The filter has to be cleaned or changed. Turn off the water supply to the humidifier and empty the water from the unit. Remove all sediment and make every thing squeaky-clean.

Replace pads if necessary.

Now that all the most important work is done, go outside and just enjoy the weather.

A good roof is worth looking up to; here's how to have one

by America's Master Handyman, Glenn Haege

Some people look for robins or waxwings in the spring. I look for roofers. In many older subdivisions, the pounding of roofing hammers is more prevalent than the drumming of woodpeckers. Just as soon as the snow melts these stalwart harbingers of spring are out pulling off old shingles and putting up new.

You don't have to climb on top of the roof to see if this is the year your home needs attention. Go across the street and look at your roof from the neighbor's sidewalk. Then, go to your back fence and look from there. If the shingles look tired and worn, and much of the surface aggregate has washed away, or the shingles are rippling or curling, it's time.

Good roofing companies get back-logged fast. Calling now, can prevent major water damage. Here's how to get the information you need to specify your roofing job and get the names of good roofing contractors.

Check to see how long the shingles have been down. If it is 15 or 20 years, you are due. If the shingles are 20 to 30 years old, take out your checkbook with a smile; you have been blessed. If the shingles are less than 15 years old, check the attic ventilation. It well may be that you are about to pay a several thousand-dollar penalty for having improper attic air flow.

If that is the case, make certain that the installation of proper soffit and ridge ventilation is part of the quote. Improper attic ventilation can cut shingle life in half and voids most manufacturer's warranties. Good attic ventilation not only extends roofing life, it can cut heating and cooling bills.

One of the most common questions I get from listeners of my radio show is, "Which is better, asphalt (organic) or fiberglass shingles?" They are almost identical. Shingle manufacture begins with a base surface called a "scrim" to which all other materials are applied during the manufacturing process. When the scrim is fiberglass, the shingle is called a fiberglass shingle. When the scrim is a thick piece of felt, it is called an organic, or asphalt shingle.

The organic shingle can resist frequent freeze-thaw cycles better. A fiberglass shingle is lighter and more fire resistant. In the Great Lakes Area, with its heavy snows and freezing rains, I usually recommend organic shingles. Where there is a great risk of fire, I recommend fiberglass.

If the roofing company has a preference between fiberglass and organic shingles, leave the choice to them. You want them to use the shingle with which they are most comfortable. The choice of quality, manufacturer, color, and dimensionality of the shingles, is up to you.

4

Dimensional shingles, using ceramic or sedimentatious material to build up the thickness, is the latest advance in design. It makes a dramatic change in the shadow line and give much the same quality look as slate, ceramic or wooden shingles.

A shingle's color and shadow line is important because it can have a great impact on the sales appeal of your home. Many homebuyers make their gut purchase decision as they drive up to the house and get out of the car. What they see first (curb appeal), can make or break, the sale.

On a single story house, roof shingles, their color and shadow line, make the largest visual impression of any aspect of the house. Shadow line is not as critical on a two or three story house, because prospects can not see as much of the roof.

Before you buy shingles, drive around your neighborhood. See what color and shadow line the other houses have, especially the newer homes and those that have been recently re shingled. If many of the homeowners have upgraded to the new raised pattern shingles, it may be smart for you to do the same.

After you've checked out the neigh-borhood, go to a wholesale roofing supply to look at the styles, quality and color selections available. These people supply professionals. Give them a call first, tell them that you are getting your house reroofed. Ask when would be a good time to stop by.

After you've gotten a good grounding on shingles, get their recommendation on roofing contractors. The wholesaler knows who has been building a good business year after year. When the wholesaler gives you the name of two or three roofing contractors, they are people in whom he has confidence.

Other good places to get information and recommendations are the contract departments at your local building materials discounter, home center and lumber yard. If a friend or relative has recently had a roofing job and is still bragging about the service and price, there is no better recommendation. When you make an appointment for an estimate, tell the contractors who recommended them.

Report R-30 lists roofing materials, manufacturers and supplies, plus maintenance suggestions. Send $2 and your name and address to Glenn Haege, Box 1498, Royal Oak, MI 48068.

(Editor Note: I included the "Roofing Report" in Appendix B at the back of this book, page 549.)

The best cleaning solution requires one part elbow grease

by America's Master Handyman, Glenn Haege

Almost no one has time for Spring Cleaning but it makes a great togetherness project; cleaning goes faster and moving heavy objects becomes do-able. If you live alone, seriously consider making it a buddy project. You help me with mine, I'll help you with yours.

Elbow grease is the most expensive cleaner in the house, don't waste it. No one gives blue ribbons or trophies for working harder than necessary. I am going to give the names of products I have found exceptionally effective for specific projects. Almost all of them can be found at your local hardware or home center.

Walls: A winter's full of dust, smoke from cooking and perhaps fireplaces has settled on your walls. Generally a good cleaning is all that is necessary to make them look freshly painted.

Use the buddy system. One person washes, the other rinses. Each should have a 2 1/2-gallon bucket and a long handled sponge mop. No one has to climb a ladder. My favorite cleaning solution is 2 ounces dry measure of Trisodium Chloride (TSP) per gallon of water. If kitchen walls seem greasy, use Dirtex® or add 2 ounces of liquid household Ammonia per gallon. Wear goggles and rubber gloves.

Apply the cleaning solution liberally with the sponge mop. Start from the bottom and work your way up to eliminate water spotting. Allow the cleaning solution to work for two minutes. Then rinse.

Change the rinse water every wall. Change the cleaning solution every room. Wipe up drips or spills immediately with a large 100 percent cotton towel. If you have to do this job solo, follow the same procedure. Wash a twelve-foot long section of wall, then rinse.

Remove fingerprints from painted walls with your favorite spray household cleaner or a specialized product like Wash Before You Paint™ by Culmac Industries. Spray the wall, then take a facial tissue and stick it on to the wet, surface. Keep the tissue moist at least 60 seconds, then use it to wipe the affected area. Use a circular motion both clockwise and counter clockwise. When the tissue falls apart, grab more dry facial tissue and complete the job. Do not use a rag. Facial tissue wicks up the moisture and allows you to clean without breaking the paint film.

Wallpaper: Vinyl wallpaper can be washed like a painted wall. The real hassle comes when you need to clean those beautiful (read expensive), hand blocked, imported papers.

Clean delicate wallpaper, lamp shades or fabric window blinds with a special rubber dry cleaning sponge you'll find at most hardware stores. It's called the Wall Brite™ Cleaning Sponge by the Absorbene Company. Start at the top of the wallpaper and gently pull the sponge down the wall. Turn the sponge over when one side gets dirty. When the entire sponge is soiled, rinse in water, wring out and let dry. As soon as it is dry you can continue the job. Never use a moist sponge on delicate wallpaper, fabric blinds, or lamp shades.

Windows: Outside: First, clean off the leaves, cobwebs and associated yuck on the sills and frames with a solution of 2 ounces dry measure TSP in a gallon of water. Sponge on, then rinse with clear water. Dry up drips with a 100 percent cotton towel.

To clean really dirty exterior glass, mix 1 level teaspoon of TSP and 4 ounces of vinegar to a gallon of water. Fold a 100 percent cotton towel and put it on the sill. Sponge the cleaning solution onto the window, then squeegee off. Mop up the water with the towel. Use an extension handle for windows that would normally be too high to reach.

Inside: Mix 1 level teaspoon of TSP and 4 ounces of Ammonia to a gallon of water. Repeat the outside procedure. Sponge on the solution, squeegee off, and wipe up any drips with the cotton towel.

Clean grease and gunk from window tracks and sliding door tracks with window cleaner or Never Dull™. If there is major oxidation, use of Peek™ metal cleaner by Tri-Peek International Inc. will make the tracks clean and free sliding.

Just cleaning the windows and walls can make a tremendous difference in your attitude. The most apparent dinghies of winter are gone. The house looks bright and smells clean and fresh. Enjoy! Next week we are going to tackle the floors.

Put some spring in your step by cleaning floors and carpets

by America's Master Handyman,
Glenn Haege

Last week we washed walls and windows, this week we're going to do the floors and furniture. By the time we're done, your home will look and smell like spring. Let's get started.

Floors: Wall to wall carpeting should be cleaned at least twice a year. A professional carpet cleaning service with big truck mounted equipment is best. The secret is extraction. Individual carpet and steam cleaners do not have the power to extract all the cleaning chemicals from the carpeting. The leftover chemicals act like dirt magnets.

If you must clean the carpet yourself, rent the most powerful unit you can. The larger equipment has more power to extract moisture and chemicals from the carpet.

Hardwood floors: Water and hardwood are not friends. Generally they should be vacuumed and dust mopped, not washed. For spring cleaning, use one of the specialty wood cleaning products, like Boen Hardwood Floor Cleaner or Total Care™ by Hartco. Wash Before You Paint™ by Culmac Industries, Polywash™ by Absolute Coatings or Simple Green™ by Sunshine Makers, all make excellent general maintenance cleaners.

If you have the energy, spray the cleaning solution on with a trigger sprayer and damp mop, then dry the floor completely with cotton towels.

Vinyl Floors and Tiles: This is a two mop, two-bucket job. Use 2 1/2 to 3 ounces of a good all-purpose concentrated cleaner like Simple Green™, Breeze™ or Clear Magic™ to a gallon of warm water. Mop on. Let stand for a couple of minutes. Then rinse with a separate bucket of clear water and a sponge mop. Change rinse water frequently. Heavy duty cleaning requires an ammoniated cleaner, like New Beginnings™, then a glaze coat, like Shine Keeper™, both are by Armstrong.

Ceramic Floor Tiles: Many of the most beautiful 9-inch ceramic kitchen and hall tiles are "single glazed," or "single fired." There were made to be non-slippery, and that means they have a non-shiny finish. Cleaning is the same as for vinyl tiles. If you want to add a little sheen, pick up a bottle of Brite™ or Future™ acrylic floor care product at the grocery store. Mix half-and-half with water and apply with a cotton or sponge mop.

For heavy scuff marks, use a waterless, non-abrasive hand cleaner like Go Jo™ or Fast Orange™. Rub the cleaner into the scuff mark with your hand until it softens the scuff. Let stand for two minutes, then take facial tissue and wipe up the hand cleaner. Repeat if necessary.

Fine Wood Furniture: Once a year your wood furniture should be cleaned and oiled. Start by washing down the furniture with mineral spirits, paint thinner or wood furniture cleaner. Spread the cleaner on liberally with a sponge. Let it stand for at least two minutes. If necessary, add cleaner to keep the wood moist. The cleaner needs time to penetrate the accumulated waxes and oils. After two minutes, wipe up with facial tissue. Repeat two or three times. Let the furniture dry over night, then treat with lemon oil.

There are many good brands of lemon oil on the market: Parker's, Hope's, Formby's, Guardsman, etc. Make certain you get lemon oil without beeswax or Silicone™. Apply a thin coat of lemon oil to the entire surface of the furniture. Do arms, legs, everything.

Now, when you think you're done, you've just begun. Only those surfaces you see have been treated. The other surfaces are raw. Once a year, all surfaces should be treated with lemon oil. Pour the lemon oil into a miniature paint tray and roll a coat of lemon oil onto all the unfinished areas with a 3-inch trim roller. Include the under side and leaves of tabletops, the back, bottom, and under sides of cabinets, armoires, dressers, and book cases, everything. You will be amazed at how your desert dry furniture drinks in the lemon oil.

By the time you are finished, you will swear that each piece of furniture has a smile on its face. The freshly oiled furniture will be very slippery. Let it stand over night before you handling.

It's time for you and the furniture to relax. Next week, we are going to tackle the stickiest jobs in the house: kitchens and baths.

The rooms in which we clean up are the hardest to clean

by America's Master Handyman, Glenn Haege

The oils, steam, soap scum and spills concentrated in kitchens and baths make them the two hardest to clean rooms in the house. The weather is too nice outside. Let's get this nasty job done and get out of here.

■ **Walls & Ceilings:** We've already talked about walls. If there's grease, don't forget to use Dirtex™ or add 2 ounces of liquid ammonia to the 2 ounces dry measure of TSP (Trisodium Phosphate) per gallon of water mixture.

■ **Counter Tops:** If the luster has gone out of your counter tops, you can deep clean, polish and seal them in one application with Hope's Counter Top Polish™ by Hope Industries. It's available at most hardware, home center and paint stores.

■ **Sinks:** Stainless Steel: To bring back the shine clean thoroughly with Bar Keepers Friend™. After the sink has been thoroughly cleaned, rinsed and dried, coat with a product like Diamond Brite™, which can be found in the automotive section of most stores. Diamond Brite™ leaves a Teflon® coating, so water drops just roll off.

For Porcelain, clean and shine porcelain sinks with bleach, Bon Ami™ and Gel Gloss®. Open the windows for ventilation, then plug the drain and fill the sink half full with liquid bleach. Fill the rest of the way with hot water. Let stand for 10 minutes. Drain the sink and clean with the bar form of Bon Ami™ (not the powder). Rinse with cold water.

When dry, apply a poly-type auto wax or Gel Gloss® to shine and seal the surface. It is always important to seal surfaces that you have deep cleaned. The sealer fills in the surface profile and makes it harder for dust, dirt and soap scum to stick.

■ **Baths:** If you have a mold and mildew problem on the ceramic tile, walls or ceiling in the bathroom, spray the affected area with X-14®. It will dissolve the mold and mildew in just a few minutes and you will be able to wipe the area clean with a rag.

■ **Showers:** To clean soap scum from ceramic tile, tub and shower doors use The Works Bath & Shower Cleaner™. This is a fairly strong cleaner so use rubber gloves. Scrub tiles with a small hand brush. Wear goggles to protect your eyes. After the shower walls have been washed and rinsed, let dry for an hour then reseal the surface with Gel Gloss™.

Also use Works™ on the shower doors and the fiberglass pan of the shower stall. Start from the bottom and work your way up. Rinse and let dry for a hour then seal the profile of the doors with Invisible Shield™ or Rain-X™ by Unelko Corp. Do not use a sealer on the shower floor. It will make the floor surface slippery and unsafe.

If the shower floor is badly stained, there is a specialty cleaning product called FSR™ Fiberglass Stain Remover developed for the boating industry and available at a good marine hardware supply store. FSR™ is a jelly. Paint it on. It will remove the most severe stains.

To shine metal shower enclosure frames and clean the gunk from aluminum tracks, use Peek™ metal polish. Never let the polish dry completely. Rub briskly, then buff with a clean rag.

If your toilet has developed hard watermarks and stains, CLR™, Calcium, Lime, Rust Remover by Jamie Industries, is worth a try. Before cleaning the inside turn off the water supply, then flush and plunge to reduce the water seal. Apply the CLR. Let stand for fifteen minutes before brushing with a very stiff scrub brush.

While empty, clean the sediment from the rim holes with a coat hanger . Check out the toilet seat and see if it should be removed and replaced. It is only held on by two bolts and a brand new replacements costs very little, so go ahead, treat yourself to a new seat, it's spring.

Clean the outside of the commode with one of the bathroom bubbling cleaners. A quick coat of Diamond Brite™ to the exterior will make it dazzle and give new meaning to the term "throne room."

Just be sure to turn the water back on before your next audience.

Good planning builds working relationships with tradesmen

by America's Master Handyman,
Glenn Haege

Every Spring, handymen, tradesmen, and building contractors sprout up like dandelions. The vast majority of them are honest, hard working men and women. Unfortunately a few use shady business tactics to fleece thousands of trusting homeowners, especially women and senior citizens, out of millions of dollars.

Not all damage is done by criminals. Many would-be builders don't know what they are doing. Your bank account can not make a distinction between being fleeced by a criminal or mugged by criminal incompetence. You're out the money either way. Use these few hints to pick a good contractor or tradesman.

When someone solicits to do repairs on your home, you do not know who they are. Take their name, company name, address, phone number, and builder's license number. If you are in a regulated state like Michigan, do not even talk to anyone who can not show you a valid Builder's or Home Improvement Sales License, complete with Builder's License number and the name of the "qualifying officer" of the firm.

If they say they are working for someone nearby, get the name, address and phone number of that person. Call the person before sitting down for an appointment. If they don't check out, call the police. Your call could save a neighbor thousands of dollars.

Always get quotes from at least three organizations for any major job. To get the names of good people, ask the folks who man the contract trade counters at wholesalers, lumberyards and home centers for referrals. They like to recommend good customers. The best time to talk to counter people is late in the morning or mid-day.

Wholesalers offer a wider selection of materials for specific types of jobs, like roofing, siding, ceramic tile, plumbing, and lighting. They get the majority of the top end business. If a broad choice of quality materials is important, make sure to seek out referrals from wholesalers as well as home centers and lumberyards.

While you're there, get a feel for the materials that will be used on your job and pick up some brochures. When you get back home, write a thorough description of what you want done. If you wish specific materials, specify them. List manufacturer, trade name, model name and number.

Never take quotes over the telephone. Set appointments in your home. When making the appointments, tell them that you want the names, addresses and telephone numbers of at least five people who have gotten the same type of job. When the contractor or sales person arrives, tell them you will not sign any agreement until after you have contacted and inspected their references.

After you have checked the references and decided on the best quote, it is time for contract signing. There is no "standard" contract. Make certain that the contract you sign contains an exact written description of the job without any abbreviations or technical terms. Never allow terms such as "industry standard" to appear in a contract. Such terms can be used to cheat you out of work or materials the sales person has verbally promised.

If a building permit is required in your jurisdiction, the contractor, not you, must apply for the contract, or you, not the contractor will be responsible for code violations.

The contract should specify all materials, including trade names and model numbers. If the materials are warranted, the contract must specify that you will be given copies of all warranties upon final payment.

It should also specify that no work will begin until you have received certificates of insurance direct from the contractor's liability and workmen's compensation insurance companies and that you will receive signed waiver of lien forms from every employee, subcontractor and supplier. Without these vital forms you could be responsible for any injury, accident or non-payment of labor materials.

The contract should also contain a promised finish date, complete with penalty clause, state who is responsible for cleanup and trash removal, and payment terms. Never pay more than 30 percent down. Always hold back at least 10 percent of the payment until you and the contractor have inspected the job and you are thoroughly satisfied with all work, including clean up.

If you need more information, a free step-by-step guide to selecting a contractor, contractor reference form, and listing of the information that should be specified in your building or remodeling contract is available. Send your name, address and $2.00 to cover photocopying, postage and handling to: Glenn Haege, P.O. Box 1498, Royal Oak, MI 48068-1498.

(Editor Note: The "How to Choose a Good Contractor Report" is included in Appendix B at the back of this book, page 557.)

MAY 13, 1995

Special steps can pave the way to a driveway free of cracks

by America's Master Handyman,
Glenn Haege

Was the winter hard on your concrete driveway, patio or walk? Have the cracks, that started out as almost invisible lines, multiplied and turned into chasms that rival the Grand Canyon? Are you afraid it is time to tear out the old and pour new concrete?

Even when the concrete has to be replaced, you still have options. Get a price on using pavers instead of poured concrete. Pavers will be more expensive, but they give a very high quality, designer look that adds value and beauty to your property.

Replacement may not be necessary. Cement cracks are caused by a combination of freeze-thaw cycles, water absorption and improper drainage. Spring is the best time for concrete driveway and walk repair. Many of the best contractors are already booked for most of the season.

There are four methods of concrete repair short of total tear out and replacement: back filling and sealing, leveling, resurfacing and repouring.

Fill small, thin cracks under half-inch in width, with a ready to use crack sealer. Just snip the top and pour. The crack sealer acts like an expansion joint.

Many crack sealers or fillers are black like traditional expansion joints. Alcoguard is considered one of the best of these. If you don't want the black lines, both Quikrete and Mr. Mac's make gray, concrete crack sealers. Sikaflex and Eucolastic make caulk like products. If you have a large area to cover, a product like Alcoguard can be the most cost-effective.

When the cracks are half-inch or wider, water will have washed a channel under the concrete. Back fill these with mason sand and tamp down with an ice chopper. Repeat the process several times. Mason sand does not clump like ordinary sand. Fill the last 1 1/2 inches in depth with a backer rod and crack sealer.

If the concrete has heaved, or sunken, or tree roots have pushed the drive out of level you can save the cost of replacement by using a mud jacking, or concrete leveling company. The company drills holes in the concrete, and forces a sand and sub soil mix under the slab, refilling all the voids where the sand has been washed away and lifting the slab to its original position.

By the time the concrete leveling company has finished, the drive, patio or walk will be as level as the day it was poured. This "fix" is usually good for at least five to seven years. After the drive has been leveled, fill all the fine cracks with crack sealer, and all the wide cracks with backer rod and crack sealer.

If the concrete has settled and broken in several areas, you can often use the old concrete drive as a foundation and repour a three or four inch bed over the old surface. If you choose this, make certain that the contractor has a good track record with this type of work.

Finally, if the drive, patio, or walk is in good condition, but just cracked, you can resurface it and beautify your property, by calling in a resurfacing specialist, like Concrete Technologies Incorporated (888) 727-6001. This company will cover the surface with a bonding coat, then apply a thin resurface coat. The textured resurface coat can be formed into patterns and tinted to look like pavers.

Even when the concrete has to be replaced, you still have options. Get a price on using pavers instead of poured concrete. Pavers will be more expensive, but they give a very high quality, designer look that adds value and beauty to your property. Once down, pavers have a 50-year guaranty. If something happens to an individual paving brick, it is a simple replacement, not a major repair.

If you decide you want to repave, make certain that the new driveway is poured on a sand base, that the concrete slab is at least 4 inches thick and composed of a six-bag mix. Specifying fiber reinforced concrete will greatly reduce chipping and cracking. Wire mesh is not required. Broad expanses of new concrete look beautiful, but crack easily. I suggest putting in several joints that run the length of the drive, as well as joints running across the width. Angle cuts at aprons are also a good idea.

Once the new concrete is poured, it should cure at least 60 days, before it is cleaned and sealed. All concrete, new or old, should be protected with a good concrete sealer. There are many good sealers on the market, including Mr. Mac's Concrete & Masonry Sealer, Olympic Water Guard, Protek Weathergard, and Thompson's Concrete & Masonry Protector. In an emergency, Thompson's Concrete & Masonry Protector can be applied after only five days.

If you need more information, ask for my free Concrete Report, # 31, and list of product names and telephone numbers. Just send your address plus $2.00 to cover photo copying, postage and handling, to Glenn Haege, P.O. Box 1498, Royal Oak, MI. 48068-1498.

(Editor Note: I included the "Concrete & Cement Report" in Appendix B at the back of this book, page 567.)

How do you get your deck and barbecue in shape for summer

by America's Master Handyman, Glenn Haege

Memorial Day marks the beginning of the summer party season. Time to get the deck and barbecue in shape. Here's how:

What you use to clean the deck is determined by what you want the final result to be. If you just want it deep cleaned, use a 50/50 combination of an organic cleaner like Simple Green or Clear Magic, or a solution of 4 ounces dry measure of TSP to a gallon of warm water.

If you want to get rid of the gray, or prepare the deck for sealing or staining, you have to use other cleaners. Graying is an indication that the wood has begun to disintegrate from exposure to the sun's Ultra Violet rays. Before you can stain the deck you have to get rid of the top decomposing layer of wood cells.

The traditional way to do this is with a strong chlorine bleach based cleaner, such as Thompson's® Deck Wash or Olympic® Deck Cleaner. For years I recommended my own recipe for this type of cleaner which consisted of 4 ounces dry measure of TSP, 1 gallon of household bleach, and 2 gallons of water. My home grown recipe was as effective as the commercial products for about one-third the price.

Recently a good deal of doubt cast as to the desirability of using a chlorine based cleaner. Bleach based products destroy the top layer of wood cells, but do not completely remove them. This results in a blurry, silvered surface, that is not a good foundation for staining or sealing.

To deep-clean and safely remove the damaged top layer of wood cells, use products that contain Oxalic Acid, Sodium Carbonate Peroxhydrate or Disodium Peroxydicarbonate. These include DeksWood® by the Flood Company, Wolman® Deck & Siding Brightener/Rejuvenator, Woodwash™ by Bio-Wash® Products (Canada) Inc., or Cuprinol Revive® Easy Deck Cleaner.

After the wood is clean, dry, and in a "like new" condition, apply a quality deck wood protector with a UV additive or semi-transparent deck stain. The clearer or more natural the look of the protective coating, the sooner graying will occur. Never use a stain, sealer or toner that does not specify that it is specifically made for decks.

Now let's make sure the outdoor grill season doesn't flare up in your face. I'm going to concentrate on gas grills because of their popularity and low cost of cooking. First, turn off the gas at its source, either at the bottle, or at the house in the case of direct gas lines.

If your grill uses lava rocks, replace them with pumice rocks or ceramic squares. Both of these products absorb drippings, making the barbecue less likely to flare up.

The Venturi is where the cooking gas is mixed with air and blows into the burners. Spiders love to lay their eggs in there, blocking air flow and causing poor flame spread. Take the Venturi off and clean it out with a coat hanger, or one of those special venturi brushes you can get at most barbecue supply stores.

Both the grate and grill need a hearty scrubbing. Soak for a half hour in a mixture of 10 ounces Simple Green or Clear Magic in a gallon of water, then scrub with a grill brush. Rinse and let dry.

Shop-Vac all the excess debris from the bottom of the grill.

Most button igniters work for only one year. Better replace it. While you're at the store, pick up a bottled gas fuel gauge. It will keep you from running out during that all-important party.

To clean the upper cooking grill, turn the gas back on and warm the grill. Turn off the gas and remove the grill from the heat. Brush down with the grill brush. Wipe with a paper towel.

If the exterior of the grill needs painting, use a special grill paint. The best have the consistency of jelly and are applied with a rag. Wash down the exterior with a solution of 10 ounces Simple Green or Clear Magic to a gallon of water. Rinse thoroughly, then let dry. Apply the paint.

Now treat your grill to a cover specifically made for that particular make and model. Don't waste time with tarps or "fits all" covers. They don't fit correctly. A proper grill cover will give sufficient protection to keep the grill looking good for years and eliminates the need to store the grill in the basement over winter.

My Deck Cleaning Product Test Report has just been completed. If you'd like a free copy, send your name, address and $2 to cover photocopying, postage and handling to: Glenn Haege, P.O. Box 1498, Royal Oak, MI 48068-1498.

(Editor Note: The "Deck Cleaner Test Report" is included in Appendix B at the back of this book, page 571.)

Many indoor problems can be solved if you just clear the air

by America's Master Handyman, Glenn Haege

You don't have to look at the almanac to know what season dis is. Just breath in (if you can) and try to keep from sneezing. People are wheezing, sneezing, and coughing at work, at home, shopping, everywhere. We can't do a thing about the pollen count, but we can do something about our home's indoor air quality. Here are a few tips to help your family get through the sneezin' season.

Furnace Filters should be cleaned or replaced. Most electronic filters have to be cleaned ever 30 days. Just because the heat is off does not mean that the furnace filter is not working. If you have an electronic air cleaner attached to your furnace and have not kept up with the required monthly cleanings, it may no longer be functioning. Have it checked by an HVAC contractor.

Drain and clean the humidifier. One thing you do not need is a humidifier tray of warm, stagnant water.

Damp basements need dehumidification, plus air circulation. Set an appliance timer to run an oscillating fan for 6 hours on, 2 hours off, continuously. Don't worry about the electric bill. These fans use only a negligible amount of power.

Damp basements need dehumidification, plus air circulation. Set an appliance timer to run an oscillating fan for 6 hours on, 2 hours off, continuously. Don't worry about the electric bill. These fans use only a negligible amount of power.

If you are also running a dehumidifier, set the two appliances across the room from one, another. Point the fan so that it directs the air current upward, not directly at the dehumidifier. This will increases the effectiveness of the dehumidifier by 30 or 40 percent.

Hang Mil-Du-Gas® Bags in crawl spaces and basements. The components in the bag vaporize slowly and kill air born mildew. This product is the most effective mildew eliminator I've ever found. They are also excellent in damp closets, and campers and second homes that are closed up for long periods of time. A 2,000 square foot basement will require five bags. Bags last 3 or 4 months. Mil-Du-Gas® bags can be found in most hardware stores or home centers. If you have trouble finding them, write Star Brite, 4041 Southwest 47th Avenue, Ft Lauderdale, FL 33314.

Consider installing central air conditioning if you don't have it. It will bring humidity down and can greatly reduce the pollen in indoor air because you are keeping the windows and doors shut.

After the pollen season is over, you will still have to control the mold, mildew and musty odors. Look around the outside of your home. Soggy soil around the perimeter of the house make the crawl spaces and basement wet and musty. Put them on a water free diet now. Build up the area around your house so that there are no damp spots and water runs away from the foundation.

Starting with this Memorial Day Weekend, pour one cup of bleach down each drain before you go to bed. Mark the day on the calendar and do it every 30 days during the musty season. Pour half gallon of bleach down the basement floor or utility room drain and another half gallon in the sump pump crock. Bleach is a great disinfectant and odor neutralizer. You will be amazed at how much odor the bleach treatment eliminates.

If you see mold stains on fabric or painted surfaces, spray them with Mildew Away by Amazon Products. There is no chlorine bleach in the formula.

The bathrooms and showers in most homes are small and damp. That makes them prime areas for mold. You can put a stop to this by repainting with Perma-White Bathroom Wall & Ceiling Paint by Zinsser. The paint is mold proof and blister proof. No sealer is needed. Two coats are required.

To dry out the bathroom, air circulation and exchange of air. An efficient ceiling fan works wonders. Installing an over the door air return also helps a great deal. Use a 3-inch-high by 6-inch-wide cold air return plate with fins pointing up on the outer wall, and another plate with fins pointing down on the bathroom side. This allows continuous free air exchange. Warm moist air goes out the vent. Dry cooler air comes into the bathroom even when the door is closed. Aiding the air supply also makes under powered ceiling fans a great deal more efficient.

For year round relief of indoor air problems, look into buying an Enviracaire portable H.E.P.A. air filter by Honeywell. Run the filter day and night and it will clean your air continuously.

JUNE 3, 1995

For Safety's sake, warm up to these hot-water tank tips

by America's Master Handyman, Glenn Haege

It is very hard to get excited about hot water tanks. They all look alike. Here are a couple hints as to when you should start shopping for a new one.

■ If the drain water is starting to look cloudy and/or contains strong traces of rust or sediment. Remember, you are supposed to drain three gallons out of the bottom of the hot water heater every three months.

■ If the water does not get very hot. Most water heaters are gas fired at the bottom of the tank. Over the years, rust, flaking, and scaling of calcium and magnesium build-up, and sediment from water born impurities settle to the bottom of the tank, insulating the water from the heat. As the sediment builds, the heater becomes less and less efficient.

■ If the hot water tanks is ten or fifteen years old. The harder the water, the shorter the tank's life expectancy. Some hot water tanks last only seven years.

Here's how to test to see if your hot water tank is operating efficiently.

■ Check to see if the water heater temperature setting is at medium. Attach a garden hose to the hot water drain.

■ Fill the laundry tub full of hot water. Don't put the stopper in until hot water is coming out. The average tub holds about 26 gallons of water.

■ Test the temperature with a meat thermometer. Do not, under any circumstances put your bare hand into this water. You can get a scald burn at 114 degrees F. The water in the laundry tub will be considerably higher.

■ If the hot water tank is operating efficiently, the temperature of the entire tub of water should be at least 120 degrees F. If it is much lower, you either have the water heater set too low, or the tank is no longer heating efficiently and should be replaced. If it is much above 120 degrees F, the setting of this high temperature should have been a conscious decision on your part. Although your washer and dishwasher operate more efficiently with water at 140 degrees F, a setting of only 120 degrees F is the recommended industry standard for safety reasons .

If you decide you need a new heater, here's what's new:

Top-of-the-line models now are more rustproof than ever. The average hot water heater is a steel cylinder with a thin glass lining, and rust creeps in through imperfections in the lining or at the welds that join the glass to the steel tank. New designs combat rust in three ways.

■ Better electric water heaters have a plastic inner tank. The water never gets to the metal tank. (Plastic can be used in electric heaters because they heat with heating elements, not direct flame, which could melt the plastic).

■ Some top of the line models have a patented turbo coil that swirls the incoming water at the bottom of the tank, keeping sediment in suspension.

■ Other new heaters have a front mounted flue, a miniature boiler, which heats water outside the tank and permits the tank itself to be of nonmetallic material that will never rust or corrode. These heaters are expensive, but the high price is offset by the fact that they have a lifetime limited warranty.

If you want to replace your household heating system and hot-water tank at the same time, you might look at the Lennox® CompleteHeat combination system. Water is heated in a heating module, and the heated water becomes both the hot-water supply and forced-air heat for the house. The manufacturer says it provides an almost limitless hot-water supply. The heat exchanger is backed by a 15-year limited warranty.

So what is best for you? For me, I buy middle of the road and change every 10 of 15 years. It all depends upon the hardness of the water in your area and the amount of water you use.

Once you have plenty of hot water, there's one last thing to think about – making sure it's not so hot someone gets scalded.

You have a couple of choices – buying new, scald-proof faucets, or installing scaldproof adapters on existing faucets. Resource Conservation, Inc. has a line of inexpensive ScaldSafe kits for showers and faucets which automatically shut off when it reaches 114 degrees. For more information and the dealer nearest you call 1-800-243-2862.

(Editor Note: The "Water Heater Report" is included in Appendix B at the back of this book, page 575.)

Newly brightened hardwood can put on a real floor show

by America's Master Handyman, Glenn Haege

If like many of us, you've been toying with the idea of converting your floors from wall to wall carpeting back to their original hardwood, the weather is perfect for hardwood floor projects right now.

It's not too hot to do hard work. You can turn off the furnace and other pilot lights without fear of discomfort. And, it is warm enough to have the windows open while the floors are drying.

The average homeowner who pulls up the carpeting and finds hardwood has a site-finished floor. That is, the wood was finished on the job site. The following instructions are useful only for this category of floors.

(If you have factory-finished flooring, it can usually be renewed with special wood restoration mixtures available from the flooring manufacturer, such as the Hartco Touch Up Kit in combination with their Total Care or Pattern-Plus Shine, or Duraseal's Renovator. These products are available from most stores that sell hardwood floor finishes. For the dealer nearest you, call Hartco at 800-4 HARTCO, or Renovator by Minwax at 800-462-0194.

Most floors do not need to be refinished. Usually, the top coat of urethane has just gotten old and yellowed.

While adding new coats of the old, oil based polyurethane's was often not successful, the new VOC finishes make it possible to add a youthful new luster and years of extra life to your floor's finish.

People are constantly asking me for an easy way to bring back the beauty to their hardwood floors. I call my secret recipe "brightening", here's how:

Materials needed: TSP, fine sanding screen for 16-inch buffer or fine grit sandpaper for Flecto SQUAR BUFF orbiting buffer, mineral spirits, tack rags, Verathane Elite Diamond, Fabulon Professional Crystal II and additive, or other VOC polyurethane finish.

Have on hand a 16-inch buffer or Flecto SQUAR BUFF orbiting buffer, sanding respirator, wet/dry type vacuum with a bag and attachments, broom, lambs wool pad applicator and extension pole.

This job can be done in a day. Sanding creates a lot of sanding dust so vacuuming is very important. The job goes twice as fast if you can use the buddy system. One person sands, the other vacuums continuously. Trade off jobs if it gets too boring.

1. Remove everything from the room. Carefully take up the quarter round moldings.

2. Clean the floor thoroughly. There should not be a hint of grease or wax when you are done. If there is any wax on the floor, it must be stripped. Wash the floor with a mixture of 4 ounces dry measure of TSP per gallon of warm water. Rinse several times.

3. When you have cleaned everything, lightly sand or screen the floor. Just cut the top surface. If you can find a Verathane Flecto dealer, renting their SQUAR BUFF vibrating sander would be perfect for this job. Many home centers carry the line. In addition to renting the sander, you would need to get 80 grit paper.

You can also use a large 16-inch floor buffer. Attach a 3M Brand Fine Grade, round sanding screen and buff lightly. Just buff until a light powder appears over the entire surface.

Sand all edges, corners, closet floors, everywhere you could not get to with the big equipment with a hand-held orbiting sander or finishing sander.

Everyone in the room should wear a respirator when sanding is going on. There will be a great deal of fine dust in the air. Turn off pilot lights and do not allow smoking in the house during the sanding operation.

Don't make this project any bigger than it needs to be. Do not sand down to the bare wood. The only reason for screening the surface is to create a profile that will enable your new finish coats to bond to the existing finish.

4. Vacuum thoroughly, floors, walls, all ledges, everything. It is important to use a wet/dry vacuum with a bag because the fine sanding dust can ruin the motor.

5. Wipe down the floor with a rag dampened with water attached to a broom. Do not let even a hint of dust remain in the room.

6. Pad on a couple of coats of VOC Flecto Verathane, Fabulon Professional Crystal II, or other VOC crystal clear finish. Pad the coats on a couple of hours apart. This procedure should make your floor look brand new. Read the can label before you leave the store. If you use Fabulon, be sure to get the additive or it will not adhere to the old surface.

If you're hot to get central air, first know the cold, hard facts

by America's Master Handyman, Glenn Haege

Whether you have central air conditioning or not, the thermometer will soon make you think about it. If you have central air, make sure the compressor is clean and ready to give you a summer's worth of service. Clear away all vegetation from within one foot of the compressor to assure a good air supply.

If you have a modern air conditioner with exposed coils, clean the coils and compressor housing with a good organic cleaner, like Simple Green or Clear Magic, and water. Use 10 ounces of cleaner to a gallon of water. Turn off the air conditioner before you start. Put the solution into a garden sprayer and gently spray the condenser coil and housing. Let the cleaner work for a few minutes, then rinse with a garden hose. Wait until the compressor is dry before turning on the air conditioner.

If you've decided to buy central air conditioning, here are a few tips.

All the major makers make good equipment. The most important part of the central air conditioning package is the person who installs and stands behind it. The contractor's work load and bidding procedure, do much to determine the final selling price.

Air conditioners are manufactured to maintain a 15-degee differential between outside and inside temperatures. On a day (or night) when the temperature is 90 degrees F outside, the air conditioner should be able to bring the inside temperature down to 75.

When shopping contractors, you need to learn about their history with the product line in addition to the standard questions about customer service. How long they have carried their present air conditioning line? What brand did they carry previously? Why did they switch?

No one can give you a quote over the phone. The contractor, or his/her representative, has to inspect the house and fill out a relatively lengthy questionnaire to determine the size of the equipment needed.

Decide what you want from air conditioning before the sales call. Air conditioners are manufactured to maintain a 15 degree differential between the outside and the inside temperatures. On a day (or night) when the temperature is 90 degrees F outside, the air conditioner should be able to bring the inside temperature down to 75. Inside temperature is measured at the thermostat, and is not level throughout the house.

On a 90 degree night, the temperature on the ground floor might be 75, but the temperature in the upper, back bedroom, might be 85. That might be unacceptable to you. The contractor can balance the air flow to correct the problem, but to do so, he has to know it exists.

If you require specific demands, such as cooling the upper back bedroom to 75 when the outside temperature is 90, get that performance guaranty written into the contract.

When getting air conditioning quotes, remember that a bigger air-conditioning system does not necessarily mean better. If your compressor is too powerful, the air can feel cold and clammy.

All of today's air conditioner's list their energy efficiency rating, called a SEER rating. The average air conditioner's SEER Rating is 10 or 11, high efficiency units are 12 - 15. The higher the SEER Rating, the higher the price. Until recently, units with a 12+ SEER Rating have been prohibitively expensive. Now, manufacturers and power companies are giving credits for the purchase of the more efficient equipment.

Check the prices on air conditioning units with SEER Rating of 10 or 11 and 12 or 12+ units. If you can get the price difference, after credits, down to the $150.00 range, go with the higher SEER Rating.

If you use propane, oil, or electric fuel, call your local electric company and get information on Geothermal. Geothermal heating and cooling systems use ground temperature to heat and cool the house. Some units even throw in a limitless supply of hot water as a bonus. Geothermal systems are so efficient their SEER Rating reach as high as 21.

If you live in a house which has never had air conditioning, because it is built on a slab, or there is no room, or you just never wanted to go through the mess of having your house torn apart to install duct work, consider a product like Space-Pak® distributed by Detroit Safety Furnace Co. (800) 682-1538.

Space-Pak® uses a compact exterior condensing unit, much like traditional central air conditioners, then disperses the cooled air from an attic mounted blower unit.

For a free copy of a report on how to choose central air conditioning, including phone numbers, send your name, address and $2 to cover photocopying, postage and handling to Glenn Haege, P.O. Box 1498, Royal Oak, MI 48068-1498.

(Editor Note: The "Air Conditioning Report" is included in Appendix B at the back of this book, page 579.)

JUNE 24, 1995

Spruce up your lawn furniture, then just sit down on the job

by America's Master Handyman, Glenn Haege

There is nothing that looks more relaxing on a summer's day than traditional wood and wicker lawn furniture.

If your patio furniture looked great last summer but is grungy this year, it's time to repair, repaint, or replace. Here are some tips on how to em-power the painter in you.

As long as it is still structurally sound, scrape and sand away the loose, flaking paint from the wood furniture, then wash it down with a solution of 2 ounces dry measure of Trisodium Phosphate (TSP) to a gallon of water or a solution of one part Simple Green to five parts water. Rinse thoroughly, then dry five or six hours. Gouge out the wood rot and replace with an Exterior Wood Filler, like Minwax High Performance Wood Filler.

Brush on one coat of a Oil Base Exterior Stain Kill, like Cover Stain. Be sure to cover the sides, edges, and bottom, as well as the top of each board. Do the bottom edges first, then the tops and sides. Let dry a minimum of four hours. When thoroughly dry, apply two coats of an Oil or Water Base Porch and Floor Paint. You're done. Enjoy!

If you have varnished wood lawn furniture that has yellowed, flaked, and gone black in spots, you can bring back the natural beauty. Sand off the old finish with a Random Orbit Mechanical Sander and 80 Grit Sandpaper.

After sanding, get rid of the wood discoloration by washing down the piece of furniture with full strength household Chlorine Bleach. Be sure to wear rubber gloves and don't let any of the bleach drain on to grass or plants. Swab the bleach on liberally.

When the wood has lightened and the dark spots have disappeared, stop the chemical action by swabbing down the furniture with plain water.

After the surface has dried, gouge out rotted areas and fill in with High Performance Exterior Wood Patch. The bleaching step raised the grain of the wood, so smooth the surface with the Random Orbit Sander and 150 Grit Sandpaper. Dust off the top, bottom and sides with a Tack Rag, then turn upside down, and apply Marine Sealer to every nook and cranny of the underside.

Stand the piece right side up and wipe down the upper surface with a Tack Rag again, and apply a coat of Marine Sealer to every surface that was not sealed when you did the bottom. Let dry about 8 hours, then apply a Marine Finish to the back, arms and seat of the furniture. Apply a second coat Within 24 hours.

If your patio furniture looked great last summer but is grungy this year, it's time to repair, repaint, or replace. Here are some tips on how to empower the painter in you.

If you have painted wicker or rattan furniture that has become worn and the paint is flaking, sand off the flaking paint, then wash it down with a solution of 4 ounces dry measure of TSP to a gallon of water. Add a cup of household Chlorine Bleach to the cleaning solution if mold or mildew has become a problem. Rinse copiously with a garden hose, then let dry four hours

Next, spray the entire piece of wicker with a Shellac Base Stain Kill, like Wm. Zinsser B-I-N. Let dry two hours, then spray on two coats of an Oil Base Exterior Enamel Paint. By the time you're done the wicker will look good enough to be on *Lifestyles of the Rich and Famous.*

If your wicker is varnished, it is a little more of a hassle, but still eminently do-able (don't even think of doing this on a day when the humidity is over 75 percent). All the basic materials come in spray cans.

Spray on a liberal coat of Paint and Varnish Remover. Follow the directions on the can to the letter. Scrape off the old varnish with a wooden spatula or a #3 Steel Wool Pad. Remove the old material from tight cracks and crevices with a BIX™ Stain Brush.

Wash the furniture down with Denatured Alcohol, then inspect carefully. If even the faintest trace of old stain and varnish remains, repeat the process.

When you're satisfied, spray on a coat of stain and three or four coats of Spray Varnish. Use light coats of a Spar Varnish or an Exterior Polyurethane. Pay particular attention to the can directions about "Tack Free" time. Wait the exact amount of time specified and then apply the second coat.

For more information on how to paint, stain or varnish all types of new and used exterior furniture, or any other exterior painting job, consult my book, *Take the Pain Out of Painting – Exteriors,* ($12.95 plus $2.00 postage & handling, from Master Handyman Press, P.O. Box 1498, Royal Oak, MI 48068-1498).

An empty house may invite some unwelcome attention

by America's Master Handyman, Glenn Haege

It's July, time to hang loose and enjoy the Water Wonderland. Unfortunately, that leaves the family house *Home Alone* without Macaulay Caulkin. Planning for a successful vacation, should include home security.

The best protection for your house is to not let it be empty. Consider a house sitter. Second-best, have a trusted neighbor park in your drive-way and also look around inside the house once or twice a week while you are gone. Next to the phone place the number where you can be contacted, along with the name of a parent, relative, or friend to whom you have delegated the power to make a major decision about the house, if you can not be located.

If you have a telephone answering machine with a remote monitoring feature, check your phone messages, and return calls while you're away. Professional burglars often call several times to make sure a house is empty.

Three weeks before you leave, give your local Police Department written notification that you will be gone and the names and phone numbers of people you have delegated to check the house and make emergency decisions. Give your friendly neighbor and the delegated friend or relative copies of the notification.

Officers at local Police and Sheriffs Departments tell me that whole-house security systems with, or without, off-site monitoring, are a good investment in home security. They advise that a good system should have a loud alarm and a re-set feature.

Of course, you'll stop the mail and newspaper delivery, and arrange to get the grass cut. That's good, but use lights to give your house a lived in look. To be effective, lights and sounds have to have random settings and be scattered throughout the house, in bedrooms, bathrooms, kitchens, family rooms, and basements.

Leave two radios on in different parts of the house with at least one tuned to a talk station.

The Honeywell Time Tracker™ is a state-of-the-art, motion activated, switch that can help you with this job. After its initial setting, the Time Tracker™ automatically adjusts for different nightfall times throughout the year. Lights go on and off at a slightly different time each day.

Each unit has up to four different on/off cycles per day, and an internal rechargeable, battery back-up, to protect against program loss and time error during a power outage. For more information on the $19.95 Time Tracker by Honeywell, call 1-800-468-1502.

Pull the plugs on the rest of your electronics, extra lights, TV, stereo, and microwave. If possible, empty the refrigerator and freezer before you leave. During a power outage, food can spoil and the appliance can absorb a smell that can not be eliminated. Turn off the water at the water meter.

Windows are a prime access for burglars. All windows should be locked. Even second and third story windows can be entered if the burglar has access to a ladder, so make certain that your ladders are put away. Door walls and sliding windows should be blocked with rods.

Don't pull the shades down in the front of the house. That just makes the house look empty. Window sheers that keep people from looking into the house are good security investments.

Lock basement windows from the inside. Consider upgrading basement windows to glass blocks with window vents. Blocks give more privacy, better light, security, and insulation.

If you have central air, turn the thermostat up to 80 degrees Fahrenheit. Maximize air flow inside the house by opening all closet and cabinet doors under sinks in the kitchen and bath.

Stop the musties by hanging Mil-Du-Gas bags in basements and major rooms and pouring one cup of Liquid Laundry Bleach down every sink (don't run any water in the sink after the bleach), and two cups of Bleach in the basement floor drain, the sump pump well, and each toilet.

Disconnect the automatic garage door opener and lock the garage door on your way out. If you have a side entrance, make certain that it is dead bolted. If there are any other entrance doors to your house, even breezeway doors, that do not have a deadbolts, today would be a good time to have them installed.

Your house is now as secure as it can be. Have a good vacation.

Home Security Checklist

■ Newspaper & Mail shut off or being picked up by neighbor.
■ Police notified when you will be away and who to contact.
■ Timers set on lights & radios.
■ Refrigerator & freezer emptied.
■ Electric plugs pulled on non-refrigerated appliances, TVs, unused lights and sound system.
■ All windows locked.
■ All doors dead bolted and sliding glass doorwalls and sliding windows blocked.
■ Arrangements made for grass to be cut.
■ Neighbor who will check house notified.
■ Security System turned on.

How to steer through the details when driven to clean your garage

by America's Master Handyman, Glenn Haege

At least once a year, we get the urge to clean and organize the garage. If the urge is upon you, here are a few tips:

First, store the bikes, lawn mower, and other treasures in the back yard under a tarp. Throw useless junk away.

Sweep down the area. Take the Shop 'n Vac hose extension and clean the cobwebs from the rafters. Wash down the walls or wood studs with a mild TSP (Trisodium Phosphate) solution (2 ounces dry measure of TSP per gallon of water). Use sponge mops. Keep changing the rinse water.

If the garage is drywalled, repair the holes that happened when the walls jumped in front of the car or tried to grab the side view mirror. Light spackling compounds, like One Time by Red Devil, work best because they do not shrink. Paint with a good Oil Based Stain Kill like H2Oil Base by Zinsser. Finish with a coat of an Eggshell Latex Paint.

Now, throw a little light on the subject. One or two, 60 watt bulbs don't give enough light to see any-thing. For all round lighting, the folks at Haig Lighting and Electric recom-mend Fluorescent Ceiling Fixtures. If the garage is unheated, order special "LT" (Low Temperature) ballasts that start in cold weather. For more information call (810) 791-2380.

Next, clean the floor. You've got three choices: simple washing, wash and seal, and painting. Simple washing is for people who just want to get the gunk off. Washing and sealing will protect the floor from being stained by oil and transmission fluids. Painting is for those who want their garage to look like a dealership service bay.

To clean, wash with a solution of 2 ounces dry measure of TSP to a gallon of water. Rinse thoroughly.

If you want to seal, and the floor is only slightly stained, use the same cleaning procedure, and remove stains with BIX™ or other driveway stain removers. Let dry 2 days, then roll on two coats of Acrylic Cement Sealer.

If the floor is older or heavily oil stained, clean with a 20 degree Muratic Acid and water solution. Proper ventilation is very important. The garage door should be open. Wear a dual canister respirator, goggles, rubber boots and gloves, wool or cotton, long sleeved shirt and slacks. No polyester or other man-made fabrics, they offer no protection.

Pour a solution of one part 20 degree Muratic Acid to three parts of water directly on the oil and rust stains. Let stand one hour. Scrub with a deck brush. Add more Muratic Acid and water if needed. Let stand 4 hours, then repeat the process. If the formerly stained area is noticeably lighter than the rest of the cement surface, brush the entire area with the Muratic Acid/ Water Solution.

After the Muratic Acid bath, wash the floor with a solution of 2 ounces dry measure of TSP per gallon of water. Rinse with a garden hose. Dry for 24 hours and roll on two coats of Acrylic Cement Sealer.

I never suggest painting a garage floor, but am constantly being asked for a recommendation. If you must paint, clean as you would for sealing. The paint I recommend is Dupont's Imron Alipatic Polyurethane Enamel. It is a two component, chemically cured paint that is resistant to salts, oils, solvents and most other chemicals. As the name implies, it is a professional paint, generally used in industrial, or dealership applications. It is seldom applied by Do-It-Yourselfers. For more information, or the names of contractors that specialize in applying Imron Coatings, call Michigan Industrial Paint Supply, (810) 774-4700.

Now that the garage is clean, and well lit, let's organize. For more traditional types, Rubber Maid has come out with storage units that sit on the floor. They don't rust or crack. If you accidentally run into them, they bounce back.

The best storage is either overhead, or on the wall, not on the floor. Every hardware store and home center has a growing supply of products that lets you use the length, width, and height of your walls, as well as the rafters overhead for storage and organization.

California Closet Co., (248) 624-1234 has specialized storage racks for golf bags, in line skates, tennis, skis, fishing and bikes. They also have a unique modular garage storage system that holds all your tools, has a work area and locks.

Using these new systems, everything, including ladders, gardening and home care tools, and supplies, can be organized and out of the way. You may even be able to fit two cars, in a two car garage. Amazing.

JULY 15, 1995

Aluminum siding's a breeze to paint, but brick can be tricky to tackle

by America's Master Handyman, Glenn Haege

In the next 60 days, more exterior paint will be purchased and applied than during all the rest of the year. Two of the biggest exterior painting challenges are aluminum siding and brick.

Aluminum provides a superior painting surface. If your siding needs to be painted, I recommend it highly. Brick provides a terrible painting surface. I don't recommend it. One painting manufacturer has created a coating that does a good job on brick's notoriously porous surface. Here are some tips on painting both aluminum and brick.

During the '60s, '70s, and into the '80s, millions of American homeowners were told that if they had their homes or trim covered with aluminum siding they could throw away their paint brushes forever. Two things the salesman forgot to tell us were that siding has to be washed every year, and although aluminum lasts forever, the color coating does not.

Now, thousands of home owners are having their aluminum siding torn off and replaced with vinyl. Repainting would be a far less expensive alternative.

The secret to successful painting of aluminum siding, lies in proper finish preparation. Power wash the siding first. This can be done professionally or as a do-it-yourself project. If you decide to do it yourself, rent a professional power washing unit that will produce at least 2,000 pounds per square inch from an equipment rental company.

Let dry for 48 hours. During the waiting period, inspect the caulking. If it has drawn away from corners, or is no longer resilient, remove the old caulk and re-caulk. Caulk can be softened with a heat gun and scraped off with a putty knife. Silicone caulk is applied after the aluminum has been painted. Apply all other caulks before the surface is painted.

When thoroughly dry, test the surface for chalking. If little chalking has occurred apply two coats of Acrylic Latex Water Base Paint. If heavy chalking has occurred, seal the entire surface with an Exterior Water Base Stain Kill like 1-2-3 by Zinsser or Total One by Master Chem, then apply an Acrylic Latex Water Base Paint. You can use a brush/roller technique, or a professional quality HVLP (High Volume, Low Pressure) spray gun. Do not use an under powered home handyman sprayer. It lacks the power to do the job properly.

If you are not an experienced spray gun user, you are better off with the brush roller combination. Amateur paint sprayers often wind up with a blotchy looking job, or use too little paint. Your final coverage should be no less than one gallon per 400 square feet.

When using a spray gun, add Flotrol by the Flood Company. This product is needed to enable the thick Acrylic Latex Water Base Exterior Paint to be shot through the nozzle of the airless sprayer. If the surface was chalking or had a mildew problem, add an anti-chalking and/or a anti-mildew additive to the first coat of paint. Do not dilute the paint with water. You will ruin it. Properly applied, you will be able to take pride in your aluminum paint job for the next 10 or 15 years.

If painted brick has become your passion, the Coronado Paint Company, has produced a better than average solution for you. The name of the coating is Final Finish. Developed as a durable film coat for exterior masonry surfaces, it can be applied to concrete walls, garage floors, or brick. It comes in both a Solvent Acrylic or an Aqua-plastic water reduced acrylic.

Both of these paints are best applied by professionals, but could be tackled by the advanced Do-It-Yourselfer. They can be applied as deep penetrating, full bodied paints, or thinned out to penetrating stains. All Paint 'N Stuff locations carry these products.

Pre-painting preparation consists of power washing, caulking and any necessary brick repair. If the surface has grown exceptionally smooth, it may have to be sand blasted or acid washed, before multiple coats of Final Finish are applied.

If you have an older home and want to try the job yourself with a more traditional coating (read cheaper), power wash and prep the brick, then let dry two days. Paint the entire surface with an Exterior Water Base Stain Kill. Let dry four hours, then cover with two coats of a premium Water Base Exterior House Paint.

For more complete directions for painting aluminum and vinyl siding, brick or any exterior surface consult my book *Take the Pain Out of Painting – Exteriors,* $12.95 plus $2.00 postage & handling, from Master Handyman Press, P.O. Box 1498, Royal Oak, MI 48068-1498.

JULY 22, 1995

How to turn up your comfort when the heat's on full blast

by America's Master Handyman, Glenn Haege

If only we could invent a way to store this summer's heat and release it a little bit at a time next winter. We can't so, we have to deal with it. Here are some tips on how to help your house handle the heat.

■ **Sweaty Toilets:** The commode's water closet is a reservoir of cold water. When the air is hot and humid, droplets solidify on the surface. The best solution is to install a rigid foam tank liner. The liners are inexpensive and available at most hardware stores or home centers.

■ **Dripping Basement Water Pipes:** Condensation also collects on the basement water pipes. Insulation is the key here, too. Install jacket style foam tube insulation over the water pipes. Do both the hot and cold water pipes. Insulating the cold water pipe stops drips now. Insulating the hot water pipes will save you a good deal of money next winter.

■ **Stale, musty, basement air:** The basement has the poorest ventilation of the house. During the hot summer days it is a reservoir of the coldest, dampest air in the house. Mold and mildew love it. This is their idea of summer fun. You can evict mold, mildew and the musties by hanging Mil-Du-Gas Bags and increasing the air circulation.

Mil-Du-Gas Bags have no formaldehyde and are very safe. They are distributed by the Star Brite Corp. of Florida. If you can't find Mil-Du-Gas Bags at your local Hardware Store or Home Center, give Star Brite a call at (800) 327-8583.

To increase the air circulation, hook up an oscillating fan to an appliance timer. Six hours on, two hours off, for a total of 18 hours out of 24. Tilt the fan toward the basement ceiling. If you have a dehumidifier, running the fan will make the dehumidifier 50 percent more efficient. If you are running a dehumidifier and fan combination, locate the fan across the room. Do not have it blowing directly on the dehumidifier.

If your dehumidifier is freezing up, the dehumidifier is dirty. You can increase its efficiency and prolong its life by cleaning it at a do-it-yourself Car Wash. Take off the case and wash and rinse the dehumidifier thoroughly. Pay special attention to the coils. Take it home, let it dry three days, and put the case back on. You will be amazed at how much better your dehumidifier operates.

■ **Hot muggy kitchen:** During the summer's hottest, muggiest, days the most uncomfortable room in the house is the kitchen. My wife, Barbara, says that the best way to beat appliance heat during the summer is reservations at a restaurant. But I'm too smart for her. I remember she said that was the best way to conserve energy use last winter. If you, like me, can't afford to eat out every night, it just makes sense not to add heat when we are trying to cool the house down. Use the microwave, or reorganize the cooking schedule during the summer. Restrict use of the automatic dishwasher and oven to evening use. Same thing for boiling water.

Remember, your refrigerator has to work twice as hard to keep food cold in the summer. Constantly opening and closing the refrigerator and freezer doors should be a definite no-no. Fill an ice bucket with ice cubes and keep it on the kitchen counter. Train the kids to go to the ice bucket and keep away from the refrigerator.

If there is too much frost in the freezer, you have the refrigerator thermostat set too cold. If the ice cubes in the freezer don't freeze, it's is not cold enough, set the thermostat lower. Dirt can cause the condenser to over heat and burn out. Be sure to clean the condenser coils under the refrigerator with a long handled condenser brush. If you don't have a brush, you can buy one at most appliance parts stores and better hardware stores.

■ **South and west sides of house:** Pull the mini blinds, shades and drapes on the South and West sides of the house during the peak sunlight hours. Windows on these two sides of the house are maximum heat producers. If you have air conditioning, the windows will, naturally, be closed. If you don't have air conditioning, open the windows, but keep the drapes and blinds drawn.

■ **You:** Your body works like an evaporative coil. Keep air moving to the maximum and evaporation will keep you feeling far more comfortable. When operating central air conditioning, the furnace fan switch must be set on the Auto Position only. Turn on ceiling fans, oscillating fans, box fans. The fans will keep air flowing even when the air conditioner is off. You will be more comfortable and may even be able to turn the thermostat up a little. The resulting reduction in the air conditioner's work load will save appreciable amounts of money on your electric bill, as well as making you feel more comfortable.

Put up a good front when you finish an outside wood door

by America's Master Handyman, Glenn Haege

The front door: No other part of the house makes such a clear, up front, statement about you. It is the center of attention from the time guests drives up, until you greet them. It is the first, often the only, part of your house, they inspect carefully while waiting for you to answer. It's color, whether it is stained or painted, says a great deal about you.

If the old front door is bowed and bent, pitted and spent, and you have invested in a new front exterior door, it is important to finish it properly to make certain that it says only good things about you.

Lay the unfinished door on saw horses and sand with 120 grit Garnet sandpaper until the wood is smooth to the touch. Remember: all doors have six sides, an inside face, an outside face, and top, bottom and sides. The top and bottom edges are the two most important areas to the overall conditioning and life of the door. They have cross grained sections which absorb moisture and sliver easily if not protected. When you finish a door, remember to finish all six sides.

Vacuum off the sand particles and wood dust, then wipe the door down with a tack rag to remove any particles.

A soft wood door made from fir should be treated with a wood conditioner. Hardwoods, like Oak, Ash or Aspen, are naturally dense and do not need a wood conditioner. Once again, make sure that you cover all six sides.

In the event that you are going to stain the door, or stain the outside face of the door, do it now. The easiest way is to over apply a good oil base stain, then, when the stain begins to dull down, wipe off the excess until you have the desired color.

When the oil stain has dried completely, apply three coats of a good spar varnish. Thin the first coat 20 percent with turpentine. Make certain that you apply the varnish to all six sides of the door. Take special care to work the varnish into the end grain at the top and bottom of the door to seal the grain. A China Bristle Brush is best for spar varnish. Lightly sand with 400 grit wet or dry sand paper to quiet the grain after the first coat. Always wipe off the wood with a tack rag after sanding.

If you would like a stained and varnished look that will turn the neighbors green with envy, the Sikkens people make a complete line of deluxe, exterior finishes that provide a magnificent, deep luster. Start with a base coat of Cetol 1 TGL Satin (for a satin finish). Cetol 1 comes in a complete range of colors (For more information call Akzo Nobel Sikkens Consumer Information: (800-833-7288).

If the complete door – or the inside face and four edges – are going to be painted, apply an oil base stain kill, like Kover Stain by Wm. Zinsser, as the primer/ sealer coat. Let the base coat dry for about two hours. Wet sanding with 400 grit sand paper at this point will assure an extra smooth, elegant finish.

To wet sand, just fill a bucket half full of water and dip the sand paper into the water from time to time.

Apply one or two coats of a top of the line, acrylic latex, exterior trim paint for the final finish. This will give an attractive, easy to clean, semi-gloss surface. For best results use a Polyester brush and flow the paint on, no short choppy strokes. Make certain that you cover all six sides. An eight hour wait is recommended before you can hang the door to close. Do not even think of cleaning the surface for at least seven days.

One of the best tips to keeping a wooden exterior door looking good, is not to bake it. If you must have a storm door, look into tinting the glass with a product like Scotchtint , or replace the glass with screens, as soon at the days reach 60 Fahrenheit. Scotchtint can cut the heat by 75 percent and block out 99 percent of the ultraviolet rays helping the door stay cooler and keeping colors from fading (for more information, call 3M: (800-480-1704). If the door is left unprotected, direct sunlight can easily heat the enclosed air to oven-like temperatures. Neither wood nor paint like that. So keep them cool.

For more complete directions on painting any exterior siding, surface, window, door or furniture, consult my book, *Take the Pain out of Painting – Exteriors* (Master Handyman Press, P.O. Box 1498, Royal Oak, MI 48068-1498; $12.95 plus $2.00 postage & handling).

Now's the time to sweat over winter's costly cold air drafts

by America's Master Handyman,
Glenn Haege

In the past few weeks there have been days when all of us have thought longingly of snow falls and icicles. Let's get real for a minute. Those cold winter drafts made you so uncomfortable you had to turn up the thermostat a couple of notches, and you wasted a lot of money.

This weekend is the perfect time to track down and eliminate those cold drafts. Go outside and look for bees climbing into mortar joints and unprotected cavities in the soffit overhangs. The cavities in which those bees are nesting, will be a big source of drafts next winter. Don't fill the chinks with mortar yet. Just write down where they are. Wait 'till fall, when the first frost has killed off the bees and you can safely remove the nests.

Next, go down to the basement and check all the basement windows. Every corner that is thick with spider webs and eggs, is a draft access. Mama spider builds her web where there is plenty of fresh air access. Clear away the webs and eggs, clean and caulk thoroughly.

Look down at the floors around doors, anywhere that you see spiders or ants crawling in and out under the threshold is a high draft area. Adjust and caulk under the threshold.

Check around the window ledges. Any sign of water leakage, or wear and tear, is a sign of draft access. Test the wood with a large nail and make certain it is still sound. If there are areas of wood rot, replace them. Small areas can be filled in with an exterior wood filler like Minwax High Performance Wood Filler. If the wood is sound, caulk or seal thoroughly. An insulating foam like Great Stuff by Insta-Foam Products (800-800-3626) is best. Using this stuff is fun. Make sure you don't get any on your hands. While you're at it, seal around the outside water faucets, and access ways for electrical, phone, and cable wires.

Carefully inspect the window glazing. Press the glaze and caulk with your thumb. If it is resilient, fine. If the glaze or caulking compound is hard, replace it. There are special caulk remover tools which will help you with this process. Use a good caulking compound like PolyseamSeal by Darworth or one of the Urethane caulks . They have a more elasticity than regular caulks and keep a tight seal while expanding and contracting with heat and cold cycles.

Keep a lookout for our flying friends, and climbing critters, like squirrels and chipmunks. If they are paying your house regular visits, they can do a lot of damage clogging vents, destroying

> *Check around window ledges. Any sign of water leakage, or wear and tear, is a sign of draft access. Test the wood with a large nail and make certain it is still sound.*

shingles and re-routing water in gutters, causing roof damage. Remove nests, clear away blockages and spray Tangle Foot by The Tangle Foot Co. (616-459-4139) around the affected areas. There is a Tangle Foot product for both birds and four footed critters.

If you have a wood-frame house, check lower boards. Press with an awl or large nail. If the wood feels soft and spongy, it is time to replace. If the wood is sound, caulk or seal. While on your hands and knees inspecting the wood, make certain that the ground slopes away from the house, so that rain water runs away from, not toward, the house.

Proper drainage will dry the boards. lower the humidity in your basement and/or crawl space, and help keep the creepy/crawly critters away. Remember, when it comes to basements and crawl space, dryer is always better.

Finally, go into the garage and check to see if any dirt or grass clippings have blown into the garage even though the garage door was down. If they did, it is a sure sign that the rubber or vinyl garage door seal, called a garage sweep, is worn and needs to be replaced.

I'd like to take space here for a personal note. Hundreds of my good readers are sending me letters asking for solutions to personal problems around the house. Folks, I love hearing from you and will gladly answer your personal questions on my radio talk show, or at my personal appearances around the country.

Unfortunately, if I answered personal letters, I would not have any time for research, writing my newspaper, magazine articles and books, or doing the twenty or so, hour long, radio interviews I do on other radio stations around the country each month. There is only one of me, and try as I may, I can only stretch so far. So please, if you've got a personal question, call the radio show from any part of the country.

AUGUST 12, 1995

What to do if leaky cellar is draining your patience

by America's Master Handyman,
Glenn Haege

The heat, humidity and torrential rains we've been having for the past few weeks have made many of us who thought we had dry basements, rethink the situation. Day after day of rain, improper drainage, and clogged storm sewers, have made many of us call for the Bail-Out Brigade.

Storm sewers should not back up into the basement, but they do. Vacuum up, mop down and sanitize. If this happens more than once, have the line from your main drain to the street snaked out. This should be done periodically. The bigger the trees near your house, the more often it will have to be done.

Some of the information that I'm going to give is late for the present problem, but please, clip this article and keep it in your "how to" file for next time.

If you have standing water, either from a leaky basement or a back up of the storm drains, vacuum up the water with a wet/dry shop vac. Make certain that the power plug is grounded, and wear rubber boots or shoes. Then, mop the entire area with water which includes a good germicide. My friends at Crandall-Worthington, the flooring and janitorial specialists, say their favorite sanitizing rinse is still 10 ounces of Ammonia to 2 gallons of water. Nothing is better or cheaper.

Take out throw rugs or removable carpeting. Professional cleaning and sanitizing is best. Otherwise, clean carpeting with a heavy duty carpet cleaner.

Because this is a multimillion dollar-a-year problem in our area, the Crandall-Worthington people have been on the lookout for years for a product that would do a good job on soaked. They finally found one. The product is Cleanitizer by Betco. It is especially formulated for cleaning and sanitizing with heavy duty carpet shampooers. Crandall-Worthington are the only people I know who stock the product. So if you've got the problem, give them a call (248) 398-8118.

If the floor has damp wall to wall carpeting, get air circulating immediately. If you have a dehumidifier, put it at one end of the room, and locate an oscillating fan at the other. Do not have the fan blowing directly on the dehumidifier. Hook up the oscillating fan to an appliance timer. Six hours on, two hours off, for a total of eighteen hours out of twenty-four. Tilt the fan toward the basement ceiling.

When wall-to-wall carpeting that is very wet and has padding, the padding may have to be replaced. In a worst case scenario, the carpeting itself may have to be replaced.

Storm sewers should not back up into the basement, but they do. Vacuum up, mop down and sanitize. If this happens more than once, have the line from your main drain to the street snaked out. This should be done periodically. The bigger the trees near your house, the more often it will have to be done.

If your sump pump has been acting up, or shuts off at a critical time, check to see why. When the electric power goes out, the electric sump pump stops working. This usually means that the sump pump is inoperative when the need is greatest.

To solve the problem install a sump pump that runs on water pressure power, not electricity. This type of sump pump, called the Home Guard, is manufactured by the Zoler Corporation. It is more expensive than electric models, but the peace of mind is worth the money. For more information, call (800) 928-7867.

You can also install a battery powered back up sump pump. This type of pump is installed on top of your regular pump and runs off a car battery. It automatically turns on, when the power goes off.

Many people with sunken window wells, had their basements flooded. Good well drainage is critical. Debris has to be cleaned out every couple of months. Some window wells have drains. The drains must be kept clear or they compound the problem.

The natural drainage in most sunken window wells is composed of various thicknesses of gravel, topped by construction sand. Natural weathering leaks silt on top of the sand, and starts clogging the gravel. Dig out and replace the clogged sand and gravel. Consider replacing the sunken windows with glass block. You will still have to keep the window wells clear, but the block will give you better protection against flooding.

Meanwhile, back in the basement, if you have a mildewy, damp, dank, smell, hang Mil-Du-Gas Bags to kill the mold spores and keep the fans circulating the air. Mil-Du-Gas Bags have no formaldehyde and are very safe. They are distributed by the Star Brite Corp. of Florida. If you can't find Mil-Du-Gas Bags at your local Hardware Store or Home Center, give Star Brite a call at (800) 327-8583.

Consider more than price when you tool around at stores

by America's Master Handyman,
Glenn Haege

How do you decide where to shop for the retail portion of your do-it-yourself (DIY) dollar? Does it make sense to go to your local mom-and-pop hardware store, or should you shop at one of the large DIY chains? How about out of town – do our local prices measure up to those in other markets?

About the time I was mulling over these questions, I picked up my copy of the August 1995 issue of Do-It-Yourself Retailing. In an article entitled "Chicago Face-Off", Michael Pecen and Walter E. Johnson did an excellent job of analyzing the Chicago market . They listed the major home centers, did a market basket survey of the major players, and queried consumers and store management on the importance of convenience, customer service, price, product information and shopping environment.

As could be expected, price was important to the savvy Chicago shoppers. But convenience and product selection were just as, if not more, important.

Both Chicago and Detroit are top ten markets, have many of the same home centers, and are among the most competitive markets in the United States. The Chicago market has Builders Square, Handy Andy, Home Depot, Menards and Sears Paint and Hardware. The Detroit Market does not have Menards, but we do have Home Quarters.

The authors market basket included 4 x 8 sheets of 3/4-inch plywood and particle board, an 8-foot length of 11/16- x 11/16-inch quarter round, a brass door handle, 5 pounds of galvanized roofing nails, a 5-gallon gas can, a 1-inch 90-degree PVC fitting, a 1/2-inch 90-degree copper street elbow, a 125 v/15 amp receptacle, a 100-foot 16/3 extension cord, a 16-ounce rip hammer, a 2-inch hole saw, a 3- x 21-inch sanding belt, a 2-1/2-inch angled sash paint brush, a quart of denatured alcohol, and utility knife blades.

We decided to survey the same products in Detroit stores and compare the two cities. We included the Damman and ACO hardware chains. Our purpose was to get a feel for our market compared to Chicago; not to tell where to save ten cents on a paint brush.

Home Centers in the Detroit Area had slightly better prices than Chicago. The overall, average Home Center Market Basket price was $105.62 in Detroit Vs $107.18 in Chicago. We pay more for plywood. They pay more for particle board. We pay more for 2 1/2-inch sash brushes and utility knife blades. They pay more for brass door handles.

Home Depot was the price leader in both markets, with a total market basket price of $97.86 in Detroit and $91.45 in Chicago. This was not a consistent, product after product, price advantage, it was on the total buy. Your results might be different if you were shopping for something else.

Home centers are so spread out, and have such a wide variety of products, that finding things can be a time killing hassle. If you are reroofing your house or rebuilding your bathroom, it makes sense to take the time to go where you can get the best combination of selection and price.

ACO had the lowest price, overall, for roofing nails. Meijers did not stock many of the items, but had the lowest prices in both the Chicago and Detroit Markets on 16-ounce rip hammers and 5 packs of utility knife blades. We were impressed at the overall competitiveness of the pricing at the hardware stores.

Price is not everything. It took an average of between 30 and 45 minutes to survey a hardware store, but even though we were professionals and knew exactly what we were looking for, it took about one and a half hours to survey a home center. Home centers are so spread out, and have such a wide array of products, that finding things can be a time killing hassle. It would have taken even longer if we had had to stand in those long Home Center check out lines.

Time is money. It has to be part of the equation. If you are reroofing your house or rebuilding your bathroom, it makes sense to take the time to go where you can get the best combination of selection and price. If you're idea shopping, go to the home centers and specialty stores with the widest selection. But when it comes to week in, week out, general maintenance shopping, don't go to one of the big boxes unless you have the extra time. Your local hardware store is usually very competitive, easy to shop, and has the trained personnel to help you fix it fast and easy.

New-products show hammers home interest in hardware

by America's Master Handyman, Glenn Haege

CHICAGO– Everyone in the industry thinks this is going to be a banner year in the hardware and building materials business judging by the recent National Hardware Show here.

There were more products and bigger displays than ever before. Retailers who ordinarily come to the show alone, brought three or four people this year. Big operations that normally bring six or eight people, brought 12 or 14. That meant close to double the number of people wedged into a thin strip of hotels bordering Lake Michigan. Temperatures hovered between 92 and 96 degrees, with high humidity. Unfortunately most of the hotels – and much of the exhibit area – had under powered or browned-out air conditioning, if any at all.

The show is really two shows: The National Hardware Show, held in conjunction with Hardware Industry Week; and the National Building Products Exposition & Conference. Both shows usually share McCormick Place, so the exposition was moved to Navy Pier's Festival Hall.

The Hardware Show had 2,500 exhibits; the expo had around 500. That's almost 3,000 exhibits extending over 12 miles, many of them huge, two-story affairs. And every square foot was jammed with humanity.

After shuttle bus trips of up to two hours – and when I was able to wipe the sweat out of my eyes – I did see some great new products that should make their way into the Detroit market by next spring or summer.

Today I'll tell you about some of the most innovative exterior products. Next week, we'll go inside.

Keep in mind, the hardware stores and home centers have not even written purchase orders for most of these products, so there is no way that I can tell you where to get them.

Various types of gutter protectors have been around for years but none work that well. The **Flo-Free Advanced Gutter Protection System** might be the solution.

The Flo-Free is a 3/4-inch thick, rigid nylon mesh that fits tightly inside any existing 5-inch gutter and completely seals the gutter system from debris and ice build up. The mesh extends all the way to the bottom of the gutter, so it will not collapse. Leaves and twigs should just blow off. Rain will flow through without opposition.

This same product cut in a larger size to completely fill the bottom of your laundry tub is called **DCI's Wash Tub & Sink Mat.** It should protect your laundry area from clogs caused by discharge from the washing machine forever.

When the filter mat gets clogged, all you have to do is take it outside and wash it out with the garden hose.

Another product worth noting is **Alumin-Nu's Power Clear Liquid Gutter & Down Spout Cleaner.**

Every home's gutter system starts to look terrible after several years. Homeowners often replace because it is the only convenient way to make them look good. Alumin-Nu's Gutter & Down Spout Cleaner could be the solution. It's good on both aluminum and vinyl. You just brush it on, rinse it off. The job's done.

Alumin-Nu is also introducing **Power Pond & Lake Restoration System.** Many people pay premium prices for lakefront homes only to have the lake become clogged with algae and organic deposits.

This product could be the answer. It was extensively tested at the lakes and ponds at Euro Disney. The environmental manager treated the lakes and ponds with power at a rate of 5 gallons per week per 10 acre-feet of pond water. Within eight weeks, the ponds went from murky green to crystal clear. The Power System introduces bacteria which out-compete the algae for nutrients. It's said to be cost-effective and environmentally friendly.

One of the biggest problem areas for decking is around swimming pools and spas because the harsh chemicals play havoc with the wood.

The **Sun Free Vinyl Extruded Vinyl Deck Membrane** could be the answer. This tough, textured, floor covering goes over concrete or plywood surfaces and provides long-lasting, skid-free protection. The vinyl is mildew, rot, fire and UV resistant.

Although it's new to the United States, it has been used in Canada for years. Sun Free Vinyl comes in 20 to 60-mil thicknesses. I expect this product to make the transition inside the house for use in kitchens, baths, and play rooms, where ever a tough, trouble-free surface is needed.

New Hardware gadgets can make living easier – and safer

by America's Master Handyman, Glenn Haege

More than 70,000 industry professionals from 100 countries attended the 50th National Hardware Show held in Chicago.

Last week I told you about some of the more interesting items for exterior use that will be unveiled in the next year.

Today we'll talk about interior items.

■ Home Security was one of the most exciting categories at the show.

So much is going on that I will be devoting an entire article to the subject in the coming months. For now, it is enough to know that the field is being revolutionized for the better. Features are going up, prices are coming down.

Security systems that would have cost $10,000 or more just a few years ago, will be in the $1,500 to $4,000 range soon.

Some of the new features will be a real blessing for older folks, or people who live alone. For instance, you will soon be able to afford to have an inexpensive video camera mounted by your front door. If someone rings the bell late at night, you'll be able to switch your TV over to the security channel and see who's there.

■ Smoke detectors have a vital place in American homes and apartments. All too often, when fire tragedies occur, fire inspectors report that the smoke detector had a dead battery. American Sensor, Inc. is introducing fire detectors with lithium power cells good for 10 years.

When a fire starts in a home, the family only has three or four minutes to get out of the house. A family is sleeping upstairs may not hear a detector going off in another part of the house.

SafeNight Technology, Inc. has eliminated this problem with a new line of smoke detectors that actually talk to each other.

When a detector senses smoke in one part of the house, let's say the basement, it flashes the word to all the other fire detectors in the house, and they all go off.

This feature could spell the difference between the family getting out in time and tragedy.

■ On the environmental scene, a 105-year-old textile manufacturer, Greenwood Mills Inc., the largest producer of denim in the United States, has introduced Greenwood Cotton Insulation.

An excellent example of turning a waste product that would normally go into landfills into a product we all need, the insulation is a 100-percent recycled cotton product that has the R value of traditional insulation. It comes in both loose and Kraft or foil-faced batting.

■ Along the same line, Unilin Decor of Belgium is introducing the Quick Step Floor into the United States.

Quick Step flooring looks like hardwood, but is really a five layer laminate. Not a single tree is cut to produce the new flooring. The core of the laminate is made of recycled wood fibers and branches that would normally wind up in land fills.

Quick Step comes in 18 different colors and designs, from oak, ash, beech and pine to eucalyptus, coral and marble.

This is a real do-it-yourselfer product with relatively easy installation. The "boards" are just cut and glued, not nailed. Quick Step is being imported into the United States by Courey Int'l. (USA), Inc. of Miami.

■ Light tubes, those stove pipe like skylights, have been making a big impression at builders shows because they give more light, are far easier to install and cost half as much as traditional "welded-in" skylights.

SunPipe, by The SunPipe Co. of Northbrook, IL. gives up to double the light of its competitors. The product's increased efficiency is due to a super reflective silver lining. One 13-inch (circumference) SunPipe illuminates up to 400 square feet.

On a sunny day a SunPipe will add up to 1500 watts of light. On an overcast day, light goes down to 200 or 900 watts.

The SunPipe is available with an optional SunScoop that almost triples winter performance.

The weather's just right to brush up on your exterior house painting

by America's Master Handyman, Glenn Haege

This is the best time of the year to paint outside. The weather is cooler and drier and many stores are having paint sales. Now is the time to get it done. Here are some tips to help you do an extra-good job.

Be sure to take advantage of the sales by getting quality paint. The difference between a promotional paint and a high quality paint is only five or ten dollars a gallon. But the difference in quality, performance, and durability, is the difference between night and day.

The choice between oil and latex acrylic paint is up to you. The vast majority of people choose latex acrylic. Oil base paint is more forgiving. If you have to paint over a surface that has a great deal of surface damage, choose oil base paint.

Don't save time by cheating on preparation. Pre-painting prep takes 65 percent of the time. If you paint over dirt, rot, peeling and cracked paint surfaces you can do more harm to the wood than not painting at all.

Always wash the surface before painting. My favorite recipe is 4 ounces of TSP (Trisodium Phosphate) to 2 gallons of water. If the surface is very dirty, use 6 ounces of TSP. If mold or mildew is a problem, add 4 cups of household bleach. TSP is a strong cleaning agent. Wear rubber gloves and goggles. If you add bleach, wear a respirator.

The best technique for washing the surface is to apply the TSP with a long handled deck brush. Rinse with a garden hose. Take special care to protect glass window surfaces.

Let dry a day before painting. While you are waiting, do any recaulking that is necessary. If you had to do a lot of scraping, fill in the scraped areas with an exterior wood filler and sand smooth. Paint all bare surfaces with an oil base, exterior stain kill.

If the paint peeled badly on one or two walls, it's usually a moisture problem. Buy ShurLine Vents at the hardware store and install according to package directions.

Painting is the easy part. Start at the top and work down. Paint in the shade, never in the direct sun. When paint gets too hot, solvents "boil off" and paint will not adhere or weather properly.

Quality latex paints are very creamy and want to spread forever. Don't let them. If you spread the paint too thinly, the job can be ruined.

Read paint can directions for spread rate (probably 400 square feet per gallon). To practice, measure off a 100 square feet (10-by-10-foot) section, and use exactly one quart of paint. This will train you to apply paint properly.

The job will go a lot faster if you use the buddy system, brush/roller technique. One person applies the paint with a long-handled roller. The second person fills in with the brush. If you do it right, the brush person will never have to dip their brush into a paint can.

Follow these simple directions and you'll have a professional-looking job you can brag about for years.

SEPTEMBER 16, 1995

Don't be left out in the cold – check your furnace now

by America's Master Handyman, Glenn Haege

Last week's cold snap was a good reminder that cold's "a coming." It's time to get your furnace ready for winter.

The furnace should be professionally cleaned and inspected every year. Make sure the humidifier tray is cleaned and the evaporator pad replaced. If you have a replaceable air filter, put in a fresh one. If you have a permanent filter, clean it. Consider upgrading to a more expensive, anti-allergy filter.

If you have an electronic filter, check to see if you have been cleaning it every 30 days. If you have let it go for 90 days or more, the filter may be permanently damaged. The service technician can not tell if the air cleaning cells are operating properly just by looking at them. Take the cells to the installing contractor for testing.

If you learn that the cells are damaged, think about whether you should pay to replace them, and repeat your non-maintenance cycle, or whether you should replace the electronic air cleaner with a top of the line, passive air cleaner, like the Air Bear system by Trion. Air Bear filters are so efficient they remove airborne particles as small as 1 micron. That is far superior to most other air cleaners. The only maintenance is replacing the cartridge element every nine to twelve months.

If your furnace was fine last year, and the cleaning technician tells you that it has to be replaced, he may be right. He may also be feeding you a sales line, so be sure to get a second opinion. I recommend you call your servicing utility. Here are a few of the signs that you need a new furnace:

1. A licensed HVAC inspector shows you cracks on the furnace heat exchanger. A faulty heat exchanger could be fatal.

2. The furnace has to be serviced regularly to keep it running during the heating season.

3. Your heating bills are a lot higher than your neighbors.

4. The furnace seems to be running all the time to keep you warm enough.

One of my most frequently asked questions is, "What is the best furnace?" There are many different brands of furnaces but only five or six manufacturers make the majority. While not exactly the same, most are similar.

The most important difference in furnaces is the installing contractor. Make sure you get at least three quotes and check references thoroughly. You want the contractor with the most satisfied customers.

Since 1992, federal regulations have required that all gas furnaces be at least 78 percent efficient. That means 78 percent of the heat is used to heat your house, only 22 percent is wasted going up the flue. Over the past few years the major manufacturers have competed to make their furnaces more fuel efficient. Today, many furnaces are more than 90 percent efficient.

It would seem that everyone would want a 90-plus furnace. Less efficient furnaces have one big advantage: they discharge air (the heat you feel coming out of the register) heated to about 125 degrees. Air discharged from a 90 percent plus model can be as low as 95 degrees. Lower air temperature makes the humidifier less efficient, causing the air to feel even cooler. Maximum energy efficiency cuts heating bills, but you feel colder longer.

Cool drafts are particularly objectionable to people over sixty. If you are sensitive to cold, you may want to stick to a 78 percent or 80 percent efficient furnace that will give you more of the heat you are used to. Conversely, you can consign yourself to wearing a sweater all winter long and get the savings.

Whichever furnace you choose, your home's chimney use will change. Ninety-plus furnaces are direct vent models. Air intake and venting is through a vent out the side of the house. Combustion air comes directly to the furnace from outside.

The 78 percent and 80 percent plus efficient furnaces still use the chimney, but require chimney liners to reduce the diameter and protect the chimney flue. The average price of a 35-foot chimney liner should be about $400 installed.

Home Show

This weekend is my Sixth Home Improvement Expo. It is the one weekend of the year WXYT-AM and I combine forces to show you all the things I talk about all year. Both Rick Bloom, host of *Money Talk*, and I, will be broadcasting from the Show and answering your questions. Joe Gagnon, the Appliance Doctor, will also be there. The show is at the Southfield Civic Center Pavilion on Evergreen (10 1/2 mile) south of I-696. Both the expo and parking is free. It starts at 8 a.m. today and Sunday. I hope to see you there.

SEPTEMBER 23, 1995

Tuck-pointing pointers and other quick fixes from the Expo

by America's Master Handyman, Glenn Haege

Last week's sixth annual Fall How To Expo was fabulous. I got the chance to talk to almost 400 people during the two-day event. Many of the questions were about adding rooms, building houses and upgrading kitchens, baths and basements. Even more were about getting the house ready for winter.

Here are the answers to some of the most asked fall maintenance questions.

■ What's the best way to replace falling mortar?

Falling mortar is not just a cosmetic problem. It's is very important. If you do not fill it in, the surrounding mortar will also shale off and the bricks will become loose. When that occurs you have to take the brick out completely, chip all the old mortar away and butter the brick back in with new mortar.

Mortar replacement is called tuck pointing. The easiest way to go about it is to buy some Mason Mix by Quikrete, a tuck pointer and a joiner.

All you need to add to the Mason Mix is water. You will be able to find all of these items at most hardware stores and home centers.

Mix up a just enough Mason Mix to do the job. Take out all the loose mortar, then refill with the tuck pointer. Compress and shape the mortar with the joiner.

When you are finished the mortar should be inset back from the edge of the brick. If it extends to the edge, the brick will be held too tightly and can be damaged during freeze and thaw cycles.

■ What are the best ways to clean and repaint T 1-11 and aluminum siding?

The standard cleaning method for both T 1-11 and aluminum siding has been to power wash the surface before re-painting. New products have come on the market that give new alternatives.

T 1-11 is a very porous surface. Both do-it-yourselfers and professionals tend to use too much power when they power wash. This often leaves the T 1-11 surface scarred and far too wet.

There are some new brushes by Schaefer Brush (800) 347-3501 with a Water Way handle that hook up to the garden hose and are especially good for cleaning T 1-11. The new brushes include everything from a wire bristle brush for removing scaling to an ultra soft brush for smooth surfaces; in many cases they make it unnecessary to power wash. They are an especially good alternative for cleaning a one-story home.

For a cleaning solution, I would recommend 3 ounces dry measure of TSP (trisodium phosphate) per gallon of water. If there is mold and mildew, add two cups of household bleach. After the T 1-11 has been cleaned and dried, use a water-base latex acrylic solid color stain or paint.

To clean aluminum siding or an aluminum sided trailer without power washing, you can use Power Aluminum Cleaner or Nice and Easy by the Alumin-Nu Corp. One or both of these products will be at your favorite hardware store or home center.

Mix the cleaner with water according to the directions on the container, then apply to the aluminum siding with a brush.

The Detroit Quality Brush Co. (800) 722-3037 makes a bi-level brush with a Water Way handle specifically for this job. It makes the job a lot easier because the bristle tips are always in contact with the surface. Work from the bottom up.

The product will suds up after application. Rinse off with a garden hose.

Quite often these cleaners do such a good job that painting is unnecessary. If you still need to paint, apply a water base stain kill. Let dry for a few hours, then apply a finish coat of a top-of-the-line water-base house paint.

Use a polyester filament brush for smoothing out brush marks

■ What's the best way to replace the joint filler in my driveway?

Go to your hardware store or building materials dealer and get a bag of mason sand, backer rod and asphalt crack filler. Pour the mason sand into the cracks. Tamp down with an ice chopper until the sand is about 3 inches from the top of the concrete.

Insert a strip backer rod and top with 2 inches of a high-quality, pourable grade, asphalt crack filler like AlcoGuard.

New energy code holds up residential building statewide

by America's Master Handyman,
Glenn Haege

We're in the middle of a cat fight folks. As of July 1, all new residential construction has to comply with a new state energy code. Because of that, construction and permit requests for houses and room additions are being held up because of non-compliance all over the state.

State Senator Mike Rogers (R-Brighton) is attempting to get legislation repealing the code on the fast track for legislative approval. This Legislation is now being drafted by the Legislative Service Bureau. This is important to you because, whichever way it goes, it is going to effect your pocket book, your freedom of choice and, quite possibly, your health.

As of today, the two primary contestants are the North American Insulation Manufacturers Association (read insulation makers like Owens-Corning) and the Michigan Association of Home Builders (MAHB).

The code requires more insulation, so, not surprisingly the insulation manufacturers are in favor of it. The contractors, whose sales are directly dependent upon giving the most house for the lowest possible cost, want to do away with the increased insulation requirements.

Briefly, the new code brings Michigan building standards up to a 1993 Federal Model Energy Code (this is *not* the almost universally recognized BOCA Code; it is another governmental bureaucracy). As I understand it, the code has five main requirements: a minimum 78 percent efficient furnace; insulated air ducts over crawl spaces; improved R value for windows; sealing off of all air infiltration openings; and basement insulation.

It would seem disagreeing with the code would be akin to being against apple pie, the American flag and motherhood. However, the issues are a little more complex than that.

By Federal mandate all new furnaces already must be at least 78 percent efficient. The old hollow core aluminum windows are a thing of the past, and the majority of today's windows have two or three layers of glass.

The sealing off of air-infiltration openings was required by the old energy code, and it was universally ignored by both builders and inspectors. (We can assume there is nothing in the new code that will cause either builders or inspectors to get religion, and for reasons I will go into later, I am very glad of that.) Air ducts over crawl spaces are always insulated by good builders and not insulated by shoddy builders. Almost no builders in Michigan insulate basements.

According to insulation industry spokesman, 95 percent of Michigan home builders already meet or exceed all energy code requirements above the basement. Therefore, this entire knockdown, drag-out fight is over basement insulation.

In an effort to get the facts, Murray Gula, a good friend of mine, president of the Michigan Construction Protection Agency and host of *Contractor Talk* on WEXL radio, arranged for me to meet last Friday with insulation industry spokesmen. Saturday I invited MAHB representatives to talk about the new code on my radio show. The two sides, and their interpretation of the code, could not be farther apart.

Insulation industry spokesmen talk about insulating poured basements from the outside. MAHB spokesmen talk about insulating basements from the inside. No one I spoke to had a good suggestion of how to insulate the exposed "collar" of concrete between ground level and the start of the siding.

Insulation industry spokesmen say insulating an average (2,000 square foot) house should cost $1,800.00 retail. MAHB spokesmen say it cost at least $4,000.00, and cited an example of a small, $60,000 Habitat for Humanity house that cost 5 percent ($3,000) more when brought up to the new standards.

I admit I do not know which side is telling the truth. I suspect both sides of fudging the figures.

The insulation industry says the new code is good because homes that comply are eligible for a 2 percent higher mortgage (which should just about pay for the insulation); spokesmen also say the investment also will earn a $2,300 bonus over 30 years.

I asked Rick Bloom, host of WXYT's *Money Talk* and Detroit News Strategy section columnist, whether he thought a $2,300 profit on a $2,000 investment over 30 years was any good. He said it didn't even keep up with inflation. Bloom says a good investment should double every five years, so a $2,000 investment should grow to $128,000.00 over 30 years. If you want to make a $2,300 profit on $2,000, invest your money in basement insulation. If you would rather make $128,000 call Rick Bloom on *Money Talk,* (248) 356-1270, and ask for the name of a good mutual fund.

Another factor supporters use to defend the new code is that all commercial – as well as VA and FHA mortgaged housing – already has to comply. Anyone who remembers newspaper reports about federal office buildings that have had to be extensively remodeled because of sick building syndrome should not be overly impressed with federal building specifications.

This is not an unfair criticism. Many believe that one of the prime causes of sick building syndrome is lack of air infiltration. Not enough fresh air is permitted to enter the building for the health of the people who have to work there. I know that air infiltration is a prime cause of residential sick house syndrome, be-

continued on next page

cause people call me with the symptoms every week. Having a plentiful supply of good, fresh air in your home may not be energy efficient, and it may not be important to the federal government. It is important, however, if you want to continue breathing.

Regardless of whether you like the new energy code, it is the law. It must be complied with and enforced. Enforcement of the code has already been held off for six months because contractors cannot be re-educated quickly enough. According to the MAHB, there are approximately 106,000 state-licensed HVAC and construction trades contractors in Michigan. When the state decides to revolutionize residential construction, a couple of press releases is not sufficient notification. To date, the state has not even sent a letter to the licensed contractors advising them of the change in the Michigan Energy Code. Repeated mailings from the state should be a minimum requirement.

In addition to notification, the 106,000 licensed contractors and approximately 1,100 building inspectors must be educated on the new requirements. According to the reports that I have received from various sources, not more than 500 people (fewer than 5 percent) have even attended classes on the two-month-old code.

Gula and his partner, Pat Murphy, are trying to solve the problem by offering a three-session class on the new code. They can conveniently teach 160 people in a class. Given 100-percent attendance by participants, it will take about 669 classes. At a rate of two sessions a day and four classes a week, that translates into 167 weeks (over 3 years) of classes to get all the trades and building inspectors up to speed.

According to Gula, currently there are only enough copies of the necessary educational materials to teach 1,000 people in the entire state.

The MAHB, which should be taking the lead in solving this problem, really only has 3,700 of the 106,000 licensed contractors as members of its association.

So even if they educated 100 percent of its membership, it would amount only to 3.33 percent of the contractors who need to be educated. Furthermore, can an association that has recruited only 3.33 percent of the potential membership into its organization claim to represent Michigan's residential contractors?

I don't know what the solution is, but we must figure it out. Your new house or addition, and your freedom of choice, depend on the outcome.

If you would like to contact the State of Michigan about this mess, call Henry Green, Executive Director of the Bureau of Construction Codes, at (517) 373-1820, or Jerry Nash at the Department of Commerce, (517) 334-7236.

If you want to get more information on the code from the insulation manufacturers, call Tim C. Grether, Manager of Owens-Corning's Technical Services Department-Insulation North America, at (419) 248-6575.

If you want to learn more about repealing the code, call State Senator Mike Rogers' office, at (517) 373-2420. If you want to learn more about the MAHB, call Janet L. Compo, president of the Building Industry Association of Southeastern Michigan, or Lee Schwartz, MAHB Government Affairs, (810) 737-4477.

And if you want to learn about classes being offered on the new energy code, call Murray Gula, Michigan Construction Protection Agency, (800) 543-6669.

OCTOBER 7, 1995

State products have a brush with success at decorating show

by America's Master Handyman, Glenn Haege

About 300 of the nation's leading decorating products producers displayed their wares at the National Decorating Products Association (NDPA) Show in Chicago last weekend. The biggest design trend is to whole wall treatments. Wallpapering and faux finishes are taking the lead. It seems the decorating industry would rather sell you a whole wall of paper or three or four gallons of paint instead of a roll of border paper.

This was a very ego-satisfying show because two of the biggest raves of the show were Detroit area products I have already featured on my radio shows and columns.

Dave Campbell's Rag Roller, which enables you to get a rag-rolled faux finish with no more effort than it takes to roll a wall, was one of the hits. After I profiled this New Baltimore resident's invention in my books and in an article in Twenty One magazine, Campbell was besieged with so many orders he couldn't keep up with production. He cut a deal with Detroit Quality Brush Manufacturing, (800) 722-3037, to take over the product's manufacturing and distribution. Soon it'll be going nationwide and we'll be able to say, "I knew him when...."

The second Michigan-based rave was by Tapco International of Plymouth. Its plastic Cove Master and Crown Master Interior Molding and Design Master Wainscoting look like fine hardwood moldings, yet can be cut with a scissors, just snap into place and can be installed by anyone. The moldings can be stained or painted just like wood. They make it possible for anyone to put the rich look of cove, crown and chair moldings in their living and dining rooms. (Call Kim Boudreau at (800) 521-8486.)

Masterchem Industries, (800) 733-4413, is introducing Kitchens & Baths Paint, a special strong, easy to clean, mildew resistant, paint especially formulated for the two biggest problem areas in the house. Their Kilz line, (800) 325-3552, is coming out with a low cost, quality, drywall primer for contractors.

Benjamin Moore, (800) 672-4686 is introducing the Pristine line of 100 percent acrylic latex coatings. The new line has no petroleum-based solvents. It is not *low* VOC (Volatile Organic Compound), but *no* VOC. No paint could be kinder to your lungs. Pristine Interior Finishes come in flat, eggshell, semigloss, and latex primer/sealer.

If cracks or nail pops in your walls are constantly appearing, getting fixed, then reappearing, Bondex International, Inc., (800) 231-6781, is introducing a flexible patch in both coarse and smooth. No bridging tape is necessary. This high-performance elastromeric paste is ready

58

> *The biggest design trend is whole-wall treatments. Wallpapering and faux finishes are taking the lead. It seems the decorating industry would rather sell you a whole wall of paint instead of a roll of border paper.*

to use. It dries to a flexible, odorless, weather- and water-resistant patch that can be primed and painted. Flexible Patch makes reappearing cracks a thing of the past.

With the increasing popularity of faux painting, Bondex is also introducing a line of Wall and Ceiling Texture Paint that makes it easy to finish a room or ceiling in stucco, swirls, combing, swirling, or other decorative textured designs. If you want an unusual finish, this is it.

Nu-Porce Products, (800) 994-9970, is reintroducing it's original porcelain repair kit. Nu-Porce is a two part, self leveling, epoxy coating that fills in chips and hairline cracks in porcelain and enamel surfaces. The finish feels dry in

just a few hours but actually remains flexible enough to eliminate cracking, peeling or blistering. It comes in 12 different colors.

Log cabin owners take note: Continental Products Company, (800) 305-5869, has just introduced Gel-Tex stain. This exterior, gelled stain is so thick, the product will not drip off the brush. It is oil-based and gives good protection against UV rays.

Come Spring Detroit Brush Manufacturing will have a new brush especially made to paint the grooves on T-1-11 boards. You paint the grooves with this new, heavy duty brush, then roll the flat portions.

Overheard: The manufacturers are listening to you folks. I can't tell you who, but I've seen the prototypes. Come spring, deck stain removers and completely clear, UV resistant, deck finishes will be on the market. Efforts are being made to get these products launched in the Detroit market because I believe you are the most aware consumers in the nation.

Hot tips eliminate your cold spots when winter invades

by America's Master Handyman,
Glenn Haege

No matter how much we enjoy the fall, winter is coming. And with winter comes cold, drafty weather.

Chances are your home has a room, or at least a corner of a room, that is always too cold. If so the time to take care of that room is now.

If the cold seems to be coming from an outside wall, or a wall between the garage and family room, check the insulation.

If the cold is coming from an exposed window, try a "shrink to fit" interior or exterior storm window kit, or have the window fitted for a magnetic, plastic, interior storm window. Sears is among the retailers that carry them.

If it's cold in the family room, or any room with a cathedral ceiling, the temperature is probably tropical two feet over your head. Put in a ceiling fan and redirect all that nice warm air that you have already paid for, down to where you live.

Check to see if enough warm air is coming out of the register in the cold room. If only a small amount of relatively cool air is coming out of that register, when lots of good warm air is coming out of the other registers in the house, you probably have a lazy furnace problem.

Remember, the furnace doesn't care if the back bedroom gets warm. It just creates heat and dumps it the first chance it gets. For most of us, this means that the furnace takes the majority of the air it needs for combustion from the basement floor. It dumps most of the heat it creates in the living room, or the first few other rooms along its air ducted path.

Your cold room is probably filled with stagnant air. Little or no room air is being drawn into the cold air return, and almost no warm air is coming out of the register. What little air exchange the room has is being drawn into the house, through the walls by negative air pressure.

Don't let your furnace get away with this. It has the ability to make more than enough heat and its blower has plenty of power to distribute that warmth throughout the house. The furnace just has to be tricked into heating the outer rooms.

Call your heating contractor. Describe the problem and tell him or her to balance the heat. This is accomplished by closing down some of the ductwork to over heated areas, and opening the ductwork to the areas you need the extra heat.

If that doesn't solve the problem, consider zone heating.

The lazy furnace has the ability to make more than enough heat and its blower has plenty of power to distribute warmth throughout the house. The furnace just has to be tricked into heating the outer rooms.

Zone heating puts you, completely in control. Your house is divided into two or three zones.

Let's say, the bedrooms are Zone 1. The living room and family room, Zone 2. The kitchen and dining areas, Zone 3.

Each zone has its own thermostat. In the evening, when the family is watching TV in the family room, increase the temperature in Zone 2. Just before bedtime, increase the temperature in Zone 1, and dial down the temperatures in Zones 2 and 3.

One of the manufacturers of zone heating equipment is the DuroZone Division of the Duro Dyne Corporation of Farmingdale, New York.

According to the manufacturer, installing zone heating equipment not only makes you more comfortable, turning down the heat in the unused zones saves between 18 and 23 percent on heating bill.

Zone heating pays for itself in energy savings in about four to five years. For more information call DuroDyne Midwest Corp., (800) 966-6446.

If you look into DuroZone and do not already have a passive air exchange system, like the Skuttle Model 216, in your house, ask the contractor whether he thinks your house requires a passive air exchange, or a powered system, like the DuroZone Dyna-Fresh Air Quality Control System.

Many of our houses are so tight that we need to import fresh air both for heath and comfort, and so that our furnaces, fireplaces and appliances can perform to the best of their ability.

If you have a relatively new house, or have recently added insulation or new windows, the air in your house could be oxygen starved and you will greatly increase quality of life and family health by bringing in a good supply of clean, fresh air.

Be a paper tiger and wallpapering won't drive you up the walls

by America's Master Handyman, Glenn Haege

The holiday countdown has begun. There are only four weekends to Thanksgiving and eight weekends before Christmas and Hanukah week.

If you are going to get anything done, it has to be now.

As I've already told you, whole wall, wall papering was one of the hot decorating trends at the National Paint and Decorating Show. Closer to home, author and paint guru, Brian Santos, told me that wall papering was the most popular mini-course he taught at the Novi Fall Builders Show.

Wall papering is meticulous work. Since you should never wall paper over wall paper, taking the old paper off, is often the hardest part of the job.

I have always been an advocate of using William Zinsser's Paper Tiger and Dif Wall Paper Remover. Brian Santos told my listeners and me how to turbocharge the Dif to make an even more powerful removal formula. His recipe will be listed in his forth-coming book *Potions, Solutions & Recipes for the Do-It-Yourselfer.*

However, the book won't be out before spring, and you need the wall paper off now. So here's Brian's recipe:

1. Remove all moveable furniture, and cluster other heavy furniture in the middle of the room.

2. Cover the furniture with drop cloths, and lay paper or canvas drop cloths on the floors.

3. Combine three gallons of hot water with one 22-ounce bottle of Dif, 1/4 cup liquid fabric softener, one cup of white vinegar, and one tablespoon of baking soda. Pour the solution in a new pump garden sprayer.

4. Go over all the old wall paper with Zinsser's Paper Tiger, The Paper Tiger perforates the paper with countless little holes so that the solution penetrates the wall paper. Spray Brian's solution on all the wall paper in the room three times.

5. Work from bottom up.

6. Take a 15-minute break to let the solution work its magic. Start pulling the wall paper from the bottom up. You may be able to pull it with your hands, or you may have to use a 1-inch to 6-inch broad knife.

Work carefully. The solution will have made the surface so soft your knife can gouge the drywall.

Hard-to-remove wall paper takes a slightly different procedure. Wet down three times, then cover the wall paper with four mil thick plastic sheeting and let it sit a minimum of three hours, or over night. The plastic sheeting will stop the solution from evaporating and keep the enzymes active. If you wait until morning, you should be able to pull the wall paper off in big sheets.

After the paper has been removed, spray the wall with Brian's solution one more time and squeegee it down to remove any paste residue that has remained on the surface.

Before repapering, make certain that all the chemicals have been neutralized by washing the walls down with the Wall Wizard's Astringent Solution, one cup of white vinegar combined with one gallon of water.

If you have a previously painted, but not wall papered surface, scrape away any surface irregularities with a wide putty knife.

Wash the walls with a solution of 4 ounces dry measure of TSP (Trisodium phosphate) per gallon of water and rinse thoroughly. Use sponge mops for the wash and rinse and you won't have to stretch or use a ladder.

Change the rinse water at least once every wall.

When the wall is dry, run your finger tips over the surface. If you find a fine white dust, the TSP was not removed and the wall must be rerinsed.

Fill in any cracks or indentations with spackling paste and sand smooth.

Roll on a coat of an acrylic wall prep like Shieldz Pre-Wallcovering Primer by William Zinsser & Co. The next day you can start papering.

If you haven't already picked out your wallpaper, select a prepasted vinyl wall covering unless you are an old pro. Solid vinyl papers are much easier to put up and maintain. Even with prepasted vinyl, you will get much better adhesion if you use a wall paper paste activator instead of water.

Now, get out and get going. What are you waiting for, Christmas?

Handy products can help keep home spotless for the holidays

by America's Master Handyman, Glenn Haege

Like it or not, Halloween is the start of the Holiday Season. For the next three and one half weeks we will be rushing to make the house practically perfect for Thanksgiving. Then, there's Hanukah, Christmas, New Years. Whew! I get tired just thinking about it.

Many of the products I want to tell you about will not only help you get ready for the holidays, they should be in your holiday emergency kit.

The first products I want to tell you about are Motsenbocker's Lift Off 1-5. This is a series of five products that lift off, not dissolve or melt like most cleaners, paint, grease, ink, adhesive, food coloring, chewing gum, or just about any splash, spray or stain that threatens to ruin the looks of carpeting, clothing, siding, brick, cement, or tile. The products are also completely biodegradable, so you can clean with a clear conscience.

Lift Off 1 Foods, Beverage & Protein Stain Remover takes care of food based stains like chocolate, coffee, ketchup, Kool-Aid, grass, blood, and pet stains.

Lift Off 2 Adhesives, Grease, Oily Stains, Tape Remover zaps chewing gum from carpets; crayons from wall paper, stickers from glass, metal, books, bathtubs; grease and soup stains from fabrics, even silk ties.

Lift Off 3 Pen, Ink and Marker Graffiti Remover lifts ball-point pen, correction fluid, fountain pen ink, India Ink, permanent marker, magic marker, and nail polish from fabric, carpet, walls and clothes.

Lift Off 4 Spray Paint Graffiti Remover lifts spray paint, enamel, semigloss, oil based lacquers, acrylics and urethanes from metal, brick, concrete, Plexiglas, vinyl, any surface with a baked on paint finish.

Lift Off 5 Latex Based Paint Remover removes any type of latex, water base, paint or stain, drip or over spray from carpet, furniture, clothes, concrete or tile.

The complete line of Motsenbocker's Lift Off products are now being carried by ACO and Handy Andy in this market. Builders Square is stocking Lift Off 1, 2 & 3.

Another product that belongs in your Emergency Kit is Harvard Chemical's Red Stainoff. Gigantic stains of red Kool-Aid, cranberry juice, wine, gravy, shoe polish, latex paint on your carpet, couch, or clothing all come off with Red Stainoff. The product comes with a towel in a pouch. You just put the towel on the stain, iron it with a steam iron and the stain disappears. Put the towel back in the pouch and you are ready for the next emergency. Harvard Chemical's Red Stainoff is available at ACO and Damman Hardware.

If the brass, stainless steel, chrome, aluminum, ceramic tile and fiberglass in your home needs a good cleaning, Peek Cleaner by Tri-Peek International, can be a lifesaver. It cleans, shines, and protects in one application. Peek is carried by Sam's Club, ACO, Damman, Meijer's, and Scrubs.

Parker & Bailey is an old line maker of wood treatment products. Their Furniture Creme is the same formula that has been in use since 1819. Now they are introducing Kitchen Cabinet Creme. Your kitchen is the dirtiest room in the house. This product was made for the job. It removes surface grime and leaves the wood looking and smelling great.

Older wood surfaces can be rejuvenated by Parker & Bailey's Orange Oil. Their Wood Floor Polish is a concentrated formula to bring back the life to hardwood floors. One warning, all these Parker & Bailey Products are extremely concentrated. Use too much and you will be wiping the stuff off for weeks. You can find Parker & Bailey at Bed Bath & Beyond, Meijer's, and Damman.

Finally, use Hope's Counter Top Polish to put the dazzle back into any kind of plastic laminate or solid counter top, from Formica to Corian. You'll find Hope's products at ACO, Damman and Meijer's.

To prevent break-ins, break out the lights, locks, pruning shears

by America's Master Handyman, Glenn Haege

How good are your doors at stopping bad guys?

The US Justice Department says that there are two million break-ins every year. That means that one out of every 50 of us will be burglarized this year.

Police can't do it all. It is up to us to make sure that we are not putting out the welcome mat for burglars.

The first thing to check is the shrubbery bordering the entrances. Bushes have been growing with abandon all summer. They are now big, beautiful and offer excellent cover for intruders. Either you or the bushes are going to get clipped.

Get out the pruning sheers and start clipping.

Next, look at the exterior lights. Standard bulbs burn out too often. If you have carriage or post lights, upgrade to something like GE's 75-watt Teflon-coated post lamp. The bulb is designed to stand up to cold and wet. Put it in now and you won't be freezing your fingers trying to change the bulb in an ice-covered lamp post this winter.

How about installing two or three Halogen flood lights and lighting the front, back and driveway?

If you want to go high tech, your local hardware, home center, lighting or electronics store has a wide variety of lamp styles, including those with light sensors that turn on automatically when it gets dark, and motion detectors, that turn on when anyone gets near the house.

Of course, lighting and security gear are only good as long as you have electricity or the back-up batteries are functioning. After that it's up to the holding power of your doors.

Today, almost every exterior door in America is equipped with a deadbolt.

However, not all deadbolts are not created equal. Locks are graded by the American National Standards Institute (ANSI). The ratings appear on lock packaging. Grade 1 locks offer good protection and are designed for light commercial and home use. Grade 3 locks are designed for light residential applications, bedroom or bathroom doors, etc. Make sure your exterior doors are Grade 2 or better.

If it's time to shop for a new deadbolt lock, check to see that the hardened steel bolt is at least 1 inch long; the lock is of all metal construction (plastic parts can be melted); and the cylinder ring spins.

Even a good deadbolt can be kicked in by a pro, but you can make your door almost kickproof.

M.A.G. Engineering & Manufacturing, Inc. makes a series of brass and steel lock reinforcers, strike and latch guards. The brass lock reinforcer is a U-shaped channel that fits over the door and makes it almost kickproof. Adding a security strike plate reinforces the frame and maximizes the protective power of the door.

M.A.G. also makes a complete line of extra-sturdy patio door locks and window security devices. M.A.G. lock reinforcers are available at Meijer, Damman and most other hardware stores (call (800) 624-9942 to get information about their complete line).

Deadbolt locks are also going high tech. The U-Change Deadbolt Lock comes with three different keys and a changing tool.

If there is a possibility the key has fallen into unfriendly hands, you can change the lock yourself in just a few minutes (800) 253-5625.

The Pease Alert-Lock combination door lock and deadbolt provides an early warning system for break-ins. This battery-powered lock is vibration-sensitive. If the door is jimmied or battered, the lock gives off a 130-decibel alarm. That is plenty of sound power to wake you up or alert you in any part of the house and scare the intruder away.

When the lock is secured, it beeps twice to let you know that it is working, and a small red light on the inside of the door lights up. When unlocked, the lock beeps every time a person goes in or out to let you know that someone is using the door.

The Pease Alert-Lock comes as standard equipment on Pease Registry Hardwood Doors. It is also available separately at some lumber yards.

For more information, call Pease direct at (800) 543-1180.

NOVEMBER 11, 1995

Home security is more affordable with the advent of new technology

by America's Master Handyman, Glenn Haege

Imagine you're sitting at home watching TV. Somebody drives into your driveway, or walks up to the front door, and they instantly appear on picture in a picture on your TV screen. If you can't recognize them in the small picture, you just push a button and their image covers the screen.

Imagine you're sitting at the office during a blizzard and worry that the power might be cut to your home or to a cottage. You call the empty house and get a complete report, everything is fine: the electricity is on, the sump pump is working, the temperature is currently 60 degrees.

Imagine you're home alone and hear a noise in the middle of the night, you just press a button and every light inside and outside the house goes on. Then, if you hear another sound and are frightened, you just press the button again and all the lights outside the house start flashing, a siren wails, your bedroom door automatically locks, and the police are called.

Imagine you're soaking up some sun in Florida and the sump pump back home stops working; your house automatically calls up to four friends and tells them about the problem so that it gets fixed before any damage is done.

Imagine your house is empty when an intruder brakes in, and the house calls you and the police and tells you about it. Then the video terminals turn on the VCR, and videotapes the intruder as he moves from room to room. If you have a TV in your office, your house can turn on your office TV and transmit the live action from your home.

If the intruder cuts the electric and phone lines, your house automatically calls police on a hidden cellular phone and tells them what is happening.

Imagine that the same technology turns the lights on and off as you move from room to room; turns your Jacuzzi on while you're driving home; locks all the doors and turns on the security system when you tell it "good night"; makes the breakfast coffee and turns on the lights and radio to wake you in the morning; and precisely monitors your heating and cooling, turning down the heat when you're away, or asleep, warning you not to turn on the dishwasher during expensive peak load periods, and saving you all sorts of money on utility bills.

This technology is already here and it's a bargain. Most people could have a good system installed in their home for $2.00 a square foot. The hidden cellular phone would cost about $300.00 extra. The number of black and white and color video cameras would alter the price, but all are affordable.

If you are a senior, or live alone, you can have a pendant or monitor that is wired for sound and will automatically call up to four different people if you push the button. Once pushed, the monitor keeps calling until one of the people responds.

There can be different programming for when you are home and when you are away and the house is empty. Passive motion and heat detectors can be paired with sound detectors which only go off when glass is broken or wood splintered.

The reason for the affordability of the new systems is the advent of Power Line Carrier, or X-10, technology which permits controllers to be plugged into wall sockets and send signals over existing 110 wiring.

This means that most of the expensive wiring is already done. Only switches and modules have to be installed.

X-10 technology is not just for new homes. Up to 60 percent of the systems being installed are in existing homes according to Steve Reno, president of Automated Electronic Systems (AES), one of the leading installers of total home control systems.

Homeowners can have as much or as little of the home monitored as desired. Some people just want to check the sump pump and furnace. Others want to be able to turn on the heat and lights at a cottage from the car phone. Once a house has been equipped for telephone monitoring, control modules can be given instructions from any telephone, anywhere.

Most X-10 systems are installed by contractors such as AES. They can tailor systems to your exact needs and select from a variety of suppliers to get the system that is best for your needs. AES completely programs the system and trains you in its operation. Honeywell (800) 328-5111 also installs complete systems.

Basic X-10 kits are available at electronics stores such as Best Buy for Do-It-Yourselfers. Radio Shack has a Plug 'n Power system. Or you can call X-10 (USA) Inc., (800) 675-3044, or Home Automation Inc., (800) 762-7846, direct.

When it comes to furnace filters, you really get what you pay for

by America's Master Handyman,
Glenn Haege

If you want to go crazy, try shopping the full range of furnace filters like I just did. A furnace filter costs anywhere from 51¢ for a cheap fiberglass filter to $600.00 for the top of the line Trion electronic air cleaner.

That leaves the consumer a lot of room to get lost.

What's the difference? What's the best? What should you buy?

There is no one answer. The place to start shopping is at your kitchen table, during a needs analysis.

■ Do you have allergies or a severe lung condition?

■ Do you want to cut down on dust?

■ Do you just want your furnace to run properly?

Clogged air filters are a prime cause of service calls. Dirty filters reduce the efficiency in today's high-efficiency furnaces and can damage equipment.

One-inch replaceable fiberglass filters are priced anywhere from 48 cents to 57 cents. You're supposed to buy them and replace them every 30 days. Many people forget and let filter replacement slip for 60 or 90 days.

You get what you pay for.

My advice is not to bother with the inexpensive filters. The next step up is to the $4 to $6 range. A $5 filter is at least twice as effective as the fiberglass kind. Some are up to seven times more efficient. Most only have to be replaced every 90 days.

There are many different brands in this price range. I am just going to include a few that are to be found in the local market. Most come in flat or pleated filter construction. Some of the flat brands include the AAF (American Air Filter) High Efficiency at $4.99; and the BP Precisionaire Washable at $3.71 to $4.31.

Quality features include electrostatic anti-microbial construction. Electrostatic means that in addition to the filter action, some of the materials in the filter are made to have a slight negative magnetic charge with the friction of air passage. This traps positively charged mold spores and other microscopic elements like dust attracted to a TV screen. Webb products has a frame and four replacement pads, for about $16.

Pleated replaceables include the Magnet 3000 at $5.99 and the Dust Guard High Efficiency at $4.99. They are electrostatic and antimicrobial. At the top of the line of this type of filter is the 3M Electrostatic Micro Particle Air Filter at $13.99.

I am partial to the pleated design and from everything that I have read, 3M's Filtrete air filter traps a greater percentage of the extremely small microbials than any but the most expensive electronic air filters. If I had allergies or a lung condition and did not want to invest in an electronic filter, this is the one that I would buy.

Regular furnace air filters also come in semipermanent and permanent styles. The semipermanent styles have permanent plastic frames you cut to measure with replaceable filters.

Air Kontrol's Static Shield costs $19.97. The filter is washed every 30 days and replaced every two years.

Webb's Adjustable Electrostatic Air Filter costs $23. It is washed every 30 days and replaced every three years.

If you have an older furnace and want to upgrade to a permanent filter, the price, at approximately $33 to $39, is very economical. Like the semipermanent filters, they have to be taken out and washed every 30 days to maintain effectiveness.

Permanent filters include 3M's Reusable Air Filter, Air Medic by Air Kontrol and the Webb Plus Permanent Air Filter. It is very easy to forget to change your filter. One brand, the Whistle Adjustable Air Filter by Newtron Air Cleaners, whistles like a tea kettle when it needs to be cleaned. This feature makes me partial to this filter in the permanent category.

None of the permanent and semipermanent filters I looked at are as effective as the 3M Electrostatic Micro Particle Air Filter at $13.99.

In a later article, I will cover the expensive, installed equipment furnace filters such as the Trion Max 4 and 5 Electronic and Air Bear Replaceable Air Cleaners.

If you are buying a furnace, and need to make the decision right now, consider whether you have a great need for extra clean air. If so, they are worth the money, and you should look into buying a furnace like the Rheem, Rudd, or Comfort Air, with a special filter speed setting, so that your air can be cleaned constantly throughout the year. If not, the filters I've written about make very good, money saving alternatives.

Santa's bag: Hardware stores for those do-it-yourselfers

by America's Master Handyman, Glenn Haege

Tis the season to go crazy looking for Christmas and Hanukkah gifts. This year, like every year, your friends and neighbors are going to go out and mob the malls. If you don't like all the congestion, or just can't stand circling one more jammed parking lot, here are some tips on gifts that you can get for that handy man or woman on your list.

You can find them at relatively uncrowded hardware stores or can still get them delivered by mail. As with all nationally branded items, prices are different at different stores.

Power tools are not just for men. But how do you know what to buy?

I asked Bill Damman of Damman Hardware what kind of a power tool he would get a kid sister who had just moved out of an apartment and into a condo.

Bill said that he would choose either a cordless screwdriver or a cordless drill. Both are extremely versatile.

A Black & Decker 2.4 volt, cordless screwdriver goes for around $23. A 3/8-inch, 7.2 volt, 2 speed cordless drill in Black & Decker's new VersaPak series goes for around $40.

Bill would lean to giving the drill because it is a lot more powerful and can be used as both a drill and a screwdriver. The deciding factor might be price.

Rubbermaid has a new tool box that is perfect for a handyman or woman who wants to get organized. One side opens up to a foam padded tool storage area, the other side opens to a divided, storage parts area. It's priced at $19.99.

You don't have to confine yourself to the tool section. Many hardware stores have excellent housewares sections. Just as women have crossed over and now do many do-it-yourself jobs about the house (or are contractors and build or remodel houses for a living), a lot of men handle a good portion of the cooking and cleaning.

Two items I think are big improvements are Ekco's air insulated cookie sheets and the Miracle Thaw. The air insulated cookie sheet is doubled bottomed, non stick, and keeps cookies from burning. Prices start at $6.99.

The Miracle Thaw is just a metal alloy block that speeds the natural thawing process of any frozen object that is placed on it. It is slower than the microwave, but thawed food still looks fresh, not partially cooked.

It's priced under $40.

I asked Bill Damman of Damman Hardware what kind of a power tool he would get a kid sister who had just moved out of an apartment and into a condo. Bill said that he would choose either a cordless screwdriver or a cordless drill. Both are extremely versatile.

Now here are three gift ideas for my favorite people: radio talk show enthusiasts. Many listeners say they love my show, but for some reason have difficulty tuning in the station. The problem is that most manufacturers have forgotten that the AM radio band exists and devote all their attention to FM.

The GE Super III portable radio, receives FM signals, but its claim to fame is that it has twice the AM reception power of any other radio sold in the United States. It is not available in most stores, but is available by mail order for under $60.

Another almost impossible item to find is the Reel Talk, extended recording, AM/FM radio with built in slow speed cassette recorder. This radio enables a listener to record up to four hours of radio on one side of a 120 minute cassette. The Reel Talk costs $129.95.

It's a real find for anyone who is really into talk.

My final radio gift idea is the Power Dialer. This is an expensive, and totally unnecessary gift for anyone who is not a talk show junky. However, if you have someone on your list who positively must get through to make their opinion heard, or someone who cannot stand busy signals, the Power Dialer will take over for their finger and dial the number 25 times per minute until they get through. The price for all that finger power is $249.95.

These last three items, should be carried by every audio store. Unfortunately the only place I can guaranty is the C. Crane Company of Fortuna, California. I consider this company to be one of my greatest "finds." The company's catalog is crammed with so much information I keep a copy on my desk at the office.

Their toll free telephone number is (800) 522-8863.

Happy holiday shopping.

DECEMBER 2, 1995

Selecting the wrong snow melter can put you on thin ice

by America's Master Handyman, Glenn Haege

It's time to get ready for all that good white stuff mother nature is going to throw our way. Buying ice and snow melters should be at the very top of your to do list. Unfortunately, almost all ice and snow melters look alike. What should you buy? How should you apply it?

According to Steve Klochko, president of Gibraltar National Corp., the local manufacturer of Quikrete products, most people pour on huge quantities of ice melter and expect the product to eliminate ice and snow. This wastes money and poisons the environment.

The purpose of an ice melter is merely to break the bond between ice or snow and the drive or walk way. Ice melters should be scattered broadly, like chicken feed, when the snow is just beginning to fall. Then, when the snow is four to six inches thick, the snow and ice can be easily shoveled or pushed away.

There are three major categories of ice melters: rock salt (Sodium Chloride), Calcium Chloride and Potassium Chloride. The great temptation is to buy rock salt. Halite, Morton Safe-T-Salt, is one of the most commonly carried brands in the Detroit Area. At anywhere from $3.16 to $4.19 per 50 pound bag, rock salt is about one third the price of Calcium Chloride and half that of Potassium Chloride. You just buy the product to throw it away. Why not buy the cheap stuff?

Unfortunately, rock salt is a marginal de-icer. Salt water run off can be very harmful to lawns and shrubs and often leaves a white residue when the brine evaporates. Salt is only effective against ice when it becomes a brine solution. It loses this ability at about 20 degrees. When the temperature is lower than 20 to 25 degrees rock salt just lies there.

Calcium Chloride, appears in the Detroit Market as Quikrete DuoFlake, Prestone Driveway Heat, and Sno Melt, among other product names. It is one of the most efficient ice melters. It is effective down to 25 degrees below zero. According to Klochko, the reason that Calcium Chloride is so effective is that when Calcium Chloride dissolves, it creates heat, which melts ice, dissolving more Calcium Chloride, creating more heat and keeping the process going. Rock salt, Potassium and Urea all need external heat to keep melting.

Calcium Chloride often is sold in 10-, 20-, and 25-pound sacks because of the cost of the product. Prices range from $4.87 for 10 pounds to $8.99 for the 20 and 25 pound sizes at local hardware stores and home centers. I saw 50 pound sacks of Quikrete DuoFlake for $11.97 at Home Quarters. That seemed a very good price.

If you have to use an ice melter around delicate trees, plants and shrubs, Potassium Chloride is recommended by most horticulturists. You'll find it under such trade names as Ice Melt Plus, Rid Ice, and Zero Ice Melt. Home Quarters carries Ice Melt Plus for $7.66 per 40 pound sack. Damman's has Zero Ice Melt for $10.49 for 50 pounds. To use in garden settings, they also carry Lake State's Ammonium Sulfate, a fertilizer that also melts snow and ice, for $5.49 per 25 pound bag. Home Depot carries Vigoro Ice Melt, a Nitrogen/Potassium based ice melter, at $12.26 per 80 pound bag, for the same purpose.

If you have a concrete patio, sidewalk or driveway that is less than one year old, do not use any chemical ice melters. Apply play sand or kitty litter for traction.

Here's two more products to help you fight the snow. First, the Sno-Ho by Michigan Brush. This very light weight tool lets you hoe instead of shoveling, greatly reducing heart and back strain . It is available in the Yankee and Good Catalogs for $19.95, (800) 225-3870. Damman Hardware sells it for $14.95. They also carry the Melnor Roof Rake. This light weight rake stores in a five foot box, but assembles to a 16 foot length for easy removal of snow from roof and gutters. It is a little bit pricey at $34.99, but well worth the money if it saves you from having to climb a ladder in the middle of the winter.

Suddenly I feel the urge to visit my folks in Florida. Want to come along?

DECEMBER 9, 1995

Get rid of condensation before your windows become all wet

by America's Master Handyman,
Glenn Haege

If there is so much condensation forming on your windows that you may have to start bailing, it is time to find out what is wrong. Windows are not wells. They do not make water. If they did, the Saudis would buy a billion of them and turn their deserts into lush farm land.

When condensation forms on a window, it is trying to tell you something. Condensation usually forms in three places on a modern window: on the inside of the window pane; on the outside of a window pane; and between the panes in double and triple paned windows. Each has a different cause and a different solution.

Condensation on the inside of a window pane is a sign that air born water is trapped in the house due to poor air circulation and exchange. This usually means that the furnace is not getting enough air for proper combustion. To test this, tape a piece of kite string to the molding above a window. Make certain that all the windows and doors are tightly closed. Wait until the furnace goes on. After the furnace has been on for about two minutes, open the window.

If the kite string goes outdoors, against the screen, you have positive air circulation and do not have a problem.

In the event the string blows in, your house has negative air pressure. You do not have enough combustible air in the house and, most probably, you do not have sufficient air exchange for good health. If you have a forced air furnace, you can probably eliminate the condensation by turning on the furnace fan for several hours.

The easiest way to actually fix the problem is to call your heating contractor and have a passive air make-up unit, like the Skuttle Model 216, installed. Do-It-Yourselfers can install the Equalize-Air by Xavier in Livonia, MI, (734) 462-1033. If you do not have forced air heat, Skuttle also makes a defuser unit to bring in fresh air.

Lately, there have also been complaints from people reporting condensation on the outside of their double pane, Low E glass windows. This is not a problem, but a sign that the Low E coating is working and reflecting heat back into the house. This condition usually occurs in the spring and fall, when there are relatively warm, humid days and cooler nights.

As the relatively warm, moist outside air comes into contact with the insulated, Low E outer glass, the pane is actually cooler than the air temperature. Condensation forms on the outer pane, like droplets of water form on a glass of iced tea on a hot summer's day. This condensation problem will correct itself as soon as the outside air temperature grows colder and less humid.

> *When condensation forms between two layers of glass in a double-pane window, it is a sign that the airtight seal has been broken.*

When condensation forms between the two layers of glass, in a double paned window, it is a sign that the air tight seal has been broken, allowing humid air to penetrate between the panes. The only way to fix the problem is to replace the glass.

Since seal failure is often caused by an error in the original installation, it will be replaced by the manufacturer if the window is still under warranty.

One final type of condensation occurs between single pane windows and exterior storms. Storm window frames are made with a breathing hole that permits condensation to escape. These breathing holes often become plugged or puttied shut over time. When this happens, moist air becomes trapped and condensation appears. To fix the problem unplug the holes.

Also consider taking off your exterior storm windows because they are really ineffective. If you have double or triple pane windows, you don't need them. If you have single pane windows, you will find interior storm windows far more effective. You can get interior storm windows installed by Sears, or call Crystal Enterprises, 248-583-4300. Do-it-yourself interior storm window kits are available from the Window Saver Company, (800)-321-WARM.

If you want to learn more about window condensation, Andersen Windows has produced two excellent brochures, "A Guide to Understanding Condensation," and "There's Condensation on the Outside of My Windows!" David McGraw, the president of Kimball & Russell, Inc., a local Andersen Windows distributor, has offered to send you a copy of these brochures free of charge. To get your copies, send a post card with your name and address to: Master Handyman/Windows, P. O. Box 1498, Royal Oak, MI. 48068-1498.

Here's how to take all those spills and stains out of your holidays

by America's Master Handyman,
Glenn Haege

'Twas the night before Christmas
and all was shining bright,
except for the windows,
and they looked a fright.

When Mom spied the windows
she screamed with alarm.
"The relatives are coming,
especially Aunt Marm!"

They'll "ooh" and they'll "ah!",
then she'll whisper like a cat:
"Her windows are dirty,
can you imagine that?"

Now Dad was a loyal listener,
so he didn't flinch.
He knew cleaning frozen windows
was a Handyman cinch.

Dad grabbed his sponge and his
bucket,
his squeegee and towel,
Then raced out to the garage
for a keen eyed prowl.

Auto window washer solvent
was the magic stuff,
If you wear rubber gloves,
it is more than enough.

He poured the solvent in a pail,
with not a drop of water.
Then he sponged and he squeegeed,
and wiped up like he ought'er.

The windows sparkled like diamonds
Mom bubbled with delight.
Aunt Marm wouldn't find any dirt
this Christmas night.

If your windows are dirty
you can do this too.
It's my way of saying,
"Merry Christmas!" to you.

The Christmas & Hanukkah Season is a fun, festive party time. That means it is a disaster waiting to happen. Somebody is going to spill something. The way to keep your cool when the inevitable happens is to be prepared in advance. Here are the ingredients to my Spill & Stain Emergency Removal Kit. Like most things, there is "some assembly required," so put the kit together now and stay calm later.

Glenn Haege's
Spill & Stain Removal Kit
1 box inexpensive facial tissue, white not colored
1 can foamy style men's shaving cream
1 bottle club soda

No substitutions. Paper toweling is not "just as good" as facial tissue. Facial tissue is far more gentle and absorbent.

Wet Spills
(wine, pop, soup, gravy):

Blot, not rub, with facial tissue. When the excess moisture has been absorbed, spray area with shaving cream. Blot the foamy shaving cream into the stain. Blot dry.

Blotting is the secret to this operation. Rubbing spreads the stain. Blotting contains the stain.

When you have completed blotting, lay a 1/2-inch thick pad of facial tissue, weighted down with a heavy book or brick, on top of the stain for at least ten minutes. You will be amazed at how much extra moisture this will absorb

Dry Spills:

Carefully remove all the dry ingredients you can, then sprinkle with club soda. Blot up with facial tissue.

Upholstery Spills:

Apply shaving cream. Do not rub. Take several tissues in your hand and blot with a pinching motion. Repeat as often as necessary. Remember, rubbing and wiping spreads stain. Blotting and pinching contains the stain to the affected area.

Candle Wax:

Finally, a use for paper toweling!

To remove candle drips from fabric or carpet, place a single sheet of paper toweling over the candle dripping. Iron the toweling with a very hot iron. Do not use a steam setting. As the toweling heats, it will melt and absorb the wax. Remove the paper toweling and repeat the process with fresh pieces of toweling until all the wax has been absorbed.

Next time, buy dripless candles.

White Rings on Furniture:

Moisten baking soda with lemon oil and mush the mix into the stain with your bare fingers. Keep mushing. If the mix becomes too dry, add more lemon oil. Wipe up with facial tissue. Do not use paper toweling, it is not as absorbent and could scratch the surface. If the white ring has not been completely eliminated, repeat the process until the stain is gone.

When the stain has been removed and all the debris has been cleared away, apply a thin coating of lemon oil to all exposed wood.

Scuff Marks:

To remove heavy scuff marks, use a waterless, non-abrasive hand cleaner like Go Jo™ or Fast Orange™. Rub the cleaner into the scuff mark with your hand until it softens the scuff. Let stand for two minutes, then take facial tissue and wipe up the hand cleaner. Repeat if necessary.

Live Christmas Tree Watering:

A Christmas tree is a natural humidifier. That wonderful pine smell that makes a natural tree so wonderful is water vapor that has been given off by the tree. The water has to be replaced or the tree will dry out and become a fire hazard. A freshly cut Christmas tree needs a great deal of water. My tree, for example, uses about 3/4 gallon a day. Water two or three times a day to make sure the tree is getting all the moisture it needs.

Chapter 2

1996 Articles reprinted from The Detroit News HOMESTYLE

Ten projects for the new year could save you money and your life

by America's Master Handyman,
Glenn Haege

If you've made a New Year's resolution to get your house in order in 1996, this is my "honey do" list for you. Some will save you time, some will save you money and some could even save your life.

1. Install a plug in, not battery-powered, carbon monoxide detector in the hall leading to the bedrooms.

Battery-powered carbon monoxide (CO) detectors have proven to be ineffective in the field and are the prime cause of unnecessary fire departments runs. Plug-in CO detectors use a different type of filter that is trouble-free.

2. Make sure there are fire detectors on every floor, change batteries every New Years Day.

ACO Hardware, in conjunction with Channel 7, are offering smoke detectors for less than $4. Every house should have several. Every apartment, every college dormitory room should have at least one.

3. Upgrade the furnace filter from cheap ($1 or less) to a top-of-the-line replaceable (from $6) or washable permanent air filter ($20 to $150).

The inexpensive variety just filters the air for the furnace equipment, not for air quality. If better air quality is your goal, start by installing a better quality furnace filter. Some people worry that installing a good filter in an older furnace may cause undue strain to the blower motor. Furnace experts tell me that blower motors are, for the most part, so overpowered that this need not be a cause for concern. So put in the better filter and breath easier.

4. Have the heating air ducts cleaned and sanitized if they have not been sanitized in the last five years.

No mater how much you filter the air in the furnace, if the ducts are dirty, the air coming out of the registers is dirty, too. Air ducts are a prime breeding ground for germs and mold spores. They should be cleaned and sanitized about once every five years and whenever a furnace is replaced.

5. Install an electric set up/set back thermostat.

Installing – and using – a set up/set back thermostat can save you hundreds of dollars a year on fuel.

If you are humidity conscious, ask about the Honeywell Perfect Climate Control Center Thermostat, model PC8900. This high-end thermostat not only lets you adjust the furnace humidity level from the hall, it has an optional outdoor temperature sensor that will automatically regulate the furnace humidity level to compensate for outside weather conditions. Call Williams Refrigeration and

Heating for more information, (888) 268-5445.

6. Install ridge and soffit vents in the attic. If the house does not have soffits, have combo vents installed.

Your attic has to breath "in" and "out." Proper air circulation will keep you home warmer in winter, cooler in summer, and will prolong the life of your shingles and roof sheathing. To learn more about combo vents call (800) 456-5649.

7. Install more roof and wall insulation.

More insulation with proper ventilation will save you money. Insulation provides the quickest return on your home-improvement dollar. You should have enough insulation in your home to have the attic qualify for at least R38 Wall insulation should be at least R11. The higher the "R" value the better.

8. Change the shower heads to a water-regulated 2.5 to 2.9 gallons per minute model.

They will give you longer, hotter showers while saving you money. Teledyne Water Pik shower heads have the necessary features at prices we can afford.

9. Install anti-scald turn-offs on hot water faucets and shower heads.

This is especially important if you have young children or older adults in the house. If it's time to replace faucets, Delta has lines of faucets that shut off automatically if the water gets dangerously hot. Otherwise, call the Reliance Co. for the retailer nearest you who carries Scald Safe faucet and shower adapter kits: (800) 243-2862.

10. Test your toilet for water leakage.

Pour food coloring (the ugliest shade you have), in the water closet and let stand for one hour. After the hour, lift the toilet lid and see if the color of the water in the bowl matches the color in the water closet. If it does, you have a water leak. Replacing the flapper ball (not the float arm), will conserve water and save big bucks on your water bill.

JANUARY 13, 1996

Stop hacking and sneezing and invest in a good furnace air cleaner

by America's Master Handyman, Glenn Haege

Everything we do seems to create indoor air pollution. Every time we cook or use a portable vacuum cleaner (a big dust polluter), paint or aerosols, shed skin cells, hair or dandruff we are adding to the problem. Our pets breath and shed skin, hair and dandruff, too. Meanwhile newer rugs, composite boards, heating elements, cleaning solutions and other household chemicals, all leach noxious stuff into the air.

Many of us are allergic to this mess. We get runny noses, irritated eyes, and hacky coughs. To make matters worse, it seems as though we have to dust every time we turn around, and walls and upholstery get dingy in no time at all. After about 20 years of hacking, sniffling and needless cleaning, many people decide to investigate a furnace air cleaner.

The Navy had a similar problem – multiplied about a hundred times over – in their nuclear submarines. They turned to electronic air cleaning technology developed by Trion Inc. of Sanford, N.C. This technology is available to you with the Trion Max 4 and Max 5 electronic air cleaning systems.

Return air is channeled through an aluminum mesh prefilter, removing most of the larger particles, like lint, hair, skin flakes and much dust. Smaller particles become negatively charged and attracted to grounded plates located in the back of the filter. A high percentage of the particles become stuck and stay there until washed away in the dishwasher. After cleaning, air passes through an optional charcoal filter to remove lingering odors and goes into the furnace for heating and dispersal throughout the house via the air ducts.

The same technology is now available from most major manufacturers. For instance it is used in the Lennox EAC12, the Honeywell F50F and the Carrier 31KAX electronic cleaners. Rheem, Rudd and Comfort Air furnaces even have a special filter speed setting, so that the air can be continuously filtered.

The other major method of cleaning furnace air is to send it through a thick-pleated, media filter that traps airborne particles like a sponge. Once every 10 months or so, the filters have to be replaced and thrown away.

This type of media filter system is available from most furnace distributors with brand names like Trion Air Bear, Research Products Corporation Space Guard or Honeywell Media Air Filter. Since the media filters are thrown away every 10 months to a year, replacement filter cost is an important feature. Prices range from about $30 to $50.

A lot of people ask me whether a media filter or an electronic air cleaner is better. The answer depends upon your lifestyle, needs and pocketbook. Price is easy. Because this is not a do-it-yourself project, you have to go though a HVAC contractor. An electronic air cleaner should range between $550 to $650 installed. The installed cost of a media filter is about $375. Options and nonstandard sheet metal work can increase prices.

Operating costs on electronic systems run just a few cents a day and use the same amount of electricity as a 40-watt bulb. The only other cost is the hot water and detergent used cleaning the system every 30 to 60 days. Media filters cost little or nothing to run but have to be replaced every 10 months to a year.

Electronic air cleaners take a great deal more care than media filters. They have to be washed in a dishwasher every 30 to 60 days. Older models specified 30 days, newer models call for cleaning every two months. If the filter is not cleaned properly it ceases to function.

If you forget to clean the air cleaner for five or six months, they are hard to bring back. Richard Frayne from Hinson Heating in Royal Oak says that most people can get the air cleaning cells working again with just an extra dishwasher cleaning. Jim Williams of Williams Refrigeration and Heating in Warren recommends soaking really dirty cells in the laundry tubs with liquid detergent, then running them through the dishwasher.

Media filters require no care. You just take out the old filter and slide in a new one, every year or so.

Media filters are effective down to 1 micron in size. Electronic air cleaners are effective down to 1/10 of a micron (.1 microns). Most hay fever and allergy sufferers react to breathing in pollen, molds, spores and pet dander, which are seldom smaller than six microns. For the majority of people, a 1-micron filter is effective. Smog, some dust, tobacco and cooking smoke particles are .1 micron or smaller. Viruses are too small to be filtered out by either type of air cleaner.

Two things you should remember when shopping:
■ A filter is good only when it is working. That means that to clean the air in your house 24 hours a day, seven days a week, 365 days a year, the blower motor has to be working constantly, not just when the heating or air conditioning is on. Therefore you have to buy, or your contractor has to adapt, a furnace to operate at an ultra-low speed, whenever the blower is not in use heating or air conditioning.

■ The filter is only as good as the delivery system. If you buy an electronic air cleaner that makes the air going into the furnace squeaky clean then distribute it around the house through dirty ductwork, you wind up breathing polluted air. Ductwork should be cleaned and sanitized every five years.

JANUARY 20, 1996

Sinking money into old bathrooms and kitchens usually pays off

by America's Master Handyman,
Glenn Haege

Many people ask me if it is worth the money to remodel a kitchen or bath if they are going to live in the house just a few more years. The kitchen and bath are the two most important rooms in your house. If the work is done well, and in line with other homes in your neighborhood, you cannot lose money upgrading.

After prospective buyers have looked at your home's exterior, including the all-important roof line, and decided they like what they see, the next things they want to see are the kitchen and bath. These two rooms are usually the deciding factors on whether prospects want to move in or move on.

When it comes to the kitchen, everything is up for grabs. Lighting is very important. If it is too dark, consider improved lighting, new windows, garden windows or sky lights.

Upgrading ventilation and electrical service is important. Consider installing the newer, more powerful ventilation units. There is no reason why the ghost of fish or cabbage past should be haunting kitchens of the present.

In addition, most kitchens do not have sufficient power. When you turn on the microwave and the TV picture gets snow flakes; or a combination of the toaster, radio and mixer blows a fuse, you know the wiring needs to be upgraded.

If the cabinets are old and not works of art, replace or reface. Be sure to include features that make it easy to access every area, and provide efficient storage for equipment and supplies .

Paint and wallpaper are very important. Borders can give a kitchen a delightful personality. Faux finishes, like ragrolling and sponging give walls a papered look that is uniquely yours and will never peel.

Consider upgrading countertops, sinks, faucets, garbage disposals, floors and appliances. Dupont Corian and other newly developed composite materials make highly attractive countertops, and because they are solid materials, they don't show wear or scratches.

Sinks now come in a wide selection of materials – not just porcelain and stainless steel. Water filters on the cold water lines to the sink and to the refrigerator ice cube tray really improve the taste of food

Top-of-the-line appliances can sell a house. Many an upwardly mobile, two-career couple has bought a house because they lusted after the gleaming, stainless steel, professional stove. Even if they have all their parties catered, in their mind's eyes, they saw themselves making breads, pastries and roasts in the huge convection ovens. These are the things of which dreams are made.

One caveat, before I convince you to invest your life savings in your kitchen: The value and features of your house should stay in proportion to your neighborhood. If you live in a hot residential area, and your neighbors are investing in paved walks and deluxe shadow line shingles, feel free to go wild. If real estate values are almost stagnant, upgrading is an investment in your quality of life, not your house. Renovate but keep it practical.

Baths are becoming mini spas. Even though you cannot expand the floor space, there is a great deal you can do to upgrade it. One of the most popular items is a whirlpool tub. Improvements in design have made it possible to replace a standard tub with a same-size whirlpool model.

Other noticeable improvements include Corian, or other composite material countertops, sinks and shower surrounds, faucets, toilets and floors. Get rid of those 1-by-1-inch floor tiles if you have them, and upgrade the ventilation.

Pressure-balancing shower controls are a must. Make all faucets scald-safe. If your bathroom windows, like most are unsightly, seriously consider glass block.

Most bathrooms do not have nearly enough power for modern electrical requirements. Hair dryers, curling irons, shavers and heaters all use electricity. If you live in an older house and the wiring has not been updated, call in an electrician and clean up the circuits. Have some dedicated to bathroom use. Install Ground Fault Circuit Interrupt (GFCI) switches and plugs.

Lighting is key. According to Essie Wells, manager at Haig Lighting and Electric in Clinton Township, (810) 791-2380, the biggest mistake most people make is choosing a light fixture on looks alone. "You have to know how much light you need, how much light a fixture can give," she said.

Too often people buy fixtures with little decorative bulbs. If real light is required for makeup, shaving and so forth, a minimum of a two-light strip fixture using 60 watt bulbs, halogen or florescent fixtures is needed.

Buy a carbon monoxide detector, but measure its readings carefully

by America's Master Handyman, Glenn Haege

We know that carbon monoxide is an invisible killer. But what does it mean when the carbon monoxide(CO) detector goes off? Probably not very much. It may mean that its a foggy day, that somebody turned on all the burners on the gas stove at one time, or that cleaning product fumes have concentrated and set off the alarm before normal household air currents whisked them away.

A CO detector measures parts per million (ppm) of carbon monoxide in the atmosphere. As little as 400 ppm can kill a person within three hours; but turning on the burner or even putting a cold pan on a gas stove can send a harmless 500 ppm spurt of carbon monoxide into the atmosphere. If the CO detector is in or near the kitchen, that could set off the alarm says Chief William Crouch of the Royal Oak Fire Department.

Many CO detectors are so sensitive that their alarm goes off when the inhabitants are perfectly safe. This oversensitivity is especially common with earlier (1- or 2-year old) battery-powered models that use a different sensor than plug-in, or hard-wired, detectors.

When the alarm on a CO detector goes off, the owner's natural tendency is to get frightened and call 911 or the gas company. The number of false alarms has become so great that it has caused concern among fire departments and power companies around the country.

In 1994, the Chicago Fire Department had more than 8,000 false carbon monoxide runs. In Michigan, Consumers Power logged 8,418 in that same year. In 1995, the number of Consumers Power calls was up 55 percent, to 12,279, according to Bob Gluszewski, CO detector program & safety manager. "In over 85 percent of these calls there was no problem or just a short-term problem," he says.

Randy Fryfogel, fire marshal of the Southfield Fire Department, says that most of his department's calls are also blank runs. Even though the firefighters test dwellings with $3,000 multigas detectors, they usually cannot recreate the problem which originally set off the CO detector and they find little or no traces of carbon monoxide.

Nationwide, the high quantity of needless runs put a strain on fire department and power company budgets and manpower. A fire engine or power company truck responding to a false alarm may not be available for a genuine emergency.

Consumers Power and Mich Con charge for responding to carbon monoxide calls. Most fire departments no longer respond to a carbon monoxide call with an emergency run, unless the call is made in conjunction with a medical emergency.

Chief Crouch and Don Stanford, assistant chief of the Royal Oak Fire Department, believe that the number of false alarms will decrease as the public becomes more sophisticated in CO detector use.

The Royal Oak Fire Department, like most fire departments, trains its dispatchers to look for fluelike symptoms and ask a series of questions to determine whether a medical emergency exists. The symptoms include headaches, breathing difficulties, nausea, dizziness, confusion or tiredness, or a cherry red skin or mucous membranes. If a caller lists any of these symptoms, the call is treated as a medical emergency – carbon monoxide exposure – according to Stanford.

Consumers Power has put together a brochure, "Make the Right Call," that explains carbon monoxide poisoning and tells what to do when the carbon monoxide detector goes off. Call (800) 477-5050 for a copy.

Here's how to respond if your CO alarm sounds:

Open doors and windows, turn down the furnace and water heater, turn off unvented appliances, and check flues and chimneys for obstructions. Check the base of the water heater for soot, and check the attached garage and basement to make sure that no vehicle or small engine is operating.

If the problem persists and the cause can't be found, the brochure recommends calling Consumers Power or another qualified contractor immediately.

Consumers Power and Mich Con sell private label CO detectors. Their prices are about $20 to $40 more than similar models in hardware stores and home centers. The added cost gives buyers free carbon monoxide service calls for five years. Otherwise Mich Con charges $44 and Consumers Power charges $45 for a carbon monoxide inspection.

If you do not have a CO detector, I suggest you put one on your shopping list. The ones with the digital LED displays that show CO levels are definitely worth the extra money.

FEBRUARU 3, 1996

If you can't stand the cold, be sure to check out these space heaters

by America's Master Handyman, Glenn Haege

Some room or corner of the house – the family room, the back bedroom, the den – is always colder than the rest. If you can't balance the heat coming from the furnace heat ducts, an electric space heater is a good temporary solution.

Initial cost is low, but operating cost is high. Space heaters pull power from the same 120-volt electric circuits you use to light the house and run the vacuum cleaner. Since they can use up to 1500 watts of power, they can starve the power supply, pop fuses and damage other household appliances.

There are different categories of space heaters: plastic, metal, ceramic, baseboard, oil-filled, radiant, quartz and parabolic. New technologies like halogen and UF elements, are also being introduced.

All use convection or radiation heating. Convection heats the area. Radiation heats the object it touches. plastic, metal, ceramic, baseboard. The new UF heater, and oil-filled heaters are convection heaters. That is, they heat the room. You get warm as the room heats up.

Quartz, parabolic and the new halogen heaters use radiation. You feel warm faster with radiant heating, but if someone or something stands between you and the heat source, the heat is blocked.

Circul*air*'s Silent Sunburst Halogen Heater uses sealed, translucent quartz tubes and tungsten heating elements filled with halogen gas to create a radiant style heater that is much warmer and more cost efficient than other parabolic or conventional radiant heaters. The Silent Sunburst retails for $100 to $130.

Vectacor's UF High Efficiency Heater uses a newly developed heating honeycomb heating element first used on Taiwanese jet aircraft. The UF (ultimate filament) element is at least 20 percent more efficient than standard heating elements. The company claims you get more heat for less money than with standard ceramic heaters. They estimate savings of $20 a month. Vectacor is a new Canadian company. Its high-efficiency heater costs about $100.

The last place in the world you want to be cold is the bathroom, yet because of the damp environment there is a fear or using high powered electrical appliances. Circul*air*'s Elite Bath & Beyond Whole Room Heater is loaded with extra safety features, like automatic circuit disruption if the unit becomes wet. Bath & Beyond lets you choose between 750- and 1500-watt power use. It turns on automatically if the temperature goes below 40 degrees Fahrenheit, and has a child-resistant control panel. Prices range from $59.99 to $79.99.

The Pelonis BathroomDisc Heater produces heat with three very efficient ceramic discs and distributes it with an industrial grade fan. Although the heater only uses 1100 watts of power, it is rated at 3700 BTUs. The Bathroom Disc Heater is equipped with a ground fault detector right in the plug, which means you could throw it in the bathtub and not get a shock. Recommended retail is $49.99.

Duracraft's Eurostyle Heater Fan has a stylish curved design, adjustable tilt feature that directs heat wherever it is needed, 1000- and 1500-watt settings, and a child-resistant switch for under $50.

Dry heat is fine. Moist heat is better. Holmes Total Comfort Heater/Humidifier combines a high-performance heater with a warm mist humidifier. Both the heater and the humidifier can be used separately. Heat is provided by a nickel-chrome multiribbon heating element. The heater has 750- and 1350-watt heat settings and Holmes' exclusive Child-Safe FlatPlug. The recommended retail price is $99.99.

Vornado made its name in fans. Their VortexHeat Model VH combines its innovative fan design with a 1500-watt heater to circulate heat throughout the room. It retails for $89.99.

For those who want a plug-in baseboard heater, Duracraft has a new 24" Space Saver that tilts to put heat where you want it for under $60. Homes has a Dual Arm Baseboard Heater that can turn around a corner for about $80.

You won't find all of these heaters in any one place. If you are looking for specific models, call the manufacturer and ask where to find them. If you are just going to shop, plan on checking out at least four or five different stores.

Here are some manufacturers' phone numbers to get you started: Circulair Inc., (800) 647-7749; Duracraft, (800) 554-4558; Holmes, (800) 546-5637; Pelonis USA Ltd., (800) 842-1289; Vornado Air Circulation Systems, (800) 234-0604; Vectacor Inc., (800) 371-0770.

FEBRUARU 10, 1996

Here is what's hot, new and snazzy at a local home and garden show

by America's Master Handyman, Glenn Haege

The first local home and garden show of the year is exciting because, no matter how many national shows I've been to, the local shows illustrate what really is going to be happening right here where you and I live. It's also a good opportunity to test the pulse of the local market.

We read a lot of national statistics, but the only building and consumer confidence statistics that affect our lives are the ones which reflect the interests of the people and businesses where we live. How excited are the people? Are they going to grab the future with both hands, or sit back and wait?

Last week's Spring Home & Garden Show at the Novi Expo Center told me two things. First, it almost seems that if you are not having your kitchen or bath upgraded this year, you are in the minority. The show was inundated with kitchen and bath remodelers and designers, and closet and cabinet specialists.

Trevarrow, Inc., the big Auburn Hills Appliance Distributor, had their top-of-the-line, restaurant quality appliances by Bosch, Sub Zero, Gagenau, and Viking on display. Just looking at those really first-class appliances can be hazardous to your pocketbook. One of my editor's best friends fell in love with a $2,000 refrigerator and will not be satisfied until it is in her kitchen. Same with the high-end fixtures displayed by Nu-Way Supply. Throughout the show the trend was definitely upscale and the displays were filled with serious shoppers, not lookers.

Which leads me to my second point: The Novi Expo Center was crowded with buyers. On one of the coldest Saturday mornings on record, people with plans to upgrade their houses were lined up and trying to get in, a half hour before the show opened.

After the show, exhibitors were almost unanimous in saying that it looks like this will be a banner year for all types of building and remodeling in Michigan. If you want or need to have something done this year, call now, so that you can get near the beginning of the line. Otherwise you may be out of luck for the '96 building season.

Spas have been a fixture at builders shows for a long time, but this year, interior whirlpool baths, many with innovative designs, took center stage. One company, Pure Water Whirlpool Systems of Warren, will even adapt your existing tub to a whirlpool.

Here are some of the other new things I saw at the show:

■ The Whistling Frog Tile Co. of Ferndale, fires tiles to the customer's specifications. If you want a one-of-a-kind floor, or wall design, they can make if for you. They also create unique tiles for use as gifts or promotions, and wall tile designs for kitchens and entrance ways as well as beautiful hand-cut, free-form, tile murals. Richard Prukler, the founder, learned his craft at Pewabic Pottery and still does design work for Detroit's most famous potters.

■ Materials Unlimited of Ypsilanti featured magnificent antique doors, as well as new, plus hardware and mantels.

■ The Rock Shoppe of Plymouth introduced a new line of lightweight, easy-to-move artificial rocks. Almost everyone likes the look of granite boulders in their landscaping. The trouble is, they take a forklift to move. You can pick up these babies with one hand yet they have the look and texture of native stone.

■ Michigan Window Tinting of Brighton and Farmington now has a do-it-yourself, cut-to-fit window tinting program featuring Lumar Window Film, which is definitely less costly than similar films. Window tinting is becoming increasingly common because of fading and glare problems.

■ Although the majority of its work is with large commercial construction, Calculus Construction Co. Inc. of Farmington Hills has developed a new technique for lifting and stabilizing foundations with helical piers that solves the problem of sinking basements. (A few builders' problems with sinking basements have gotten a great deal of media play in recent months. If you are unlucky enough to be that one in 10,000 homeowners confronted with the problem it can be a nightmare experience.) The same technique is an effective, relatively low-cost way, to put a stop to basement and retaining wall bowing. I hope you never have the problem. But if you do, this new technique definitely warrants your consideration.

Naturally, there were a hundred other displays that showed innovative new materials and techniques that I do not have room to write about. You can only get the real flavor of a show only by walking the show floor. If remodeling your home or building a new one is in your plans and you missed the Novi show, make it a point to go to the upcoming shows Feb. 29-March 3 at the Pontiac Silverdome and March 16-24 at Cobo Center.

Brush away the February Blahs by repainting a room or two

by America's Master Handyman, Glenn Haege

OK, so the winter's got you down. You looked into the mirror this morning and could not think of a place where you would rather not be. The dingy, dirty walls are crowding in on you. The house that seemed so bright and festive just two months ago, is tired and old. The furniture is old. The paint is old. The flooring is dingy.

You have a case of the February Blahs. The Builder's Shows give a short time high, but when you get back home, the house looks even worse. There is nothing wrong, with you or your house, that a couple gallons of paint can't cure. We can have you proud of yourself and smiling again in 48 hours.

It used to be that you couldn't paint in February without being driven from the house or forced to open the windows and let in the frigid air. The fumes from oil based paint could make you feel light headed. Water based latex paints gave off a painty smell that hung around for weeks.

At least two major paint manufacturers now have no, or low, odor Acrylic Interior Latex paints. Kurfee's (800-626-6147) has their Fresh Air line and Benjamin Moore (800-344-0400) has just introduced their Pristine line in a flat, eggshell, semi-gloss and primer sealer. In addition, Atlanta Sundries (now Lily Industries) has Odor Zapp Paint Odor Eliminator (800-253-3957), a special additive, which, when added to a conventional paint, makes the majority of the odor causing ingredients to sink to the bottom of the paint can.

Using any one of these three products you can paint without fear any time of year. Here's the most efficient way to do it:

Clear the room of as much as possible. Then man-handle the big stuff into the center of the room. If you uncover any really dirty/dusty spots on the floor, sweep or vacuum up so that you don't start spreading dust. Cover tables, chairs and book cases, with cheap plastic drop clothes. Use only paper or canvas drop clothes to cover the floor.

Wash down the walls with TSP and water, Dirtex, or Wash Before You Paint. TSP does a great job. If you are cleaning the kitchen, or a room in which a smoker puffs away, use Dirtex because it includes both TSP and Ammonia.

To wash down the walls use from 2 to 4 ounces of TSP or Dirtex in a gallon of water depending on the amount of dirt. When you use either of these products you have to rinse thoroughly after washing. Change rinse water every wall. The buddy system with one person washing, the other rinsing works best. If you use sponge mops you won't get a sore neck. If you would prefer not having to rinse, use Wash Before You Paint.

After the washing, let dry four hours. Mask all areas which need to be protected with 3 M Blue Painter's Tape (800-364-3577) or Daubert Chemical's EZ Mask (800-634-1303). They both also have some excellent tape and plastic combinations for masking large areas that need to be protected.

Now you are ready for painting. Start with the ceilings because they are the hardest. Paint the corners first. Start in a corner and paint a three or four inch wide border around the ceiling with a 2-inch trim brush. Be sure to paint right up to the wall edge with your initial stroke. Use this as a guide when you paint the wall.

Now, use a roller with a Mr. Long Arm or other long handle to paint the rest of the ceiling. The roller you choose depends upon the texture of the surface. A smooth section requires 1/4-inch to 3/8-inch nap. A lightly textured wall requires 1/2-inch nap. Semi-Rough surfaces require 3/4-inch nap. Rough surfaces require 1-inch nap.

Roll across the narrow not the long angle of the room. You will have tendency to cover too large an area. If you do that, the paint will appear streaky and you will have to repaint.

When you finish the ceiling, do the walls. Use the paint brush or a Shur-Line paint pad (716-683-2500) to paint a 4 inch border around the walls. Then finish off with a roller.

The actual painting takes far less time than the preparation. After you paint, the surfaces will probably be dry to the touch within four hours. Let the paint cure for a seven day week before you wash.

You've got the time and you're not going anywhere, so February is also great time to experiment with faux finish painting. If you need some guidance, look through a copy of my book *Take the Pain Out Of Painting – Interiors* and faux finish one wall. Sponging, feather dusting, combing, are all very interesting, relatively easy faux finish techniques. Next month, Dave Campbell's rag roller will have area wide distribution and you can rag roll your walls. Call Detroit Quality Brush (800-722-3037) for the dealer nearest you.

Dirty ducts can cause illnesses, but cleaners can clear the air

by America's Master Handyman,
Glenn Haege

Until about twenty years ago, very few people even knew about air duct cleaning. Now it's a growth industry. My friend, Mike Palazzolo, at Safety King, also runs a duct cleaning school and is getting inquiries from as far away as Malaysia.

The reasons for the sudden interest are that houses are getting tighter, increasing the prevalence of indoor air pollution, and consumers are getting smarter.

Inside air is far more polluted than outside air. Efforts to lower energy consumption through tight construction and energy efficient HVAC systems, often create concentrations of pollutants ten to 100 times greater than that found out doors. That's one of the reasons why I demand that higher air quality standards be built into new energy codes. I don't care how well insulated your house is, if you can't breath, you can't listen to my radio shows or read my columns.

Most people spend about 90 percent of their time indoors. About half of that time is in our own homes. Infants and elderly people send virtually 100 percent of their time in their homes. The quality of the air we breath at home is a matter of life and death importance.

Stachybotrys, a nasty little member of the mold family, can be found in about 5 percent of American homes. Generally it is in homes with a chronic moisture problem, i.e. where drywall or ceiling tile has been damp for an extended period. The mold breeds in the wet cellulose, then gets into the duct work and spreads through the air.

Connie Morbach of Sanit-Air, showed me research reported in the October '95 issue of Indoor Air Quality Update, linking Stachybotrys with neurological disorders, such as memory loss and sleeplessness in adults and death in infants. A recent study in Cleveland linked it with 11 infant deaths.

Aspergillis, another member of the mold family spread through dirty ductwork, is related to chronic infection in the respiratory system. There are also dust, dust mites, human and pet hair, and various other forms of allergens, that often accumulate as an up to 15 pound, 2-inch thick layer of debris lining the air ducts in many houses.

To find out if you need to have your ductwork cleaned Morbach suggests taking off a cold air return register to see how much debris has collected. If it looks dirty, go to the furnace room and bang on the air return duct work.

If you hear rattling, that is chunks of concrete and drywall, nails, etc., the duct work should be cleaned. If it sounds like a dull thud, it means debris is lining the ducts, and needs to be cleaned out. If you hear a hollow booming sound, the duct work is clean.

Not all cleaning is equal. Some firms just open the registers and clean a short way into each opening. Other firms vacuum, then spray a petroleum based concoction into the ducts to immobilize the rest of the crud.

The only form of duct cleaning I recommend is Source Removal. Firms using this technique usually use truck mounted vacuums that generate 20,000 cubic feet per minute of cleaning power. They go to the furnace area, cut holes in both the cold air return and heating ducts, and clean the entire length of the duct work, then clean the furnace.

If you decide that your home's duct work should be cleaned the next decision is whether it should be sanitized. If your family suffers from chronic flu-like symptoms: headaches, runny noses, malaise, difficulty breathing, or suffer from allergies, sinus, or bronchial conditions there is a good chance that the duct work should be sanitized.

Your home is also a good candidate for sanitization if it has undergone remodeling, flooding, or fire; or if there are unusual or unpleasant odors. There are two primary methods of sanitizing duct work: chemical and the ozone. Both work. I'll write more about duct sanitizing in my next column.

When looking for a duct cleaning company, check out its bragging rights. Make sure they use source removal techniques. Mike Palazzolo (the friend with the duct cleaning school) has a list almost 60 companies that do duct cleaning in this area, but there are only 12 companies in Michigan with certified duct cleaners according to the National Air Duct Cleaners Association in Washington, DC. If you'd like a recommendation from the association, call (202-737-2926).

Sanit-Air (888-778-7324) is a duct cleaning company that also does indoor air quality assessments, and specializes in the ozone method of sanitizing. They have a certified ozone technologist on staff and are members of the International Ozone Association. Safety King (800-972-6343) is one of the oldest specialized companies in the business. A-1 Duct Cleaning (800-382-8256), Dalton Environmental (800-675-2298), and Sterling Environmental (888-992-1200) are other companies that specialize in duct cleaning. Flame Furnace (313-527-1700) and Bergstrom Heating & Plumbing (313-522-1350) are heating contractors that also do duct cleaning.

You'll probably breathe a bit easier after sanitizing your home's ducts

by America's Master Handyman, Glenn Haege

Recently I explained how mold's, mildew's and microbe's food sources can be eliminated from ductwork in your home. However, simply cleaning ducts does not decontaminate them. If you or anyone in the house has allergies or breathing problems, sanitizing may be a good idea.

The two main methods of duct sanitizing are chemical application and ozone generation. Chemical application is the traditional approach. Oxyne, the chemical of choice for duct cleaning, is effective against a very broad range of microorganisms, says Michael Palazzolo of Safety King, a duct cleaning specialist.

During chemical sanitation, Oxyne is fogged into the ductwork. All chemicals strong enough to sanitize, are strong enough to harm, so it is recommended that people – especially chlorine sensitive people – and pets leave the house during application. They may return safely an hour after the ducts have been treated.

The chemical method destroys 99.99 percent of all mold, bacteria and spores with which it comes in contact. The chemical agents become inactive within four or five minutes of application and degrade into a non-volatile substance after drying.

The second sanitizing method, ozone generation, decontaminates the entire house, not just the air ducts. Drapes, carpets, basement – everything is sanitized. The procedure takes 24 hours. All pets, plants, and people must be absent during that time.

During the Ozone sanitizing, an ozone generator creates Ozone molecules by using an electrical charge or ultra violet light. All the happy little microbes get zapped and become harmless CO_2 molecules.

This process is becoming an increasingly popular method of sanitizing and odor removal. It is used extensively in medical, fire and flood repair. Some companies rent ozone machines to the general public. To my mind, ozonation is definitely not a do-it-yourself project. It should be done by a specialist company, like Sanit-Air, that has Certified Ozone Technologists.

The ozone method of sanitizing is chemical free and 100 percent effective, says Connie Morbach of Sanit-Air, who has a Masters Degree in Hazardous Materials Management, recommends it for allergy suffers, chemically sensitive individuals, and for use in homes that have water damage.

Central Vacuum Systems

I have a vacuum cleaner on each floor of the house, a shop vac in the basement, and a hand held for all those little odd jobs. You may have more.

The question is, "Why?" Granted, vacuum cleaners pick up dirt, but they also spread dust. They have to be cleaned out regularly and make a terrible mess if the replaceable bag bursts. Vacuum cleaners cost anywhere from $85 to $1,400. Most homes have at least $300 to $500 of them hanging around taking up valuable storage room.

There has to be a better way. There is. It's called the central vacuum system, and its been around for 40 years. A central vacuum system is about eight times more powerful than a portable and all the clutter and dust is eliminated. Inconspicuous hose connections connect to a central power plant located in the basement or garage. When you want to clean the carpets, or drapes, or stairs, you just connect the vacuum hose to one of the outlets and clean to your heart's content.

It's smart. It's logical. So why aren't we using it?

Our Canadian cousins are a lot farther ahead of the game. According to Dan Zimmerman of Zimms Vacuums (800-664-1105), 75 percent of all the new homes built in Canada are prepped for central vacuum cleaning systems. Only a small fraction of US construction is prepped for centralized systems.

Here are a few facts: Even the best portable vacuum cleaners spread dust. Central vacuum systems, like the Vacuflo and Beam, the two major brands, maintain up to 98 percent cleaning efficiency, and exhaust the remaining 2 percent of small dust particles outside not inside the house.

With a central vacuum system, the heavy equipment is eliminated. All you carry is a cleaning wand attached to a vacuum hose. The systems have all the standard vacuum cleaner tools.

I like the central vacuum systems primarily because they reduce dust and improve air quality, but they also cut down on noise because the power unit is not located in the living area.

Any house can be fitted for a central vacuum system. An average size house can be retrofitted for about $1,000.

If air quality is a priority in your home, duct cleaning, sanitizing and a central vacuum system may make you breath a little easier.

MARCH 9, 1996

Make sure the spring add-on really adds on to your home's beauty

by America's Master Handyman, Glenn Haege

Two sure signs of Spring are crews punching holes for new homes and laying slabs for room additions. New homes mean people have faith in the future. Room additions mean that people are happy with their communities and want to grow with them.

If you plan to "add on" this year, make sure that your addition fits the architecture of the house and the surrounding neighborhood, or you may not get your money back when it comes time to sell your home.

The exterior look of an addition is just as important as the interior. No matter how nice and snug it is inside, if it takes away from your home's appearance, it will reduce its salability.

If you have a brick home, try to match the brick when you build a ground level addition. If the home is Tudor or Californian, make sure that the addition is a complimentary style. Don't add a California Modern addition to a standard colonial.

Sun rooms can add an interesting look, and are accepted on most types of architecture. If the reason for the addition is to shelter a spa, it's a great idea. But be careful, an enclosed spa area should have its own heating, cooling and ventilation or it will spread an amazing amount of humidity throughout the home.

Dormer additions can enhance or destroy the look of a house. Skillfully done they turn a bungalow into a colonial. Badly designed, they can give a house an unbalanced look that makes you think it may collapse in a stiff wind. Your modernization salesman may not be the best advisor here. His or her job is to sell you, not to be concerned about resale.

If you only need to add one bedroom, don't just perch a lump on the left or right side of the house. Center the room, or better still, extend the addition to include the entire width of the house.

If you want, you can finish only the interior of one room leaving the other side vacant. Even unfinished, the extra room will be a big selling point.

It is usually quite easy to extend the plumbing service to a new addition, but electrical, heating and cooling systems may be a problem. Make certain that the new addition has plenty of electric circuits. If the rest of the house is under powered, this might be a good time to upgrade the electrical service for the entire house.

Check with a heating and cooling contractor to make certain that your home's present heating and cooling plant has sufficient capacity to extend to the addition. Your home's existing systems may well be maxed out and not be able to handle the additional load.

So far your decision has been based on need and emotion. "The kids are getting older and *need* a room of their own." "The house is too confining, we *need* a family room and an extra bath." "Mother is coming to live with us and *needs* a bedroom, sitting room, kitchenette and bath." "We like the schools, community and neighbors, and *want* to stay here."

It is wonderful that you have a stable community and a happy home. But before you sign on the proverbial dotted line, check the alternatives.

Find out what your house is worth in the present market. Add the price of the addition. Let's say your present house is worth $185,000. The addition will come to $50,000. Doesn't it just make good sense to see how much house you can buy for $235,000 before committing to the addition?

You may find that you couldn't duplicate the house and addition for $275,000. That makes the addition one heck of a deal. On the other hand, you might find that you could get the house of your dreams in a brand new subdivision for the same money, or that there is a house a mile away with everything you need for only $200,000. In that case, even if you pay $5,000 to move, you can still save $30,000. Wouldn't that money look better in your retirement fund than the builder's bank account?

Mother-in-law additions, like the one I described above, are expensive. At time of resale they are hard to get a dollar for dollar return, because they are atypical. If you are lucky, and some one is selling, at the same time you need the additional room, you may find that you can duplicate most of the features of your present house, plus the mother-in-law wing, and still save $25 to $35,000 over the cost of building. That, of course, is sad for the seller, but if someone has to loose money, wouldn't you prefer that it be the other guy?

You may decide that regardless of the money, you choose to stay where you live. I applaud that decision. Just make sure that you have all the facts before you decide. Then brag about it!

Seminars offer you the know-how for many home projects – all free

by America's Master Handyman,
Glenn Haege

Anyone who has listened to my radio show for more than a month knows that my three favorite expressions are: "Learn all you can before you do;" "The most important tool in your tool box is your check book;" and "Glenn Haege's favorite price is free!" That's the gist of this week's article.

The early birds among you have already begun the process, reading newspaper and magazine articles, watching and listening to TV and radio shows, and attending the Spring Builder's Shows. Novi was great. The Silverdome was a blast. The Cobo Hall International Builders Home, Flower & Furniture Show and the Michigan Kitchen & Bath Show, today through March 24, is the last and the biggest of them all. This is the first year the Builders Show and the Kitchen & Bath Show have been combined, so it should be spectacular.

Now come the Seminars. Joel Helfman and his son, Adam Helfman, of Fairway Construction led off with a top flight remodeling seminar at the Southfield Civic Center, Tuesday, March 12. It was attended by about 400 people who saw two hours of presentations on home remodeling, and then had a chance to network one on one with Fairway's builders, architects, designers and craftsmen, plus financial people, Murray Gula, Pat Murphy and myself.

I emceed the event and talked about the remodeling process. Murray Gula, president of the Michigan Construction Protection Agency, spoke about the protections and pitfalls of the Michigan Lien Law. Franklin Building Inspector, Pat Murphy spoke about construction permits, contractor qualifications, job sites and the various other pressures of remodeling. Financial advice was given by representatives of Harris Financial and Green Tree Financial.

Topics were designed to help consumers make the best use of their hard earned dollars. All at Glenn Haege's favorite price: Free.

Even if you missed the Fairway Seminar, and the earlier builder's shows, you don't have to loose out. If there is a major how-to project in your future, one or more of the area's finest retailers has probably scheduled a seminar that will give you much of the information you need.

For the most part these are fast paced information events led by professional crews and manufacturers representatives. Here is a listing of some of the seminars occurring in March and April. When you go, take your plans with you, grab as many brochures as you can, and don't be afraid to ask questions.

If you want to attend one of these seminars and I have listed a telephone number, call ahead so they can be certain there is sufficient room for all interested parties.

If you don't find a seminar that covers a subject you want to learn more about, call your local retailer and ask if he is having a seminar on the topic. There is a good chance that he is, and I haven't heard about it, or that he will be if he gets a couple of more calls from interested, prospective customers, like you.

■ ABCs of Remodeling Seminar: Michigan Association of Home Builders-Remodelers Conference; 9:30 a.m. today and March 23, Cobo Hall, (810) 737-4477.

■ Building Your Own Sun Room; TEMO Sun Rooms, April 6. Clinton Township, (800) 344-TEMO.

■ Buying Or Selling Real Estate: Century Twenty One – Royale. 7-8:30 p.m. March 26 in St. Blaise Hall, Sterling Heights, (810) 268-2244.

■ Construction Financing: N. A. Manns. 9:00 a.m. today and 7 p.m.. April 17 in Canton Township, 7 p.m. Tuesday and

April 16 in Monroe, 9 a.m. Thursday and 7 p.m. April 11 in Trenton, and 7 p.m. April 23 in New Boston, (800) TRY MANS.

■ Deck Building: Dillman & Upton will have programs 7 p.m. March 28 and April 25, Rochester (248) 651-9411. N. A. Manns will have clinics 7 p.m. Monday, Tuesday and Thursday, Down River (800) TRY MANS.

■ Decorating On A Budget with Virginia Ficaro: Builder's Square. 1-3 p.m. April 20 in Dearborn, May 5 in Sterling Heights and May 18 in Waterford.

■ Faux Finish Painting: Mercury Paint. 1-2:30 p.m. Monday in Flint (810) 733-8810, March 25 in Livonia, (313) 421-6830, Mach 27 in Madison Heights, (248) 585-0990.

■ Lawn Care: Area Home Depot stores, 11 a.m. Saturdays in March.

■ Measuring and Installing Anderson Windows: John's Lumber 7 p.m. April 20 in Clinton Township, (810) 791-1200.

■ Pipe Connecting: Area Home Depot stores. 2 p.m. Saturdays in March.

The real world of remodeling isn't pretty, so look before you sign

by America's Master Handyman, Glenn Haege

So much remodeling and building are already underway that I predict the flower of the year will be the "spike". A spike grows when a builder tells you, "Sure, we can start right away. Just give us 50 percent down so we can start."

You pay the money and, sure enough, the materials are delivered. Legally the job has started. Days, then weeks go by and little or nothing gets done. Your phone calls don't get answered, or they turn into marathon shouting matches. Your job has been officially "spiked."

Some people in the building trades are afraid of saying "no". You want your job done now. If they tell you that construction won't start for 30, 60, or 90 days, you will get someone else. So the temptation is sign contracts, take deposits, and start many more jobs than can be completed within a reasonable amount of time.

The result is the "spikes of spring," irate customers with lonely piles of materials that have been dropped (delivered) to legally start jobs, but may wait for weeks or months before they are actually used.

Over the years, Fairway Construction, has tried to educate the public about the "spikes of spring" and other potential remodeling hazards. Tuesday, the 12th of March, Fairway sponsored a free remodeling seminar given by independent experts at the Southfield Exhibition Center.

Two of the experts discussed topics that bear keeping in mind – Michigan's Lien Law and the real world of remodeling.

"Under Michigan Law, if your contractor does not pay sub contractors and suppliers for work or materials on your home, then they can lien your property and make you pay, even if you have already paid the contractor," said Murry Gula, president of the Michigan Construction Protection Agency and host of *Construction Talk* on WEXL-AM (1340). Gula owns the company that processes many of the liens against people's property so his advice is golden.

To make sure this doesn't happen, Gula advises doing everything in writing. "Have the contractor include a breakdown of work to be performed by value, and verify that he or she has a valid builder's or trade license before signing a contract," he said.

Gula told homeowners that building contracts have start and stop dates, with penalty provisions for late completion. He also advised requiring a list of every sub contractor doing work on the job, including their name, address, phone number and insurance carrier.

To ensure that jobs are protected by insurance and the law Gula said that Contractor's Workmen's Compensation and Liability insurance certificates should be sent directly from the company to make sure the insurance is in force, Gula said. Also make certain the contractor applies for the building permit. "If you, the homeowner, take out the permit, you, not the contractor, are responsible for making sure the job is built to code.

"Never pay for work that has not been completed, and always hold back a percentage until all corrections have been made. When you pay, exchange lien waivers signed by the sub contractors for payment. No waiver, no payment."

Gula publishes *"The Homeowner's Lien Kit"* which contains all necessary forms and explains the Michigan Lien Law. For more information, call the Michigan Construction Protection Agency, (800) 543-6669.

Pat Murphy, Franklin City Building Inspector, and president of Pat Murphy, Inc, echoed Gula's advice that homeowners never apply for a building permit unless they are going to do the work themselves. He also cautioned against trying to save money by not taking out a permit. "If the work is not approved, the Building Department can order you to tear open the job, so that they can make the required inspections," he said.

Known as the building inspectors' building inspector, Murphy retired recently as the Building Inspector for the City of Birmingham, and has taught inspection classes throughout the state. His company does plans approval for many municipalities in the area. No other person is better qualified to tell you what is likely to happen on your remodeling job.

"One of the biggest causes of homeowner remorse, is that they try to save a few dollars by cutting the size of a room and wind up with a cramped area that just makes them unhappy," he explained. Murphy cautioned homeowners that living through remodeling was the acid test of a marriage. "Expect severe stress. If you can't live with it, don't remodel."

And he added, "expect a mess, no matter what they promise, the building trades never clean up after themselves."

Murphy's final bit of advice was never to assume that a proposed remodeling job is in compliance with zoning laws just because the contractor, or designer, says it is. "Every municipality is different. What is perfectly legal in the next town, may be against an ordinance where you live," he said. "If the job is out of compliance, you need to get a variance from the Zoning Board. That can set back your job four or five months, and there is no guaranty that the variance will be granted."

I've covered many of these points on my radio shows and articles, but they bear repeating because they are critical if your remodeling project is going to be a success.

MARCH 30, 1996

Your basement is the hole problem when it comes to flooding

by America's Master Handyman,
Glenn Haege

April showers may bring May flowers, but after the big snow and late freeze we've had this year, they will also bring flooded basements. If your basement tries to make you the not-so-proud possessor of an indoor swimming pool, there are a number of things you should know before you take action.

The first thing you should understand is the inevitability of it all. Every basement is a puddle waiting to happen. Your basement is just a hole in the ground. When it rains, holes are supposed to fill with water. The only reason yours doesn't is that your builder lined it with eight to ten inches of concrete, put in some drainage tiles and built a house over it.

Mother Nature has eternity. Over time, fill land settles, poured and block concrete walls crack, drainage tiles are invaded by roots, plugged by debris, and crumble with age. Mother Nature works to regain the upper hand and make your basement the puddle it was meant to be.

If you don't want Mother Nature to turn your basement into a palace for pollywogs, the price is eternal vigilance. You have to keep your basement on a water free diet. Walk around the house and look for signs of bird bathing (indentations in the ground near your foundation which are perfect for puddles). If you find them, fill them.

Always build up the ground around the foundation so that it slopes away from, not toward, the house. A misplaced down spout can direct water toward the foundation or wash ground away. Housing in many older cities has roof gutters with down spouts connected to the city storm drains by ceramic tiles.

These tile systems break after a number of years and cause basement problems. If your home has down spouts that connect to the ground, disconnect them and direct the water away from the house.

Cement drives and walk ways can heave or settle, directing water toward the house. If your walks or driveways have settled they must either be built up, or mud jacked so that so that water drains away.

If you have done everything you are supposed to on the outside and still have a water problem, it is time to look at the basement itself.

The average house has two sets of tiles. The one that runs around the outside of the basement or foundation is called the weeping tiles. The tiles underneath the concrete slab are called the sanitary drains and storm sewer lines. Houses with sump pumps have bleeder lines that drain into the sump crock. Over years these tiles become clogged or break. The first step in the repair process is to get professionals to snake out the storm and sanitary sewer lines all the way to the street.

When the weeping tiles and bleeder lines are so broken or clogged that they no longer drain, they may have to be replaced. Different companies have different ways of doing this.

If you have a 45-year old house and are getting leaks on one side of the house, I only recommend fixing the drain tiles on that side of the house for two reasons: First, this type of repair is very expensive. Second, if you just fix the problem on the leaking side, you probably won't have a problem on the other sides of the house for another ten, twenty or thirty years. There may be many new, less expensive solutions by then.

If the basement drains must be repaired, one of the systems I like works from the inside of the basement. They cut through the basement floor and install new tiles or PVC perforated drains. Two companies that use this procedure are the B-Dry System (800-875-2379) and Affordable Dry Basement (800-310-5700).

There are other businesses in your area that also do quality work. The Yellow Pages is full of them. As with any contractor, one of the best places to find them is where they buy their supplies. Ask masonry supply stores and major lumber yards for a recommendation.

If your basement water problem is caused by a crack in the poured concrete, Mr. Sponge (800-491-4686) uses an advanced high pressure injection technique to stop seepage.

If you have a concrete block basement, water may have gotten into the cavities. You may have to drain the blocks. To do this put some old towels on the floor and drill a few 3/4- to 1-inch holes in the bottom tier of blocks. If the flooding of the block cavities was severe, the water may come out with quite a bit of pressure.

Let the blocks drain for a week or two. When seepage stops and the blocks are dry, fill the drain holes with a product like Quikrete Water Stop Cement.

If you don't like the idea of doing all this, join the club. Build your next house on a slab or find a building site on well-drained sand.

APRIL 6, 1996

Clearing all decks of dirt is a simple matter with a bit of elbow grease

by America's Master Handyman,
Glenn Haege

This article is only for you if you are champing at the bit to get out doors and start using the deck. If you don't wear walking shorts while there is still snow on the ground, clip and save the article until June.

As always, I am going to name, names. Just to keep us legal, I need to say that all of the manufacturer and product names are copyrighted or trade marked and are the sole property of the companies that manufacture them.

This has been a real rough winter on your deck. The late freeze didn't help. The deck wood is very weak right now. Let it dry before you do anything to it.

Don't rush out and buy the first deck cleaner you see. What you use depends on the present condition of your deck, what you've done to it, and what you plan to do to it this year.

I maintain my own test deck on which I test different finishes and cleaners. I wrote a book reporting the results, and best application techniques, called *Glenn Haege's Complete Deck & Paver Guide.*

To my knowledge, it is the only book on the market that not only tells you how to take care of your deck, but gives actual test results. I also sweet-talked my friends at Akzo Nobel into giving me a Sikken's Deck Surface Thermometer for every book. That means that you can actually tell the temperature of the surface of the deck.

The secret to having a beautiful deck is applying the proper product at the proper deck surface temperature, not air temperature. Applying a deck stain, sealer, or toner when the deck wood is either too cold or too hot keeps the product from being absorbed properly and ruins the job. It is one of the main causes of deck treatment failure. I'll talk more about temperatures next week when we go into toners and sealers. Right now, let's clean the deck.

I used to recommend a mixture of TSP, chlorine bleach, and water for deck cleaning. Many of the most common deck cleaners are also Chlorine based. Research has shown that Chlorine based products do real damage to the wood. If you had a microscope and looked at a wood surface cleaned with a Chlorine based product you would see that the wood fibers have been badly burned and mangled. The wood is more prone to water damage and has a difficult time accepting a stain or sealer.

The type of cleaner that you should use, depends upon the present condition of your deck. If you have a grayed, pressure treated pine, a grayed cedar, redwood or other grayed wood deck that has not been sealed or stained, I suggest a cleaner that uses oxalic acid, or a carbonate such as disodium peroxydicarbonate or sodium carbonate. These cleaners remove the top layer of old, dead cells and return the deck to "like new" condition. The cleaners can also be used to rehabilitate wood that has been "burned" by a chlorine based cleaner.

On the off chance that you did not major in chemistry at college, this means you should look for cleaners like Wolman Deck Brightener, Flood Dekswood, Cabot Stains Problem Solver, and Cuprinol Revive. The use of these products also prepares the deck for staining or sealing.

For our older, grayed, test deck, in all cases, we needed twice as much cleaner as the directions called for, and all needed power washing for really good results. The problem with power washing is that inexperienced people can tear up their decks. I do not recommend that you ever use more than 800 PSI (pounds per square inch) when deck cleaning.

Don't believe the words "no scrubbing necessary." Even if you are using a pressure washer, you must work in all cleaners with a brush for best results. DQB (Detroit Quality Brush) has introduced a long handled, specially shaped deck brush that makes the scrubbing job easier and more efficient. If you have a big deck, it is definitely worth the investment. You should be able to find it at most Home Centers or call 800-722-3037 for the dealer nearest you.

If you have a dirty treated or untreated deck and just want to clean it, use Simple Deck by Bio-Wash, Dirty Deck Cleaner by Citrus Strip, or brew your own with cleaners like Simple Green or TSP. (Hint: We found that, on previously stained or sealed surfaces, TSP was the least expensive of all the cleaners tested by a factor of five or six to one, yet gave the best results.)

For Simple Green the recipe is 1/2 gallon of Simple Green per gallon of water. For TSP the recipe is 4 ounces dry measure per gallon of water.

If you have an older stained, sealed or varnished deck and want to remove the old surface, use Stripex Wood Stain Stripper by Bio-Wash.

After cleaning let the deck dry for at least 48 hours and get ready for next week's article on staining and sealing. Make certain that your deck is really dry. Feel the under side of the deck. If it is wet, the wood needs longer drying time. Do not put on a stain or sealer when the night time temperature is going below 50 degrees.

Check the temperature before you hit the deck with stain or sealer

by America's Master Handyman, Glenn Haege

When staining or sealing your deck, don't make the mistake of thinking the air temperature is the same as the deck's temperature. Deck woods get the direct rays of the sun. They absorb and store heat. During the day, air temperature may vary only a few degrees, but deck surface temperature may change 30 degrees or more. This variation in temperature can be crucial to your success in staining or sealing.

When we charted our test deck's surface temperature during the heat of the day in March, air temperature was only 60 degrees Fahrenheit, but the deck surface was already over 90 Fahrenheit. This was almost too hot to apply stain safely! A few hours later it was too cold. Too hot and the solvent in the stain or sealer "boils off," and the product does not penetrate the wood. Too cold and the stain or sealer just becomes gooey.

To show the difference between air and wood surface temperature, we took the surface temperature of our test deck with Akzo Nobel's Surface Temperature Thermometer every three hours on a rather cool day at the beginning of June. Air temperature was 55 Fahrenheit at 6 a.m., 70 at noon, 72 at 3 p.m., 71 degree at 6 p.m., and 68 by 9 p.m.

By contrast, deck surface temperature was 55 F at 6 a.m., 90 at noon, 100 at 3 p.m., 75 at 6 p.m. and 70 by 9 p.m. The air temperature only shifted 17 degrees.

The deck surface temperature shifted 45. By Noon the deck was almost too hot for staining or sealing. By 3 p.m., the solvents would have "boiled off" as soon as the product was applied and the job would have been ruined!

For best results, work early in the morning or late in the day after the deck has cooled. Apply stains or sealers when the deck surface temperature is between 50 F (10 Celsius) and 95 F (35 Celsius).

Deck surface temperature is so important, I talked the Akzo Nobel Sikkens people into giving me a deck surface thermometer for each one of my *Glenn Haege Complete DECK & PAVER GUIDES* and packaged the thermometer inside the book (see end of article for purchase information).

Buying the proper product is just as important as doing the work at the proper temperature. Deck care products come in all price ranges from $10 to $55 a gallon. The more you pay, the more "guts in the bucket." It makes good sense to pay for quality. I'm going to name some of the good ones. Keep in mind that all of the manufacturer and product names are copyrighted or trade marked and are the sole property of the manufactures.

If you have a brand new deck (less than sixty days old), put a coat of Seasonite by the Flood Company, Wolman RainCoat, Wolman F & P Clear Wood Finish, Cabot PTW Stain or other product that specifies that it can be applied to new wood.

If you like gray, weathered decks, look for Cabot Bleaching Oil. Apply it as is, or mixed 50/50 with Cabot Weathering Stain for an enhanced gray look.

If you just want to keep your deck looking like when it was new, you are out of luck. Regardless of what TV commercials imply, clear sealers do not stop graying for very long. The best you can hope for is a clear wood sealer with UV (ultra violet) Protection. The UV additive darkens the deck slightly but helps hold the color for a season. In really harsh climates you may have to seal the deck in Spring and Fall.

The next step up is a sealer/toner that gives an attractive, honey nut color. Quality sealer/toners provide approximately 18 to 24 months of protection. There are many on the market. One of my favorites is Penofin Cedar/Marine Penetrating Oil Finish. It uses rosewood oil for superior penetration and provided excellent results on my test deck.

Stains come in semi-transparent, semi-solid, and solid varieties. Each step up gives more solid color and greater wood protection. Semi transparent stains provide the most "natural" colors. I recommend them highly for beautiful deck woods like cedar, redwood and Jarrah.

If you want a "furniture finish", no product made comes close to Sikkens Cetol DEK by the Akzo Nobel company. Not just a stain, this is a deck treatment system. The first year, apply two coats of Cetol DEK Base. Every year thereafter, top it off with a coat of Cetol DEK.

If you're into easy care, look at Wolman RainCoat Water Repellent, and Wolman F & P Clear Wood Finish and Preservative. You can apply both products with a garden sprayer and even them out with a deck brush.

For a strong, solid color, look at Sikkens Rubbol DEK. It gives a paint like finish that breaths and wears like a quality deck stain.

Choosing a deck care product determines how you will spend your springs for the next several years. Take time to study the labels. Never buy any product that does not say that it is for decks prominently on the label.

AIR TEMPERATURE Vs DECK SURFACE TEMPERATURE		
Time of Day	Air Temperature	Deck Surface
6:00 a.m.	55° F	55° F
9:00 a.m.	64° F	75° F
12:00 p.m.	70° F	90° F
3:00 p.m.	**72° F**	**100° F**
Too Hot To Apply Sealer or Stain!		
6:00 p.m.	71° F	75° F
9:00 p.m.	68° F	70° F

Get cookin' – now's the time to clean lawn and barbecue equipment

by America's Master Handyman, Glenn Haege

I've played my first league golf game. The paver people are working on my pavers. Tony V's people have got my spa sparkling. Barbara keeps pushing me out the patio door with plates of ground round patties and chicken breasts.

I guess it must really, finally, be spring. That means it's time to brush down the barbecue and wash away the winter grime from the lawn furniture.

The best way to clean the barbecue is to strip it down and degrease it. If you have a gas grill, turn off the gas or remove the propane tank. Take out the grills, burners and lava rock or pumice.

If you are a charcoal traditionalist, shovel out any of the old ashes (there should not be any, because you should have stored away your charcoal burner, clean and dry). The rest of the directions are for all types of barbecues.

Wire brush the top of the burners. Clean out the loose debris with a Shop Vac or wet/dry vacuum cleaner. Clean and degrease the barbecue and grill.

To get last year's grease and gunk off, wash down the grills and barbecue with full strength Simple Green or Wesley's Clear Magic. Wear rubber gloves for this job. Spray down the grills and barbecue with water, then apply the concentrated cleaner. If they are very greasy, let stand for several minutes, then brush with a stiff bristle brush. Rinse with clear water. Repeat if necessary.

While waiting for the cleaner to do most of the hard work, make a decision on the lava rock or pumice. If you have old lava rock, throw it away. Pumice is worth cleaning. Ceramic rock is best but expensive.

To clean pumice or ceramic rock, soak in a bucket filled with a 50 percent solution of Simple Green or Clear Magic. Let stand for a couple of hours. Stir with a stick from time to time. Then discard the cleaner and rinse the pumice or lava rock with a garden hose and water. Let dry.

Spiders love venturi tubes. Evict them and their webs with a venturi brush or a coat hanger.

Reassemble the barbecue, hook up the burners, and attach the propane tank. Turn on the gas and ignite. Check the color of gas flame. If it is blue, the burners are fine. If the flame is yellow, you have a burner problem.

Turn off the gas and reclean the burners. Then check the gas again. If the flame has turned blue, go to the head of the class. If it is still yellow, replace the burners.

If the barbecue's paint job needs to be touched up, use barbecue paint. I prefer a spray can for this job. Paint the exterior only.

The final job is to tighten all loose bolts and put back the freshly cleaned grills and rock.

Treat yourself to the grill cover you were going to buy last year. Buy it now while the size you need is still in stock. It will give the grill years of extra service.

Now, let's clean the furniture. I suggest cleaning unfinished, natural redwood or cedar tables, chairs and benches with a good, non-chlorine base deck cleaner, like Wolman's new Cedar and Redwood Cleaner.

If you want to add a finish this year, let the furniture dry for three or four days and finish with two coats of Cetol DEK Base-Cedar.

If the furniture is painted or varnished, give it a bath with a 10 to 1 solution of Simple Green or Clear Magic. Rinse well with the garden hose and let dry.

Wood furniture is left to the mercy of the elements. You will add years to the service life if you buy vinyl covers to protect patio furniture when not in use.

Wash down painted aluminum furniture with a 10 to 1 solution of Simple Green or Clear Magic. Rinse with the garden hose. When dry, apply a coat of Diamond Brite Paint Sealant. Clean glass tops with a good glass cleaner. When dry, give the glass a coat of Diamond Brite, too.

Plastic Resin outdoor furniture can get really dull, dingy, and almost uncleanable. First, clean like wood or aluminum. If that doesn't work, try Meguiar's Mirror Glaze Professional Clear Plastic Cleaner #17, before you throw them away. Wipe on, let dry to a haze, then wipe off and coat with Diamond Brite.

To clean padded Texiline furniture, wash with a 25 percent solution of Simple Green and water. Scrub with a scrub brush, then rinse with lots and lots of water and let dry.

Finally, don't forget the umbrella. Open it up and lay it on the grass. Dampen with the garden hose, then spray with a 10 to 1 solution of Simple Green. Brush gently. Clean inside and out and rinse with a garden hose. Do not close the umbrella until it has dried completely.

You should be able to find Simple Green, Clear Magic and Diamond Brite at Damman's, Murray's or most other good hardware and automotive supply stores. Look for Meguiar's products at automotive supply stores.

Now, that you are ready for your first garden party, where's my invitation?

New Michigan-made products should interest avid do-it-yourselfers

by America's Master Handyman, Glenn Haege

Last Saturday, I devoted almost my entire radio show to new, primarily Michigan Made products being introduced this spring. This newspaper article goes to four times as many people as my radio show, so I figure I should bring all of you up to date, too. One product is for the roof. Two are for the basement. One is for the storage shed. And one for your tool box.

Let's start with the tool box because the item weighs less than an ounce, but will give you many pounds of torque. A company called Pockrandt, Inc., of Warren, MI, has introduced Stiction Sure Grip. Put just a little dab of this product on a screw or bolt that doesn't want to come out and you will greatly increase the torque of the screw drive or wrench. The formula works instantly and will not harm fasteners or substrate, the material that anchors the screw.

Pockrandt has come out with an line of tie in products. (Ed: unfortunately Pockrandt no longer makes these products. The line was sold to Frebar, Inc., 248-634-8278.) Belt Grab is a friction enhancing formula designed to increase drive belt grip for cars, compressors, lawn tractors, winches and furnace motor belts. Sure Grip 750 is a heavy duty formulation developed to hold large coarse thread fasteners, like push broom handles. I am currently testing this out myself. If it works as advertised and stops my push broom from loosening every couple of sweeps, I will tell the world about it.

Now, let's get down to the basement and work our way up. The popularity of basement remodeling runs in cycles. One year everyone is doing it. The next year, everyone is into sun rooms. This year, basements are big news. Two handy products that will make your basement remodeling easier are Tree Tech Fine Wood Pole Enclosures and Environmental Cushion Industries Enviro Cushion.

Undoubtedly the most ugly things in the basement besides the laundry tub, are the metal stanchion poles which support the floor. You can't eliminate them, but now, thanks to Tree Tech, you can turn them into beautiful wood pillars.

The pillars, which can be installed by the company or by the Do-it-yourselfer, come in your choice of red oak, walnut, cherry, knotty pine, mahogany, birch and maple. They are real wood, not some composite imitation. Costs range upward of $150. When you compare the time and trouble usually wasted boxing the stantions, Tree Tech's Fine Wood Pole Enclosures represent a good value. To learn more, call Tree Tech in Royal Oak, at 248-543-2166 (Ed: no longer in operation).

Now, look down at the floor, the coldest part of any basement. Many families want to use the basement for their children's play area but are afraid of the cold. Tile doesn't help. Carpet helps a little bit, but you need something more on a cold winter's evening. Carpet padding doesn't list an R factor. Now ECI, Environmental Cushion Industries of America, has introduced Enviro Cushion, a pad so dense that it has a 4.5 R factor.

The new Mexican made product is 100 percent odorless. 100 percent non-toxic and 100 percent waterproof. Not even dog or cat urine can soak in. It should make the basement a far more comfortable place. I would seriously consider this new padding if I were remodeling my basement. For more information on the Enviro Cushion, call Fairway Tile and Carpet in Clawson, 248-588-4431.

Now, from the bottom of the basement to the top of your roof. Roman Tafelsky started out in the lumber yard business at the ripe old age of nine. In the great tinkerer/inventor tradition, Tafelsky has patents on a steel baler and a 2-foot-by-2-foot deck system, called the Modula Decks System.

Now he has improved upon the Black Max Vent Shield originally invented by Frank Nievelt, to stop roof vent pipe roof leakage. The new Critter Control vent shield, not only shields the vent, it stops birds, leaves and small animals from falling down into the stack and plugging the sanitary stack.

Since plugged sanitary stacks are one of the main causes of slow moving drains, this makes the Black Max Vent Shield with Critter Control big news. The product is being carried by most major hardware stores and lumber yards. if you have any difficulty finding it call the manufacturer, Capital Building Supply Co., Detroit, at 313-836-8000 or 800-836-3325.

Now lets organize the garage. Knape & Vogt Manufacturing has developed a new shelving system that is a Do-it-yourselfer's dream. The shelving system comes in a kit that includes the fasteners, brackets and materials list. You just give the materials list to your lumber yard and they cut the necessary 2 x 4's and Particle Board to size. All you have to do is take it home and assemble. Not only is it easy, since it is basically 2 x 4 construction, it is the strongest shelving you are likely to find anywhere. Various size kits are available at ACO and other fine hardware stores. To find the dealer nearest you, call Knape & Vogt, Grand Rapids, at 800-253-1561.

MAY 4, 1996

Committee hammers out the finishing touches on state energy code

by America's Master Handyman,
Glenn Haege

The following information is only important to you if you presently live in a house, ever expect to buy, build or pay for a house, or have a room addition built. The rest of you are excused.

The Model Energy Code is a federally sanctioned insulation standard. It outlines the energy efficiency and amount of insulation needed in home construction. The Code is a recommendation only. It does not have to be adopted by the Sovereign States of this great Republic. As is the case with every voluntary federal standard, the first thing the bureaucrats in Washington do is think up ways to blackmail the serf sand citizens of the Sovereign States into conforming to their demands. The particular form of blackmail the congress put into the Model Energy Code legislation was that no federal money (VA, FHA or HUD mortgagees), would be doled out for housing that was not built in conformance to Model Energy Code.

Informed citizens may remember the "brouhaha" this caused in Lansing. After months of hearings, the State adopted the 1993 Federal Model Energy Code so its citizens could get the federal bucks. Then some of the State's most influential builders rose in open revolt, claimed they had been sandbagged and convinced the Legislature to take another look. Other folks pointed out that only a very few homes are federally financed in Michigan so the federal arm twisting would have very little effect.

The result was that the Legislature did an about face and not only rejected the 1993 Model Energy Code, but went all the way back to the State's (Neanderthal) 1970 Code. The new/old energy code is as close to state of the art as a Ford Model T is to an Indy racer.

This, of course, created a backlash from just about every environmental group in the State (as well as a good number of lobbyists), so our representatives decided to make a stand, come to the hard decisions, and do the right thing. They appointed a committee.

The purview of the 1996 Energy Code Ad Hoc Committee is to make a recommendation on what Michigan's residential insulation code should be in the future. This is a very important committee because what they decide will directly effect every home buyer and every rent, mortgage and energy bill payer in the State for the foreseeable future.

Lucky for us, the folks in Lansing appointed a pretty good committee. Under the very effective leadership of Henry Green, Executive Director of the Michigan Department of Labor's Bureau of Construction Codes, the group is attempting to thrash out a practical energy plan. There is a lot of disagreement among members, but they are committed to come up with a code that is cost-effective for the consumer. That means that any recommendation has to pay for itself in the seven or eight years that the average consumer stays in a house. According to the latest estimates by the National Association of Realtors, the median time frame is now six years.

One of the committee's biggest problems is determining what is fact and what is propaganda. Even the smallest things, such as the cost effectiveness of the various types of insulation and R (Insulation Rating) Factors, or how many states are actually in support of the Federal Model Energy Code, have to be questioned because the committee has found much of the information to be biased or wrong.

In a recent committee meeting, one of my representatives heard Ron Burton, Vice President in charge of Energy Code Compliance for the National Association of Home Builders, tell the committee that the National Energy Code has provided more problems than solutions on the national level.

He said that everybody trying to enforce the complex code is having difficulty because builders are finding it impossible to comply. "The new code has created so many problems that the states of Ohio, Pennsylvania, Kansas and Vermont are trying to roll back the code," he said.

Burton concluded his observations to the Committee by warning the members that "something that promotes more hardship than gain is not an advantage to anyone. To be effective the new code has to be cost effective and affordable."

Not everyone agrees with Burton, but sounds like good advice to me. Michigan needs a good, economically and environmentally sound energy code. We have to pull together to make sure that future construction is energy-wise, livable, healthy and affordable.

The 1996 Energy Code Ad Hoc Committee only has four more meetings before it is scheduled to make its recommendations. The committee meetings are open to every one. I especially urge members of the remodeling and construction industry, who's livelihoods may very well be dependent upon the Code, to get involved.

The next meeting is May 8, 9 a.m. to 5 p.m. at the ING-Bureau of Construction Codes Conference Room. Why not call Henry Green at 517-322-5247, and tell him you want to come to the next meeting?

MAY 11, 1996

Give Mom a break from household drudgery this Mother's Day

by America's Master Handyman,
Glenn Haege

OK, you forgot that Sunday is Mother's Day! Fear not. There is still time for the Handyman to turn you into a hero by doing a few extra chores and letting mom see you understand and appreciate her.

Housework is more fun when it's shared. If you can, convince a buddy, or brother or sister to do the work with you. The work gets done faster and quicker. You can actually do more. When you're done, go over to your buddy's house and repeat the procedure for his/her mom. You will make two mom's feel very special.

Let's start, in the kitchen. You can clean the kitchen cabinets with products like Simple Green or Clear Magic. Use two buckets. One has a mixture of one part cleaner to every ten parts of warm water. The other bucket is filled with clear water. Wipe the cleaner on with a sponge. Let stand for a minute. Rinse with clear water. Dry with a towel, if necessary.

If mom has real good wood cabinets and you don't want to use water, use Parker & Bailey's Kitchen Cabinet Creme. It's especially made for fine wood cabinetry. Pour a little polish on a damp, 100 percent cotton cloth and rub into the surface. Buff to a shine with another clean cotton cloth.

Vinyl floors can be nicely cleaned with a 50 to 1 solution of Simple Green or Clear Magic. That's about 2 ounces of cleaning solution in a bucket of hot water. Rinse with clear rinse water. Dry with an old cotton towel.

How about the counter tops? Hopes makes a great Counter Top Polish. Dab on with a damp cloth, then buff it off. The counter tops will look like new.

Clean and shine stainless steel sinks with Bar Keeper's Friend, or Parker & Bailey's Stainless Steel Polish. After the sink has been cleaned, rinsed and dried, coat with Diamond Brite to eliminate water spotting.

Clean porcelain sinks with Bon Ami. When dry, apply a poly-type auto wax or Gel Gloss to shine and seal the surface. The sealer fills in the surface profile and makes it harder for dust, dirt and soap scum to stick so mom will have a shiny sink for a long time.

You can also use the Stainless Steel Polish to clean and shine the stove, refrigerator and dishwasher. Use the same product to clean and shine the aluminum or steel storm doors.

Now let's go to the bathroom. If there is mold or mildew on the ceramic tile, walls or ceiling, spray with X-14. Wait a few minutes, then wipe with a rag.

To clean soap scum from ceramic tile, tub and shower doors use The Works Bath & Shower Cleaner. This is a fairly strong cleaner so use rubber gloves. Scrub tiles with a small hand brush. Wear goggles to protect your eyes. After the shower walls have been washed and rinsed, let dry for an hour, then seal the surface with Gel Gloss.

Also use Works on the shower doors and the fiberglass pan of the shower stall. Start from the bottom and work your way up. Rinse and let dry for a hour then seal the profile of the doors with Invisible Shield or Rain-X by Unelko Corp. Do not use a sealer on the shower floor. It will make the floor surface slippery and unsafe.

To shine metal shower enclosure frames and clean the gunk from aluminum tracks, use Peek™ metal polish. Never let the polish dry completely. Rub briskly, then buff with a clean rag.

If the bathroom floors are covered with easily removable carpeting, take them to the Laundromat and use their commercial carpet cleaning machine. Don't clean them in your automatic washing machine.

If the bathroom has a tile floor, this is your chance to be a major league hero. Wash the tile, but more importantly, clean the grout with a commercial tile cleaner like Aqua Mix or Tile Pro. Let dry for four hours, then seal with like Aqua Mix or Tile Pro penetrating grout sealer.

Aqua Mix and Tile Pro are specialized products look for them at places like Beaver Tile Distributors or Fairway Tile and Carpet.

You can use the same technique to deep clean the tile shower walls.

Look at all the hard work you did in just two rooms. Mom is responsible for the whole house, 365 days a year. No wonder she is tired.

PS: I have checked with my wife Barbara. She says it is in perfectly good taste for mothers to clip this article and post it on the refrigerator. Clusters of cleaning products make dramatic kitchen table center pieces. Photo copies also make great place mats and can be used monthly. High lighting most needed projects is perfectly acceptable.

MAY 18, 1996

Low-cost, low-tech security devices can help prevent break-ins

by America's Master Handyman, Glenn Haege

Next week is the long, Memorial Day Weekend. The beginning of Michigan's camping and cottage season. Millions of us will be packing the car and going up North or just visiting. Hundreds of us will be coming home to houses and apartments that have been broken into while we were away.

The loss of property is painful, but the feeling of violation is worse. After you've had your home broken into once, you never feel completely at ease when you go away. That being the case I thought a few words about an easy way to increase your home's security might come in handy.

There's a great deal of high tech talk about home security. The trouble with many home security devices is that they take so much extra effort, or demand that we change our life style so much, that we don't use them even if they're installed.

If you are a low tech type, don't leave the welcome mat out for burglars. You can greatly increase your home's, and your family's, security with very inexpensive, low tech items that do not surround you with television camera's, heat and motion detectors, or monthly payments to security services.

In 1994, the latest statistics on file with the Michigan State Police Data Center, Michigan residents suffered 88,214 cases of breaking and entering. Many of them could have been prevented if the homes were protected with the relatively low cost, low tech, items I am writing about today.

We make burglar's work too easy. According to the Kwikset Lock people, in over 40 percent of residential burglaries, the thief enters through an unlocked door or window. So the first thing you should do to improve your security is lock your doors and windows.

If the perpetrator does have to break in, he usually gets in within eight seconds. He doesn't pick the lock. He doesn't try to force the deadbolt back. He just walks up to the front door and kicks it in. Bam! Eight seconds and he's in. He then carefully closes the door and goes about his business. From the street, the door looks like nothing has happened. In all probability, no one will notice until your mail is delivered or you come home.

So you should prevent the burglar from being able to kick in the front and back door. If you do this the amateur burglar will usually give the door a few swift kicks, get disgusted, and go away. The professional will take one look and leave for easier pickings.

If you are a low tech type, don't leave the welcome mat out for burglars. You can greatly increase your home's, and your family's, security with very inexpensive, low tech items that do not surround you with television camera's, heat and motion detectors, or monthly payments to security services.

The first thing you should do to make your door tough on burglars is check the deadbolt locks. The deadbolt should be of hardened steel and at least 1-inch long. The lock assembly should have no plastic parts. If the deadbolt is shorter than an inch or plastic is used in the assembly, replace the lock.

Now comes the part that makes your doors invincible. A small California Company, but the name of M.A.G. Engineering & Manufacturing, Inc. makes a line of highly attractive door lock and frame protectors.

The Install-A-Lock Door Reinforcer is a clip made of solid 22 gauge brass, bronze or stainless steel. The Door Reinforcer comes in a large variety of sizes to fit most door and lock combinations. It fits over the door and protects and reinforces the handle and lock mechanism. Another clip, the Uni-Force Door Edge Guard fits over the door and protects the deadbolt area.

The strike plate area of the frame can be protected with a Strike 3 Strike Plate with a deep drawn metal box that surrounds the extended dead bolt in metal. Used in combination with the Door Reinforcer and Door Edge Guard it will make your entrance doors impervious to kick-ins.

Prices vary, but all three parts should not cost more than about $24 a door. Once you get the supplies, installation shouldn't take more than 30 minutes. Most good hardware, home centers and building supply stores carry at least a limited selection of M.A.G. security products. You can call the company direct at (800) 624-9942 to find the store nearest you.

Pave the way to a long-lasting new driveway by hiring a contractor

by America's Master Handyman, Glenn Haege

If your driveway looks like a World War II battle zone, you have three replacement choices: concrete, asphalt or pavers. The cost for residential-grade asphalt can be less than concrete, but more scheduled maintenance is required.

Paver driveways can make a very elegant statement, are almost indestructible, and initially cost a great deal more than concrete. There greatest strength is also their greatest weakness. Because they are imbedded in sand or slag, rather than cemented together, pavers move with freeze/thaw cycles and almost never crack. Because they are not cemented together they can shift with the seasons, requiring regular maintenance to remain flat.

If you are not particularly fond of hot or cold tar emulsions, and are allergic to even the thought of a $30,000 or $40,000 paver driveway, you will probably decide on concrete.

Since concrete driveways can last fifteen to twenty-five years or more, you probably have never shopped for one before. I asked Steve Klochko, President of Gibraltar National Corp., one of the nation's leading concrete manufacturers, what he would recommend.

Klochko says although do-it-yourselfer can feel perfectly qualified to mix and pour a concrete patio or walkway, they shouldn't even think about pouring a concrete driveway unless they have a great deal of expertise, equipment and a skilled labor force.

Here's what Klochko recommends: The concrete in your new driveway should be at least 4 inches thick. Actually, the thicker the better. If you are going to park a heavy truck on the driveway, or have an in-home business and get occasional deliveries from a semi-trailer, or have any type of truck traffic heavier than a light pickup, increase the thickness of the slab to 6 inches.

The composition of the concrete used in the drive should be a 5 1/2 to 6 bag mix and contain 5 to 8 percent entrained air. Entrained air is little air pockets that give concrete the flexibility to withstand freeze/thaw cycles, Klochko says.

The concrete mix should have what is called a 4- to 5-inch slump. The slump is a measure used by professionals to determine consistency. A 4-inch slump is preferred. A 5-inch slump is the maximum permissible. To get an idea of what this means, imagine filling a coffee can full of concrete, then turning it upside down like you were building a sand castle.

At first, the pile of concrete would be twelve inches high. After about fifteen minutes the pile might have spread out and only a height of eight inches. Subtract eight from twelve and you get a 4-inch "slump".

When the concrete is poured you want as little troweling as possible. Making a driveway extra smooth, makes it slippery and destroys traction.

If the driveway will receive heavy traffic, it is a good idea to reinforce the 6-inch depth with mesh. While the new fiber reinforced concrete is excellent for patios and walks, the extra strength of metal mesh is still preferred for driveways.

If you have an existing drive, removal of the old concrete will usually take a day and cost between fifty cents and a dollar per square foot. This cost can vary greatly depending upon the complexity and size of the job.

The average size of a driveway is 16 feet wide by 30 feet long, and can be prepared and poured in a day. The cost for a laying a four inch thick slab is usually $1.75 to $2.50 per square foot. Mesh or fiber reinforcing is extra. The additional cost for fiber reinforcing is usually eight to ten cents a square foot additional. The cost for mesh is approximately ten cents a square foot.

Speaking from experience, I believe expansion strips are critical to the survival of concrete driveways. The average con-

tractor will run a vertical, fiber-filled, cut down the center of the pad. I suggest adding several horizontal relief cuts as well as angular relief cuts where the driveway meets the garage and at the end of the driveway apron.

As with any major remodeling project, the most important single ingredient is the skill of the contractor. I asked Klochko how a person would make certain of getting a good contractor. "The best way to find a good contractor is still word of mouth from friends," he said. I would also suggest calling masonry supply houses, such as National Block (734-721-4056) in Westland and J. C. Cornelli (810-293-1500) in Roseville, for recommendations.

Naturally, you should ask for references and visit several recent jobs and talk to the homeowners before signing a contract. Since the work is completed very rapidly, homeowners can often negotiate payment upon completion terms.

Once the job is done, the best way to assure a long lasting driveway is proper maintenance. Let the concrete cure for sixty days, then apply a water repellant concrete sealer. Do not use an acrylic sealer on the driveway because it will make the surface too slippery.

JUNE 1, 1996

When ants invade your home, it's definitely no picnic – fight back

by America's Master Handyman,
Glenn Haege

The invasion has been going on for weeks. Ants are everywhere: single-mindedly crawling across floors and countertops, climbing refrigerators, swimming in dishwashers, even invading your bed or favorite chair. The same thing is true about Indian meal moths and Mosquitoes. They come. They're a bother and they never pay rent.

This week I am going to write about the battle against ants. Next week, we will take on two of my least favorite flying fiends, Indian meal moths and Mosquitoes.

A long line of ants does not necessarily mean that a colony is living in your home. The colony could be located in a tree or your neighbor's rotten fence post. On the other hand, there may be several colonies in your home that you will only discover by accident.

If the ants have moved in, they will be located in old, water damaged wood. Colonies are often found inside hollow doors, in the rotten wood below windows, in roofing boards, behind fireplace mantels, or any place leaking water has caused wood rot.

The reason for their appearance in the living area of your home is usually the search for water. Forager ants go out looking for food and water. When the first forager ant finds a good source of supply, he loads up and heads back to the colony.

On the way home he excretes what is called a pheromone trail. This chemical trail acts like a sign post directing all the other forager ants to go to your house and get a load of good stuff. This is why you often see a single line of ants going in one direction. They are all following an invisible pheromone trail.

The best times to exterminate ants are in the Spring and Fall when the forager ants are most noticeable, says Paul LaBuhn of Maple Lane Pest Control of Sterling Heights. These are also the two busiest times of the year for pest control businesses.

If you have seen a large number of ants a careful inspection of the inside and outside of your house is warranted. Small piles of sawdust inside a fireplace or dishwasher are a good indication that carpenter ants have taken up residence. Try to see where the ants are coming from and what their line of march is once they are out in the open.

Don't forget to look overhead. Two prime ant highways are tree limbs that touch the roof and telephone and cable wires connected to your house. Wires may be a traffic jam of ants going to and from the house. Inside, ants often have colonies in the roof boards.

Ant colonies are often discovered when roofs and windows are replaced. Old shingles and windows are both prone to leaks creating water damage to underlayment and wood supports. LaBuhn says that it is a good idea to give a can of ant killer to the roofing or window contractor and ask them to spray any ant colony the crew finds while working.

Ant colonies are often difficult to find. Tom Thompson, of Thompson Pest Control in Plymouth, has a specially trained dog, named Molly, who is one of only 25 dogs in the United States trained to sniff out ant colonies. The dog can climb ladders, get into confined areas humans can not even think about, and sniff out her quarry behind paneling.

Once found, all the ants in the colony, the queen, the larvae, and the eggs should be killed. The most effective pesticides are dangerous and only available to licensed pest control companies. If you have a significant ant problem, contact a quality pest control company like Thompson or Maple Lane. For more information consult your Ameritech Yellow Pages or call Paul LaBuhn at Maple Lane Pest Control (800-870-7096) or Tom Thompson at Thompson Pest Control (800-934-4770).

If you have only a slight problem and want to tackle the job yourself, you'll find a number of Dursban- and Diazinon-based products on the market. Both Raid and Ortho make specific interior and exterior ant control products. Meijer private labels 5 percent Diazinon granules for exterior use that are a very good value.

The real trick to success and safety according to both LaBuhn and Thompson is to follow pesticide label directions to the letter. Do not use twice as much because you think it will be twice as effective. An ant only dies once. Twice the dosage means twice the danger to people and pets.

If the label directions say the product will be effective for two weeks, believe it. Do not reapply the product in a week. Even when dry and invisible to the human eye, many of the spray products adhere to the ant's feet and kill when they clean their feet.

Most important, if the directions say to keep away from food, children, and pets, don't take chances. That even goes for goldfish. Air borne toxins can poison a fish tank. The smaller the person or pet, the more sensitive they will be to toxins. You can never go wrong by playing it safe.

Flying pests don't have to drive you out of town – exterminate

by America's Master Handyman,
Glenn Haege

Flying pests are one of the most irritating parts of Spring and Summer. Ants you can step on, and if you listen carefully they give a nice, satisfying, crunch. Flying insects just laugh at you. Swatting hands, rolled up newspapers, even fly swatters just make empty eddies in the air and all we usually get is frustrated. Two of the flying fiends that bug me the most are Indian meal moths and mosquitoes.

Indian meal moths are those half inch, mottled colored, flying insects that we increasingly see hanging out in kitchen cupboards. They were never really rare, but they were not usually much of a problem, either. Most home makers could afford to be pretty smug knowing that Indian meal moth infestation was a problem that "other people" had.

In a well meant effort to protect us from carcinogens, the Federal Government has cut down on the amount of pesticides used in food preparation. That means that the stuff they used to put in the flour to make sure it didn't become a Indian meal moth maternity ward isn't there anymore and suddenly Indian meal moth infestation is everybody's problem.

Once they have invaded your home, your kitchen can be literally crawling with them and you won't get rid of them until you have clean and sanitize the kitchen area.

Empty kitchen cupboards and put everything on the table. Look through all the opened packages of grain products: cereal, rice, flour, pasta, etc. Anything in which you see worms, cobwebs, as well as all open flour that may have little eggs in it has to go. Get rid of every product that you even think might have been contaminated.

Dump all the loose stuff into a plastic garbage bag. Seal the bag carefully, then take it outside to wait for garbage day.

Seal all uncontaminated products in heavy zip-lock plastic bags, or burp-top plastic containers by Tupperware or Rubber Maid. Once everything is sealed, clean and sanitize the cupboard area completely before putting things back on the shelves.

If you have removable shelving, pop the shelves and wash them down. If you have fixed shelving, clean carefully. Wash down with a product like Simple Green and water. Paul LaBuhn of Maple Lane Pest Control suggests that you use a tooth brush to get into all the cracks and get all the worms and pupae.

"Jam your head in the cupboards and look into the back side where the doors are hinged and places like that because they will pupate into the smallest of cracks. You really have to work to make sure that you have sanitized every possible area or there may be moth larvae lurking there ready to hatch out," he said.

Once you've cleaned up the area, be on the lookout for more moths and re-sanitize if there is the slightest hint of re-infestation.

Now, let's get outside and tackle the mosquitoes. This year was unseasonably cold during the spring, then we got rain and very warm weather. The combination of warmth and moisture was perfect for hatching mosquito larvae. Now there are legions of mosquitoes waiting to pounce on you.

The best way to control mosquitoes is to eliminate their environment. Standing water is nothing but a breeding ground. If you have ponds, keep the water flowing. Don't bother fogging. Try as you will, you can't kill off the entire mosquito population. Five minutes after you fog an area, the wind may blow in a whole new mosquito population.

If you're going to have a party, cut the grass extra short and apply a mosquito repellent like Mosquito Beater by Bonide Products, Inc. of Yorkville, New York to the outdoor party area.

Mosquito Beater is not new but it is quite effective. It is a granular, Naphthalene based product that works on the same theory as moth balls. Mosquitoes and black flies stay away because they can't stand the smell. You will notice a moth ball smell when you first put it down. That smell goes away in about a half hour.

To apply, spread one half cup of Mosquito Beater per ten square feet. You can just broad cast it or buy the sifter canister. One bag or canister treats 5,000 square feet, and costs about two cents a square foot. Don't waste the product by spreading it where there won't be any people. If no one walks down the side of the garage, don't treat the area. Let the mosquitoes congregate there and have their own party.

Apply the repellent about one hour before the party starts. It will be effective for up to eight days, but rain or even a heavy dew dissipates the product and makes it ineffective. Don't try to save money and not use the repellent until mosquitoes become a problem. Once mosquitoes get the taste of blood, they go a little crazy and repellent won't stop them.

You can find Mosquito Beater at many ACE, ACO, True Value, HWI, Servistar and Damman hardware stores, Home Depot and most independent garden centers. If you have a problem finding the product, call their rep at (800) 552-8252.

JUNE 15, 1996

Before you purchase a gas grill, consider all the grate options

by America's Master Handyman,
Glenn Haege

Here's a little vignette that is being enacted in countless homes around town. Mom decides to have a Fourth of July barbecue. Dad gets to do the honors. He starts out strong, beginning to clean the old gas grill a week early. Unfortunately the gas grill has turned into a rust bucket.

The paint is flaking. The burners are disintegrating. The cart is on it's last legs. The cooking grate is rusty, yucky or chipped. Maybe a combination of all three. The redwood shelving is weathered, greasy and rotten.

Dad has to get rid of the old grill and get a new one set up before the big day. If this vignette sounds like your real life story, here are a few things you should consider before buying your next gas grill.

Big decision: Do you want to buy a light duty, disposable or a heavy duty, long life grill? Gas grills are a lot like light bulbs. Disposable bulbs are cheap but have to be replaced every thousand hours or so. Heavy duty bulbs last far longer, but are several times more expensive.

Light duty, gas grills cost between one and three hundred dollars and usually only operate effectively for two or three years. After that, everything starts going bad. The paint job looks terrible. The burners and support legs get rusty. The igniter button just laughs when you push it.

Heavy duty gas grills start at about four hundred dollars. The support base, usually called the cart, and the hood are made of much heavier duty metal. Some of the pricier models may even use stainless steel. The burners are made of heavy gauge stainless steel. The igniter switch is usually the more durable, rotary type.

A giant step above the heavy duty grills are the professional models designed for restaurant use, or for the movie star who has everything. They run from $2,000 to $5,000 or more. If you're going to buy one, and have the chef to go with it, consider adding Barb and I to your party list. Now back to the real world.

Whether you should buy a light duty or a heavy duty grill depends on you. Over a nine year period, you may buy three light duty gas grills. If you pay an average of $250 per grill, that would amount to $750 over the nine years. For the same amount of money you could buy a very good Weber, Ducane or other top of the line grill.

There are some very good reasons for buying low priced grills. If you are a little short of cash, or live in an area where someone may requisition your grill in the middle of the night, you only lose $250 with a light duty grill. If you only use a grill two or three times a year, it doesn't make sense to pay top dollar. Another advantage is that you always have something new. Every three years you get to go shopping and get yourself a new toy.

If you buy a heavy duty grill, you make the entire investment at one time. Properly maintained, the product can last a lifetime and you will have a vastly superior appliance to make those all important steaks and burgers.

The first things you notice with a heavy-duty gas grill – as with a new Cadillac, Continental or BMW – are the look and feel of strength and quality. You also get a certain prestige of ownership.

Makers like Ducane and Weber have a tradition of quality and leadership. The MHP (Modern Home Products) and PGS (Pacific Gas Specialties) grills have a lineage that goes back to the very beginnings of the outdoor grill industry, and have never lowered their standards. The PGS grill, for example, is so strongly built you can jump on it without causing damage. Try that with a $189 special.

You also get many quality features you won't find on light weight models. Heavy duty stainless steel or porcelain-coated steel grates provide a superior cooking surface. The bars are more closely placed, so that you actually can grill vegetables as well as beef, fish or fowl.

If you choose the elevated rear burner option on the Ducane, MHP or PGS grills, you can use indirect heat to cook roasts, chickens, and turkeys to succulent perfection. The same feature makes it possible to grill hamburgers and steaks so effortlessly you don't even have to turn them.

After the quality decision, you have to decide what size grill to buy. Most manufacturers make two sizes. If you are only cooking for you and your significant other, or if it is just mom, dad and two kids, get a smaller, one or two burner, model. You will still be able to make burgers for that occasional party of ten.

If you do a lot of back yard entertaining, invest in the larger model.

If you often entertain 25 or more, look at dual grill models by MHP, PGS or BroilMaster.

The final decision is whether to buy a natural gas or propane grill. Most of us automatically opt for propane. If you use your gas grill a great deal, don't like unsightly propane tanks hanging around, or don't ever want to run out of fuel, consider a natural gas hook up.

Installation of the gas line varies from house to house, but will probably cost between $150 and $200. This may be offset by savings on fuel costs over the years. Natural gas is the most economical fuel you can buy, and eliminates lugging those heavy propane tanks around town forever. Propane, purchased in small tank sizes, is one of the most expensive fuels.

If you decide to shop for a long lasting grill you can find Weber grills at better hardware stores and home centers all over town including Damman Hardware and Home Depot.

Ducane, MHP, and PGS are harder to find. There is a good selection at Jimmies Rustics or call Ron Hunkins at Thermo Fire (800-878-7000) for Ducane, or John Botsford at Ameri-Flame (248-546-3214) for the MHP and PGS dealers nearest you.

If rains have left you with mold and mildew, then wring out the air

by America's Master Handyman,
Glenn Haege

I don't have a crystal ball, but let me describe your house. You discovered that mold is growing in one or more corners of the basement. The cold water pipes are sweating. Condensation on cold glasses are making puddles on counters and tables. The air conditioning just makes the air feel cold, not dry.

Mold, Mildew and the Musties, three guests you didn't invite, are making the air rank, dank and dreary. Extra cleaning doesn't help. Even turning the air conditioning on high just changes the air from hot and humid to cold and clammy.

The reason this condition exists is that this past week's downpours have super saturated the clay soil, wicking moisture through your home's basement walls and slab, adding to the humidity already in the air. Add the natural heat making ability of your house and the warmth and moisture you and the rest of the family release into the atmosphere, and you have a prime breeding ground for mold, mildew, and the musties, and any other bacteria that might be hanging around.

If you recognize these signs you need to wring out the air in your house with air circulation and dehumidification. The best place to start is the basement. If you do not have a basement, start on the first floor.

Position a box or oscillating fan at the farthest end of the house, aimed at the center ceiling. Attach the fan to an appliance time set for six hour on, two hours off. Keep the fan running for several days.

Position a dehumidifier at the other side of the room. Turn it on the low setting and keep it running continuously. If the dehumidifier condensation coil starts to freeze up, turn it off immediately. There is nothing wrong with the dehumidifier that a good cleaning will not fix.

To clean it, take the dehumidifier outside. Take off the casing and wash down the dehumidifier with a garden hose. After cleaning, air dry the dehumidifier for several days.

When you are certain that all the wiring on the dehumidifier is perfectly dry, take it back to the basement and run according to the instructions I just gave you.

Since I am talking about a great deal of fan use, you may be tempted to turn the furnace blower fan setting to constant running. Do not do this. Let your air conditioning unit decide when the furnace blower should be on. If you keep the furnace blower running when the air conditioner is not running, you will just circulate cold, damp air throughout the house and actually work against the furnace drying process.

After running the oscillating or box fan and dehumidifier for several days you will notice a marked improvement in the basement humidity. When it feels relatively warm and dry, leave the fan running, but take the dehumidifier upstairs. Put the dehumidifier in the largest room. Make sure it is out in the open, not buried behind some furniture.

Turn the dehumidifier on and let it do its job. In addition, place a oscillating fan on the other side of the room and keep it running until you are comfortable. You will find that this procedure will do wonders.

Last winter I suggested that you buy a BT-254 F Hygrometer (humidity tester) by Bionaire. During the winter, you use this tool to make certain that there was sufficient humidity in your house. During the summer you should use it to see where there is too much humidity. (I checked with Damman Hardware and they keep them in stock.)

Now is the perfect time to whip out your trusty BT-0254 F and look for pockets of high humidity in your home. When you find one, fight it with a fan. Turn it on for three or four hours, then recheck with the Hygrometer. Stagnant air is the prime ingredient for mold, mildew and the musties.

Homes with a high vaulted ceiling should have a ceiling fan to keep the air moving. If you don't not have one, installing a good quality ceiling fan should be a top priority. Joyce Begnoche, the manager of Haig Electric in Canton (810-791-2380) recommends that when the ceiling is over eight feet high, you should get at least a five or six blade, 52 inch or longer, fan.

Some fans blades only have pitches of 9 or 10 degrees. To really move air, the pitch should be at least a 14 degrees. The low speed setting should develop between 70 and 90 Revolutions Per Minute (RPM) and move 1300 to 1500 cubic feet per minute (CFM). Keeping a fan moving during the summer doesn't cost money, it saves you money. A gentle breeze of cool air, will cool you down, and let you be comfortable with the air conditioner turned to a higher temperature.

JUNE 29, 1996

Take the pain out of painting with the right tools and techniques

by America's Master Handyman,
Glenn Haege

In the next two months American homeowners probably will buy and use more outdoor paint than they will in the rest of the year combined. You may be one of those lucky homeowners.

This article is designed to give you pointers to make the ordeal as pain-free as possible.

What kind of surface can you paint? Wood, aluminum, vinyl, concrete, brick? I don't recommend painting brick because it's a very porous surface that was never meant to be painted, but paint stores have specialized paints that will do a good job.

Properly cleaned, aluminum siding provides an even better painting surface than wood. But chalking must be removed, or a product such as Emulsibond should be added to quality latex paint before starting the project.

Paint or stain?

Your first decision is weather to use paint or stain.

When painting a new house or garage, I recommend using a stain for the first few coats. Most people paint, but stain protects the surface just as well and adds far less "mil build" (coating thickness) that will eventually have to be sanded and scraped.

You can always stain or paint over a stain, but you can never stain over paint.

When staining over a previously stained surface, choose a solid-color stain that will cover any imperfections. When staining, use long strokes, try not to overlap and never stop in the middle of the wall. Short strokes, overlaps and starts and stops will all be noticeable after the stain dries.

Latex or oil?

The majority of Americans choose to paint rather than stain. Oil-based paints are worked into the wood, forming a rigid water-tight film. Water-based paints dry to form a tough but not water-tight membrane that "breathes," letting air and moisture pass in and out.

Oil-based paints – because they are far more forgiving – require less surface preparation; dry slower; and adhere to dirtier, shinier, more weathered surfaces.

Water-based paints dry faster, have less odor, are more tolerant to humidity, and require only a soap-and-water cleanup. Water-based paints outsell oil-based paints about 10 to one. If you have to paint over an older paint job and you can't do proper preparation, seriously consider oil-based paint.

If rainy weather or extremely high humidity are problems, choose water-based paints. On a high humidity day, water-based paint just takes longer to

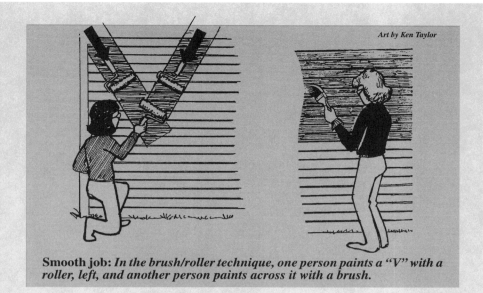

Smooth job: *In the brush/roller technique, one person paints a "V" with a roller, left, and another person paints across it with a brush.*

dry. Water-based paint also dries and skin coats faster protecting the paint job from a shower.

Which paint to buy?

All paint manufacturers make high-quality, long-lasting paints. If they didn't, they would be out of business in no time. But almost all of them also make the promotional stuff that you should not buy.

The difference in quality paint and cheap paint is the amount of guts in the bucket, the quality and quantity of the pigments and binders.

The paint industry is very competitive. The higher the price, the higher the quality. The higher quality the paint, the easier it goes on, the longer it lasts, the less it fades and the better it protects.

According to the Rohm and Haas Paint Quality Institute, top-quality acrylic latex paint has about 50 percent more paint solids and dries about 50 percent thicker than ordinary latex paints.

For most exterior paint jobs, I recommend water-based latex flat outdoor paint. Enamel's gloss rate makes it easier to clean, but magnifies and imperfections in the wood or paint job.

The only time you need to use a primer is when you are painting wood for the first time.

What else do you need?

A Painter's tools are his or her arsenal. The best paint, applied with poor equipment, is going to result in a sloppy looking job. Cheap brushes fall apart fast and spread unevenly. High-quality brushes will practically last forever.

To paint a house, you need a 2-inch or 2-1/2-inch brush for small areas, a 3-inch or 3-1/2-inch brush for large expanses, and a 1-1/2-inch notched (angular) brush for window sashes.

Use natural bristle or nylon/polyester bristle brushes with oil-based paint. Use

continued on next page

nylon or nylon/polyester bristle brushes with water-based paint. (If you are painting T 1-11 a type of siding), Detroit Quality Brush (800-722-3037) has developed a special Groove Brush for those long grooves that drive painters crazy.

Your roller should be a quality 9-inch five wire cage model with a handle that is specially threaded for use with an extension pole.

Roller covers have become a commodity item. Good rollers cost $4.50 to $5 and have a good phenolic core and the proper trimmings, filament design and nap needed to give long-lasting service and flow the paint on evenly You will also need a wood or metal extension pole such as a Mr. Long Arm. A 4-foot wood is plenty for the average ranch type.

By the way, a good ladder is important, so important that I will try to write a column about ladders and proper ladder selection in the next couple of weeks.

When using a roller to paint your house, don't be limited by the roller tray. For fast and furious roller work, try a gallon of paint in a 1-1/2-gallon bucket fitted with a roller screen.

If you want to use a paint sprayer, rent an HVLP (high volume/low pressure) model from your neighborhood paint or equipment rental store.

If you do not have spray painting experience, use a brush or the brush/roller technique. Your house is no place to learn to use a paint sprayer.

Canvas drop cloths are excellent for professional or people who remodel houses for a hobby. Do-it-yourself painters should stick to inexpensive, disposable products.

Exterior prep:
Most important step
The best paint in the world is only as good as the surface preparation. Paint won't stick unless you put it on a firm, clean, dry surface.

Firm means that all loose, peeling and scaling paint has been scraped away and rotten wood has been replaced.

Clean means that the surface has been washed and all dirt, mold, mildew, nests, etc. have been removed. I usually use a TSP (Trisodium phosphate) solution for exterior cleaning before painting. If the surface is only slightly dirty, use a 4-ounce dry measure of TSP per 2 gallons of water. If the surface is very dirty use an 8-ounce dry measure of TSP. If mildew is a problem, add 4 cups of household bleach.

Many people use pressure washers for this step. Pressure washing strips much of the loose paint. It also puts a great deal of pressure on wood and forces water into cracks and crevices, possibly ruining some insulation.

Whichever way you decide to clean, wear long sleeves and slacks, goggles and rubber gloves. Clean in the cool of the morning. Never work in the direct summer sun.

After hand washing, you can usually paint the next day. Power washing may require several days drying time.

This is when you reputty the windows and recaulk areas where the caulk and putty has become old, hard and cracked. If you press the caulk with you thumb and it doesn't give, replace it.

To replace, soften with a heat gun, then scrape away with a chisel or putty knife. Final cleanup can be accomplished with mineral spirits. If you have a lot of putty to remove, try to track down a Prazi Putty Chaser by Prazi U.S.A. (508-747-1490). This new product attaches to your 1/4-inch or 3/8-inch electric drill to remove hardened putty in seconds.

When you find a raw wood surface under the caulk or putty, coat the surface with Penetrol by the Flood company.

You should allow 24 hours drying time. If you don't have the time, use a water-based stain kill such as Zinsser 1-2-3 and you will be able to recaulk in four hours.

Painting techniques

When painting, always remember that spread rate is more important than the number of coats. With a water-based paint, you are trying to apply a finish that will be 5 mils thick when dry. That is very thick and means that the paint has to be oozed on.

To train yourself, measure out 100 square feet and put 1 quart of paint into the roller tray. Force yourself to use the entire quart on the 100 square feet. That's how the entire job should be done.

The easiest and best way I know of Painting a house is the brush/roller technique. This is a two-person job. The first person transports the paint to the wall with a roller and paints a large "V." The second person "tips in" the paint by brushing across the "V" with a 3-inch or 3-1/2-inch brush. You will be amazed by how fast this goes.

If the surface was especially chalky after cleaning, add Emulsibond to the paint. If there was a mold or mildew problem, add a mildewcide such as Sta-Klean to the final coat. If spiders and ants are a problem, use an antibug additive such as Bug Stuff.

You should be able to find most of the items I've recommended in the paint departments at better hardware and home centers and at all full-service paint stores.

There is a lot more that I believe you should know about exterior painting, but I've run out of room and it took me a 224-page book to explain it all. This will get you started. Follow the steps I've outlined and you will earn bragging rights big time.

JULY 6, 1996

Take careful steps in choosing a long-lasting ladder for your home

by America's Master Handyman,
Glenn Haege

Whether getting the family cat out of a tree, cleaning the eaves troughs, changing a hallway light bulb or painting the dining room, ladders are an indispensable part of most households. They can also be a fast ticket to the hospital.

Ladders are definitely not one size fits all. You or your house may have outgrown the ladder. A conventional home requires a 6 foot high stepladder. If you have a newer home with cathedral ceilings, you'll also need a 12 footer.

If you do outside work, you may need an extension ladder. The average ranch type home is 11 feet from ground to roof line, 17 feet from ground to peak, and requires a 20 foot extension ladder. The average two story home is 19 feet to the roof line, 25 feet to the peak, and requires a 28 footer.

There are a lot of choices. Leno Corradi, owner of the area's leading ladder supplier, National Ladder & Scaffold Co. (800-535-5944 or 248-399-0984 in Detroit). The company lists 70 different sizes and styles of wood, aluminum or fiberglass extension ladders and 89 different sizes and styles of stepladders in their catalog and maintains a complete inventory at their Madison Heights, Canton and Grand Rapids locations.

In addition to step and extension ladders, there are many special purpose ladders, including trestle ladders (a combination of a two sided stepladder and an extension ladder); tripod ladders (a three legged step ladder that is very good for use in corners and uneven ground); platform ladders; shelf ladders; stocking ladders, and attic ladders.

Ladders come in wood, aluminum, and fiberglass. Wood is often the least expensive and does not conduct electricity when it is clean and dry. But wood ladders can crack and warp and are the most perishable.

Aluminum ladders are strong, rugged, and light. Unfortunately, they conduct electricity and should never be used where they can come in contact with electrical cables. This makes them a no-no for inhome use.

Fiberglass is very strong and non-conductive, but is not as rugged as aluminum. Treated with care, a fiberglass ladder can last practically forever, and is my favorite for in home use.

Ladders are rated by grade, type and duty rating. There are four different grades: household, commercial, industrial, and extra heavy industrial. Each grade has a type number. Both grade and type number indicate a duty rating which is the maximum weight of the person plus clothing, tools and materials, that can be safely carried by the ladder.

Confused yet? Don't try to remember this. Clip the article and save it for when you need to buy.

Wood and Aluminum ladders come in all four grades. Fiberglass ladders are premium and just come in the top three grades.

Household grade (type III) ladders have a duty rating of 200 pounds. No one heavier than an ant should buy this grade ladder.

Commercial grade (type II) has a duty rating of 225 pounds. This is still not heavy duty enough to give the safety edge you need.

Industrial grade (type I) has a duty rating of 250 pounds, the minimum acceptable for most homes. Remember most Americans are over weight. Many men are carrying 30, 50, 75 or more extra pounds. Few of us are getting lighter.

A good ladder can easily last 20 years. The ladder you buy today should be the highest grade you will ever need, not the minimum you require.

Extra heavy industrial grade (type IA) has a duty rating of 300 pounds. This is the best quality ladder that you can buy and is the minimum acceptable if any person using it would even think of shopping at a big & tall men's store.

I buy extra heavy industrial grade (IA) fiberglass ladders. Although they are the most expensive you can buy, they meet or exceed every requirement my family will ever need. It costs a couple of extra bucks to get the best but it is well worth the money.

Ask yourself this before you buy: Why do you need a ladder? Why do you need to store a 23-foot extension ladder in the garage 50 weeks out of the year? If you decide to buy an extension ladder, also get a stand off/stabilizer by Werner. It attaches to the top of the ladder and makes the ladder a great deal more stable and safe to use.

Most equipment rental stores specialize in short term ladder rental. Specialist stores like National Ladder & Scaffold, deal in long term rentals.

If you are going to paint the outside of a two story house, consider renting scaffolding. National Ladder will rent a 20 foot high, 10 foot long, 5 foot wide, scaffold, including safety bracing and guard rails, for only $110 a month. And you can fit the whole thing in the back of your buddy's pick up truck. This amount of scaffolding will let you work safely up to a 26 foot height. You don't have to worry about stretching, tipping, or moving a heavy ladder every couple of feet.

Whatever you choose. whichever equipment you rent or buy, make safety your first concern. Don't over stretch. Don't take chances. Don't pinch pennies. Your body is not made for bouncing. Besides, good readers are hard to find.

JULY 13, 1996

New home test can tell you if there's more than air in your ductwork

by America's Master Handyman, Glenn Haege

Is there something in your ducts that's bugging you? If you suspect there is, Sanit-Air of Troy, Michigan, has just introduced a way for you to find out for only $37. For this small amount of money, they will send you a test kit which you attach to an air vent for 15 minutes, then seal and mail back to Sanit-Air.

Sanit-Air technicians grow the culture, then put it under the microscope and send you a complete report. The findings may surprise you.

My editor at Master Handyman Press had her home tested before and after she had her home's ductwork cleaned. She received both good and bad news. The good news was that Terry Baker, the chief scientist, at Sanit-Air did not find any bacteriological growth in the duct work. However, he found that the ductwork culture had a 13 rating of cladosporium fungus. Anything over a 10 rating is considered severe contamination. So my editor really had a problem and immediate action was required.

Twenty-four hours after duct cleaning and sanitizing, the test was redone, and the cladosporium count was down to 1. This level of contamination is typical of the average house.

According to Connie Morbach, owner of Sanit-Air, seven types of fungi found in homes: aspergillus, penicillium, cladosporium, yeast, epicoccum, chrysosporium, stachybotrys, trichoderma, trychophyton, fonsecea compacta.

Fungi are not exactly the kind of folks you want to invite to your house and stay the duration. According to Morbach, you do not want them anywhere near your home if someone in the house has allergies, asthma, diabetes, or is on any immunosuppressive drug.

For example, members of the aspergillus genus cause a group of diseases known as aspergillosis. These diseases can take the form of an allergic reaction, or an invasive infection in individuals with lowered resistance due to an underlying debilitating disease or prolonged treatment with immunosuppressive drugs. People with diabetes or who are recovering from burns are particularly susceptible to aspergillosis.

Fungi from the Penicillium family can cause allergies and chronic asthmatic-like conditions to hyper-sensitive individuals. Definitive studies have not yet been done, but there is also some speculation that people who get a reaction from penicillin, may have had the condition worsened by penicillium in their home.

Gladosporium, like that found in my editor's duct work, is very common on decaying plants and can cause allergies and chronic asthmatic-like conditions.

Stachybotrys can release a neurotoxin associated with memory and hair loss, sleeplessness, and infant death.

Trichoderma can cause chronic asthma-like conditions.

Fonsecea Compacta is rare but can cause a chronic infection with wart-like tumors.

The common bacteria found in ductwork are staphylococci, bacillus, and micrococcus. Staphylococci and micococcus can cause diseases in human beings.

"Most of the spores of these microbials are commonly found in the air we breath. In themselves they do not cause problems," Morbach says. "They need nutrients and moisture to become active."

This is where your ductwork comes in. Dirty ductwork is loaded with a vast banquet of things on which microbes like to dine: common household dust, drywall dust, dead insects, and common household dirt. If your home's ductwork has never been cleaned, it probably has a half inch thick layer of dust on the bottom, assorted collections of newspaper, drywall or plaster, small pieces of wood that were swept into the ducts during construction. My editor found fifty year old newspapers, mini-boulders of plaster, and an assortment of nails and wood in hers.

All of these contaminants turn the ductwork into a vast Petri dish just waiting for moisture before exploding into a microbial Garden of Eden. During summer, the humid, air in the ductwork, gets chilled rapidly by fresh cooling air from the air conditioner, causing condensation. The condensation provides the moisture necessary for the microbials to become active and multiply.

The June 1996 issue of Indoor Air Quality Update reports a NIOSH (US National Institute of Occupational Safety and Health) study that indicates that occupants of buildings where the ductwork has not been cleaned are more than twice as likely to develop respiratory ailments.

I have done my level best to spread the clean air gospel for years. The air in our homes is often the most polluted air we breath. The two prime causes are insufficient air infiltration and dirty ductwork.

Thanks to Sanit-Air's new service, it is cheap and easy to find out. Every home in America should be tested. You can get the kit by sending a check or money order to Sanit-Air, 966 Livernois Rd., Troy, MI 48083 or charge on your Master or Visa Card by calling (888) 778-7324.

Following the '12 commandments' can increase success of projects

by America's Master Handyman, Glenn Haege

I didn't really get them off a mountain top, but these commandments deserve to be carved in stone. Follow them and you will never get into trouble on your Do It Yourself projects. Ignore them and your body or your bank book will pay for the oversight.

1. Learn all you can before you do. There is no excuse for not knowing all about a job before starting. Consult my and many other people's books, newspaper and magazine articles, tapes, radio and TV home improvement shows. Get free handouts and attend seminars at paint and hardware stores, home centers, and builders shows.

2. Plan all jobs well in advance. Don't try to hire a roofer in the middle of summer, or buy a furnace when the first snow flies. Back time your projects so that you have time to organize, comparison shop, check references, and still be one season ahead of when everybody else is doing that kind of work. Don't stand in line, start the line, and you will get work done by the best professionals at very good prices.

3. Always read the directions. Women are way ahead of the game here. Women read directions and are not afraid to ask. Many men just open a can, box, or bottle, and start working, then wonder why the job goes wrong.

Call the company, a buddy, the hardware store, or a radio show like mine, and ask for clarification if everything is not perfectly clear. You will be amazed at how much time and money this saves you.

4. Never bite off more than you can chew. Do It Yourself is one of America's greatest building trends. The more you do, the greater your skills become.

If you become a really good carpenter, go ahead and remodel the kitchen yourself. There will be some "iffy" moments, but you can do it. I can guaranty that you will be an even better carpenter after hanging all those new cabinets and cutting those counter tops.

On the other hand, if you hit your thumb, almost every time you try to hammer a nail, and are proud when you saw a straight line, hire a professional. An amateurish job can cost you many thousands of dollars when it comes time to sell your home. Be smart. Stay within your skill level.

5. Never tear up more than one room at a time. I know that if you are going to paint, it sounds smart to wash the walls in the dining room and family room at the same time. Unfortunately, if we tear up two rooms, the family has no place to go. Mess up one room at a time. Get the job done fast. Clean up right away. And brag about the results.

6. Never learn to use a major tool on a big job. Practice on something small. The use of every major tool, a new saw, a power washer, a paint gun, is a little different. You need to experiment and get the feel of the equipment.

This is especially true with power washers and spray painting equipment. With power washers the tendency is to tear up wood. With spray painting equipment, uneven coverage is the major failing. Either can ruin a job.

7. Never climb a rickety ladder, or any ladder you do not feel comfortable climbing. Birds fly, people fall and break things. You are not made for bouncing. Cheap, light weight, or rickety ladders have put many people in the hospital.

8. Never get careless around anything electrical. Just brushing against the wrong wire can kill you, or cause you to drop a power tool, or ruin a paint job. Keep yourself, and your ladder away from wiring. Always make certain that the power is turned off before you attempt any electrical repair.

9. Never over build for your neighborhood. "Don't move, improve" is a great slogan and good advice. Just don't go overboard. A 4,000 square foot palace in a cozy neighborhood of 1,200 square foot bungalows will never provide a decent financial return on the dollars invested. If financial return is of prime importance, do not over-build.

10. Never be afraid to turn a job over to a professional. Too many men (thank heavens this is not usually a female failing) have this macho thing, and refuse to believe a job is above their skill level.

My editor's husband ruined three plastic drain repair kits before he gave up and called a plumber. You are too smart for that.

11. Always check references and get a completion date. Checking references is the only way you can find out if a professional really has the skill to do a job. Putting a completion date in the contract is the only way you can be assured the work will be done on time.

Don't sign on the dotted line until you have checked the references and gotten a completion date in writing.

12. Remember, your check book is the most important tool in your tool box. The power of a checkbook is an awesome thing. Use it properly and it can build you the home of your dreams. Waste it and you will be a very dissatisfied customer.

Danger level for radon in the home is still up in the air

by America's Master Handyman,
Glenn Haege

"We know that radon can cause lung cancer. We just don't know how much, what level of radon gas is necessary to create a dangerous environment."

John D. Boice Jr.
Scientific director of the
International Epidemiology Institute

Newspapers throughout the United States carried a brief stories about radon gas, reported by the Associated Press. The story, datelined Washington, DC, reported that a major scientific study conducted in Finland, showed no correlation between low levels of radon gas in homes and lung cancer. The study was conducted by the Finnish Center for Radiation and Nuclear Safety.

There was little or no follow-up on the study in local media, so I had John D. Boice Jr., the gentleman quoted in the article, on my radio show 8 a.m., last Saturday. Boice, who is currently Scientific Director of the International Epidemiology Institute, was former chief of radiation epidemiology at the National Cancer Institute.

He is one of the best people to discuss the hazards of radon gas because he doesn't just talk about the problem, he has years of experience overseeing large radon gas studies in the United States and other countries.

The Finnish test, which Boice thought was very well done, analyzed the residential radon exposure of 1,055 lung cancer patients, and compared the results against a control group of 1,544 non lung cancer patients. Very importantly, the people selected for the study were all long term residents of the houses in which they lived so that radon-related lung cancer could be directly attributed to gas found in the house in which they lived and the exact residential radon level that had caused the cancer could be measured.

It was a great study, but there were no residential radon-related cancers found. There was no statistical difference in the radon gas level in the homes of those people with lung cancer and those people without.

Boice is quick to point out that although no relationship between residential radon and cancer was proven, 85 percent of all the people with lung cancer smoked cigarettes. Even the most hardheaded of my cigarette-smoking friends has to recognize that link.

The new Finnish study is corroborated by similar studies in the State of Missouri, Canada and China, which also showed no correlation between residential radon exposure and lung cancer. The only study to date which has found a possible correlation is one conducted in Sweden.

Still more tests that Boice is involved with, currently underway in Connecticut, Utah and England, may hold the key to definitively answering the question of radon level danger, he says.

Boice, who says that in all his years of study, he has never found a single case of lung cancer connected to residential radon gas levels, nevertheless considers in-home radon a potential problem.

"We know that radon can cause lung cancer. We just don't know how much, what level of radon gas is necessary to create a dangerous environment," Boice says.

Radon is a clear, odorless gas that forms from the decay of uranium and radium in nature. It is measured in picocuries per liter of air (pCi/L). In nature, radon raises from the ground and is dissipated in the air. In his book, *Radon The Invisible Threat,* published (Rodale Press), Michael Lafavore, reports that .2 pCi/L radon level is the average in outside air.

In homes, radon usually seeps into the house through the basement and becomes trapped inside the home until dissipated by normal air circulation. The problem is that the tighter and more energy efficient we make our homes, the harder it is for naturally appearing radon to dissipate.

In the 1980s, the Environmental Protection Agency pegged the action level (when something should be done about radon exposure) at 4 pCi/L. There was no scientific reason for this. It is just a government number.

Most other countries have higher action levels. Canada lists 10 pCi/L. Sweden lists 11. The National Council on Radiation Protection lists 8.

No one knows what the danger level is, yet according to the Associated Press, Americans have spent about $400 million testing and repairing homes with higher than EPA recommended radon levels.

I have long maintained that the EPA's radon action level was too low. The Finnish test seems to confirm my "don't be alarmed – go slow" approach to radon.

If you are concerned that you may have a radon problem in your home, you can find radon test kits at almost every hardware store and home center. For preliminary testing, I suggest buying an inexpensive carbon test kit. Put it in the basement. If the carbon kit shows a higher level of radon than average, invest in an Alpha Track test kit and send away for a definitive reading.

If the Alpha Track results come in high, there is still no reason to become frantic. The problem can usually be solved by merely increasing fresh air exchange in your basement.

Do-it-yourselfers find new creativity in the arts and crafts world

by America's Master Handyman,
Glenn Haege

Where would you look if you were renovating your bathroom and wanted the sink to be exactly the same color as your hand glazed, ceramic floor tile? Or were redecorating the family room and wanted to replace the tired old, switch plates and electrical outlet covers with, dare I say it, switch plates and outlet covers that actually had personality?

Where would you shop for a one-of-a-kind, handpainted mailbox, that included likenesses of Uncle Joe, Aunt Martha and their kids?

Who could be relied on to make you a unique mini pond you could put on the deck so you wouldn't have to dig?

Millions of do-it-yourselfers could give you the answers because they are among the loyal fans who attend arts and crafts fairs around the country. They have turned what started out as a group of do-it-yourself hobbyists an exploding business phenomenon.

Someone tuned into arts and crafts would search out a ceramic painter to glaze the sink. He or she would select from a host of ceramic artisans and wood workers for the switch plates. The personalized mail boxes could be commissioned from a skilled wood crafter or metal worker. The unique minipond would come from a metal sculptor. You can find many of these wonderful craftspeople hanging out together at the many arts and crafts fairs you'll find throughout the country.

In the '70s and '80s, the trend was for homemakers to buy magazines like Better Homes & Gardens and House Beautiful to try to duplicate the look of the fabulous homes pictured. Then came the do-it-yourself revolution, and innovation and exploration became the order of the day.

Homemakers found that do-it-yourselfers didn't have to limit themselves to pounding nails and painting the garage. Jean and Joe Average gained the courage to experiment, renovate, and decorate rooms that were uniquely theirs. Along the way they discovered arts and crafts, distinctive hand made items, often made by do-it-yourselfers just like them.

They liked the fact that these artists and artisans would discuss their work, show how it was done, give a novice a helpful hand, or offer to make a piece just for the customer, to their specifications.

Arts and crafts went from being oddities shown at neighborhood fairs and festivals, to extravaganzas that took over entire cities the size of Ann Arbor, or filled giant football arenas like the Pontiac Silverdome.

Today, the field is so big that it has its own magazines with titles such as American Craft, the Crafter, Crafts 'N Things and Craftworks for the Home. Even one of the big boys of the publishing business, Better Homes & Gardens, has a whole series of craft magazines for the Do It Yourselfer, including BH&G's Decorative Woodcrafts, American Patchwork & Quilting, and Craft & Wear.

For my money, one of the best of the magazines is Country Folk Art, published right here in Holly, Mich. According to its distribution director, Mary Ellen Krause, Country Folk acts as a year-round link between many of the craftspeople found at the best shows and the homeowner and collector.

Careful study of the magazine can show the enterprising do-it-yourselfer which way the industry is heading. According to Krause, cows and ducks are still strong but seemed to have topped; Angels are ever popular and multiplying in variety; Snowmen and Santas are coming on strong; and the Western Motif is so big that Country Folk Art is bringing back a twice a year magazine, Yippy Yi Yea Western Lifestyles.

Country Folk Art magazine also shows variations on decorating themes that can make a home extraordinary. One ex-

ample is Cliff and Barbara Bliss' handmodeled geese with granite, quartz, flint and other types of crushed stone that give the birds colors and textures unlike the cast concrete birds you normally see. A story about the geese will be in the magazine's pre-Christmas issue that will be mailed Sept. 3.

Another example is combination ironing boards and step ladders from Grandpa's Crafts, pictured in the September issue. The unique combination turns a mundane item you might try to hide in a closet or basement, into a conversation piece you'd want to be the center of attention.

The magazine acts as nation-wide communications network between crafters (as the practitioners of arts and crafts call themselves) and their fans. It is so popular with advertisers and readers that its Pre Christmas issue will run 200 pages. The issue should be in bookstores by Mid September. If it is like most issues, it will be sold out within two weeks.

Should you be a do-it-yourself type of person, but not yet an arts and crafts enthusiast, you can learn a lot about the phenomena by getting a copy of the magazine.

AUGUST 10, 1996

Get the key items in writing before committing the job to any contractor

by America's Master Handyman,
Glenn Haege

I've spent years telling readers and listeners how to find a good modernization contractor. But once you've found one, what do you do?

The modernization contract becomes the key ingredient to assuring that you will get a good job. The "standard contract" you may receive to sign when the contractor asks for your down payment may not be in your best interest.

First of all, there is no "standard" modernization contract. If your contractor paid good money to have a "standard" form printed, you can be sure it has been fine tuned, and is loaded with paragraphs designed to protect the contractor, not you. If a contractors association has put together a "standard contract", it often means that a bunch or high priced lawyers have gotten together to create a document that gives the contractor loads of weasel room and severely restricts the homeowner's rights.

How do you make sure that there is enough good stuff in the contract you sign to protect your interests and assure a good, hassle free, job?

The following information should be in every remodeling contract to give you the information you need and protect your rights. The contractor, or his sales representative, may say that there is no room for this information on their contract form. That's OK. You don't need a printed contract form.

Let the contractor retype the contract, putting in all the required information. His doing this also gives you a legible typewritten version of all the contract's fine print.

If the contractor protests, make me the bad guy. Give the contractor a photo copy of this article on the meeting before the contract signing. On the day of the signing use this article as a check off sheet. Don't sign until every point is covered. Don't let the contractor bully you. If the contractor refuses to put any of this information in your contract, he or she should not be given the job.

Here's the information you need.

1. Complete name of the modernization company.

2. Name of the head of company, the qualifying officer (the person who holds the builders license number for the company), and the name of the production manager.

3. Address of company.

4. Statement that the company will obtain all necessary building permits and blue prints, and what the costs shall be for these items.

5. Listing of Company's Workmen's Compensation and Casualty Insurance Company names and policy numbers and a statement that you will receive certificates of insurance from the insurance companies or their agents before work begins.

6. Builder's License number of both the company and the qualifying officer.

7. Exact description of the work to be done, including all dimensions.

8. Drawing of work to be done showing location of all doors, windows, stairways, or special features. In the event of a simple modernization, such as furnace replacement, this item can be eliminated.

9. Listing of all special materials or equipment to be used in the modernization. This listing must include the Manufacturer's name, trade and model name, model number, and exact dimensions. Never allow the term "industry standard" to be included in your contract. It will usually be used to short change you.

For example, if a door is being installed, list who makes it, what the name and model number of the exact door is, and the dimensions of the door. If it is an exterior door, also require the name, description, and model number of the lock set.

10. Clean up and trash pick up is part of the job. Make certain that the contract lists who will be responsible for what, when.

11. Statement that you will receive Full Unconditional Waivers stating that all construction lien rights to your property are being relinquished by the sub contractors, employees and/or building materials suppliers, before you are required to pay their bills.

In other words, if concrete work is done, you pay for the concrete work after the concrete company and the subcontractor who actually did the concrete work, have been paid and supplied, signed, Full Unconditional Waiver of Lien Forms to the builder.

This is not too much to ask. Your down payment assures that the builder has the money to do this. The builder gives you the Full Unconditional Waiver Forms along with his invoice when he or she asks for payment.

"Full" and "Unconditional" are the two most important words. A Full Conditional, or a Partial, Waiver means that there may still be work not done, materials not delivered, or bills not paid, and you could still be on the hook.

This is one of the most critical parts of the entire agreement. In many States, including Michigan, if you do not get Release of Lien forms signed by the materials suppliers and the subcontractors,

they have a right to lien your property if they do not get paid by the builder. This means that even though you have already paid the builder in full, you could be forced to pay for the job twice in order to clear the title on your property.

12. Statement that you will receive copies of all product or equipment guarantees or warranties used in conjunction with the job after it is paid in full.

13. Statement that all work shall be done in compliance with, or exceeding applicable state, city, and county building codes, and that all work will be inspected and approved by the appropriate inspectors.

14. Guaranteed start and completion dates. The completion date is most important. A penalty clause should be included, specifying money to be paid to you if the work is not completed by the completion date. Likewise a bonus extra payment should be specified that will be paid the builder if the work is done before date.

15. Itemization of how additional costs shall be determined if unforeseen, but necessary, work is needed once the job has begun.

16. Payment terms. I don't care if the builder is your brother, never pay more than 30 percent down. Payments should always be linked to task completions and the receipt of release of lien forms signed by the pertinent subcontractors and building materials suppliers. Always hold back at least 10 percent until the job has been finished to your satisfaction, all cleanup has been completed, and all trash taken to the dump.

This may sound like a lot of work, it is. Would you rather do the work and be sure of what you are getting, or not do the work and run the risk of getting into trouble later? Play it smart. Get the information you need written into your modernization contract. Then sit back and brag about the results!

Companies focus on subtleties to satisfy our nation of nesters

by America's Master Handyman, Glenn Haege

It is difficult to describe a hardware show attended by some 70,000 people at Chicago's McCormick Place Complex, as having a "mellow mood," but so help me, it did.

The National Hardware Show, which was held in conjunction with the National Building Products Exposition and Conference, had the complacent feel of an entire industry which was basically pleased with itself, wanting to hold on to what it already had, and just fine tune their products to make sure they felt the public's mood.

The show's feel reflects the yuppie generation comfort with approaching middle age. The generation is not looking for revolution; it's more than content with evolution.

The new products being offered tell me that buyers want to hunker down, feather their nest, and personalize their environment to make their home express themselves. This may not sound like wild eyed adventure, but most of us don't want to push away the snack table, and leave the home theater to go out anyway. After all, if we wanted to go out, why would they have bothered to put the Discovery and Travel channels on cable.

Most of us want to be able to take a door, a wall, a window, a floor, a piece of pottery and make it a unique expression of our own personality, created with our own hands. Here are just a few examples of how different manufacturers are trying to fill our demands.

Stanley Door Systems' (800-521-5262) new Select Entries Systems of doors are shipped individually so that the retailer can offer the widest possible range of styles. Instead of just having a selection of doors, you can pick the door, then choose the special features, like decorative etched glass, buy them separately, and install them yourself. The result is the widest possible selection and personalization, at the lowest possible cost. The new Stanley Select Entries come in both steel and fiberglass models.

If security is your major demand, the Stanley Steel Security Door, has a unique, multi-point lockset that secures the door at the top, middle and bottom of the jamb and can resist force entry pressures of up to 300 pounds. All three bolts work simultaneously with a single lever action.

And while we're talking about doors, Weiser Lock (800-677-LOCK) introduced the Powerbolt Keyless Entry System at the show. The ultimate in personalization, the Powerbolt has an electronic deadbolt with a touchpad numerical control. You never have to carry a key while jogging, or worry about losing a key again. Once you key in your personally chosen security code, just input the security code, and the door unlocks.

The lock even has a provision for a second, temporary security code, that would allow you to give the code to a neighbor, for a one-time entry, then erase the code without interfering with, or divulging, your personal number.

If you want to change the look of a metal or fiberglass door to a stained, natural look, you can do it with the new Minwax Gel Stain line, introduced by the Minwax Company (800-526-0495), at the show. I have often recommended using a gel stain for giving a wood stain look to metal or fiberglass surfaces but the product was exclusively manufactured by a small company which had sufficient market clout to gain the distribution necessary to meet demand. Now, with Minwax, I will not only be able to talk about it, you will be able to find the product.

Minwax also debuted its Minwax Home Decor line at the show. The new, integrated, line includes an entire spectrum of paints, glazes, tools and accessories for faux finish techniques on wood.

Our own Detroit Quality Brush, (800-722-3037) had one of the most attractive exhibits at the show, highlighting Dave Campbell's rag roller. The Rag Roller, which makes it easy to give any wall that custom, rag-rolled look, was gaining a great deal of interest from national companies. (That-a-way guys; you are making us proud.)

Shaped Edge Borders by Forbo Wallcoverings (800-366-7700) also were designed to give walls a customized appearance. The new self-stick borders jut into the wall and look like they were painted there. There's no paste, no water, no mess. If you prefer, you can give an antique look with embossed, paintable, Profile Moldings from the same company.

Get the idea?

Fast, easy, personalization techniques are coming on strong. Not just by these, but by hundreds of different companies, covering many different areas we have not covered today: floors, shelves, windows and window treatments, decks, pavers. You will see all of these ways to personalize your home at your favorite paint, hardware and home centers by next Spring. If you want something sooner, use the phone numbers I have listed and see if they are already at a store near you.

AUGUST 24, 1996

Start planning before-winter projects now

by America's Master Handyman, Glenn Haege

Let's get it out of our systems. All together now: *"Where did the summer go?"*

One look at the calendar tells us that this is the weekend before Labor Day. The summer that was has done got up and went. End of summer does not mean the end of the home improvement season. On the contrary, it means that we have seventy, maybe eighty, days of prime do-it-yourself time before the winter winds blow.

But it does mean that planning is critical. Here's how the Handyman looks at the calendar: Dec. 25th is Christmas; Nov. 28th is Thanksgiving; Oct. 31st. is Halloween. Today is Aug. 24th.

It's up to you to fill in the blanks, to decide what you want to be done by these dates. Prioritizing and back timing are absolutely essential. The first thing you have to do is decide whether it is realistic to try to get what you want, when you want it. For instance, if you wanted to have new windows installed before Thanksgiving, you're already behind the eight ball. The next two or three weeks are critical. The time to start a thorough shopping and selection process is now.

Even seemingly realistic goals take a lot of planning. If you decide that by Oct. 31 you want the kitchen painted, new curtains up, a new light fixture and vinyl floor installed, here is what you should be doing.

Right now, Aug. 24th, look for sales on high quality flooring, curtains and paint. Shop tough. Pick out the flooring first, then the curtains, then the paint color.

Taking on too many projects is a common error. So look at the calendar. How long is it going to take you to find the items?

How long will it take you to get that flooring installed? The actual work may be done in a day, but it could take two months for delivery.

How long to paint? Depending on the condition, an average room can take two or three complete days. Two days for preparation. One day for the actual painting and clean up. If you are going to faux finish one of the walls, add an extra day.

How long to get the light fixture installed? Sure, it should only take an hour. But is the fixture you want in stock or does it have to be special ordered? Are you going to do it yourself or do you need an electrician? Can you even find an electrician who will do such a small job? If you don't know of someone, get the name of several small job electricians from the electrical department or electrical supply store where you are buying the fixture. If they can't help you, don't buy the fixture from them.

150

Now, throw in some "wiggle" time. You can bet all the money in the coffee fund that something is going to happen. Screw-ups will occur.

Ask yourself if you can realistically get all the work done in the time you have allotted? Don't think you are suddenly going to be able to paint until 2 a.m., then get up at 6:30 a.m. and work the full day. It won't happen and bosses get ugly when they see that work is being short changed because of your favorite DIY project.

If you don't have the time to do all you want, revise the plan. Prioritize now before you tear the place apart. A little extra planning now can save a lot of heart break later.

Even if you are not planning anything major this fall, you are not off the hook. Now is the time to take a look around and do any exterior work that needs to be done. Earth is easy to move now. It is next to impossible once the freeze has set in.

Look at the landscaping. Does a bush or tree have to come out? Take it out now and see how that effects the water flow around your house. Remember, water has to wash away from, not toward the foundation.

This is also the perfect time to check the caulking and window putty. Remember the rule, if the caulk gives when you push in with your thumb nail, it's fine. If it's hard, it isn't doing the job and has to be replaced. Replace old caulk and putty now, while the weather is fine and the caulk and putty work smoothly.

Plan now for a fall season filled with accomplishment, and you may even have time to watch the Sunday afternoon football games.

A Personal Note
Starting September 7th, 1996, 10 a.m. 'til Noon, Eastern, the Ask the Handyman Show will be syndicated by Westwood One Entertainment, the nation's largest radio syndication company. That means that if you live out of the Metropolitan Detroit Area, and want to listen to my show or call me with a question, you can.

Radio syndication, even with the best and biggest companies is really a DIY project. That means that if you want to listen to me, your best bet is to call your local news or talk station, ask for the General Manager, and tell him or her that you want to hear my show. Tell them they can get all the details by calling Westwood One, (703) 413-8550.

These two independent groups help put the labor in Labor Day – salute them!

by America's Master Handyman,
Glenn Haege

I want to use this Labor Day Weekend Article to pay tribute to two hard working groups of people. They work harder, longer, for less money than most. They put their entire lives and fortunes on the line to make our lives better, our homes more livable, yet they get little respect and next to no loyalty.

I am writing about the independent paint and hardware retailers and the independent building and modernization contractors. I stress the word independent with both of these groups because it gets to the very essence of who they are, and what they lay on the line to serve us.

Most of us are wage slaves. We put in 35 to 50 hours, complain about the increase in hospitalization or pharmacy co-pay, live for our vacations, and day-dream about the glories of a worry-free retirement. The two groups I am honoring today feel guilty if they just put in 50 hours, often can only afford to wish for hospitalization, and are too worried about making this week's payroll to bother about retirement.

Most independent paint or hardware store owners work a six and a half to seven day week. Like many mom and pop businesses, it is often a family affair. Mom may do the books, place many of the buys, man a cash register, and be called in as a decorator consultant.

Dad "manages" the store; that means he does his best to make sure 10 to 30,000 items are in more or less logical order, hires and trains the personnel, answers customers' questions, gives impromptu "how to" lectures, and is thought to be personally responsible if some manufacturer includes one too few bolts in a "some assembly required" kit.

In addition to the locally hired and trained staff, Junior, Julie, Uncle Bob and Cousin Sally often also help out at the store. All put in long hours and work for surprisingly little money.

Most or all the family savings is tied up in inventory or upgrading the store. And the ROI, that is Return on Investment for you non-entrepreneurial types, is so limited that even looking over the books is enough to give most bankers a bad day.

Customer loyalty is such that when the paint or hardware store owners go out to check the competition, they can usually count on running into a relative or high school chum ducking into Sears or one of the big boxes in an attempt to save 10 cents on a bag of screws.

Customers seem to forget that the big chains usually only stock the 20 percent of products that comprise 80 percent of sales. Independents specialize and stock product lines in depth, but they can only afford to keep the inventory we need if we also buy the day in, day out, items there.

So join me in honoring the independent, hardworking, individually owned and operated paint and hardware store owners on this Labor Day. They work hard, risk much, and make our lives a whole lot better.

The next group of men and women I want to honor are the independent building and remodeling contractors. Their luxurious offices usually consists of the bench seat in their pickup truck. Their filing system is a wad of papers that tend to blow around the cab when the windows are open, and their scientific, computer controlled estimating system is often of the seat of their pants variety.

Independent contractors are overworked, undermanned, usually under capitalized, and absolutely indispensable to our way of life. They are in charge of bringing back, or adding on, everything our homes need to function properly. Ask yourself what you would do if the roof started leaking, or the basement was flooding, the house needed painting, or the electrical was shorting out, and you phoned for help, and there was no one there ... ever.

The independent building and remodeling contractor's day begins at the crack of dawn, when he or she plans the day, well before their crew assembles and materials are picked up. The contractor works throughout the day, matching the crew, pounding nail for nail, shingle for shingle, pipe for pipe and cable for cable, pausing only to answer questions and solve problems.

Then, when the crew has gone home exhausted, independent contractors get their second wind and go out to make the calls, and sell the jobs that keep their company's afloat, their employees working, and our homes livable.

We often bargain them out of their profits, bicker about the job if everything doesn't go exactly our way, then complain about the fact that there are not enough of them.

The independent paint and hardware store owners and building and remodeling contractors are some of the hardest working groups of people I know. If you are among their number, I salute you. Keep the faith. We need more of you. Have a great Labor Day.

As for all the rest, have a great day; but please, take a minute to reflect on how important these people are to all our lives, and give them a little more respect, understanding and loyalty.

Now's the time to cast a cold eye on the state of your insulation

by America's Master Handyman,
Glenn Haege

Don't let drafts give you a cold second story bedroom anymore, or a family room that feels like a meat locker, or the bathroom that specializes in freeze dried wash cloths, for the last ten or twenty years. This the fall to solve the problem, unless you really enjoy paying high heating bills to keep the pigeons warm while you shiver.

Homes built before the 1960s, had only a little insulation in the attic and no insulation in the walls. Homes built in the '60s and '70s, were only a little better. Even homes built 15 years ago may have little or no insulation between the garage and the adjoining family room.

The result is cold, drafts and high heating bills. I have always recommended increasing the insulation in attics in ranch houses and attics and walls in two or more story homes. Over the past year, I have seen enough studies to make me modify my recommendations and suggest that everyone, whether living in a single, or a multi-story home, up grade the wall as well as the attic insulation.

Michigan is in the process of revising insulation requirements on new homes and additions. The insulation requirements will increase to R19 for walls and R30 for attics. It makes sense to retrofit existing homes as close to the new specs as possible. In fact, I recommend that homeowners increase attic insulation to R45.

When you do this, you have to make certain that the attic has proper ventilation. Proper air flow requires soffit vents for air infiltration and roof or ridge vents for air exfiltration.

If you are not certain whether your home requires additional insulation, if you have recently upgraded the insulation in your home and still have cold spots, or have problems heating or cooling your home, it is a good idea to call in a company like Monroe Infrared Technologies (800-221-0163) to do an infrared energy inspection. The cost is only about ten cents a square foot with a $175 minimum. An infrared inspection will show you where your home is "leaking" heat. The same technique can demonstrate potential water leakage sites. Bill Fabian or one of his technicians, makes a visual infrared recording of both the inside and the outside of your house. It shows where insulation may be settling or non existent, where stapled insulation may have broken away and fallen, and where moisture is collecting.

After the house has been inspected you'll receive a copy of the recording, and a technician will interpret it for you. One of the best features of having a company like Monroe do an infrared energy inspection is that they are inspection specialists and have no vested interest in your buying insulation. If insulation is required, you can bring in bales of insulation and install them in the attic, or you can have a company that specializes in blown-in fiberglass or cellulose insulation.

A key advantage of blown in insulation is that, properly installed, it can go everywhere and fill in every nook and cranny. Done improperly, the insulation can get hung up on braces or wiring and leave air pockets.

Charles Akers of Ace Insulation (248-642-4311), a cellulose specialist, says that even the best contractor can leave an air pocket, so service after the installation is critical. He is so concerned that every one of his jobs is done correctly that he does an infrared inspection of every wall job after the insulation has been installed. If any pockets have been missed, the crew will fill the cavity.

Constant monitoring is the path to success in the insulation business. Bob Mackie, of Macomb Insulation (810-949-1400), a fiberglass insulation specialist, assures quality by going out on many of the jobs himself. He says that many newer homes have family rooms sharing a wall with an unheated garage and need to have the common wall insulated.

What is the difference between fiberglass or cellulose blown-in insulation? Owens Corning produces the majority of the fiberglass sold in Metro Detroit. Slightly more expensive than cellulose, it is an excellent quality, noncombustible product. Because the fiberglass is installed with a larger-dimension hose, work can be completed in a shorter time.

Cellulose insulation is made from wood chips and newspaper. In my opinion a real benefit is that it uses materials that would otherwise be clogging land fills and transforms them into a product we need. Cellulose is slightly less expensive and provides slightly greater R value by volume than fiberglass.

When installing blown in insulation into aluminum or vinyl sided walls, installers usually remove strips of siding at the top and immediately below any window or support framing, then blow in the insulation through holes drilled between the studs. After the insulation has been blown in, the siding is replaced.

When installing blown-in insulation into brick walls, fiberglass installers have to remove entire bricks from the walls because of the size of the fiberglass hose. Skilled cellulose installers, working with smaller hoses, can often blow in the insulation through holes in the mortar, leaving an almost invisible job.

As you can see this type of work can be pretty tricky. Reputation and references are everything. Be sure to check them before you sign on the dotted line.

Fixing caulking and mortar in the fall keeps a house warm in winter

by America's Master Handyman,
Glenn Haege

This is the best time of year to go around the house and really check the caulking. If you have brick walls, also check all the brick work for loose mortar. Look at the chimney as well as the walls.

Caulking is a prime factor in protecting you and the rest of the family from cold winter drafts and it really cuts down on the heating bills. Loose mortar allows not only wind and cold, but rain to get behind the brick surface. Fixing the problem takes only a little time and a little bit of hydraulic cement. Left un-corrected, the problem can degenerate the entire brick wall and result in astro-nomical repair bills.

Look everywhere. Around the windows. Around the doors. Around the electrical outlets. If the caulk has pulled away from the corners and edges it is supposed to be sealing, or has lost resiliency, it needs to be replaced.

Don't just look, give it the old thumb test. If the caulk doesn't give a little when you push in, get rid of it. The best way to remove old caulk is to soften it with a heat gun or Burnsamatic Torch. The Burnsamatic Torch is a lot faster, but if you don't like open flame, use the heat gun.

When the caulk gets pliable, scrape it away with a hook nose linoleum knife or a chisel point putty knife. Be sure to scrape away all the caulk. Leaving any residue will adversely effect the set of the new caulk. After you have scraped away everything, clean the surface thor-oughly with mineral spirits or paint thin-ner.

Now you're ready for recaulking. Know this. All caulks are not created equal. Do not shop for the cheapest price. Three of the many new elastromeric caulks are Sika Flex, Sashco Big Stretch and Vulkhem. They cost more, but will give years of extra use. You should find these top quality products at any home cen-ter, hardware store or lumber yard.

If it has been a while since you caulked, you may also be in the market for a new caulking gun. Believe it or not, a Cali-fornia company, called Dripless, Inc. has developed a new, improved caulking gun that is, well, like the name says, dripless. When using the gun you get a smooth, steady bead, not any of those spurts or drips common with the old type of caulk gun. The professional model also fea-tures a hex rod that can be used as a lad-der hook, a spout cutter built into the handle and a spout punch. For more in-formation or the store nearest you that carries the new Dripless caulking gun, call (800) 960-1773.

Now, let's get to the brick work. Replacing loose, damaged or missing mortar is very important. Make certain that you check all the brick on your house, that includes the most important brick that any home has: the chimney. If you can't see your chimney brick clearly, don't be too shy to bring out the old binoculars and walk to the sidewalk so you can get a good angle. Loose mortar on chimney brick may be symptom of a far more serious problem. You probably don't belong on the top of the roof trying to do cement work and hold on at the same time, so if you see loose mortar, seriously consider calling in a professional chimney cleaning company, like Mary Poppins, or ask the Masonry Institute of Michigan (734) 458-8544 for a referral for someone to repoint the chimney and do an interior chimney brick inspection. Moisture may have gotten into the chimney and started degregating the interior brick. When that happens it can cause the entire chimney to have to be replaced. So don't kid around. Call them in.

If the loose or missing mortar is close enough to the ground for safety, you can easily do it your self. First, spray down the entire brick area with a garden hose. This both helps clean the area and dampens the surrounding brick so that it will not draw moisture from the new mortar.

Clear all the old loose mortar from the joint between the bricks. You may need to use a cold chisel and hammer to get some of the damaged mortar out. Chisel out the damaged mortar joint to a depth of at least one-half inch. If you do, be sure to wear goggles. Clean out the joint by blowing or brushing away with a whisk broom.

To fill in the joint, mix up a very small batch of Mason Mix by Quikrete. Use only a little water. You want the mixed mortar to be a plastic-like consistency. Put the mixed mortar on a small board that you will use as your pallet. Using the bottom edge of a mortar trowel, pick up a small amount of the mortar and carefully push it into the cracks. Be careful not to get the mortar on the surrounding brick work.

When you've done a few bricks and the mortar is thumbprint hard, finish off the joints by drawing a jointer or piece of dowel rod across each mortar joint at a 45 degree angle to match the old mortar joint. Make sure you do this after you have finished each area.

If an entire brick has become loose, take out the entire brick and chisel away all mortar. Then butter the top, bottom and sides of the brick with mortar and push it into place. Remove excess mortar immediately and finish off the joints as soon as the mortar gets thumbprint hard.

Home expo in Southfield has everything for do-it-yourselfers

by America's Master Handyman, Glenn Haege

All year long you read my columns and/or listen to my radio shows. This is the one time of the year that you actually get to see what I talk about. This weekend, my originating station, WXYT-AM 1270-Detroit, the city of Southfield, Hansen Marketing, Fireplace and Spa, Flame Furnace, and Westshore Estates, combine to put on Glenn Haege's Home Improvement Expo. The show is at the Southfield Civic Center Pavilion, Evergreen at 10 1/2 Mile, from 8 a.m. to 6 p.m. today and 8 a.m. to 4 p.m. Sunday

To my knowledge, I am the only how-to talk-show host and newspaper columnist to have his own home-improvement show. There are three big differences between my show and most of the other ones.

1. My show is primarily educational. You come to Glenn Haege's WXYT Home Improvement Expo to learn. You will find more education per square foot than any how-to, home improvement expo in the world. That's why the City of Southfield has given us so much help over the years. City officials know this is the public's best chance to get hands-on home improvement information, and they want to be involved.

2. You get to see, touch, and learn first hand about all the things I talk about all year long. As much information as my show gives, there is no better way to learn something than to experience it first hand. Here are just a few examples of what I mean:

I talk about testing and cleaning the ductwork in your house for Microorganisms. Sanit-Air has a display explaining testing procedures, plus a new UV device that can safely remove microorganisms from your home 24 hours a day, 7 days a week. Connie Morbach, Sanit-Air's owner, will be on hand to explain everything to you. To give even more information, several of the best duct cleaning companies in Detroit will be there .

With our recent cold snap, heating questions are on the rise. Several companies will have answers. We have everything covered – from the latest in high-efficiency furnaces and the new Complete Heat design that provides an unlimited supply of hot water, to heat-producing direct vent and ventless fireplaces. Flame Heating and Fireplace and Spa will bring major educational displays.

Added insulation and improved windows are often needed to keep the heat in and the cold out. Ace Insulation and Weathergard Windows are on hand to show how they can help. Motor City Services has created a display to show how just about everything I talk about in heating and cooling interconnects.

Kitchen and bath remodeling are the most popular home modernizations. Nu-Way Supply, Universal Plumbing, Budget Electric, and Val-Tile, as well as two bath tub relining companies, Bathtub Liners of Michigan and Bath Fitter Tub Inserts, will be on hand to answer your questions.

Concrete cracks and painting are a constant problem. Gibraltar National, the Quikrete people, and Epoxyseal, the revolutionary water born concrete people, both have displays.

Not a week goes by without leaky basement and deck questions. Everdry Waterproofing, Insta-Dry Waterproofing, Mr. Sponge, S.A.S. Basement Waterproofing have educational displays. Roto Rooter shows how to keep the drains from plugging up and flooding the basement. On the deck side, Damman Hardware, Paint 'N Stuff, Painter Supply, Superdeck, Hansen Marketing and Coy Construction all have displays.

A gentleman by the name of Uli Walther has invented a revolutionary fastening system with far greater grabbing power than traditional screws and fasteners. Hansen Marketing is bringing the inventor all the way from Germany to answer your questions Saturday. The creators of Leafguard gutter systems will be on hand both days.

Since our homes are not just places to keep out the cold, the little touches that add quality to life are becoming more and more important, so Audio Video Systems is showing the latest in home theater, Gallery Animato will show fun decorations, and Tony V's, Four Season's, and Palm Spring Soft Tubs will demonstrate my favorite way of relaxing and getting away from it all.

To answer your questions on new home construction, Westshore Estates is giving seminars with their leading subcontractors between 11 and 12 noon on Saturday and Sunday. Reddi-Wall will be answering questions on new, insulated basements and foundations. Fairway Construction will have design teams on hand to show you how to put it all together, and several mortgage companies will show you how to get the money to pay for what you want.

See what I mean? Just about everything you ask me about, the Skuttle Model 216, Space-Pak air conditioning, Square Buff Sanders, Multi speed switches for blower motors, whole house vacuums, carpet cleaning, all the stuff you need to solve problems around your house, plus the new Parker & Bailey products I introduced on QVC Sept. 13.

3. Just as important is what the show does not have. There is no admission or parking fee. There are no nick nacks, no clog dancers, no carnival-type pitch people. All it costs is the gas it takes to drive your car.

Detroit News columnist and WXYT Talk Show Host Rick Bloom and I will be doing our shows from there. I'll be on hand during and after my show to answer your questions. So come, bring your brain and learn all that you can or be confused for the next 12 months.

Fall Home Improvement Show clears the deck for new product

by America's Master Handyman, Glenn Haege

One of the nicest things about having a builders show with a reputation for buyer sophistication, is the number of new products that manufacturers and distributors display. They actually want to hear what the consumers think and, consumers get to see products and services that are cutting edge. Here are a few examples we saw at my Fall Home Improvement Show last weekend.

One of the most difficult parts of painting is getting rid of the left over paint. Last weekend, Bio-Wash Products Inc. of British Columbia, Canada, gave away free samples of their new Latex Waste Paint Hardener at the Damman Hardware Display. It solves the left over paint problem: All you do is add the crystals to the excess paint and stir. Within two or three minutes, the paint turns solid and you can throw it in the trash. The hardener is available at Damman Hardware and Paint 'N Stuff.

One of my most frequently asked questions is "What is the best way to remove the old finish from my deck, so I can start from scratch?" Until now, deck stain and finish removers have been specific. You had to know whether the old finish was oil or water based, or you wouldn't get good results. If you remembered wrong, or just guessed, and got the wrong product, you had to re-do the entire project, doubling the work and the expense.

Last weekend, a local company, the Specialty Group (which makes Citrus Strip), showed a new product, Deck Stain & Finish Stripper, that removes both oil and water base stains and finishes. You simply apply the product, agitate with a deck brush, then spray away with a garden hose. The product contains no chlorine or other harsh chemicals, so it will not injure grass, trees, flowers or shrubs. Call (248) 340-0400 for more information or the dealer nearest you.

Two big improvements in indoor air quality control were demonstrated at the show. Most people who buy electronic air cleaner attachments to their furnaces get far less than they bargain for. It doesn't matter how effective an air cleaner is, if it only works when the blower motor is running, you only get air cleaned and filtered about 10 percent of the time.

On most furnaces, if you turn the blower motor on manually, the motor runs too fast and costs too much. Motor City Services president, Art Grace, designed an almost universal, after market, constant speed, blower motor switch and displayed it at the show. The new, extra low speed will enable most homeowners to turn their electronic air cleaners into 24 hour a day, 7 day a week air cleaning devices. For more information call (800) 292-1311 (Ed: unfortunately Motor City Services is out of business and we have not been able to locate another supplier.)

The second advance in indoor air quality control was a new UV air sanitizer demonstrated by Connie Morbach of Sanit-Air. Her company has started installing the new product in homes where elimination of airborne microorganisms is critical

Being a scientific type, she is doing in-depth testing in some of the new installations. The results so far have been so impressive that Ms. Morbach is planning a scientific paper on the subject. If air quality is critical in your home, Motor City's new switch, Sanit-Air's new UV air cleaner, or a combination of the two may improve the quality of life in your home.

For more information on the UV air cleaner call Sanit-Air at (888) 778-7324.

Anyone who has listened to my show during the winter knows that I often recommend the installation of interior magnetic storm windows. Far more efficient than exterior storms, they actually seal in the heat and make older, single pane windows almost as energy efficient as the newer double glazed models. Interior Storms also seal out a great deal of street noise and dust penetration.

The only negative with interior storms has been that there really was no competition.

Now there is: Diversified Energy Control, Ltd. demonstrated a new Magnetic Interior Insulating Window at the show. It features a wider magnetic strip, optical grade acrylic panes, and an I-Beam frame construction that flexes with freeze-and-thaw cycles to maintain a constant airtight seal.

I also like that Diversified Energy Control will install the storms, or sell materials so that the do-it-yourselfer can make and/or install their own. Call (800) 380-0332 for more information.

There were a great many other new products at the show. Uli Walther made such a big hit with his star-headed fastener system that he stayed an extra day (call Hansen Marketing for more information: (800) 552-4877. Mr. Sponge (800) 491-4686 introduced the first scientifically designed poured concrete tie rod hole filler, the Tie Reinforcement Sealer Kit.

I don't have the space to write about them all. You should have been there. Make plans, to come see it all at my Fall Home Improvement Show, next year.

OCTOBER 5, 1996

You shouldn't water down the importance of a high-quality valve

by America's Master Handyman,
Glenn Haege

"When is a faucet not a faucet?" Simple, when it is a valve. The exterior "faucets" that you use to water the garden or wash the car are valves. If they have a drip or a leak, you have to repair or replace them now, or hold off until next spring. The water turnoffs under the sink, by the commode, running to the water tank and to all exterior lines are also valves.

There is a big difference between valves and faucets. Faucets are turned on and off constantly. They are relatively expensive, heavy duty items. Valves are cheap disposables. They are used where a water shut off is necessary, but seldom used.

Since they only cost about $5.00, they are a throw away, not a repairable item. The theory is that since valves get very little use, it is not worth installing expensive faucets. Instead, you install valves, use them for 20 or 30 years and throw them away when they need to be replaced.

The idea is better in theory than practice for three reasons: Some valves, like silcocks (the outside water "faucets"), are used quite frequently. In older homes with galvanized pipe, one pipe screws into the other, requiring that all pipes between one end of the line and an offending valve be removed before the

valve can be replaced. Valves in homes with copper pipes are soldered into place and cannot be removed easily.

These factors combine to often make replacement of a $5.00 valve a very costly item, so your best bet is to try to extend their life as long as possible. I discussed the problem with Jim Kronk of Universal Plumbing (248-542-3888). Jim and all the people at Universal are very DIY friendly folk and spend a great deal of time telling weekend warriors how to get the job done. Here are a few of the tips he suggested to prolong valve use.

If you lose a valve handle, don't try to turn the valve on and off with a pair of pliers. The pliers will ruin the soft brass valve stem. Since replacement stems are not made, the entire valve will have to be replaced.

If the valve is dripping from the spigot, turn off the shut off valve feeding into the leaking valve, remove the handle and stem as you would from an ordinary faucet and replace the washer. Reassemble and turn on the water. If there's no drip, the problem is fixed; if there's a drip, replace the valve.

If the valve is leaking from the stem, the packing has been compressed. You may be able to solve the problem temporarily by tightening the packing nut with a pair of channel lock pliers. If that doesn't work, add some packing. Packing string is available at any hardware store.

Turn off the shutoff valve feeding into the leaking valve. Remove the handle and packing nut, pull out the stem and add three or four turns to the packing string. Replace all of the string if it is in bad condition. If packing string is unavailable, you can make do with mop string but it won't last as long. A length of Teflon tape spiraled into a thin rope is an ideal substitute. Reassemble the valve and turn the water back on. If the leak is over, you won. If not, replace the valve.

If the screw holding the handle is so worn that it can't be unscrewed, all is not lost. The cast-iron handle can be broken apart. If this is necessary, remove the upper portion of the valve with a wrench. Then break the handle into pieces with a pair of channel lock pliers. Do not King Kong it. If you bend the stem, the valve is done for.

You should wind up with the core of the handle held in place by the damaged screw. Saw a groove into the side of the core and knock it off the screw with a mallet and cold chisel. This should allow you to remove the screw with pliers. Disassemble the valve and replace packing and washers.

If the stem leak is on an outside valve (silcock) or any other valve that is used a great deal, remove the stem, take it to a plumbing supply store and buy preformed, original equipment packing for the valve. The heavier duty, preformed packing is well worth the extra time and money.

Many people ask if they can buy a new valve and use it for replacement parts instead of replacing a valve. Unfortunately, valves are commodity items. They are imported from all different parts of the world. There is no standardization and therefore no interchange ability of parts.

If you find that the valve has to be replaced and it is at the end of a run, the hose silcock on the outside of the house is a good example, you can probably replace it yourself. Just turn off the water. Twist off the valve with a wrench. Clean off the pipe. Put plumbers putty on the pipe and attach the new valve. Turn the water back on.

If the leaking valve is not at the end of a run you have to start from the end of the run and remove every pipe until you get to the offending valve.

Unless you actually enjoy this kind of thing, call a plumber.

When replacing a valve you will find a very wide variety of prices. If the valve is for a location that will never be used, you may be able to get by with a cheap import.

However, if you are buying a highly used valve, like the silcock, or a very important valve, like those underneath the sinks or in the laundry room, buy a Mansfield, or other heavy duty, American made product. There is about a fifty percent difference in price, but far more than a fifty percent difference in quality.

OCTOBER 12, 1996

When checking out a contractor's referrals, ask the right questions

by America's Master Handyman, Glenn Haege

You did your homework. You got the name of three to five good contractors. You had them stop by the house and discuss the job. You even had them issue a written quote and give the names, addresses and phone numbers of customers who have had the same type of work done by the contractor. Now what do you do?

I asked some highly regarded contractors and suppliers what questions they recommend you ask a referral before buying.

Eric Schultz, Director of the Roofing Industrial Fund (810-759-2140), is so concerned about the buyer's need to know before buying that he teaches a roofing information course at the Birmingham Community Center a couple of times a year.

"Most homeowners know nothing about the subject. The first thing that he or she should do is learn a little about roofing. Then go look at the referral's roof and see if it looks like a good job," Schultz said. If the appearance of the job isn't up to your expectations, you won't be pleased with your job. Don't even bother talking to the referral. That contractor should be on your dead letter list. If the roof passes the appearance test, Schultz says the only question you have to ask

is: "Would you hire this contractor again?" If there is any hesitation, you don't want that contractor.

When checking out window installers, you should ask the referral about the time frame of the job, says David McGraw, of Kimball & Russell (800-686-2300), a big Andersen Window distributor. Did they start and finish when they said they would?

Next ask if the referral experience any difficulty during the window installation? Were the workmen considerate? Did they respect the property, protect the area not affected by the installation and clean up after themselves?

McGraw's final questions relate to service after the sale. Has the referral noticed anything unusual since installation? Are they feeling more drafts? Are the new windows hard to operate or the screens hard to put in? These problems show that the windows were not installed properly and are not level.

Steven Toth, Cadillac Window Co. (248-352-5404), has a slightly different spin. His first tip is to ask for referrals with jobs that are at least 5 years old. "All new windows work. You want to talk to people whose windows have stood the test of time." The five-year limit also tells you that the installation company has been in business at least that long.

Toth also suggests that you ask referrals the length of their window's warranty and whether the installation company or the manufacturer is supplying it. "The manufacturer's warranty is the only one that means anything because many installation companies are out of business before the buyer has had any chance to get value out of the extended warranty the company used to get the sale," he says..

Dan Bergstrom, of Bergstrom Heating & Cooling (734-522-1350), says the shopper should ask for referrals who live in their immediate area. If they live within a few blocks, you may know them and can really get the skinny on the contractor.

Questions Bergstrom recommends asking referrals are: How do you know the contractor? If they are a friend or relative, treat everything they tell you with a grain of salt. How long ago was the job done? Did they keep their promises as to installation date, time, and price? Did they clean up after themselves? Finally, if the referral has had a service call since the installation, was the work done promptly and to their complete satisfaction?

"Also remember, choosing a service technician, is as important as shopping for a new furnace or air conditioner. The service technician comes into your home and you rely on the information he gives you as to the safety and reliability of the furnace. He has to be honest," Bergstrom says.

Jim Kronk, president of Universal Plumbing (248-542-3888), doesn't believe that tracking down referrals on plumbing jobs makes much sense. "Many jobs are very small, like installing a new commode, garbage disposal, or water tank. People are just too busy to track down referrals on that size job. This makes the plumbing wholesaler or parts supplier the most important part in the information loop. The supplier knows who is doing a good job and who has the time to actually do the work," he said.

What about the most important contractor purchase of them all, a new house? Susan Krall, a partner in Westshore Contracting (313-692-0044), says that with a custom home, or a major renovation, the most important question to ask the referral, is whether they were satisfied with the work.

"With every major construction, there are going to be problems. I warn prospective customers that they should expect them. But the important thing is, did the builder stick to his time and price lines? Did he handle problems promptly, fairly and efficiently? Krall says. "If the subcontractors did not come through and stand behind their work, did the builder do the work himself?"

If the referral says yes to these questions, Krall believes that you have found a good builder, and that you too, will be pleased.

Listen: Creating a home theater system in the living room is a blast

by America's Master Handyman, Glenn Haege

I learned that the average single family home in America is 28 years old. That means that at least half of us are living in homes built in the '40's, '50's, '60's, and '70's, for life styles of the same periods. And, believe me, they sound that way.

Many homeowners cannot even remember the '40's, but their plumbing can. For quite a few the '50's takes on the tone of ancient history, so does their homes wiring and lighting. For many younger Yuppies and older Generation X-ers, the '60's and '70's seem just plain old and out of date, just like their bathrooms and kitchens.

The modernization industry is booming because our population is trying to adapt older housing stock to the needs and lifestyles of the year 2,000. Nowhere is this more evident than in the not-so-quiet revolution in sound systems. Homes in the '40's and '50's were built for a world of radios and phonographs. The '60's and '70's had 8 tracks, components, cassettes. Sound went from monaural to stereo, but no one ever thought of, no home was every built for, surround sound. And the home theater concept is completely beyond the pale of all but the most sophisticated builders even today.

Al Stewart, owner of Audio Video Technologies (248-853-2170), is leading proponent of updating out of date houses for present day sound and entertainment systems. One very successful technique is to turn the least used room in the house into an utterly awesome, surround sound, home theater.

The home theater concept seems beyond the pale for many people, but the fear-factor can be taken away once you get up close and personal. At it's most basic, a surround sound home theater system integrates a series of five speakers with your television and VCR to make your sight and sound experience mimic what you would see and feel in a fine motion picture theater. As a side light, Yamaha even has an integrated component system (the Digital Super Surround) that will let you change the sound in your room to sound like Carniegie Hall, a cathedral, or an intimate jazz club.

Now back to home theater. About 85 percent of the sound, information and dialogue comes from the three front speakers (one center, two stereo). Two smaller "surround" speakers are mounted in the back of the room and serve to trick your senses into believing that you aren't just viewing the action, but are actually in the middle of it.

The real magic of a surround sound, home theater is a big speaker called a subwoofer that sits next to the video. This base unit usually just sits there like an unconcerned citizen, but when the bomb blasts, the jet takes off, the bat cracks, or the monster roars, the subwoofer leaps into action and gives the gut wrenching, timber shaking, low level sound, that makes your pulsating body feel like you are actually there.

This kind of sound and sight experience is not for everyone. I personally love it, but I have to admit it gets hard for the person sitting next to me to read a book while I'm grabbing onto the arms of my chair to keep from being blown over-board as a jet fighter takes off from my carrier. Having kids try to study in the same room would be flat out impossible.

That's why Stewart started champion-ing the idea of converting the living room into a home theater. To get the right effect, furniture has to be pushed away from the walls. Stewart tells people that couches are upholstered on the back as well as the front. For many this is a deco-rating revelation.

Creating a home theater in the living room accomplishes two things, Stewart says. The living room actually gets used, and the TV stops being the focus of the family room. Just think of that for a minute. The fireplace gets used. Family members get to read, talk and interact, with nothing more than a stereo in the background. Hey, that sounds so good it might catch on.

Reading about surround sound, home theater, and how it differs from the av-erage TV and stereo setup, is one thing. Actually experiencing it is another. If you'd like to hear, feel and see what I'm writing about, Audio Video Systems, on Rochester Road, just past M-59, has a series of integrated rooms in which you can get the total experience. It's a good place to begin learning about the sub-ject.

If you decide to get serious about the subject and start pricing out systems, make serious inquiries about who is go-ing to actually install your system. Most retailers do not have enough qualified installers to set up the equipment prop-erly. Remember, like I always say, you want to brag about your results.

Today's stain removers can clean up almost any devilish trick

by America's Master Handyman, Glenn Haege

Devil's Night and Halloween can be pretty scary. Kids in costume don't frighten me, it's what you sometimes find the day after. Even in the best of neighborhoods, little horrors tend to happen on Devil's Night and Halloween – egg and spray paint on the brick.; soap and wax on the windows; crayon and ink on the aluminum or vinyl siding; maybe even sticky candy and bubble gum in the hair. If you're really lucky, you may even have a combination of all of these on your car.

Manufacturers had developed specialized products to keep tricks from turning into permanent disasters. If the little devils have sprayed or splattered paint, scrawled crayon, or thrown tar on stone, concrete, brick, vinyl or aluminum siding, glass, fiberglass, and varnished or oil based painted surfaces, the staining can be removed with Atlantic Sundries' Graffiti Remover. An additional benefit of using this product for removing a stain, is that if the surface has to be repainted, Graffiti Remover is self-sealing, it acts like a sealer and the final finish coat can be painted directly over the cleaner.

If you have a wall that looks like it has been stained with latex paint, you can also try Oops! Latex Paint Remover by Rhodes/American.

You may already have Goof Off by Guardsmen Products of Grand Rapids in your home. It will also remove old latex paint, grease, crayon and tar based products. Goof Off will even get chewing gum and sticky candy out of the kid's hair so that you don't have to cut it out.

Other common household products that are good graffiti fighters are De-Solv-it Citrus Solution by Orange-Sol, Citra-Solv by Chempoint Products, Inc., and Goo Gone by Magic American. All three of these citrus based solvents and cleaners are excellent for removing oil, tar, lipstick, crayon, candle wax, grease, adhesives, decals and tape residue. Work the cleaner into the stain, blot out, repeat if necessary, then rinse with clear water.

You probably have a first aid kit hanging about the house, if you like the idea of getting a first aid kit for your house in case tricksters hit. I'd suggest Motsenbocker's new LIFT OFF Five Pack. The Five Pack contains 2 ounce bottles of all five of the company's specialized stain removers.

Motsenbocker's LIFT OFF No. 1 is specially designed to remove food, beverage and protein based stains, like chocolate, coffee, fruit juice, ice cream, ketchup, Kool-Aid, pop, wine, perspiration, grass, pet stains, even blood. One of the things that makes this cleaner so special, is that it actually neutralize the stains. It works on cloth, walls, countertops, tile.

LIFT OFF No. 2 removes all greasy, oily stains, stickers, adhesive residue, chewing gum, crayon, lipstick, even shoe polish from fabric, walls, aluminum and vinyl siding, floors and tile.

LIFT OFF No. 3 removes ball point pen and fountain pen inks, high lighters, magic markers, even permanent marks, nail polish and pencil marks from most fabric and exterior surfaces. If the stain is especially obstinate, use an old tooth brush or scrubbing brush to clear up the stain, then rinse off with clear water.

LIFT OFF No. 4 removes aerosol paint, enamel, semi gloss, oil based lacquers, acrylic, urethane, all oil based paints, even stain killers from concrete, plastic, brick, stucco, metal, vinyl and aluminum siding or rock.

LIFT OFF No. 5 removes all the other kinds of paints and stains including latex, wood stains, linseed oil, acrylic latex stains from the same surfaces.

If the surface has been sprayed with paint and you don't know which kind, start with No. 4. If that does not work, use No. 5. Most of the stains will come off with No. 4.

All these products also come in larger containers, but they are all highly concentrated and a little bit of cleaner goes a long way. If a wide area has been spray painted, you can get 16 ounces and even gallon sizes.

You can find most of these products at Mr. Scrubs on Greenfield and 10 and a half mile, Damman, Aco and many other fine hardware and home centers. There is plenty of help out there. If you have a really tough graffiti problem that you just can't seem to solve, call these special problem help lines: Motsenbocker's: 800-346-1633; Citra-Solv: 800-343-6588; Goo Gone: 800-321-6330; or Orange-Sol: 800-877-7771.

Before the big night arrives, do yourself and all the little ghouls and goblins a favor and put a little extra light on the subject. Change any outside yellow bug lights to clear lights.

My apologies

Readers living outside the 810 and 313 area codes who wanted to learn more about the Magnetic Interior Insulated Storm Windows that I wrote about a few weeks ago, but could not dial through the localized 800 number. The national manufacturer is a.1 Technologies Incorporated. Their 800 number is: 800-533-2805. Hope that helps.

NOVEMBER 2, 1996

Guide clues you in on how much value a home project will return

by America's Master Handyman,
Glenn Haege

One of the first questions anyone even remotely considering remodeling his or her home asks is, "Is this a good investment or money down the drain?" Remodeling salesmen are not usually the best sources for an honest answer, but who can you ask?

Every year Remodeling Magazine tries to give unbiased answers by publishing a Cost vs Value Report which analyzes the construction cost of typical remodeling jobs in different parts of the country, then reports what local real estate agents estimate the resale value of the remodeling would be if the home were sold within twelve months. This is priceless information for the homeowner. Keep in mind that these numbers do not reflect what I like to call the ROE, Return Of Enjoyment, or the increased salability the project gives the home.

The Detroit Area real estate agents who participated in the study this year were Vivian Wilson of Max Brock Real Estate in Bloomfield Hills (248-647-2200), Eric Pilarcik of Coldwell Banker in Clarkston (248-625-1333), Douglas Mason, Coldwell Banker in Plymouth (313-271-6300), Cecily C. Bliesath and Lavern Rusk, Century 21 in Birmingham (248-642-8100), and Irene Kraft, The Michigan Group in Brighton (810-227-4600).

Remodeling Magazine's study makes it easy to see the inflation cost of Detroit's current building boom. The job costs are uniformly higher in Detroit than the national and Midwest averages. Offsetting this slightly, we tend to recoup a trifle more of our remodeling dollar at resale. As you can see, Detroiters really like the idea of new windows, with an estimated return of 119 cents on the dollar if the home is sold within one year.

To my mind this is one of the most valuable annual studies in the home improvement field and a great service to the buying public. Anyone who makes a living in hardware, home improvement, building or real estate fields who does not yet have a copy of the study should get one.

The publishers of Remodeling Magazine make the report available for $8.95 including postage and handling. To get a copy, send a check or money order to Cost vs Value Report, One Thomas Circle NW #600, Washington, DC 20005, or call (847-291-5221).

How Detroit stacks up

Here's an abbreviated idea about how Detroit compares to the rest of the country and the Midwest in some of the categories. For a complete description you need the Cost vs Value Report. The national average is a compilation of the results of sixty cities. The Midwest average is a tabulation of fifteen cities including Chicago, Cleveland, Kansas City, Milwaukee and Minneapolis.

Two-Story Addition

A 24' X 16' wing over crawl pace. The first floor consists of a family room with fireplace. The second story has a bedroom with full bath. Separate heating and cooling system.

Area	Job Cost	Resale Value	Cost Recouped
Detroit	$59,646	$46,137	77%
National Average	$55,687	$46,236	83%
Midwest Average	$55,087	$40,622	74%

Family-Room Addition

Add a 16' X 25', light-filled room over crawl space with new foundation and wood joists, match exterior siding and fiberglass shingle roof.

Area	Job Cost	Resale Value	Cost Recouped
Detroit	$34,936	$30,409	87%
National Average	$31,846	$26,483	83%
Midwest Average	$31,773	$21,968	69%

Minor Kitchen Remodel

Update a 200 square foot kitchen with 30 lineal feet of cabinetry and countertops, including refinishing existing cabinets, new mid-priced sink, faucet, wall covering and resilient flooring.

Area	Job Cost	Resale Value	Cost Recouped
Detroit	$8,821	$8,406	95%
National Average	$8,507	$8,030	94%
Midwest Average	$8,170	$7,095	87%

Bathroom Addition

Add a second 6' X 8' full bath to a house within the existing floor plan.

Area	Job Cost	Resale Value	Cost Recouped
Detroit	$12,322	$11,560	94%
National Average	$11,645	$10,593	91%
Midwest Average	$11,648	$8,840	77%

— Source REMODELING magazine, October 1996. © Hanley-Wood, Inc.

You get what you pay for – and then some – in a furnace inspection

by America's Master Handyman,
Glenn Haege

Ten years ago, the mother and father in law of my Editor at Master Handyman Press had their furnace cleaned and checked with one of those $29.95, too-good-to-be-true, telephone solicitation deals. The technician found that the heat exchanger was cracked and was leaking potentially lethal amounts of carbon monoxide. The furnace needed to be replaced at once or the old folks might die in their sleep.

Because of the urgency, the head of the furnace installation company said he would put the old couple's job at the head of the list and install a new furnace the very next business day (Monday) as long as they signed a contract and gave the technician a check for $4,800, the furnace installation replacement cost. The old couple couldn't afford the $4,800, but they didn't want to die, so they signed a contract and gave the man a check.

Luckily, my editor heard about the problem. She knew this sounded like one of the oldest scams in the business.

Using my name and the executive director of Detroit's Department of Consumer Affairs as her battle cry, she called the company and quashed the contract. Then she called in a good local furnace contractor.

The new furnace technician found there was nothing wrong that a good cleaning wouldn't fix. If the furnace had needed to be replaced, a same size replacement would have cost only about $2,000.

The first company's representative had not only lied about the condition of the furnace, he had charged the old couple over double the fair market value! If my editor hadn't stopped by, the technician and his company would have gotten away with it.

Ten years have passed. The old couple, already high in their eighties when the incident happened, have passed on to their reward. But the furnace is still going strong. It's heat exchanger has not cracked, and it is not leaking carbon monoxide.

Every year hundreds, maybe thousands, of innocent people, very often senior citizens who can least afford it, are snagged by the same furnace scam. How can you make sure this doesn't happen to you?

As always, knowledge is power. Before you shop you should know the rules of the road. Dan Bergstrom, of Bergstrom's Plumbing, Heating and Cooling in Livonia (734-522-1350), says that you should choose the company that gives your furnace its annual cleaning with the same care that you would use if you were buying a new one.

You cannot expect to get something for nothing.

"A good furnace cleaning and check should take about one to one and a half hours and cost between $70 to $100. Some promotional contractors will occasionally sell cleaning and checks for $50 to $80 as a loss leader, he says.

According to Bergstrom, a thorough furnace inspection and cleaning includes a check and possible adjustment of the thermostat, controls, heat exchanger, blower, belts, pilot light, safety equipment, and air conditioner. The furnace should be tested for carbon monoxide and other harmful gas. The inside and outside of the furnace should be cleaned and the filter cleaned or replaced.

The humidifier should be checked to see that no water is dripping, and that the humidistat is operating properly. If the humidifier has to be cleaned it will usually cost an additional $20 to $40, Bergstrom says.

Once you get a report that your furnace needs major repairs or replacement, proceed with caution, he warns. Furnace heat exchangers do crack and are one of the major causes of furnace replacement.

"But even in the case of a cracked heat exchanger," Bergstrom says, "you have a few days to shop and get a second opinion."

Gary Marowske of Flame Furnace (888-234-2340), a large southern Michigan heating and cooling contractor, is running a furnace cleaning and safety check special. To make sure that no one takes any shortcuts on furnace cleaning and safety checks, he has issued a page-long explanation of standard operating procedure that itemizes every step of the program.

Marowske echoes Bergstrom's warnings about low priced specials and the need to get second opinions. "There is no way someone can go out to a house and clean and check a furnace for $15 or $20.

"If carbon monoxide or other gas leakage is found it has to be reported on the front of the invoice at our company. Anytime there is a leakage report, we send a second person out to recheck at no additional cost."

I believe that Bergstrom and Marowske are right on in their advice. Check up on the contractor before you invite them into your home. Don't expect something for nothing. Always get a second opinion before you make a major commitment. Remember, your check book is the most important tool in your tool box, use it wisely.

Hot high-tech grills will tempt you to cook the turkey outdoors

by America's Master Handyman,
Glenn Haege

Remember how sleepy you got after that big Thanksgiving dinner last year? If you used a gas stove to cook the bird, there is a good chance that sleepy feeling was as much due to oxygen depletion as it was to that third helping of turkey or the second piece of pumpkin pie. All the hours the oven and stove top burners are on, boiling potatoes, heating vegetables, baking pies, cookies, yams and turkey, you are burning up oxygen big time.

If you don't want to saturate the house with turkey smell, or burn up five or six hours of oxygen needlessly, you can show Mr. Turkey the door and still have him over for dinner by cooking the bird on the Barbecue. Some of the leading manufacturers have developed their equipment to the point where the gas barbecue grill is now a year-round cooking machine.

Two Columbia, S.C. manufacturers, the Ducane Co. and Thermal Engineering Corp., have developed highly specialized, though completely different grill designs for the serious enthusiast. Both grills are highly efficient, using lower BTU's than the average gas grill.

Ducane grills are designed from an even, slow cooking philosophy. This approach, can turn anyone, even an infamous backyard burner, into a backyard gourmet.

Thermal Engineering, uses unique twin Infra-Red burners, to instantly sear meat, sealing in the delicious juices while cooking very rapidly. A TEC burner uses only 16,500 BTUs an hour, yet operates with a surface temperature of 1,650 degrees Fahrenheit on "high fire". This is so hot, it can cook a 1-inch steak rare in four minutes, medium in six minutes. TEC's professional Searmaster line is used in some of the best steak houses around the country. The TEC Patio I puts the same technology within the range of the serious backyard enthusiast.

I'm writing about these grills today for two reasons. First, there is still time to get them before Thanksgiving. Second, neither of these grills are inexpensive, but they would make fabulous Christmas gifts for anyone who is serious about outdoor cooking. Clipping this article, underlining the one you want, and stuffing it into your wife's "honey do" jar, could have miraculous results.

Cooking a bird on a rotisserie gives it a taste you cannot duplicate. It can be stuffed, the only limitation is that it cannot weigh more than ten to fourteen pounds. Other than that, you can make a bird that you'll be bragging about for years.

The Ducane Company has developed a unique tri-burner grilling system that utilizes a separate vertical burner, called a Rotis-A-Grate. This special burner is very efficient. Although it uses only 12,500 BTU's an hour, it rotisseries the bird faster than the TEC speed grill.

With the Rotis-A-Grate, the bottom burners are not used. All the cooking is done from the vertical back burner. This allows you to put a drip pan holding the basting liquid underneath the bird. The pan collects the drippings and combines them with the basting solution to create a gravy base to die for.

Ducane recommends using an apricot basting sauce made from 1 cup Kahlua Liqueur, an 8 oz jar of apricot jam and 1 1/2 cups of water. For a less sweet taste, try their beer basting sauce recipe made from one 12 oz bottle of beer, 12 oz of water, and 1 stick (1/4 pound) of butter. Figure 15 minutes of preheating time and about 2 1/2 hours for cooking the bird. With the Ducane you rotis (their term) with the hood closed, basting the bird every twenty minutes. A Ducane Model 2004 with Rotis-A-Grate retails for about $ 850. For more information call ThermoFire at (800-878-7400) for the dealer nearest you.

With the TEC Infra-Red gas grill, you cook from the bottom. To rotisserie the bird, remove the cooking grids and position the BBQ tray under the bird. The tray should be partially filled with water, or a mix of fruit juice, apple cider vinegar, or beer and water. Close the top and cook for about 3 1/2 hours. Check every 45 minutes. Refill the liquid as needed. Use a dry tray for the last 15 minutes to make the skin crispy.

The TEC Patio I retails for $1,199 and is sold exclusively by Michigan Fireplace and Barbecue, Long Lake just East of Dequindre, in the Detroit Area (248-689-2296). Call Thermal Engineering Corporation, (803-783-0750), in other parts of the country.

If you are like me and love rotisseriing fowl, but hate trussing them, take a look at Broilmaster's Hugga-Rack Rotisserie attachment while you're at the store. Instead of a rod and meat hooks, this unique system features two, half basket-like metal frames which clamp together, securely holding the bird, making trussing unnecessary. Michigan Fireplace and Barbecue stocks them, or call Broilmaster (800-255-0403) for the dealer nearest you.

No matter which method you use to prepare the bird, test the inside with a meat thermometer and make sure the temperature is at least 175 degrees Fahrenheit before you stop cooking.

The hottest innovations in vent-free gas fireplace designs are, well, cool

by America's Master Handyman, Glenn Haege

It doesn't take a lot of cold to get me hot footing it over to the fireplace. I have always been a fan of wood fires. I still am. For my money, if you are a wood fire fanatic, there is no finer heating system than a Fuego fireplace, or fireplace insert. The Fuego is easy to light. It's flame is magnificent, and combustion is so complete that very few ashes remain.

Unfortunately, most of us no longer have a lifestyle that is conducive to savoring even the most efficient of wood fires. Wood still has to be stacked, stored, split, and brought into the house. Ashes have to be shoveled and fireplaces cleaned.

We have become more of an instant-on, instant-off, no maintenance please, society. Over the years this has led to the increasing popularity of natural gas fireplaces and logs. Today, gas fireplaces and logs by companies like Heat-N-Glo, Hunter, Napoleon, Fuego and FMI (Fireplace Manufacturers Incorporated), are so natural looking, you expect, but never have, to shovel ashes.

To learn what is leading edge on log and fireplace design, I went to the only place I know that always has 25 to 35 functioning fireplaces on display, Atlas Fireplace and Veneer, 2212 Livernois, in Troy (248) 524-1020, and spoke to the owner, Al King.

The two hottest innovations are very realistic vent free logs and fireplaces and electric fireplaces so real you can see the fire burning.

Vent free logs and fireplaces are definitely the stars of the show. King recommends FMI vent free gas logs to people who want to install gas logs in existing fireplaces. He suggests vent free gas fireplaces for no hassle basement installation. "When you install ordinary gas logs in a conventional fireplace, the damper has to be permanently set so that it is never totally closed. This means that you always have heat loss up the chimney," King says. With FMI vent free gas logs, the damper can be closed, doing away with heat loss; yet enough air seeps through the closed damper, to virtually eliminate gas smell when the burner is first lit,"

Vent-free gas logs are also quite economical and throw a great deal of heat. The logs retail for about $275 to $500 and can be installed for about $125 including gas hook up. Barb and I were very impressed and bought a set. The heating unit is so effective that I had to push my chair farther back from the fireplace.

A vent free gas fireplace in the basement, simplifies installation because it requires no chimney. In addition to making the rec room cozy, it eliminates the excess humidity usually found in the basement.

FMI Vent free fireplaces are available in one, two, three and four sided models. Prices range from around $1,000 to $3,500, installed.

For years condominium owners, and apartment and mobile home dwellers have asked me for a way to have a fireplace when no gas or wood burning installation is permissible. Until this year electric alternatives have never been realistic. Now a Canadian Company, Dimplex North America Limited (888) 346-7539, has created an electric fireplace called the Symphony. The flame is so realistic I was on my hands and knees looking for the fire. When you turn on the blower, it will heat a room at a cost of a dime or less an hour.

The Symphony isn't cheap, it costs about $1,000, installed. But it plugs into a wall socket. When you move, you can pull out the plug and take the fireplace with you! Wow!

Of course, if you live in a conventional house, and want to add heating efficiency that will warm that freezing family room and a large part of the house, you cannot do better than a direct vent gas fireplace or insert by companies like Napoleon, FMI, and Heat-N-Glo.

These units are certified as furnaces and perform at about 75 to 80 percent efficiency. They have sealed glass fronts and combustion air comes from outside, so their is never any heat loss. Their cost usually ranges from $2,000 to $3,500.

You can find working models of everything I've written about so far at Atlas Fireplace in Troy. Fireplace & Spa (248) 353-0001 is another big dealer with locations in Southfield, Utica and Canton. Or you can call the manufacturers for the dealer nearest you at the following numbers: FMI: (800) 888-2050; Heat-N-Glo: (800) 669-4328; Hunter: (800) 634-0233; Napoleon: (800) 461-5581.

If you are in the market for gas logs, or want to beautify your existing fireplace with unique, custom designed, fireplace doors, check out the selection at Michigan Fireplace and Barbecue, 18 Mile just West of Dequindre (248) 689-2296.

Don't be green when it comes to a fresh-cut or an artificial tree

by America's Master Handyman, Glenn Haege

It's time to put up old Tannenbaum. For many this will just mean dragging the artificial tree box out of the basement. Some will shop for a new artificial tree. Traditionalists (like Barbara and me) will go out and get what we call a live, but is really a fresh-cut, tree.

I wouldn't miss my annual trip to the tree farm for the world. We'll select our tree, have it cut, and, bring it home. But how should we shop for a tree? To find out, I went to see Robert Wilk at Evergreen Home and Garden Center (810) 791-2277 on Groesbeck South of 16 Mile in Clinton Township. Evergreen also has a store on East Eight Mile in East point.

I picked Wilk because Evergreen is a garden center that goes all out for Christmas. In a 2 1/2 month period they change over 90 percent of the merchandise in the store. The Clinton Township store has over 13,000 square feet devoted to Christmas Trees and decorations. And that doesn't include the live trees outside.

Dave, the live tree manager, says that the first thing you should decide is whether to get a live, or artificial tree. "You can't beat the look or smell of a real tree, but they have limitations. If you just want the tree up for a week or two, a live tree is a good choice. If you want a tree on display for over 18 days, you are better off with an artificial tree," Dave said.

Six different types of trees are commonly sold in Michigan. They are: Blue Spruce, Green or White Spruce, Scotch Pine, Douglas Fir, Fraser Fir, and Balsam. A seventh variety, the Con Color, which looks like a Scotch Pine with swirled branches, is being introduced, he says.

Scotch Pine has the best needle retention, closely followed by Fraser and Douglas Fir. Blue Spruce is among the most beautifully shaped, but is notorious for shedding needles.

Dave believes that the best time to choose a live tree is in the two weeks after Thanksgiving, when selection is at its best. "The tree is better off stored in your garage. Make a new angle cut at the bottom to help the tree absorb water. Store it in the garage standing in a bucket of warm water.

"When you bring it in, cut the trunk straight across, about an inch above the angle cut," he says. "Mount the tree in a sturdy tree stand. Fill the stand with water and add a commercial tree preserver."

Most stands are of light construction and have little room for water. Evergreen carries a new, American made, solid steel tree stand that has both the weight and the water capacity to do a good job. The stands range from a cost of about $40 for an average size tree, to $100 for trees taller than 12 feet.

I price checked both Evergreen and Franks Nursery & Crafts and found that fresh cut Christmas tree prices ranged from $15 to $60 in the popular 6- to 8-foot heights.

Artificial trees are a whole different ball game. Most come from China, some brands, like Hudson Valley, are still made in the United States. Evergreen has the biggest selection I've seen locally.

Artificial trees are classified according to how the limbs are attached when the tree is assembled: hook, hinge and combination hook or hinge. Trees are also classified by the total number of branch tips and the diameter of the bottom layer of branches. The different diameters are classified as Slim Line (about a 40-inch diameter for a 7-foot tree), Mid Girth (58-inch diameter), and Wide (up to 70 inches). Slim Line trees make it possible to have a tall tree in a smaller room. Most artificial trees have the stands included with the tree. These stands are usually fine for trees up to 8 foot tall. If you go for a taller tree, buy a heavy-duty tree stand.

Comparison shopping at Evergreen and Franks, I found that both had roughly similar prices for similar trees, but only Evergreen had a good selection of artificial trees over 9 feet.

Take care of sudden spills and stains quickly so you can party on

by America's Master Handyman,
Glenn Haege

If there's one thing that is guaranteed to take the "Ho, Ho" out of the holidays it's a glass of burgundy on the carpeting or a nice round "O" where a wet glass or coffee cup soaked through the table cloth. It is best if these, and any other stain, are taken care of immediately.

Here's a listing of how you should take care of the most common party-related emergencies.

Glenn Haege's All Purpose Emergency Party Pack: First keep on hand Club Soda, Facial Tissue and Shaving Cream. These three items can whisk away a grease, food or beverage stain from an expensive tie, silk blouse, velour top, party dress, table cloth, upholstery or carpeting.

Buy the cheapest brand or look for sale prices on these products.

Do not substitute paper towels for facial tissue. Tissue has many times the absorbency of paper toweling. This extra absorbency can spell the difference between success and failure.

When cleaning a tie, expensive party dress, or blouse, start with two handfuls of facial tissue. Pour a little cold soda on one handful, then using the other wad of tissue as backing underneath, or behind the fabric, gently blot away the stain with the soda dampened tissue. Use more tissue if needed. Always blot, never rub. Rubbing can set the stain.

If you stain a couch or deep pile carpeting, gently blot up the excess with tissue, then work in some shaving cream with your fingers. Do not spread the stain. After you have worked in the foam, scoop up the residue with wads of facial tissue. Do not rub.

Now let's go to regular stains.

Gravy and all grease stains: Use the emergency kit I just wrote about, or Motsenbocker's LIFT OFF #2.

If there's a grease mark is on carpeting, my new daughter-in-law, Julie, recommends sprinkling baby powder on to the stain and working it into the carpeting with facial tissue. The tissue and baby powder will absorb the stain.

Cranberry, coffee, red or orange Kool Aid, or red wine: Use Motsenbocker's LIFT OFF #2. If you are going to launder the garment or piece of color safe fabric, daughter-in-law has another good tip. Make a paste using dry dishwasher powder and water. Scrub it into the stain, then launder. The stain will come right out.

Water or Coffee rings on wood: The best solution that I have found is the Wood right Deep Cleaning System by Parker & Bailey (F. O. Bailey on the East Coast). Pour a little Wood right on a clean, dry, cotton cloth, and work it into the wood. If the ring persists, wipe with a Teflon pad using a circular motion. After the ring is out, the area will look lighter because it is now the cleanest part of the table. To balance the color, clean the entire table top. The table will love you for it, and the surface will look beautiful.

Scuff marks on floor: Use a little dab of Fast Orange by Permatex on the scuff mark, then rub with a wad of facial tissue. I prefer the Fast Orange because it has a nice citrus smell, not the greasy garage odor of most other heavy duty hand cleaners.

Blood stains, Jell-O, vegetable coloring, or just about any protein stain: Use Motsenbocker LIFT OFF #1. If you don't see the stain until the party is over and you are tired, rub in Stain Stick by DOW and just toss the garment into the dirty clothes hamper. The Stain Stick will block the stain, and actively protect the fabric for days.

Adhesive marks, stains, or smudges on walls: Use your favorite countertop cleaner, Fantastic, 409, Clean Away, or Wash Before You Paint by Culmac Industries, and facial tissue. Spray the stained area with the cleaner. Stick a piece of tissue onto the dampened area. Keep the area moist for a couple of minutes to let the cleaner work, then lightly wipe in half circles. Use more tissue and cleaner if needed.

Kitten or puppy accidents: Don't lose your temper and swat or shout, you'll just frighten the poor thing. Scoop up any solid. Use facial tissue like a blotter to absorb the liquid. To clean, use Motsenbocker's LIFT OFF #1, or any citrus based cleaner. Both will do a good cleaning job, but the citrus based cleaner will leave a residual orange smell that the animal will not like. When dry, spray the area with SMELLS BEGONE by Punati Chemical. The odor eliminator effectively removes the pet's calling card, so they will not get the idea the area is a good place to do their dirty work.

You can get Motsenbocher's LIFT OFF at Aco, Damman, Home Depot and Mr. Scrub in Oak Park; Parker & Bailey Wood right at Damman and Bed Bath & Beyond; Permatex Fast Orange at Mr. Scrub and most hardware and auto supply stores; SMELLS BEGONE at most hardware stores.

DECEMBER 14, 1996

Hardware store workers suggest great gifts for do-it-yourselfers

by America's Master Handyman, Glenn Haege

Finding that something special for the handyman or woman on your list can be puzzling. To find out what's hot, I asked owners and store managers of some of the area's leading hardware stores and home centers, for help with DIY (do-it-yourself) gift ideas.

Dennis DaPra, COO of ACO Hardware (248) 471-0100, the country's largest independently owned hardware store chain, recommended Stanley's seven-piece tool set. "This neat little kit contains the basic tools you need for most common repairs. It has a hammer, tape rule, utility knife, three screwdrivers and a mini hack saw", DaPra says.

"We cut the price to only $12.84 for Christmas, so it's a great gift or stocking stuffer for any new homeowner, apartment dweller or college student," he adds.

Scott White, the manager of the Home Depot in Roseville (810) 415-9620, says that, the "can't miss" item this year is what is probably the most advertised hardware item in America: the Snake Light by Black & Decker. It has hundreds of different uses, and at just $18.74 it won't break Mrs. Claus' or even the elves' budgets.

Larry Sambaugh, of Hilzinger's Ace Hardware, on Main Street in Royal Oak (248) 541-2003 recommends the new, one gallon Shop Vac. "The big wet/dry vacs are good, but they are just too heavy to haul around.

"The 1-gallon size is easy to carry and perfect for draining a plugged sink, cleaning the car, stairs, ceilings or other high areas," Sambaugh says. It comes with a full sized wand, crevasse tool and brush for only $34.49.

Scott Rollis, the store manager at Sear's new Hardware & Paint store at 18 Mile and Ryan, Sterling Heights (810) 795-4408, says that the "hottest Christmas Hardware item at all eight Sears Hardware locations is the three piece Craftsman Professional RoboGrip Set."

The RoboGrip pliers lock in place and can serve as that "second set of hands" when the job requires that you have at least three. The RoboGrip set includes 9-inch V-Notch, 9-inch Straight, and 7-inch Curved Jaw Pliers, and is Special Purchase priced at $49.99.

Bill Damman, of Damman Hardware (248) 399-5080, said that "the Black & Decker Versa-Pak Kit" is a great gift for the handy man or woman, even if he or she has other tools." The Versa-Pak kit includes a 7.2 volt two speed cordless drill, a multi-purpose bayonet type saw, a snake light and two Versa-Pak batteries with charger.

"It's a winner of a gift, because the battery power allows the handyman complete mobility to do almost any job. Damman's has reduced the price to just $99, a $40 savings, until December 22 Damman says.

Gary Patterson, of Plum Hollow Hardware on Lahser, West of 9 Mile, in Southfield (248) 356-4014 says, "everything is cordless this year." His pick is the Makita Cordless Drill. "They run anywhere from a 4.2 volt model for the first time buyer, at $50, to the heavy-duty 9.6 volt, $130, cordless drill for the experienced handyman," he says.

Ron Pederson, of Marsh Power Tools in Livonia (248) 476-7744, has a hot suggestion for furniture refinishers. "The Porter Cable's Profile Sander kit. The kit includes the 6,000 stroke-per-minute sander, standard triangle pad, 17 different profiles for sanding spindles with different concave and convex radii, and different angled surfaces, and other accessories, and it's specially priced at just $119."

Doug Mans, of N. A. Man's Building Center in Canton (734) 981-5000 says that his choice for he year's best DIY Christmas Gift is the DeWalt Cordless Drill/Screwdriver. At $239, the 12-volt model is not cheap, but Mans says, "If you only own one power tool, this is the one to have."

If you'd rather let your fingers do the walking and the handy person on your list doesn't have a copy of my most popular book, *Fix It Fast & Easy!*, QVC says they still are taking orders for the F. O. Bailey Furniture Care and book kit. The kit contains 16 oz sizes of Kitchen Cabinet Creme, Wood Furniture Creme, and Wood Right Deep Cleaning System, plus 8 oz sizes of Woodenware Conditioner & Protectant, and Appliance & Countertop Polish, and my book for just $21.84.

The Wood Right Deep Cleaning System, Woodenware Conditioner, and Appliance & Countertop Polish, are brand new products, not yet available in stores. Since the retail value is well over $40, and you get break through, state-of-the-art products, it is a heck of a deal. QVC's phone number is (800) 345-1515, item No. V7796.

If you are a Do-It-Yourselfer, and see something here that belongs under your Christmas tree, here's a DIY tip from the Handyman: Cut out this article, circle what you want in red, and attach it to the refrigerator door. If subtlety doesn't work, consider pulling the plug on the kitchen stove, or putting an "Out of Order" sign on the commode.

You've gotta be tough. Remember, Christmas comes but once a year. Make the most of it.

Chapter 3

1997 Articles reprinted from The Detroit News HOMESTYLE

Builders have a difficult time keeping up with the housing boom

by America's Master Handyman,
Glenn Haege

When I talk about the '96-'97 building-and-remodeling picture, I sound like Dickens in his opening to *A Tale of Two Cities:* "It was the best of times. It was the worst of times."

On the one hand, mortgage rates have seldom been better. David Seiders, chief economist for the National Association of Home Builders (NAHB), expects the good times to continue. His crystal ball shows fixed-rate mortgages hovering in the 7.7 to 7.9 percent bracket through 1998.

And today's housing can be exciting. Break-through ideas; new product innovations like surround sound, home theater, X-10 home automation; and trends like insulated block basements, geothermal and hydronic radiant floor heating are no longer just written about in newspapers and magazines. You can actually buy a house today that architects could only dream about five years ago.

Builders, building product manufacturers and the building trades all reported record or near-record sales in 1996. On the local level, Scott Jacobson, newly elected president of the Builders Association of Southeast Michigan, expects a 15 percent increase over 1996. Figures aren't in, but at his own firm, S.R. Jacobson Development Corp., December sales are 60 percent ahead of the previous year.

1996 was so big in the Detroit building and remodeling market that if you could lift a hammer and were vaguely interested in working, you had a job. If you actually reported for work, a construction supervisor from a competing firm would try to recruit you during your coffee break.

Almost everyone in the business can tell you about slow-paying contractors who had their entire crew disappear because they were recruited during their lunch hour. That's a good laugh unless those guys were working on your house.

This brings us to the "worst of times." Whenever demand outstrips capacity in the building business, quality nosedives, time to completion lengthens and prices escalate.

All three are happening while you are reading this. Basic materials needed for construction, like lumber and drywall, are going up in price and developing shortages.

Canadian lumber quotas caused prices to skyrocket so high in November that the NAHB and the National Lumber and Building Material Dealers Association held a joint press conference, trying to calm market jitters.

Thankfully, prices are going down. We're told the lumber quota price increases were just a temporary end-of-year spike, so we shouldn't worry. According to an article in the Nov. 25 National Home Center News, NAHB estimated that the quota spike increased the cost of a new home by just $2,000.

Even if you are lucky enough not to be influenced by the price spike, an eyeball estimate of 1995 vs. 1996 prices shows last year's lumber prices averaged about 25 percent more than the previous year's (about $450 vs. $375 per 1,000 board feet).

Meanwhile, drywall, the stuff that covers the 2-by-4's to make walls, is in such short supply that it has been sold on allocation for the past year. The gypsum factories are already working at about 97 percent capacity, and no new capacity is expected to come on line for the foreseeable future. In simple English, that means that if construction increases (and it is), unless homes get smaller (and they aren't), additional housing would have to be built without walls. I consider that highly unlikely.

Construction workers are in such short supply that construction on a house can be held up for weeks or months waiting for a critical subcontractor. And there is little the builder can do. Carpenters, electricians, bricklayers and plumbers are independent subcontractors. The builder can yell, offer extra money, whatever, and the trades will show up only when they want to, when they can't make more money on another job.

According to Jacobson, the Builders Association is trying to solve the problem. It is starting a program to train new people in the trades and hope to add 100 rough (entry level) carpenters this year. The trouble is, builders need 2,000. Until labor and supply problems are solved, consumers wishing to buy, or even remodel an existing home, should proceed with caution and expect price increases and delays.

The latest indoor air cleaners will help keep your family healthy

by America's Master Handyman, Glenn Haege

If it seems like breathing is getting hazardous to your health, you're right. And it's not just an American phenomenon. The January 3, 1997 edition of the Journal of Science included a study showing that asthma rates have doubled in the developed nations of the world over the past 20 years.

They hypothesize that it may be that a decrease in childhood infections blunts the body's sensitivity to allergens. In other words taking your kid to the pediatrician, getting him all his shots, and keeping him healthy may actually make him sicker in the long run. Am I missing something?

The scientific investigators might want to consider two phenomena which occurred in the same twenty years: 1) Our children are a generation of couch potatoes. They sit inside, in front of the TV, Nintendo, or computer, instead of being pushed out of the house and into the fresh air, running, playing, laughing and doing all the things necessary to exercise their lungs and the rest of their bodies. 2) Every advanced country has sealed houses tight against heat loss, making them far more energy-efficient but noxious places in which to breath.

These two factors mean that we have sedentary children (and adults), with weaker bodies, spending increasing amounts of time in an unhealthy atmosphere (our homes). No wonder they're getting sick.

It did not take an international study to tell me that; more people are calling my show to learn how to improve indoor air quality.

Many already have top-of-the-line electronic air cleaners like the Honeywell, Lennox, or Trion Max 4 or 5; mega media filters like Space Guard and Air Bear; or are using HEPA filter air cleaners like those produced by Bionaire, Homes, Honeywell and Vornado. They are already doing everything normal people do and still need more.

If you need to maximize your home's air quality, here are a few suggestions.

Air ducts, carpeting and drapes are breeding grounds and hiding places for dust, dust mites, dirt, bacteria, fungi etc. Eliminate them. Move to a house with an electric, geothermal, or hydronic heating system that does not have air ducts and do without carpeting, rugs and draperies.

If your needs are not that extreme, maximize the effectiveness of what you already have. The air in your house is not being cleaned the majority of the time. Furnace filters and air cleaners only work when the blower fan is running. Motor City Services (Ed: Sorry, they are out of business) builds a filter speed blower switch which keeps the blower running at a very low speed constantly.

Seal the windows and install a Skuttle or Equalize Air air to air exchanger. Whenever your home needs it, a plentiful supply of fresh air will be directed through the furnace air cleaner into your house.

Clean and sanitize air ducts on a regular basis. All air duct cleaning services are not created equal. The most sophisticated air cleaning contractors, like Mike Palazzolo at Safety King (800-972-6343), use high tech equipment to analyze for air duct and carbon monoxide contamination.

Most duct work only needs to be cleaned every six years. If your family is experiencing breathing problems, test the air every six months, then clean and sanitize as indications suggest. Connie Morbach at Sanit-Air (888-778-7324) in Troy is still providing Microbial Culture Test Kits to people in my listening and reading audience for only $37.

Install a central vacuum system. Regular vacuums do a better job of spreading dust than eliminating it. Central vacuum systems, like the Vacuflo and Beam, maintain up to 98 percent cleaning efficiency, and exhaust the remaining 2 percent outside the house. According to Dan Zimmerman of Zimms Vacuums (800-664-1105), an average size house can be retrofitted with a central vacuum system for about $1,000.

Even if you don't have carpeting, hardwood and composition floors, book cases, window moldings, and blinds are all best cleaned by vacuuming on a daily basis.

You can even try to eliminate dust from the air itself. As far as I am concerned, this is still in the experimental stage.

Morbach at Sanit-Air, is having good results installing a specially designed ultraviolet (UV-C) probe light kit in the return duct of problem homes. The probe activates every time the heating or cooling system goes on, theoretically eliminating germs and odors.

Ozone and Ionization air cleaners attack the problem in a different way. Ozone occurs naturally. It is an unstable $O3$ instead of the usual $O2$ molecular grouping. In theory, when you use an Ozone/Ion air purifier, the extra Oxygen molecules and ions attach themselves to contaminants and eliminate them.

John Perry, the sales manager for Pure Air Plus (800-455-5247), says that Alpine Industries produces a portable unit, the XL-15, which can clean homes up to 2500 square feet. David Zimmerman of Zimms Vacuums is also a believer.

Your basement isn't truly finished until it's as inviting as the upstairs

by America's Master Handyman, Glenn Haege

If you need additional living space, sitting on top of an unfinished basement is like living in a tent pitched on top of buried treasure. Getting your basement finished costs only about $15 to $25 a square foot. Building up, or out, starts at a $100 a square foot.

Unfortunately, most finished basements are just that, finished basements. They never become an accepted, fully functioning part of the house. Since they do not become true living space, they add only marginal resale value to the home.

To find a way around these problems, I talked to Mike McCoy of Coy Construction Inc. (248-363-1050). Coy specializes in building decks and finishing basements. McCoy expects the company to build 800 decks and finish 50 to 60 basements this year. I do not know of any other contractor that does that kind of volume.

The secret to getting full use and resale value out of a basement is to change the look and feel from a basement to that of another living level, McCoy says.

"The standard way to finish a basement is to put in furring strips and paneling, install a drop ceiling with ugly ceiling tiles, and lay vinyl on the floor," McCoy says. "You would never live in a house with a living room that looked like that. How can you expect to use a basement that looks that way?"

To get maximum "living appeal" from a basement, McCoy says you have to start at the top of the stairs and rethink the entire situation.

"When a contractor builds a house he separates the unfinished basement from finished living space with a door at the top of very utilitarian stairs," he says. "The door and the stairway combine to tell you 'Stop. You don't want to go down there.' "

To change your basement into living space, get rid of the psychological stop signs. Take out the door and door trim, and open up the staircase by removing as much of the stairway wall as possible. Replace it with a top-quality banister that looks exactly like one you would choose for a stairway leading from the front vestibule to the second floor.

By doing these things the staircase becomes a natural progression to a lower living level. You can continue this feel by making the finished portion of the basement look and feel as much like the first floor as possible.

To do this, McCoy recommends drywalling both the walls and the ceiling; carpeting, not tiling, the floors; adding a full, not half, bath; installing recessed lighting and upgrading the electrical by installing at least three additional electric circuits.

By drywalling, instead of installing a drop ceiling, you change the look from industrial to living area; gain 3 to 4 inches in height, giving the basement a much more livable feel; and replace expensive ceiling tiles which are likely to go out of style and become irreplaceable. You also gain the flexibility of being able to build around duct work, and you'll save about 60 percent on materials.

Installing drywall instead of paneling on the walls accomplishes much the same thing. Since McCoy believes that straight walls are important, he recommends using full 2-inch-by-4-inch studs with bottom and top plates, instead of just using furring strips tacked to poured or block basement wall. Naturally, because there is always a potential for water, the bottom plates have to be pressure treated.

"This not only gives you a perfectly level drywalled surface, instead of the wavy wall usually associated with paneled basements, it also gives extra room for insulation," McCoy says.

Drywall has other advantages. In the event a leak develops, drywall is replaced easily and inexpensively. If paneling is used, it becomes almost impossible to duplicate after only a few years.

If you prefer to use furring strips instead of 2-inch-by-4-inch construction, Wallmate insulation by Dow USA is especially made for this purpose.

If you want to add extra warmth, install Envira Cushion imported by Fairway Tile and Carpet (248-588-4431) instead of normal padding. It is waterproof and is the only padding made that lists an R Factor.

Here are a few other tips for making a finished basement into a natural-feeling living area.
■ Lay out the floor plan so that metal stanchions are hidden inside walls.
■ Use the same floor and ceiling moldings in the basement that are used on the first floor.
■ Think about putting in a large fixed window between rooms to provide an open feel.
■ Don't finish the entire basement. Remember, unfinished storage space is a valuable commodity.

Learn waterproofing lingo to get to the bottom of basement leaks

by America's Master Handyman,
Glenn Haege

Although 60 percent of all leaky basement problems can be solved by reestablishing proper water drainage, every homeowner lives in fear of the other 40 percent. Many put off even trying to solve the problem because they are afraid to talk to a salesman.

This article will give you the basics you need to talk to the basement waterproofing contractor or salesman on an equal basis. To make sure that I was up to speed, I talked with Ben Ciccarelli, owner of Affordable Dry Basement (800) 310-5700, one of Detroit's leading basement waterproofing companies.

I picked Ciccarelli for four reasons: His company does every major type of basement waterproofing. He makes a legitimate effort to be cutting-edge and give homeowners the latest technologies. He provides easy-to-understand literature explaining the waterproofing process. He agrees that homeowners should be conservative in their fixes.

That means, if the basement has a corner, part of a wall or a crack that leaks, fix the corner, part of the wall or crack. Do not get talked into fixing the rest of the basement for a problem it might never have.

The one time you might want to go overboard is if you are about to invest in extensively remodeling your basement and fear a leak may occur and ruin expensive carpeting, paneling or drywall and furniture. In this case, you may choose install an interior drain tile system as a preventative measure.

Before refinishing the basement, inspect the walls and floor minutely. If you find efflorescence, signs of previous water leakage, cracks or other signs of damage, call in a couple of professionals to get quotes. Make sure water problems are corrected before the basement is finished.

The most common basement problems are tie-rod holes, wall cracks and crushed or blocked drain tiles. The worst problems are collapsing walls and shifting slabs. The latter two problems will be covered in a future article.

In the cost hierarchy, fixing rod holes costs the least, followed by cracks repaired by urethane injection, basement de-watering and interior drain tile systems. Exterior repair is more expensive than interior repair and generally includes extensive relandscaping. Reconstruction of walls and slabs is the most expensive.

As with any construction problem, the effectiveness of the repair depends on discovering and correcting the true source of the problem.

Leaking tie-rod holes are holes left in poured concrete after the removal of rods that held together the wooden forms during construction. They can be fixed by the do-it-yourselfer or they can be professionally repaired. The traditional way to fix rod holes is to push a cork in about 3 or 4 inches, then fill the remainder of the hole with hydraulic cement.

Doing the job yourself will cost a dollar or two per hole. If you call in a professional, the company will charge you $100 to $150 for five holes. If the company already has someone at your house doing other basement work, it may charge only $10 or $15 a hole.

Dean Teaster of Mr. Sponge Waterproofing has introduced a new rod-hole-filler insert kit. The high-tech products expand to fill rod holes. Mr. Sponge Tie Reinforcement Sealer Kits cost $18.99 per pack of five at Damman Hardware stores. That's about $3.80 a hole.

The next most common problem in poured concrete walls is cracks. Cracks may run the entire depth of the wall. Many homeowners try to solve the problem with hydraulic cement. This is not usually a permanent fix because the repairs are improperly made or wall settling cracks the cement, and the leak returns.

In poured concrete walls, the preferred solution is injection of urethane resin. The urethane fills the entire crack and reacts with water forming a flexible waterproof gasket. Both Mr. Sponge (800) 491-4686 and Affordable Dry Basements do injection waterproofing. Costs start at about $350 per crack repair.

Block wall cracks can be more serious. If you have a block wall basement and see a crack on the upper half of the wall, "you can be pretty sure there's a crack on the outside of the block," Ciccarelli says.

The best way to repair exterior block cracks is from the outside. Concrete blocks are hollow, providing excellent channels for water flow. The exterior crack may be at the opposite end of a wall from the interior leak.

This problem is often solved by the installation of a basement de-watering system that collects leaking water in a hollow baseboard and channels it to the sump pump. The cost of this type of repair is about three quarters that of installing an interior drain tile system.

Basement leaks often develop when the brittle, relatively fragile, clay exterior drain tiles become clogged or broken. This can be repaired by digging around the walls and replacing broken tiles, installing an interior drain tile system, or installing a basement de-watering system that rechannels the water but doesn't fix the problem.

All three solutions are expensive. At about $30 to $40 a running foot, the interior drain tile repair is the most cost-effective. Interior drains use 4-inch PVC drain pipe with fittings and clean-outs making them easy to snake out.

Humidity, temperature and poor air circulation make windows all wet

by America's Master Handyman,
Glenn Haege

When I used to do interviews on 10 or 20 stations a month, I was always amazed at how similar the questions were. Now that I am syndicated and talk to listeners in about 100 different markets every week, I find the similarities incredible.

Right now, the most common questions from people in the Midwest, East and Northwest are "Why are my windows wet or freezing? And what can I do about it?"

There can be several reasons. One has to do with indoor humidity vs. outdoor temperature. When the outside temperature is 40 degrees F or above, the recommended indoor humidity is 45 percent. When the outside temperature drops to 0 degrees, the indoor humidity should be 25 percent. Anything above 25 percent will steam up your windows. The steam turns to water, then, if the pane is cold enough, ice.

If you have forced-air heat, you should continuously reset the humidity control on your furnace in accordance with the outside temperature. Honeywell (800) 328-5111 makes a deluxe thermostat, the PC 8900, that can hook up to an outside sensor to automatically reset the humidity control to the outside temperature. In our area, Jim Williams of Williams Refrigeration (888) 268-5445 is a big advocate of this system.

Whether you have a furnace-mounted humidifier or not, you should buy a digital hygrometer, like the Bionaire available at Damman and many other fine hardware and home centers, and test the humidity levels in the different rooms in your house. If the humidity is too high, you get wet windows. If it is too low, you get electric shocks when you touch metal, as well as dry-skin problems.

Don't laugh. Desert-dry indoor conditions are bad for your skin, your family's and pet's skin, bronchial cords and sinuses. The general health of houseplants

THE BEST HUMIDITY

If you have forced-air heat, you should continuously reset the humidity control on your furnace in accordance with the outside temperature. Here are recommended humidity levels. Temperatures are Fahrenheit.

Outdoor temperature	Recommended humidity
40 degrees and above	45 percent
30 to 39	40 percent
20 to 29	35 percent
10 to 19	30 percent
0 to 9	25 percent
-1 to -10	20 percent
-11 to -20	15 percent

suffers in such dry air. It also causes cracking of wood floors and fine furniture.

If you find that you cannot increase humidity sufficiently using the furnace mounted humidistat setting, buy a warm mist portable humidifier and take it from room to room. Your houseplants, lungs, nasal passages and floors will thank you.

Another cause of wet windows is insufficient air exchange. In other words, your house is exfiltrating more air than it is bringing in. Every fall we try to seal our houses against the cold. We add insulation, new shingles, improved windows. This makes our houses more energy efficient. It also seals out much of the air we, and our houses, need to breathe. Then, when the furnace or clothes dryer goes on, the blowers push more air out of the house than can come in and creates negative air pressure. A clothes dryer uses up 200 cubic feet of air a minute.

Partial vacuums cannot exist in nature. This means that air will be sucked into the house through the weakest parts. This usually includes the windows. Frigid, dry winter air is sucked in, super chilling the window pane and frame. The cold window chills the relatively hot, humid, indoor air, causing an immediate chilling and release of moisture on, you guessed it, the windows. If the pane and frame are cold enough, this moisture turns to ice.

A temporary fix for this problem is to increase air circulation. Those with central air can turn the furnace blower motor to the continuous "on" position. Another solution is to place a fan where it will circulate a stream of air on the offending windows. The real solution to the problem is to increase air infiltration with a Skuttle Model 216 or Equalize Air (734) 462-1033 by Xavier.

A third and final reason your window panes may be wet or frozen is that you have leaky, old windows or loose-fitting window panes. This is often the case with older homes, mobile homes and apartments and condominiums. The instant fix to this problem is the installation of interior storm windows.

Interior storms are magnetically framed, acrylic windows and are far superior to exterior storm windows. They insulate the windows from the warm interior temperatures and eliminate drafts. Interior storms are so effective that they even seal out a high percentage of road noise.

My bookkeeper has a basement office with two sunken, full-size, metal framed windows. The windows were cold, drafty and continuously wet. I had Diversified Energy Control install two interior storm windows, and they completely eliminated the problem. For more information on interior storm windows, can call DEC (800) 380-0332 or Crystal Enterprises (248) 583-4300 in the Detroit market. For information outside the metro market, call the manufacturers: A.1 Technologies Inc. (800) 533-2805 or Magnetite (800) 624-8483. Interior storm window kits are available from DEC and the Window Saver Co. (800) 321-9276.

Regardless of the reason for your wet windows, they are an engraved invitation to airborne mold and mildew. You can wash the mold and mildew away without damaging your window frame with Mildew Stain Remover, a nonbleach product by Amazon Premium Products (800) 832-5645.

Novi show suggests that homeowners are on a quest for quality

by America's Master Handyman, Glenn Haege

You know how PR and advertising people are always saying something is the biggest and best? Well, with 350 exhibitors, this year's Spring Home & Garden Show was definitely the biggest show the Building Industry Association of Southeast Michigan ever crammed into the Novi Expo Center. That the show had that many exhibitors without feeling crowded is a credit to Rosalie Lamb and the rest of the show's planners.

As for the best part, it was the quality of the wares the exhibitors brought to the show. Things such as Amish carpentry, marble and granite tables, hand painted tiles. There are always some of these at every show, but at this year's show, the quality was everywhere.

Since the year's first show sets the tone for the rest of the year, I predict that this is the year that the homeowner's quest for quality will be king. This was especially apparent in the kitchen and bath displays. The kitchen and bath are the two most expensive parts of the home. This year, they will be even more so.

Merillat, the nation's largest cabinet manufacturer (and a Michigan company), is famous for its beautiful magazine ads. H.J. Oldenkamp's display brought one of those ads to life, so you could open all the cabinets and pull out all the drawers to see what's inside.

Kurtis Kitchen & Bath Centers featured drawers with quality design elements like glass fronts you can fill with things such as multicolored pastas and still have storage space; cabinets that open onto two and three pullout shelves; drawer fronts that pull out to become 3- and 4-foot-long tables. They also were giving away a free "How To Measure Your Kitchen" guide that was very good. If you missed the show you can pick up the guide at any of Kurtis' nine stores.

The kitchen displays were great locations for name droppers. The Northpointe Design Group's exhibit had an AGA commercial gas cook stove. At about 1,200 pounds, it was so huge it made any other stove look like a paperweight. Trevarrow's featured top-end appliances from Bosch, Gaggenau, Sub-Zero and Viking. Wholesale Builders Supply had Wolf, Jenn Air and Blue Creek, while Specialties Showroom had Five Star and Dacor.

While all these food-preparation vehicles were impressive, Nuway Supply Co. had one appliance that was even more so: a 1.6-gallon toilet that actually works. Anyone who has had performance problems with the new crop of toilets knows what I mean. The new Briggs' Whisper Vac is based on a unique Fluid Master "vacuity" concept that uses a superior vacuum force to rid the line of waste matter. That to my mind is quality.

Extensive – perhaps we should make that expensive – tile work is the kitchen and bath design trend of the year. Last year, the show had good tile displays. This year, the displays were phenomenal. So much so that within the next few weeks I plan on focusing an entire article on designer tiles.

Virginia Tile Co. displayed tumbled stone, marble and terra cotta mosaics from Italy, hand painted tiles from England, Finland, Italy and Portugal, as well as the good old U.S.A. It also had three-dimensional tiles with fish and frogs jumping from lily pads.

There were top-quality ceramic, marble and granite displays by the Bloomfield Design Center, Cera-Mex, Novi, T.J. Marble and Granite and Uro Tile. Stewart Specialty Tiles showed custom-designed, hand painted golf, aquarium and just fun tile murals. Booms Stone Co. had a massive finished marble display.

Naturally, unless you are one of the favored few for whom price is no object, entire rooms of designer tiles can get pricey. But using them as accents or a centerpiece could set the tone of a room.

Speaking of accents, look for glass to be big. Not just plain glass. Mirror & Glass Magic and other glass exhibitors had magnificently etched glass, glass tiles, layered and beveled-glass tables and mirrors within mirrors. All items that transformed what could have been commonplace into works of art.

See what I mean about quality? Add Amish and other custom-built cabinetry, and indoor and outdoor furniture. Peter's True Value even had an Amish Noah's Arc playset.

I'm sure that the Novi show was just the tip of the iceberg. If you saw it, we shared a wonderful experience. If you didn't, I hope that I have made you decide you have to see the next show.

The Michigan Home & Garden Show is at the Pontiac Silverdome Feb. 27 and 28 and March 1 and 2. The International Home, Flower and Furniture Show will be at Cobo Hall March 14 to 23. WXYT's Home Expo will be at the Macomb Center Campus April 19 and 20. Look for me at all these shows. I hope to see you at least at one of them.

Bragging rights

I want to share one little brag with you. Two weeks ago, while I was on vacation, Westwood One signed the 100th affiliate for my syndicated radio show – WZAN in Portland, Maine. Thanks Westwood. Thanks to all of you.

FEBRUARY 15, 1997

Manufactured homes gain respect with lower costs and less hassle

by America's Master Handyman, Glenn Haege

It used to be that manufactured housing left a lot to be desired. Not anymore. Today, one out of three single-family homes sold is factory built. The majority are erected on private property, not in trailer parks.

Variety and availability aren't limited, either. According to Manufactured Home Merchandiser, some 150 manufacturers produce more than 1,000 brands of manufactured housing in 39 of our states and seven of Canada's provinces.

Michigan is getting more than its fair share of the action. Thanks to mergers and consolidations, Champion Enterprises is one of the two largest producers of manufactured housing. Fortune magazine named the Auburn Hills company one of America's 100 fastest-growing companies. Champion has a network of 3,200 retailers nationwide.

The reason for the increased popularity is a no-brainer. The Feb. 12, 1996, issue of Forbes magazine sums it up by saying despite our long love affair with home ownership, "after figuring in taxes, maintenance and mortgage interest costs, a house has become a lousy investment. But it's less lousy if you pay less."

According to U.S. census data, in 1994 the national average per-square-foot construction cost of multisection, manufactured housing (top-of-the-line, double-wide and above) was $27.41. (That doesn't include land cost.) Compare that with $54.65 for site-built housing. Even if you add another $50 dollars to each figure for inflation and land costs, that still gives manufactured housing a 25 percent advantage over site-built.

As prices for on-site construction go higher and the scarcity of quality trades people gets worse, the competitive advantage of manufactured housing increases. This is especially true since the buyer is no longer limited to pedestrian plain. Paneling has made way for drywall and, in many models, you can see Corian countertops, deluxe appliances, sunken baths, fireplaces, even hardwood floors.

Other advantages include guaranteed completion dates (usually within two months, not two years); the major plumbing, wiring and roofing already done, so the on-site contractor is not at the mercy of building trades; and construction built to rigid national codes that equal or exceed local codes.

Manufactured housing can be divided into three categories: mobile, modular and panelized. Mobile homes are towed on their own chassis. Modular and panelized constructions are loaded onto trailers for the trip between factory and erection site.

I've been an advocate of modular housing for years. My folks in Florida live in a modular house. During assembly, I found dealing with the contractor a snap.

With all their advantages, manufactured housing is known to have a few squeaky little problems. In fact, that is one of their biggest problems, floors quite often squeak or bounce slightly when a person walks across a room.

The primary reason for the squeaks is that the components were hauled a couple of hundred miles over potholed roads before being assembled. If you took a stick built house and gave it the same treatment, you would be lucky to have a pile of kindling at the end of the trip.

One local company, the consumer products division of E and E Engineering (800-323-0982), has capitalized on the squeaks and sags with products that eliminate the problems. They solve the same problems on site-built housing as well. I have been recommending one of the products, Squeak-Ender, for years.

All three of these products work from under the floor and improve the bonding between the subfloor and joists. Each is a two-person fix, but easy for the do-it-yourselfer.

According to Ken Shore, E & E Consumer Products' national sales manager, floors start to squeak when the subfloor loosens from the joist. Once the location is identified by walking over the area, a Squeak-Ender is attached to the subfloor and joist and draws the subfloor down tight, eliminating the problem.

The Sag-Ender eliminates sags, dips and weak spots in floors by bracing up the affected area with a metal reinforcing plate braced between the joists.

Occasionally, one piece of subflooring will rise and become wedged above its neighbor, causing an unseemly seam or "pop" in the flooring. The Seam-Ender is attached to both pieces of the subfloor and draws them into alignment.

As I said, all of these problems also occur in standard, site-constructed houses. If you have the problem, you now have the solution. The products are available at Damman Hardware. The Sag-Ender is also available at Builders Square, Home Depot and many independent hardware and home centers.

Decorating with tile is as old as the pyramids, as new as tomorrow

by America's Master Handyman, Glenn Haege

The newest decorating trend in town has a lot in common with the oldest. In fact, if you're redecorating or building a new house and want the very latest, your decorating will have a lot in common with the pyramids and Pompeii.

Extravagant use of tile is in. Of course, you can put up the same tiles that your Aunt Mable did 40 years ago. You can even go space age and put in Baker Ceramalite for a conventional tile look at a fraction of the cost in product or installation time. If you already have tile and just want a new color, you can have a bathtub relining company bond a new, easy care, acrylic surface in your choice of colors.

Or you can decide that this is the year you are going to create a work of art, and work with decorators and tile designers to make your kitchen, bath, family room, floors, patio, maybe your entire house, something that people will talk about for years.

When you talk designer tiles, you share one thing with those guys who built the pyramids and the houses and baths of Pompeii: You are designing for the ages. Tile is an artistic expression that should last as long as the house. If you are the type of person who likes to redo the look of a room as often as you change your hairstyle, put tile in your bad idea file and stick with paint and wallpaper.

If you decide to make the commitment to designer tile, you will find a breadth of selection that would make Pharaoh whip his whisk with envy.

Trips to the showrooms of companies like Beaver Tile (248-476-2333), Ceramic Tile Sales (248-356-6430) or Virginia Tile (800-837-8453) will open your mind to design approaches that you could never get from newspaper or magazine articles.

Tile can be made using advanced, scientific, production techniques or it can be laboriously hand made using techniques that have been handed down for hundreds, sometimes thousands, of years.

Tile comes from all over the world. The basic production procedure of mixing the clay and other ingredients, molding, drying, glazing and firing it varies slightly depending upon the traditions of the craft. The combination of local materials and production techniques accounts for distinctive qualities of the tiles from the various regions. Tiles from India, Mexico and Portugal could never be confused.

Ceramic tile comes in two basic styles: glazed and unglazed, also called quarry, tile. Glazed tiles come in matte, gloss and satin finishes. Each of the different finishes reflects light differently and gives a different cast to the tiles. Some tiles are made in a combination of glazes, providing a variegated-finish pattern.

The texture of a tile can be anything from porcelain smooth to coarse, depending upon the materials and molding process used. They can be mass produced or hand molded. Naturally, the mass produced has a more exact look. The hand-molded tiles have a greater variety.

Different design patterns can be put into the molds, providing a three-dimensional relief. After firing, these same designs can then be hand painted with different glazes. Other popular hand-painting techniques include filling in a charcoal sketch (like paint by numbers), and outlining a design (like you would decorate a cake) and then filling in the pattern with translucent glazes.

Choices in tile are infinite. Some tile companies, like American Olean, are not content to just let tiles look like tile. They also create tiles that look like slate, marble, and granite. Of course, if you like that look, you might as well go for the gusto and buy real slate, marble and granite. You can get all three cut to tile sizes or in slabs.

If Ancient Rome is your design inspiration, you can look at Country Floors' Tumbled Stone at Virginia Tile.

Country Floors gives you perfectly new quarried stone that has been tumbled in a mixer (like prewashed jeans) until it looks like it has been in use for the last four or five hundred years. If Byzantine is more your style, the same manufacturer makes terra cotta mosaics that can make your bath look like it was lifted from Constantinople way before the Turks arrived.

You don't have to settle for the choices offered by the big showrooms. Thanks to Pewabic Pottery, Detroit has a rich tile tradition of its own.

Trips to places like Dianne Stewart's Pond & Landscape Solutions (248-680-TILE) or Dick Pruckler's Whistling Frog Tile Co. (248-542-1112) or many other crafts people in the area will enable you to talk to the designer/artist/artisan and get the color, the glaze and the design motif you have in mind. To do that, of course, you have to investigate and know what you want.

Take your time. See all you can see. Learn all that you can learn. It will be a great trip.

Pipe systems avoid the draft and dust of forced-air heating units

by America's Master Handyman,
Glenn Haege

It used to be that a natural gas forced-air furnace was the only game in town if you were building a new house. Electric heat and propane have always been expensive. Oil was subject to big price swings. Natural gas forced-air heat was relatively cheap and efficient.

Like everything, natural gas forced-air has some negatives. Super heating air makes it desert dry. Forced-air furnace blowers do an excellent job of blowing dust around the house. With the most efficient models, the circulating air becomes a relatively cool and annoying draft. We cope by adding humidity, trying to eliminate dust with furnace filters and dialing up the thermostat.

I am not trying to pan natural gas forced-air furnaces. I have one in my home by choice. However, if you are going to build a home in the next couple of years, you should know that there are good, viable alternatives. Hydronic and geothermal are two of them.

Hydronic heating systems

Hydronic heating is a combination of a gas or oil-fired boiler and a subsurface hydronic (water) heating system. Hot water is circulated through piping loops under flooring to provide draft-free heat. It can be laid under floor surfaces, whether concrete slab, hardwood, carpeting, vinyl or ceramic tile. The system eliminates cold spots and rooms that are too hot or too cold. Because there is no duct work, it also cuts way down on dust.

The water, which circulates continuously through polybutylene tubing at a temperature of about 180 Fahrenheit, heats continuously. Since the heat is rising from the floor, maximum heat is at body level, not collecting at ceiling height. The hot water circulates through a sealed loop system, eliminating heat loss through holes in duct work. Manufacturers claim a savings of 20 to 40 percent compared to conventional heating methods.

The biggest problem with hydronic systems is that they are slow. Forced air heating systems are fast. You can walk into a cold house, dial up the thermostat, and have heat almost instantly. Hydronic heating takes hours. When you turn up the thermostat, the boiler goes on and gradually heats the water. The hot water circulates through the hydronic system and heats the flooring. Heat from the flooring gradually heats the air. Once it's warm, it's wonderful, but don't take off your coat right away.

A big plus is that hydronic heating is versatile. You can easily use it to heat the garage, or keep ice and snow off sidewalks and driveways by extending a loop system under the area you wish to remain cleared before the concrete is poured.

Once constant loop is not used throughout the entire house. A manifold directs different amounts of heated water to different areas. If you want a specific room in the house to be 10 or 20 degrees cooler than the rest of the house, so be it. If you would like heat to be directed under the driveway to keep its surface at a nice ice-and-snow-melting 33 degrees, that is what will happen.

Geothermal heating and cooling

Geothermal heating makes electric heat cost competitive. It uses Mother Nature to heat and cool your house. She also pays 40 or 50 percent of the heating bill. Up to four times more efficient than propane, a geothermal system doesn't really create heat. It just shifts heat from the ground to your house, or to the ground from your house, depending whether the system is being used to heat or cool.

The heart of the geothermal heating and cooling system is the earth loop. Loops of high strength plastic pipe are buried either horizontally, or vertically in the ground (or in a lake or pond). A heat pump is used to direct heat from, or to, the ground.

The Department of Energy likes geothermal systems because they are efficient and restrict pollution to a single source, the electric power company, rather than a hundred million homes. This not only makes pollution easier to monitor, it cuts it down drastically.

Homeowners like geothermal systems because they are clean and cost efficient. They also can save money on hot water. A conventional geothermal heating and cooling unit assists on hot water heating about 40 percent of the time. Add a desuper heater option and a geothermal unit gives you a virtually limitless supply of hot water.

Both hydronic and geothermal heating systems require a bigger initial investment than natural gas forced air, but annual operating costs are lower, so they pay off within five years.

They are both specialized systems, so make sure that your heating contractor has the necessary experience before you sign on the dotted line. For more information about hydronic heating, call Hartford & Ratliff (800-466-3110) or Heat Link USA (800-968-8905). For information on geothermal systems, call Detroit Edison (800-833-2786) or Wholesale Heating Supply (248-338-6454) in the Detroit area, or Water Furnace International (800-222-5667) or Climate Master (800-922-3045).

After the basement dries out, turn the tide against mold and mildew

by America's Master Handyman,
Glenn Haege

> *As soon as the muscle work is over, put your brain in gear. Track down why the flooding happened and what you can do to prevent similar problems in the future.*

The rash of flooding in Westland shows another reason why Michigan is called the Water Wonderland. Fast action by the city, sending in people to pump out, mop and decontaminate resident's basements resulted in a mollified, if not happy, citizenry.

What happens if your city, municipality or unincorporated whatever does not have the brains, brawn or budget to help with the cleanup when flooding happens? You better start to plan now. Since flooding started in February, this may be the kind of year that puts Cadillacs in the driveways of a lot of basement waterproofers.

When the water settles, your work starts. If you still have a little standing water, vacuum up the residue with a Wet/Dry Shop Vac. Make certain the power plug is grounded, and wear rubber boots or rubber shoes.

Mop the entire area with a mixture of germicide and water. Nothing I know of is better or cheaper than 11 1/4 ounces of household bleach in 5 gallons of water. This is strong stuff, be sure to wear a respirator.

Take out throw rugs or removable carpeting. Professional cleaning and sanitizing is best. If you can't send them out, clean the carpeting with a heavy-duty carpet cleaner.

My friends at Crandall-Worthington (248-398-8118) suggest that if you fear fecal or other organic contamination, sanitize with a microbial such as New Push by Betco or Enzym D by Big D Industries. These products contain living, nonpathogenic microorganisms that consume any organic matter that may be on the floor or in the carpeting. Mix approximately a half gallon to 5 gallons of water and apply with an extractor.

If the carpeting is just wet, they recommend Betco Cleanitizer to clean and decontaminate the carpet. You'll find other carpet cleaning and sanitizing products at Scrubs (248-569-5995) or your local janitorial supply.

Get air circulating immediately to dry wall-to-wall carpeting. If you have a dehumidifier, put it at one end of the room and place an oscillating fan at the other. Hook up the oscillating fan to an appliance timer. Six hours on, two hours off, for a total of 18 hours out of 24. Tilt the fan toward the basement ceiling.

Padding, under very wet wall-to-wall carpeting may have to be replaced. In a worst case scenario, the carpeting may have to be thrown out, too. Upholstered furniture that has been contaminated also has to go.

If the water damage is severe, your best bet is to have the basement ozonated. When you do this, professionals come in and set up heavy-duty ozone-making equipment in the basement. The ozone eliminates odors in the house by killing mildew and microbes. Ozonation takes 24 hours. All pets, plants and people should be out of the house during that period.

You can rent ozonation equipment from Guaranteed Furniture Service (248-545-1130), or call a company like Sanit-Air (888-778-7324) to have the work done for you.

If the basement has only a slight mildewy, dank smell, circulate the air with fans and hang Mil-Du-Gas Bags to kill the mold spores. Mil-Du-Gas Bags, made by Star Brite Co. (800-327-8583), now come in a new formulation, called MDG-2, that has no formaldehyde and is very safe. They are stocked by Damman, ACO and most good hardware stores and home centers.

As soon as the muscle work is over, put your brain in gear. Track down why the flooding happened and what you can do to prevent similar problems in the future.

Many people with sunken window wells have flooded basements. Good window well drainage is critical. Debris has to be cleaned out at least every spring and late fall. Some window wells have drains. The drains must be clear or they compound the problem.

The natural drainage in most sunken window wells is composed of various thicknesses of gravel, topped by construction sand. Weathering leaks silt on top of the sand, and clogs the gravel. Dig out and replace the clogged sand and gravel.

Consider replacing the sunken windows with glass block. You will still have to keep the window wells clear, but the block will give you better protection against flooding.

Storm sewers should not back up into the basement, but they do. If this happens more than once, have the line from your main drain to the street snaked out periodically. The bigger the trees near your house, the more often it will have to be done.

If your sump pump has been acting up or it has shut off at a critical time, check to see why. When the electric power goes out, the electric sump pump stops working. This usually means that the sump pump is inoperative when the need is greatest.

Consider installing a sump pump that runs on city water pressure, not electricity. Water-powered sump pumps are manufactured by the Zoler Corp. (800-928-7867). They are more expensive than electric models, but the dependability is worth the money.

It's costly, but improving a home's air can help you breathe easier

by America's Master Handyman, Glenn Haege

If you read my columns or listen to my radio show regularly, you know that indoor air quality is one of my big concerns. I know I sound like your grandmother, but I can't help it. Ten out of 10 medical studies agree that breathing is absolutely essential to good health.

That may sound stupid, and I admit that I wrote it for comic effect, but it's true.

As our homes become more energy efficient, they are increasingly like Baggies. Humidity levels from cooking and breathing increase, causing mold and mildew. Carbon monoxide and carbon dioxide levels increase. Harmful chemicals, leached from construction materials, furniture, carpeting, padding and household cleaners drawn by the overly moist atmosphere, contaminate our air supply.

All types of bacteria and other microorganisms, many of them potentially lethal, think they have found Nirvana and propagate profusely in the ductwork, basement, garbage, drain areas and every other dark, dank place.

During the winter, the furnaces in most homes aggravate the problem by pumping internal air out of the house, causing negative air pressure.

We get cranky, headachy, nauseous, we develop sore throats and sinus conditions. And, the final straw, our windows steam up. I believe steamy windows are a sign of direct intervention by the Almighty because most of my listeners are able to ignore all the other symptoms, but they call me when their windows steam up.

My quick fix is to install the Equaliz-Air by Xavier (734-462-1033) or the Skuttle Model 216 (800-848-9786). These products use the home's negative air pressure to open air channels into the house and bring in fresh air when needed.

The good thing about the Equaliz-Air and the Skuttle Model 216 is that they are relatively economical ways to fix the problems. The EqualizeAir is easily installed by the do-it-yourselfer and readily available at Damman and many other good hardware stores for about $65. The Skuttle Model 216, which costs about $300, ties directly into your heating system, and is usually contractor installed.

A good heating contractor will tell you these systems have three weaknesses: 1) Since they are mechanical, not powered, they function only when there is negative air pressure. 2) In the dead of winter, when they function most, they bring in dry, frigid air causing decreased humidity and increased strain on the furnace. 3) They do only half the job, bringing in fresh air, but not exhausting stale air.

If you have a good heating contractor, he or she can tell you about equipment that solves these weaknesses.

The heart of the system is the heat recovery ventilator (HRV). The HRV draws fresh air into the house and exhausts stale air out of the house. In the winter, the outgoing stale air heats the incoming fresh air as the two air streams pass by opposite sides of multiple layers of media inside the heat exchange core. In the summer, the air conditioned exhaust air, cools the hot incoming air.

Most companies higher-end models of the HRV (sometimes called ERV for energy recovery ventilator) are made with humidity-absorbing cores that humidify the dry incoming air during the winter, and dehumidify moist incoming air during the summer.

Lennox has a really neat optional air sensor, called the Air Sentry, that continually monitors air quality and automatically increases air exchange when it detects a wide range of pollutants. Honeywell often ties its HRV into its Perfect Climate Comfort Control System to automate the entire procedure. It also recommends exhausting the air from the kitchen, bath and utility rooms, eliminating noisy exhaust fans, and directing incoming air into the bedrooms and living areas.

Now, if I know this, why didn't your heating contractor tell you when he sold you a furnace? As consumers, we can expect to receive quality information from contractors, or any other retailers, only when we behave like quality buyers. Most contractors are afraid to talk about materials that will increase costs. They know most buyers are price-, not quality-oriented, and do not want to risk losing the sale.

I'm not selling anything, so I'll tell you about the equipment, then you can bring it up to your heating contractor if you want to breathe easier. An HRV system can add $800 to $1,500 or more to the cost of the furnace. A separate installation costs around $1,500. While an HRV costs a big chunk up front, by preheating winter air, and precooling summer air, it saves money on your total energy bill at the same time it increases your home's air quality. That makes it a darn good investment.

You can get more information about HRVs from Flame Furnace (888-234-2340), Williams Refrigeration (888-268-5445) or any good contractor. You also can call the manufacturers. Major manufacturers of HRVs are Broan (800-548-0790), Honeywell (800-345-6770, ext. 775) or Lennox (972-497-5000).

MARCH 22, 1997

It's time to take a stand and flush away those 1.6-gallon toilets

by America's Master Handyman, Glenn Haege

Toilets aren't talked about in polite company. It is my duty to break this taboo and tell you that it is essential for you to keep your present toilet in good working condition. The honored 3.5 gallon reservoir commode is becoming a thing of the past thanks to size limitations inflicted on us by the Energy and Conservation Act of 1992.

This prime piece of potty legislation mandated that toilets be limited to 1.6 gallons per flush and that showers have a flow rate of no more than 2.5 gallons per minute. Typical of legislation created by people who make laws while giving no thought to their results, there are problems. New law-forced toilets do not flush and pin-point showers may make people sick.

Since most of the mandated 1.6-gallon toilets do not work the first time, you have to keep flushing and flushing. If you buy a 3.5-gallon model for new construction on the black market because you want a toilet that works, you can be fined $2,500 for willful procurement of a restricted toilet. (I am not joking).

The 2.5-gallon-per-minute showers are worse. The restricted shower heads don't just make you mad because you aren't getting wet; a University of Cincinnati study shows that the smaller nozzle holes create inhalable droplets which can cause us to breath Chlorine and other contaminants from our water supply deep into our lungs (much like a mini poison gas attack).

Rep. Joe Knollenberg, of Michigan's 11th. District, is on the case trying to roll back the legislation with House Bill HR 859. Personally, I would prefer that we kept the legislation and rolled back the legislators who were dim witted enough to foist this kind of law on us.

If you want to learn more about the proposed legislation, Congressman Knollenberg will be on my radio show today, between 11 a.m. and noon EST. If you can't listen, but demand the right of free men and women everywhere to flush the toilet of your choice, send your congressperson a section of toilet tissue with the words: "Get the Government out of my toilet, vote for HR 859."

In the meantime, if you want a 1.6 gallon replacement that works, you will have to replace your hundred dollar commode, with a four, five, or six hundred dollar model. If you don't want to spend that kind of money, keep your present toilet in tip, top, condition.

I talked with Jim Kronk of Universal Plumbing in Berkeley (248-542-3888) about toilet maintenance. Kronk says that the average toilet or commode lasts about 30 years.

The two biggest causes of commode replacement are unseen firing flaws and clogged water passages. Hidden cracks inside the ceramic work their way to the surface over the years. When that happens it's replacement time.

Hard water will also cause mineral deposits to form on the inner passageways slowing water flow to a trickle. This is especially true of the narrow passageways that conduct water from the water tank to the small holes that surround the bowl. If this is happening in the bowl of your commode, take a coat hanger wire and clean out the holes, the next time you clean the bowl.

One of the most common problems do-it-yourselfers bring to Universal Plumbing is the slow flushing toilet. When that happens make certain that the problem is with the commode not with some other element of the plumbing system, like the pipes or roof vents. Wad up some toilet paper, drop it in the bowl, then pour in a pail of water.

The bowl should react as if the commode had been flushed. The paper will be flushed, the water level will go back down to its normal level, and you will hear that satisfying "glug, glug" that signifies that the commode has gone through a complete flushing cycle.

If it doesn't happen, the line and/or the roof vent have to be snaked out. If the flushing cycle is successful, check that the water in the tank is up to the water line. Then flush the tank to see that the flapper is not dropping prematurely cutting off water flow from the tank. When the water cuts off prematurely, adjust the ball cock mechanism.

The next possibility is that mineral deposits may be blocking the water holes around the rim of the toilet bowl. Shut off the water supply and stop up the rim holes from beneath with moist paper toweling held in place by wet rags. Pour Lime-Away by Benckiser (800-284-2023) or Lime Buster by Whink (800-247-5102) into the overflow tube and let the chemicals soak away the mineral deposits for about an hour. You should be able to find these chemicals at ACO, Damman, Quality, Spartan, and many other independent hardware stores and supermarkets.

If this doesn't solve the problem, it's replacement time. Pray that Joe Knollenberg's Bill HR 859 has been successful and we can buy affordable toilets that actually work.

MARCH 29, 1997

Sooner or later something is sure to give, so let's pump you up

by America's Master Handyman, Glenn Haege

Basements are nothing but seven or eight foot deep holes in the ground. Simple physics says that a hole that deep, below the water table, has to fill with water sooner or later.

The final line of defense for our basements is the drain tile system that directs the invading ground water into the sump crock where it is pumped out of the house by the sump pump. This valiant little rascal works twenty-four hours a day, patiently bailing out the basement.

The purpose of this article is to give you the information you need to know about sump pumps before you have a problem.

Sump pumps come in three different styles: pedestal, submersible and torpedo. The pedestal sump pump's motor is out of the water and actuated by a ball cock mechanism. The submersible sump pump is located inside the sump crock. The torpedo style sump pump is most commonly used when a house was not originally built with a sump, and is in the drain tile cleanout.

All of these pumps are actuated by a rising water level. When the water in the sump rises to a pre-set level, the switch clicks and the pump turns on and pumps the water from the bottom of the sump up a pipe and over to a discharge outlet.

Residential sump pump motors are usually .3 to half horse power (hp). The Zoeller .3 hp submersible sump pump can pump 34 gallons a minute, or 2040 gallons an hour, up a ten foot lift and get it out of your house. The 1/2 hp submersible model is rated at 61 gallons a minute, or 3660 gallons an hour. Wayne Pump's 1/2 hp submersible is rated at 3000 gallons an hour.

According to Jim Kronk, of Universal Plumbing (248-542-3888), bigger does not necessarily mean better. In real life, a sump pump almost never runs for an hour. Quite often, it will only run five or ten minutes in five or ten hours and may not even turn on for months at a time. The longer sump pumps run, the more efficient they become. So Kronk believes that, unless you have a definite need to move a great deal of water, the .3 hp may be a better choice.

Sump pumps are very reliable, easy to maintain, and will serve you for many years. Their switches may have to be changed five or six times during those years. If the switch breaks, the pump won't turn on.

Maintenance should include regular inspections during the wet season. Look into the sump for debris. Brush off calcium deposits. If you haven't heard the pump go on in a while, pour some water into the sump crock to see if the pump goes on. If it doesn't, the switch probably needs to be replaced.

Scoop out the muck from the bottom of the sump at least once a year. A good way to keep the crock clear of accumulated debris is to run a garden hose from your laundry tub and turn on the cold water. This churns up the gunk and gives the pump a chance to get rid of it.

Since sump pumps are powered by electricity, when the electricity goes out in a storm, the pump stops working when it is needed most. You can install a backup sump pump to guard against a power failure.

Most back up pumps are battery powered. On the better ones, like the Ace In The Hole (so help me, that is the name of the pump and the company that makes it), when the electricity goes out, an alarm sounds and the battery-powered backup starts pumping. A battery powered backup sump pump costs in the $250 range not including the auto-style battery.

When the power failure is of short duration, everything is fine. As soon as the electricity goes back on, the battery pump stops and the battery recharges. If a power failure lasts for a long time, the battery pumps for about 24 hours. Even if you install a second battery attachment, that just saves the basement for another day.

A completely different kind of backup sump pump uses water power from the city water line. If your house is hooked up to a city system, a water powered backup pump gives unlimited protection. It will keep working as long as the water lines have pressure.

Water powered back up sump pumps are made by Zoeller (800-928-7867) under the Zoeller (heavier duty contractor model) or HiLo brand names, and by a local company, Sumpvac, Inc., of Lathrup Village. Most water powered back up sump pumps range in price from about $119 to $285. The installed cost runs between $600 and $700 for a regular pump depending on the pump. Saginaw makes a brass and copper unit that costs around $500, plus installation, and will last longer than your house.

That's a lot of money for a back up pump, but it is very cheap insurance when you consider that, in most homes, the furnace, water heater, washer, dryer and electrical hook up are all in the basement, to say nothing about the irreplaceable things most people store down there. If you have remodeled part of the basement into rec. room or office space, keeping it safe and dry is even more important.

Sump pumps and battery powered backup pumps are available at most hardware and home centers. Water powered backups are available at Universal Plumbing, Damman Hardware, or your plumbing contractors.

Renew or replace outdoor furniture to be sitting pretty this spring

by America's Master Handyman, Glenn Haege

Spring! Everyone wants to be outdoors but the only problem is that your patio furniture has seen better days.

If it's just dirty and dull looking, clean it with a good all-purpose cleaner like Simple Green or Clear Magic and water. Scrub vigorously, then rinse with a garden hose. When dry, follow up with a coat of Diamond Brite or a Teflon paint sealant for that "like new" look.

If it's time to replace, and you want the replacements to be really special, here are a few tips.

Start your voyage of discovery at a specialty store. The home centers and discount stores have patio sets, but they don't specialize in them. Only a specialty store has buyers who spend weeks analyzing which pieces are best for our particular market and can afford to deal with small designers and manufacturers who do not produce in a year what major chains sell in a week.

Just as important, the specialty stores are set up to do special orders. If you want "this" chair in "that" color, with "those" pillows, you got it.

To see what's hot this year I went to two specialists, Evergreen Home and Garden Center (810-791-2277), on Groesbeck South of 16 Mile, and Jimmies Rustics (248-644-1919) on Woodward in Birmingham. Both have more than one location, so look them up in the yellow pages or give them a call before you go shopping.

For nice five piece sets, with a 48-inch round table and four chairs, prices range an average of $500 to $1,500, but you can go as high as your comfort level allows. For instance, I saw a 36-inch round marble topped table with two chairs preseason sale priced at only $2,184 at Jimmies. I want you to go out and buy it this weekend because I don't know how long I can keep my lovely bride away from that store.

The top color is green, but taupe is coming on strong. Bar-height tables and chairs, that give you the extra height you need to look over the hedge, are becoming very popular. So are market umbrellas, you know, the super sized versions of the ones you saw carried in Madam Butterfly. Market umbrellas used to be exclusively of the sash cord variety. Today, some of the pricier models come with cranks, so you can have the style and the convenience.

Outdoor furniture is classified by construction materials. Aluminum furniture can be either tubular, or cast. Tubular or extruded construction accounts for 60 percent of all US outdoor furniture sales. It is durable, light weight and, sometimes, the most economically priced. The biggest drawback of tubular construction is that the light weight makes it easy to blow over in high wind areas.

Tubular does not necessarily mean round. It may be oval or rectangular with inner support panels. If you go the tubular route, inspect the welds when shopping. If the welding material is ground down so as to become almost invisible, the weld may not be as strong. Robert Wilk of Evergreen says that a slightly puffy weld on an aluminum chair is a sign of quality and insures greater strength.

Cast aluminum outdoor furniture is usually the most expensive category you will find in the store. The molds are often intricately cut duplications of classic designs. The newer designs are far less busy than those that were originally introduced. Since the furniture is solid, it is a great deal heavier than tubular construction.

The two most basic materials, hard wood and wrought iron, still hold their places of honor on the patio. Jim Sica of Jimmies Rustics believes that teak is superior and the best looking hardwood for outdoor furniture. He has found that the lesser woods discolor more rapidly and are more difficult to maintain.

When looking for wrought iron, inspect the paint job very carefully. Iron is prone to rust, its only defense is the paint job. Whenever you get a scratch, apply touch up paint immediately.

Indoor/outdoor wicker ware is another great look. The "wicker" is really acrylic on a steel or aluminum frame. It's pricey, but very attractive and comfortable.

The Woodard company of Owosso, Michigan, (517-725-4500) makes high quality outdoor furniture in both tubular and cast aluminum as well as wrought iron. Brown Jordan (800-743-4252) and Tropicana, the most famous names in outdoor furniture, do beautiful work in all the materials we've talked about today.

One final tip from Bob Wilk, whatever you choose, protect your investment from the elements with covers. A reinforced vinyl patio umbrella cover by Daya costs $20. A sombrero cover, shaped to fit an umbrella, table and chairs, costs about $95 at Evergreen, and is well worth the investment.

For a grate and long-lasting love, stick with a high-quality grill

by America's Master Handyman,
Glenn Haege

Little girls may play with Barbie dolls, but real men play with *Barbies*. I can still remember my first fling: a charcoal-burning Weber Orange. For her time, she was wonderful. Easy to light. Even burn. Great for slow cooking.

But times change. I started running around with a snappy little propane number. Instant gratification. Just turn on the propane, push the igniter button and she was ready to start cooking. It didn't last. She was flashy, but cheap. Her igniter stopped working, then the rattles and warping started. Rust began to show.

After a few years, I got one with a see-through, tempered glass pane in the hood. After one steak, I couldn't see more than a glimmer through the glass, no matter how often I cleaned.

I should have listened to my mother when she told me "never fool around with anything cheap." I'm not the only man that has learned this painful lesson. Today's outdoor barbecuer is on a quest for quality. The manufacturers have listened and laid out lines of long lasting, heavy duty grills. One little warning: Quality costs money.

Jim Sica of Jimmies Rustics, says outdoor grills have made the transition from outdoor barbecues to outdoor appliances. "When you consider the quality of construction, premium outdoor grills are very good values. A top-of-the-line indoor cooktop can cost $1,200 to $1,800, and you would never think of leaving it out in the rain," he says.

The trend is to bigger, heavier grills. Stainless steel is the exterior of choice. You can pretty well tell the quality of a grill by lifting the top. If it lifts solid, like a high priced car door, you are looking at a grill that was meant to last. If it lifts light, it probably will warp from the heat of cooking and may not weather well.

Stores that specialize in these products usually have the best selection. Robert Wilk, of Evergreen Home & Garden, (Groesbeck South of 16 Mile, 810-791-2277) displays everything from charcoal burners to some of the most expensive, built-in models. He says a good natural gas or propane grill starts at about $500 and should last for ten years.

That's a good opening price. But if you don't want to spend that much money, Evergreen has a Weber Performer, a high bred charcoal-propane grill that I first saw in Chief's Catalogue. The propane is used to light the charcoal. You have the ease of propane, and the unmatched cooking quality of charcoal. Evergreen's price is only $389. Of course, if you want to spend one or two thousand dollars, Evergreen also carries six-burner, stainless steel, Weber Summit 650's, and top of the line Broil-Masters and Ducanes.

Another moderately priced grill that is a real conversation starter is the Holland Grill at Jimmies Rustic's Livonia store (Six Mile West of Middlebelt, 248-644-1919). The Holland grills, steams, and smokes, yet costs only $535. You can bake a bread and broil a steak at the same time. It has two little smoke stacks on top that look ridiculous; but it can cook a twelve pound turkey in two to three hours.

If you tend to burn, rather than broil, your chicken breasts, fish, or steak, check out the Ducane line at any good outdoor store. While other manufacturers brag about their cooking power (up to 60,000 BTUs for the Weber Summit), Ducane's burners are so efficient, they burn only 12,500 BTUs an hour. This makes it almost impossible to burn a steak, and you will get rave reviews cooking medleys of raw vegetables directly on the grill. Prices range from $450 to $1,800.

If speed is your thing, TEC (Thermal Engineering Corp.) grills, use a unique, Infra-Red burner system to instantly sear meat, locking in all the natural juices. You can broil a chicken breast in less than four minutes. TEC grills range from about $1,100 to $3,000. They're available from Michigan Fireplaces (Long Lake just West of Dequindre, 248-689-2296).

If you grill outside a lot, need to feed an army, and want to have something that will leave everybody standing in the dust, stop by Jimmies Rustics and look at the stainless steel, DCS (Dynamic Cooking Systems Inc.) grill. The heavy gauge stainless-steel housing says quality. The massive, porcelain-coated side burners, make other grill's side burners look like toys. The rotisserie spit and motor are big enough for a 20-pound turkey. You can have all this in your back yard for only $4,320.

Two final thoughts. One: It is rumored that Viking, one of the most famous names in indoor food preparation, is coming out of the kitchen. It's first outdoor grill is supposed to be at Jimmies Rustics some time in May or June. Two: No one, not even the distributors and manufacturers stock the more expensive grills in great depth. If you want the best of the best, order early. By June, they will all be gone.

Show and tell

My first ever East Side Modernization and Building Show, sponsored by WXYT Talk Radio Detroit, will be at the Macomb Center, M-59 (Hall Road) and Garfield next weekend, Saturday, 8 a.m. to 6 p.m., and Sunday, 8 a.m. to 5 p.m.. Both the show and parking are free.

APRIL 19, 1997

Despite building frenzy, there are few house-hunting nightmares

by America's Master Handyman, Glenn Haege

A few years ago, Michael and Debbie Ward got involved with a horror story of a house. What was supposed to be the home of their dreams, turned into a nightmare. Their home had been built on land that never should have been approved for construction, and it started sinking into the ground.

They eventually got the situation resolved, but it took a great deal of effort, including innumerable calls to the City Building Department, the State, insurance companies, and contractors, as well as picketing, radio and TV broadcasts and newspaper articles.

Shortly after solving his problem, Ward contacted me, saying that he would like to put on a seminar, so that other new homeowners would not have to go through the same ordeal. I agreed to help.

Michael Ward is a real go getter, who runs a training organization, called BEST Solutions. His stock in trade is coming up with ideas and executing them. Within months of our initial contact on the seminar, Ward had gotten a site, Switzer Elementary School in Shelby Township, and had enlisted the aid of township building and planning officials, real estate and insurance agencies, builders, contractors, home inspectors.

The New Home Buyers Forum was held last Thursday. Frankly, I was filled with trepidation when I drove to the event. The seminar, which was billed as an open forum to educate prospective home buyers and solve problems of people who already had difficulties, was an invitation to disaster.

We are in the middle of a building boom. Labor shortages are critical on almost every job. Even the best builders could easily have legitimate problems. I feared that I might be stepping into a swarm of unhappy homeowners and wind up with an event which would give South East Michigan Home Builders an unjustified black eye.

My worse fears seemed about to come true when I drove up to the school. The parking lot was so crammed with cars that I almost didn't go in. I finally parked in a tow away zone and sheepishly crept into to the Switzer Elementary School gymnasium.

The gymnasium was set up with 200 almost empty folding chairs. The cars that jammed the parking lot belonged, not to irate homeowners, but soccer moms and dads. I breathed a sigh of relief. This might not be a bad evening after all.

By the time the Seminar started, about 150 people from all over the Greater Detroit Area were in attendance. The great news about the Homeowners Forum was that there was no news. Only about five of the attendees had problems with their new homes. I had known about most of them for months.

The rest of the audience consisted of people considering buying a new home who had come to "learn before they did" something that I have been preaching for the past fourteen years.

You may have missed the significance of what I just wrote. We are in the middle of a building boom which is stretching the construction trades up to, and beyond their limits, and we didn't have any new home building problems reported at the New Homeowner Forum.

This means that South East Michigan Builders, working under the most trying conditions, are putting out a product they, and the new home buyers, can be proud of. This kind of information should be a real confidence builder if you are in the market for a new home.

Speakers at the Forum were all people who worked in the trenches. They approved the plans, or inspected, built, insured, sold, and even liens against the jobs when something went wrong. Here is some of the advice they gave.

■ If you are house hunting, decide on the community before you pick the house.

■ When you know where you want to live, get out of the car and walk the streets. Talk to the owners of new homes that look a lot like the kind in which you want to live.

■ Ask them about their builder. "Was he on time?" "Did he let you come on site and check things out throughout the period of construction?" "Did he have problems with the trades?" "Was he amenable to change?" "Was the final price close to the original estimate?" "Are they pleased with the quality?" "Does the builder come over right away and solve problems they may find?"

■ After you find the names of a few good builders who do a lot of work in the area, make appointments and get references.

■ Check with the City Building Department and the State Licensing authority to make certain that there are no bad marks against the builders and their qualifying officers.

■ Check all references thoroughly. That includes banks and building supply companies as well as home buyers.

■ Choose the builder, before you select your site.

■ *Don't sign anything until you have selected the lot and checked out the covenants of the deed, easements, and zoning ordinances.* Never think that just because there are no restrictions on one lot, that it will be the same for the lot across, or down, the street. Restrictions often vary from lot to lot.

■ Don't spend so much on your lot and architect that you no longer have enough money to build the house.

Come see me – free

For more information on home improvement or new construction directly from experts, come to my free WXYT Modernization and Building Show, at the Macomb Center, M-59 (Hall Road) and Garfield this Saturday, 8 a.m. to 5 p.m., and Sunday, 8 a.m. to 5 p.m..

Suppressors have the power to protect your home against surges

by America's Master Handyman, Glenn Haege

When I was a boy, it seemed as though there were almost never any problems with electricity. We never thought about power surges. Unless there was a direct lightning strike, you didn't have to worry.

That is no longer the case. I asked Don Collins of Budget Electric (800-400-8941) about power surges. Budget Electric pulls more residential electric permits than any other contractor in the State, by a ratio of about 2-1 over their next biggest competitor.

Unlike most electrical contractors, Budget Electric specializes in residential work. I figure Collins should know about residential power problems, because he's the guy that fixes them.

Collins says the spiking problem is even worse that I thought. Quoting a recent, year long, national study of 1,000 homes, he explains that the average home has about 2,000 foreign surges every year. Only surges that were large enough to burn out appliances were counted.

Think about that. In an average year, your home's electrical system gets 2,000 power surges powerful enough to fry your refrigerator, television set, or air conditioner. That's six to eight power surges a day.

When I tell Collins the statistics seemed high, he asks me if I'd seen the lights in my house flickering recently or if I'd no-ticed that I had to change light bulbs more often. I've noticed both; you probably have, too. I'd figured that, like everything else, the light bulbs were just being made more cheaply.

Bulbs being manufactured today are actually made to closer tolerances, than bulbs made 20 years ago, Collins says. The flickering and the more frequent bulb replacement are caused by power surges.

The increase in power surges is due to increased electric power consumption. Houses are closer together. Air conditioning used to be a rarity, now it can be found in almost every home. Hot tubs, home theatre, and other luxuries we need today all pull a lot of power.

Every time a neighbor's air conditioner goes on, or a compressor is turned on, a surge could be created – to say nothing about surges caused when the power goes off mysteriously due to new construction or problems with the lines.

During the middle of summer when almost every air conditioner in the neighborhood is on at the same time, if five or six turn off at the same time, there is a sudden jolt of power that can hit every home in the neighborhood.

The delicate electrical components in garage door openers, furnace transformers, and appliance touch pads are especially vulnerable to local power surges.

The best protection against power surges is the installation of a whole house surge supressor. Surge supressors vary in price from $50 to about $250. The $50 are a little light. The average price for a good surge supressor is about $149, Collins says.

The supressor protects appliances by intercepting the surge and turning off. During normal surges, a good surge supressor, like the Ditek 120/240-CM (made by Diversified Technology Group, Inc., 800-753-2345), automatically resets itself and continues to give protection.

In the event of a very powerful surge, a nearby lightning strike, for example, the supressor sacrifices itself, burning out, and tripping the specific breaker to which it is connected. If you see that the circuit breaker is tripped, and will not reset, the surge supressor has burned out protecting your appliances and must be replaced.

Nothing, according to Collins, can protect your wiring in the event of a direct lightning strike. When that happens, the surge supressor will be fried and the power surge may still be powerful enough to blow the circuit breaker box off the wall.

Naturally, at times like that, major electrical repairs are needed. That is one of the reasons I recommend pulling the plugs on all electrical appliances during a major storm.

Installing a whole house surge supressor does not mean that you can disconnect the individual surge protectors and multiple outlet surge receptacles around the house. These receptacles are necessary to protect your appliances from surges that are created inside your house. Since these surges are within your homes wiring, the whole house surge supressor can not even sense that they are happening and offers no protection.

In-house surges can be created whenever the washing machine, dryer, air conditioner, high powered vacuum cleaner, micro-wave oven, hair dryer, or any high powered appliance is turned on or off.

On an ordinary wash day you may create a dozen or more electric surges. Every one of them is powerful enough to fry the touch pad controls on your microwave or electric stove, or the circuits in your garage door opener or furnace transformer. This is especially true if your home's electrical system has not been upgraded to meet modern power needs and major appliances are not on dedicated circuits.

If this describes your home's electrical system, Collins recommends three things:
■ First, go out and get individual surge protectors for all your major appliances.
■ Second, make the commitment to having your home's electrical system upgraded to meet modern conditions.
■ Third, request that your electrical contractor install a whole house surge supressor as part of the job. If your house already has sufficient power, an electrical contractor can install a whole house surge supressor for just a few hundred dollars.

Very clear installation instructions are included with the surge supressor, so a moderately skilled handy person can install it themselves, but I don't recommend it.

Hottest kitchen designs dish up high-end cabinets and convenience

by America's Master Handyman, Glenn Haege

Every April the National Kitchen & Bath Association (NKBA) has their Annual Show. I couldn't make it this year because of other engagements, but Dennis and Dave Pink, the owners of Cabinet Clinic, (734) 421-8151 agreed to be my spies and tell me about the new trends. They made their report on one of my April radio shows. Here's a brief rundown.

The most expensive ingredient of your kitchen design, and the single feature that most determines the look of most kitchens, is the cabinets. Over the years European look and country-kitchen look and many other "looks" have held sway. A good real estate agent can walk into a kitchen and date the kitchen by the cabinets. Even though you may have the most up to date appliances, if the cabinets have an out dated look, the kitchen is old. Therefore if you are remodeling your kitchen, it is important to have the newest styles, so your kitchen stays "newer" looking longer, maximizing the return on investment when you eventually sell your home.

As a people, we are feeling good about ourselves. The leading cabinet trend at this year's NKBA show was the affluent, "high end" look. Maple is the most popular wood with cherry and hickory running a close second and third. In accordance with the "high end" look, glass in doors and drawers is very popular, along with fluted fillers, ornate mullions, and dentic, batteen and crown moldings.

As a society we are getting older and busier. Kitchen designers are compensating by raising dishwashers so that they are easier to get to. Our hectic lifestyle has made microwave ovens such an indispensable part of the kitchen that now there are often two of them in the modern kitchen. One is located above the stove, another on the counter. The small one is for warm ups. The larger one for major cooking projects.

Another critical addition is added lighting, especially task lighting so that you can read a recipe clearly, add ingredients easily, and find even the most seldom-used pot, pan, bowl or china. The lighting is not obvious and doesn't take up a lot of room. Most are located inside or under cabinets.

I believe that it is time for my good friend, Joe Gagnon, to take a bow. He has led the crusade against touch pad appliance controls since they first appeared on the scene. They are easy to burn out with even a moderate power surge and almost impossibly expensive to repair or replace. Old-fashioned knobs are much easier to use and last practically forever. Now Joe's battle seems to be won and knobs are reappearing on upscale appliances. Appliance doors are also being beveled to make controls more visible and easier to use.

Corian and other solid surface counter tops are becoming even more popular. For those unwilling to spend $4,000 to $8,000 on their countertops, there are more special edges and solid surface veneer edges. Using solid surface veneers you get the solid surface look at a lower cost. Also, remember the option of using designer tiles for counters and back splashes. The cost of solid surface countertops can make a unique designer tile design a money-saving alternative that is certain to grow in value over the years.

Solid-surface sinks have come down in price. Under-counter sinks are even more popular, not only for their good looks, but because they make kitchen cleanup easier. The role of the sink area has expanded so that now the best designs are not just cleaning, but food preparation centers greatly enhancing ease of cooking.

Laminated floors from Pergo, Wilsonart, Bruce, and Formica are getting very popular in this country. They combine the look of wood with easier clean-up.

That wraps up the Pinks' report.

Along the same line, I have been searching the World Wide Web a good deal recently. One of the best sites I've found for anyone designing or remodeling their kitchen is the Masco Corporation at masco.com. It includes information on Delta and other faucet lines, plumbing fixtures, and most important, their Merillat and KraftMaid cabinets. Both the Merillat and KraftMaid sites give design help, show their different cabinet styles and materials, as well as offer free Kitchen Information Kits loaded with cabinet and design ideas.

Merillat's on-line designs are so attractive that one, almost made Kathy, my editor, tear out the wall between her kitchen and dining room so that she could have a great room.

You can sign up for both the Merillat and KraftMaid information kits at their Masco Web sites or, if you're not tuned into the Web, you can get the kits for my favorite price (free) by calling Merillat at (800) 575-8759 or KraftMaid at (800) 571-1990 .

Honey, pick up some Pringles when you're at the hardware store

by America's Master Handyman, Glenn Haege

Last week, since my blushing bride was going out of the house anyway, I asked her to go by one of my favorite hardware stores and pick up a cleaner that was perfect for a nasty job she had assigned me. I, after all, am America's Master Handyman. I know the exact product for each specific chore. While she was gone I sat back in my easy chair thinking how impressed she would be when I whisked open the top of the cleaner, and in just a few swift flourishes removed a stain that would have caused her hours of hard work.

I knew that this particular store had the product because over the years, I had not only seen it there, but had directed thousands of people to the store to get it. Imagine my surprise when Barbara came home to report that they no longer had room to stock the product. But, not to worry, they had plenty of Aunt Jamima Pancake Mix and Syrup.

I rushed out of the house. She had to be wrong. Naturally, she was right. It's been 28 years, and she still has that annoying habit.

I decided to check Dammans and see if they were also infected with non-hardwareitus. Dammans is famous as one of the "new, new product stores." If you've developed an innovative product, Dammans buyers will often lend a sym-pathetic ear and buy it for their entire chain. Even the big nationals, shop Dammans to see which new products are going well.

During my inspection tour of Dammans I picked up an Arizona Iced Tea for the trip, but passed on the Pringles. There was a nice little Radio Flyer miniature wagon for $4.99 that I thought Barb would like for her nostalgia collection. The Magic Goo at $3.59 was a pretty good buy, but the Chem Slime at $3.99 seemed a little bit pricey.

At Trevarrow Hardware, on Long Lake at Livernois, one of North Woodward's biggest and best stocked hardware stores, I went immediately to the Crystal display, but was soon distracted by the Potpourri section. At $4.99 the Potpourri seemed like a nice way to handle the stench of my golf shoes in the trunk of the car, but I couldn't find the proper container so I gave up on the idea. One of those big $18 Yankee Candles caught my eye, but I decided that a couple of wax potpourri tart candles would probably be more practical for the work bench.

Trevarrow's had a metal ACE Hardware scale model Chevy Truck bank for $17.88 and a 1929 Lockheed collectable, Do-It Express Plane for $24.88. Just looking at that thing reminded me of when the Cunningham's News Ace would zoom into our homes to bring us the latest news.

Back from the nostalgia kick, I stopped off at Costello Hardware, on Rochester Road in Troy, but couldn't find a thing but hardware, plumbing and electrical supplies. The sales clerks were too buy with customers for me to even ask if they had anything else. How can those people expect to survive!

ACO they didn't have any "sheer energy" in my size. Ditto on the sandals. The Cheese Puffs were out of stock, but Circus Peanuts were 88 cents and the Toasted Coconut Marshmallows were 99 cents. At $1.95, the Noxema shaving cream looked like a good deal, so I picked up a can. I bet Ted Trascos is in line for the 50 Year Platinum Shopping Cart Award to go along with all of his other 50th Anniversary Honors. Congratulations Ted!

Two hardware stores in the Dearborn/Livonia Area are famous for their side ventures. At Murray's Ace Hardware, Plymouth and Inkster, I could not only get 6 tooth brushes or 1,000 cotton swabs for $1, I could get a 14-karat gold bracelet for $16.99, 1/2-karat diamond earrings for $99, or Timex watches for as low as $15.95. I have a sneaking suspicion that Murray's makes more on their huge jewelry department than they do on the rest of the store.

Hanses Ace Hardware, Warren and Schaefer, in Dearborn, has a toy train department that may be the biggest department in the store. Don't tell anyone, but, if you act fast, Hanses has a Lionel Southern Pacific, G 54 Steam, 4-8-4 with Sound, for only $995.99, marked down from $1,499.99! But, like I said, you got'ta act fast.

In between hardware stores, I stopped off at some local home centers. I couldn't even pick up a box of Sugar Pops, but there were loads of people in the hardware, tools, plumbing, electrical, K & B (Kitchen & Bath), and garden sections. Funny thing, the Lighting and Electrical stores just had lighting and electrical. The Paint & Wallpaper stores just had paint and wallpaper. The Plumbing Supply stores just had kitchen, bath and plumbing supplies. I guess these companies are all way behind the times. But most of them sure have a lot of customers.

All of the hardware stores I've mentioned in this article are excellent independent stores or highly successful chains. I wouldn't mention their names if I didn't think they could take a little well meaning fun. At the same time, I couldn't help but remember my football coach at Warren High School, exhorting us to "Focus, focus, focus!" My golf pro always tells me, "Haege, this time try to keep your eye on the ball."

But hey, what do they know about hardware?

Get your spring cleaning done now so you can enjoy next weekend

by America's Master Handyman,
Glenn Haege

We all know that the long Memorial Day Weekend is your special time to run around like a crazy person trying to do all the things that need to be done outside. How about getting the projects done this weekend, so that next weekend, you actually have time to kick back, relax, take in a parade, fire up the barby and burn some burgers?

The first step is to find out what needs to be done by walking around making notes on what needs to be fixed, cleaned or painted. I call this "manage by walking around." Golf widows can do this by themselves and wind up with enough "honey do" slips to keep the love of your life busy all summer.

Get a pad and pencil and walk around the house four times. First trip, look at the roof for loose shingles, sagging gutters, or other winter damage. Second trip, look at the face of the house, check out windows, screens, siding, vents, and exterior lights. Third trip, check out the foundation, exterior valves, make sure the ground is sloping away from the house and that no bird-bathing has occurred. Fourth trip, look away from the house at your property. Are there broken tree limbs? Has a tree sagged against a power line (call your power company, don't try to fix this)? Have moles invaded the lawn?

Next, turn on all the exterior lights, the front and back door lights, the flood lights, the coach lights, everything that is outside and burns electricity should be turned on. Bulbs may need to be replaced. Some are probably broken. Bring out all exterior hoses and sprinklers. Turn them on to make sure that everything is working and you don't have any costly water drips. If you have a lawn sprinkler system, check to see that each sprinkler is functioning and aimed properly.

OK, you're done. By now you may have a very long "To Do" list, or if you're lucky, you may have just a few notes on general cleanup. Here are a few window clean-up tips that everybody needs. I'll follow up with more in-depth solutions for specific outdoor repairs in later articles.

Window Cleaning

For fourteen years I have recommended TSP based window washing formulas. The problem with TSP is that it is an even better fertilizer than cleaner, helping the algae to grow like wildfire in lakes and streams. Today, there is very little of the super cleaning agent, Trisodium Phosphate, in TSP. So I have changed my window washing formula.

You need different window cleaning solutions inside and outside the house. What is fine for greasy inside windows, will not do the job outside, and vise versa.

Outside Window Cleaning Solution: 1 gallon water, 4 ounces vinegar, 1 teaspoon liquid hand dish washing detergent. Do not put in more than one teaspoon of the dish washing detergent to clean extra dirty windows. Any change in formula can ruin the effectiveness.

Inside Window Cleaning Solution: 1 gallon water, 4 ounces of nonsudsing household ammonia, one teaspoon liquid hand dish washing detergent. Don't change the proportions. Indoor windows need ammonia to cut household grease (All windows in buildings inhabited by people are covered with grease. Besides you probably fry, boil or broil foods, and do other messy procedures that spread air-born grease). Outside windows are caked with hard, dried-on dirt and need vinegar to clean and shine. Both solutions use a tiny bit of detergent to break down surface tension allowing the cleaners to clean, and the water to rinse away the dirt.

Your warrior tools include a couple of old cotton bath towels, a plastic bucket, sponge, and squeegee. You may want an extension pole so you don't have to use a ladder.

Place a rolled-up towel on the window ledge or sill. Wash down the entire window with cleaning solution. Squeegee the water into the towel. Wipe up remaining moisture with the towel then wring it out and go to the next window. Using this procedure, you should be able to clean an entire inside or outside window in less time than it took to read this paragraph. If you want to use a premixed solution on your exterior windows, Armorall has a very good cleaner called Armorall Home Care Window Wash. The Armorall container hooks up to a garden hose for easy use.

Use either the Armorall or my exterior cleaning solution to clean your screens. With my solution, take out the screen and brush it down on both sides with a brush filled with cleaning mixture. Rinse with a garden hose. Air dry or wipe off screens and frames with a cotton towel.

Both the upper and lower tracks of sliding glass door walls and screens need to be cleaned at least two or three times a year. Vacuum out the tracks. Spray Peek Metal Cleaner in both the door and screen tracks and the threshold. Rub the track and threshold with the 00 steel wool. Wipe up with paper towel. Repeat if necessary. Remember to do both the bottom and the top tracks to clean all the gunk and oxidation out of the tracks and free up the rollers. If the rollers still hang up, get replacement parts.

All the products I mentioned here are available at most good hardware stores and home centers.

Maintenance of exterior lighting makes your house more attractive

by America's Master Handyman,
Glenn Haege

Exterior lighting is the finishing touch for many beautiful homes. It can make your home more attractive and secure if the lights are good-looking, working properly, and set up correctly.

To keep coach or post lights looking good, they need periodic cleaning and shining. If this is on your To Do list, here are a few tips: When the light is above your head, stand on a ladder, not a chair. Make sure that it is set securely, and don't climb any higher than two feet from the top.

Put any parts you need to take down in a plastic pail stuffed with an old towel. That way you won't be dropping, losing, or breaking parts on the lawn or walkway.

Clean and shine the entire lamp with Peek in the foam can by Tri-Peek International, Inc. (800) 465-8994. You should be able to find the product at most good hardware and home centers. Peek is made with jeweler's rouge. It is strong enough to cut through the worst tarnish, but does not include chemicals that will take off the lacquer coating. This product will not scratch the lamp surface. I have seen company representatives actually use it on the lenses of their eye glasses. For most cleaning, just have to spray on the foam, then polish off with a soft 100 percent cotton cloth.

If you have an extreme tarnish condition, use brass wool in addition to the Peek. You can find brass wool at boat supply and many good hardware stores. Spray on the Peek, polish with the brass wool, then buff with a clean, 100 percent cotton rag. The same cleaning and shining technique works with wrought iron, stainless steel, aluminum or any exterior metal surface.

When the exterior lighting is too far gone to bring back with a good shining, it may be time to replace. I went to see Steve Cartier, at Illuminations Lighting, to get some replacement suggestions. One of the things I like about Illuminations is that their light fixtures are displayed with enough separation so that you can actually see them. The store, on Oakland Avenue a quarter mile North of Wide Track Road in Pontiac, used to house an automobile dealership, so there is plenty of room. Exterior lighting is displayed inside, in a garden setting complete with waterfall and pond. The setting makes it easier to visualize what the lighting will look like in your patio or yard.

The three biggest reasons people re-do their exterior lighting, according to Cartier, is that they don't like the constant maintenance required by copper and brass; they started with inexpensive underground line and found that it falls apart when they move it; or they didn't plan ahead and find that their landscaping has outgrown the lighting system.

"If your readers don't like shining brass, they should consider the new, very durable, powder coated cast aluminum lights. The new lights are warranted up to 25 years and there is nothing to polish," Cartier said.

Cast aluminum fixtures come in a wide variety of colors that vary from maker to maker. The fixtures in the Focus line Illuminations carries (Focus Industries, Inc. (949) 830-1350), come in black, white, antique bronze, hunter green, and weathered brown.

"We also get a lot of traffic from customers who purchased less expensive exterior accent lighting kits and find that the plastic line connecting the lights is so fragile it breaks apart when the home owner tries to pick it up and reposition it after two or three years. It's better to pay a little more up front and get cast aluminum rather than plastic. Aluminum stays strong and can be easily picked up and repositioned," he said.

Landscaping changes can also necessitate a new lighting scheme. All too often a homeowner plants small shrubs and trees, then installs lighting that highlights them. As soon as the landscaping grows, the lighting is wrong. It may be so overgrown it disappears. When lighting is installed with new plants, it should be placed to highlight the adult, not the young, plant, Cartier said.

"The most important part of a homeowner's first exterior lighting purchase should be the transformer. Many people just install a small transformer to meet their initial needs. Then, when they expand the landscaping and want to add more lighting, they find that they have to tear out the old transformer to fill the new electrical requirements. It's far less expensive to install a transformer that will meet all your requirements, right away. Then you can add lighting as your budget permits or new landscaping requires," Cartier said.

He also suggests that the best way to keep the finish looking good on big exterior lamps is to bring the lamps indoors and let them come to room temperature, then apply a good carnuba wax based automotive wax. "The wax will extend the factory-new look for months. Rewax poles and fixtures every three months," he advises. Like everything else, the more preventative maintenance you do, the longer your investment lasts.

A lawn sprinkler system needn't be a drain on your time or wallet

by America's Master Handyman, Glenn Haege

Some people enjoy watering their lawn. Since neither Barb nor I likes playing in the water, our home's sprinkler system went in as soon as the landscaping was planted.

Installation of lawn sprinkler systems is a highly generational phenomenon. Most people over 50 don't have sprinkler systems. Most Yuppies do. Similarly, older homes usually do not have lawn sprinkler systems. New homes, in new subdivisions, usually do. In the not-so-distant past, sprinkler systems were very expensive, so only the very affluent had them. Today, according to John Schmatz, who runs Aqua-Flo Enterprises, (248) 524-1511, with his partner Richard Gregor, sprinkler systems are relatively inexpensive, so up to 95 percent of the homes in new subdivisions have sprinkler systems installed.

"An average six zone system on a 70- x 130-foot lot, in a new subdivision, only costs about $1,500. The same installation in an older subdivision, where the installer has to work around entrenched trees and other landscaping, would cost about $300 more," he says. The reason sprinkler systems are relatively inexpensive is that the old metal sprinkler heads have been replaced by heavy-duty plastic. Plastic heads are less expensive and last longer because there is no mineral build up.

There are only two times in the year when having a lawn sprinkler system is not an advantage – when you open the system for the first time in Spring and when you shut it down in the fall. Opening the system is something you can do yourself. If you don't know how, you will by the end of this article. Closing down the system is something most people want professionals to do.

Closing down the system is usually done by the original installation company, so it is a good idea to make sure the company that installs the system has staying power. The majority of the money in sprinkler systems is in installation. Service is quite often a break-even at best proposition for the contractor. That means he or she doesn't really want to service other company's installations. If you get a heck of a deal on installation, and then the sprinkler company goes out of business, you may have a hard time finding another company willing to take over the service.

When I mentioned that I was doing this article, my sprinkler guy thought it was a great idea, but adds, "Please don't give anyone my name or phone number." When I asked why, he told me that he and his partner were already booked through the middle of August on new installations, and they just didn't have time for free-lance turn ons. When they get a call from a homeowner on a system they didn't install, they usually just tell the caller to contact the original installer.

"People don't realize that every sprinkler system is laid out a little bit differently. If we didn't install the system, there's no way of telling exactly how it is laid out. That means that if there is a problem, we can be out there for hours, mucking about with a shovel, looking for the sprinkler lines," the installer says.

Secondly, they have found that people hate to pay $40 or $50 for something that they think should be as easy as turning on a water faucet.

The bright side of the issue is that if your system has wintered well, opening it up for the year is almost that easy. Here's how: Go to where the main sprinkler water control valve is located (usually by the main water supply valve), and turn on the sprinkler water control valve.

You should hear a rush of water that lasts ten or twenty seconds. The sound is made by water going to and through the sprinkler system's Back Flow Preventer (sometimes called the Vacuum Breaker). If you can't find the sprinkler water control valve in the basement, it is sometimes located, on the Back Flow Preventer.

On the very rare occasion that the rush of water does not stop within a minute, it means that you have a leak in the system and need to call the sprinkler installation company.

If the rush of water stops on time, it means that your sprinkler system has weathered the winter successfully. Run each sprinkler zone, one at a time. As each zone goes on, check that all the sprinkler heads have popped up and are covering their proper area.

When a sprinkler does not pop up within a few minutes, it means that there is a loss of pressure or that the head has become clogged with debris. The first step is to clear away the debris. If it is a rotor sprinkler head, pop it out and clear away any clippings or dirt that may have lodged inside the unit. Some sprinkler heads need a special key to adjust the unit.

If the sprinkler head still does not function properly it probably mans that it got hit by a snow plow or shovel over the winter, and will have to be replaced by your installer. Ninety-five times out of a hundred, all your sprinkler heads will pop up and operate beautifully. You will have saved the price of a service call. It's that easy!

JUNE 7, 1997

There's no crystal-clear answer to picking windows, but here's a start

by America's Master Handyman,
Glenn Haege

The official start of summer is only two weeks away. That means that in the next four months, approximately 2.5 gallon windows will be sold in the US. I don't know the exact number, but I do know that about 15 percent of all the questions I get on my syndicated radio show will be about windows.

All these questions could be classified into two categories: "What's the best window?" and "What type of window should I buy?"

For those of you who are in a hurry to get to the comic section, I will answer these questions at the top of the article, and save you some reading.

What's the best window? It's the one that is installed correctly. No matter how well a window is made, if it is not installed correctly, you bought a problem, not a solution.

What type should you buy? I haven't got a clue; it depends upon your personal taste, needs, and economic circumstances.

Like everything else, the more you know before you make a window buying decision, the more likely you are to get what you are looking for. I went window shopping to save you a little time, get you some basic facts, and provide an unbiased foundation of information.

Remember, these are basic facts only. If you are window shopping you should use the information in this article as a beginning, not the end.

There are many different national, regional, and local, window brands. Most are pretty good. Some are great. I confined my search to replacement windows available at two major lumber yards in this market, Dillman & Upton (248-651-9411), in Rochester, and N. A. Mans Building Center (734-981-5800), in Canton. Mans also has stores in Trenton, New Boston, Monroe, and Maumie, Ohio.

Both of these organizations have served the market for generations, carry a large supply of windows, and can provide the shopper with product and installation.

They are not unique. We are blessed with many quality lumber yards in southern Michigan. You can find the same, or similar quality windows at a good lumber supply store near you. There are also a large number of independent window specialists. Some sell direct to the consumer.

Window replacement can be a need or a want. You may want to get rid of your perfectly serviceable windows because they are more trouble than they are worth – they have 20 coats of paints of them, they're drafty and they stick. All these problems are repairable. Paint comes off, drafts can be sealed, tracks can be cleared to eliminate sticking.

Therefore, the first thing you have to decide is if your windows really need replacing. Many original wood windows could remain in service for another 20 or 30 years, with proper repairs.

If you decide that the windows are worth saving, give Don Keiper at H & R Window Repair (248-366-8282), a call. Don repairs all types of windows, and has built a national business based on the fact that he has, or can find, the parts to fit any window since the ark. If you are lucky enough to have Andersen windows, call your local distributor. Andersen maintains an active inventory of every part for every window they have made in the past 50 years.

If your windows are fine, but you want to upgrade from single to double paned windows, Bi-Glass Systems of Southeastern Michigan (248-729-0742) specializes in this procedure.

If you want or need to replace your windows, here are some basics. Tony Reedy, at Dillman & Upton, says that they sell about 40 percent double-hung windows, 40 percent casement windows, 20 percent sliding windows. For the purpose of this article, I compared same-size, double-hung windows.

Quality range
Windows, like automobiles, have many different price points. A Ford Taurus and a Lincoln Mark VIII both provide good transportation, but parking lot attendants tend to give better service to someone driving a Mark VIII. Likewise, if your home is in a middle or upper-priced neighborhood, a real estate agent will probably not hype vinyl windows, but Andersen or Marvin windows could increase your home's sales appeal.

In increasing price order, Dillman & Upton carries Carefree Vinyl, Caradco, Andersen, and Marvin Windows. Carefree is a good Vinyl replacement window. Personally, if I were going to buy a vinyl window, I would go to one of the local manufacturers like Weathergard (800-377-8886) or Wallside (800-521-7800). They aren't limited to standard sizes. Each window is made to fit the exact dimensions of the opening.

Nelson Wood says that N. A. Mans carries Louisiana Pacific vinyl and wood replacement windows (Ed note: Louisiana Pacific is out of the window business. They sold their window division to American Weather Seal, (800-468-4996) as their lower price point, plus Andersen, Marvin, and the St. James Composite Window made by Hoosier Windows.

All of the windows in this comparison are good windows. They all:
■ Have double panes.
■ Have Low E glass standard (on the Andersen) or available as a very low cost, or no cost, option.
■ Have low conductivity spacers (the metal or plastic piece which separates and supports the two panes of glass.
■ Are made by extremely reputable manufacturers.
■ Are available with complete lines, many different options and upgrades. Caradco, for example, offers 12 different grille options (the little pieces of wood, plastic or metal that divide windows in different designs), and 16 different glass, insulation, and tempering options.

continued on next page

231

Vinyl windows have vinyl frames and sashes. Andersen windows are vinyl-clad exterior, wood windows. Caradco and Marvin are wood or aluminum-clad exterior, wood windows (Marvin, naturally uses a heavier gauge extruded aluminum). The Saint James Hoosier Composite window has an aluminum exterior, and vinyl interior surfaces over a urethane interior core.

Louisiana Pacific, Carefree, and Andersen, come in a wide assortment of standard sizes. But if you have an odd-sized window, it will have to be fitted with a smaller standard size and built out to fill the window cavity. Caradco, Marvin, and Hoosier windows can be custom made to fit your exact specifications.

The bottom line

I mentioned price points at the beginning of the article. Since we live in an automobile town, I'll continue with the automotive analogies. You could consider Louisiana Pacific and Carefree Vinyl replacement windows to be Fords or Chevrolets. Caradco or Louisiana Pacific wood windows could be high end Buicks or Mercuries. Andersen is a Lincoln or Cadillac. Marvin and Hoosier Composites are definitely in the Rolls Royce league.

Your final decision may well come down to how important the interior window trim is to you. Vinyl is a relatively shiny material that comes in only a limited number of colors, usually white, beige, and brown. This material can not be painted or stained successfully. If you want to paint or stain the window frame inside, you have to buy a wood or wood-clad window.

Like all major purchases, it pays to shop. Be on the lookout for truck load sales. During these special events you can save an honest ten percent.

Money-saving option for D.I.Y.'ers

If the frames of your windows are in good shape, Louisiana Pacific (LP), Caradco and Marvin have sash only window replacement options. LP calls theirs the Smart Kit. The Caradco is called the Zap Pack. Marvin's is called the Tilt Pack. Sash only packs can cut $75 to $100 off the window price and are quite easy to install. The first window should take about an hour. After that, your speed should increase to one window every 45 minutes. Think of it, you can have top-of-the-line Marvin wood replacement windows for less than the cost of vinyl.

Should you need a little instruction, Marvin has a video that takes you through the entire procedure. If you want personal instruction, hire an installer to do the most difficult window with the understanding that you can help and ask questions. Learn all you can during that original window installation. Then do the rest yourself.

If you have trouble tracking down some of the windows mentioned in this article, here are some phone numbers to get you started: Andersen: (800-426-4261), Caradco: (800-238-1866), Internet: www.caradco.com; Hoosier: (800-344-4849), Marvin: (800-346-5128).

Looking at costs

Here are some cost comparisons minus salesman's hype. Costs are for what is called a basic 32" X 24" double hung window with double pane Low E glass. It's outside dimensions would be about 3'2" wide by 4'9" tall. I've included average prices for the window only, and the window plus approximate labor. The prices are "street" (what you'd actually pay), not list prices.

Brand	Window Cost	Labor	Total
Carefree vinyl	180	150-250	$330-$430
Louisiana Pacific Vinyl	225	200-250	$425-$475
Caradco	250	240	$490
Louisiana Pacific Wood	235	200-250	$435-$485
Andersen	295	240	$535
Marvin	260-340	200-250	$460-$590
St. James Hoosier Composite	305	200-250	$505-$555

Source: Glenn Haege

JUNE 14, 1997

Canada's amazing wood care products finish ahead of the pack

by America's Master Handyman,
Glenn Haege

I have been hearing whispers about revolutionary products in wood care. To learn more about it I made a pilgrimage last week to the land where wood is king, British Columbia, Canada. I centered my search on Whistler, two hours Northwest of Downtown Vancouver, and the home of Bio-Wash Products (Canada) Inc..

Whistler is a land of mountains, forests, waterfalls and fjords. To see just how seriously Western Canadians take their wood, I went on a tour of 19 different houses. One of the first was a two-year old, three-story, 3,400 square foot log home. When I write log home, I don't mean log cabin. The only log cabins in Whistler are on pancake syrup containers.

This entire house, including an additional 2,000 square feet of decking, floors, kitchen cabinets, window frames, even the threshold, matches perfectly, because all the wood came from the same 300 year old red cedar tree. The windows are so finely fitted, there are no nails in them. The house is valued at $2,500,000 Canadian ($1,700,000 US).

Remember, this is a log home. One of many similar homes I saw on that tour.

Many of the houses were beautiful from the street, but they looked gray to black, worn and weathered on their most windward sides. Some three- or four-year old log homes were completely discolored and peeling.

To find out if this was a common problem I went to the best research center for local building conditions that you can find in any town: the ham and eggs joint most favored by the building trades. In Whistler, that emporium of fine food is the South Side Deli.

Most of the guys were already on their second cup of coffee at 7:30 a.m. When I started asking around, their horror stories were legion. "Yes," cedar natural log was the favored manner of construction because it blended in with the natural look of the area. "Yes," the prices were gawd-awful. "Yes," no matter what they did, the finish on the logs started peeling, blistering, discoloring, and the logs, turned black, gray and ratty looking after four to seven years.

Where most people saw unsolveable problems, Brian Morse and Peter Palkovsky of Bio-Wash Products (Canada) Inc., saw opportunity. Brian is a brilliant chemist who used to jam with the Beetles. Peter is a dedicated conservationist, committed to creating and promoting earth-friendly products.

First they tackled surface preparation problems, getting new wood in the proper condition to accept stains and sealers so that the wood would be protected better, longer; removing old coatings that had begun to disintegrate; and reconditioning and reviving wood to look like new.

When I first learned about these products four years ago, I was amazed at their performance characteristics. Bio-Wash Mill Glaze Away opens up the compressed pores of new lumber so that the wood surface absorbs wood treatments evenly. Simple Wash gently cleans moderately soiled and weathered wood surfaces. Woodwash washes away black and gray dead wood cells with gentle scrubbing and water from a garden hose.

Stripex Wood Stain Stripper removes deteriorated solid color and semi-transparent oil-based stains and water sealers. Another product, Stripex L removes latex stain, varnish and clear coat wood finishes. Both Stripex and Stripex L remove, not only the finish, but also the damaged and discolored wood fibers, so that the remaining wood surface looks almost like new.

To understand how unique these products are, you have to realize that although the best wood brighteners remove disintegrated old wood, they cannot penetrate wood sealers. Paint strippers, remove coatings, but do nothing about damaged and discolored wood.

Not content to rest on its laurels, Bio-Wash started test marketing a completely new, water borne, two step wood coating system, called Supernatural Protective Wood Finish a year ago. The first coat forms a water block foundation. The second coat provides a UV block and finish. Supernatural is both an interior and an exterior finish. It can be tinted almost any color and was designed to give lasting protection to those beautiful log homes I've been telling you about. A second new product, Natural Deck Oil, is designed to give the same type of protection to decks.

Now, why have I wasted all this time telling you about Whistler, BC, when we don't have any one and two million dollar log homes in this area and probably never will. We do have a great many smaller log cabins and homes – no less precious to their owners – and natural wood surfaces such as decks. Products that win in Whistler, will breeze through even the most rugged Michigan weather conditions.

We have many good products made in the United States, but none that I know about tackle this many problems, this thoroughly. If you have similar problems, the Bio-Wash line may be the answer.

Bio-Wash products are available at Dillman and Upton (248-651-9411) in Rochester and at all N. A. Mans Do-It Centers (734-981-5800) in Canton, Down River and Maumee Ohio; and Paint N Stuff stores (out of business) throughout the area.

For a dealer near you call Bio-Wash, (800-858-5011), or look them up on the internet at WWW.biowash.com.

Realize quality doesn't come cheap in any remodeling project

by America's Master Handyman,
Glenn Haege

Did you read Bev Clark's "On The Homefront" article last week? I thought it was wonderful. If you didn't read the article, I hope the June 14 issue of Homestyle is not on the bottom of the bird cage yet, because it belongs in your clip-and-save file. I want you to re-read it every time you even think about starting a major remodeling project.

In the article, Clark talks about purchasing an older home in Detroit, and thinking she and a girlfriend could fix the whole place up in a week. She started doing minor stuff to the kitchen and found that the week turned into a week plus evenings and weekends, into a nightmare, and she couldn't even put her dishes into their proper place, until eight months – count 'em – eight long months, went by.

Clark is typical of most Do-It-Yourselfers in that she grossly underestimated the time and money home repairs and upgrades cost. She and her fellow DIY'ers are not alone. Professional remodelers underestimate all the time. That's why there are so many arguments, work stoppages, unpaid bills, liens, lawsuits, and bankruptcies in the home improvement field.

Luckily, Clark was able to afford the time (if she's like me, she's too tired when she gets home from work to go out anyway) and money (who wants to spend money on travel or clothes when you can invest in the finer things of life such as wallpaper, fixtures and power tools?).

If Clark is like most purchasers of "fixer-uppers", she won't complete all of her fix-up tasks until shortly before she is ready to move. I don't know if it will be any consolation to her, but according to the National Association of Home Builders , average home buyers spend $6,500 decorating and furnishing their home in the first year.

This year, all of us together will spend $125 billion on home repair and improvements in the United States. Maintenance and repair will amount to $45.3 billion, home improvements and upgrades will account for the other $80 billion. By the way, American Express says the total is really $135.4 billion, but I think they include furniture.

NAHB says that a good portion of that money will go into the kitchen and notes that last year (and most years), kitchens were the most popular remodeling job. (According to Am Ex, the most popular room to remodel was the living room, No. 2, was the master bedroom, but they consider adding drapes or getting a new bedspread a home improvement).

Remodeling Magazine pegged the cost of an average kitchen tune-up at $8,507 in their 1996-1997 Cost Vs Value Report. A major kitchen remodel averaged $21,262. That seemed cheap to me. With such upgrades as Corian countertops and sinks, hand-painted tiles, deluxe cabinets, fixtures, hardwood floors, and appliances, it is very easy to spend $50,000 in the kitchen.

According to the new Am Ex home improvement survey, Bev Clark is part of the majority of homeowners who opt to do the job themselves. Two-thirds of consumers (78 percent of the men, 54 percent of the women) plan on swinging a hammer or wielding a paint brush. She is also in the majority (65 percent) who admit that if price were no object they would prefer to hire it done.

Unfortunately, the necessity of saving money goes along with product selection because 69 percent of shoppers listed price as the most important characteristic they were look for in a home improvement store. Quality was only a consideration for 49 percent. They should take a tip from the Handyman – quality is far more important than price. Low prices may make the initial cost less, but quality materials make sure you have a job that lasts.

Clark was also among the vast number of people (46 percent of women, 55 percent of men) who think the job will be done quickly (in less than a month) and relatively cheap. The average home improvement budget was $2,660 according to the Am Ex Retail Index.

Unfortunately, most homeowners remodeling budgets do not reflect reality. According to Remodeling magazine the average cost of upgrading a bathroom last year was $8,423. Replacing 10 3-by-5 foot windows was $6,112, and just adding a 16-by-20 foot pressure-treated pine deck was $6,172. Adding a 16-by-25 foot family room was $31,846.

Is it any wonder our credit cards get maxed out real fast when we get bitten by the home improvement bug? As high as these prices are, they won't stop the 62 million of us who love our homes from improving them. NAHB says that we will spend $3 billion more in 1998 than we are in 1997, and $2 billion more than that in 1999. Personally, I believe these amounts are underestimated.

No less an American than Abraham Lincoln said that "The strength of the nation lies in the homes of its people." So Bev, Clark and all the rest of you out there, do the patriotic thing: Take out your credit cards and CHARGE!

Insulate yourself against high air-conditioning bills this summer

by America's Master Handyman, Glenn Haege

Insulation is not something you aspire to possess. No one ever races home to tell the family, "Man, you should see Frank's attic. He has a double thickness of Owens R-15 Pink, and those rafter baffles are out of sight!"

The desire for insulation is far more subtle. It grows during the winter when we get cold from drafts and hot under the collar from heating bills. The rest of the time it just lies there. But we really should pay a lot more attention to our home's insulation during the summer, because it can save us big bucks on air conditioning.

But just how much insulation do our homes need? Where should we put it? And can it really save us money?

According to the Department of Energy, Michigan homes should have enough insulation to provide an insulation value of R-30 in the attics; R-21 or R-19 in exterior walls with 2-by-6 studs, or a minimum of R-15 or R-13 with 2-by-4 studs. Floors over unheated space should be R-19 or at least R-11. Basement walls should be R-11.

Your favorite lumberyard, building supply wholesaler, or home center has many different kinds of insulation. What you select is up to your needs and pocket book. Fiberglass comes in batts, blankets, and loose. Some batts are backed with kraft paper or foil to act as vapor barriers. Some are encapsulated in po-

rous plastic bags. According to a report by the National Association of Home Builders, fiberglass batt insulation has an R-factor of from 3.1 to 4.3 per inch.

Fiberglass and cellulose (old newspaper and wood chips), can be blown into wall cavities or on the attic floor. According to NAHB, wet spray blown insulation has an R-Factor of 3.0 to 4.0 per inch. The R-Factor of dry spray cellulose and fiberglass varies from 3.2 to 4.8 per inch.

Urethane and other spray foams can be used to insulate cavities. According to NAHB, their R-Factors range from 3.6 to 6.2 per inch.

Expanded polystyrene (EPS) foam sheathing has an R-Factor of 4.0 to 4.5 per inch. Extruded polystyrene (XPS), like Dow Styrofoam and Wallmate, has an R-Factor of 5.0 per inch. Urethane and isocyanurates sheathing has an R-Factor of 6 to 7 per inch.

All good stuff, but is it really worth the money to bring your house up to DOE recommendations? To find out I estimated the energy savings for an average 2000 square foot house upgraded to current DOE specifications.

There's no magic to my calculations. The National Association of Home Builders Research Center does a great deal of research on this sort of thing. With the support of the U.S. Department of Energy and the National Renewable Energy Laboratory, they have prepared a series of reports entitled: Energy Efficiency in Remodeling. The different reports cover topics like foundations, walls, roofs/ceilings, windows, ducts, water heating, and appliances. As of June 12, 1997, these reports were available on their website at www.nahb.com/research. You can also call the Research Center at (800) 638-8556.

Their calculations were for Baltimore, MD, with fuel prices of 8 cents per kWh and 55 cents per therm (British Thermal Energy Unit). According to their charts, if you had a moderate 80-percent efficient Furnace and a 6.5 SEER (Seasonal Energy Efficiency Ratio) air conditioner you could make the following annual savings.

If a 2,000 square foot house had ceiling insulation with an R-Factor of R-8, and was upgraded to R-30 as recommended by the DOE, the savings would be $7.80 per year/per 100 sq. ft. in heating and cooling costs, or $156 per year. If the attic already had fairly good insulation, let's say an R-Factor of 15, you'd save $3.30 per hundred square feet, or $66 a year.

I'm going to fudge a little bit here because I will figure 8-foot-high walls and a 40-by-50 foot house and not make allowances for windows and doors. This would give our house 1,440 square feet of wall space. If we figured that the current walls had no insulation and were brought up to DOE recommendations, savings would be approximately $17.45 per year/per 100 sq. ft., or $251 per year. If our house already had some insulation in the walls, lets say R-7, we would save $4.75 per year/per 100 sq. ft., or $68 per year by increasing the wall insulation

If the basement height was 7-1/2 feet, our house would have 1,350 square feet of uninsulated basement walls. By bringing them up to an R-Factor of R-11, we would save $14.55 per year/per 100 sq. ft., or $196 per year.

This means that if you owned a badly insulated 2,000 square foot house, you could reduce your heating and cooling bills by $603 a year. The owners of even a moderately well insulated house could save $330 a year.

If you need to learn more, the Pink Panther prowls at www.owenscorning.com (one of the best laid out sites on the internet) or call (800) GET-PINK; Certainteed is at www.certainteed.com or call (610) 341-7000 ; Dow is www.dow.com or call (800) 441-4DOW; Johns Manville/Schuller is www.johnsmanville.com or call (800) 654-3103; and the National Association of Home Builders, is at www.nahb.com or call (800) 638-8556.

Blowing insulation into walls is an art. For local information on cellulose, call Charles Akers at Ace Insulation, (248) 642-4311. For information on fiberglass call Bob Mackie, of Macomb Insulation, (810) 757-8521.

Soulliere family has paved its way to success using concrete

by America's Master Handyman,
Glenn Haege

Have you noticed the popularity of concrete pavers this year? I am just putting the finishing touches on my latest book, so I drive over to my editor's Royal Oak house all the time. In just two blocks of that very old, stable, neighborhood, five new paver jobs are under way. Over the next two weeks, I'm going to take a closer look at pavers and their imitators, what I call the fabulous fakes.

In my 1995 deck and paver book (sorry, it's out of print until next year), I predicted a 400-percent increase in the use of pavers in the US and Canada, and I think we are already half way there. There are four reasons for this increase.

■ Wood deck prices keep increasing and we don't like the constant maintenance.

■ Real estate values have increased so much that relatively expensive add-ons, like pavers, make economic sense. They add to our home's resale value and "curb appeal".

■ Pavers have increased versatility. New designs by Unilock and Versa Lok, make building paver patios two, three – even ten feet above grade level – easy.

■ Pavers have become popular Do-It-Yourself projects. Installation is hard work, not brain surgery. Manufacturers are at builder's shows, work hand in glove with contractors and retailers, hold clinics, and supply installation brochures.

Top Canadian paver manufacturers like Lafarge (800-876-6257) and Unilock (800-UNILOCK) were already going gang busters in Windsor. When they looked across the river at Detroit, they saw a State with 25 percent of the population of Canada. They decided to gamble on the possibility that we might want to buy some product, and built paver factories here. It was a good gamble.

Our own Fendt Builders Supply & Pavers, makers of the original Michigan Brick, expanded their line to include all the most popular paver shapes and sizes. The race for your mind and pocket book was on.

The rise in fortunes of the Soulliere family has paralleled the explosion in paver popularity. The Soullieres started out landscaping and building walks. They were especially good at pavers. Building contractors and landscaping buddies started saying, "Hey, we're doing a big job. Can you put in a walk here, or build a retaining wall over there?" The Soullieres didn't mind helping others, so they said, "sure."

Soon, they had so many crews working, that it became more efficient to have their own supply yard and not get every order delivered from the factory. A few avid D-I-Y'ers saw the stacks of pavers, and mounds of gravel, slag, and sand, and wanted to know if they could buy some of the stuff. "Sure."

"Oh, by the way, could you deliver it and show us how to put it in?" "Sure."

"The pavers are beautiful, could you tell us if there is anything we should do to keep them looking good?" "Sure." "Could you do it for us?" "Sure."

"This paver installation is hard work. The equipment is expensive and not worth buying for just a job or two. Could we rent some from you?" "Sure," again.

A couple weeks ago I saw the full flowering of Soulliere's good neighbor policy on Twenty-Two Mile Road, between Ryan and Shelby. It's a great success story to celebrate on this Fourth of July Weekend because it shows that here, in the good old' US of A, if you're willing to work hard and give good value for service, you don't need an MBA from a highfalutin business school, or a million-dollar bankroll to be successful.

Today, under the direction of Roger Soulliere, Soulliere Decorative Stone Inc., (810-739-0020), designs and builds large and small paver walks, drives, patios, and retaining walls around the state. He, his mother, father, uncles, aunts, nephews and nieces have also built an empire on 22 Mile Road.

Right next door, Mike DeFrane, manages Stone City Products (810-731-4500). Stone City has the broadest paver display you will find in Michigan. "We wanted to put all the different paver designs and colors by Fendt, Unilock, and Lafarge where people could see them in one place, in a natural outdoor setting," DeFrane said. The displays are not just samples, but big sections of walkways and patios, along with Pisa and Versa Lok retaining walls. The display area is backed by acres of inventory for contractors and D-I-Y'ers.

Next door to that is, you guessed it, Michigan Skid Loader, Inc., (800-770-GEHL), the family's equipment rental company, that, according to Julius Ledbetter, the manger, "will rent anything from a bag of hand tools, or a mechanical tamper, to Gehl skid loaders."

In case you need any paver sealer, they recommend the Soulliere family's Protek brand of paver sealers and cleaners. Protek, managed by David Anthony (810-739-0020), is a regional supplier that has products in home centers and hardware stores. Naturally, you can also buy the family brand from any of the family's stores. If you don't want to do the work yourself, just ask, they'll be glad to do it for you.

This Soulliere family's success story is not unique. Over the past ten years, the paving industry and our free enterprise system have created the opportunity for hundreds of similar stories in Detroit, Chicago, Minneapolis, the East Coast, Atlanta and Texas. It's a great country, isn't it?

JULY 12, 1997

You can get the paver look without tromping all over your budget

by America's Master Handyman, Glenn Haege

The paver look is taking over Michigan. Everywhere you look folks are putting in paver patios, walks, even drives. The look is beautiful, and so long lasting that when you buy pavers, you are definitely buying for generations to come. Pavers are available in many different designs and colors. Their only problem is that they can be rather pricey. If you like the paver look, but not the paver price, there are alternatives. Today's article is going to list some of them.

First, if you have to have pavers but the pocket book just isn't big enough, consider doing the job yourself. If you've been quoted $14 a square foot, you can realistically figure that, with a lot of sweat equity, you can do the job yourself for $7 a square foot. That includes base, pavers, sand, tools, delivery, everything, according to Mike DeFrane at Stone City in Utica, (810) 731-4500.

If you don't have the back or the free time to do the job yourself, you still might be able to afford the real thing. This is no big brainstorm. Start by getting another couple of quotes. Right now labor is very tight, but, if you have a relatively big job, even the big boys – especially the big boys – can really cut the price big time if they want to. Some persistent shoppers get driveways installed at only a 20- or 30-percent premium over Do-It-Yourself prices.

If you have only a small job, it's Quikrete to the rescue. Gibraltar National the big concrete and masonry mix supplier has introduced the Walkmaker Line of inexpensive forms you use with Quikrete Sand Mix. Just lay the form on the ground, mix the Quikrete with water, and pour into the form. As soon as the concrete dries, move the form and make a new batch.

You can double the speed of production, by buying two forms. They are relatively inexpensive and a good way to build a small walk or small patio. The Quikrete forms come in field stone and paver styles, and are available at many hardware and home centers. Call Gibraltar National, (800) 442-7258.

For larger jobs there are faux paver alternatives installed by three different companies.

If you have a big driveway that has cracked, but you don't like the idea of having to pay to get all the old concrete broken up and pulled out and new concrete poured, you can resurface it in a multitude of different paving styles, textures and colors, by calling in a resurfacing specialist, like Concrete Technologies Incorporated, (888) 727-6001, Nation-Wide. This company covers the surface with a bonding coat, then applies a thin resurface coat. The final result looks exactly like pavers.

If you need a new drive or patio, Vento Masonry & Cement Co., (734) 513-2242, will come out to your home, tint the fiber reinforced concrete just before it is poured, then hand stamp the still wet cement into your choice of designs using highly specialized Stampcrete tools. Your design choices range from Fieldstone and Slate, to Wood Plank, to Mexican and South American Tiles, as well as the traditional Brick and Cobblestone paver designs. For more information on the Stampcrete system, call Stampcrete Decorative Concrete direct, (800) 233-3298.

The Concrete Technologies and Stampcrete products are basically concrete that look like pavers. They are priced at a substantial premium over poured concrete, but a good deal less than true pavers. They have the same strengths and weakness that poured concrete has vis-a-vis pavers. That is, while no single "paver" will shift during freeze/thaw cycles, slabs of concrete are still subject to the cracking.

The newest faux paver look, doesn't involve concrete. If you like the feel, and the pricing of asphalt, but want the look of pavers, you are in luck. Integrated Paving Concepts Inc., (800) 688-5652, nationwide, has developed a process called Street Print Pavement Texturing. This process makes an asphalt road or driveway look like it was made of pavers in your choice of an off-set brick, soldier course, herringbone, or decorative arch design.

Jill Cheff, Street Print's local rep, says that the street grade asphalt is laid, textured, then bonded and sealed, and a colored epoxy modified acrylic coating is added. The procedure takes heavy equipment, so it cannot be used in backyards or on small jobs. The surface is warranted for three years, but the job will probably not need to be touched up more than once every five years. If you can't believe that asphalt can look like pavers, drive by the Grosse Pointe War Memorial on Lake Shore Drive.

Which of the three faux paving solutions would I choose for my drive? I'd call all three and get people out to my house to explain the pros and cons.

If I were a residential paving contractor, and couldn't offer one of these alternatives to my customers, I'd see the writing on the wall and start looking. There could easily come a day when contractors who just offer the plain old flat stuff, will be in the same category as buggy whip manufacturers.

JULY 19, 1997

On the job: Michigan toilet firm is flush with success of its system

by America's Master Handyman, Glenn Haege

We're all proud that when people think of Michigan, they think of the Motor City and cars. But Michigan's reputation may be going down the toilet, and from the perspective of the folks at Sloan Flushmate in Wixom, that's a pretty good thing.

Many of you have heard me rant about the double flush and plunging problems with the new 1.6-gravity fed toilets foisted upon us by Congress. They save water, but about 40 percent of the time, they do not do the job until you flush two or more times. Sometimes you even need a plunger.

You may also recall that I recently played Sancho Panza to Joe Knollenberg's Don Quixotelike efforts to reverse the legislation. We were able to paper Washington with a blizzard of toilet tissues proclaiming, "Get the government out of my toilet, vote for HR 859," but have not yet gotten the necessary movement out of Congress to pass the roll-back legislation.

Luckily, Flushmate, is manufacturing a unit that solves the problem and may make Michigan the seat of power for pressure-assisted toilets. Sloan Flushmate, a division of the Sloan Valve Company, makes football-sized tanks that fit inside a toilet's water closet. When flushed, each tank expels 1.5 gallons of water through the toilet system at a speed of 70 gallons per minute. According to Joseph Bosman, Flushmates chief operating officer, that is almost three times the power of a normal, gravity-fed toilet and is sufficient to clear the toilet and the waste vent line with less water than required by law. There are no left-overs.

I went to the factory to see the ANSI (American National Standards Institute) flushometer tests that compared a Flushmate-powered toilet to a standard 1.6 toilet. The tests flush 100 specially made, marble shaped balls, out the toilet and down a 100-foot clear plastic waste vent line.

The tests were very eye-opening, because they showed that even when it looked like all the balls had been flushed out of a 1.6 gallon gravity-fed toilet, up to half of the balls remained in the toilet system. In your home, that would be waste material, lying hidden inside your toilet – not a very antiseptic situation.

The Flushmate-equipped toilet flushed all the balls out of the toilet and completely through the 100 feet of pipe.

Industry leaders have tried to persuade me that 1.6 gallon toilets are fine. They tell me that the first 1.6 gallon toilets had problems because they were rushed into production, and improperly designed and glazed. I believe that many of the newer gravity-fed designs, created in conformance with more difficult specifications, are better. But I keep remembering those ANSI test balls that stayed in the toilet system even after it looked like the toilet had been evacuated.

Toilets equipped with Sloan Flushmate pressure tanks are impressive because they don't run the risk of having that kind of performance problem. They are certified for 150,000 flushes – that's about 20 years. The significant drawbacks to the Flushmate are that although a high pressure flush only takes about four seconds, it is louder than a much longer lasting gravity-fed toilet flush; and the toilets are pricey – in the $200 to $250 plus area.

As of now, there is no perfect solution. A little sound-proofing bathroom insulation should be able to be taken care of the noise, and competition will bring prices down. As the situation now stands, I see nothing but good things for this Michigan manufacturer.

Flushmate systems are presently included in such toilets as American Standard's New Cadet, (800) 223-0068; Crane Plumbing's Economiser, (606) 678-5131; Eljer Plumbing's Aqua-Saver, (662) 566-2363 Gerber Plumbing's Ultraflush, (847) 675-6570; Kohler's Pressure Lite, (800) 4 KOHLER; and Mansfield Plumbing's Quantum, (419) 938-5211.

You can see these innovative products locally at Giant Plumbing & Heating Supply in Hazel Park, (800) 959-0827; and Madison Heights Plumbing Supply in Madison Heights, (248) 588-4690. If you're out of the Detroit-Area, call Flushmate direct, (800) 875-9116, for more information or the name of a dealer near you.

For those of you who are replacing an existing toilet, it is still legal to replace a 3.5 gallon toilet with a 3.5 gallon toilet. The problem is that there are not many left. Most of the suppliers I've talked to, say that they will be completely out of stock by Fall and, as the law stands, manufacturers will not be making any more. If you want one of the last of the 3.5's the time to act is now.

The following suppliers have contacted me and said they still have some 3.5 toilets in stock. P stands for Plumbing, P & H stands for Plumbing & Heating: Advance P & H, Walled Lake, (248) 669-7474; D & C P & H at Bloomfield Design Center, Walled Lake, (248) 624-1336; Giant P & H, Hazel Park, (800) 959-0827; Kitchen & Bath Gallery, Ann Arbor, (734) 761-8820; Mt. Pleasant Supply Co., Mt. Pleasant, (800) 968-8857; Pousho P & H, Highland, (248) 887-7561; Universal P, Berkley, (248) 542-3888; Wagner P & H, Kalamazoo, (616) 349-6608.

Here's the smart way to nail a builder who leaves you in the lurch

by America's Master Handyman,
Glenn Haege

The vast majority of Michigan builders are hard working people who, day after day, and year after year, go out of their way to see that their customers are well served. Unfortunately, there is a building boom going on, and the job market is so tight that almost anyone with a hammer can get a job on a construction crew. And two months later will know enough to pass themselves off as a builder to some unsuspecting soul.

Imagine this scenario. Your house has been torn up for six months. The crew disappeared months ago and the builder hasn't even had the courtesy to return your calls for 60 days. Or what's worse, his phone has been disconnected. The job was supposed to be done by May, but you don't see how it can be completed by winter. You can't sleep at night. What do you do? What is your legal standing?

I'm not a lawyer and this article should not be considered legal advice, just suggestions from a friend who hears horror stories every day and is often called upon to recommend solutions to almost impossible problems. Nothing here is going to make you feel good. Reality is often a bitter pill.

To start with, don't do anything rash. What probably got you into this dilemma was jumping into a contract before you checked out the builder's references properly. If your builder has a legal contract and you improperly give the job to someone else, the original builder could sue and force you to pay him for work he did not do.

Every State is different. The specifics in this article are for Michigan. The general principles will work everywhere.

Two of the first things you should do are to take photographs and make a phone call. If the matter ever goes to court, your saying the builder left a gaping hole in the wall, or that materials were strewn all over the yard, will not make nearly as big an impression on the judge as photographs of those conditions.

The phone call I recommend is to Murray Gula at the Michigan Construction Protection Agency (MCPA), (800) 543-6669. Order his Home Owners Lien Law Kit and, while you're on the phone ask him to check and see if your builder is licensed by the state of Michigan. The Kit explains the building process from the legal point of view, includes legal forms that should be filled out every step of the way, and lists state phone numbers you may need to call. The kit only costs a few dollars, the licensing check is free.

If your builder is licensed, builders laws apply, you can file formal complaints, the state Department of Commerce has investigators to help you, and there is a trust fund that can be used to pay to have work completed. If your builder is not licensed by the state of Michigan, none of these extra protections apply.

If at all possible, you want the work to be completed by the original builder. The next step in this process is to write what I call a fifteen day letter. In the letter spell out exactly what is wrong and give fifteen days to respond before you take legal action. Send the letter to your builder by Certified Mail, Return Receipt Requested. If the letter gets the necessary action and the matter is resolved within fifteen days, fine. If not, call your family lawyer. He or she may want you to consult a specialist in building law.

Always be realistic. Being virtuous may get you into heaven, but being right will not necessarily get your job completed. Do not expect your lawyer, the local building inspector, or the state of Michigan to wave a magic wand and make the problem go away. Going to court may get a judgement in your favor. Unfortunately, no one, no judge, no jury, can make a builder perform work he does not know how to do, or pay money he does not have.

Try to meet with the builder and a friend who can be called in as a witness. Go over the job listing your complaints and get the builder's solution. Try to find out what the real reasons behind the work stoppage are. Is he experiencing cash flow problems? Are the workers being paid? What about the materials?

Contact your local building inspector and report the problem to him. Find out if he knows whether the builder is having similar problems on other jobs. Ask the inspector's advice. See if he will call the builder.

Analyze your contract. See what work has been done as compared to what work has already been paid for. Are you about even, or has the builder already received far more money than he has earned? The more money you have paid the builder, the less reason he has to finish your job.

Call the building materials supply company. Find out if the materials that have been delivered to the job have been paid for. If not, the supplier will probably lien your house and you will have to pay for the materials directly, even if you have already paid the builder for them.

If you have done all this and not gotten satisfactory results, ask your attorney (not you) to have the contract terminated, so that you may safely have the work completed by another builder.

Remember, there is only one letter difference between "hire" and "fire". If you hire properly, you won't have to fire.

Keep a cool head as the furnace duct cleaning business heats up

by America's Master Handyman,
Glenn Haege

One day last week I heard this tremendous banging sound, Thump, Thump, Thump! It was Mike Palazzolo banging his head against the wall. I said, "Mike, what's the matter? Are you trying to kill ants or just trying to get attention?"

"I think I've created a monster, Glenn. I must have trained half the duct cleaners in Detroit, Now, they're suing each other. Worse, they're suing me," he said.

Palazzolo was out of sorts because a recalcitrant ex-student, who is now one of Detroit's most successful duct-cleaning business owners, sued Mike for saying the business owner had been one of his students. Palazzolo's attorney proved that the man had indeed been one of Mike's students and the judge dismissed the case. No big deal, but a very bad symptom.

Twenty years ago, duct cleaners never squabbled. They were a band of brothers who stuck together and helped each other. It was them against a world that didn't even know their ducts should be cleaned.

Palazzolo is one of the grandfathers in the duct-cleaning business. His company, Safety King, not only cleans ducts around the entire city, it also trains people from around the country.

So what caused kindred spirits who would loan equipment back and forth, to become dues paying members of the litigious society? Too much success can be a terrible thing. Duct cleaning has become big business as homes grow older, we make them more air tight, and central air conditioning and the blower motors of newer, more efficient furnaces' send air (and dust) spewing out at a higher velocity.

First, just a few pioneers cleaned ducts. Safety King, (800) 972-6343; A-1 Duct Cleaning, (800) 382-8256; Dalton Environmental, (800) 675-2298; and Sterling Environmental (888) 992-1200, blazed the trail. Then Sanit-Air (888) 778-7324, became the first company to combine air quality testing with duct cleaning. I believe they are still the only company in the area that has a Certified Ozone Technologist on staff and is a member of the International Ozone Association.

The business looked pretty good and the duct work looked bad in most homes, so leading furnace companies, like Flame Furnace, (888) 234-2340, and Bergstrom Heating & Plumbing (734) 522-1350, added duct cleaning to their services.

Leading contractors got together and created the National Air Duct Cleaners Association (202) 737-2926, for training and testing. If you are unsure about who to call, the Association will provide a list of area members and certified duct cleaners.

Over the past few years, many companies have gotten into the business. Some, like Vent Corp. (248) 473-9300, are thoroughly trained and have good equipment. This is not true with everyone.

Today, a person can buy a glorified vacuum cleaner for $3,000 or $4,000 and be in the duct cleaning business. There is no way an inexpensive machine, even with a HEPA filter, can do the same job that you will get from one of the big forty or fifty thousand dollar truck mounted units that utilize 20,000 CFM (cubic feet per minute) of cleaning power.

You, the consumer, have to be more sophisticated. Carpet cleaners, chimney sweeps and even a bait shop owner have recently entered the duct-cleaning business. This does not mean that they are not very good duct cleaners, but it does mean that you have to do your homework and be very careful about checking references. Don't say yes on the first sales call. Contact all the referrals and see if people were satisfied with the job. Did it make a noticeable difference? Were the people well trained and professional? Did they sanitize as well as clean the duct work? What type of sanitizer did they use?

During the sales meeting some of the questions you have to ask are: How long has the company been in business? What type of equipment do they use? Where did they learn the trade? Are they certified? By whom? When they clean the ducts, do they actually cut holes in the duct work for cleaning, then reseal after the work is completed, or do they just pop open a register or two and hope for the best?

Is your house a problem house? Do you have medical symptoms that may have been caused or aggravated by microbes breeding in your duct work? According to Sanit-Air's Connie Morbach, Stachybotrys, a species of mold found in 5 percent of homes, can be attributed to severe neurological disorders like memory loss and sleeplessness. Another potentially dangerous mold, Aspergillis, causes a chronic infection in the respiratory system. Then again, you may just be allergic to those clumps of cat hair that have accumulated over the years.

If you are unsure, you may want to have your home's air quality tested by firms like Sanit-Air or Christopher Cote's Air Analysis & Consultant Company, Inc. (800) 416-2323.

Don't hold off cleaning your ducts until the dust settles. It never will. Duct cleaning is now just like any other business. It is up to you to be a smart consumer. Learn all you can before you do. Your check book is the most powerful tool in your tool box. Use it wisely.

Act quickly and cleanly when cats and dogs leave their marks

by America's Master Handyman, Glenn Haege

Spring and summer may be the best times to get a new puppy or kitten, but what happens when Fido or FeeFee forgets? Or has not quite gotten the hang of what a litter box is for? Or starts marking their territory, and their idea of eminent domain is different than yours?

Like every proud parent, you want puppy to have friends, but what do you do when he or she comes in contact with the wrong end of a skunk? Also, although it's very sad to contemplate, what happens after Fido or FeeFee have gone to that great pet farm in the sky, but their memory lingers on and on? Especially when it rains.

I do not have pets and am not a qualified dog or cat trainer. My expertise comes after the fact.

It is very important that you get to droppings and drenching fast. For droppings on solid surfaces like vinyl or hardwood, pick up and get rid of the evidence with paper toweling. Then lightly spray the area with a good universal cleaner like Simple Green. Rinse and remove all moisture with a wad of tissues. Finish off by spraying with an odor eliminator, like Punati Chemical's Smells Begone; call (800) 645-2882 for information.

If the problem is urine on carpeting, do not use cleaning solution, wick it away. Start by placing a stack of facial or toilet tissue on the spot, then literally stand on the tissue. By pressing down with your full weight, you compress the carpet and padding allowing the extremely absorbent tissue to wick up the moisture. Throw the moist tissue away and repeat until the carpet is dry. Do not use paper toweling. It does not have the absorbency of facial or toilet tissue.

If a stain remains, Club Soda to the rescue! Lightly sprinkle Club Soda on the carpeting, then repeat the paper procedure. For odor control in a small area, spray with Smells Begone.

About 60 days after you think your pet has been thoroughly house trained, have the carpeting cleaned and sanitized professionally. You may think you cleaned up after every accident, but your pet out smarted you many times.

Marking territory comes naturally. Homeowners paint the front door a different color, male animals spray. All cats and dogs have urinary accidents. If you find an area that has been marked repeatedly, or have purchased a house and find the ghost of a pet lingers on, it is time to get out the heavy artillery. To track down every area that has been effected, send the person with the most delicate nose around the house with a misting bottle filled with water. Moisten the walls, low corners, flooring and trim, and holler every time you smell even a hint of urine.

Do not confine the efforts to one floor, check everywhere from basement to attic. Everywhere you find a urine smell has to be decontaminated. Carpeting must be lifted and the flooring cleaned and encapsulated with a quality alcohol-based stain kill such as Bulls Eye B-I-N. Floor trim in the affected area has to be removed carefully, cleaned and encapsulated with B-I-N. This product can be found at most good paint and hardware stores and home centers. It comes in both the liquid and spray can. Get both. Spray corners and where flooring meets the wall.

You must also encapsulate the walls in the effected area. When using a stain kill, cover twice the size of the effected area. If you think the area is as big as a bread plate, cover the size of a dinner plate. If you think the smell only goes 2 feet high on the wall, cover 4 feet up.

After everything has been encapsulated with the B-I-N, top coat with an oil based paint. Do not use a water base or latex. Encapsulation is the name of the game and you need oil paint's water-tight properties.

This particular job is best done during summer. The smell of alcohol-base stain kills is terrible. You really want to be able to have the windows open.

If the odor and possible discoloration problem is with a hardwood floor, and you can't paint, there is no easy solution. Many flooring refinishers tell me that you will be time and money ahead by fixing the walls, then replacing the affected section of hardwood. The only other solution is to completely sand down and refinish the entire floor. Even then, you will not be certain that you have eliminated the problem until a year has passed without the smell's return. There will often be a heat register or cold air return around the effected area. I have seen occasions where repeated spraying drenched, then almost rusted through, the ductwork, so complete the job by having the ducts cleaned and sanitized.

Finally, what do you do when Fido comes off second best from a confrontation with Mr. Skunk? There are many home remedies, including washing down with tomato juice. My suggestion is that you go a little more high tech and have someone hold the animal while you spray it down with Smells Begone. Wash thoroughly with a good pet shampoo. Dry. Then re-apply the Smells Begone. This stockyard strength odor eliminator will do the job and you do not have to worry about poochy getting sick licking off the product. It is a perfectly benign anti-microbial that can even be sprayed into an open wound without harmful results.

AUGUST 16, 1997

Water products make a splash at an otherwise dry hardware show

by America's Master Handyman, Glenn Haege

Do your eyes tend to glaze over when you are looking for something in a home center's overwhelming amount of stuff? Now, try to imagine yourself in the middle of a home center as big as Cobo Center. Mind blowing, isn't it? Now, upgrade the picture to five Cobo Centers.

That's about the size and feel of the combined National Hardware Show and the National Building Products Exposition at the McCormick Place Complex in Chicago, this past week. The expanded facility now has three gigantic buildings. This year's show utilized five humongus floors for exhibits, three floors for meetings, and two floors for eating, storage, and maintenance.

This year's 1,200,000 square feet of exhibit space may not sound mind boggling, but my aching feet tell me it was! The Official Show Directory required 724 pages just to list the names and addresses of some three thousand exhibitors displaying over 250,00 products. The new products directory had 112 pages.

What did I see that was really new? Comparatively little. In former years there would often be a star of the show that everybody talked about. The biggest star was aggravation on the part of foot sore attendees who traveled around in circles unable to find specific displays or became weary and saw only half the show.

In fact, there was so little going on that the non-hardware press jumped on the fact that the American Medical Association sold their endorsement to Sunbeam. When meaningless advertising drivel becomes the headline grabber you know very little of substance is to be found. This year, there simply wasn't any newer-than-new, stand out products. Almost everything in the new product showcase, for instance, was "new" only because it was an incremental improvement: A rake with a more ergonomically-designed handle; a charcoal smoker with a stainless steel, rather than a sheet metal, cover; a furnace filter that screens out slightly smaller impurities; a remote-controlled fan.

I'll go over consumer products briefly this week. Next week, we'll talk about some of the new tools that were on display.

The biggest trend was in water and air treatment products. Bionaire, Hunter, Lasko, and others showed new air cleaners and single room humidifiers. Bionaire (recently bought out by Rival-800-253-2764) introduced a HEPA air filter that also includes a VOC (Volatile Organic Contaminants) component that filters out paint or new carpet odors. Bionaire's top-of-the-line, whole house humidifier has been greatly reduced in size, yet still has the power to humidify a 2,900-square-foot ranch style home.

Lasko Metal Products, Inc. (800-394-3267) is introducing a pump-driven humidifier that utilizes cascading, rather than wicked water, for increased efficiency. Culligan (888-CULLIGAN) bought Amtek Filter (800-645-5426) and is now joining companies such as the Omni Corp. to lead the charge for water filtration. While water filters aren't new, Culligan brings the marketing clout and name recognition necessary to create public awareness of the benefits of the different types of water filtration. They showed a water filter pitcher, much like the Brita filter pitcher, at the show, in addition to a whole line of Culligan label and Amtek label faucet, sink, below sink and whole-house filters.

Continuing the water treatment theme, Field Controls introduced the ClearWave microprocessor and IDC/Intermark (800-453-2101) introduced the Mineral Magnet. Both claim to sonically or magnetically treat the water to prevent mineral build up.

While I'm talking water, Peerless Faucet (800-GET MORE) has brought out a new Do-It-Yourself double-handle kitchen faucet. FLUIDMASTER (714-774-1444) brought out a new line of toilet repair kits. Innovative Manufacturing Company (800-488-7177) brought out new additions to their line of toilet flappers and flush valves and introduced a leak stopper kit for corroded flush valves.

Another trend was home security. Kwikset (714-535-8111) seems to be on the verge of bringing out some very innovative lock sets. Their Titan Technologies' NightSight utilizes a motion detector that automatically illuminates the keyway at night, eliminating fumbling with keys. Their LockMinder uses a battery-powered light to let you know when the deadbolt is locked. And a new technology that may be out in 1998 or 1999 will allow you to use your car door opener to open the front door.

Supra Products (800-225-2974) showed their line of combination KeySafe key boxes, that let you store door keys outside for use by children, housecleaning services and repair persons.

The Home Equipment Manufacturing Co. (800-854-6415) displayed some very innovative lighting fixtures. One timed light socket adapter turns on lights at dusk, then turns them off six hours later. Their Smoke Alarm Emergency Light turns on when the smoke alarm sounds or the electric power goes off.

The Ice Alarm, by EasyHeat monitors exterior water pipe temperature from the inside the house. While the alarm's hardly earth shattering, it was a nice little nuance. That goes for the whole show. Nothing earth shattering but a lot of nice little nuances that will upgrade a broad spectrum of hardware products.

Power sanders and shorter saws make it tool time in Chicago

by America's Master Handyman,
Glenn Haege

First I have to tell you that I was energized by Crystal Bernard.

A month before the Hardware Show at the McCormick Place in Chicago, I received an expensive radio-activated car controller and a note saying that I had been scheduled to race miniature cars with Wing's star Crystal Bernard at 10 a.m. Monday morning. That seemed like the best offer I'd had all month so I hustled over to the fifth floor of the McCormick Place South at the appointed time.

Bernard is a nice young lady and I am now a believer in Energizer batteries. As far as I am concerned, what makes them decidedly better than the competition is that they are endorsed by the actress.

Thoroughly energized, I began to prowl the hallowed halls of hardware. One of the most noticeable aspects of the show was the tremendous influx of Far Eastern companies that now display their wares. There was an entire book for of Taiwanese products and their main land compatriots were not far behind.

For instance, the official Directory of the Hardware Show listed sixteen companies with corporate names starting with the word Zhejiang. They ran the gamut from the Zhejiang Machinery and Electronic Co., Limited, that displayed office chair parts and casters; to the Zhejiang Yuyao Great-Wall Measure Tape Company, that displayed a line of – you guessed it – measuring tapes. I have never met Mr. Zhejiang, but he must be a heck of a businessman.

Now, let's talk tools. Power tools are glitzy, but many of us still work by hand. In the hand tool department, Tajimo (a good Irish name) introduced one of the new, short bladed trim saws that use a pulling rather than a pushing motion.

This is a Japanese concept that has been in the East for ages, but is comparatively new to the West. The pulling motion makes it easier on the arm muscles and gives far superior control. The Tajimo saw comes with three interchangeable blades and, like the Ginsu knife of late-night TV fame, can cut through almost anything.

Nobody gets blue ribbons or trophies for sanding, but this procedure is involved in almost every home repair project. It has to be done right, or the entire job can be ruined. The NicSand Company of Berea, Ohio, has created a new category of products that may revolutionize sanding.

We all know what steel wool is. We all know what sandpaper is. The NicSand Company combined the best features of both categories and created a new product that is almost too good to be true. I've used NicSand Power Wool and it is almost impossible to wear out. It fits all contour and orbital sanders and you can also use it by hand. Miracle or miracles, you don't have to wait for this new product. It is already at ACO and Damman, so you can still use it this summer.

Power sanders (Belt, finish, palm, random orbit) are an exploding category. Every power company from Black and Decker to Makita to Milwaukee displayed new sanders at the show that offered minor improvements over prior models.

A new generation of the contour sanders that were just introduced a year ago last Christmas, has arrived. The new Dremel contour sander has decidedly more shape-sanding units, more sizes, more power, and more control, than the first generation units. Look for them at your favorite hardware or home center in time for this Christmas.

Absolute Coatings, the floor coatings company, introduced a new hardwood floor sanding machine for the rental market that is especially made for refinishing factory-finished flooring. The machine is imported from England and utilizes a two-inch wide, 3M sanding strip attached to an orbital buffer. It's designed to just cut the finish enough so that you can recoat without stripping the flooring down to raw wood.

The new unit weighs only 95 pounds, so it is 40 pounds lighter than its biggest competitor. It also breaks into two pieces for easier carrying. Both features should make it popular with the DIY crowd. Unfortunately Absolute Coatings is beginning this product roll out in Texas, so it will be a year or more before it becomes available in our part of the country.

Zircon, the Stud Sensor company, introduced a wide number of new, high tech, products at the Hardware Show. I especially liked two of them. The first was the Zircon Repeater, a 25-foot tape with a built-in digital voice recorder so you can record measurements as you work. The other was the Zircon Metalli Scanner. This newest addition to the Stud Sensor line, gives a video read-out of what is behind the wall. It can identify hidden rebar rod and wiring through a six-inch slab of wood, drywall, even concrete.

Black & Decker was another big hitter at the Show. Talk about power to the people. They introduced enough of the highly popular VersaPak tools to bring the product line up to 35, plus standard electric and VersaPak versions of the Wizard Rotary tool that can cut, sand or shape anything small.

This wraps up my report from the Hardware Show. Next week, we'll get back to work on end of summer projects. Think about it folks. Next week the summer is over.

Showroom has ideas on easy ways to make a home look elegant

by America's Master Handyman,
Glenn Haege

Making your home look like you are either made of money or are the world's greatest handy person just got easier. I'm talking heavy duty, mansion-style great looks, not the usual handyman special variety. Things like coved lighting, metal and wood paneling, even embossed plaster ceilings.

These looks are not only Do-It-Yourself do-able these days, they're affordable, too. This revelation started for me with a trip to Acoustical Distributors, Inc., (810) 465-2010, on M-59, between Romeo Plank and Groesbeck, just East of Lakeside Mall.

Although the company has been a distributor for more than 14 years, they have been a rather closely kept secret of the higher echelon architectural and contracting tradesmen. Now the owner, Kim Laenen, has opened his showroom to folks like us.

What does this mean to you and me? Let's say you want to add a little extra light and a lot of charm to the kitchen. How about coved lighting all around the circumference of the room? Doing something like that with drywall is a major project. No matter how they look to the naked eye, corners aren't square and walls aren't straight. Gordon Architectural Aluminum Specialties Inc., (800) 747-8954, makes the job easy with a line of positive locking, extruded aluminum light coves.

All the major work is already done. You just hang pieces and snap them together. Corners are mitered at the factory. So are a wide selection of angles and curves. Once installed, you fill the joints with caulk and they become invisible. Light cove pieces can be painted to match your room. Even the electrical is a no brainer because the hanger brackets double as shelving for standard tube lighting strips.

Want to do something really different in a living room or family room? How about an historic embossed metal ceiling or walls? The look can be turn of the century or art nouveau. The Interfinish Division of Chicago Metallic (800) 560-5758, has a line of decorative embossed metal panels and cornices that give a hundred year old look, but are very easy to install. If you like the look, but not the sound reflecting characteristics, perforated panels and acoustical pads are available.

Let's talk suspended ceilings. We all know what acoustical tile looks like. Anyone who frequents the big home centers has seen the same four or five acoustic tile styles a hundred times. What most of us don't know is what we've been missing. If you have recessed lighting, modern suspended ceilings can take as little as 2-1/2 inches from the height of the room. Even fluorescent fixtures only require a 4-inch drop.

If you have a big old barn of a room that is hard to light, you could make the entire ceiling look like one vast skylight with Interfinish Astralume luminous acrylic panels.

How about plaster? If you are doing a really luxurious remodeling job, you can make the ceiling look like it was plastered with the kind of craftsmanship that hasn't been around for fifty years. Imagine 2-by-2-foot square designs in a Victorian Poppy, Bell & Flower, French Flower, or Bamboo pattern. Or perhaps you'd prefer classic Roman Squares? All these ornate, intricate designs are made of 2-by-2-foot glass reinforced gypsum panels by the Specialty Interior Products Group of Chicago Metallic, (800) 323-7164. The look is classic, but easy to attain because the panels hang from a standard suspended ceiling grid.

If wood paneling is more your fancy, Acoustical Distributors has already received their first shipments of the new wood paneling just introduced two weeks ago at the National Hardware Show.

If allergies are a problem or you have an area that must be kept very clean, traditional acoustic panels are out of the question. Just look at them with a wet mop in your hand and they start to crumble. Now, Chicago Metallic's Endure and Endure Plus panels have sealed vinyl surfaces that can be cleaned constantly.

Many of these acoustic panels come in an assortment of colors. This is very important because if you paint acoustic panels you destroy their sound suppression characteristics.

All of these modern technologies are on display at Acoustical Distributors and nowhere else that I know of in Michigan. If you want to do it yourself, you can. Kim Laenen and his crew will provide you with step by step instructions, and the few specialized pieces of equipment that can make the job easier are available for rental. If you decide that you don't want to do the job yourself, Laenen has craftsmen that will do the work for you or can recommend contractors. If you are already working with a contractor, they will gladly work with them.

I am certainly not saying that these new ceiling tiles are the solution to every ceiling problem. If you have a low basement, a standard drywall ceiling with recessed lighting, is probably a better answer. What I do say, is that before you do any project, it makes sense to learn all you can. If you are going to do a major home improvement, stop by the store, look at the selection, and get some brochures. It is the job of Laenen and all the other distributors to provide the information you need to make a wise buying decision.

The fall season is ideal for tackling those home painting jobs

by America's Master Handyman, Glenn Haege

This is the prime-time painting season. You have 60 days of great weather. The sun is a little lower on the horizon. The siding is at its driest of the year. Some stores are having paint sales. The brushes are calling so put on your grubbies and paint.

Here's a brief primer.

■ Exterior wood siding: Scrape away all loose paint, then wash with 2 ounces dry measure TSP per gallon of water. Rinse thoroughly, let dry one day. If very dirty, increase the TSP to 4 ounces. If there is mildew, add 2 cups of household bleach per gallon. This is powerful. Wear a respirator, goggles, and rubber gloves, plus a long-sleeved shirt and slacks. Whenever you add bleach, drench all flowers, lawn, shrubs and trees that may come in contact with the bleach solution or run off water before and after cleaning. Cover any delicate plant with a tarp before cleaning.

Let the house dry for at least a day, if the old paint was badly weathered, apply a water base stain kill like Zinsser Bulls Eye 1-2-3 or Master Chem Kilz 2, then two coats of a high-quality water-base house paint. Follow the spread rate on the can religiously. Remember, a good water base acrylic base paint is very creamy and wants to spread. You want to put it on thick.

If chalking is a problem, make certain that the label on the paint you buy says it will hold up against chalking. If mildew is a problem, mix in a mildewcide additive like Super Mildex by Atlanta Sundries or Sta-Clean by Envirochem into the final coat of paint.

If the wood is in really bad condition, use a premium oil base wood primer, then finish off with your favorite oil or water-base top coat.

■ T1-11 Siding: Your siding may be stained, not painted. If so, you probably will want to restain with a quality water-based solid exterior wood stain. The color of water-based stains lasts longer than oil-based stains.

If you have decided to go from stain to paint, or to recoat an already painted T1-11 surface, clean first using exterior wood siding directions. Let dry, then apply one coat of a water-based stain kill and one coat of a good acrylic water-base paint. Do not exceed a spread rate of 400 square feet per gallon.

■ Vinyl or Aluminum Siding: Vinyl and aluminum are actually better painting surfaces than wood. Wash with a good aluminum or vinyl cleaner like Alumi-Nu, Power, or Armorall Vinyl Siding Cleaner. Let dry, then apply a coat of water-based stain kill and one or two coats of a premium water-based acrylic house paint. Do not exceed a spread rate of 400 square feet per gallon of paint.

■ Cement Block: Wash down with a 4-ounce dry measure of TSP and 2 cups of chlorine bleach per gallon of water. Wear protective clothing, goggles, respirator, and rubber gloves. Scrub the surface with a hard bristle brush and rinse with a garden hose. Let dry 24 hours. Apply a water-based stain kill. If there was a mildew problem, add a mildewcide. Finish off with two coats of a good water-based acrylic paint. The spread rate should be no more than 300 square feet per gallon of paint.

■ Shingle Siding: If you have asbestos shingles that are beginning to crumble, they have to be removed and discarded according to hazardous waste regulations. Call the city and ask how to discard the shingles. Please don't try to get rid of them on the sly. I have to share this planet with you. If the siding is still in good condition, wash, using exterior wood-siding directions. Let dry, then apply Zinsser Cover Stain, an oil-based stain kill for exterior use. When dry, recoat with two coats of a good water-based acrylic paint.

■ Brushes: Apply water-base paint with a good nylon or nylon-polyester brush. If using an oil-based paint, use a china bristle or a polyester bristle brush.

■ Paint Sprayer: Use an airless or HVLP (high-volume, low-pressure) paint sprayer. Rent a good one, don't try to use one of those amateur sprayers. They are not designed for big jobs. If you are going to spray a water base paint, add Flotrol, by the Flood Co., to prevent the sprayer from plugging. Do not thin down the paint with water. You will ruin the paint, if you do.

Announcement:

WXYT-CBS Detroit and I would like to invite you to my Annual Fall Home Improvement Expo next weekend, September 13 and 14, at the Southfield Civic Center Pavilion, Evergreen at 10-1/2 Mile. Come see all the things I write and talk about all year long. The hours are 8 a.m. to 6 p.m. Saturday and 8 a.m. to 4 p.m. Sunday. Thanks to the cooperation of the great people in the Southfield Department of Parks and Recreation, the show and the parking are my favorite price, free. With a little bit of luck, advance copies of my new, 416 page book, Fix It Fast & Easy! 2, Upgrading Your House, will be available. Call WXYT, 248-455-7350, for show information.

SEPTEMBER 13, 1997

Protect your deck now to help it weather another Michigan winter

by America's Master Handyman, Glenn Haege

This is the weekend of my Fall Home Improvement Expo at the Southfield Civic Center Pavilion. I will not only broadcast from the show, but spend hours answering individual questions from listeners and readers who stop by. It's fun for me to talk to people face-to-face. Many will bring snapshots or blue prints to make it easier to explain technical questions. If you're a homeowner with a problem, or just want to learn more before you are, come on down.

After all these years I feel a little bit like a father confessor. He hears the same sins over and over again. I get the same questions. One of the biggest categories of questions will revolve around decks. The three most often repeated questions will be:

■ "I've just had a deck built, do I need to do anything this year, or should I just wait until next spring?"
■ "What should I put on my new (fill in the blank: pressure-treated, cedar, redwood, or hardwood) deck?"
■ "My deck is badly weathered, how do I bring it back?"

The answers are all in my *Complete Deck & Paver Guide,* but in a rare display of brilliance on my publisher's part, the book has been sold out since April. It will be back in stock by spring, but you need the information now. Since no other book I know of contains the answers, I want to use the remainder of this article to give you the highlights. Besides my publisher's *faux pas,* there are some very good new products on the market that will make your job easier.

Regardless if you have a new deck, or an old, weathered deck, the time to protect that deck is NOW. Winter is the toughest time of the year for decks. In many parts of the country decks will go through 40 or 50 freeze-and-thaw cycles. Other parts of the country will have monsoon-like rains that can do just as much damage. Protecting your deck now will protect your investment through a tough winter.

Recent U.S. Department of Agriculture Forest Service research by William C. Feist and R. Sam Williams of the Forest Service Forest Products Laboratory, in Madison, Wis., revealed that the sun's rays are so harmful to raw wood that a deck or other outside structure should be protected immediately. Unprotected wood begins to deteriorate within two weeks.

Even brand new decks need to be prepped before they are treated. Bio-Wash Total Wood Care Systems (800-858-5011 or www.biowash.com on the Internet) has developed a new product, called Mill Glaze Away that actually changes the pH of the wood and prepares it for coating. Using this product before any stain application evens out the absorption of the stain and assures a uniform appearance.

One the most convenient things about using the Bio-Wash System is that you don't have to waste a day drying out the wood after it is prepped. Another of their products, Natural DeckOil, can be applied in as little as two hours after the Glaze Away; enabling you to get the entire job done in one day.

There are many other deck stains on the market. Be careful about what protective coating you choose. Only specially formulated products like Timberseal, Super Deck (800-825-5382), Penofin (800-736-6346) and Wolman (800-556-7737) RainCoat Water Repellent and Wolman F & P Clear Wood Finish and Preservative can also be used on new wood.

Many people ask me if they need to have their gray decks power washed before applying a sealer or stain. The answer is a resounding "No." New products make power washing unnecessary. If the deck wood is weathered and grayed, you can clear away the old dead wood with products like Bio-Wash Woodwash, Wolman Deck & Siding Brightener/Rejuvenator, or DeksWood by the Flood Company.

There are many other, often less expensive, deck-cleaning products on the market, most are made with chlorine or sodium hypo chlorite (NaOCl). All chlorine-based products do lasting damage to the wood grain and make it almost impossible for deck stains to be absorbed into the wood properly. This will give the deck an unappealing blotchy appearance.

If the wood has been previously treated with a sealer or stain, the remaining stain and sealer can be cleared away with Bio-Wash Stripex or Stripex-L. Stripex removes oil based stains. Stripex-L removes latex stain and clear coat wood finishes (810-773-1200).

You can find most of these products at Damman Hardware, N. A. Mans, Paint 'n Stuff and many other good hardware and paint stores.

If you've got a personal question, don't be a stranger. Drink your last cup of morning coffee in the car and come see me at the Expo, 8 a.m. to 6 p.m. today and 8 a.m. to 4 p.m. Sunday, held at the Southfield Civic Center Pavilion. Evergreen at 10-1/2 Mile. You'll find more than 30,000 square feet of home improvement products and information. Parking is free.

What's new under the sun (and down in the basement) for home

by America's Master Handyman, Glenn Haege

Last weekend's Fall Home Improvement Expo was a fun learning experience. Quite a few new, or new to our market, products were introduced. Here are some of the highlights.

Lifetime Exteriors, (248) 669-1452, displayed Lifetile light-weight concrete shingles. The shingles look like tile, slate, or wood, but wear like pavers. Lifetile shingles can't burn, won't curl, and last as long as the house.

Chimney liners are the law of the land, but nobody has taken the time to give a good explanation. Best Chimney & Roofing, (248) 549-8311, showed the Flexi-liner and distributed literature that explained what chimney liners do, why they are necessary, what they look like and how they are installed, better than anything I've seen.

From the input I got at the show, last week's article on fall deck care struck a chord with a lot of people. Timber Seal, the one product I recommended for which I did not have a telephone number, was exhibited at the show. Timber Seal is unique because is it is made with synthetic, not natural. oils. This means there are no nutrients to attract mold and mildew. For more information, call Woodtec Products Group, (800) 338-3175, nationally, or Howard A Davidson Lumber, (800) 543-0469, in Michigan.

Both Reddi-Wall, (810) 752-9161, the polystyrene-insulated, concrete-wall system people, and Mr. Sponge, (800) 491-4686, the basement waterproofers, were sporting impressive new air quality studies by Sanit-Air, on the elimination or reduction of fungi and bacteria through the use of their systems.

While these studies are not broad enough to be conclusive, they offer important indications as to the importance of dry basements to health.

When you consider that the Reddi-Wall system can reduce energy costs by as much as 70 percent, at the same time it eliminates damp basements, the study would make me consider the system for a new house. The Mr. Sponge study goes a long way toward convincing me that even tiny basement leaks can have a big effect on family health and should be eliminated.

Call the companies for information

While Connie Morbach of Sanit-Air, was distributing copies of her first news letter, Indoor Archives; her husband, Tom, was showing off the company's new Golem advanced duct cleaning system. The newsletter does a thorough job of describing mold, what it is, how it grows, and how to get rid of it.

For a free copy, send a stamped #10, self addressed envelope to Sanit-Air, 966 Livernois, Troy, MI 48083.

The new Collom duct cleaner was developed in Sweden. It is several times more powerful than conventional duct cleaners and will travel two or three floors straight up, greatly reducing the

> *The Mr. Sponge study goes a long way toward convincing me that even tiny basement leaks can have a big effect on family health and should be eliminated.*

need for access openings. This is more power than most residential customers need.

However, if you have a commercial building, a really big house, or any building where cutting multiple access holes into duct work would be a problem, the new system could be the answer. Call (888) 778-7324 for information.

While on the subject of air quality, Button's Rental, (248) 542-5835, has started carrying Ozone Generators for the elimination of mold, mildew, and all odor problems.

The use of Ozone is very effective. It is also very powerful. A good rule of thumb is to get the family, pets (even goldfish), and plants, out of the house while the generator is on. Don't bring them back until about two hours after the generator has been turned off.

A nightmare of many homeowners is coming home after a trip, and finding that the water heater has let go, or the toilet or washing machine has malfunctioned, and the house has been flooded.

Hartford and Ratliff, (800) 466-3110, introduced a new water security product at the show. The FloodStopper uses sensors to detect leakage and automatically shuts off the water in an emergency.

Illuminations Lighting, (248) 332-7500, introduced the Radio Ra radio-controlled dimmer switch by Lutron Electronics, (800) 523-9466. Just a press of a control panel button can light up your house with a preprogrammed lighting format that varies from room to room.

I was glad to see that both Flame Furnace, (888) 234-2340, and Williams Refrigeration, (800) 538-6650, displayed Lennox Complete Heat Furnaces. These innovative furnaces double as water heaters and give a limitless supply of hot water.

Although Damman Hardware had dozens of displays including Rag Roller and Bio-Wash deck care demonstrations, the Doozy Furniture Polish caught my eye.

Mr. Furniture Finisher. (888) 851-8500, has made Doozy for 45 years, but it has been a fine furniture store item until now. The polish contains no waxes, petroleum distillates or other oils. It just makes your furniture look very, very good.

Hallmark Paints displayed Yenkin-Majestic's new Majic Kidproof Fire Retardant Wall Paint, (800) 848-1898. This very scrubable, eggshell paint can be tinted to 2100 different colors.

More important, it contains an ingredient that slows the ignition and spread of fire. That could be a life-saver.

Another lifesaver, for me and my publisher was the fact that David Williams and Anistasia Tomassi were manning the Stress Busters of America booth, right next to me.

Their massages made both my publisher and I feel almost human and eliminated his constant back pain. I know he'll be a regular at their Lakeside location.

New building methods make basements warm, dry and comfortable

by America's Master Handyman, Glenn Haege

Lifestyles are changing. Basements are not just dark, dank places to store unwanted furniture and hide the furnace and water heater. They are living, recreating, and office areas. That means they can no longer be overlooked when house hunting. The method used to build the basement of your next home will play a big part in its livability and versatility.

The seldom discussed "new" methods of basement construction are Wood, Structural Insulated Panels (SIPs), Pre-cast Insulated Panels, and Modified Polystyrene Block Systems. All speed construction and make basements warmer and drier.

Pressure-treated wood and modern plywood sheathing made wood basements feasible. They were developed, and most often used, in the West and are best in sandy, well-drained, soil. The average wood basement comes with a 20-year guarantee. They are warmer, roomier, and airier, than conventional basements.

In 1980, Carl Campbell, a retired Pershing High School teacher from Detroit, first read about wood basements in a builder's magazine. He is now considered the grandfather of wood basements in Michigan. His 21st Century Superior Wood Basements (248) 350-9510, web site: www.woodbasements.com) are shipped to as far as Poland.

Campbell's insulated wood basement panels are built on a 2-by10 or -12 Footing Base. The outer skin is a sheet of 1/2-inch R .60 Wolmanized plywood. The inner skin is a minimum 1/4-inch sheet of Wolmanized plywood. Depending on the amount of insulation, there are 2-by-6 or 2-by-7 studs. The hollow core is filled with Applegate Cellulose insulation, giving walls an R (insulation) factor of 30, effectively eliminating heat loss through the basement.

21st Century Superior Wood Basements have a 100-year guaranty. Erection of their standard basement takes a four-man crew about one day. According to the company's web site, the total cost of an insulated wood basement is about $500 less than a traditional concrete basement that has been insulated.

SIPs (Structural Insulated Panels) are an offshoot of wood basements. This engineered construction technique is increasingly used in the construction of walls, roofs and basements. SIPs were developed by Alden B. Dow, an architect and the son of the founder of Dow Chemical Co.. The first houses to use the new technique were built in Midland in 1952, and are still occupied. Today, the use of SIPs is promoted by the Structural Insulated Panel Association, (253) 858-7472.

Team Industries, Inc. of Grand Rapids, (800) 356-5548, builds SIPs. Their standard permanent wood foundation building panel has a 1/2-inch R .60 pressure-treated plywood outer skin, a 1/2-inch OSB water board inner skin, .60 pressure treated studs, and a 5-1/2-inch thick rigid foam insulated core. On-site basement construction time is about the same as regular wood basements.

Both wood and SIP panels are so light they can be put into place by two workers. Both need good drainage and are not recommended in areas with a great deal of clay. The biggest drawback is that since 4-by-8 sheets of plywood are used in their construction, they are limited to an 8-foot basement height.

Precast Concrete Insulated Structural Panels, like those made by Superior Walls of America (800) 452-9255, are made with 5,000 psi concrete, and solid concrete studs. The exteriors have 1 inch DOW Styrofoam giving an R-5 insulation value. Putting an additional 7 inches of insulation in the stud cavity brings the R-value up to 26. Manufactured locally by Michigan MFG Foundations, (888) 925-5641, the precast panels come in 8-foot, 9-foot, and 10-foot wall heights.

Precast Concrete Panels must be erected by crane. Contractor David Levi of West Shore Contracting, (313) 692-0044, says that he believes this system is a little more expensive, but since he was able to build a 3,000 square foot basement in only 1-1/2 days and shaved three weeks off normal construction time, it is a real winner.

"I'll never build a traditional basement again. Precast Concrete Panels allow me to give my homeowners 9 and 10 foot ceiling heights and basements that are guaranteed not to leak for fifteen years," Levi said.

Rigid Foam Blocks, like those manufactured by Reddi-Wall Inc., (810) 752-9161, of Oakland, and installed by Benchmark Insulated Concrete Walls (248) 853-9400, use hollow blocks of dense expanded polystyrene foam filled with concrete to provide a very versatile basement wall system.

Since the blocks are set into place on site, then filled with concrete on a layer-by-layer basis, one or two well trained men can build a basement wall, and the wall can be any height the builder desires. In many houses, all exterior walls are made of Reddi-Wall blocks creating a very solid, well insulated wall system with an R-value of 22. Such homes have been found to cut energy costs up to 70 percent over traditional construction.

OCTOBER 4, 1997

The way some companies treat retailers doesn't paint a pretty picture

by America's Master Handyman,
Glenn Haege

Consolidation in business is a fact of life. I don't shed many tears when Kmart decides they are losing money on Builder's Square, and Hechingers decides they are losing money on Home Quarters, and both sell out to a "turn around" specialist. That's OK by me.

What I don't like to see is when big business seems to go out of its way to knock off a little guy. Case in point: One of the most successful, most innovative, paint retailers in our area is Paint 'n Stuff, owned by the Schwartz family. Smart, service oriented, competitively priced – they did just about everything right.

More than just good retailers, I always saw the Schwartz boys, father, Leonard, and two sons, Paul and Steve, at every national and regional paint show. They were always on the lookout for something new. Something that would make your and my job easier, or help us get done faster. You rewarded them by making them one of the area's biggest paint retailers.

The great American success story, right? Wrong.

If you are a paint manufacturer, there's a lot to be said about owning your own retail stores and maximizing profits. In addition, knowledgeable, independent retailers demand a great deal of service for their customers. They don't buy everything the big boys want to sell them. They can't be forced to stock dog items in depth.

Many independents operate under archaic billing and payment terms which are becoming increasingly expensive to manufacturers. This is especially true now that an ever-increasing sales volume is going through mass merchants and discount stores, cutting traditional profits.

As the retail scene changes something has got to give. I worry that that "something" may be the independent retailer.

About a year ago, Benjamin Moore bought out the most successful paint retailer in Chicago. Not to worry, they assured us, they had just done this to gain the owner's expertise, so they could help their retailers more. Not even the Handyman believed that one.

Soon, Leonard Schwartz, received a telephone call from a top exec at Benjamin Moore. Over the years, Paint 'n Stuff had become Michigan's largest retailer of Benjamin Moore paint. This one manufacturer's line amounted to about 60 percent of Paint 'n Stuff's total sales.

The Benjamin Moore telephone call was short but not sweet. The manufacturer was revoking Paint 'n Stuff's credit line and expected immediate payment.

The paint industry practice is to sell spring dating orders for paint requirements at the beginning of the year. They ship in the early spring and receive payment throughout the year. Benjamin Moore and the Schwartz family had been doing this for years. The Schwartz's had never failed to settle in full by the end of the year and were considered one of Benjamin Moore's prime accounts.

In the paint industry, Benjamin Moore's phone call would be considered a death sentence. But not to sharp, smart retailers like the Schwartzes. Leonard called his number two and three paint suppliers, Pittsburgh Paint and Coronado Paint, and explained the situation. To their credit, they stepped in and gave Paint 'n Stuff the extra credit terms the Schwartz family needed to survive.

Schwartz expected a 40-percent drop in sales when he lost Benjamin Moore but his customers were so loyal the company experienced only a 10-percent decline. Then Schwartz received another telephone call. This time from Pittsburgh Paint. It seems companies like Paint 'n Stuff were no longer "in the manufacturers marketing plans." Pay now.

Not even the best retailer can survive two hits like that. Paint 'n Stuff will soon be out of business. Leonard, his wife, their two sons, and their employees will be out on the street and looking for a place to rebuild their dreams.

Nothing in this story should make it seem like the big paint companies did anything illegal. I am certain they dotted all the "i"s and crossed all the "t"s. To them, I'm sure, it was just a sad but necessary part of business. But I'll always remember the Schwartz family's exuberance as they ran from display to display at the paint shows looking for something new, and their pride and joy when they brought that "something" home for us. They were the American Dream.

Consumers must realize there is no reason for big chain employees to look out for the customer or give the same kind of service as hard-working entrepreneurs. Each of us will pay for Paint 'n Stuff's demise with a less competitive marketplace, lower quality service, less innovation, and more limited selection. Fewer little guys will be willing to go out on the hook to serve us.

This isn't a story that will make headlines, but we should all be concerned. I know the remaining Benjamin Moore and Pittsburgh Paint dealers will be.

The ideal Sweetest Day gift?
How about power tools – for her

by America's Master Handyman,
Glenn Haege

Two weeks ago I broadcast my show from the Rick Bloom-WXYT Financial Expo at Walsh College. After the show I stuck around for a while to answer readers and listeners questions and sell some of my books.

I will always remember one woman. She not only bought two complete sets of my books, she confided that although her husband loved to shop at Saks Fifth Avenue, she preferred Home Depot.

This woman is not all that unusual. Sixty percent of my radio audience is female. These women are not sidewalk superintendents or straw bosses. They are intimately involved, very often the main man (oops, sorry) on a household job.

Next Saturday is Sweetest Day. For many of these women, candy is no longer dandy, the appeal of flowers has faded, and perfume may well be *passe.* What, would be the ideal gift for these do-it-yourself women?

Frank, one of the store managers at Home Depot in Southfield, thought the ideal gift would be a copy of Home Improvement 1-2-3, Home Depot's home improvement encyclopedia. It's a $34.95 book that sells for $24.97 at their stores.

Russ, at Mr. O'Tools in Shelby, thought a DeWalt or Makita 18-volt Cordless Drill would be a primo gift for Ms. DIY. The most powerful cordless drills on the market, these tools can do almost anything. Drill, charger, and battery, plus case cost about $250.

I like cordless tools as gifts, because once you know what make and series they prefer, there is a wide array of companion tools that work off the same power source. If that special someone already has a cordless drill and likes it, you can get one of the matching saws or sanders. If you don't know just which to pick, an extra battery pack is guaranteed to start the love-lights gleaming in her eyes.

Jim Mans, from N. A. Mans in Trenton, thought a heavy duty DeWalt Saber Saw would be a good choice for the serious Do-It-Yourselfer.

"It's very versatile and says 'you are not just playing games, you are serious,'" he said.

The folks at both Tool Traders in Royal Oak and Marsh Power Tools in Livonia said that getting the proper tool is such a personal thing they would recommend gift certificates. We're all stuck with budgets. When I get a gift certificate it makes me feel like a kid in a candy store. You can't beat the feeling.

While all of these were excellent answers, I was blown away by the response of Bill Damman of Damman Hardware. It seemed like I was listening to the keynote speaker at a sensitivity seminar. Here is some of what he said:

"If you really know someone you have a insight into what they want. It well may be that there is a special pair of earrings or an outfit that she really wants, but has held off buying because the family budget is only so big, and she needs the money for the kids or the house. Sweetest Day is a wonderful time to fulfill her secret desire.

"I shop my stores all the time and am constantly amazed at how many young, very well dressed, women stop and ask me how to do a certain job, or what tools they need to complete a specific project. It's very obvious that these women are not just bringing the fixings home to the guy in their life. They are going to do the project themselves.

"I don't think this is because they have to, they want to. They are thrilled by the sense of accomplishment they get from doing the job themselves. I can appreciate this because I, and most other weekend warriors, get the same thrill.

"A man shouldn't be afraid to give a woman a tool for Sweetest Day, or any other day of the year. If he knows a lady like this, then a carefully selected tool can be a very loving gift. There have been tremendous advances in tools. They do more, work better, harder, faster. Modern tools are lighter weight and ergonomically designed. This is especially important to women because most do not have the muscle mass and weight of a man.

"The gift doesn't have to be big. It can be as simple as a fiberglass shafted hammer, or as high tech as one of the new video stud finders that can see through six inches of concrete. Modern screwdrivers have special handles that make gripping easier. Pliers lock better. There has been so many advances in drill sets that if her drill set is over five years old it should be thrown out and replaced with a new one.

"Then there are the new tools. One of those new Dremmel tools that are excellent for crafts and small places or Black & Decker Cordless tools would make an excellent gift.

"Whatever it is, she'll love it, and not just because of the tool. She'll love it mostly because you had the insight to give her something that will continue giving her the reward of accomplishment year after year."

I couldn't have said it half so well. I think I've got a good idea why after 24 years and three kids, the love light still shines so brightly in both Bill and Debbie Damman's eyes.

I think I'll rush out and try to find a Coach purse that's big enough to hold a basic tool set.

Happy Sweetest Day!

EZ Wall Panel System lets you have real brick look without the cost

by America's Master Handyman, Glenn Haege

Last week, I discovered a new wall system by Williams Panel Brick that makes installing brick, tile, even marble and granite so easy, anyone, even an entry level handy person can do it with no sweat.

But first, are Nancy Szerlag and I a team or what? Last week we had two tool articles in one Homestyle issue. It was like we planned it. In my story, Bill Damman talked about how the new ergonomic tools are lighter weight and easier for women to handle. Then Nancy proved it with the new Ames Ergo Concept Rake that enabled her to rake her lawn even though she had a strained neck.

Nancy's article was so convincing that, even though my editor at Master Handyman Press has a lawn service, she rushed out and bought the rake and the Black and Decker electric Super Vac 'N' Mulch Blower. After reading my article, my editor's husband, Captain Klutz, snuck out and got a Makita 18-volt cordless drill. Are they going to have a romantic Sweetest Day at their house or what?

Now, back to this week's article. I was over at Williams Panel Brick talking to the owner, Bob Francis, last week. Most people think of Williams Panel Brick as a retailer, but the same store front on

Eight Mile, just East of Inkster Road, (800) 538-6650, serves as the headquarters for the family's American Brick Company that does business throughout North America, and will soon hop the pond to Europe.

On my way out of the store I saw a guy plopping bricks on a wall display so fast I thought my eyes were deceiving me. Francis told me that this was their new EZ Wall Panel System. The system uses 29 gauge, hardened G-90 (very high quality) galvanized steel back support panels. This new metal brick-mounting system is very durable and fireproof. The 2-by-4-foot and 4-by-4-foot steel panels are perforated throughout with a pattern of tabs that act as interlocking ties for placing 1/2-inch thick veneer bricks.

The G-90 galvanizing gives the steel excellent corrosion resistance. Since the tab design provides instant vertical and horizontal brick alignment, all you have to do is attach the metal panels to the wall studs, dab adhesive on the panels and place the brick. The company recommends an SBR (Synthetic Butyl Rubber) adhesive for Do-It-Yourselfers, because it can be used over a broader temperature range than silicone. When the bricks are in place, apply a latex modified grout and you're done. The look is that of a solid brick wall, but the cost is only about $5 a square foot. You can use the same system for both interior and exterior installation.

Using brick veneer – rather than more expensive, full-face brick – has been a standard commercial building technique for years. The new EZ Wall Panel System is an excellent product for DIY use. The smaller 2-by-4 foot panels are versatile and light enough for a woman to handle easily. And it costs just half the price of the 4-foot panel, so the female Do-It-Yourselfer doesn't get stuck paying a premium for something that is sized for her use. I think this is just one sign of the recognition of the power of women in DIY projects.

According to Ray Henry, vice-president of operations, four of the 12 largest brick companies are presently making thin brick for Williams Panel Brick. That means you can get a very complete selection of thin brick veneer in almost every style and color brick and should have very little trouble adapting their inventory to your design requirements.

The same EZ Wall system can be used for installing tile in the kitchen or bath, or marble around a fireplace. The hardest part of all these jobs has always been aligning the brick or tiles properly. The perforated tabs on the EZ Wall panel make it easy to have perfect horizontal and vertical alignment every time. No matter whether you are using brick, or tile, or marble, the only difference in the backer panel, is the pattern of the tab perforation. For veneer bricks the pattern is 2 inches by 4 inches plus grout line. For tile, marble or granite, the pattern is 4 inches by 4 inches, 8 inches by 8 inches, or 12 inches by 12 inches, depending on your size requirements.

The new EZ Wall Panel System means that if you were not concerned about insulation and wanted a brick wall look for your basement, you could anchor the panels directly to the concrete. If you wanted to add insulation, you can install 2-inch firing strips or hang 2-by-4-inch studs and fill the cavities with insulation.

For exterior use, the new EZ Wall Panel System can be applied over any structurally sound substrate. Since no footings are required, the veneer may extend all the way down to the ground. Being fast, versatile, and easy to install makes this new system a winner.

OCTOBER 25, 1997

Air purifiers make our homes safer places to live and breathe

by America's Master Handyman, Glenn Haege

You may think that you and your family are safe, but if you knew all the concentrated "yuck" that you breath, drink, and absorb, into your body, you would be frightened to a frazzle. And not just on Halloween.

Over the years, my columns have covered air quality, VOCs (Volatile Organic Compounds), water quality, and sick house syndrome. I have been investigating these subjects in even more depth, and will give you the results over the next few months. The more I learn, the more I think you need to know.

Individually, you and I can do very little about the fabled ozone hole. We can't clean up the world's environment by ourselves, but we owe it to our families to clean up our own personal environment. We can keep the air we and our families breath and the water we drink clean and contaminant free. This is an individual responsibility. My job is to give you the information. Your job is to make the important decisions.

The most vital thing we do each day is breath. We would not like it, but we could do without water for four or five days, maybe even a week. Ten minutes without breathing and we're on our way to discovering a whole new reality.

According to the Environmental Protection Agency (EPA), indoor air can be up to 40 times more polluted than outdoor air. As we close up our homes and add new windows and insulation, our homes become more efficient places to heat and cool. That's good. We also cut off the majority of fresh air from coming in. That's bad.

To work around this, we improve air infiltration with electronic and media filters, clean and sanitize the ductwork and bring in fresh air with air infiltration devices like the Skuttle Model 216 or Equalize Air units.

The best high-efficiency media filters, such as the Air Bear, only filter down to 0.1 microns. An electronic air cleaner operating at peek efficiency only filters down to 0.01 microns. That's good, but increasingly it does not seem good enough.

According to the Center for Disease Control, allergies and aggravated respiratory problems are caused by particulates (35 percent of the time), by Bioaerosols (34 percent) and VOCs (31 percent). Particulates in a home come from dirt, dust, and pollen. The most common Bioaerosols are microorganisms like dust mites, mold spores, bacteria and germs from sneezes and coughs. VOCs are fumes off-gassed from the artificial products in homes (carpeting, furniture, insulation, composites and other products, household chemicals, cooking, grease and wood smoke, combustion gasses, etc.).

Particulates from dust, insecticide, smog, fumes, even cooking and wood smoke can be as small as 0.0001 microns. That means that many of these particles can just walk through even a properly functioning electronic air cleaner. Many electronic air cleaners are not properly maintained and are therefore close to worthless.

VOCs are even smaller. VOCs, various household odors, and gas molecules, can be as small as 0.000001 microns. Realistically, these fine particulates cannot be filtered. They have to be zapped.

Enter the ozone machines and ultra violet air purifiers. Information on Ozone machines is available locally from Pure Air Plus, (800) 455-5247. Ultra Violet systems, such as the Second Wind distributed by Lennox are available locally from Williams Refrigeration, (888) 268-5445, and Flame Furnace, (888) 234-2340; and Steril-Aire by Steril-Aire USA, (800) 2-STERIL, is available from Sanit-Air, (888) 778-7324.

Ozone is a very effective sanitizer. The ozone machine creates 03, a very unstable molecule which oxidizes (zaps) the contaminants in the air. The new Pure Air Plus has an automatic sensor and switch that turns ozone creation off if the ozone level gets to .04 parts per million. This is very important. When Sanit-Air sanitizes a home using ozone machines, they insist that all the people, pets, and plants be out of the house. So if you decide to use an ozone air machine, make certain that the ozone creation can be limited.

Ultra Violet light systems use ultra violet rays to sterilize the air. Although new to the consumer, Ultra Violet purification systems have been used to sanitize the air in hospitals and prisons for years. If they are effective in these environments, purifying the air in your house is a piece of cake.

Ultra Violet systems operate in the duct work. Since they are completely enclosed, they can do no harm. All you get is pure air. Both the Steril-Air and the Second Wind systems are priced in the $800 to $1,000 range. Ultra Violet systems require no maintenance, but bulbs have to be replaced about every 12 to 16 months.

Jim Williams, of Williams Refrigeration, says that the change in air quality is so noticeable, that if a Second Wind air purifier is installed in a person's home, and they go out for breakfast, they will be able to tell a difference in the air when they walk back into the house.

Sanit-Air, does complementary air checks before and about three weeks after installation, so that customers can see the scientific difference in their air quality. The company's testing shows about a 90 percent reduction in the ambient fungi and pollutant air levels over a six week period. That means that a home with a fully functioning Ultra Violet air purifier has very clean, safe, air.

Now, you can breath easier.

NOVEMBER 1, 1997

More Americans set their sites on off-site manufactured housing

by America's Master Handyman, Glenn Haege

Ken and Marleta Eason will move into their new home in Salem Township a couple of weeks before Thanksgiving. Depending on how you count, that is either five weeks late, or seven months early.

The five weeks late is because even though the Eason's modular, two story colonial home was built just eight weeks after the order date – yes eight weeks, your eyes are not playing tricks on you – the final siding and finish crews didn't show up until a month later because demand has been double company's projections.

The seven months early is because if the Eason's had chosen traditional, site-built construction (in the industry we call it stick built), rather than modular, they would be lucky to be moving in by next June.

Building efficiency and labor availability are the reasons for the wide time differential between modular and traditional construction. With a site-built house, all the parts are literally dropped off at the building site, then the crew puts the bits and pieces together. That's where qualified trades come in. The average builder does not have his own crews, so that when he sells a house, he just prays that the plumbers, electricians, roofers and the like show up on time. Quite often they can't fit schedules into the builder's plans, and the builder can't find anyone else, resulting in months of delay.

As site-built construction grows increasingly expensive and slow, manufactured housing of all types is becoming increasingly popular with the home buying public. There are four different subdivisions in the category: mobile homes, a successor of the "trailer homes" of yesterday; true manufactured homes, which are built in the factory to HUD building code specifications, then trailered out to the site; modular housing, which is built to BOCA building codes like a stick built home, then trailered out to the final site in sections and erected by crane; and panelized construction, which consists of walls, prebuilt in the factory, then trucked out to the site and assembled by crane.

According to the Manufactured Housing Institute, the four types of manufactured housing account for about a third of all new single-family homes sold. Today, approximately 18 million people, over 7 percent of the U.S. population, live in manufactured homes. Of that total, Automated Builder, the magazine of record for the modular building industry, estimates that in 1996, 112,000 homes, approximately 6 percent of all new single family homes sold, were modular construction.

Modular homes are built in sections, each of which weighs about 36,000 pounds. The sections are trucked to the building site, and put in place by a 110-ton crane. Upon completion, they are indistinguishable from site-built homes.

When the Easons started house hunting, they were not content with existing homes in the area they wanted to live. They thought about building a house themselves. Because of the excellent experience Marleta Eason's cousin had building a modular home in Pennsylvania, they decided to explore the modular route here in Michigan.

Since not every builder is knowledgeable about Modular construction, they "let their fingers do the walking" and found their builder, Sierra Modular Homes in the Ameritech Yellow Pages. Tom Grady, the owner of Siera Associates, which is the parent company of Sierra Modular Homes. He's also secretary of the Automated Builders Consortium, Headquartered in Buffalo Grove, Ill., (847) 398-7756, the modular building industry's trade association. Grady suggested a modular home built by Active Homes of Marlette, (800) 228-4834.

"Before agreeing, we toured the factory and were very impressed with the quality of construction," says Marleta Eason.

The couple's new home was built at Active Homes factory in Marlette, then trucked to the home site in Salem. Since the house is modular construction and built to national BOCA code, rather than Michigan construction code, the home has superior insulation, R-19 Walls and R-39 attic ceilings.

In fact, the new home is state of the art. It has a Blue Maxx expanded polystyrene concrete basement wall system and Geothermal heating and cooling. The Blue Maxx wall system is waterproof, stronger than standard poured concrete, and gives the basement walls an R factor of R-25 rather than R-5 or less for standard concrete walls. For more information call Thermal Wall Construction, (810) 346-2070, locally, or AAB Building Systems, (800) 293-3210, nationwide.

The open loop, geothermal system provides heating, cooling, and the majority of hot water. Compared to today's 80 and 90 percent efficient natural gas furnaces, geothermal is 350 to 400 percent efficient, according to Jerry Goetz, Detroit Edison's Geothermal Marketing Specialist. This type of heating and cooling system provides a 25 percent savings over natural gas annual heating bills, and a 60 percent savings over liquid propane bottled gas.

If you are interested in learning more about Geothermal, Detroit Edison is hosting a free seminar at the Macomb Community Center, Garfield and Hall Road, Nov. 9. For reservations, or a free copy of their Geothermal magazine, call their consumer hot line at (800) 833-2786.

If all this is new to you, and it is to most people, you don't have to just read about it. This weekend, you can see how the whole thing comes together. Sierra Associates is holding an open house at the site, 7663 Sleepy Hollow (a perfect address for Halloween weekend), off Six Mile, just five miles West of Northville. Call (248) 399-7062 for directions or a free modular housing brochure.

Brush up on the latest tools from paint and home products companies

by America's Master Handyman,
Glenn Haege

I didn't see anything revolutionary at this year's Paint & Decorating Retailers Association Show in St. Louis. Since this was the fiftieth anniversary, I expected a couple of the big paint companies to use the event to introduce something spectacular. They didn't.

However, there were, some nifty, little improvements that will soon be coming your way. Here are the top ten:

1. Finally, someone has discovered that wood skirted portable spas need help. Superdeck's (800-825-5382) new Spa Saver Care Kit includes everything you need to care for wood that has been damaged by sun, rain, or spa chemicals. The kit includes Superdeck Exterior Transparent Stain, Deckdocktor Tannin Stain Remover and Wood Brightener, as well as brushes, sanding pads, complete step-by-step directions, a small matching can of stain for touch ups later, even a stirring stick. Way to go guys.

2. If you've ever tried to patch a ceiling painted with rough textured acoustic paint, you know that it is just about impossible. Now, Spray Tex (800-234-5979) has introduced a Popcorn Ceiling Patch in a spray can that makes matching much easier.

3. It has always been difficult to caulk around tiles and bath tubs. Sure, do-it-yourselfers can use those cheap little caulk shapers, but the shapers don't do well around corners. The Vancouver Tool Corp. (604-255-6953) has just introduced the Caulk-Rite tool with a soft, pliable tip. The pliable tip gives you perfect control even when caulking around an oval or a 90-degree angle.

4, 5, and 6. Sasco Products, Inc. of Novi made as close to a home run as any company at the show. They introduced three great little products – the Invisible Corner Guard, "Wet Paint" Brush & Roller Bags, and the Invisible Wire Fastener.

Ending wallpaper at a corner has always been a nightmare. The wallpaper edge is an open invitation to peel or tear. The only solution has been clear plastic corner protectors which often come off and don't look very good. Sasco's Invisible Corner Guard consists of self-adhesive, clear vinyl film which folds around the corner and is as invisible as 3M patching tape.

Sasco's Wet Paint Brush & Roller Bags are an absolute no-brainer that you look at and say, "Why didn't I think of that." Unfortunately, you didn't. They did. The package consists of little draw string clear plastic bags, just big enough to fit a paint brush or paint roller. When you are in the middle of painting and want to quit for a few minutes, or even a few days, you simply plop your wet brush or roller into the appropriate bag, pull the drawstring tight, and you're done for the day. It works. The wet paint brush they sent me has been sealed for a week and is as pliable as ever.

Our homes are increasingly dominated by electronics. We string wires everywhere for speakers, computers, TV sets, and soon Christmas Tree Lights. They all look messy and disorganized. Sasco's self-adhesive, clear plastic Invisible Wire Fasteners can make the tangled mess a thing of the past. Just string the wire, wrap a fastener around it, and stick it to the wall.

7. Anyone who has ever tried to roll a matching color on two adjoining walls will bless the Nordmark Group (956-423-9556) for introducing the Nap Cap Corner Painter.

The Nap Cap is a frizzy little wheel cover that snaps into the end of a standard size paint roller and paints a 1-1/2-inch wide strip on the adjoining wall at the same time you roll the last panel on the first wall. No splatters. No scraping. No brush marks. It's perfect.

8. What do you do if you've got a nice, big picture window overlooking a junk heap in the neighbor's back yard? Or perhaps you've got sliding glass door walls in a room you want to decorate formally? Maybe you just want to do something really neat with the glass in your front storm door? Etch Art Inc.'s Wallpaper for Windows to the rescue.

Etch Art (800-320-8439), is a thin, clear plastic in an etched glass design, that makes windows look like etched glass. It can be installed on any non-porous surface. Once installed, it cleans easily with soap and water, and can be removed and re-installed any time you want. Call for a catalog.

9 and 10. The Metabo Corporation of West Chester, Pa., (800-638-2264) is introducing two unusual, heavy-duty power tools. Although the tools were designed for the professional or tool rental companies, they are so special I had to tell you about them. The Metabo 6.4 amp Paint Remover is a mechanical stripper that cuts away paint and varnish from flat wood surfaces.

If you ever buy that 100-year old farm house that has about 50 coats of paint on the floors and stairs and cabinets, this tool could be a life-saver. It does the job about 70 percent faster than conventional methods.

The Metabo 3.8 amp Electronic Variable Speed Random Orbital Disc Sander is a two-orbit sander. You use the large orbit for heavy stripping, the small orbit for smooth, finish work.

NOVEMBER 15, 1997

Got an extra bedroom? Sleep on all the choices before you remodel

by America's Master Handyman,
Glenn Haege

Don't tell anyone, but as we grow older, our homes go through change of life, too. It used to be that when the kids left, their bedrooms became miniature shrines to what had been. Son John could come back to his room ten years later and find it just like he left it, only cleaner.

Today's big question is, "do I have to wait 'til the kid graduates, or can I change the room as soon as he or she leaves for college?"

Extra bedrooms can be heaven sent. Suddenly you have the room for the home office, computer room or study you need to get organized, get informed, or get on with your life. You might also feel the need for a sitting room to get away from it all; an exercise room to help you get in shape; a hobby room or a home theater just for the joy of it.

A word of caution. The room has to fit the use, or you are just kidding yourself. If the room and the size match, great, but usually there are modifications that have to be made before the magic can happen.

Sitting rooms are easy. All you need is paint and wallpaper. New carpeting would be nice, but not really necessary. Comfy furniture and a couple of floor or table lamps and you have your own private world.

Now, let's get to the tough stuff. A too-small bedroom does not a home office make. It could be a cozy study or maybe a computer room, but a business-related home office needs all the space necessary for you to function effectively.

If you don't have the space you need for lots of filing cases, book cases, supply storage, your desk, credenza, table and at least a couple of chairs, forget it or locate the office in some other part of the house. If your office is going to be computer driven, you need more space for the computer, printer, scanner, and fax machine.

Sure, you can have the fax and phone-answering machine in your computer or a combination fax/scanner/printer, but I only recommend these machines for severely limited spaces. Before you buy a multipurpose machine, remember how helpless you feel when the printer or fax breaks down. A combo machine makes it three times as likely that that all important proposal will not be printed, or the emergency fax will not be sent.

How about electrical? A home office cannot run on the shared circuit allocated to most bedrooms. It should have at least two dedicated circuits. The computer needs one circuit. The rest of the office equipment takes the other circuit. It's also important to remember the dedicated computer circuit even if you are just creating a computer room. Big computers are delicate and take a lot of power. So do big printers. The temporary brown-out that can occur when some other family member turns on a hair blower, microwave, or clothes dryer, is enough to knock out your expensive equipment.

While your electrician is adding circuits and surge protectors, make certain that he also upgrades the lighting. You will be spending long hours in this room, you need enough lumin power to eliminate eye strain.

That's enough work for one day. Let's have some fun and install a home theater.

I continuously upgrade the home theater and surround sound system in my family room. It is my favorite room in the house. Many other people turn there seldom-if-ever used living rooms into home theaters.

Whichever room you choose, it should be large enough for proper acoustical dynamics and provide a sufficient distance between you and the big screen TV for proper viewing.

Sound travels in all different directions. Isolating the sound to the home theater room is very important. If you don't deaden the sound, that jet fighter taking off the carrier won't just make you feel like you are standing on the flight deck, it will rattle the crystal in the dining room, and scare the day lights out of some poor soul taking a cat nap in the rear bedroom.

Al Stewart of Audio Video Technologies, (248) 853-2170, says that the best way to tackle the problem is by installing insulation with a sound transfer co-efficient (STC) rating in all interior walls and the ceiling. The floor underneath the carpet should also be isolated using Homasote 440 Boards, (800) 257-9491, nailed or glued into place.

Some new wiring will be necessary. One word of advice. An electrician is not necessarily a sound technician. Make certain the person stringing your wires knows the requirements. Don't just install the basic minimum, and don't go cheap. You probably won't be able to buy everything you want right now, but you can make certain the wiring is ready when your wallet is.

Speakers should be elevated so that they are not sitting behind chairs or plants that can muffle their sound. They don't have to be big. Bookcase speakers have come a long way and now give a big-quality sound while taking up very little space.

Now get some popcorn, grab the remote, lean back in the old easy chair, and let your spirits soar. Brag about it!

NOVEMBER 22, 1997

Fireplace users warming up to energy-efficient, vent-free gas logs

by America's Master Handyman, Glenn Haege

A few evenings ago, the Catalog Queen of Macomb County (my lovely wife, Barb) noticed that it was snowing and opined that it would be nice to have a fire. It only took me about two seconds to get out of my chair, step over to the fireplace, and turn on the fire.

If I wasn't the athletic type, I could have just picked up the remote from my Lazy-Z-Boy and accomplished the same thing in even less time.

A wood-burning purist will say that Barb and I don't have the real thing. I agree. Although the manufacturers of gas logs have made fantastic strides, nothing can surpass the constantly changing shapes and colors of a real wood fire. Gas logs come in second, but are more in accord with our busy life style.

At the same time, I am happy to report that wood-burning fireplaces are regaining their popularity. Al King, owner of Atlas Veneers and Fireplaces, reports that his wood burning fireplace business is up 25 percent over last year. Larry Jonas, Sales Manager of Williams Panel Brick and Fireplace, says that their wood burning business is more than holding its own.

I have gotten so much good information on wood-burning fireplaces recently, that I will write an article on the subject soon. Unfortunately, I don't have space for it here.

Many, people already have a hole in the wall they call a fireplace. They don't use it very often because it's too much of a hassle. It doesn't have to be that way. The purpose of this article is to show you two good alternatives.

There are two types of fireplaces: heat wasters and heat makers. Most conventional wood-burning fireplaces and fireplaces with gas logs are heat wasters. They look good while burning and throw a little bit of heat, but waste energy big time.

There are three reasons for the energy loss.

■ They burn so inefficiently that almost 75 percent of their potential BTUs (British Thermal Units) of heating energy go up the chimney.

■ This creates a true "chimney effect" sucking much of the heat out of the house and causing the furnace to turn on.

■ In the case of a wood fire, after the burn is complete, the chimney flue must remain open until all the embers have burned out. This means that the flue often stays open all night and the heat continues to go up the chimney.

Because conventional gas logs have pilot lights, building regulations mandate that chimney flues have clips installed that keep flues open one inch at all times. This keeps gas from being trapped, but also means that heated air is continuously lost up the chimney.

These heat users can be turned into heat producers by installing vent-free gas logs or 0 clearance, direct-vent fireplace inserts. Vent-free gas logs are 99.9 percent energy efficient. When used in an existing fireplace they do not need to be vented and can be operated with the flue damper opened or closed. In the fall, you might choose to have the vent open, so that you have the beauty of the fire, but most of the heat went outside. In the winter, you could have the flue closed so that all the heat stayed inside. All vent-free logs and chimneys have Oxygen Depletion Sensors and will turn off automatically if there a fuel interruption of a change in air quality.

Two of the companies that manufacture vent free gas logs are FMI (Fireplace Manufacturers Inc., (800) 888-2050, and TEMCO Manufacturing (800) 753-7736. If you do not have an existing fireplace, but like the concept, these manufacturers also make vent free gas fireplaces.

Al King's favorite way to turn a conventional fireplace into a heat producer, is to install a 0 clearance, direct vent, gas fireplace insert. This makes the fireplace 70 to 80 percent efficient. Cool air is drawn off the floor, heated and recirculated; but the fire is sealed within the firebox and combustion air comes from outside.

The same companies that make 0 clearance inserts, also make direct vent fireplaces that make it relatively easy and economical to install a fireplace in any room. Some of the major manufacturers are Hunter, (888) 823-4328; FMI; Heatilator, (800) 843-2848; Heat & Glo, (800) 669-4328; Majestic, (800) 842-2058; Napoleon, (800) 461-5581; and Temco Manufacturing, (800) 753-7736.

An impressive side benefit of most gas logs and fireplaces is that, unlike central heating, they will continue to function when the electric power goes out. This means that, in an emergency, they could keep your house warm enough to keep the pipes from freezing and be a real life saver if there is an invalid in the house.

If you want to take a look at these logs and fireplaces, Williams Panel Brick, (800) 538-6650, in Detroit, is the largest Heatilator dealer in Michigan. They also carry the Temco and Peterson lines of gas logs and fireplaces. Fireplace and Spa, (810) 726-7100, are major Heat & Glo and Temco dealers and have stores in Livonia, Utica, Canton and Southfield. Atlas Veneers and Fireplaces, (248) 524-1020, in Troy, has the widest collection of fireplaces, logs and free-standing gas stoves that I have seen anywhere. They have 32 burning units and 48 assembled fireplaces and stoves on display.

Winter's coming. Time to get cozy.

NOVEMBER 29, 1997

Wood fans get all fired up about new and efficient fireplaces

by America's Master Handyman, Glenn Haege

I heard so much from the wood burning contingent after last week's article on gas fireplaces and logs, that I decided to do the wood-burner article right away. If you would like even more information than is contained in these two articles and you are on the internet, the Hearth Products Association answers 500 of the most commonly asked questions and has hot links to many of the major manufacturers at www.hearth.com.

No one can duplicate the sight, sound, and smell of a wood fire. The problem with conventional masonry wood burners is that they don't give much heat, are a lot of work, and make a mess. When the fire is over the ashes have to be cleaned out and there is always the worry about creosote build-up in the chimney.

After all the work, 80 percent to 100 percent of the heat goes up and out the chimney with a conventional wood burning fireplace. You may have made the birds on your roof happy, but did next to nothing to heat your house. In fact, the chimney effect of the fireplace draws heat from the rest of the house and causes the furnace to work harder and burn about a third more fuel. Then, while the fire is burning down, and the embers are slowly dying, the open chimney flue keeps letting more and more heat out. In a worst case scenario, if your house is negative, cold air can actually be sucked into the house filling it with cold air that has a musty, burnt wood smell.

The good news is that it doesn't have to be this way. Modern wood burning fireplaces and fireplace inserts – by companies like the FMI, (800) 888-2050; Travis, (425) 827-9505, which makes Lopi, Avalon and Fireplace Xtrordinair; Fuego, (800) 445-1867; Heatilator, (800) 843-2848; Heat & Glo, (800) 669-4328; Hunter, (888) 823-4328; and Napoleon, (800) 461-5581 – are far more efficient.

These fireplaces can be real heat producers. As an example, the Fuego Flame uses only one third the wood, provides up to 50,000 BTU's per hour of heat, and returns up to 250 cubic feet per minute of heat through its built-in natural convection blower system. It's flue is closed up to 95 percent, so little or no heat is lost up the chimney. The big Fireplace Xtrordinair can heat up to 3,000 square feet and has an output of up to 75,700 BTU's per hour.

The difference between a conventional fireplace and a modern fireplace like the Fuego Flame is that air flow is controlled to provide ultimate burning conditions. Only a limited amount of air is admitted into the firebox for burning. The fire in a conventional fireplace burns at a relatively cool 500 degrees Fahrenheit. In the Fuego, the fire burns at about 900 degrees or more. This creates a phenomena called secondary burn. The volatile gases which, in a conventional fireplace, go up the chimney as black or gray smoke to form creosote and pollution, are burned inside the fire box in the Fuego. This means that the fireplace creates three times the heat, and little or no smoke or pollution.

Additional quantities of room air are drawn in under the firebox, heated behind the firebox, then re-circulated into the room through vents at the top of the fireplace. This air gets warmed by the fire, but never enters the combustion chamber.

In addition to fireplaces, there are also wood stoves by manufacturers like Travis, FMI, Napoleon, HearthStone (800) 827-8683, Jotul (207) 797-5912 Lopi and Waterford. Most also create fireplace inserts.

You can pick a wood stove to fit your decorating scheme. Waterford and Jotul have very traditional looks. Waterford also makes wood-burning cook stoves. Avalon and Lopi have a more streamlined look. HearthStone stoves are made with a combination of metal and soap stone or granite. The stone not only looks beautiful, it absorbs heat, then releases it gently.

The type of wood you burn is just as important as the type of fireplace. Atlas Veneers & Fireplaces gives away free wood comparison charts. A full cord of dry Shagbark Hickory provides 24,600,000 BTUs of heat energy. That's the equivalent over a ton of anthracite coal, 251 gallons of fuel oil or 30,800 cubic feet of natural gas. Other good burning woods are Apple, rated at 23,877,000 BTUs; White Oak, 22,7000,000 BTUs; and Maple, 21,300,000 BTUs. All of these woods have very good heating value and gives off very few sparks, but are fairly tough to split. Al King, the owner of Atlas, recommends buying a mixture of seasoned fruit and hardwoods.

Soft wood such as Aspen and White Pine are only about half as effective as heat producers. They provide between 12, 000, 000 and 12,500,000 BTUs, and are only the equivalent of about half ton of anthracite coal, 125 gallons of fuel oil, and 15,000 cubic feet of natural gas. Although very easy to split, they are considered to be fast burners and poor heat providers, and they give off lots of sparks.

You can find wood-burning fireplaces at most of the places you'd look for gas burners. Two of the best places to see a really broad selection of both wood-burning fireplaces and stoves are Atlas Veneers and Fireplaces (248) 524-1020 in Troy and Emmett's Energy (248) 674-3828 in Romeo and Waterford.

Clean up your act – and 'most everything else – for Christmas

by America's Master Handyman,
Glenn Haege

I'm not going to try to tell you who to invite or what to make for your party, but I thought a checklist of some of the basics might come in handy. First, the work savers:

If you have silver, chrome or copper, Siege Chemical, (602) 265-3200, makes a special Power Cleaner for each surface.

Soap scum can be cleaned off shower walls with The Works Tub and Tile Cleaner by Lime-O-Sol, (800) 448-5281. You'll find it at most good hardware stores and super markets.

If the kitchen counters are looking dull, try Counter Top Polishes by Hope's, (800) 325-4026, or Parker & Bailey, (888) 727-6547. Both will put the dazzle back into laminate or solid counter tops.

If the outside windows look dirty and its too cold to use your conventional window cleaner, use automobile windshield washer fluid straight from the container. Apply the undiluted cleaner with a sponge. Squeegee off, then wipe up the drips with a towel.

You can get inside windows and mirrors brilliantly clean with a mixture of 4 ounces if liquid household ammonia, and one teaspoon of liquid hand dishwashing soap, in a gallon of warm water. Use the squeegee just like outside.

If someone spills some wine, soup, pop, or whatever, don't scream, faint, or even bite your lip, just make sure that you have my emergency spill kit on hand. One bottle of club soda, one can foam-style shaving cream, and one or two boxes of bargain white facial tissue. Always blot up spills with facial tissue.

When the spill happens, apply about an inch thick wad of tissue to the spill and press down gently. Replace the tissue as it gets filled, and keep increasing the pressure until all the moisture is absorbed.

If the spill was on the carpet, you may want to stand on the last few wads of facial tissue so that all the moisture is pressed out of the padding.

Should any stain remain, sprinkle some club soda on the stained area and let it foam away the stain, then repeat the facial tissue steps and absorb the stain away. If any residue remains, repeat the procedure.

If the spill turns out to be baked beans, or ravioli and meat sauce on your new oyster-hued carpet, no problem. Just pick up the solid with facial tissue. When the bulk is gone, spray enough shaving foam to cover the soiled area. Gently work the foam into the carpet fibers. Let stand for a minute or two, then take two or three sheets of facial tissue, lift the foam out of the fibers. Don't wipe, use a grasping motion. Repeat as needed. When the stain has been removed, you can get rid of the last of the shaving foam by sprinkling with club soda and whip up with tissue.

Really bad stains, like cranberry or Kool-Aid, can usually be cleaned with Motsenbocker's Lift Off #1 Food, Beverage & Protein Stain Remover, (800) 346-1633. You can find it at Aco, Damman and most good hardware stores and home centers.

Now the scoop on snow.

You will want to have the sidewalks free from ice and snow. Not all ice melters are created equal. When it is relatively warm, above 20 degrees Fahrenheit, a salt based product, like rock salt, Halite, Morton Safe-T-Salt or the new Snow and Ice Melting Crystals by Gibraltar can be used. The Gibraltar Melting Crystals, (800) 442-7258, are new this year. They are very competitively priced and do a better ice melting job than plain rock salt.

When the temperature drops below 20 degrees Fahrenheit, salt is no longer effective and a calcium chloride product, like Gibraltar DuoFlake, should be used.

Remember, ice melters are just meant to break the bond between the walking surface and the ice or packed snow. You still have to shovel.

Finally a few tips on the interior comfort level at your party.

On the day or night of the party, dial the furnace down and the water heater up. All the cooking you are doing and all the extra people that are coming into the house add heat and moisture. Every person adds about 700 British Thermal Units (BTUs) of heat. Twenty people equal an additional 14,000 BTUs per hour. That is a lot of hot air, so dial the thermostat down before the guests arrive.

Those guests will also be using extra hot water. If you usually have the water heater turned to the economy setting, dial up to meet the added demand for the party. While you're downstairs, make sure the power humidifier is set correctly for the outside temperature.

If the temperature is 40 degrees or above, the humidity should be set at 45 percent. Between 30 and 39, 40 percent; 20 to 29, 35 percent; 10 to 19, 30 percent; 0 to 9, 25 percent; -1 to -10, 20 percent. Any humidity above these settings will cause water and/or ice to form on the inside of the windows.

Now you can have a great party you can brag about.

Temperature/Humidity Chart	
If the outside temperature is:	The humidistat should be set at:
Above 40 degrees	45%
Between 30 & 39	40%
Between 20 & 29	35%
Between 10 & 19	30%
Between 0 & 9	25%
Between -1 & -10	20%

Guess what area do-it-yourselfers are getting for the holidays?

by America's Master Handyman,
Glenn Haege

Let's face it. Buying presents for the do-it-yourselfer can be tough. He/she already has boxes and boxes of those little tools and things, and the hardware stores and home centers are filled to bursting with all sorts of other manual, electric and gas driven "things." How are you supposed to know what the D-I-Yer on your list needs or wants?

You are not alone. Even the spouses of intrepid D-I-Yers like Bill Damman, Mark Champion and Mike Clark of radio's *Drew & Mike Show* have thrown in the sponge.

Debbie Damman, wife of Bill Damman of Damman Hardware fame, says she sticks to "cookies, brightly colored ties and anything golf related."

Mark Champion and his wife, Wendy, decided to forgo exchanging personal gifts this year and sponsor a less fortunate family's Christmas instead. It sounds like something a lot more of us should do.

I know that Drew and Mike, the top-flying morning drive radio team on WRIF-FM, are do-it-yourselfers, because they talk about me and call me with personal "How To" questions all the time. When it comes to Christmas, however, Mike Clark won't have so much as a monkey wrench in his stocking. His wife,

Patricia, has learned from long experience to "avoid anything that requires assembly. Mike's no handyman!" Sorry, Mike. Maybe next year.

Here's what some of Detroit's other notables are getting their handy spouses this year.

■ Geoffrey Feiger will probably get more tools that he was looking for. His wife, Keenie, says that since they have just purchased a new home in Anguilla in the Caribbean, she will get him something he can use down there.

■ Elisabeth Barrett, the new bride of WXYT-AM talk show host Jimmy Barrett, is planning on getting him something to keep warm this winter.

■ Jennifer Wendland, the wife of WDIV-TV and WXYT-AM *PC Talk Show* host Mike Wendland, says she thinks he spends too much time sitting in front of a computer, so she's going to give him a treadmill to get some exercise. I could have told her that all she needs is a "honey do" list to provide all the exercise a man can stand.

If you're still looking for ideas, think about giving a gift certificate to a hardware store or home center. A handy person with a gift certificate is like a kid in a candy store.

The best solution of all could be the gift of knowledge. Leading the pack are three magazines: Fine Homebuilding by Taunton Press, Old-House Journal and the Family Handyman by Readers Digest.

Each issue of Fine Homebuilding is filled with informative photos and in-depth articles on building and remodeling using the best materials and finest craftsmanship. When you read the magazine, you learn not just what you need to get by, but what you need to do to make the job the best it can be.

That kind of editorial attracts advertising for many of the best and most unique products and services. The magazine is published seven times a year. A year's subscription costs $29. Call (800) 888-8286.

Old-House Journal is like a Fine Homebuilding for old homes. The articles and advertising are all directly for the heritage home market. If that describes your D-I-Yer, you couldn't find a better gift. The magazine comes out quarterly and is priced at $4.95 an issue, or $27 for a year. Call (800) 234-3797.

Family Handyman, the last magazine on my "must have" list, shows a more down-to-earth side of the building process. Quality, yes, but real-world solutions that everyone, not just Mr. and Mrs. Megabucks, can afford. This magazine is clearly illustrated, gives step-by-step instruction and state-of-the-art answers. It costs $2.95 per issue, or $17.97 for 10 issues. Call (800) 285-4961.

If magazines are too impersonal, but you still like giving information, how about making it up close and personal? Many specialized stores teach classes. If your significant other would like to get into wall papering or faux finishing, there is a good chance that, with a little digging, you could sign that person up for classes at a store near you.

Woodworking stores also teach classes but are a little harder to find. If your do-it-yourselfer would like to think about becoming a carver, the Wood Crafters Store, (810) 268-1919, has a class starting Jan. 3, in which participants will make a carving knife, then go on to create their own Scandinavian wood carving. Your significant other gets the knife, the carving, and the class for only $95. What a very sweet deal.

The store also has upcoming classes on setting up a wood shop, furniture refinishing, basic router techniques, wood burning a relief carving, even checkering and carving wood gun stocks. Great classes, fine-tuned to your do-it-yourselfer's exact interest.

What more could anyone want for Christmas? Happy shopping.

DECEMBER 20, 1997

It takes very little money to protect your home from burglaries

by America's Master Handyman,
Glenn Haege

Christmas time is a wonderful time of year. Many of us are away from home more than usual. We're shopping, going to parties, visiting relatives or taking a well-earned Christmas vacation. Unfortunately, not everyone is thinking about chestnuts roasting by an open fire. December is the second most popular month for forcible entry. It's not usually that jolly old elf bounding down the chimney with a bag full of toys. It is far more likely to be the neighborhood vandal kicking in your door to grab whatever looks valuable.

Police forces around the country report that there's a burglary once every 10 seconds in the United States. If we just consider reported burglaries, this means that about one in 15 homes are burglarized annually. Many in the police and insurance fields believe this number is vastly under reported, and that the actual figure should be about one in four.

Up to 42 percent of all break-ins are through unlocked doors or windows. Residential and commercial burglaries are entirely different types of crime. Commercial jobs are usually well-coordinated, the thieves leave with a great deal of value, and they take place at night. The average residential burglar doesn't stay long, probably less than 10 minutes. The "take" is under $1,000, and the burglary usually is accomplished during weekday, daylight hours.

The residential burglar usually is not a pro, and he or she is definitely not old. In 1986, the most recent year for which I have statistics, 49.8 percent of burglary arrests were of people 19 years old or younger; and 34.8 percent involved people in their 20s. Only 15.4 percent of burglary arrests were for people 30 or older.

So what do we do-it-yourselfers do to the handle the situation? According to Kevin Jamison, a district manager for Ademco, the word's leading manufacturer of security devices, there are four tiers of home security devices: No cost, low cost, moderate cost and substantial investment. He recommends that you start with no-cost or low-cost security devices and progress to higher levels as your situation dictates. We'll cover no cost and low cost today, then cover moderate and substantial cost devices in the new year.

No cost

The simple way to cut burglaries by almost 50 percent is to lock your windows and doors, trim the shrubs, put ladders inside the house and stop hiding a key under the mat. The first choice of burglars is to walk through an unlocked, preferably a back or side, door. When we say lock doors, we mean all doors, including garages, patios, and breezeways.

The burglar's second choice is a convenient, ground-level window. They especially like windows that are hidden by trees or shrubs so that no one can see them going in. If you don't like uninvited guests, trim back the shrubs. Remember that an unattended ladder is an open invitation for someone to climb into an unlocked second-story window. Stop hiding a key outside. If you can find the key, the burglar probably can also. If you must have a spare key, leave it with a trusted neighbor.

If you're going away for any period of time, don't talk about the fact all over town. Don't change your answering machine message to say you'll be away for a while. That's like advertising for a burglar. Make sure that you have canceled the newspaper and made arrangements with a friendly neighbor to pick up the mail and cut the grass or shovel the snow.

Low cost

Upgrade locks on doors and windows. Cylindrical, key-in-knob locks are easy to force open by even an amateur burglar. Doors should have deadbolt locks with a minimum 1-1/2-inch bolt. Make sure that all windows, especially on the ground floor, have good, secure locks, not just the skimpy variety installed by most window manufacturers. Sash locks on double hung windows, which use a nail or screw through the top of the bottom window into the bottom of the upper window frame, can prevent the window from being forced. All sliding and track windows and doors should have broom handles or bars in the track that will prevent opening even if the rather fragile lock is broken.

I'd like to take the final paragraph to wish you all a Happy Hanukkah and a Merry Christmas. Enjoy the season, but don't overstress the wiring and never leave Christmas lights on unattended or with children or pets. I'll be running my annual Glenn Haege's Phone Book the next two weeks, so if you are going to be away, make certain someone saves those articles for you.

Chapter 4

1998 Articles reprinted from The Detroit News HOMESTYLE

A little TLC and WD-40 will keep garage door going this winter

by America's Master Handyman,
Glenn Haege

Winter is the toughest season of them all. And this is as true for garages and garage doors as it is for people.

If you have a garage that is not connected to the house, you may not care how cold it gets in there as long as it keeps the snow and ice off the car. However, many of us have attached garages that have to be heated occasionally with portable electric or kerosene heaters when we are engaged in a project that has to be done in the garage. Much of this heat is wasted because it goes straight up and out the roof.

The best way to stop that heat loss is to attach drywall directly to the garage rafters to create a ceiling. Then, insulate the ceiling with 12 inches of rolled insulation (R-38), and put a minimum of three pot vents on the roof to allow trapped heat to escape and keep the shingles from cooking and curling during the summer.

The next decision is whether to have an insulated garage door. The rule of thumb is that if your garage is drywalled, attached to the house, or used for any type of work during the winter, an insulated garage door is a good value.

Garage doors are operated either manually or with an attached garage door opener. Garage door openers are worth-while because they make life more convenient and provide a lot of added security for a small investment. Many different makes and models of garage door openers are available at Sears and most hardware and home centers or specialized door stores. Specialized stores often have a larger selection and more knowledgeable sales people.

You can install garage doors and door openers yourself, or have them installed by professionals. Making sure that the garage door opener is attached and balanced properly is an art. Most manufacturers, like Stanley and Lift-Master, give longer warranties to professionally installed garage door openers.

Two of the broadest selections of garage door and door openers in Metro Detroit are Home and Door Products, (248) 399-3667, Coolidge and 11 Mile in Berkley, and Tarnow Doors, (800) 466-9060, at 23701 Halsted Rd. in Farmington Hills. Both service all of southeast Michigan.

The biggest problem with garage doors and door openers is that they are prone to break down during winter. This often means being late for work and dislocating the family budget with an expensive service call. I recently had Dione Murray, the customer service rep from Home and Door Products, on my WXYT radio show to discuss the best way to keep garage doors maintained properly.

Murray says the most common problem with most garage doors is the lack of lubrication or improper lubrication. This is what causes the door to squeak, squeal and break down during the winter.

He stresses that all lubricants are not created equal. "Thick, greasy lubricants become as sticky and hard to move as molasses in extremely cold weather. The best overall lubricant is WD-40. This penetrating oil lubricates as well as cuts through grease and grime," he says.

"There are 19 barrel hinges on most garage doors. Lubricate each with WD-40. When finished, you should be able to turn each barrel easily with your fingers."

The two torsion springs located on the door frame above the garage door also should be lubricated lightly. Tension springs do not last forever. The average work life of torsion springs is eight to 10 years. After that they break and have to be replaced. "Lubricating the springs with WD-40 eliminates much of the rubbing between the coils and extends their life," Murray says.

All folding doors have metal guide rails and either nylon, plastic or metal wheels that go up and down the rails. Nylon and plastic wheels need little or no lubrication. Metal wheels should always be lubricated. Here again, "WD-40 does a great job," Murray says. "Heavy grease can actually stop the door from functioning."

When it comes to chain, track, and tube guide poles, lubrication is different with every manufacturer. Stanley has a tube guide, which needs no lubrication. Lubrication can stop it from working.

Craftsman, Liftmaster and all garage door openers that use T-rails should be lubricated with a small amount of lithium grease.

Garage door openers like Genie, which have screw drives, should be lubricated only with the lubricant specified by the manufacturer for that specific use, or the product will break down and drop on your car, Murray says.

If the barrel hinges, track or rails have been improperly lubricated with thick, sticky grease, the old grease should be removed. Because WD-40 is a penetrating oil, the grease can be cleaned easily by spraying the area with WD-40 and wiping away the residue with paper toweling.

That's the complete garage door lubrication story from a top professional. With a little TLC and WD-40, most of us can make it through the winter without an expensive service call.

JANUARY 17, 1998

Space-age marvels come down to earth at Chicago housewares show

by America's Master Handyman,
Glenn Haege

Chicago was the center of the Housewares Universe earlier this week. All the biggies from Wal-Mart, Kmart, Target, Home Depot, True Value, Ace and Sears, plus all the specialty stores such as Williams-Sonoma, Bed Bath & Beyond, gathered Sunday through Wednesday for the National Housewares Show.

I would say the two biggest trends were:
■ the adaptation and use of high technology from our Space Program, and
■ the attempt to make products more environmentally friendly.

Here are some of the hottest products I saw at the show:

The Wells Lamont Co., (800) 323-2830, is best known for work gloves. Their representatives showed me a couple of prototype gloves that will not be out for six to 12 months. One uses NASA technology to create a glove that is so effective against cold that I was able to hold a large piece of dry ice with a temperature of -140 degrees Fahrenheit and my hand didn't even get cold. Anyone who has ever had to handle frozen pipes or ice-cold equipment on a frigid day will know what a find these new gloves will be. I also saw a protective glove for slicing and fine food preparation work that was able to withstand 4,000 slashes with a razor blade on the same spot without damage.

Another space-age product was the Clean Touch Plus, an anti-bacterial wash cloth by the Daikyo/Palt Group of Japan, (800) 797-7007. This light-blue cloth has ultra fine copper micro fibers embedded in the cotton and rayon fabric. The copper mesh disrupts the molecular balance of bacteria and destroys it, so just wiping off the kitchen counters with the cloth creates a germ-free environment. The Clean Touch Plus cloths should start showing up in stores around April. Each cloth will cost between $14 and $19.

Another new high-tech product was Un-Du by Doumar Products, (888) BUY-UNDU. This product comes in a little 1-ounce clear plastic bottle with a scraper attachment. It safely removes labels, stickers, tapes or anything that is stuck to another surface with any kind of an adhesive. The demonstrations were almost magical. Un-Du does not destroy the adhesive, it releases it. So if you opened a sealed envelope, the flap of the envelope would remain sticky, and you could use the envelope again. This product should retail for $4.99 and will be carried in stores such as Office Max.

Perhaps the most innovative product at the show was a totally nonelectric, water-powered waste disposal made by Hydro Maid, (888) 82-HYDRO. No electrical hook-up is required. All parts, instructions and an installation video are shipped with the product. The Hydro Maid disposal is presently sold direct and costs about $299.

Since I brought you down to the garbage disposer with the last item, we might as well clean it. Who has not wanted to clean their garbage disposer? The trouble is, whatever you pour down into it, just goes down and does not clean the entire upper portion of the disposer. Scot's Tuff by Scot Laboratories, (800) 486-7268, solves the problem. The product will come in mousse form. Just shake it up and spray. When it reaches the top, your work is done. The rest of the job is done by the mousse. It will not attack rubber or plastic and is environmentally benign. Scot's Tuff has not been priced yet, but the company promises it will be in hardware stores and the big home center and supermarket chains by the time the ice melts.

Sticking with that environmentally friendly theme, Whink Products, (800) 247-5102, has introduced some great ones. Top of the list is the company's Rustguard/Protector, an environmentally friendly, toilet bowl-cleaning tablet that does not contain chlorine. Most of the toilet bowl products you see advertised have a high chlorine content that adversely affects rubber flapper balls. This product works like a charm.

Whink is famous for its Rust Remover. Now it has introduced a Rust and Lime Remover in gel form. It hangs on to be really effective on vertical surfaces.

Hardwood floors are highly popular, but wood and water don't mix. Quickie Manufacturing Corp., (800) 257-5751, will roll out the Home Pro Dust & Shine, a complete wood-cleaning kit, in the middle of April.

One true handyman item you have to know about is the Hang 'n Carry pegboard system by Zag Industries, (800) 283-8959. The pegboard looks like an ordinary pegboard, but when you want a bunch of tools for a job at the other end of the house, you just take the pegboard off the wall, fold it up, and take it with you. When finished, just hang it back up. You stay organized all the time.

Since the last product was almost "all boy," I want to finish off with a product that is most assuredly almost "all girl." Painted Potties, (888) 767-0404, are toilet bowl decals that are easy to apply. Hey, don't laugh. These decals have water-resistant adhesive. They can give everything in your bathroom – sink, commode, waste basket, soap dish, everything – a hand-painted look. I can definitely guarantee your commode will be the talk of the neighborhood.

JANUARY 24, 1998

Builders' Show offers the latest in technological comforts of home

by America's Master Handyman, Glenn Haege

I go to a lot of industry shows. The National Hardware Show, the Housewares Show, the Paint Show and so on. But I haven't been to the big one, the International Builders' Show, put on by the National Association of Home Builders, for several years. That's why I was delighted to broadcast my radio show from the convention floor this past weekend, Jan. 17 and 18.

An army of 2,000 workers was needed to erect the displays of more than 1,000 exhibitors in the eight days leading up to the show. The exhibits covered 499,000 square feet of exhibit space (slightly less than Cobo Center).

More than 150 buses were used to shuttle attendees to and from the various demonstration sites, where houses, up to the 4,573-square-foot Home of the Future (see the story on Page 18D), showcased the most advanced architectural design and construction techniques.

There were 170 educational programs on subjects ranging from sales techniques, the economy and the environment, to housing for seniors, design and construction technology. The Honorable Margaret Thatcher gave the keynote address, and more than 15,000 movers and shakers attended the opening ceremonies.

If you tried to reach your builder last weekend and couldn't, there was a good reason. More than 65,000 people attended the four-day event. John Bollan of Bollan Building in Bloomfield Hills, the chairman of the Michigan NAHB show committee, told me that approximately 600 Michigan builders were registered for the show.

Size aside, if anyone asked me to tell the difference between the NAHB show and other industry events, I would say it was the quality of the people. At the other shows, it is often hard to find someone willing to talk to you who knows enough about the products to explain them to you. At the NAHB show, every man and woman staffing the displays was a seasoned professional. They not only knew what they were talking about, they were anxious to tell you. Quite often, they were senior company staff who could give straight-from-the-shoulder answers to every possible question.

As a born and bred Michiganian, I am proud to say that for sheer size, scope and people, the most impressive display was the 30,000 square feet inhabited by the Masco Corp. and a selection of its operating companies. I could easily write a month's worth of articles on the beautiful furniture, fixtures and appliances they displayed. Suffice it to say, a little grade school arithmetic tells me that their display took almost 1/16th of the total exhibit space. Most Metro Detroiters do not realize that this company, based in Taylor, is truly one of the giants of the building and home improvement industry.

All very impressive. But what did I see at the show that was truly innovative? Here are a few of the items; keep in mind that each of these items is a category killer worthy of an article all its own.

■ Weiser Lock, (800) 677-5625, introduced the Powerbolt 3,000, a remote, keyless entry system that works like a car door opener to unlock a house's doors and turn on the lights. With this system, you never have to fiddle around with your keys or worry about entering a dark house.

■ Continuing the high-tech theme, three companies, Mod-Tap RCS, (800) 779-6770; Lucent Technologies, (800) 344-0223, ext. 8001; and AMP Building Systems, (800) 321-2343; introduced different versions of a revolutionary home wiring system. The system uses a low-voltage cable, much like the heavy wire used to hook up a cable TV, to manage the home's power needs and make any room instantly upgradable to any future communication or power need.

■ Mod-Tap calls its system the Mod-Tap Cabling System. Lucent Technologies, the Bell Labs Innovations People, call theirs the HomeStar Wiring System. AMP calls theirs OnQ. Although primarily for new construction, the cables also can be installed in existing homes. If you are really into home theater, heavy cable TV, computer, Internet or other communications use, the new system could solve a lot of future problems.

■ If you are heavy into luxury, Jacuzzi Whirlpool Bath introduced the J-Allure, a combination whirlpool, deluxe shower and steam bath for two, complete with stereo/CD system and optional TV monitor. The ultimate in hedonistic living, the entire ensemble fits into a relatively tiny area just 52 inches long and 52 inches wide.

■ Moving from the bath to the kitchen, In-Sink-Erator introduced the Septic Disposer, a food waste disposer designed especially for Septic Systems that automatically injects superconcentrated enzymes each time the disposer is used. The enzymes instantly begin breaking down the food waste chain and greatly increase the efficiency of the septic system.

■ Therma-Tru, (800) 843-7628, introduced an exclusive finishing system for staining fiberglass doors and giving them a beautiful wood appearance.

■ SmartDeck introduced a synthetic lumber decking material made entirely from oak and recycled materials. The decking and posts look like wood and have a pleasing honey-nut color, but resist moisture, UV rays and insects, and will not rot, warp, split or splinter. Since the composite is 70 percent wood, it will gray, but company representatives say the gray can be easily removed with standard decking brighteners.

I'd love to tell you more, but there is no more room this week. The show was great. I wish you could have been there.

JANUARY 31, 1998

Michigan products were a hit at the International Builders' show

by America's Master Handyman, Glenn Haege

The National Association of Home Builders International Builders' Show is the biggest building and construction show of the year. According to Ignacio Cabrera, NAHB Vice President of Expo Sales, 21 of nearly 1,000 exhibitors were from Michigan – eight from Greater Detroit, 13 from outstate.

The five Michigan "biggies" at the show:
■ Masco Corporation of Taylor, Michigan and several of its operating companies occupied 30,000 square feet of floor space, the largest show exhibit. Two Masco Michigan based companies included in the Masco exhibit were Merillat of Adrian, the nation's largest cabinet maker, and the Alsons Corp. in Hillsdale, a maker of premium shower heads and hand showers.
■ Chevrolet displayed its trucks.
■ Ford Motor Co. had a truck exhibit, too.
■ Dow Chemical of Midland was showcasing their usual fine insulating and building wrap products.
■ Whirlpool Corporation of Benton Harbor showed – what else? – appliances.

Other Metro Detroit companies represented in Dallas were Ecopic Corporation, of Birmingham; McCoy Sauna & Steam of Novi; Detroit Radiant Products, Warren; Tapco International, Plymouth; and the ABT Co. of Troy.

Outstate companies included Acorn Window systems, Quincy; Baron's Window Coverings, Lansing; Great Lakes Insulspan, Blissfield, Laser Alignment, Grand Rapids; National Nail Corp., Grand Rapids; PrintComm, Flint; Real Brick Products, Perry; Simplex Products Division, Adrian; and Windquest Companies, Holland.

This year, builders were on a quest for quality. The new Brilliance finish products, which Alson shares with sister companies, Weiser Lock and Delta Faucets drew much interest, says Stan Speerstra, Alson marketing director. He says the finish changes brass from a beautiful but hard-to-keep-shiny surface, to one that is permanently shiny and almost scratch proof.

Larry Wilson, director of marketing services for Merillat, echoed the quality theme. "It's like people are saying, 'I'm not going to move for a while, and I want to put in what I really want, not something that is purely value-oriented.' This desire translates into greatly increased interest in the upscale Amera line of fine wood cabinets on the part of the upper echelon of new home builders," Wilson says.

This same quest for quality was reported by Windquest Vice-President Barry Walburg. "There was a great deal of interest in our laminated wood closet organizing systems, and one of the stars of the show was our wall bed with a pneumatic frame that makes the bed easy to raise and lower. When not in use, the bed looks like wall cabinets," he says. It's great for multi purpose rooms that have to do occasional duty as a guest room.

Gary Moody, general manager of McCoy Sauna & Steam, was surprised at the amount of interest in the company's new wine racking display. "Our major business is saunas, but builders were showing a lot of interest in wine racking systems for upscale homes," he says. McCoy is exhibiting at this week's Spring Home Show at the Novi Exhibition Center. You can go and see their complete line at the show.

Russ Livermore, marketing communications manager of ABT Co., said that inquiries were up about 20 percent at this year's show. Again, the focus was on quality. The biggest attention-getter was a new fiber cement siding that has an extra deep wood grain finish.

Acorn Window Systems' vice president of sales and marketing, Ralph Pfeiffer, said their new, multiple-window designs for vinyl windows caused the most excitement. The new technique makes it possible to design and build a single window that looks like a large, multiple-paned window. "This technique is stronger, easier to install, and more cost efficient, than standard multiple window treatments," he says. Pfeiffer says the consumer gets the look he wants at a cost he can afford, while the builder keeps his costs in line and gets a product that is faster and easier to install.

Solange Dubeauclard, the general manager of Ecopic Corporation, a distributor of French-made products, says the leading attraction at her display was a line of bird control devices. The devices, which consist of stainless steel rods sticking out of a plastic base, deny the use of ledges to our fair-feathered friends, but are almost invisible from ground level.

Detroit Radiant Products, a long time radiant heating specialist, introduced infrared ceiling heating tubes at the show. According to Scott Fleet, their primary residential use will be heating two- and three- car garages. The completely sealed system draws combustion air from outside and exhausts outside. This can be a life saver for hobbyists who have a wood or metal shop in the garage because the possibility of combustion of air-borne chemicals is eliminated.

The quest for quality approaches to basic construction was also apparent. Frank Baker, CEO of Great Lakes Insulspan, a leading innovator in SIPs (Structural Insulated Panels) says interest in SIPs for use in standard construction as well as modular and manufactured housing has greatly increased. The combination of higher cost and lowering of quality in traditional wood framing, have made SIP technology highly attractive to today's builders.

Steel studs must also be increasingly popular because Brian Dekkinga, marketing director for National Nail Corp., reports the fastener that received the most interest in their display was their steel stud plastic top screw which is used exclusively for attaching Styrofoam insulation to steel studs.

I've got lots more to tell you but no more room. If you want to know more, come see me. I'll be broadcasting at the Novi Home Show this weekend.

Good home security doesn't have to cost you an arm or a leg

by America's Master Handyman,
Glenn Haege

No doubt about it. A home break-in can make your life hell. Even if very little was taken and all you have to replace is a broken window, you feel violated. It's not just losing stuff, regardless of what the police say about crime statistics, you know that you and your family are no longer safe.

My article on Dec. 20, 1997, talked about no-cost and low-cost things you can do to improve your home security. That's the most important half that will stop the vast majority of home burglaries. If it is already thrown out, it is on The Detroit News web site: www.detnews.com.

Today, we are going to go over the moderate-cost category of home security. Keep in mind that investment in home security is in inverse ratio to effectiveness. That is, the no-cost and low-cost items give the majority of the protection. Moderate cost is middle of the road. This category maximizes traditional home security. The substantial-cost category is high end and involves electronics, monitoring and computers.

Moderate cost

The first thing to check is that your windows and doors are in good condition. If the door is so warped that you have to bang it shut, or really jiggle it to set the locks securely, it can no longer do the job and needs to be replaced. Same thing with windows.

All exterior doors should be solid hardwood or metal. Hardwood is the most beautiful, steel is the most secure. If you have hollow core exterior doors, replace them immediately. Doors are not cheap, but they are your first line of defense against home intruders. Your best bet is a solid hardwood or metal door, outfitted with a wide angle spy glass, so you can see anyone standing on your porch, but they cannot see in.

We're not done with the doors yet. Since the vast majority of B&Es are the "kick in the door" variety, the more you can do to make your doors kick-proof, the better.

If you invest in new doors, you will naturally have good dead bolt locks installed. With just a little added investment, you can make these doors absolutely kick-proof by adding lock and frame protectors by M.A.G. Engineering & Manufacturing Inc. The Install-A-Lock Door Reinforcer is a clip made of solid 22-gauge brass, bronze or stainless steel that fits over the door and protects and reinforces the handle and lock mechanism. Another clip, the Uni-Force Door Edge Guard, fits over the door and protects the dead bolt area. The strike plate area of the frame can be protected with a Strike 3 Strike Plate.

These clips are very attractive, but highly visible. The young tough who just wants to smash and grab will break his knee before he breaks in your door. The professional will take one look and leave for easier pickings.

Most good hardware, home centers and building supply stores carry at least a limited selection of M.A.G. security products. You can call the company direct at (800) 624-9942 to find the store nearest you.

As with all major investments, the exterior door installer is just as important as the manufacturer. If he or she doesn't want to add the extra items that give impressive additional security for very little cost, or downplays them, you may want to look for another contractor.

You don't want the best price, you want the best craftsman. Check out his references with as much detail as you would if you were buying a furnace or windows.

Windows are next

Let's start with the basement. For the most part, they are a waste. My advice is to have the traditional basement windows torn out and replaced with glass block. Glass block offers maximum security and increases the amount of light refracted into the basement. At least one window on each wall should have an air vent.

After you have upgraded the basement windows, check the rest of the house.

We all want windows to last forever. They do not. A window over 20 years old is past its prime. Many older wood windows have become so warped they do not close securely. That not only lets in drafts, it makes you easy prey for burglars. From a security point of view, this is especially important on the ground level.

Aluminum-framed sliders are no better. They were never meant to be high-security devices and have little energy efficiency. Upgrading old windows for energy-efficient new windows with good locks is a good investment. They not only increase your home security, they eventually pay for themselves in savings on heating and cooling costs.

The final moderate-cost home security area is traditional exterior lighting. I'm not talking about the high-end stuff – that will be covered in a later article. Walk around your house at night. All the major entrances to the house and garage should be lit with halogen lights. For just a little more you can get the kind with light sensors that will turn on automatically when someone passes.

These outside lights help give the impression that your home is protected and give you a feeling of security. But keep in mind that most home burglaries are during daylight hours and through the doors or windows. So if you are on a budget, upgrade the doors and windows first.

An attack plan helps gain useful info at spring building shows

by America's Master Handyman, Glenn Haege

I go to a lot of shows. It's my business. I work each show to get the maximum information in the minimum time.

Now, we're into your show season. Most of the important building shows are concentrated into two and a half months. This year, with labor so tight, if you have a major project and don't have a firm direction by the end of the show season, you may well be out of luck until next year. That means you don't have any free time – just time well spent or wasted. Here are some tips on how to work a show.

Plan your attack before you go.
Prior planning pays big dividends. Plan your attack before you go. List what you want to learn on a sheet of paper.

If you have major projects that must be done this year – windows or a furnace that needs to be replaced, a kitchen or bath upgraded, the installation of a deck or paver patio – list them. If you're interested in getting more information on something, but not yet ready to act – let's say installing a sun room, or buying a vacation site – add that to your list. If you just want to learn more about something, let's say building a log home or geothermal heating, put that down too.

On the day of the show, prioritize.
One, two, three, four. This is your action plan.

Do not mindlessly shuffle up and down the aisles collecting bags full of brochures you will never read. That's browsing (Cattle browse, not people). Get a program and plot your course. List the booths that have the information you need.

If you (1) need to replace a furnace, (2) are thinking about a paver patio, and (3) want to collect information on log houses, look up all three categories in the program. If there are five heating-and-cooling displays, you probably want to see all of them. Mark where they are on the floor plan in the program.

There may be five or six deck and paver guys and a couple of manufacturer displays. You need to see the manufacturer displays and as many of the deck and paver people as possible. One or two names will be familiar because you have seen their trucks in your area. Add them to your "must see" list.

As for items you are just vaguely interested in, put them on the bottom of your "must see" list. Mark them on the floor plan. Try to see them, coming or going, to the more essential exhibits on your list.

Now, go directly to the highest priority location. In this example it would be a heating manufacturer or large heating contractor.

Ask smart questions.

Once you get to a display, ask the person attending the booth, "What's the most technologically advanced furnace (or whatever) you have here? Why is it better? How much more economically will it operate than less advanced equipment? What's the Warranty? Is there a show special?"

If the product looks interesting, you also want to know "If I place an order in the next three weeks, when will the job be completed? What are the payment terms? If I sign up for an appointment today, when will you or a representative from your firm be out to see me?"

You also want to know "Is the owner or general manager working the show? What's his or her name? What's his direct phone number?" If the owner or manager is at the show and you are interested in the product, go over to see him. Introduce yourself. Ask him if you sign up for an appointment today, when will he or one of his representatives be out to see you?

In today's tight labor climate this type of information can put you at the head of the pack. Many show leads are never called. You not only want to be called, you want to be served. Being on a first-name basis with the boss can make the magic happen.

If you need to make any measurements or notes, take them. Collect the product literature you need and go to the next exhibit on your list.

After about ten stops you will be more informed about the products than most of the sales people in the field. You will also be tired, you feet will have begun to hurt, and your eyes will be glazed over.

Take a break at show seminars.

Here's a professional secret. Every show has seminars. Most people never go to them, but they can be life (and feet) savers. Pick a seminar about a subject that interests you that is being held in the middle of the time you have allocated for the show.

When your eyes start to get glazed and your feet hurt, go to the seminar. You will probably learn some useful information. More important, you will have spent 30 to 45 minutes sitting down. By the time the seminar is over, you will be rested.

Go back to the show, finish off the items on your "must see" list, then relax and roam around. Treat yourself to a hot dog. You've earned it.

The next day, go through the brochures. Wait a couple of days and see if the businesses you want to do estimates, call. If they don't, call them. If you don't get the response you want, contact the boss. Tell him Glenn Haege suggested you call.

Enjoy the shows!

If you're interested in windows, mark those exhibits on your home show floor plan. For information on Andersen's new Frenchwood outswing patio door, which features tempered insulating glazing, call (800) 426-4261 Ext. 2542.

Snow birds can free their Florida homes of mold and mildew

by Glenn Haege,
America's Master Handyman

Both Kathy, my editor at Master Handyman Press, and I, had the occasion to go to Florida and stay with relatives in the past month. Her mom goes for the winter. My folks moved and have made Florida their permanent home base. Both of us came back and told each other about the problems snow birds have with dampness, mold, and corrosion.

Since friends in Boca Grade tell us that March is second only to Christmas in popularity for visits to Florida and other southern climes, and the planes are already booked to full capacity on most air lines, I suspect that quite a few of you will be heading south over the next several weeks. I decided to make a listing of solutions to problems that plague folks in our southern coastal states.

If you're going, take this article with you, high tail it to a nearby hardware store, fix the problems, and be a hero. If you're not going, or have already been, send a copy of the article to all the snow birds on your list.

The biggest problem is humidity. Many days the air is so heavy with moisture it feels like you could wring it out. Alligators love high humidity and it makes the tropical plants grow. It also makes wallpaper peel, clothing smell musty, and mold and mildew grow everywhere. The mildew problem gets so bad that the owner of one of the big homes in

Sarasota, named his estate, Mildew Mansion.

Let's take the mold and mildew problem first. Mildew, mold, and musties can usually be cleared away by air movement. Closing the windows, turning up the thermostat, and keeping the fan running constantly would be a good Northern solution to the problem. Unfortunately, one of the major reasons folks go South is so that they can have their windows open in the middle of winter and feel the balmy breezes that blow in. One hour of balmy breezes can undo a whole day of closed windows and constant air movement. The Northern solution just doesn't work as well in the south.

If the problem is really bad, pull the plants, pets and people out of the house for a day and run an ozonator. You can rent them at some equipment rental places, or call Pure Air Plus and ask about those distributed by Alpine Industries, (800) 455-5247. At the end of the day you will have zapped every microbe in the place. The problem will start up again when you open the windows, but at least you'll be starting from ground zero.

In less extreme cases, you can usually get by with constant maintenance. Chlorine kills mold and mildew, but is bad for everything it touches. Clean off the mold and mildew with Mildew Stain Remover by Amazon Premium Products, (800) 832-5645.

Hang Mil Du Gas Bags II, by Star Brite Corp., (800) 327-8583, in closets, storage lockers, crawl spaces, boat galleys, and any other confined area that you can think of. The Mil Du Gas Bags will control the mold spores and does not contain Formaldehyde.

Another favorite hang-out for mold and mildew is the caulk around the tub or shower. You can clean off the mildew with Mildew Stain Remover, or try wiping with a rag soaked white vinegar. In the worst case, you may have to completely remove and replace the caulk.

Peeling wallpaper can easily be solved by reattaching the paper with a border or seam adhesive like Stan Fix or Golden Harvest Grip. You'll find one of these at any good wallpaper and paint store, or better hardware stores. Since peeling wallpaper is an open invitation for mold spores to set up housekeeping, roll back the paper and clean the wall surface and wallpaper thoroughly with Mildew Stain Remover before applying the adhesive on both the wallpaper and wall surfaces.

The final problem on our list is corrosion. Fog, coming in from the ocean, contains salt and other corrosive materials. It bathes each surface, seeking any little imperfection in the surface coat so that it may rust and degrade the materials beneath.

In this type of condition, it is very important that cars, patio furniture, or any steel or iron finish, be continuously repaired with touch up paint, or rust will develop within a short period of time. Kathy's brother-in-law from Wyoming had what looked like an excellent finish on his older four wheel drive vehicle. After two weeks in Florida, the car was pitted with minute rust spots where tiny, almost invisible, chips in the finish had exposed the bare metal to the salt laden air.

If that happens to you, clean the car's painted finish with a clear gloss polishing compound. Then follow with a good carnauba-based paste or cream wax like Mother's Carnauba Gold or Meguiars. You'll find one of these products at any good auto supply store. In a climate like Florida's it will be necessary to recoat about every 90 days.

After you've done all this, it's time to take a walk along the beach, or laze around the pool and brag about it. Have a great time. You've earned it.

PS Send oranges.

El Nino's raises cain on the coast and renovation prices in Michigan

by Glenn Haege,
America's Master Handyman

If you're having a new house or major renovation built, and start having unexpected delays, there is a good chance that the contractor will be able to throw up his hands and say, "It ain't me. El Nino did it."

When we look at the nightly news it is easy to see the devastation brought on by floods, tornadoes, and mud slides on the east and west coasts, and believe that the El Nino just effects "those other guys."

Not true. We don't live in a vacuum. The construction industry throughout the United States and the rest of North America is interrelated. When ice storms hit the east coasts of Canada and America, power and phone companies from throughout Canada and the United States scramble and send emergency crews to restring the lines and bring power and phone service. The same thing holds true when any natural disaster hits.

The companies and the personnel do a great job. But guess what? All those linemen and women were not surplus personnel. When a Michigan Lineman is stringing wire in Quebec, he isn't stringing wire in Michigan. That means Michigan schedules have to be pushed back to conform to the new reality.

The same thing holds true in a less formal way for all manner of construction crews. If they need tree trimmers in Maine and are in such short supply they are paying double time, the word gets around and soon a whole bunch of tree trimmers who aren't getting double time in Michigan, Minnesota, and New Jersey wind up going to Maine. Ditto for carpenters, plumbers, electricians, you name it.

Making the problem more severe, economists working for the National Association of Home Builders (NAHB) and others, had already projected that new home construction in 1998 would drop 4 percent from 1997's record figures because of a lack of labor.

In other words, insufficient numbers of qualified tradesmen and women are already beginning to curtail housing supply. What actually happened in the month of January, according to NAHB figures, was that single family new home starts rose 7 percent above December's record figures, further increasing the demand on labor and accentuating the problem.

Labor is not the only ingredient that is going to be in short supply. There were lumber shortages at the end of last year. Dry wall was already on allocation and no increase in dry wall production capacity is projected for the next 10 years.

Now, let's look at El Nino. When I look at a beautiful home destroyed by a mud slide or tornado, or a family's home being swept down a river in a flood, my reaction is the same as yours, "Oh those poor people."

Then the professional part of me kicks in, and I don't just see a family's hopes and dreams being washed away. If it's just a small, 2,000 square foot home, I see 13,127 board-feet of framing lumber, 6,212 square feet of sheathing, 2,325 square feet of exterior siding, 3,100 square feet of roofing material, 3,061 square feet of insulation, 6,144 square feet of dry wall, 15 windows, 13 kitchen cabinets, etc., being destroyed. And each one of these homes has to be replaced with materials that are already short supply. This means that even greater shortages will occur around the country, and, as the supply/demand spiral kicks in, prices will go up.

I don't have a solution to the shortages of labor and materials. But I think we'll all be better off if we at least know why they're happening.

Now, I'd like to take a few paragraphs and go from a problem we can't do anything about, to one we can fix easily.

Congressman Joe Knollenberg, of Michigan's 11th. District, has been trying to reverse the 1.6 gallon toilet standards included in the Energy and Conservation Act of 1992. The reason for the 1.6 gallon standard was to save water. Unfortunately many of the newly mandated toilets do not flush satisfactorily and require two or more flushes to do the job, thereby wasting, not saving, water.

Knollenberg is trying to bring back personal choice, the ability of the consumer to buy what he wants, with House Bill HR 859. I've backed him and suggested that you send me, or your congressional representatives, a piece of toilet paper with "Get the Government out of my toilet. Vote for HR 859" written on it. If you don't know your congressman's address, just send the toilet paper to me and Representative Knollenberg's office will see that your congressman gets it. Send it to Master Handyman Press, Toilets, at Master Handyman Press, Inc., PO Box 1498, Royal Oak, MI 48068-1498.

The legislation is doing well and currently has 60 co-signers, but has not yet been reported out of the Commerce Committee. Representative Knollenberg will be on my radio show on March 7 to give us a progress report.

The idea that our drinking water is safe can be hard to swallow

by Glenn Haege,
America's Master Handyman

I can remember when the water in Lake St. Clair was so clear, you'd think you could drink direct from the lake. That probably wasn't a good idea then. It certainly is not a good idea now.

Although some of us have well water, most have "city water." We feel that it is the responsibility of the water department to provide us with a constant supply of clean, fresh water. It doesn't take a rocket scientist to know that this has become an increasing challenge. Our natural water supply has become more polluted. The water supply lines are often antiquated. Many of us live in houses that are 30 or more years old, with plumbing and fixtures that are as old as the house.

The city water system treats the water with chlorine to make it safe. I know that chlorination is a life saver. But I also know that chlorine is dangerous. It was dangerous when they used it as a gas in World War I. It's dangerous when used to kill mold or mildew on decks or bathrooms. If you inhale large amounts of chlorine impregnated steam, it can also be dangerous in the shower. All danger aside, I personally don't like drinking water that smells and tastes like disinfectant.

No matter how clean water is when it leaves the treatment plant, by the time it reaches my house, it could have picked up all sorts of trace elements and contaminants. A Water Resources Education web site, called WETnet, hosted by Purdue University, lists the amount of lead leached from lead-based copper-piping solders and brass fixtures as potentially dangerous.

Add to this the dangers of waterborne bacteria, such as cryptosporidium and giardia, and volatile organic chemicals (VOCs) such as methylene chloride, benzene, and pesticides, that sometimes find their way into the drinking water supply.

Like most Americans, I am not content to just turn on the tap. I want to do something to give my family that extra ounce of security. The question is what?

There are two different types of household water purification – whole house and point of use. A whole house system treats all the water used in the house. A point of use system is a filter attached to the dispensing device. Whole house systems are the way to go for people with wells and, in special cases, for people with city water.

Most of us on city water will find point-of-use filters fit our requirements. A filter system directly connected to the kitchen sink will cover 90 percent of the family's water consumption for cooking and drinking, but would not provide any help removing the chlorine from the shower water. If you are sensitive to chlorine, you would be better off with a whole house system. I'm going to write about point of use filters for the rest of this article. Whole house systems will be covered later.

Whenever I want to know about water, I talk to Nick DiSalvio of Environmental Water Service (800-371-PURE). To DiSalvio, water treatment is not a business, it is a vocation. When I asked DiSalvio about point-of-use filters, he said that there were two types: true filters and reverse osmosis (RO) systems. The first is the most common and is what most people think of when they talk about a filter. It attaches directly under the kitchen counter, or stands on top of the counter. It may be attached to the faucet, or may include a special faucet just for the treated water.

This type of filter can have many types of filter inserts, is made by many different manufacturers, and comes in many different price ranges. The most effective filters are made of activated carbon. The top of the Culligan line, for instance, is the UC-1A. It has a 1,500-gallon capacity and protects against lead, cryptosporidium and giardia bacteria, chlorine, and improves taste and odor. This type of unit has to have the filters replaced every 1,500 gallons. If this is not done, filtration stops and previously filtered impurities may actually be added to the drinking water.

A hybrid of this type that combines a carbon filter with UV and ozone. Ozone, like chlorine, is a powerful oxidizer and destroys contaminants. UV destroys the bacteria and viruses. The activated carbon filter traps lead, chlorine, etc. UV/carbon filters are made by several manufacturers. The filter made by Alpine Industries uses a process called photo-oxidation to make the UV and Ozone even more effective. It is marketed by Pure Air Plus (800-455-5247) and other distributors in this market.

Although very effective, carbon based filters can't be effective against carcinogens like arsenic or nitrates. To protect yourself against these types of problems, choose an RO system. An RO system uses reverse osmosis to purify water. A good RO system, like the Hydrotech, distributed by Environmental Water Systems, processes about 45 gallons of drinking water a day. In an RO system, surplus water washes away impurities and very little maintenance is needed.

Any of these systems will make your water taste and smell a lot better. Once you get used to good tasting water, you'll never want to drink any other kind. Be sure to read the installation and service manual and follow instructions to the letter.

Odorless paints make it easy to give your house a new spring look

by Glenn Haege,
America's Master Handyman

Two weeks ago it was Spring. As of this writing, we're back to winter and it's a great time to be painting. There is nothing like a coat of paint to make a room, or even a whole house, come alive. Just like crocuses, a freshly painted room can be a harbinger of spring.

It used to be that painting when the house was closed meant that you had to live with that tell-tale "new paint" smell for weeks or months. Not any more. ICI, Glidden, Kurfees, Sherwin Williams, and Benjamin Moore, all have low or no VOC (volatile organic chemicals) paints that are almost odor free.

These paints are not wall flowers that sacrifice holding power for low VOCs. They are strong enough to even stand the wear and tear in junior's room. Benjamin Moore's Pristine paint, for instance, is a premium quality, 100 percent acrylic latex, with both excellent hiding and scrub resistance. You can not only cover the scuffs, you can wash with confidence after junior has made a mess. Pristine comes in flat, eggshell and semi-gloss.

The company also makes a companion low-odor, solvent free, interior latex primer sealer. These paints are available at Shelby Paint & Decorating, 810-739-0240, Utica, Rochester Hills, and Grosse Pointe Woods stores, and other Benjamin Moore dealers. For the dealer nearest you call Benjamin Moore, 800-672-4686.

After I checked out the Pristine line, Tim Eisbrenner, president of Shelby Paint, showed me Special Effects, a new line of specialized faux finish paints. The new line, made by McCloskey, definitely looks like it has a great deal to offer the consumer. I have been an advocate of faux finishing for years. But even my Editor at Master Handyman Press, has to admit, that unless you are very artistically inclined, mixing glazes leaves a lot to luck.

If you have not mixed the exact color and glaze proportions before, you can not be certain what the final color will be. When my editor, Kathy, and her husband, Captain Klutz, sponge painted their bathroom, they were trying for a mysterious, muted beige. The actual final result was a mixture of misty bronzes and golds. Beautiful, but a surprise.

McCloskey's Special Effects line of faux finish paints takes the guesswork away and makes faux finishing almost fool proof. The paints are premixed, have well-laid-out, step-by-step brochures and, for the first time ever, color swatch cards that show exactly what the final faux-finish look will be. No more surprises.

McCloskey's Special Effects line includes a base coat that can be tinted in any color, translucent color, opal and pearl glaze, porcelain-crackled and weather-crackled glazes, aging and metallic glaze, sand and suede paint. Of the last two, suede paint looks and feels like suede; sand paint looks and feels like . . . you guessed it, sand. Both are used alone and come in a wide variety of colors.

McCloskey's free, step by step, four color brochures cover sponging, rag rolling, color washing, stippling, dragging, crackling, and marbling. Some are amazingly detailed.

The marbling brochure illustrates a nine-step procedure, then shows the final results in nine different color combinations. Each of the color combinations lists a recipe book of the paints and finishes used to create the effect. What looks like a beautiful black marble we learn, started with a base coat called Black Earth. Then, in successive stages, Pickling White Aging Glaze, Pine Green Translucent Color Glaze, and Asphaltum Aging Glaze were applied. The veins in the marble were created by applying White Aging Glaze with a feather.

Don't be intimidated. Eisbrenner has been conducting faux-finishing seminars with the new McCloskey line at his Shelby Paint stores, and says customers have been getting amazing results. His March Seminar is already filled, but he will be conducting four free seminars at my WXYT Spring Building Show, at the Macomb Community College, Garfield and Hall Road Campus at 11 a.m. and 4 p.m. March 28 and 11 a.m. and 2 p.m. March 29. (For more information or directions on how to get to the show, call WXYT. For dealers who stock the Special Effects line of faux-finish paints call the McCloskey Division of Valspar, 800-345-4530.)

As the owner of a highly regarded, full service paint store, Eisbrenner sees a lot of people who come to complain after purchasing bargain paints at home centers and non-specialty paint stores. You'd think it would be a time for him to gloat, but Eisbrenner doesn't do that.

"After hearing their stories, I usually have to tell them that it is not the paint" he says. "Most people get bad results because they don't prepare the surface properly. Even the best paint will not adhere to a dirty, greasy surface. No paint will stand up if it is applied too thinly, or if a second coat is applied at the improper time."

Conversely, if you obey the rules, clean the surface thoroughly and apply paint according to label directions, you'll get good results every time. So why don't you go out today and give your favorite room a new spring coat. Then brag about it.

Builders shows rack up successes – for vendors and consumers

by Glenn Haege,
America's Master Handyman

Going to the builders shows is a good way for me to scope out the market. They are where you, the public, let your money do the talking.

So, what are you saying?

For starters, you are more interested than ever in home improvement. To fill your need for knowledge, more of you are going to builders shows and there are a lot more shows for you to attend.

This spring, the Building Industry Association of Southeastern Michigan is putting on four. Two at the Novi Expo Center, one at Macomb Community College and one at Cobo Center. Showspan, a large regional exposition company, was doing so many shows they had to put on two of their biggest, one in Grand Rapids and one at the Pontiac Silverdome, simultaneously.

Secondly, exhibitors are telling me that they are talking to many of the same people at the different shows. That's good. Many of you are going to several builders shows, scoping out the field, and learning all you can before you buy.

Show managers are providing more and more information. This includes free seminars by top professionals on every home improvement topic from kitchen design, gardening and back yard barbecuing, to painting, insulation, and how to hire a contractor. Murray Gula, Joe Gagnon and I gave a dozen seminars at the Silverdome Show. The crowds were bigger than ever. Homestyle columnists Nancy Szerlag, Janet Macunovich and others were also pulling in big audiences.

At the Cobo show: Steve Thomas, of *This Old House* fame; nationally known kitchen designer, James Krengel; America's Master Gardener, Jerry Baker; and those two crazy barbecue guys, Mad Dog and Merrill; were all playing to standing room only.

My hat goes off to the people who laid out the Builders Home and Detroit Flower Show this year. Seminar theaters were thoughtfully placed inside the exhibit area making them easy for you to get to. If you were just plain tired and needed to rest your feet, it was easy for you to find a seat, revive, and go back to the show.

Thirdly, you are buying big time. There may never be a good statistical way to track the amount of sales a builders show generates. The leads an exhibitor receives are often used throughout the year.

I get to see the shows from the inside. I talk to the men and women working the shows. There are a lot of smiley faces this year. I can't remember when so many people told me that they were having a banner year.

How good is business? My publishers, Master Handyman Press, sold five times more books at the Silverdome Show this year than they did the last year. We don't sell books at the Cobo Show, but the WXYT booth was barraged by people who wanted books. Sorry, we can't be everywhere. Come see me at my last builder's show of the season, the free WXYT Spring Building Show at Macomb Community College, Garfield and Hall Road Campus, Friday through Sunday, March 29.

We were certainly not alone. A large landscape designer confided that he was getting half of his entire year's business from the Silverdome Show. The owner of a small water treatment company told me that by Saturday evening at the Silverdome he had sold thirty portable RO (Reverse Osmosis) units. That may not sound like much, but it was one guy in an 8-foot by 10-foot booth, who had already sold thirty $450 units – $13,500 of cash business – before Sunday, the historically best-selling day of most builders shows. That's a tidy profit for a one man band.

But it was just the icing on the proverbial cake. It didn't take into consideration all the leads on the big water purification jobs that were the real reason for his being at the show.

Another little guy, Gerald Reimann, of Retired Pet Swings of Edgerton, Wis., was at the Cobo show. He and his son had already sold almost their entire truck load of very innovative children's pet swings made from used tires, by 1:30 p.m. Saturday. Do you relate to that folks? Truck load, Saturday afternoon. Most of the rest of the weekend sales were mail-order only.

Now, if the little guys were doing that kind of business, can you imagine what the big guys were doing?

I talked to managers who had such big smiles they couldn't keep from chuckling. One contractor told me that the most qualified leads he had ever gotten in one day was 240. Saturday at Cobo he got 401.

Kitchens, baths, decks, solariums, spas, grills, paver patios, windows, you name it. All were being sold in record numbers.

One old pro confided, "we need years like this. Usually we get beat down so bad over price it's hard to make a profit. This year there is so much business that if you don't like the price, we'll go on to someone else. I almost feel sorry for the consumer. I don't see how we can possibly build all the work we are getting."

Those words should be carved in stone. It's a great time to for the building and home improvement industries. It could be a great time for you. But make sure you have a completion date in your modernization contract or you may not have much to show for it.

Water, water everywhere … but can you make it more fit to drink

by Glenn Haege,
America's Master Handyman

Depending on whom you talk to our water is: A) perfectly safe; or B) not fit to drink. When it comes to something as important as water, I prefer to err on the side of caution.

On March 7, I gave a brief run down on "point of use" water treatment systems. Today's article is on "Whole House Systems."

The first thing you have to decide is whether you should bother with a whole house system. Here are several questions to ask:

■ Is someone in your house is especially sensitive to allergies or chemicals, such as chlorine? Then you are a candidate.

■ Do you want treated water from every tap and do not want to install a separate filter at each drinking source? You should consider a whole house system.

■ Do you drink well water? You are not just a candidate, you are on the must-have-now list.

■ Do you have city or well water? City water sites take less equipment and are less expensive.

■ What do you want to filter out of the water? The best way to decide this is to have the water tested to see what's in it. Many of the water treatment professionals test the water automatically before recommending a system. Independent tests are done by companies like Absolute Analytical Laboratories, (248) 435-5100.

■ What about cost? Most homeowners are comfortable in the $200 to $800 area. Unfortunately a good whole house system, especially one designed to purify water from a well, lake, or river, can easily cost $3,000 or more.

To find out what works, I talked to three people I respect. Nick DiSalvio, Environmental Water Service, (800) 371-PURE; Jim Reynolds, Reynolds Water Conditioning Co., (800) 572-9575; and John Perry, Pure Air Plus, (800) 455-5247. DiSalvio and Reynolds are water specialists. Perry works on air and water decontamination.

Specialists like DiSalvio and Reynolds, look at each water treatment job and recommend highly individualized solutions. They use a combination of filters and water treatments, to create the final product.

Reynolds Water Conditioning started in 1924 and is the oldest water treatment company in Michigan. Now in its third generation, it may be the oldest family owned and operated water treatment company in the nation.

According to Jim Reynolds, Michigan has almost every type of water condition found in the country. Monroe has heavy sulfur. Detroit and the Northern suburbs have iron and hardness problems. St. Clair County has naturally salty water. Add to this the known and unknown pollutants from land fills and over fertilization.

For homes on city water, Reynolds uses several whole house water treatment systems. The least expensive is an industrial grade cartridge that has 20 times the capacity of residential cartridge filters. The filter is made from powdered activated carbon and reduces solids down to one micron in size. Cartridges have to be changed between four months and a year depending on water consumption.

For well, lake, or river water, Reynolds uses a combination of at least two different cartridge filters and ultra violet.

For city water, Nick DiSalvio of Environmental Water Systems, uses a combination of cartridge filters, water softening, and ads an RO (reverse osmosis) point of use filter for drinking. Like Reynolds, he prefers potassium chloride to salt brine in the water softener.

In plotting his attack against water-borne contaminants in well water, DiSalvio uses a very extensive collection of county maps which show land fills and the possible danger of contamination each may represent. He prefers a water purification method that utilizes hydrogen peroxide to totally destroy all the contaminants, then a series of filters and a water softener and an RO system for drinking water.

DiSalvio's unique Peroxide water purification unit will be on display at a free WXYT Spring Builders Show this weekend at the Macomb Community College, Garfield and Hall Road Campus, from 8 a.m. to 6 p.m., today, and 8 a.m. to 4 p.m., Sunday. If you have a water problem and want to talk to one of the areas top experts, you couldn't do better than stopping by this display.

Pure Air Plus recommends their POE-10 and 15 systems for homes with well water. These systems use heavy duty ionization machines, called corona discharge ozone generators, to create ozone and purify the water. The ozone kills any bacteria, viruses or mold spores.

Three different companies. Three very different ways of tackling the same problem. I can't tell you which is best. Every method I described will give you better tasting water than you have now. Most will kill the microbes that may infect our water supply. Some will take out the lead. If you worry about nitrates or arsenic, your best bet is an RO filter or distillation.

This is definitely a case where you have to learn all you can before you buy. Do your homework, then brag about it!

APRIL 4, 1998

Gaps in an electronic home security system could prove alarming

by Glenn Haege,
America's Master Handyman

Americans take home security very seriously. Last year, we shelled out 314 billion on professionally installed electronic security products and services. The year before it was $13.2 billion, according to the National Burglar & Fire Alarm Association. By the end of 1997, 1-in-5 homes were electronically protected.

Even so, most of the people I talk to are still in the dark about the subject. They ask these questions:

■ What kind of security do you need?
■ How much is enough? What's over-kill?
■ How much should it cost?

I covered inexpensive and mid-cost level ways to increase your homes security in articles on Dec. 20 and Feb. 7. This article is designed to give you a basic primer on electronic home security.

To get the answers I called Kevin Jameson, the business Development Manager, National Accounts, for ADEMCO Group. That's a mouthful but trust me on this. ADEMCO is to home security, like grass is to dirt. They manufacture the equipment that is in many of the home security systems manufactured throughout the world.

I asked Jameson what a basic electronic security system should contain and he answered:

"The three basics are complete perimeter door protection, interior trap protection, and fire protection.

"Most illegal entries are through the door. So if you are trying to get by as inexpensively as possible, make sure all the doors are covered. If you have a little extra money and like to open your windows during the summer, look into getting electronic security screens for all the ground floor windows. Security screens look and act like regular screens, but they have fine wires embedded in the mesh. If some one removes or cuts a screen the alarm will go off.

"Once a person gets inside the house, you need some kind of interior trap, either a motion detector or an alarm keyed to the very important interior doors, like the master bedroom.

"A burglar goes to where the goodies are. That means the first place a he goes after breaking into a house is usually the master bedroom. He knows that most people store their valuables in the master bedroom, den or home office. The first thing he takes is a pillowcase into which he stuff valuables as he rifles though the house.

"The psychology behind putting an alarm on the master bedroom door is that if he penetrated the house without the alarm going off, he thinks he is home free. When the master bedroom door alarm goes off, he's out of there.

316

"The reason for a fire protection monitor in addition to a standard smoke detector is that smoke detectors are only effective if someone is in the house. If you are out for the day or on vacation, the smoke detector can be sounding the alarm, but no one will know about it until the fire has burned through the roof and the house is already gutted," Jameson said.

There is a difference of opinion as to whether monitoring is necessary if you have an electronic security system. After all, if you had the system installed and the burglar was frightened away as soon as the alarm went off, why pay a monitoring company?

Jameson believes that the best type of home security would be a house sitter. Failing that, you should have a friend, neighbor, or relative check the house once a day, not once a week or every few days. If that is not possible, a monitored alarm system is necessary.

"The real reason for monitoring is to safeguard your property after a burglar has entered. If a burglar broke in and the alarm system did its job, the burglar has been frightened away, but your house is now completely unprotected.

"Once the alarm has cycled, it goes off, and the door, or maybe a window are wide open. Another burglar, an animal, or anyone off the street could walk in and make themselves at home. The house may also open to snow, wind, rain, and all sorts of weather-related damage.

"If you do not have someone to house sit for you, and most of us don't, it is the job of the monitoring service to be that friend and safeguard your home," Jameson says.

As far as costs are concerned, a good basic package for a 2,500 square foot house should cost between $1,000 and $2,000. If you add security screens, the cost will be run between $100 and $150 per window, because each screen has to be custom-made to fit the particular window.

If you would like to know more about home security, and what to look for in a home security system, you can get a very informative brochure, entitled *Safe & Sound* free from the National Burglar & Fire Alarm Association. Send a self addressed, stamped #10 envelope to National Burglar & Fire Alarm Association, 7101 Wisconsin Ave, Suite 901, Bethesda, MD 20814.

The same association also provides the names of qualified home security installers. For the names of some installers near you, write or call the Association at (301) 585-1855. Or look them up on their web site at www.alarm.org.

Take my advice and do it today. It's important to your security.

Different deck problems will call for different cleaning solutions

by Glenn Haege,
America's Master Handyman

Since we didn't have any winter to speak of, you are probably anxious to get outdoors. The only thing between you and the great out doors is a dirty deck. That poor thing has been at the mercy of the elements all winter long. You probably didn't even shovel away the snow with a plastic snow shovel last as you were supposed to.

Now, depending on its prior condition, you have a dirty, dirty and gray, or dirty, dull and peeling deck. There may also be mold and mildew.

Each of these conditions calls for a different solution. If you use the wrong application, you will not get the results you want regardless of how hard you work. In a nutshell:

■ A dirty deck can be cleaned with a good general cleaner. This is the most gentle procedure.

■ A dirty gray deck with mildew can best be cleaned with an oxalic acid cleaner.

■ A dirty, dull, and peeling deck must be stripped. This is the most harsh and time-consuming process.

Be sure you have the proper tools. A deck brush, like that manufactured by Detroit Quality Brush (DQB), (800) 722-3037, or the Wolman Woodworx Deck Brush, (800) 556-7737, will really help get the job done. Also be sure to wear rubber gloves and goggles. Since brighteners and strippers are caustic and can burn the skin, wearing an old, long sleeved shirt and slacks is required when doing either of these procedures.

To add confusion to your shopping, Bio-Wash and Wolman, two top deck treatment manufacturers, have renamed their product lines this year. I am using 1998 product names. If your store is still selling stock from last year, the names may be different. The products I mention here are not the only solutions. Your hardware store or home center may have different products. Before you buy, make certain the products contain the essential ingredients I list in this article.

General Cleaning

All decks get dirty. If the deck is just dirty and stained with a little bit of cooking grease or leaf stains, all you need is a general all-purpose cleaner. Follow label directions, but remember, you need a strong cleaning solution. For organic cleaners like Simple Green, Clean Away or Clear Magic, I recommend 1/2 gallon of concentrated cleaner to one gallon of water. The solution for a Trisodium Phosphate (TSP) solution, a strong, proven alternative, would be 4 ounces of TSP per gallon of water. Bio-Wash Simple Wash is specially made for deck cleaning. Follow label directions. Make sure you clean everything including the railings. You should not have to power wash.

Photo courtesy Bio-Wash Products

Dirty Gray Decks

When a deck made from pressure treated wood gets dark, the gray/black is quite often mold. To clean effectively, you have to use a cleaner that says it removes mildew on the label. I do not recommend cleaners that have bleach. Household bleach kills mold and mildew, but is dangerous and destroys the cell structure of the wood surface making it almost impossible to apply a uniform stain coat. To deep-clean a dirty gray pressure treated deck, use a cleaner/brightener like Cabot Stains Problem Solver or Bio-Wash Wood Wash.

With pressure-treated pine, cedar, redwood, or hardwood, the gray may also be caused by ultra violet destruction of the top layer of wood cells. If this is the case you have to use a cleaner/brightener that has an acid base, like Oxalic Acid. Cleaners of this type include Bio-Wash Wood Wash, Behr Wood Cleaner Brightener Conditioner, Cabot Stains Problem Solver, Flood Dekswood, Natural Wood Brightener, Superdeck Deckdoctor, Timberseal Rescue and Wolman Deck & Fence Brightener. Wolman makes two different products for this job – Deck & Fence Brightener for pressure treated wood and Cedar & Redwood Deck & Fence Brightener Liquid for cedar and redwood.

Each of these cleaners has specific mixing instructions. Pay attention and follow the rules.

Dirty, Dull, & Peeling Decks

In addition to regular dirt problems, if your deck was stained or sealed a couple of years ago, the finish may have begun to disintegrate. When this happens, you need to strip the deck surface. Oxalic acid based cleaners won't do anything

continued on next page

to solve this problem, so a specialized stripper is needed.

Timberseal Rescue II, Wolman Deck Strip Stain and Finish Remover, and Behr Quik-Fix Deck Finish Remover, can be used on both oil- and latex-based finishes. Bio-Wash makes Stripex for the removal of oil-based products and Stripex L for latex finish removal. If you can't find a specialized deck stripper, or the surface is especially tough, use an environmentally friendly conventional wood stripper, like Citristrip.

Most manufacturer specifications say that you do not need to use a pressure washer with their product. You may find a power washer will help you get the job done faster. If you do use a pressure washer, use the lowest possible setting. Start at 400 or 500 psi (pounds per square inch) and work your way up. Never use more than 1200 psi.

Make sure you rinse away all the gunk that hides in cracks, corners and crevices.

Now, take the rest of the day off. You've earned it. Most deck sealers have to be applied only to thoroughly dry surfaces and temperature should not drop below 50 degrees Fahrenheit while the deck stain or sealer is drying.

Next week I'll talk about staining and sealing.

Photo courtesy Bio-Wash Products

Product list
Cleaners
Simple Green
Breeze
Clean Away
Clear Magic
Bio-Wash Simple Wash
TSP

Brightners
Bio-Wash Woodwash
  Weathered Wood Restorer
Behr Wood Cleaner
  Brightener Conditioner
Cabot Stains Problem Solver –
  removes mildew
Natural Wood Brightener
Flood Dekswood
Superdeck Deckdoctor
Timberseal Rescue – Oxalic Acid

Touch 'n Spray Wood Deck &
  Fence Renewer – Pre-Mixed,
  Contains Butyl Cellosolve
  & Potassium Silicate
Wolman Cedar & Redwood Deck
  & Fence Brightener Liquid
Wolman Deck & Fence Brightener

Strippers
Behr Quik-Fix Deck Finish Remover –
  Contains Sodium Hydroxide
Stripex Wood Stain Stripper
Stripex-L Latex Stain
  & Varnish Stripper
Timberseal Rescue I – Contains
  Sodium Bicarbonate
Wolman Deck Strip – Contains
  Sodium Hydroxide
Citristrip

APRIL 18, 1998

Read product labels before using a stripper, sealant on your deck

by Glenn Haege,
America's Master Handyman

Last week I talked about cleaning decks. But maybe your wood deck needs more than cleaning.

Does it need resealing? Or do you need to move up to a semitransparent, or solid-colored stain? You may not have to do anything. If the deck looks dull, but rain water still beads up, it probably just needs cleaning.

After you have cleaned the deck and it has dried at least four hours, you may decide it looks fine for another year. If it still looks gray and grungy, fill a 4-ounce glass with water and splash it on the deck. If the water breaks up into tiny beadlets and just sits there, too much sealer remains on the deck to proceed further without stripping.

If the water lays around in a puddle, then disappears through a combination of evaporation and absorption into the wood, the sealer has worn off and the wood can be resealed, preferably with a seal coat that is a few shades darker than you used two or three years ago.

This is the big decision point. How you proceed must be determined by:
■ the type of deck wood
■ the condition of the surface
■ your choice of deck sealer or stain.

If your deck is made of pressure-treated pine, cedar or redwood, you can reseal or stain as soon as the deck is thoroughly dry.

If it is pressure-treated pine and the deck surface is that black/gray color that connotes cell death or mold, or if it is grayed cedar or redwood, possibly with tannin stains and nail rust marks, the deck has to be brightened before re-sealing. In the event that the deck was previously stained or sealed, and the protective surface has begun to disintegrate, the deck must be stripped. I gave directions for stripping and brightening in last week's Homestyle.

When choosing products, don't just go for the bargain brand. You will notice that all the big deck stain and sealant companies also have their own lines of brighteners and strippers. You might want all the products you buy to be in the same "family".

Bio-Wash has designed their entire line to work as an "integrated system", that works best when used together. Wolman has done the same thing. So has Behr, Cabot, Flood, Osmose, Penofin, Olympic, Pittsburgh, Superdeck, Thompsons, as well as many smaller or regional companies such as Silvertown Products' Rhinoguard, American Building Restoration Products, and Menco Corporation's Men-Wood brand. I've talked to many of the chemical engineers who make these products. Most of them readily admit that the products are "tweaked" to give best performance when they work in conjunction with the rest of the product line.

Every company's sealers and stains are a little bit different. If a company also makes a cleaner, brightener, and stripper, it makes sense to formulate those products to do the best possible job preparing the wood for the company's products.

Read the label of the stripper or brightener before you leave the store. Many of these products require that you perform another step before applying the stain or seal coat. For instance, after using Bio-Wash Woodwash, Stripex, and Natural Wood Brightener, you should apply their Mill Glaze Away to restore the wood's pH to neutral, before applying their Natural Deck Oil or any other stain or sealer.

After using Behr's Quik-Fix Deck Finish Remover or Deck & Mildew Stain Remover, the company advises applying their Wood Cleaner, Brightener, Conditioner to restore the wood to its natural color before applying a seal or stain coat. On the other hand, Wolman's brighteners and strippers are made so that no intermediate step is necessary before applying one of its toners or stains.

I can't list all the different companies' do's and don'ts. It's up to you, what ever you buy, to read the label before leaving the store.

If you are unsure if an extra step is required between cleaning or stripping and sealing, consider playing it safe and applying Bio-Wash Mill Glaze Away before the finish coat. This product brings the pH level to neutral and assures maximum coating adhesion and penetration.

Now that we've got you ready to seal or stain, what should you buy? The clearer the seal coat, the less protection it gives wood from Ultra Violet (UV) Rays. The more pigment in the stain or sealer, the more uniform the final look. What you choose depends upon the condition of the wood. If you have a new deck, most people choose a clear sealer. After a couple of years, they progress to a sealer/toner that adds a little pigment for more protection, yet highlights the wood's grain and texture. It gives the wood a honey nut look.

When a few more years go by, a semi-transparent stain is an excellent choice. Still later, decks that have proved the test of time have earned the right to the extra UV protection of a solid-colored stain. Every major stain company makes all or most of these. If you want your deck to look like furniture, choose Sikken's Cetol Dek.

Proper preparation is the key. So take a little extra time now, then sit on your deck and brag about it.

Innovative new products could become fixtures in your bathroom

by Glenn Haege,
America's Master Handyman

It's time to talk about the bathroom, which on a square-foot basis is the most expensive room in the house, the bath.

Ever since I first saw KorStone, the new solid countertop product at the Silverdome Home & Garden Show in March, I have wanted to write an article about bathroom innovations. I scouted out other new products a week ago, the Kitchen/Bath Industry Show at McCormick Place South in Chicago.

My good friends at H. J. Oldenkamp, the local Corian distributor, tell me KorStone is not Corian. It does not look like Corian. And it doesn't work like Corian.

They are 100 percent right. Corian looks like Corian. KorStone looks like KorStone. It costs about half the price of Corian and is designed for all the people who like the look, but not the price, of most solid surface countertops.

KorStone is a quality product that is so practically priced you can get a 31- by 21- inch vanity counter top cast with a beautiful molded sink, and a 4-inch coved back splash, for around $165. A custom six foot double bowl, solid surface counter top runs about $550. A competitive model would be in the $1,000 to $2,000 range.

KorStone is easy enough to work with that it can be a do-it-yourself project. For more information, call the inventor, Bob Bordener, at Talon Surfaces, (877) 567-7866.

Now that you've saved all that money on a solid surface counter top, you can splurge on truly top-of-the-line faucets and hardware. There are two new looks – Satin Chrome and Satin Nickel. They give fixtures a sort of Western, worked metal look. The finishes are being introduced on Franklin Brass fixtures, (800) 829-0089, Alsons hand showers and shower heads, (800) 421-0001, and Delta faucets, (800) 345-DELTA. The new finishes should be in our part of the country in about 90 days. Call the companies for more information.

If you have children who can turn on – but forget to turn off – faucets, or just want to add ease of use, AquaTouch USA is introducing a battery operated automatic faucet that senses when a person puts their hand under the faucet. Take your hand away and the water turns off. One 9-volt battery powers the sensor all year. The AquaTouch is being introduced in New Jersey, and will spread Westward from there. To learn more, call AquaTouch, (800) 220-3036.

You may have read about, or sadly experienced, the trouble many people have with the 1.6 gallon reservoir toilets mandated by Congress. Many need two flushes to adequately do the job. The Flushmate, sold by the Sloan Valve

Company, was introduced to solve the flushing problem, with a high powered flushing system. The product works well but is a little noisy.

Now, Bruce Martin, Flushmate's inventor, has invented a refined product, the PF/2, which is being introduced by a newly formed Masco company, W/C Technology Corporation. The new product works on the same principle, but very quietly. The pressure units are presently on some toilets made by American Standard and Eljer. For more information, call Martin at (888) 732-9282.

According to the inventors of the Clair-Flo Direct-Thru Toilet Exhaust System, every time a toilet is flushed, germs spread throughout the bathroom onto toothbrushes, towels, razors, etc., in an aerosol-like air movement. AdVent International's new Clair-Flo Exhaust System sucks the germs and, bathroom smells into the toilet bowl and exhausts them out of the house though a special venting system. For more information, call AdVent, 888-5ADVENT (888) 523-8368).

We're not done getting rid of the malicious microbes yet. Aqua Glass, the shower stall and bathtub makers have introduced an easy-to-clean, gelcoat finish with microban antibacterial protection. Microban technology has no effect on humans, but it is impossible for microbes to live on the surface. I was very impressed when I heard about this at the National Association of Home Builders show earlier this year in Dallas. Now the products have made their way through the distribution channels and are available for you, the consumer. To learn more, call (901) 632-0911.

If you want more anti-microbial power, Formica has introduced a new line of counter top laminates with the same Microban Antibacterial Protection built into the surface. You can't see it, taste it, or scrub it away. Again, Microban protection is perfectly safe. It has been used in hospitals for years, but is just now working its way onto the consumer stage. For more information, or the dealer nearest you, call (800) FORMICA.

If you get turned off, every time you turn on a ceiling exhaust fan, Broan has introduced a the Ultra Quiet line of ceiling fans and fan/light/night lights. The new fans range from 50 cubic feet per minute (cfm) to 110 cfm. In ninety days they will be introducing a 150 cfm model. These exhaust fans are top quality, but you won't find them everywhere. Call (800) 558-1711.

Heck, we're out of room, and I haven't even told you about the solid wood sinks and bathtubs, yet. Hint: If you really would, soak in wood, call (718) 729-3686. But don't blame me if your bank account gets splinters.

MAY 2, 1998

Your home could be a casualty in this costly biological warfare

by Glenn Haege,
America's Master Handyman

There's a war going on in our homes. And it's up to you to make sure you are not one of the casualties.

The battle is against mold and other microbes that grow wherever there is moisture, sufficient heat and a food source. Problem areas include leaking roofs, walls, basements, sewer back ups, dirty duct work, too-tight houses (we make moisture just living, breathing, cooking, growing house plants and having aquariums), and leaking or sweating plumbing.

The problem is so serious that on April 20 busy professional took off an entire day to talk about mold and other microbes at a Mold Seminar at the Troy Holiday Inn. It was sponsored by Connie and Tom Morbach, the owners of Sanit-Air, Inc. and Environmental Compliance Solutions, Inc., the duct cleaning and environmental testing companies (888) 778-7324.

This was not just a biology class. It was a take-no-prisoners seminar attended by doctors and lawyers, as well as technical and maintenance professionals, modernization and heating, Ventilating and air conditioning contractors and duct cleaners.

To me, the most newsworthy aspect of this seminar was that it was held at all. The director of a retirement community was there, so were representatives of various school systems, a representative of the American Lung Association, leading building and modernization contractors, and many different duct cleaning organizations. They came from Maryland, Indiana, Ohio, and Canada, as well as from all parts of Michigan.

These people would not have been there unless they believed there is a serious problem. Lon Grossman, president of Technihouse Inspections, (248) 855-5566, and one of the speakers at the seminar, said is that 85 percent of the houses he has inspected have a mold or microbial problem. In the 1970's and '80's the government and all the building inspectors were telling people to tighten up their houses. Now, houses and people are getting sick, so they have started telling home owners to do the opposite, he said.

"The majority of houses with stucco siding are rotting in the walls," Grossman said. One house he inspected had $200,000 worth of damage.

Ductwork and walls are excellent incubators for mold and other microbes. You and I are surrounded by potential contamination.

According to Terry Baker, president of T. Baker & Associates, (810) 732-9602, a company that specializes in microbiology and laboratory testing, a single mushroom produces 16 billion spores and can release 8 million spores per hour. Each spore has got everything it takes to grow a colony. Other fungi have

326

similar procreative capabilities and release spores at different times of the day and season depending upon maturity, temperature and moisture.

All fungi and bacteria are not evil. We could not live without the various microbes which help us digest our food and break down organic materials. But some microorganisms like stacybotrys, alternaria, cladosporium, and aspergillus, can be down right dangerous.

How dangerous? According to Dr. George Riegel, president of Healthy Homes, Inc., (248) 358-3311, they are so hazardous that when he has a crew clean up a source of major contamination he uses the same procedures he would use in asbestos removal. That includes cutting the contaminated area off from the rest of the building and installing a three-air-lock system with a portable shower and negative air machines. The crew wears Tyvek suits and power air-purified respirators, goggles and gloves.

Professional remediation is very expensive. Procedures include pretreatment with an antimicrobial, tear out, double bagging of debris, scrubbing down with antimicrobials, and encapsulation.

After reading about the clean-up procedure, you are probably thinking the area must have been attacked by a malicious foreign power using insidious bacteriological weapons. Not so. One emergency job Riegel discussed at the seminar was caused by a leaky shower valve behind the bathroom wall. Contamination was so bad it was considered an emergency. The cost of the clean up was $25,000.

According to George F. Curran, III, of Cummings, McClorey, Davis & Acho, PC, (248) 737-3333, these types of clean ups are seldom covered by insurance. Although commercial buildings have a better chance then residential of getting coverage, the outlook is not good. If you have a problem you need the advice of a high-powered insurance legal specialist like Curran.

One place where the outlook is getting better for the homeowner is in cases where damage is caused by the backup of sewer water into basements in cases where city drains are not able to handle storm water. According to Philip G. Bozzo, (810) 776-0306, an attorney who specializes in water damage class-action suits, while cities and their insurance companies used to be successful claiming governmental immunity from such sewer damage, cities now are being held liable for their mistakes through the "trespass nuisance" exception in Common Law. Bozzo said he and colleagues from another specialist firm, Macuga, Swartz, and Liddle, have already won cases against several municipalities.

It's up to you and I to do everything we can to make certain our homes are healthy. That includes duct cleaning, thorough cleanup and decontamination after water backup, continuous inspection, and testing when ever there seems to be a problem.

This is all the room I have today. I'll go into more detail about microbial growth and what you can do to keep your house and family healthy in a later article.

Thanks to El Nino, ants and mosquitoes launch an early offensive

by Glenn Haege,
America's Master Handyman

Your house is under attack and are going to have to get out of that chair and start doing something right now, if you hope to win the battle of the bugs this year.

One downside to the nice warm winter we've been having in Michigan and many other parts of the country is that insect development is 30 to 45 days ahead of normal.

The invasion started early. Pest control companies have already started getting calls on ants. Warm weather, plus the large amounts of rain we have received in the last few weeks, mean mosquitos will not be far behind.

Few things are more upsetting than walking into the kitchen and seeing a hundred winged ants doing their best the to take over the place. The usual reaction is: "Oh no, the house is infested with carpenter ants. They'll eat through the walls and floors. The house could collapse."

Luckily, most of the relatively large black ants that you may have already begun to see swarming are acrobat ants, not carpenter ants, says Paul LaBuhn of Maple Lane Pest Control, (800) 870-7096, in Sterling Heights. Both acrobat and carpenter ants nest in wood or fiberglass, but an acrobat ant needs softer wood and generally do much less damage.

To find out which type of ant is invading your house, look on the back of the ant. The thorax at the rear of the acrobat ant is shaped like a heart. Another way to tell the difference between the two is that acrobat ants will eat bait and will go in to ant traps. Carpenter ants will not.

Seeing ants inside the house does not mean you have an ant colony. The colony could be in a neighbor's fence or tree. Forager ants are on a constant quest for food and water. When they find these treasures, usually in the kitchen, they go back and tell their friends, laying a chemical trail for them to follow to the food or water source. Soon, a hundred ants can be on their way to pick up groceries at your place.

Diazinon granules scattered around the perimeter of the house or spraying with a Diazinon or Ortho Dursban spray will help keep the insects out. Diazinon granules are time release, but only contain a 5 percent concentration of the active ingredient. Ortho Dursban Spray, available at most hardware, garden and home centers, has a 20 percent or 25 percent concentration but is only effective for about two weeks

"Before you use any pesticide, read the directions thoroughly. Don't spray all over – just around the windows, doors, and any openings to the house, or cracks and crevices," LaBuhn says. "If you see mounds of sawdust in the house, you have found an ant colony and can probably eliminate that entire ant population with a good aerosol." Aerosols you can buy over the counter are Black Flag or Raid Ant and Roach Killer.

Mosquitos also are getting their marching orders early this year. A warm winter and a wet spring have prepared the way. Another warm spurt will hatch the larvae and we will have legions of mosquitos.

Once a mosquito is in the air, wind currents can bring it from miles away and there is little you can do to stop it. The best way to control mosquitoes is to eliminate their environment in the larvae state.

Brian Sass, of Maple Lane Pest Control, has written papers on what homeowners can do to eliminate pests like ants and mosquitos and keep critters from invading the house. Since standing water is needed by mosquitos in the larval stage, Sass suggests getting rid of all extraneous items that can collect water. That includes old tin cans, jars, bottles, and tires. If you have a flat-topped roof, check it five days after a rain. Any standing water creates a mosquito farm. Fix the roof.

You also should drain or fill low-lying areas in the yard, and empty the eves troughs to eliminate standing water.

By eliminating the water, you will be doing everything you can to eliminate the mosquitos in the larval stage. Once they start flying, they can come from anywhere, so there is no such thing as total elimination.

If you are going to have a party, however, and just need to eliminate mosquitos for a short period of time, there are a few things you can do.

Cut the grass short. Short, dry grass is no fun for mosquitos. Shortly before the party, apply a mosquito repellent such as Mosquito Beater by Bonide Products, (800) 552-8252.

If the party is really important, a wedding, college graduation, call in a professional pest control company to spray the area.

The series of papers Sass wrote to help home owners get rid of the insects and varmits without calling an exterminator is available at no cost to Handyman readers and listeners. To get a copy, send a number 10, stamped, self-addressed envelope to Maple Lane Pest Control, 6020 Chicago Road, Warren, MI 48092.

Get rid of the bugs by yourself, then brag about it!

MAY 16, 1998

Don't hit the roof when it comes to costly repairs of shingles

by Glenn Haege,
America's Master Handyman

If you need a new roof, don't think the hard part is done when you've picked out the shingles. Shingles are just the outer shell. You still have to make the hard decisions that will determine the longevity of your shingles and much of the heating and cooling efficiency of your home.

First, there's the question of the roofing contractor. This late (yes, mid May is late) in the season, most companies are working at full capacity and you will be at the wrong end of a very long line. You might think they could hang up a "now hiring" sign and add crews. Unfortunately, because of the big "L" (lack of labor) many contractors have scraped the bottom of the barrel when it comes to trained or trainable personnel. This is especially true for the hard jobs, like roofing, concrete and carpentry. Finding somebody good, dependable, and willing to break their backs in the hot sun, is hard to do.

As a roofing customer, you may find yourself in the position of having to wait six or eight months, or holding off until next year, to get a good contractor.

An alternative to reroofing, is extending the life of your present roof. If the shingles are not in bad shape, you can apply a waterproof shingle repair coating like Roof Guardian by Oregon Research and Development Corp.: (800) 345-0809. The product is about half the price of shingles and will usually extend shingle life by seven to 10 years.

If you don't want a temporary fix and need new shingles, make certain that everything necessary is specified on the contract. Most contractors do not have time to educate you. They want to get the job, get it done, and get out of there. If you want any extras, you have to make certain that you put them in the specifications.

Good roofing contractors will always install 7/16-inch oriented strand board (OSB) when they have to replace decking. Most will automatically install, or at least ask if you want, snow and ice shield. However, it is up to you, the home owner to make certain you get these basic minimums.

OSB is especially manufactured to withstand the moisture and extreme heat and cold conditions to which deck boards are subjected. Make certain OSB is on the contract.

Snow and ice shield is a waterproof membrane that should be installed under the building paper in high ice and snow areas like Michigan, the North East, North West, Northern, Great Lakes and all of Canada. It extends from the drip edge up, and protects the final three feet of roof line, so water does not penetrate the roof.

Your attic has to breath, so make certain you specify the installation of both soffit and ridge vents. If you presently have pot vents and are having a complete tear off of the old shingles, seriously consider replacing them with a ridge vent. The ridge vent is more attractive and does a better job.

The other half of the equation is soffit vents. Soffit vents are openings, usually placed in the roof overhang, that permit air to come into the attic area. Without soffit vents it is impossible to have proper ventilation in the attic. They keep the attic and actually the entire house, cooler in summer, and dryer in winter.

Not having proper ventilation in the attic leads to sweating, rusty roofing nails, deck board decomposition, curling and crumbling of shingles, wet insulation, and potential ceiling and wall leaks.

Should your house not have a deep enough overhang for soffit vents, call the Globe Materials Company, (800) 456-5649, and ask for literature on Combo Vents. These unique products have a metal top flange that creates the space necessary for venting.

If the attic has blown-in insulation, The insulation may plug the venting. Install soffit baffles to keep the air free flowing. Soffit baffles are made by most insulation companies and are available at home centers and roofing wholesalers.

Don't let the roofer tell you that you have gable vents and do not need soffit vents. He is only saying that because he doesn't know the benefits, or doesn't want to do the extra work. Gable vents make turbulence inside the attic and interfere with proper air exchange.

If you are in a heavily wooded or very moist area and the roof usually develops a mildew problem, have the roofer install Shingle Shield by Chicago Metallic, (800) 323-7164.

Not really part of a roofing job, but usually added to the job, is the installation of new aluminum or vinyl gutters. New products, like Gutter Helmet, that virtually eliminate clogged gutters, are available. They are installed locally by Joy Company, (800) 378-1924. Although not cheap, they are well worth it if you do not like climbing ladders. Special prices are available when gutters and Gutter Helmet are installed at the same time.

Be a well-informed consumer. Take a trip to your local roofing or building supply wholesaler. Ask questions. Look at the materials I have suggested. Learn all you can before you do.

MAY 23, 1998

You can still get that outside furniture ready for Memorial Day

by Glenn Haege,
America's Master Handyman

Big plans! You're having the family over for a Memorial Day barbecue. You've got steaks and fish. All the new spring flowers are in, and the outdoor furniture looks like . . . yuk.

It didn't seem that bad last year. But looked at it from a guest's point-of-view, Memorial Day could be a disaster.

The beautiful varnished picnic table has turned into a scaly monster. The cast-iron furniture has turned to peeling paint and rust. The padded outdoor pillows that looked so cool now are dirty with black mold spores. The shiny plastic chairs are pitted and dull.

With one day's work, we can turn this disaster into something we can brag about.

Wooden furniture

Let's start with the scaling picnic table, or swing set, or any shiny wooden outdoor thing you got talked into. If the wood is unsound, get rid of it. If the wood is solid, the furniture should be looking good in a day.

Let's try the easiest method first. Get a gallon of Stripex-L by Bio-Wash, or Woodpal Deck Stain and Finish Stripper by Specialty Environmental Technologies. I'm listing the Bio-Wash, (800) 858-5011, and Specialty Environmental Technologies, (800) 899-0401, products because they are fast, easy to use, and environmentally friendly.

Scrape off the loose, scaly film, then apply the stripper to the surface as thick as possible. Use an old polyester or nylon polyester brush for this job. Keep the surface moist for up to one half hour. You can moisten the surface with a fine mist from your garden hose or apply more stripper. I'd apply more stripper.

After a half hour, wash the stripper off with the garden hose. With luck, you should wash off most of the old varnish. If this is the case you can either reapply more deck stripper to the few varnish hold outs and repeat the process, or let the table dry for a couple of hours and sand off the spots.

If the varnish is still hanging tough, go back to the store and get a stronger stripper, like Citristrip Paint & Varnish Stripping Gel by Specialty Environmental or Rinse or Peel Water Rinse Paint Stripper by Bio-Wash.

Unfortunately, this fix adds more time to the project. Spread the products on thickly and cover the entire surface with cheap, thin plastic drop cloths. After 24 hours, you should be able to wash all the gunk away with a garden hose.

A picnic table takes the same beating the sun gives a deck, so clean off the gray wood cells with a wood brightener. Both the Woodpal and Bio-Wash deck stripping products may have wood brightener attached. Just dissolve the contents in water according to package directions, and apply with a garden sprayer. Wait fifteen minutes and rinse away the gray with the garden hose.

Apply Bio-Wash Mill Glaze Away or Woodpal New Deck Prep Mill Glaze Remover. Wait about four hours until the surface is dry to the touch and apply a coat of Bio-Wash Supernatural Protective Wood Finish. This is a water borne soft sheen finish that can be applied to wood without waiting for several days of drying time. The picnic table should be ready for use in about four hours.

Painted furniture

Now let's get to the rest of the furniture. If the furniture is painted it may just be dirty, wash down painted wood, aluminum, iron or steel furniture with a 10 to 1 solution of Simple Green or Clear Magic. Rinse with the garden hose.

Cast-iron furniture

If rust spots are developing on your cast-iron furniture, spray on OxiSolv Rust Remover by OxiSolv Inc., (800) 594-9028 to dissolve the rust and remove oxidation. OxiSolv leaves a zinc phosphate residue that provides an excellent base when you repaint later. It is distributed locally by Painters Supply & Equipment Co., (800) 589-8100.

Plastic furniture

Plastic resin outdoor furniture is relatively soft so it can get looking dull and dingy fast. First, clean like wood or aluminum. If that doesn't work, try Meguiar's Mirror Glaze Professional Clear Plastic Cleaner #17. Wipe on, let dry to a haze, then wipe off and seal the finish with a coat of Meguiar's Clear Plastic Polish. Look for these products at auto parts stores like Murray's or call the manufacturer at (800) 347-5700.

Padded furniture

To clean really dirty, padded outdoor furniture, wash with undiluted Simple Green. Scrub with a brush, then rinse with lots of water and let dry. If the padding is only slightly dirty, use a 30 to one solution (1/2 cup to a gallon of water).

Don't forget the vinyl umbrella. Open it up and lay it on the grass. Dampen with the garden hose, then spray with Westley's Bleche-Wite and rinse. Do not close the umbrella until it has dried completely. You may have used this product in the past to brighten white wall tires. It's made by Blue Coral, (800) 416-1600.

Have a good holiday.

Hit the deck: Outdoor wood requires regular cleaning, stripping

by Glenn Haege,
America's Master Handyman

Judging from the emergency deck calls I get on my radio shows, and despite the fact that I've written two deck articles since the beginning of April, a lot of you have deck disasters and still need a little help.

Home items such as roofs, water heaters, and floors, only need intensive care once every 10 or 20 years. But decks are not like that – they need constant maintenance. There is no way around doing the work to keep it looking good.

Decks should be regularly cleaned and completely stripped and resealed at least once every two years. Trying to apply new stain or sealer on top of old stain or sealer is one of the prime causes for splotchy-looking decks and finish failure.

People are frustrated with the amount of work deck care takes and the lack of results they get from many of the products they use. Believe me, I understand your problems and frustrations because my publisher, Master Handyman Press, maintains a pressure-treated wood test deck. We give multiyear tests to many of the deck stains, sealers, brighteners and strippers. We don't just read press releases, we experience the same problems and frustrations you do.

Neither I, nor my publisher, endorse products, but many of our results are reported in my book, *Deck Care Fast & Easy*. Here are some of the things we learned. Keep in mind, our tests are subjective and many of the best products on the market today did not even exist five years ago. Don't hold it against your favorite product if it is not mentioned. Use the following as background information to direct you to general classes of products, not necessarily brand names

We used five of the leading strippers on deck and railing surfaces that had been treated with four deck stains or sealers. Two deck surfaces were clear and two were pigmented. All four surfaces were five years old at the time they were stripped.

On the clear sealed deck surfaces, the clear coat that called for a two coat application, Penofin Cedar Marine, Performance Coatings, (800) 736-6346, outlasted the one coat application by at least two years. Remember, 65 percent of the work is preparation. You save time and money applying a second coat.

The pigmented stains used on the deck were Wolman Rain Coat, (800) 556-7737, and Sikken's Cetol DEK, (800) 833-7288. The Wolman product was sprayed on with a garden sprayer and brushed out with a push broom, per manufacturer's instructions. The Cetol DEK is a two coat system requiring the application of one coat of Cetol DEK Base, then a follow up coat of Cetol

DEK the first year. The second year a single coat of Cetol DEK was applied per manufacturer's instructions. The instructions actually called for an additional coat being applied every year. We did not apply coats after the second year. The Wolman Rain Coat got lighter as the years passed, but deck color was satisfactory through the third year. When it came time to take off the stains and sealers, Rain Coat was the easiest to strip of any product tested.

Cetol DEK has a furniture-like oil base finish. It is a lot of work to apply but was the most durable finish. When stripped completely, the wood underneath the Cetol DEK was in the best condition of any wood on tested.

Almost all deck strippers and brighteners claim that a pressure washer is not required so none was used for finish removal or brightening. However, if you have access to a pressure washer, use it. The fellow who actually did most of the work, swears he will never strip a deck without a pressure washer again. Using a pressure washer would have saved about 75 percent of the time and at least one-third of the product used.

Two of the three most effective strippers were citrus based: Bio-Wash Stripex L, (800) 858-5011, and Specialty Environmental Wood Pal Deck Stain and Finish Stripper, (800) 899-0401. Wolman DeckStrip Stain & Finish Remover, (800) 556-7737, which contains Sodium Hydroxide, was also very effective. Both the Bio-Wash and Wood Pal products are two-stage strippers. You strip the deck, then use the ingredients in the attached packet to give the wood a light acid bath to remove discolored, dead wood. The Wolman product label warns that cedar and redwood may need a brightener to remove discoloration after stripping.

Almost all the strippers and brighteners we tried could remove light mildew growth, but none were effective removing really intense mildew staining. X-14 Mildew Remover, Block Drug, (800) 365-6500, was used on a small portion of the deck to make certain that the discoloration was really mold and mildew growth, not common outside dirt. The X-14 was effective. A strong Trisodium Phosphate (TSP), chlorine bleach and hot water solution was also found to be effective when used with a scrub brush. I am not recommending either procedure. If you must use them, be sure and apply a wood brightener to remove damaged wood cells before re-staining.

This is a case where using a powerwasher might have made a big difference. I will report back to you when I can confidently recommend a mildew stripper.

Regular boat upkeep can prevent damage from water and sun

by Glenn Haege,
America's Master Handyman

Boats are big around here. And why not? According to the Great Lakes Commission, we are in the middle of six quadrillion gallons of fresh water. This is 94 percent of the U.S. supply of fresh surface water. Michigan alone has 3,200 miles of shoreline.

The Great Lakes Region has 3.5 million registered boats. That's a lot of boats and a lot of boaters. From the Handyman's point of view, that's also a lot of sore arms and backs as you clean and shine the deck, hull and cushions.

Here's hoping this article will make things a little easier for all you weekend sailors.

I love teak trim. Unfortunately teak gets old-looking rapidly. Your job, as captain, is to keep the trim looking good. Most of the sealing and stain products on the market cannot with stand the deadly combination of water and sun. Akzo Nobel Sikkens, (800) 833-7288, has created a finish exclusively for this challenging environment.

The product called Cetol Marine is either a three-coat or a four-coat system depending on whether you want a satin or a gloss finish. If you want a satin finish, strip the teak or other wood trim and sand lightly. Then apply three coats of Cetol Marine. If you want a gloss surface, strip and sand, then apply two coats of Cetol Marine and two coats of Cetol Marine Gloss.

The surface will have a rich furniture finish. To keep it looking good, clean annually with a hand dish washing detergent like Palmolive and a Scotch Brite sanding pad. When dry, apply one coat of Cetol Marine or Cetol Marine Gloss.

Luckily the day of wood boats is long past for most of us. Today's boat owners live in a world of fiberglass and aluminum. For general maintenance, clean with good biodegradable cleaners like Simple Green by Sunshine Makers, (800) 228-0709; Clear Magic by Blue Coral Inc., (800) 545-0982; or Krud Kutter by Supreme Chemicals, (800) 466-7126.

When fiberglass gel coat becomes stained, you can often clean the surface easily with a gob of waterless hand cleaner, such as Gojo, Fast or D&L that you will find at any hardware store. Just sponge on and wash off. No scrubbing required.

If your fiberglass boat has gotten dark brown, algae-covered, and grungy-looking, you can clean it off with OxiSolv Fiberglass Boat Cleaner by OxiSolv, (800) 594-9028. This product comes ready to use. Just spray on the soiled surface and spray off with a garden hose or pressure washer. If you have to do the entire hull, start from the bottom and work up to avoid streaking.

One of the best things about this product is that, although very strong, it is biodegradable and will do no harm to our water ways. OxiSolv Fiberglass Boat Cleaner also does a good job cleaning stainless steel and chrome.

Pontoon boats are a good value and fine for fishing and family fun. Unfortunately, the aluminum pontoons get weathered-looking rapidly. The weathered appearance is a combination of oxidation, algae growth and staining. The OxiSolv company has created Aluminum Pontoon Boat Cleaner for this specific problem. The product is strong enough to bring back the luster, but biodegradable, so it won't hurt the environment. Apply with a brush or roller, let it set 10 or 15 minutes, then rinse off with a garden hose.

If a boat bottom is very fouled with barnacles and zebra mussels, the Star brite Company, (800) 327-8583, makes a very strong hydrochloric acid based cleaner – Star brite Boat Bottom Cleaner – that will remove everything. This is really strong stuff, so read the directions very carefully and follow all the safety recommendations.

Deep cleaning fiberglass or aluminum surfaces establishes a rough profile. That means that it has made the surface easy for dirt, mildew and all the other bad guys to grab on and make the surface dirty again. To help slow down the procedure give all non walking surfaces a coat of Gel Gloss by TR Industries, (800) 553-6866. It contains a unique mixture of carnauba wax and silicones that provides a long-lasting, smooth finish.

Boats, water, mold, mildew, and the musties, go together. Your boat is the perfect breeding ground for mold, mildew and their accompanying dank smells. Punati Chemical Corp., (800) 645-2882, has just come out with Smells Begone Odor Absorber in a solid form. Open the product and place it in the boat cuddy or full cabin, it will absorb all odors including gasoline and keep the area smelling good for about 90 days. Smells Begone Odor Absorber is completely biodegradable.

To kill the mold and mildew hang a couple of Mildew Gas Bags II by Star brite in the cuddy or cabin. This is especially important when you store the boat for any period of time because moist enclosed spaces are perfect breeding grounds.

To spot clean mildew off of cloth, fiberglass, wood, or vinyl use Enviromagic by Amazon Premium Products, (800) 832-5645. Spray on and wipe off.

The bilge of most boats collects oil and fuel spills. To remove the pollutants, get a Bilge Hawg mini-boom by Applied Science Corp., (813) 899-0707. Just throw the Bilge Hawg in the bilge. It will absorb the oil and fuel but repel water, and is impervious to humidity.

You've done enough for one day, Captain – let's take the boat out and go cruising.

JUNE 13, 1998

Preparation is the most important step when painting your house

by Glenn Haege,
America's Master Handyman

If the outside of your house looks like the setting for an Adam's family reunion, it's time to paint.

Unfortunately, there is no such thing as a no-maintenance finish. Even if you have brick or stone, you still have to worry about windows and trim. Eventually even brick and stone should be sealed.

For the next two weeks, I am going to concentrate on exteriors that have to be stained or painted. If you need more information look for a copy of my book, *Take the Pain Out of Painting – Exteriors,* at your library, book or hardware store.

A good looking paint job requires attention to the Three Ps:
■ Preparation
■ Paint
■ Performance

Since 60 to 65 percent of the work is Preparation (getting ready to paint and surface preparation) I'll concentrate on that this week. Next week I'll cover paint and performance.

Exterior painting and/or staining is not a one-day job. Applying the paint is like frosting a cake – it is something you do after the majority of the work is already accomplished.

Inspect the surface

Take a walk around the house and write down what needs to be done. Carry a broom with the bristles covered by a rag to brush away the cob-webs. You may find that you have nests with baby birds that cannot yet be moved. If so, be a good neighbor and put off the job until they are ready to leave home.

If you find bee or hornet nests, have them removed by a pest control expert. Trying to remove the nests yourself could put you in the hospital. If you see them entering a hole in the siding, DO NOT CLOSE THEM IN. Trapped insects can escape into your house and make it uninhabitable.

During your inspection, you will find that the surface is not uniformly bad. The past 10 years or more have had different effects on different areas. Mold and mildew on the northern exposure. Blistering or peeling on the south and east. Perhaps the wood looks soft under the living room picture window (better get an awl and check it). Or maybe the caulk is dry and beginning to pull away.

You can prep and paint a house by yourself, but togetherness is a wonderful thing. Whether it's carrying an extension ladder, assembling scaffolding, cleaning, or painting, two people get the job done far more efficiently. Besides, it's more fun.

Painted areas

OK. Let's start. Scrape away all the loose paint. Then sand smooth with 80 grit sand paper.

When the surface is very dirty or the paint is in especially bad condition, you may want to power wash before you sand and strip. The power washing will do much of this work. Wear goggles, gloves, long sleeved shirt and slacks. Keep the pressure below 1500 PSI (pounds per square inch). Power wash in the cool of the day. If you are going to wash down the surface by hand, hold off until the rest of the prep work has been done.

All deteriorated paint has to be removed. This may require that you sand or strip it away with the aid of a heat gun, or a tool like the Bernz O Matic Portable Paint Stripper, by Bernz O Matic, (800) 654-9011.

Remove all rotten wood. In some cases you may have to remove entire pieces of siding. At other times you can just remove the damaged wood with a chisel and fill with Minwax High Performance Wood Filler, (800) 462-0194, or other product that plainly states that it is for exterior use.

Windows

To check the condition of the caulk, press into it with your thumb nail or a dime. If it bounces back, fine. If the surface is stiff, or has pulled away in some areas, replace it. Remove old caulk with a hook billed linoleum knife and clean with mineral spirits or paint thinner. This is not a fun job, so re-caulk with one of the new urethane caulks, like Vulchem. They stay supple far longer.

If you are going to work on the windows, sand the frame surface and remove old putty. Brush clean, then apply a coat of Penetrol by the Flood Co., (800) 356-6346, on all raw surfaces. Wait at least eight hours before you re-putty.

Hand-washing

You're almost done. If you are hand washing the surface, now is the time. Clean the exterior and window frames with a solution of 2 ounces (dry measure) of trisodium phosphate (TSP) per gallon of water. If there was any mold or mildew on the surface, add 2 cups of household bleach. If the surface is especially dirty, double the amount of TSP. An entire house usually takes about three to five gallons of cleaning solution.

If possible, use the buddy system. One person uses a long handled brush and big bucket and washes. The other person rinses with a garden hose. TSP is strong stuff, be sure to wear goggles and rubber gloves. If you have had to add bleach, drench the ground and all plants before you start to clean. Protect sensitive plants and bushes with plastic tarps.

Next week we'll paint.

Take these steps for a paint job your home will wear with pride

by Glenn Haege,
America's Master Handyman

Last week I told you that the three "P's" – preparation, paint and performance – are the secret to a great-looking paint job. Last week we prepped. This week we'll take care of the Paint and Performance.

There are cheap paints and top-of-the-line paints. Cheap paints are a waste of your time. Top-of-the-line paints are manufactured with all the properties needed for a strong, long lasting, surface. Performance – how much paint you apply, how you follow instructions – is the final ingredient needed for a good-looking, long-lasting paint job.

I am going to concentrate on the most common exterior surfaces. If you need more information, look for a copy of my book *Take the Pain Out of Painting – Exteriors* at your library, book or hardware store.

Ladders

Falling from ladders is a leading cause of serious injury. The R. D. Werner Co., one of the country's leading ladder manufacturers, has established the following guide lines.

Working Load/Type Ladder
(Combined weight of User, Tools & Materials)

Over 300 pounds	Stay off ladder
Up to 300 pounds	Type I A
Up to 250 pounds	Type I
Up to 225 pounds	Type II
Up to 200 pounds	Type III

You and your family will be safer if you invest in a good, heavy duty, class I or IA step ladder.

If you only use extension ladders occasionally, you are better off renting a good one than buying a cheap one, or borrowing some rickety old thing from a neighbor.

If you are going to paint a two or three story house, consider renting scaffolding. National Ladder & Scaffold, (800) 535-5944, will rent a homeowner a 20 foot high, 7 foot wide by 5 foot deep scaffold, for only $100 a month. That is a lot of safety for very little money.

Paint Application

There are four basic ways to apply exterior paint: brush, roller, brush/roller combination and airless spray. I prefer the brush/roller method. One person applies the paint with a roller, the other person brushes it in.

If you decide to use an airless sprayer, rent a professional quality unit from a full-service paint store or equipment rental company. Jim Hay at Harrison Paint, (810) 268-0808, will rent a professional Airless Co. spray unit for $60 a day. At United Paint the rental rate is $65 a day plus $500 deposit. This type of equipment will give you a much better job than what is available at a hardware store.

Before you spray, check with your significant other and nearby neighbors. Airless spray guns use an atomizing pressure between 1200 and 2800 PSI (pounds per square inch), and have a minimum dispersal rate of 1/2 to 3/4 gallons per minute! You better know where all that paint is going. Practice your technique on some old boxes, not the side of your house.

OK. Let's paint.

Wood Surfaces
Big question: Should you paint or stain? Any wood surface can be stained or painted. That includes regular siding, T-1-11, and staccato board. Stain allows the texture of the wood to show. Paint bridges the surface and gives a smoother look.

The general rule is that if you like the look, you are better off using a solid color stain the first few times. There is less film build and pre-painting preparation is therefore easier. Water based stain holds its color longer than oil-based.

T-1-11 that is more than 12 years old should be painted.

If you paint, most people buy a premium acrylic latex paint. Apply a water-based stain kill, like 1-2-3 by Zinsser, (800) 899-1211, or Total One by Master Chem, (800) 325-3552, to bare spots before painting.

Aluminum Surfaces
Aluminum is actually a better surface to paint than wood, but the surface must be very clean and all chalking removed. There are many excellent paints on the market especially formulated for aluminum siding such as Valspar Aluminum Siding Paint, (800) 345-4530, Pittsburgh Manor Hall, (800) 441-9695, Benjamin Moore Mooreguard, (888) 236-6667, Sherwin Williams Super Paint, (800) 474-3794, etc. Follow label directions to the letter and you will be a winner.

Other Surfaces
You should not have to paint vinyl surfaces, but if you want to change color, apply a water-base stain kill, first, then use a premium acrylic latex for the finish coat.

As for asbestos shingles, concrete block, stucco, & masonry surfaces, clean them thoroughly then coat with a premium acrylic latex paint. Encapsulate the surface completely.

Performance
The final "P." No matter how good the paint, it can not provide the protection your house needs unless you apply it properly.

Good paint, especially premium acrylic latex is very creamy. It is very easy to apply too thin a coat. The new surface needs to be 5 mills thick when dry. That usually means two coats applied at 400 square feet per gallon.

If the surface is especially rough or porous, like rough sawn cedar or stucco, the first coat should be applied at a rate of 200 square feet per gallon.

If you are dealing with a painting contractor, the number of coats of paint means nothing. The contract should specify the square footage of area to be covered and how many gallons of paint will be used on the job. The formula is: Square footage to be covered divided by recommended square feet per gallon, equals gallons per coat. If you have a 2,000 square foot surface area, divided by a 400-square-feet-per-gallon spread rate. You would need five gallons per coat. Two coats would require 10 gallons.

Follow the rules and you will have a great looking job.

JUNE 27, 1998

New machines can make sanding your hardwood floors easy

by Glenn Haege,
America's Master Handyman

You pulled up the worn out carpet and found old, ratty looking, hardwood flooring. Should you cover it back up or can you breath new life into the thing?

The good news is that solid hardwood flooring is rated for life of structure. It could last as long as the house does. It does not mean that it will look good all that time without proper care.

In my book – *Glenn Haege's Complete Hardwood Floor Care Guide, How to Refinish & Care for Your Wood Floors* – I mention an easy way to bring back the gloss to a floor. The procedure, called "brightening," consists of cutting the surface of the old finish, cleaning thoroughly, then applying another couple of finish coats.

Brightening is a good technique, if done every three to five years. If the hardwood surface has had major wear, complete refinishing is necessary. Usually, a hardwood floor has to be refinished every 20 years.

No one wants to think about refinishing a floor in July, but this is a good time to do the job. You can work with the windows open and family members not involved in the project can go up North for a vacation and stay off your floor.

Refinishing is not nearly as hard as it used to be, thanks to the Clarke EZ 8 Floor Sander, Alto US, (800) 253-0376. A standard drum sander weighs 200 to 300 pounds. The EZ 8, at 150 pounds, is a light weight. The beauty is that it can do just as good a job as the big boys, and is a great deal more maneuverable. It's available locally at Buttons Rental, (248) 542-5835, and Crandall Worthington in Ferndale, (248) 398-8118.

Another lightweight sander, the Squar Buff by Flecto Co. Inc., (800) 635-3286, is available at Dammans, Builder's Square, Home Depot, and many other fine hardware and home centers.

In addition to the big sander, you will need a respirator; a professional 16-inch edging buffer/sander; a heavy duty, wet/dry bag vacuum; sanding block; scraper; and putty knife. You should also wear a dual cartridge-style respirator. Don't cheat on the vacuum cleaner – if you don't use the bag style, the fine dust will ruin the motor.

The materials you'll need for the sanding procedure are rolls of open-faced coarse, medium, and fine grit sanding belts for the EZ 8, disks for the edger, nonmetallic steel wool pads, and wood filler.

The trick when sanding is to take off the all the finish, but almost none of the wood. A professional only removes about 1/16-inch of wood.

Here is the general procedure:

Safety first. No smoking, and turn off the furnace and water tank pilot lights. Turn the air conditioner off.

Remove the quarter round molding and protect wall molding with painters tape. Clean the floor thoroughly.

Make certain that the flooring is firmly attached to the sub floor. If you have to replace entire strips of wood, countersink the nails before sanding.

Sand the entire area. Begin with the coarse grit paper. Sand with the grain, never across the grain of the wood. Start at the far right wall, 2/3 of the way across the width of the room. Just before you reaching the far wall, lift the sanding drum from the floor. Gently lower the sanding drum to the floor and pull the sander back to its original position. When you have returned to your original position, gently raise the sanding drum and stop.

Move the sander 4 inches to your left and repeat the process. You will overlap 2 or 3 inches. Overlapping helps you judge the depth of the cut. Continue the procedure until the entire width of the floor has been sanded. When you reach the opposing wall, lift the drum, turn the sander 180 degrees and repeat the procedure, until you have sanded the entire room.

Use the power edger to sand to the walls and other areas too small for the EZ 8. When using the edger start at the wall. Work with the grain to the edge of the sanded area. Then pick up the edger, go to the left and repeat the process. Overlap the drum-sanded area slightly.

The coarse grit paper removes the old finish and a whisper's depth of wood. Do not let sanding dust collect on the floor. Vacuum constantly.

Repeat the procedure with medium, then fine grit paper. The medium and fine papers remove scratches created by the rough grit paper. Remove final swirl marks where the edger and the EZ 8 overlap with the sanding block.

When sanding is completed, vacuum meticulously, including window sills and door ledges. Then wipe down the floor with a slightly damp rag. Let dry thoroughly.

Now you have a completely new surface. Stain and finish with the products of your choice. Every good lumber yard, home center and hardware store have good collections of stains and finishes. Crandall Worthington, specializes in do-it-yourself refinishing and can give you some very good tips.

Put on at least three or four finish coats. Many finishes, especially the new waterbornes, dry so rapidly that you need only 2 or 3 hours drying time between coats.

A lesson in smart parental management: Hire a student (yours)

by Glenn Haege,
America's Master Handyman

Most of the students who are going to have summer jobs, have them. If yours missed out, not having a job can mean a prolonged bout of utter boredom: sleeping late, watching TV, marathon phone calls, needing money desperately.

You, as the father/mother, are the automatic chairman of the entertainment committee. You will be expected to provide the funds for summer fun.

Here are a few summer projects designed to help your child earn extra money, while doing work that needs to be done. These are all equal opportunity jobs and can be performed by any boy or girl from the tenth grade on up.

Garages

A good project is to clean and paint the inside of the garage. Give the garage drywall a strong, water-proof surface with two coats of latex basement floor paint or Permawhite by William Zinsser, (800) 899-1211. After painting give the floors a good cleaning. Sweep, vacuum, and dust. Use Goof Off II, Atlanta Sundries, (800) 253-3957, to remove grease spots and paint – just spray on, rinse off.

Windows and deck

These two jobs should be done monthly.

Remove all screens and clean with a garden hose and a medium soft bristle brush. A car cleaning brush is ideal. Set aside to air dry, and replace after washing windows.

Wash windows outside with a solution of 4 ounces of vinegar to 1 gallon of water. Your teen should use a sponge, squeegee and old cotton towel. Put the towel on the sill. Sponge cleaning solution on. Squeegee off. Wipe up drips with the towel. If your home has storm windows, clean debris from the sill between the storm and regular window.

Inside windows are cleaned with the same technique, but use a solution of 4 ounces of vinegar and 1 teaspoon of hand dishwashing detergent to 1 gallon of water.

To lightly clean the deck use a 10-1 solution (about 1-1/2 cups of product per gallon of water) of an environmentally friendly cleaner like Simple Green or Clear Magic. Brush on with a deck brush. Rinse off with the garden hose.

Exterior of house

Though few of us do it, a home's exterior of a house – whether wood, aluminum or brick – needs to be washed. A teen can give a one story house a bath. I don't recommend they wash two-story homes; climbing extension ladders can be dangerous. However, they could use the garden hose to rinse off the second story; then wash as high as they can reach from ground level. Detroit Quality Brush, (800) 722-3037, makes a Bi-Level brush just for this purpose.

Use the same 10-1 solution I recommended for the deck to lightly clean all types of siding. If more power is needed, increase the solution to 1/2 gallon of cleaner to 1 gallon of water. Make certain your teenager wears goggles and rubber gloves.

Chain link fencing

If your kid would like to look like the Tin Man in *The Wizard of Oz,* he or she may actually like painting the chain link fencing. Wear old throw away gloves, shoes and clothes. Since you are only interested in painting one side of the fence, check with the neighbors before starting. They may want to do their side at the same time. If your child has an entrepreneurial spirit, he or she might want to offer to do the job for the neighbor for a fee.

Cut the grass short near the fence. Pull out all weeds and trim the shrubs. Brush away loose dirt with a garage broom. Aluminum paint should not be shaken, so it will have to be mixed at home. The best way to do this is to "box" the paint. That means pouring the paint back and forth between containers until all the paint is thoroughly mixed.

When ready to paint, pour a gallon of paint into a five gallon bucket and insert a roller grid available at any paint store. Roll on the paint with a fence roller. Don't clean up until completely done. If the bucket and roller are warped in Saran Wrap they can still be used the next day.

Household inventory

Have your student walk around the house and take pictures of every item of value. That includes the TV, microwave, stove, dishwasher, radios, tools, jewelry, everything. The photos can be shot with a still camera or video taped. If video taped, a verbal description can be made at the same time as the visual.

Get two copies of the photos, or duplicate the video tape. One set goes into your bank security deposit box or is given to a friend or relative. The other should be stored in a secure spot in your house.

If your child is a decent typist, get your address book and those scraps of paper you've been saving, and have your teen transfer the data to your computer. This will make your relatives believe you're really organized. Most word processing and spread sheet programs can sort alphabetically.

Isn't telling someone else to do the work fun? Try it more often. The kids need the money and actually working to help keep up the house and do something the family needs builds feelings of self worth. In other words, *they can brag about it.*

JULY 11, 1998

Protect your home from power surges, blackout – and burnouts

by Glenn Haege,
America's Master Handyman

Electric power is a two-edged sword. It is absolutely essential for modern life, but it can destroy your appliances and burn down your house.

Electric power surges, spikes, black outs, brown outs, and what we can do about them is such a big subject that I am splitting it into two parts. This week I'll cover spikes and surges.

Next week's topic will be what we can do when the power goes down.

For the last few years Don Collins, of Budget Electric, (800) 400-8941, and I have been preaching about the need for surge protectors. Collin's company installs more whole house surge protectors than any other company in the state. However, the vast majority of our homes are unprotected.

Most problems relating to electricity and electronic devices can be traced to line noise, over-voltage, and under voltage. Examples of over-voltage are spikes and surges. A spike is a very short over-voltage condition, usually less than a millionth of a second. Spikes usually don't harm electronic equipment.

Surges last much longer – usually last several thousandths of a second – and are often more powerful. This, in electronic terms, is long term over-charging. It can overcome internal protection and burn out (fry) delicate electric circuits.

A spike can be created from something as innocuous as one person turning on

the electric clothes dryer, while another person is on the computer.

A surge can be created from a squirrel chewing through an electric cable, two or three neighbors turning on their air conditioning at the same time, a lineman shutting off, then returning the power to a line, or lightening hitting a tower and sending a couple of hundred thousand extra volts down the line.

Surges can also be transmitted through the ground for considerable distances and cause a great deal of damage.

In our parent's day, most electrical equipment had manual switches that simply turned off and on.

Spikes, surges – even low power situations – seldom caused major damage. With the introduction of ever more delicate micro-electronics, our electric products are becoming far more sensitive.

Computers and products with touch pads are especially vulnerable to power variations.

Most whole-house surge suppressors are connected to the inside electric power.

Some rural power cooperatives provide a surge protection device, called the HomeGuard, that connects directly to the electric meter and stops major surges from entering the house.

If your electricity is provided by a power co-op, contact them to see if they are supporting this NRTC (National Rural Telecommunications Co-Operative) program.

Whole-house surge protectors only protect electronic equipment from one third of the potential problems. Spikes and surges can also travel along cable and telephone wires. Your electronic devices need to be protected from them, too.

Ditek, a surge suppressor manufacturer, (800) 753-2345, has created a series of telephone, cable TV and Whole House surge protector kits that retail from $178 to $298. The more expensive kit provides a surge suppressor that has about four times the energy dissipation capacity of the lowest-priced kit. It also provides a $25,000 electro mechanical warranty against damage to connected equipment.

Individual pieces of electronic equipment, should be protected with specialized surge protection devices. Full-line protection companies like Ditek and APC, American Power Conversion, (514) 369-4919, make specialized surge protectors for everything from computers, medical, and high performance devices, to sump pumps and satellite systems.

Different types of equipment require different amounts of surge suppression and different clamping speeds. Clamping speed is the term that denotes how fast the equipment reacts.

A surge suppressor with a low clamping voltage (good) but also a slow clamping speed (bad), is not sufficient to protect delicate equipment like computers.

Most good surge suppressors have a 1449 UL Rating with a 330 volt rating. This rating requires that the suppressor will let through no more than 330 volts of electric power. Actual let-through voltage may vary from 180 to 330 volts. The lower, the better.

The vast majority of our homes are unprotected.

Many computer stores carry surge protection devices especially designed for computer equipment. Some suppressors protect both power and modem phone lines.

When you consider how costly it can be to lose the information on your hard drive, surge protection devices are very cheap insurance.

Collins, of Budget Electric, warns that although he always recommends surge suppressors, there is no fool-proof system.

"If you have to be away from home for long, make certain that a friend or neighbor checks the house regularly.

"Just walking inside and turning on the lights is not enough. The power may have come back on after a black out and the home may seem to be in good condition, even though critical appliances have burned out.

"The person looking after your home should go down to the basement and check the sump pump. If it has burned out, your basement could be ruined. Then check other major appliances, like freezer and refrigerators" he advises.

During an electric or wind storm, Detroit Edison, suggests you unplug all sensitive electronic equipment and appliances, but leave incandescent light bulbs on. When the lights stop flickering and go back to full power, the danger is past and the electronic equipment can be plugged back in.

Next week, we'll look at what we can do to put ourselves in control of our power supplies.

JULY 18, 1998

Want more power to the people? Generate a backup energy source

by Glenn Haege,
America's Master Handyman

It's so hot the lights are growing dim. The refrigerator is giving off a funny "click, click, click" sound. That sound could be a death rattle. It means your electrical appliances are in a brownout condition and may be minutes away from burning out.

It used to be that all we could do was shut off the air conditioning, TV, computer, refrigerator, and freezer. Pull the plugs, sit down and prepare to sweat it out and say, "Welcome to the good old summer time."

When we need it most, our electric power is in the shortest supply. The power companies have over-use conditions, have to reallocate electricity, and may automatically decrease the power flowing through your residential lines.

If you don't pay attention, the power decrease could cause your electrical equipment to burn out.

Sags, brownouts, and blackouts, are all under-voltage conditions. A sag is a momentary dip in the electric power supply, like when the air conditioner or dryer goes on. A brownout is reduced power due to over-usage. A blackout is the complete loss of power.

You can protect your house from under-voltage, but it is an expensive proposition. However, once you have installed an alternative power supply, like an electric generator, you can take your house off-line during brownout or dangerous weather conditions and make it completely safe from electrical power line problems.

Don Collins, of Budget Electric in Roseville, says that the proper way to use an electric generator is to go "off line" and start the generator as soon as you think that blackout or brownout conditions may start.

"All motors should be run occasionally. Turning the generator on is good for the equipment, and once your house is off the utilities power grid, you are safe," he says.

When buying a generator, the majority of us get gas-powered equipment. Diesel, propane, and natural gas motors are usually restricted to very expensive, megawatt installations in hospitals and factories.

Collins says a 5,000-watt generator is enough to provide the basics for most homes. This includes sufficient power for the furnace, refrigerator, freezer, micro-wave, TV, VCR, radio, and basic lighting.

If you have a home office or medical equipment, your requirements may be in the 7,000 to 10,000-watt range.

Phil LaCoursiere, owner of Discount Air Compressor and Generator, in Pontiac, warns that people with wells have to be especially careful to get a properly sized generator.

"Most folks can get by with 5,000-watts, but if they have a deep well or a shallow well with a big motor, they will need extra power," he says.

This is because motor loads require three to four times the wattage (or amperage) ratings on the nameplate. LaCoursiere believes load factors to be so important that he will not sell a generator until he has done a needs assessment with the customer.

Prices of gas-powered generators have come down greatly over the past few years. The cheapest I found was a Coleman Powermate 5,000-watt for $599 at Builders Square.

Collins of Budget Electric, (800) 400-8941, says that if you shop for the generator carefully, his company can install a basic 5,000-watt system for around $1,500 to $1750, including generator and switches.

This type of generator has to be turned on and off manually. Hooking one up is definitely not a do-it-yourself project. Improper installation can not only kill you, it could electrocute power company employees trying to restore electric power to your neighborhood.

Not everyone believes in low-cost generators. The savings usually come from lighter weight materials.

The people at Weingartz Lawn and Garden, (810) 731-7240, of Utica and Farmington Hills, and Discount Air Compressor and Generator, of Pontiac, (248) 338-2255, swear by heavy-duty Honda Powered equipment. Both companies sell to contractors and people with a medical or other critical need for continuous power.

There is a great deal of difference between similarly rated equipment. Weingartz sells a light weight 5000-watt Honda generator for $999. Heavier duty models of similar wattage cost far more.

Discount Air Compressor and Generator carries a wide range of equipment, much of it created to LaCoursiere's own design.

The store's entire catalog is on the internet, (www.gohonda.com), and it is one of the most informative generator sites I have visited.

The store's A-50, 5,000-watt Honda Generator is on sale for $1,199. One of LaCoursiere's exclusive designs, the 10,000-watt Thunderbolt multifuel generator, runs on gas, propane, and natural gas. It is rated for critical load micro-electronics, fire/rescue, and life support. List priced at $4,886, it is on sale at $3,495.

That may seem expensive, but if you have high power requirements or need rugged equipment that can run on almost any fuel, it could be a life saver.

Regardless of what you buy, LaCoursiere says that the most critical factor for long term performance is the quality of the gasoline. He says that most of his generator repairs are caused by gummed up carburetors and impurities from the gasoline and recommends high octane lead free from a high-volume national retailer like Amoco, Mobil, or Shell.

The right settings will keep your air conditioner running smoothly

by Glenn Haege,
America's Master Handyman

It's either so hot and muggy you can't lift a toothbrush without perspiring, or it's so hot and dry the grass is dying and there's is a water ban in place. Add to the mix that it is probably an Ozone Action Day.

Isn't summer wonderful?

Larry Kaufman, a product manager for Detroit Edison, was on my radio show last Saturday discussing summer-related electric power problems and what you can do about them. Edison has a free brochure on summer energy use. You can get a copy of the brochure by calling (800) 833-2786, or look it up on the web at www.detroitedison.com.

Here are a few tips to help you keep your cool.

Almost all of us have central air conditioning or window units. During the summer, these appliances are the hardest-working ones in the house.

Central air conditioning systems are designed to lower the temperature in the building by conditioning (dehumidifying) and cooling the air. They are limited to lowering the air temperature by a difference of 15 degrees Fahrenheit. If it is 98 degrees outside, the maximum the air conditioner has been built to do is lower the inside temperature to 83 degrees.

Setting the thermostat for 70 degrees on a 90- degree-plus day will keep the unit straining trying to accomplish an impossible task. Compressor repair during a heat wave is not only expensive, it could easily take days or weeks to get a service person out to do the repair.

In other words, be kind to your air conditioner, or it won't be around when you need it most.

If you are starting to feel cool or want the air conditioner to stop running for a short period of time, turn the thermostat setting up. The air conditioner will finish it cycle and shut off. When you want the air conditioner to start up again, return the thermostat to its normal setting.

During the summer, always set your thermostat at the highest comfortable temperature. Then, when leaving home for more than five hours, raise the thermostat setting an additional 5 or 10 degrees. This will make the air conditioner's job much easier.

The same thing holds doubly true for window air units. Window air conditioners are built to cool a confined area. Do not expect one or two units to cool the entire living area, unless you live in a very small apartment. Don't have them running on high all the time.

Keep the compressor clean on both window air conditioners and central air units. Clean or replace the air filters at least once a month.

Everything has been growing like wild outside. That includes all the plants around the air conditioning unit. These plants cut off the compressor's air supply and can cause overheating.

Cut down and pull out all the offending plant life. Move any lawn chairs or other obstacles that may be impeding air flow. Do the work in the cool of the morning when the air conditioner has been off for several hours. When you are done cutting and moving, take the garden hose and spray the accumulated lawn clippings and air borne contaminants off the compressor.

Give the air conditioners a helping hand. You are cooled, not just by cold air, but by wind, so keep the fans going. A gentle breeze causes the perspiration on our bodies to evaporate. This causes us to feel cool and comfortable at a warmer temperature. The fan also extends the reach and power of the air conditioner by decreasing the humidity in the air and making the compressor more efficient.

So turn on ceiling fans and oscillating fans. They don't have to be turned on high, just a gentle breeze will make you feel a lot cooler.

By turning on a fan, you are decreasing, not increasing, the electric bill. Fans run very inexpensively. Air conditioners are the biggest users of electricity in the house.

Any cooling you can get from a fan instead of an air conditioner, is money in the bank.

Remember, air conditioners work by dehumidifying air. Once you start using the air conditioner, keep doors and windows closed. When the temperature goes down, it is very tempting to open the windows and let the good cool air in. But this hurts the air conditioner and costs you money because outside air is filled with moisture. When you open the windows you let moist air in. The moisture is absorbed by the carpeting, draperies, all fabric in the home, and also sinks into the basement, making it extra cold and damp.

When it comes time to turn the air condition on again, it will have to work twice as hard and twice a long, dehumidifying the air in your home. The longer the air conditioner has to work to cool the air, the harder it is on the equipment, and the bigger your electric bill.

My final tip is for all you business owners. These tips work really well in offices, too.

Your days are numbered if you expect home remodeling this year

by Glenn Haege,
America's Master Handyman

Welcome to 1999. What's that? You say this is the first weekend in August and you haven't even taken your summer vacation yet? Well, if you need a major home improvement and haven't started yet, you could be looking 1999 square in the face before anything starts happening.

One roofing and siding company I know has been operating under "sold out" conditions since the end of June and has been writing all contracts for 1999 since then.

I checked with a leading remodeling company last week and learned that if all the decisions were made and the contract signed, the earliest they could start would be 12 weeks. Since this is the first week in August, that means work couldn't even start until the first week in November, with little hope of the job being completed by Thanksgiving.

A Midwest lumber supplier is reporting a sales increase of over 50 percent so far this year. And they've been in business almost 100 years!

Why is that?

I have a lot of opinions on the subject, but to make certain that I had all the facts, I recently had three builders on my radio show: Mark Guidobono, CEO of Cambridge Homes and president of the Builders Association of South East Michigan; Adam Helfman, president of Fairway Construction, and president of the National Association of the Remodeling Industry; and Don Martin, 1998 President of the National Association of Home Builders.

All three men agreed that thanks to a strong economy, low interest rates, and high consumer confidence, 1998 is going to be one for the record books. Nationwide, we should build 1.2 million homes, many of them far larger than was usual 5 or 10 years ago. As an example, Guidobono's company, Cambridge Construction, specializes in homes of 5,000 square feet or more.

Guidobono says that the building surge translates to 17,000 single family home permits being issued this year in southeast Michigan. That's a lot of houses.

The remodeling part of the equation may even be bigger. According to Helfman, "1998 is going to be the biggest remodeling year on record."

The downside of all this building is that the entire industry is operating in a "stress mode". Helfman says that for a builder or remodeler, this means they have to be careful, "not to take more work than they can handle; not to promise the 'unpromisable'; and to deliver on time."

The trouble is, it's very hard for companies in a seasonal business like construction to say "no." When they get overbooked, some contractors start "spiking" jobs. That means that they get a deposit, deliver materials to the site, maybe even start work, and then just let it sit until they have time to complete the job.

It also means that many new companies go into business and try to snap up the work that is going begging. That's fine if they know what they are doing. If they don't, it spells trouble.

Murray Gula, president of Michigan Construction Protection Agency, warns that the large number of building licenses being issued may well relate to a high number of builder bankruptcies later.

"Just because a person gets a builder's license does not mean that he or she knows anything about the building business. With a little coaching, my cat could probably get a builder's license," Gula says.

This does not mean that I think you should put off getting that new house, or contracting for the new roof, windows, kitchen, or room addition, you need.

I don't see the building boom ending soon. In the Metro Detroit, the situation is going to get a worse before it gets better. Once commercial construction starts on the casinos, good trades people will gravitate to higher paying commercial work and be in even shorter supply.

What all this means is that you have to be extra careful choosing your contractor. Guidobono says that if you want to build a new house, your best bet is to find a subdivision you want to live in and start knocking on doors of the houses you like.

"Go up to the door, and ask the people who their builder was; whether they did a good job; how fast construction was completed; whether the house was completed when promised, and how quickly the builder came back to make necessary repairs," Guidobono says.

If you get good answers to these questions, you know you may have found someone who can do a good job for you. Do a thorough job of checking references and get everything in writing, complete with guaranteed completion dates . This is also very important when looking for a remodeling contractor.

The Michigan Construction Protection Agency, (800) 543-6669, is publishing a new edition of their Lien Law Kit booklet. This booklet goes through the complete construction process, and gives examples of the forms you need completed by the contractor as he or she builds the job. The booklet is very economical and can save you thousands of dollars if something goes wrong.

If you do your part, check out the contractor, follow the rules, and are realistic in your expectations, you'll get a job you can brag about.

Teach your home to run by itself with smart house technology

by Glenn Haege,
America's Master Handyman

How'd you like a house that just about runs itself and will even call you at the office if anything goes wrong? Or how'd you like a house that became as impenetrable as Fort Knox, dims the lights and starts soft music playing when you felt romantic, and even starts dinner when you were run late? It's all possible with X10 smart house technology.

X10 should not be confused with expensive, hard-wired systems. Since X10 runs on your home's 120-volt lines, you are already hooked up. All you have to do is add equipment to hook into the system

Today, I'll introduce you to X10. Later articles will concentrate on home security, home automation, and home theater and family entertainment.

The entire industry is only around twenty years old. In the early 1970's scientists at a Scottish company, Pico Electronics, discovered that they could send short 120 Kilohertz (Khz) radio signals over the 120-volt electric power lines in our houses. That meant that if you had a signaling device connected to your home's power grid, you could send a short signal to some other object connected to the power grid, if it were equipped with a receiver.

Pico Electronics began developing and shipping products using X10 technology in 1979. For the past 20 years all products utilizing X10 technology have been produced by X-10 Ltd. or licensed by them. The Pico patent ran out in 1997. Since the expiration, many more companies have entered the business.

You may have noticed that I have written "X10" and "X-10". "X10" refers to the technology; any can use the term. "X-10" is a copyrighted name of X-10 Ltd. and refers only to products produced by the company or one of its divisions, such as X-10 USA.

When you count everything from plug-in lamp or appliance modules that turn the lights or power on and off, and controllers, which turn things like computers, phones, or timers, on and off via remote control, X-10 Ltd. and its divisions have an installed base of 100 million home automation systems. If you have a TV remote that also turns on the VCR and cable, you are probably on the X10 band wagon and don't even know about it.

In addition to their own retail sales, X-10 is an original equipment manufacturer for IBM, RCA, Leviton, GE, and Radio Shack.

Installing X10 technology for home automation and security can definitely be a do-it-yourself project. The biggest problem in the past has been that setting up the equipment called for buying lots of little, relatively inexpensive parts. Inventory control for retailers was next to impossible and usually only very technically oriented people got involved with sorting through all the stuff.

Now, X-10 USA, has started selling kits that contain everything you need for various levels of Home Automation installation. Their basic Activehome Kit, sale priced at $49.99, includes $127 worth of equipment, including a CD so that you can integrate your home computer into your X-10 system instead of just using a controller; a 6-in-1 remote; a PC interface; keychain remote control; a lamp module and a transceiver module that you can use to control an appliance. You can get the entire kit connected, up, and running in 15 to 20 minutes, says Alex Peder, the retail division president.

For $100 more, their Activehome Superdeal contains four additional lamp modules, three appliance modules, a wall switch, a motion sensor and a $100 off coupon for security equipment of your choice. That is a $353 value. You can buy the kits by calling (800) 675-3044, or find a complete description of their product line on the internet at x10.com.

If you want so see the broadest range of home automation products, call Home Automation Systems, Inc., (800) 762-7846, and ask for their free catalog. The 126-page catalog gives an excellent description of what home automation is and lists every conceivable product you can imagine.

Home Automation System's website (smarthome.com) is one of the most informative I have seen. It features a guided tour which shows everything from the standard motion detectors, heating and cooling automation, video cameras, and driveway sensors, to products like a mailbox sensor which tells you when the mail is in, pet feeders for your dog, cat, or aquarium. There is even a scarecrow motion detector that shoots a 35-foot stream of water at any critter that invades your garden and an electronically controlled pet door which will let your dog or cat in, but keeps uninvited guests out.

If you like the idea of X10 and smart home technology, but don't like the idea of setting up the system yourself, my friends at Detroit Edison, do a lot of work with Steve Reno at Automated Lifestyles, 248-926-0740, in Ferndale. Reno says that his company can install a basic X10 system in a home for as little as $1,000. A good system can be had for under $3,000. (Ed. note: unfortunately we tried calling Reno five times for this book and were not able to get an answer or find another phone listing.)

Whether you do it yourself, or have it done, X10 technology, can do a lot for your home.

With the right products you can easily patch wood and concrete

by Glenn Haege,
America's Master Handyman

What do you do when good exterior wood goes bad, or a perfectly good concrete drive or steps start spawling? Both can be patched, but how do you make sure it lasts?

First the wood. Decks, porches, and window sills are constantly exposed to the elements. Sooner or later, moisture penetrates at least one area, and the wood begins to get soft. When it comes time to refinish, the first task is to fix the underlying problem. Why did moisture collect there?

Once that problem is solved, patch or replace the wood. When patching, make sure the wood filler's label says that it was made for exterior use. Most wood patching material will not stand up to water and winter's freeze and thaw cycles.

The best known product on the market is Minwax High Performance Wood Filler by the Minwax Corporation, (800) 462-0194. It can be found at almost any hardware store or home center. Minwax Wood Filler comes in a can with a mixing lid. Before you buy the product, remove the mixing lid and make certain that there is a little tube of hardener enclosed. If you go home and find that the hardener was not included, the product is worthless.

Gouge out the rotten wood with a screwdriver or chisel. Clean out the area thoroughly. If the surrounding fibers are a little soft, apply a coat of Minwax or other company's Wood Hardener to strengthen and reinforce the wood and provide a solid surface for the filler.

Once the surface is prepared, open and mix the Wood Filler and the Wood Hardener in the lid. The wood filler will dry to a rock-hard consistency in 15 minutes, so make sure you only mix small amounts. Slightly overfill the indentation. When the product has hardened, it can be sanded and shaped just like wood.

When dry, the product can be stained or painted. Painting will be very successful. If you are staining don't hope for too much. Areas we filled on my test deck have never accepted stain well enough to become unnoticeable. The deck looks like a stained deck with holes filled with stained wood filler. On the plus side, the areas that have been filled have gone through several years and many hundreds of freeze/thaw cycles and the Minwax Wood Filler is still hanging tough.

Wood filler isn't just a cosmetic fix. Rotten wood in load bearing columns or pillars can also be replaced. Once the column has been braced, the rotted section can be sawed out and replaced with a good wood filler epoxy. One company that specializes in this type of product is Abatron, Inc., of Kenosha, WI, (800) 445-1754. They make a two-part Liquid Wood hardener and filler, and WoodEpox, a two-part structural and decorative wood substitute, especially designed for repair of exterior wood.

Retail distribution of these products isn't too good. The closest location is James Lumber in Flint and Grand Blanc, (810) 232-1107. Abatron also sells direct. These products can be purchased independently in sizes ranging from one pint to five gallons. The company also makes a wood restoration kit that includes LiquidWood resin and hardener, pints of A and B the WoodEpox, and a pint of Abosolv solvent cleaner. The pint-sized kit costs $63.25 plus shipping. If you have a big job, a gallon-size kit is priced at $245.90.

Quikrete, (800) 442-7258, makes patching concrete easy with Quikrete Vinyl Concrete Patch. Just make certain that the area to be patched is clean and dry. The product is self-leveling so as soon as you fill the hole, you're done. If you have a large surface that has to be restored, use Quikrete Vinyl Concrete Patch or Ardex Concrete Dressing, (888) 512-7339.

When working with either concrete or wood patching compounds, make certain that every tool you use is cleaned before the product dries. All of the products I listed here dry as hard as concrete.

A personal note

I'm sure I am not the only one who felt a tear trickling down their cheek when they read Nancy Szerlag's column last week. The tribute to her husband, Hank, and the plans for the memorial garden she and her children plan to build, were lovely and loving. Every man who read that column could only hope that, when it's his turn, his life will have made him worthy of so much love.

Though I never really knew Hank, I felt like I did. Regardless of their specialty, Homestyle columnists give us more of themselves than mere technical knowledge. They share so much of themselves that all of us, fellow columnists and readers alike, feel like members of an extended family.

I felt the separation pangs when Marge Colborn's eldest moved out of the house and flew across the country to her first job. Last week, I felt like I was helping decorate her youngest daughter's studio apartment at college. I know Janet Macunovich's family well, even though I only see them on the weekends.

Nancy's loss and her love touched me profoundly. I am certain that when she works in that special garden, she will feel an extra pair of hands helping her there. The love that she and Hank have, they will forever share.

For builders, 'Dream Cruise' was along aisles at hardware show

by Glenn Haege,
America's Master Handyman

Last weekend we had the "Dream Cruise" of classic cars up and down Woodward Avenue. But to anyone in the Hardware Business, the real "dream cruise", or maybe it should be the "Dream Hike", was up and down 18 miles of exhibits at the National Hardware Show and National Building Products Expo this past week at McCormick Place in Chicago.

Some 3,000 exhibitors displayed their wares over 1.3 million square feet of space. More than 1,600 new products were displayed at the show. Most of these new products do not yet have distribution in Detroit, or any other U.S. market. Some were just on display in prototype form. But all of them combined to quicken the pulse of any building professional or do-it-yourselfer lucky enough to attend.

Over the next two weeks I'm going to report on some of the new items that caught my attention. I'll discuss exterior items today, and report on inside items next week.

Three new items that may actually be available to consumers this fall were American Metal Products, Gutter Helmet do-it-yourself packs, Werner Ladder's QuickClick Stabilizer, and Security Product Company's Moss and Mildew Killer.

The Gutter Helmet by American Metal Products, (888) 443-5638, is a solid metal shield that keeps leaves and debris out of gutters. Previously, this product has been exclusively contractor installed. Now, the company is coming out with a do-it-yourself version that will enable the home handy person to save 60 percent or more over contractor installation. If you are somewhat this is a very do-able money saver.

When you install the Gutter Helmet, you need to use a ladder stabilizer on the extension ladder so that you do not lean against the gutters. Up until now all ladder stabilizers have been attached to the ladder with rather unhandy metal brackets. Now, Werner Ladder Co., (724) 588-8600, has come out with the QuickClick Stabilizer that just snaps onto the top ladder rungs. One click and you're ready.

Once you climb up the ladder, you often see moss and mildew starting to grow on the shingles. The Security Products Company, (888) 241-9547, has developed Moss & Mildew Killer a product that can just be sprayed on the roof to destroy the Moss in three to seven days. A handy optional hose-end sprayer sprays the up to 30 feet, so you can reach the top of the roof without being on top of the roof.

Keeping up with the "fall available" theme, Homelite John Deere Consumer Products, (704) 588-3200, introduced the YardVark Gas Blower. Gas blowers are excellent for fall yard clean up. Wheeled blowers are heavy, awkward, and cumbersome to maneuver. Hand held versions get heavy. The YardVark Gas Blower is lightweight and can be wheeled around on an easy to use, two-wheeled dolly. If you have to clean off stairs or a deck, just lift the blower off the dolly and use it as a hand-held blower

All of these products I have written about so far are supposed to be in retail stores this fall. The manufacturers said that they had orders and were either shipping now, or would be in the very near future. Start looking for them in major home centers and cutting edge hardware chains sometime after the middle of September. I don't look for a true national rollout until next year.

One summer/fall season product that will begin shipping as soon as the product is delivered from Finland, where it is made, is the EZ Reach Pruning Stik by Fiskars, Inc. (800) 500-4849. The tool consists of a high quality, hand powered pruning head attached to a lightweight aluminum tube. Using the EZ Reach Pruning Stik you can cut branches up to 1-1/4 inches in diameter, up to 12 feet in the air, without a ladder. Since the cutting head rotates 240 degrees, you can use the same tool to trim ground level shrubs and branches without bending.

The next item could be used by a do-it-yourselfer, but is probably most affordable for the professional deck builder or sub-flooring installer. Nail pops are a perennial problem. Freeze and thaw cycles assure that you have to get down on your knees and pound many nails back in, or you run the risk that some one will run over the deck in bare feet and gouge the sole of their foot quite badly.

One alternative would be to fasten the deck with screws, but that is a very labor-intensive proposition. First you drill, then you nail, and "Oh my aching back."

Now, Stanley Bostitch Fastening Systems, (800) 556-6696, is introducing the ScrewMatic coil-fed screw system. The ScrewMatic system combines one of their Screw Guns with a CST-EXT Extension Pole. No bending is required. Just push down and the screw goes straight in. As soon as this combination gets popular, you will see a lot more screwed decks.

The final new and notable exterior product for today is Perma-White Mildew Resistant Paint by William Zinsser, (732) 469-8100. It comes in a nice selection of white and pastel colors and has a five-year mildew proof warranty.

Oh my aching feet. Next week, we'll go inside.

AUGUST 29, 1998

New hardware on the cutting edge will make your life easier

by Glenn Haege,
America's Master Handyman

How important is hardware?

According to figures released by the National Association of Home Builders, 86 percent of all the homeowners in the Northeast plan to remodel their home. And we in the Midwest are not that far behind.

This creates a tremendous market for hardware and housewares. Many of the best of these products were on display at the National Hardware Show in Chicago.

The show included over 1,200 semi-trailer loads of contractor and exhibitor materials. Among this mass of products and equipment, show spokesmen reported that there were 1,600 new products.

Last week, I described some of the exterior products at the show. This week, I'll report on some of the products and tools meant for interior use. I get paternalistic toward many products because I've see them grow from an idea to a category killer.

One product I first saw in prototype form at the National Houseware Show is now in final design and will soon be in hardware, home center and super market stores. It's called Dispos'l Clean. Produced by Scot Laboratories, (800) 486-7268, the product is an antibacterial foam cleaner. Just spray it into the garbage disposer and it foams up and cleans, disinfects, and deodorizes the area.

Wells Lamont, 800-323-2830, has also developed complete new lines of work gloves. When you have a really tough job, there is nothing better than leather gloves. Unfortunately, you can't wash them, so they get yucky looking fast. And when they get wet, they become so stiff they are only good for dog chews.

Now, Wells Lamont is coming out with a whole line of washable leather gloves. They've also developed lines of cut resistant gloves that will protect your hands from knives, broken glass and sheet metal. The gloves are lightweight, yet give two or three times more protection than leather.

For people who are allergic to latex, Magla Products, Inc., (800) 727-1757, has introduced the Magla Nyplex line of washing and cleaning gloves.

I get a lot of questions about home security. Most burglars don't do anything exotic. They just kick in the door. MacLock, (888) 622-5625, stops that problem with the MacLock 1500. The product adds a 28-inch steel blade and 31-1/2-inch steel strike, giving 28 inches of steel on steel protection. The MacLock 1500 can be attached to any wood, metal or fiberglass door

To lighten up a little, let's talk light. The dark, gray days of winter will soon be with us. To make us see and feel better, Verilux, (800) 786-6850, is introducing the Happylite, a bright, full-spectrum light that they claim may help overcome the feeling of withdrawal, depression, gloom and sadness, we get from light deprivation and seasonal change.

Not to leave our four-footed, feathered, or wiggly friends out, Verilux also has Instant Sun fluorescent pet lighting. These fluorescents provide simulated sunlight for dogs, cats, birds, and reptiles.

Think I'm crazy? Westinghouse, (888) 417-6222, has a complete line of ReptileLites for your snakes, and MarineLites for your fish.

Speaking of lights, the IntelaVoice switch by Vos Systems, (800) 596-0061, will turn a light on or off just by telling it "Lights." You can also use it to turn other small appliances on or off.

If you're doing a project that makes you wish you could see through walls, now you can. SLI Lighting, (800) 533-7290 offers the ProVision 100, a flexible fiber-optic scope, that enables you look between the walls, or inside a garbage disposer, or other inaccessible place.

You may not actually be a superman, but now you can see like one.

When redecorating, nothing adds a better finishing touch than a border. Unfortunately after the first few feet, you need an extra pair of hands to get the job done. Now Dripless, (800) 960-1773, is introducing the Border Hold-Up, a unique tool that holds a whole roll of wet or pasted border paper and instantly attaches to any wallboard surface, enabling you to use both hands to brush and paste.

While you're adding nifty accents, why not give some items a decorative metal finish with water based Metalcoat by Metal Paint Incorporated, (310) 447-1841, Paint & Coating International Magazine called it "the most significant breakthrough in coatings technology this century." You'll call it beautiful. (Ed. Note: unfortunately this company no longer seems to be in business)

Chicago Metallic, (800) 638-5192, has introduced Real Wood ceiling panels and ceiling grid covers. Red Devil introduced caulks that can be painted in 30 minutes.

I've got a stack of press releases and spec sheets about products that I'd like to tell you about that is at least a foot high next to my computer. Unfortunately, I'm out of room. We'll sneak in other product mentions throughout the year.

How to buy winning windows

Beauty and energy efficiency are top considerations when you go shopping

Photo Courtesy Semco Windows & Doors

by Glenn Haege,
America's Master Handyman

Marian Lam's 1950's house had old aluminum windows and she hated them. Every winter the frames got freezing cold and condensation sent streams of water onto the sills, causing the paint to peel. this was the year she decided to get new windows.

Sue Boitos of Livonia had already replaced 13 windows in her Livonia home. The final two large family room windows still needed to be done. since she already had bought windows from Cadillac Windows in Southfield and they had been very good about warranty work, she called them in again.

Marlene and Greg Kehoe's home in Beverly Hills had been built in 1965. they knew they needed new energy-efficient windows and saved up for them. This fall, their old single pane windows will be replaced with a combination of vinyl and wood windows.

"Even though our windows won't be installed until the end of October, I'm really excited about them. I think the look will be very attractive," Marlene Kehoe says.

Every year, millions of homeowners from around the country are confronted with the same problems and decide to take the plunge. If your house has old, drafty, single-pane windows, they are costing you money. This might be your year to join Marian, Marlene and Sue, and go window-shopping.

"What window should I buy?" or "What's the best window?" is always among the top ten questions people ask me. David McGraw, president of Kimball & Russell, the Wixom-based Andersen distributor, says "tell people that when they are choosing windows they should pick a company that has been in business at least as long as their guarantee."

There is a lot of truth to that. My standard answer to window shoppers is: "The best window is the one that is installed correctly." The installing contractor is very important. Improperly installed, the most expensive window will make you unhappy.

Now, let's get down to the core question of what to buy. In most people's minds the choice is between wood and vinyl-framed windows. You might also consider windows framed in metal or composite materials. But remember, the glass in the windows is more important than the frame. Your choice is between single-pane, clear double-pane (double-glazed), double-pane with low-E, Argon filled, or triple-glazed.

Finally, if you are window shopping for a new house, you have to decide whether you want hinged windows, like casement or awning styles, or double hung or sliders. Casement and awning style windows are more expensive but are more energy-efficient. Double hung (the standard window that goes up and down) and sliders (windows that slide side to side) are less energy efficient and cost less.

Confused?

Fear not. Your government now has not one, not two, but three quasi-governmental committees and councils working to make your window selection easier.

The first is the National Fenestration Rating Council. It was mandated by the Energy Policy Act of 1992 to establish a window-rating program. The majority of the work has now been done and some major manufacturers have started to display the council's Energy Performance labels.

Windows can be tested to determine the U-Factor, the solar heat gain coefficient, visible transmittance, air leakage, and annual energy performance. In the future, the council even plans to rate the durability of the window.

The first labels may only show U-Factor and solar heat gain figures. Visible transmittance will soon be added.

Still Confused?

The NFRC rating sticker shows the U-factor, solar heat gain and other rating characteristics of the particular window line

Don't worry. The new Energy Star Program will add a second label to the window. The purpose of this new label will be to translate the National Fenestration Rating Council ratings on the first label. Don't laugh, this is serious.

Your government and mine is doing this to help you.

The Energy Star label will show whether a particular window comes within the energy efficiency guidelines for the northern, central or southern climate regions of the United States. These labels were actually supposed to be out this spring, but I haven't seen any yet.

Personally, I am very excited about the new labels. because translating them for the general public should give me at least ten years more job security.

What type of windows is best for your house?

Before you buy, walk around your neighborhood and check what your neighbors are doing.

continued on next page

363

Most of us live in subdivisions of houses built at roughly the same time. The chances are good that many other folks have replaced their windows before you. If they are replacing their windows with wood, you had better follow suit or it may work against you when it's time to sell your home. If the replacement window of choice is vinyl, it would be a good choice for you, too.

If you live in a neighborhood where each house stands on its own, the decision is up to you. Here are a few facts about the different window framing materials.

Wood Windows

Wood is the natural alternative. Windows are considered to be 20- to 25-year replacement items. A good wood window, properly maintained, will last for several generations.

Kathleen, my editor at Master Handyman Press, has 47 year old, single-pane, wood windows. The frames are still good, but the windows should be changed to make them more energy-efficient. I am confident that quality wood windows of today are capable of lasting at least as long as Kathleen's have lasted.

When choosing among wood windows, you will often have the choice of wood, or wood clad with aluminum or vinyl on the exterior.

Vinyl and aluminum clad windows cost a little more but they eliminate exterior maintenance and are well worth the investment.

You have three options when replacing a wood window. You can replace just the sash and glazing (glass). This is the

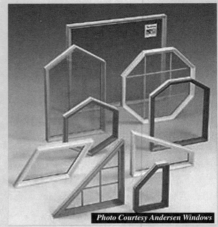

Photo Courtesy Andersen Windows

Windows can be made in any shape or size. Even the largest companies, such as Anderson, have design flexibility if you give them extra time.

cheapest and easiest way to go. Many of the large wood window manufacturers have sash packs. If you are handy, it could be a do-it-yourself project that would save you $250 to $350 a window.

The next alternative is to remove the old sashes from an existing window and install a new window complete with frame, in the opening. This is called "frame in frame" installation and is the standard of the window replacement industry. Since the window now has two frames, total glass area is reduced.

Finally you can take out the entire old window, frame and all, and replace it with an entirely new window. Complete replacement is the most expensive. McGraw of Kimball & Russell says that even though Andersen makes Narroline windows for frame in frame replacement, the company recommends full frame replacement for wood windows. Most other quality wood window manufacturers agree.

Vinyl Windows

In the past 10years vinyl replacement windows have gone from wood's poor relation to contending for top honors. In the June 8 issue of National Home Center News, Jason Gonzalez reported that in 1991 wood had a 48-percent share of the prime window market. Vinyl and aluminum windows were neck and neck with about 25 percent each. Today, he says, vinyl is poised to take over the top spot.

Modern vinyl windows are far superior to early models. The multi-chamber frame design found in some of today's vinyl windows greatly increases the frame's insulation value, rigidity, and strength. These improved windows are gaining a lot of respect in the building industry.

Metro Detroit vinyl window manufacturers, Weathergard and Wallside, are at the cutting edge of American vinyl window technology. Weathergard, has just installed the country's first Sturtz four-head double stack welding machine. According to Dave Fishman, the company's general manager, the new $250,000 machine "cuts frames and sashes to a computer-set tolerance, then simultaneously welds all four corners of two frames or sashes."

Fishman credits the company's new machine for his company's ability to cut the time between measurement and window installation down to three to four weeks.

Composite Windows

Composite, or hybrid, window frames are combinations of several materials. Some composite frames have an aluminum core, surrounded by vinyl. Others are completely new materials developed exclusively for the window industry.

Although composites do not have a major market share, they are one of the most exciting trends in the window industry. Each composite window is different. I'm only going to list two examples, but if you are window-shopping, you should definitely check them all out.

Fibrex, a new composite made from pine wood fibers and a thermoplastic polymer used in the new Renewal replacement window line by Andersen is so strong that it is able to have a far thinner frame than either vinyl or wood.

According to McGraw "the extra strength of the Fibrex composite enables a Renewal replacement window to have a 35 percent larger glass surface than a comparable vinyl product. Even when replacing an older Andersen window, a Renewal replacement might provide a larger glass surface than the original."

Renewal windows can be ordered with an optional pine veneer interior surface that can be stained or painted just like wood.

Owens Corning's new Generations composite window has a frame that is filled with the company's pink foam insulation This should provide an unbeatable insulation factor. Generation comes in white, light oak or medium oak interior finishes.

continued on next page

**Modern
2-pane window**
(Low-E double glazed)

—— Interior pane

—— Air- or argon-
filled center

—— Low-E
glass coating

—— Exterior pane

—— Space bar

Art by Ken Taylor

Aluminum Windows

The strength of the metal means that aluminum window frames can be very narrow, maximizing the glass surface. While very popular for industrial and commercial use, aluminum framed windows have almost faded from the residential scene. Metal frames have great thermal conductivity. If it's cold outside, the frames will be cold inside. This leads to heat loss and condensation. Manufacturers have tried to alleviate this weakness by separating the aluminum inner and outer frames with a thermal break often made of plastic. The improvement does not seem big enough to increase aluminum frame popularity.

Glass

Regardless of how much hype the window companies put on the frames of their windows, you do not buy a window for the frame, you buy it for the glass.

Modern glazings are far superior to the single pane windows of yesteryear. Some of the important variations you can have include double-pane windows, low-E coatings, triple-pane, gas-filled, and warm edge spacers.

Double-pane means that the window is glazed with two sheets of glass. In order to tell you whether this is a good idea or not, the U.S. Department of Energy has sponsored another group through their Windows and Glazings Program. This one is the Efficient Windows Collaborative. They have a very informative web site (efficientwindows.org).

The U-Factor for a single pane of glass is 1.30. Adding another pane of glass cuts heat loss more than half. The U-Factor goes down to .49. Adding a low-E coating cuts the U-Factor down to .33. Filling the space between the panes of glass with an inert gas, like Argon, would reduce the U-Factor, still further.

How about cost?

Getting a good price comparison is tough. Stephen Toth of Cadillac Window Corp. says "each company tries to make their product as unique as possible … many product brochures appear to offer the same things but prices vary greatly."

Toth points out that buyers have to read the fine print.

As an example, one national company charges $405 to prime the interior side of a window. Another company charges only $100 for the same task. Other things being equal, a shopper could save $305 per window.

To get a general idea about window and installation costs my staff and I priced out a 38-inch by 57-inch double-hung window. That sounds like an odd size, but it is actually one of the most popular windows made. The glazing was double pane, low-E glass.

How much do different types of windows cost?

To get a general idea about how much a window costs in the Detroit market, Glenn Haege got quotes on windows and installation from several different organizations. Prices on some windows varied widely. Some windows were quoted on window cost plus installation. Many quoted window and installation as a package. The window he priced required a rough opening of 57 1/4 inches in height and 38 and 1/8 inches in width. This is one of the most popular double hung window sizes. We also specified that the window include double-pane, Low-E glass.

Manufacturer	Window	Installation	Total
VINYL WINDOWS			
Weathergard			$250-$350
PolyTex from Cadillac Window			$357
Great Lakes from Cadillac Window			$372
Sunrise from Cadillac Window			$379
Home Depot Custom Line	$130-$158	$100	$230-$258
Builders Square Survivor	$161plus Install		
Ajax from Custom Vinyl			$370
Vinyl window average price:			**$320.75**
WOOD OR WOOD CLAD			
Andersen Tilt	$280-$300	$250 (est)	$530-$550
Andersen Narrow Line	$260-$280	$200 (est)	$460-$480
Marvin from Cadillac Window			$529
Weathershield from Cadillac Window		$421	
Andersen from Cadillac Window			$546
Pella from Cadillac Window			$629
Pella ProLine	$348	$250	$598
Wood or wood clad window average price:			**$527**
COMPOSITE WINDOWS			
Renewal by Andersen – frame in frame installation			$628
Renewal by Andersen – full frame installation			$873
Composite window average price:			**$750**

The average cost for a vinyl window, including installation, was: $321. The average price for a high quality, good window, including installation, was $527. The average price for the Andersen Renewal, the only composite window we quoted, including installation, was $750.

No one would buy a single replacement window. However, if you assume 11 to 15 windows, some bigger, some smaller, some casement, my handy hand calculator tells me that a very rough average for a house full of vinyl replacement windows would be $3,531 to $4,815. Wood replacement windows for the same house might average $5,797 to $7,905. A house full of composite replacement windows might cost $8,250 to $11,250.

To get these numbers we just multiplied 11 or 15 by the average window costs. Your windows will vary. This is a very

continued on next page

rough guesstimate. With careful shopping, windows for your home might cost far less. On the other hand, depending on the size of your house, and the extras you might want, they cost could be far more.

Windows for a single room with a glass wall, French doors, and bay windows, could easily cost more than I estimated for an entire house.

How Much Would This Save?

Based on a study of a house in Madison, Wisconsin, the Efficient Windows Collaborative determined that by converting from single pane to double-pane clear glass windows, an average homeowner would cut his or her heating bill by 25 percent. By converting to Argon filled, double-pane windows with a low-E coating, the heating bill could be cut 34 percent.

How soon could the windows be installed?
If you act fast you could have them in your house before Thanksgiving. Weathergard is promising installation in three to four weeks. Renewal by Andersen can do the job in six weeks. Cadillac Window is promising their customers eight to ten weeks.

Unfortunately, some of my favorite remodeling companies are already booked through the end of the year. This article should start quite a few people thinking about windows, so start calling now.

It's been great window shopping with you. If you have any questions, come see me at my annual free fall home improvement show next weekend.

How to Choose a Contractor

- Always check out the window contractor carefully.
- Make sure he or she has a showroom.
- Look at life-size examples of the company's windows.
- Call the Michigan State Department of Commerce builder hotline, (900) 555-8374, and ask the following questions: 1.) Does the company have a builders license?
  2.) Does either the company or the licensed contractor have any violations?
  3.) If so, what were the violations?
- Get references. Ask for name, address, and phone number.
- Go to the houses and see if you like the look of the windows.
- Ask the owners if they were satisfied with the job and if they had any service problems with their windows.

Sources

Some of the sources used in this report:
Anderson Corp.: (800) 426-4261
Kimball & Russell (Andersen Distributor): (248) 624-7000
Builders Square: (810) 826-8330
Cadillac Window Corp.: (248) 352-5405
Classic Window Builders Supply: (248) 437-5861
Custom Vinyl Windows: (810) 574-1700
Dillman & Upton: (248) 651-9411
Fairway Construction Co.: (248) 350-3460
Home Depot: (248) 423-0040
Marvin Windows: (800) 346-5128

Pella Corp.: (800) 847-3552 (In
 Lathrup Village: (248) 594-8801
Pine Building Co.: (248) 539-9600
Renewal by Andersen: (800) 426-4261
 (In Michigan (888) 537-3639
Weathergard: (248) 967-8822
Windows Plus: (810) 754-2060

Windows on the Web

■ **Efficient Windows Collaborative:**
www.efficientwindows.org

Beautifully designed. The explanation
of U-Factors and glazings is outstand-
ing.

■ **National Wood Window and Door
Association:** www.nwwda.org
Very classy. Biased in favor of wood,
but so am I. The site has some
excellent design articles. The glossary
is nicely illustrations.

■ **National Fenestration Rating
Council:** www.nfrc.org

This site explains all he whys and
wherefores about the Council and
NFRC testing and labels. It even lists
testing software, and how to get in
touch with testing companies.

■ **Energy Star Program:**
www.energystar.gov

Well-organized. Explains the NFRC
labels and new Energy Star Label. It
shows the three energy rating regions
of the United States.

■ **Andersen, Inc.:** www.andersen.com

Very comprehensive. Lists major
energy ratings for all their window
lines.

■ **Pella Window:** www.pella.com

Explains window lines and has a good
glossary.   .

What Do NFRC Ratings Mean?

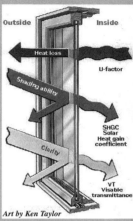

Art by Ken Taylor

The U-Factor measures the way the
window transmits heat created from
sources other than the sun. It tells
how effective a window is at keeping the outside temperature outside,
and the inside temperature inside.
The lower the U-Factor, the less energy goes through the window. A U-
Factor of .32 is better than a .50.

The Solar Heat Gain Coefficient
(SHGC) measures the way a window
absorbs heat from the sun. The lower
the better. A .45 SHGC is better than
.60.

The Visible Transmittance (VT) measures the percentage of visible light
that comes through the product. The
higher the better. A .60 VT is better
than .54.

Just to tease, the NFRC lists two ratings for each category: Residential
and Non-Residential. Only look at
the residential rating.

SEPTEMBER 12, 1998

You'll be more than over-heated if you fall for a furnace scam

by Glenn Haege,
America's Master Handyman

If your household is anything like mine, telephone solicitors besiege you – especially at dinnertime. I am not psychic, but I will guess that a large number of the calls you receive over the next three months will be from heating companies that are running a furnace cleaning special and just happen to be in the neighborhood.

There is nothing wrong with a furnace company running a legitimate special. If you need your furnace cleaned, go for it. But be careful, all too often these specials are too good to be true.

A so-called technician may come into your house on a $40 cleaning and suddenly discovers that the heat exchanger is cracked. Quite often he has to make an emergency call to his supervisor (salesman) or the owner (salesman) to rush out and confirm his worst fears. You and your family will be in deadly peril unless you have an immediate furnace replacement to the tune of $5,000 or so.

By the time they have finished, you are afraid for you life, sign on the dotted line. This con works on anyone but is particularly effective on the people who can afford it least, single women and older folks.

I hate the scum who perpetuate this kind of a swindle. My feelings are benign compared to what the many legitimate heating and cooling contractors would like to do to these scoundrels.

To make certain that I had all the facts I called Gary Marowske, General Manager of Flame Furnace, and asked him what you should look for in a furnace inspection and cleaning. I chose Marowske because Flame Furnace, (888) 234-2340 is one of the biggest and oldest heating and cooling contractors in Michigan. The company has offices all around the Detroit Area.

Marowske said that before you set an appointment, you should call the State of Michigan, (900) 555-8374, and make certain that the company is a licensed heating, ventilation and air conditioning (HVAC) company. While you are at it get the name of the man or woman who is on the license and is the person who actually passed the State's HVAC exam.

According to Marowske, if the furnace is over five years old, it should be inspected annually. He suggests that the following items be included in a furnace inspection and cleaning.

1. Check the entire house, not just the furnace area, for carbon monoxide leaks.
2. Check furnace burners to make sure they are burning properly. Adjust if necessary.
3. Replace the furnace thermocouple.
4. Change or clean furnace air filters.
5. Clean the humidifier thoroughly and replace the humidifier pad.

6. If the furnace is a high efficiency (90 percent efficient or above) check intake and exhaust pipes to make certain they are clear and free of debris.

7. Shut down the air conditioner.

8. Check condensate drains and make sure they are working.

Marowske said that his company charges $74.50 for a furnace cleaning like this. Some other very legitimate companies charge a little less for the inspection, but add a separate charge for cleaning the humidifier.

If you are looking for a legitimate cleaning special, you'll have to look very hard. September starts the busiest time of the year. Few companies are going to reduce prices when they already have more work than they can handle.

If you want a legitimate special, Marowske suggests waiting until January when business slows down. "Many people think that the furnace has to be cleaned in the fall. Usually the furnace doesn't have to be cleaned at the very beginning of the season. If the homeowner waits for a slow period, there is a good chance that they can save money."

When the technician is inspecting the furnace, if he tells you that the furnace has to be replaced, do not be stampeded. Get an estimate in writing, then call another furnace contractor and get a second opinion. If you are told that the furnace has a bad carbon monoxide (CO) leak, you may want to go down to your local hardware store or home center and buy a plug-in style carbon monoxide detector. Take it down to the furnace and see if the alarm goes off. The technician may have more sensitive equipment, but a residential CO detector will tell you if you have a major problem.

If CO detector's alarm goes off, you may have an authentic emergency. Call the gas company's emergency phone number immediately and tell them you have a carbon monoxide leak. The Consumers Power emergency number is (800) 889-1252. Michcon's emergency number is (800) 942-5571. Consider having the family sleep over at the in-laws or a nearby motel. When everyone is safe, get furnace quotes right away.

If you wait until January for the furnace inspection, you'll have to close down the air conditioner yourself. Don't cover the out door unit in plastic. Marowske says that the air conditioner needs air circulation. He suggests just putting a board on top to keep leaves from falling into the fan area. You can also call your HVAC contractor and order a custom-made condenser cover. For more information on covers, call Connie at AC Covers, (313) 541-7770.

Learn about home's dangerous fungi and you'll breathe a lot easier

by Glenn Haege,
America's Master Handyman

Stachybotrys is not on the FBI's Most Wanted List, but this ferocious fungus belongs there. You can have the cleanest house in the neighborhood and Stachybotrys can be silently working away, making your house a horror.

Connie Morbach and her husband, Tom, run Sanit-Air, a Troy based Duct Cleaning company, (888) 778-7324. Since Ms. Morbach has a Master of Science in Hazardous Waste Management, and is a Certified Hazardous Materials Manager (CHMM), she and her husband are often called in to investigate "sick houses" in addition to their company's duct cleaning work.

Since she has found a number of Stachybotrys-related air quality problems in houses that were probably a lot like yours and mine, the following cases belong in your need to know file.

Case No. 1: Three years previously, the basement of a Farmington Hills house flooded. As soon as the water receded the basement was professionally cleaned, carpeting removed and all surfaces sanitized.

According to Morbach, although everything was spotless in this meticulously clean house, a damp, moldy smell permeated the area and the occupants were experiencing pulmonary difficulties.

The Morbachs were stumped until Tom found half-dollar sized greasy black spots behind a piece of basement floor molding. When all the molding was pulled away, they found the entire house was surrounded by the greasy black mold. Moisture had wicked up 6 inches and the inner side of the drywall was contaminated.

Morbach performed a swab test and found that the black spots were Stachybotrys. Stachybotrys fungi are potentially lethal. According to Morbach, Stachybotrys fungi are really quite rare. Usually many other microorganisims have made their appearance before these fungi appear. Once there, Stachybotrys spores travel through the air and attack the cilia in the lungs, often causing severe lung damage. The fungi have been associated with infant death.

In this case the entire basement had to be gutted, sanitized, and sealed before the family could return.

Case No. 2: Improper drainage surrounding a house built on a slab in Clinton Township enabled water to wick into the house from moist soil. Drywall and insulation soaked up the water making the lower walls a breeding ground for Stachybotrys. Remediation consisted of tearing away and replacing insulation and drywall, sanitizing and sealing affected areas.

Case No. 3: An expectant mother in a northwest suburban home was experiencing breathing difficulties. Although there did not seem to be anything the matter with the home, a full air quality investigation discovered that a small plumbing leak in the master bath, had saturated the drywall. The space between the outer and inner walls was saturated with Stachybotrys. The entire bathroom had to be gutted and sanitized before the home was livable.

Case No. 4: Improper attic ventilation in a Roseville house caused severe condensation during freeze-and-thaw cycles. Moisture soaked through attic insulation and settled in the ceiling and wall drywall. The wet drywall became a breeding ground for Stachybotrys. Insulation and drywall had to be removed, and the entire area sanitized and sealed before restoration could begin.

Last year Dr. George Riegel described the procedure necessary to correct the kind of problems I've listed at a seminar on mold infestation problems sponsored by Sanit-Air. Riegel is the president of Healthy Homes, a highly respected environmental inspection and remediation company headquartered in Southfield, (248) 358-3311.

He told us that remediation jobs like Morbach described often cost between $14,000 and $25,000. Crews have to use extreme safety measures. The entire contaminated area must be completely contained. This includes installing an air lock entry system, portable showers, and negative air machines. Personnel wear Tyvek suits, gloves, hard hats, goggles, and half face power air purified respirators.

The contaminated area must first be treated with an antimicrobial, then all contaminated materials are torn out, double bagged and taken to the dump. Before restoration begins, the area is sanitized, dried, and encapsulated with a stain kill like B.I.N. or Kilz.

The first step to avoid these problems is not to create them. Make certain that your home has proper drainage and that the attic has sufficient air circulation through a combination of soffit and ridge or pot vents.

In the case of flooded basements, speed is essential. Carpeting must to be removed, cleaned and sanitized. Carpet padding, wet drywall and upholstered furniture must be removed and discarded immediately. Then the entire area must be sanitized with a very strong household bleach solution, dried and sealed.

This can be very dangerous work. Every case in this article had progressed beyond the stage where remediation could be accomplished by the homeowner.

Sanit-Air does some sophisticated culture lab tests on a mail-order basis. If your home has a mysterious mold or a moldy smell that you cannot get rid of, Morbach said that Sanit-Air would perform a mail-in swab test for $95. This is one case where learning all you can will let you breath a lot easier.

SEPTEMBER 26, 1998

Grab a notepad, go take a walk, and get home ready for winter

by Glenn Haege,
America's Master Handyman

When I wrote the first draft of this article it was as warm as a summer's day. BUT the past week's cool weather reminded me. It is only five weeks to Halloween, 9 weeks to Thanksgiving, 11 weeks to Hanukkah, and 13 weeks to Christmas.

It may feel like summer, but it's fall. Blink an eye and snow will be falling and this winter is supposed to be especially long and cold. We have to get our homes ready now.

Let's start by getting organized. Walk around the house with your clipboard and write down what needs to be done.

■ Check the landscaping. For adequate drainage, ground should slope away from the house by at least one inch per foot.
■ Do you have any exterior painting yet to do? This is perfect painting weather.
■ Check the caulking. Jam a fingernail or a dime into the caulk. If it is no longer springy, it needs to be replaced.
■ How are the windows holding up? Cracked windows need reglazing. Check the putty on single glazed windows. Stiff or cracked putty should be replaced. If windows need repairs, H & R Window Repair Co., in Detroit, (248) 366-8282, has a huge selection of replacement parts and crews that will do the work.

■ Consider replacing damaged basement windows with block windows. They give better security and insulation value.
■ Check the mortar on brick siding and chimneys. If any is missing, penetrating moisture and the freeze-thaw cycles of winter can do a great deal of damage. Fix it now.
■ Use a pair of binoculars to inspect the roof. Old Man Winter will soon be trying to tear the shingles apart. Missing or damaged shingles must be replaced now. Pay particular attention to valleys. If there is eve a hint of cracking, patch now to avoid major water damage.
■ Look at your drives and walk ways. Any cracks in the concrete or asphalt will cause severe heaving and thawing throughout the winter.

Here are some hints to get you started.

Caulk removal and replacement

Make the old caulk pliable with a heat gun, then scrape it out with a hook nose linoleum knife or a chisel point putty knife. Clean the surface thoroughly with mineral spirits or paint thinner. Recaulk with an adhesive style caulk like Poly Seam Seal, Sashco Big Stretch, or Vulchem. You'll be able to find at least one of these at any good hardware store or home center.

Window reglazing

Soften old putty with a heat gun, then scrape out with a large screwdriver or putty knife. Brush away all loose putty and wood slivers. Brush on a coat of Penetrol by the Flood Company, (800) 321-3444 and let dry. Insert new glazing points and reglaze with fresh putty. Press in, then smooth down to a 45-degree angle. Paint with an oil base stain kill like XIM, (800) 262-8469, or Cover-Stain by William Zinsser, (732) 469-4367.

Mortar replacement

Mortar or brick problems may be a sign of a far more serious problem. If just a little tuck pointing needs to be done, you can probably do it yourself. Spray down the brick with a garden hose, then clear away the loose mortar. Put on goggles and use a cold chisel and brick hammer to chisel out the damaged area, then brush out with a whisk broom.

Fill in the joint between the bricks with Mason Mix by Quikrete, (800) 442-7258. Mix to a plastic like consistency, pack it in to the cracks with a mortar trowel. When the mortar is thumbprint hard, finish off by drawing a special brick tool (a jointer) or piece of dowel across the joint at a 45-degree angle. If the job is bigger than you can handle, stop by J. C. Cornillie, (810) 293-1500, in Roseville, or call the Masonry Institute of Michigan, (734) 458-8544, for the name of a masonry contractor in your neighborhood

Roof cracks

This is an ideal time for small roofing repairs. The shingles are still pliable enough to be relatively easy to work with. Broken shingles must be replaced. Pry them up and wedge in the replacement.

Cracks in valleys take a little more work. The best system I've found is Roof Guardian by Oregon Research and Development Corporation (ORD), (800) 345-0809. You'll use three different products: Elastoseal, Contour Seam Tape and Roof Guardian. Make sure the surface to be patched is clean and dry. Put on one primer coat of Elastoseal over the valley. Let dry. Then apply another coat of Elastoseal. While it is still wet, cover the entire length of the crack with Contour Seam Tape and apply another coat of Elastoseal. When this has dried, put on two coats of Roof Guardian. You should be able to find all of these products at Meijers or Builders Square, or at most Ace or True Value hardware stores.

Cracks in asphalt, concrete drives

Fill cracks and tire depressions in asphalt drives with Professional Cold Patch by Quikrete.

Concrete cracks under 1/2-inch wide can be filled using Quikrete Gray Crack Seal. Fill wider cracks with Mason sand and tamp down. When you get to within 1-1/2 inches of the top, place a backer rod with a wide enough diameter to fill the crack, and cover with crack sealer.

OCTOBER 3, 1998

Improper care of septic systems can affect whole neighborhoods

by Glenn Haege,
America's Master Handyman

Septic tank systems have been going bad for years. Even if you don't have a septic system, if you're a taxpayer, what happens to your neighbor's septic system, is important to you. Various communities have converted from septic to community waste treatment systems. Usually at great expense.

While connecting to sewers sounds good, I'm a little leery for two reasons. First, every time it rains, many houses have flooded basements. The drain and water treatment systems can't handle the work they already have. Increasing the load on the sewer systems may just increase taxes without solving the problem.

Second, I have found that the government solution to any problem is usually the slowest, most frustrating, and most expensive, form of resolution. If at all possible, I am usually better off solving the problem myself, or at the least, working on a mutually agreeable resolution with a few of my neighbors.

In the best of all possible worlds, a single, perfectly working sanitation system would be best. Unfortunately, none of us live in the best of all possible worlds. So I am going to devote the rest of this article to other possible solutions.

The most important thing septic tank folks should realize is that they are not alone. People from all over the world

are working on solutions and there is a wealth of information on the internet. If you and your neighbors are looking for a solution, your home computer, or your local library, can link you to government, university, and manufacturers' sites from around the world.

If you have a septic system, you have to treat it properly. According to the National Small Flows Clearing House, a program of the National Research Center for Coal and Energy at West Virginia University, septic tank users should never flush coffee grounds, dental floss, disposable diapers, kitty litter, sanitary napkins, tampons, cigarette butts, condoms, gauze bandages, fat, grease, or oil, or paper towels.

Just as important, never flush chemicals that will kill off the helpful bacteria in their system and possibly contaminate surface and groundwater. Among the "never flush" chemicals are: paints, varnishes, thinners, waste oils, photographic solutions, and pesticides.

A septic system begins to deteriorate the very first day it is used. Regardless how careful you are, small particles, grease, and soap scum begin to clog the drain system. Over time drainage becomes restricted and water has a harder time flowing downward. The result is that the drainfield often becomes water logged, and ceases to be able to do its job. The result can be contamination of surface and ground water. This is not good for you, me, or the rest of the animal kingdom.

If a septic system is failing, it can sometimes be resurrected with a septic system cleaner like Septic-Scrub by Arcan Enterprises. The product is introduced into the distribution box located between the septic tank and the drainfield. The product contains chemicals which form a chemical reaction with grease, sludge, and slime, producing a non-toxic material which can be digested by the soil's bacteria. To learn more about Septic-Scrub, look up the company's website or call (888) 352-7226, and ask for a brochure.

When you believe your septic system is beyond the point of remediation, consider upgrading to an improved septic system, like the FAST Wastewater Treatment System by Bio-Microbic, Inc., (800) 753-3278, or a high-tech sewage system, by MicroSeptic Inc., (714) 367-8686. Either of these systems are feasible for a single home-owner, a group of neighbors, an entire subdivision, or a commercial establishment.

Bio-Microbic's FAST system was first developed for the U.S. Coast Guard. It utilizes activated sludge treatment technology and reduces nitrogen levels by over 70 percent. The final product is clear, odorless treated water. The system is compatible with dishwasher and garbage disposer use and is virtually maintenance free. Bio-Microbic's FAST system fits into a septic tank and as its name implies, can be installed very rapidly.

The MicroSeptic "EnviroServer" System is an alternative to both septic and large sewer systems. The complete system can be installed in just a few hours, and while not cheap, MicroSeptic offers one solution to a septic problem. Computer controlled, the system uses a combination of microwave dehydration, controlled combustion, fluid processing, filtration, and UV water purification. MicroSeptic reduces liquid and organic refuse to harmless ash and clean, filtered water.

If you or your neighbors have a septic system problem, there is a solution. Only you can decide the best solution for your home. As in all modifications to your home, I suggest that you follow my First Commandment: Learn all you can, before you do. Don't take what you read on the internet as gospel. Get references and make certain you always know the sources of the information, before you act upon it.

OCTOBER 10, 1998

If your skin is drying up, you need to check furnace and humidifier

by Glenn Haege,
America's Master Handyman

Furnaces and fireplaces are going on all over America. This is the beginning of the sneezing/wheezing season. As soon as that furnace gets going your throat is dry when you wake up in the morning and your eyes start itching. Ever wonder why?

The problem isn't with you – it's the heating system. After the first cold snap when the heat stays on three or four days in a row, the sneezes and wheezes begin. That's because the air in the house becomes desert dry. All the moisture in the floors and carpeting evaporates. Carpet dust and dust mites start whirling around the house every time the furnace blower motor goes on.

Inside your head, the mucus membranes that luxuriated in the lush moistness of summer become raw and dry. Your eyeballs become dry and irritated. Even your skin becomes scratchy and sore.

The first thing to do is give your body some TLC. Get Vicine or some other drops for your eyes, moisturizer for your skin, and drink lots of water. Extra water for the pets and plants is also important.

Next, go down stairs and make certain that the humidifier is in top operating condition. If the drum humidifier belt is old and stiff, replace it. Humidifier trays should be cleaned or replaced. Check with your hardware store or heating contractor, they may have tray liners that can just be tossed out when they become covered with sediment.

When the temperature outside is 40 degrees or above, the interior humidity should be at least 45 percent or your mucus membranes will start drying out. Check the humidity in various parts of the house with a hygrometer. If you don't have one, Damman and other fine hardware stores sell Bionaire hygrometers for about $25.00. It's a good investment.

Check the furnace filter. Replace it if necessary. If you have just been using cheap $1 or under filters, upgrade to the $5 to $15 variety. The less expensive filters give minimum protection to the furnace. The more expensive replaceable filters like the Precisionaire or the 3M Filtrete Electrostatic Micro Particle Filter actually filter microbes out of the air.

If you have electric air cleaners be sure to take them out and give them a washing in the dishwasher. Flame Furnace, (888) 234-2340, now has an electronic air cleaner service. The service technician takes the electronic air cleaner cells out, takes them to the shop where they are chemically cleaned, then brings them back and re-installs them. The cost is $42 for one air cleaner, $52 for two air cleaners. The service can be scheduled monthly or quarterly.

Recommended indoor humidity levels

Outdoor temperature	Indoor humidity
+40	45%
+30	40%
+20	35%
+10	30%
0	25%
-10	20%
-20	15%
Below -20	Move to Miami

Most vacuum bags are so porous they blow dust around. If your vacuum cleaner, uses replaceable bags, treat it to an anti-bacterial bag. A good bag traps the dust, dust mites, and miscellaneous spiders. Vacuum your carpets and floors thoroughly twice to get all the loose dust that has been tracked in over the summer.

Have you cleaned the carpets lately? If it's been a while, you might as well call and get the carpets cleaned for the holidays. Two cleaners that I often talk about on my radio show are Modernistic Carpet Cleaning, (800) 609-1000, and Duraclean by Maryann (800) 372-5427.

Modernistic has one of the most advanced cleaning systems I've seen. They are so big, they train and supply many of the smaller guys. When my companies moved into their new offices, Modernistic cleaned 3,500 square feet of very dirty carpet in one afternoon and the carpeting was dry enough for the movers within a couple of days. Maryann Zukosky has one of the largest Duraclean franchises in the world. Both companies got where they are today by putting the customer first.

If it has been five or six years since you had the furnace air ducts cleaned, call and schedule an appointment now. The cleaner the ductwork is the less dust you have in the house. If you don't know who to call, contact the National Air Duct Cleaners Association (NADCA), (202) 737-2926, and ask for the name of a certified technician near you. In the local Detroit Area, some of the good ones are Safety King, (800) 972-6343, Sanit-Air (888) 778-7324, A-1 Duct Cleaning (800) 382-8256, Dalton Environmental (800) 675-2298, and Sterling Environmental (888) 992-1200.

If your wooden chairs start to squeak and moan it is because they have been losing moisture. Go to the hardware store and get some Chair Loc. It's not a glue, just a wood sweller, and will solve the problem for you.

After you've done all this the air in your house should be clean, fresh, and a pleasure to breath.

OCTOBER 17, 1998

Let in the light with improved skylights and new tubular designs

by Glenn Haege,
America's Master Handyman

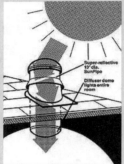

The rooftop dome of SunPipe captures sunlight and directs it down a reflective pipe to light the room.

If you have a room that is too dark and believe that the Almighty does a better job of making light than the light bulb manufacturers, a skylight may interest you.

You have two choices:

■ Traditional square or rectangular skylights make a strong architectural statement while also giving light and heat. While plastic or acrylic domed skylights are still available, they have been supplanted by clear glass glazing in popularity.

■ New, tubular skylights do not make much of an architectural statement, but give more light with less heat.

Don't limit your thinking to conventional uses. Skylights can be used instead of dormers to bring air and light into a converted attic. They create a very modern look while actually providing greater light.

If you need a skylight that can double as an emergency exit, the Velux Model GPL and the Roto Roof Door were specifically designed for that purpose. The GPL opens 45 degrees, while the Roto Roof opens a full 90 degrees.

If you have an upstairs room and wish you could change a slanted roof into a balcony, the amazing Velux Cabrio was made for just you.

People usually have three worries about skylights: leaking, heat build up, and condensation. Skylights do not leak. The flashing around skylights sometimes does. The flashing package is just as important as the skylight.

As with all windows, proper installation is the key. If you are going to do the installation yourself, make sure that the company brags about the installation package.

Heat buildup can be a very real problem. Venting skylights provide an excellent solution. Open the window and the heat escapes. If too much sun is a problem, better manufacturers have a low E glass option. You can also get skylights with built-in screens, pleated shades, and venetian blinds. There are even powered units that enable you to open the skylight or pull the shades with a press of the remote control.

Wherever you have heat without ventilation, condensation can be a problem. Heat rises, so unventilated skylights are prime candidates for condensation during winter months.

If you want the natural light of a skylight, without the hassles of heat buildup or condensation, a tubular skylight could be your answer.

Greg Miller of Oakbrook, Illinois, invented the SunPipe in 1989. The SunPipe, (800) 844-4786, consists of a roof mounted acrylic dome that captures sunlight and spirals it down a super-reflective circular pipe to a ceiling-mounted diffuser.

At about the same time Miller and his family invented the SunPipe, the Sun Tunnel was invented in Australia. It soon made its way to the United States.

The Sun Tunnel, (800) 369-3664, and several other tubular skylights use flexible tubing mounted on an angle, rather than rigid vertical tubing. One benefit of flexible tubing is that the interior fixture does not have to be directly under the roof dome.

ODL of Zeeland, Michigan, makes a Vista brand tubular skylight that is available at Home Depot and other home centers and building supply stores.

Tubular skylights have several benefits. They actually give more light, more evenly, than a similarly sized traditional skylight. A 13-inch diameter SunPipe gives up to 1500 incandescent watts of light. That's big enough for a 12- by 20 foot room. A 9-inch diameter SunPipe gives up to 900 watts of light. A 21-inch can provide up to 3000 incandescent watts of light – all with very little heat, and with not one dime going to the electric utility.

SunPipes and Sun Tunnels cost in the $300 to $500 range, depending on the size, plus installation

Not every tubular skylight is as efficient as the Sun Pipe, so check out lighting efficiency before making your purchase.

The only negative to this type of lighting is that as soon as the sun goes down, the light goes out. Doug Wozniak, the local Sun Tunnel distributor, reports that his product can get around this problem by having a light fixture installed in the tunnel. During daylight hours, you get free light. When the sun goes down, flip a switch and you still have light.

One final benefit of tubular skylights is that since at least 25 percent of them are sold direct to homeowners for do-it-yourself installation, the companies have done everything they can to make installation easy. That means that if we want, we can buy direct, install it ourselves, and brag about the results.

Sources

Acrylic skylights: Made by many manufacturers, including Allied Plastics of Pontiac, (248) 338-3830, Wasco Products, (800) 866-8101, and ODL of Zeeland, Michigan, (800) 253-3900. ODL and Allied also make acrylic skylights in circle, pyramid, triangle and ridge designs.

Glass-glazed skylights: Traditional square or rectangular, glass glazed skylights are made by a host of companies including Velux, (800) 888-3589, Andersen, (800) 426-4261, Roto Frank, (800) 243-0893, and Wasco Products. All make fixed and opening (venting) models. Velux makes a fixed skylight with a vent flap that lets in a limited amount of air for ventilation. According to Brad Upton at Dillman & Upton in Rochester, (248) 651-9411, a 2 foot by 4 foot Velux fixed skylight costs about $240. The same size venting model costs $425.

The Sun Pipe: It is installed locally by Al Walker & Sons in Dearborn Heights, (800) 844-4786.

The Sun Tunnel: It is installed locally by Michigan Sunlight Systems, Shelby Township, (800) 369-3664.

Get the lowdown in this sneaky guys' guide to selecting carpeting

by Glenn Haege,
America's Master Handyman

Men have made great strides to partial equality with women on the home front. We now get to shop for groceries and even pick out some of our own stuff. We get to help straighten the house, bath the kids, cook meals, wash floors, do the laundry (except delicates), and paint and wallpaper – but not pick out the colors.

One of the big "no nos", is carpet selection. Oh sure, we get to go along and maybe even pull out the charge card; but any man who has been married more than a week knows that our roles in the selection process are strictly relegated to saying, "Yes dear"; "I think you're right dear"; and "It looks good to me, dear."

We are kept in our place by constant feministic reminders that "Men don't know anything about carpet or color"; "Men have no fashion sense"; "If you let a man do it, the house would look like a barn."

Most women never realize how cutting these remarks are to a man's more sensitive side. In an effort to level the playing field, I decided to publish enough information so men could discuss the subject with their wives almost as equals.

I am convinced that women have this information imprinted in their genes at birth. We guys don't. But we can learn. To get the facts I sneaked over to see

Paul McEachern at A. R. Kramer's in Livonia, (734) 522-5300.

As any woman can tell you, most men have male order attention deficit disorder (MOADD), and it is very hard for us to keep our attention on something important like carpeting for a prolonged period of time. For those guys of you out there who have MOADD bad, here's a quick course. About two thirds of all carpeting made is nylon; two thirds is beige; one third is a looped weave called Berber.

If you get cornered by your wife and have to give an opinion on what carpeting to buy, you are probably safe looking thoughtful for a moment, then saying that you think a beige, nylon, Berber would be nice. Even if that is not what she is going to buy, you will get points for having given the subject serious consideration.

For those men who are a more retentive, I'll give more facts over the next two weeks.

Roughly 97 percent of all carpeting is made from synthetic fibers. Two thirds of the carpeting in the U.S. is nylon. Nylon is very strong and can last almost forever. It holds colors very well and is quite stain resistant. Major manufacturers' branded nylons, like Monsanto Wear-Dated, Dupont Stainmaster, and Allied Anso, can be even better because they are especially "tweaked" to have specific features, like wear or stain resistance.

About 30 percent of the carpet fiber made is Olefin (polypropylene). It is very colorfast and easy to clean. Often used in indoor and outdoor carpeting, Olefin can cost up to 30 percent less than nylon.

Two other synthetics are polyester and acrylic. Polyester makes a very luxurious, thick pile carpet. Acrylic gives the appearance and feel of wool, without the price.

Wool – the great, natural carpet fiber – is very luxurious and durable. It hides dirt because of its light scattering characteristics. Unlike synthetic fibers, wool does not melt when exposed to fire, it chars. Wool makes a very high quality, but pricey, carpet.

Carpeting comes in several different textures. With level loop piles, like Berbers, the yarn is looped at the top. Multi-level loop pile carpeting is merely looped carpeting with two or three different loop heights. Looped carpeting is excellent for high traffic areas because it shows wear very slowly. Foot traffic is on top of the loop, which is really the side of the fiber.

Because they bear up to traffic so well, Berbers are very good for family rooms, halls and stairways. They are also an excellent choice when you want the entire house to have the same carpeting.

In plush pile carpeting, the top of the loops are cut off. The most popular are Velvets and Saxonies.

Velvets have very smooth, luxurious surfaces. They show foot traffic because the areas that are walked on lean to one side and reflect light differently from the rest of the carpet.

In a textured Saxony weave, the top of the yarn is cut at different angles so that traffic and wear patterns are not as noticeable.

According to McEachern, cut pile carpeting is best for low traffic rooms like bedrooms, living rooms, and dining rooms.

A relatively new texture of carpeting, called Frieze, combines the strength of a level loop pile with the look of a plush pile. A Frieze carpet has had the top of the loop cut off, but the top of the yarn is then crimped over to one side so that you get almost the same wear characteristics as Berber.

There are also various textured and cut and loop combinations and patterns but these specialized weaves take only a very small proportion of carpeting sales.

I can see your attention is beginning to wander, guys, so we'll get into color selection, padding, pricing, and how a Do-It-Yourselfer can save money next week.

Floored by carpet choices?
Here is our smart guide for men

by Glenn Haege,
America's Master Handyman

When you set out to buy carpeting, you are really buying three things: carpet, padding, and installation. If you are sold short on any of the three, your carpeting purchase will be a money-losing proposition.

Last week we discussed the different fabrics and styles of carpeting. What about color?

There isn't a man alive who is going to win an argument about color with his wife or girlfriend. Even though 65 percent of all carpeting sold is beige, if you are a man and a rebellious "non-beiger," here's how to sound intelligent while you lose.

According to the professionals, light colors open up a room and make it look larger. They also show footprints less. Dark colors make a room seem warmer and cozier. Dark and multi colored carpets are also good at hiding soils and stains.

While you're deciding on color, check the highlights of the yarn. Shiny carpet yarns accentuate defects. They show footprints and soiling more than dull carpets.

John Greenough of Fairway Tile & Carpet in Clawson, (248) 588-4431, says that higher quality yarns reflect less light. The higher the quality, the duller the carpeting will be.

His colleague, Gene Pearlman, says that another way to tell inexpensive from better carpeting is to make a close-up inspection of the fibers. The thinner and more tightly packed the threads, the better the carpet. If all else fails, turn the carpeting sample over. Better quality carpet will have both the name of the chemical company that produced the yarn, usually Mannington, DuPont, BASF, or Allied, in addition to the name of the mill that actually wove the carpet.

"If the name of the chemical company is on the sample, both the mill and the chemical company are standing behind the warranty. If only the mill's name is on the carpet, only the mill is standing behind the warranty," Pearlman says.

The padding under the carpet is so important that installing an improper cushion can void the warranty, according to Paul McEachern of A. R. Kramer, in Livonia, (734) 522-5300. The five most common types of padding are synthetic hair, prime Urethane, rebond Urethane, flat rubber and ripple rubber.

Prime Urethane is very good but expensive. Unlike a fine wine, you are not going to impress anyone, even the carpeting, by ordering a prime Urethane. Consider it only if you are buying a very expensive wool.

Carpet padding for the rest of us is usually synthetic hair or rebond Urethane. They commonly come in 2-, 4-, 6-, and 8-pound weights. Eight-pound padding is the best and well worth the money for heavy traffic areas. Never accept less than 6-pound padding, McEachern advises.

There are really three types of rubber padding: flat, rippled, and bubble rubber. Flat and rippled rubber are excellent. They are waterproof and often used in basements and other cement slab installations.

Bubble rubber padding does not have sufficient density and thickness and can cause premature aging of the carpet. Using it can void the manufacturer's warranty.

If you are going to install carpeting on a concrete slab or in the basement and want a warmer floor, consider the Envira Cushion imported from Mexico by Fairway Tile & Carpet. It is environmentally friendly, waterproof, and lists an R factor of 4.5. If you don't like cold feet, it is worth the premium.

How much should all this cost? Carpeting is sold by the square yard. Before shopping, measure the rooms. Length times width gives the square feet. Divide by 9, then add 10 percent for waste. Multiply that number by the installed carpet square-yard price and you will get a fair cost estimate.

Naturally, you can pay as much as you want. Some exotic wool carpeting weaves cost $145 a yard. A very good quality nylon carpet, with good padding and expert installation, should cost between $20 and $40 a square yard. Usually the price will be between $25 and $30. If you are quoted a price significantly under this amount and the person does not look like Santa Clause, be skeptical. Make certain you are getting quality carpet and padding and expert installation.

Do not try to install the carpet and padding yourself. Expert installation is so important that amateur installation often voids the carpet warranty.

You can usually save one dollar a yard by moving the furniture yourself and another dollar a yard by pulling up the old carpeting. Do not remove the old carpet tack strips. Tearing them out can ruin the wood underneath. Besides, the older strips are wider and better than those with which they would be replaced.

Removing the old carpeting yourself is a good idea for a couple of reasons. First, you get to give the floor a thorough cleaning and can make any necessary repairs. Second, you can fix any squeaks in the floor before the carpeting goes down.

See, fellas, we made you a carpeting expert in just two weeks. Next week: do-it-yourself lipo suction.

NOVEMBER 7, 1998

Remodelers Show had many nice improvements worth mentioning

by Glenn Haege,
America's Master Handyman

Remodeling is big business. According to the National Association of Home Builders, 66 percent of us own our own homes. Many need fixing because their median age is 28 years. Forty-three million are more than 40 years old.

Every year the NAHB holds a Remodelers Show with seminars and displays especially skewed to the industry. The 1998 Show was held at the McCormick Place in Chicago, October 23-25.

While there were not any revolutionary advances displayed, I saw a lot of nice little improvements that are worthy of mention.

The show marked the formal introduction of American Metal Products' new Do It Yourself Gutter Helmet package, (888) 443-5638. I've talked about the new, money saving product in a past Homestyle article. It's now available locally at selected Damman hardware stores, (248) 399-5080. (Ed. note: The DIY version of this product is no longer available.)

The biggest area of improvement that I found at the show was in the replacement window field. Weather Shield was promoting their pocket Custom Shield replacement window. The window can be installed without tearing up any interior framing. You just pop out the old window sash, and pop in the new Custom Shield window.

Weather Shield, (800) 477-6808, also has true divided lites (the little trim pieces that often divided single pane windows). Most producers do a very unsatisfactory job of faking window lites by attaching little pieces of wood or plastic to the double or triple pane windows.

Weather Shield makes true lites available by making double pane windows that fit each lite. Naturally, it's expensive, so simulated divided lites, airspace and perimeter grilles, are also available.

Pella, (800) 847-3552 is making its exterior window cladding in 14 different colors. The colors range all the way from black and renegade blue to boysenberry and bright red. The company says its new EnduraClad finish resists fading. If so, it will make a big improvement for those not content with the standard white, cream, and brown window frames.

Both Velux, (800) 888-3589 and Andersen, (800) 426-4261 are bringing out skylights especially designed to replace the old fashioned bubble plastic that has turned into eye sores on so many roofs.

The world is getting smaller and S.A.C. Industries of Hickory Hills, Ill., (708) 430-8274 is importing French-made windows and doors. The Janneau window has one design feature that should be a big hit with folks who want to turn their homes into a fort. The window is available with an exterior roller shutter which can be rolled down to encase the entire window. Granted, when the shutter is down you can't see out of it, but no uninvited guest can crawl in, either.

I'm sure that the Portes Bel'm French door line S.A.C. is importing is a quality product. It comes in some very distinctly French (naturally) designs and the doors have names like Sirocco, Suroit, et Grand Vitrage.

But the thing that hooked me into reporting it, was that the company's elaborate 44-page color brochure is all in French. An English translation is provided on see-through vellum. The final cost of the brochure must have been enough to break a medium-sized bank. Just looking through the brochure is a French lesson.

Inside the house, KraftMaid Cabinets, (800) 914-4484, the nation's largest maker of semicustom cabinetry, has added more custom look features. Among them are four additional glass inserts, new deluxe crown moldings, and porcelain and chocolate glaze finishes.

Many homeowners are having difficulties with their home's exterior. I am going to devote an entire article to solving T-1-11 problems in the near future. Because of these troubles we are beginning to see new exterior building products. Two examples from the Remodelers Show were Custom Brick by Dryvit and Cedar Look Design Essentials by Owens Corning.

The Dryvit Company's Custom Brick, (800) 556-7752 looks like brick, but is really a custom formed finish that can be applied over almost any sub-strait. The forms come in seven different brick designs.

Owens-Corning's Cedar Look Design Essential Shakes and Scallops siding designs (800) 438-7465 are exactly what their name implies. The flexible Polyvinyl Chloride siding styles look like cedar shakes and scallop shingles. They are so close to the real thing that you see every impression and ridge. The marketing people assure me that they are available locally, so just call your local building supply.

Finally, if you have absolutely had it with refinishing your deck, DeckRite, (501) 945-1919, is importing a vinyl sheet decking product which applies over 5/8 inch exterior grade plywood. Glue it on and all you have to do is sweep and wash for the rest of the life of your deck.

There, you've seen the show and you didn't have to get any blisters on your feet.

Not all of these products are available in our market at present, but if you're interested, call the producers and tell them the Handyman sent you. They will do their best to get the product to you as soon as possible.

NOVEMBER 14, 1998

Is there life after T-1-11? Only if home is properly primed, painted

by Glenn Haege,
America's Master Handyman

This story is so scary you should be reading it on Halloween.

Imagine that you are Bill. You bought a nice 2,400 square foot colonial in 1992. Originally built in 1987, the house is one of those English colonials with brick, beams, and T-1-11 siding. The exterior paint job didn't look that good, but you figured that you'd repaint in a few years.

After three years, the exterior paint job became a peeling, blistering, scaling mess. It was definitely time to repaint.

Now comes the interesting part. You are not just anyone. Your day job is as a senior paint specifier for one of the big three car companies. When you buy paint you really know what you are doing. You choose a premium grade exterior house paint.

You go the whole nine yards selecting a painter. You get references, call people, and inspect some of the jobs. To make certain the house is prepped properly, you power wash all the flaky old paint off and wait three weeks drying time before prep and painting.

The painter spends days preparing the exterior walls. By the time he has finished painting, you have the best looking house in the neighborhood.

Side of house with improperly prepared T-1-11 siding. Paint will not adhere, causing peeling.

Two years later, the paint is peeling and blistering on the T-1-11 exterior wood veneer siding, the framing, and the window sills. Despite all your efforts, you must have gotten a bad batch of paint! Here is where you might expect me to start slamming the paint company. Nothing could be further from the truth.

Paint is made in huge 20,000 to 100,000 gallon batches. If your paint were bad, there would be thousands of other homeowners with the same problem, and everyone in would know about it. Paint companies do not release batches of bad paint; their reputations are too important and the market is too competitive.

Paint companies also know that exterior house paint is their best form of advertising. If you get a great looking paint job, friends, neighbors, even passers-by will say, "Great looking job, what kind of paint is it?" When you say, "It's Sherwin Williams," or "Pittsburgh," or what-ever; it's like money in the bank.

"OK Glenn, then what's wrong with the job?"

Remember, the homeowner is a professional paint specifier. He doesn't just say, "Oh well," and repaint. He drags the retailer out to his home. The retailer calls in the paint company's technical rep. No one has an answer.

Finally, the technical rep sends a 4-inch by 4-inch siding sample to the company's lab in Chicago. The lab report shows that the T-1-11 was so saturated with moisture, no paint made would adhere to the surface. Furthermore, the T-1-11 had been wet so long, it was beginning to delaminate. When Bill stripped off the siding he found that even the 2 by 4 studs were soaked and many had to be replaced.

I wish that Bill's horror story were an isolated problem, but I get T-1-11 paint problem questions from all parts of the country on my radio show.

"Why does this happen?" If you go to any good lumber yard, and ask about T-1-11 or any other plywood or veneer exterior siding, you will be told that all exposed surfaces of the siding have to be sealed properly.

Home Depot has a huge sign mounted right on the T-1-11 bin saying "All veneer exterior grade plywood siding has to be primed and painted." The sign actually repeats it three different ways: "primed/painted," "with primer and paint," and finally "It is important to prime and paint all exposed surfaces."

Despite the warnings, one of the places where new home builders and painters fall down the worst, is in priming and painting exterior sheathing. No matter how much they may charge for a house, many builders want the painting done fast and cheap. The result can be a horror story just like Bill's.

Here's what happens. If you look at T-1-11 carefully, you will see that the board is really a series of almost paper-thin strips of laminated wood. Thoroughly sealed, then painted, the siding will bear up relatively well. Improperly sealed, T-1-11 has the water repellency of a blotter. Every laminated edge is like a sign saying, "Come on in." Once inside the laminated wood, capillary action draws the water throughout the sheathing. The water is then trapped between an inner waterproof house wrap and the exterior coating.

When the sun beats down on the siding, it draws the water through the exterior surface, blistering and destroying the paint. Once the siding has been improperly prepared and becomes permeated with moisture, I do not know of any "quick fix." Eventual replacement of the siding may be the only sure solution.

Bill wound up tearing out all the siding and many of the 2 by 4s. Since he wanted to retain the look, he opted to have his house sided with Certainteed (800-345-1145) Cedar Impressions. Owens Corning (800-438-7465) has just come out with a similar line called Design Essentials. Both siding products have the look of cedar shingles in shake and scallop designs. This work was not cheap.

Like I said, this story is pretty scary.

NOVEMBER 21, 1998

Practical shopping tips for the handyman or woman on your list

by Glenn Haege,
America's Master Handyman

Every year during the holiday season I do at least one article on shopping for the Do-It-Yourselfer (DIY-er). Usually I ask some of my friends in the hardware business to give tips. This year I decided to give some of my own gift ideas.

These suggestions are not just for men. They are for both handy man and handy woman or for someone who may have just moved into a home and needs everything.

My idea of a great gift is not necessarily something that is showy. It is something that will definitely be used, and that the person might not think to buy.

Another thing, since I don't know whether you are a kid on an allowance or Ms. Megabucks, my suggestions run from $1.99 on up. Most of these gifts are available from your local hardware store or home center. Here's my Top 10 (actually eleven).

1. At the top of my list is a hard hat. These plastic, one size fits all, helmets can be found at almost any home center and only cost $6 or $7. A roofing or flooring nail can be a lethal weapon. You can't even go out on most commercial building sites unless you are wearing one, yet most DIY-ers don't think about getting a hard hat until they cut their head on a nail or bang it so hard they get a concussion.

2. I found high quality, OSHA compliant, safety glasses by Ruff Work Eyegear for only $39.99 at the Contractors Clothing Co. division of National Ladder, (800) 383-1117, in Madison Heights.

3. A dual cartridge respirator can save the lungs you love. Damman carries the AO Safety Economy Dual Cartridge Respirator with charcoal cartridges and dust filters for only $23.28. Home Depot carries Aero Eastern Model 355X Dual Cartridge Paint Solvent Respirator for $28.97. Both have optional replacement filters you can use for other contaminants.

4. Electric saws, lawn mowers, shop vacuums, and power equipment of every kind make too much noise. Home Depot has Aero Hearing Protectors for $11.97 with a noise reduction rating of 21 Decibels. Damman's has six packs of ear soft foam earplugs by AO Safety. They have a 29-decibel Noise Reduction Rating and cost $1.99.

5. A good back support belt is something every DIY-er needs. Medalist Pro Value Back Support Belts are available at almost any hardware or home center for between $15 and $16 (Fashion tip: they also come in female sizes and can be worn under outer clothing so that no one has to know you are wearing one.)

6. Work gloves. Every DIY-er has some, but puts off buying more because the old ones aren't worn out yet. Put a bow on a pair and they make a gift that is sure to be worn and appreciated. Best of all they are eminently affordable. I found some Wells Lamont lined work gloves with Hob-Nob, non-slip palm and finger, for $6.00 at Contractors Clothing. Lined pigskin gloves were $12.00. You can find similar values everywhere.

7. A good ladder can save thousands of dollars in hospital bills, yet too many DIY-ers buy cheap. Good 1A Class fiberglass 6-foot step ladders run from $87 to $146.50 at National Ladder & Scaffold, (800) 535-5944, in Madison Heights, Canton and Grand Rapids. A 1A Class ladder is rated to support 300 pounds.

Home Depot and many other home centers and hardware stores also carry good ladders. But Werner makes a 6-foot, 1A Class, exclusively for National Ladder that has heavy-duty rail shields and rung supports, yet costs only $98.65.

The National Ladder salesman I was talking to bought this step ladder for his own father last Christmas. Leno, one of the owners of National Ladder, said that it "was heavy duty enough to hold the Handyman." That is saying a lot.

The next three suggestions come from the C. Crane Company, (800) 522-8863. I don't have any stock in the company, it's just the only place I've found that carries these neat items.

8. Most of my stations (like WXYT, 1270) transmit on the AM band, therefore AM reception is very important to me. The CC Radio is the ultimate AM/FM radio. It has special circuitry for high-quality AM reception. It also receives FM, weather and TV signals. Priced at $159.95, this is a great gift for someone who likes Talk Radio.

9. Select-A-Tenna is a special antenna designed to bring in weak AM signals. Most antennas are made for FM. This $57.95 antenna will make a cheap AM radio out perform a $1,000 model.

10. The LED Flashlight just takes three "AA" batteries, but gives an ultra strong, ultra bright LED light. The waterproof bulb is rated at 100,000 hours, $34.95, three for $29.95 each.

11. In the true spirit of the season, my publisher has a special offer on two my own books. Now through Dec. 31, you can get both *Fix It Fast & Easy!, the Most Asked How To Questions,* and *Fix It Fast & Easy 2, Upgrading Your House,* for just $25 including sales tax, shipping and handling. That's a $42 value. To order, call (888) 426-3981 or send your check or money order to Master Handyman Press, PO Box 1498, Royal Oak, MI, 48068-1498.

It's the power-shopping season, but sure to be appreciated gifts, remembered and used, don't have to be expensive. So use this list, get out your credit cards and "Charge."

NOVEMBER 28, 1998

Advances in faux wood fireplaces should heat up burning interests

by Glenn Haege,
America's Master Handyman

I admit it. When you hear the expression "a boy and his toys" they are talking about me. I am the kind of guy who wants state-of-the-art everything. My car. My spa. My home entertainment system. Even my bathroom fan and shower head.

When they come out with a legitimate improvement, after the president of the company, I want to be No. 2, or worst case, No. 3 on the list.

Two years ago, my fireplace had the best gas logs on the planet. They looked so real you wanted to open a bag of marshmallows and cuddle up to the fire. Light the wood smoke incense, and it was like the real thing, only I never had to haul in the logs or shovel the ashes out of the fireplace.

Now, the Robert H. Peterson Co., (626) 369-5085, has come out with the Peterson Real-Fyre Ultimate Series Charred Oak log set, and these ceramic logs look so real that they leave my old log set in the dust. The fire twirls around and in front of the logs. The embers glow, and, so help me, you can see where little patches of the logs are just beginning to catch fire. Amazing.

Two of the retailers who carry Peterson logs in the Detroit Area are Williams Panel Brick, in Redford, (800) 538-6650, and Fireplace & Spa, (248) 353-0001, with stores throughout the Detroit Area.

Bob Frances of Williams Panel Brick, explained that the realistic look is created with three "secret weapons" in addition to the beautifully crafted gas logs. A front flame director directs some of the flame to the front of the logs. Then artistically placed vermiculite granules are glued on to the logs where-ever you want them to "catch fire".

The realistic look is completed with carefully placed Lava-Fyre granules on the bottom of the hearth. You can also add wood chips, branches, extra logs and ceramic pine cones. All these extras mean that every Real-Fyre gas log fireplace can have its own distinctive look.

Another very realistic log set, is the Best Fire by American Gas Log Co., (888) 484-7293, carried by Al King at Atlas Veneers & Fireplaces, in Troy, (248) 524-1020. King says that directing the flame on gas logs is an art. If the flame is too low, or directed directly at a log, carbon build up may result. A strong, hot flame is needed to burn off the carbon.

All this reminds me that the gas log and fireplace industry is really growing and maturing. Larry Jonas of Williams Panel Brick points out that there is now a Hearth Technician Certification Program, by the Hearth Education Foundation of Batavia, N.Y.

The Ultimate Series Charred Oak Real-Fyre gas logs by Peterson look like a mature fire with burned-through front logs, multiple flames and glowing embers.

The Foundation even has its own web site where the public is supposed to be able to get a listing of the certified technicians in their area. The only problem is that when we called up the site at hearthed.com, we found that even though all of Williams Panel Brick's fireplace technicians have been certified for a year, the only technicians listed for this area were from Fireplace & Spa!

Certification is an excellent idea, but the Foundation still has a few bugs to work out on their web site. Something tells me that the telephone lines will be sizzling between Detroit and Batavia next week.

Another proof that the industry is maturing is that Williams Panel Brick has begun to offer annual tune-ups for vented or direct vent gas fireplaces and logs. The service is not available for unvented gas logs and fireplaces.

I am really glad to see this new service because it is sorely needed. Gas fireplaces and logs are not toys. They are furnaces installed in fireplaces. As such, they can have the same problems as any other gas furnace.

The fireplace and log tune-up consists of a thorough check of all the working parts such as the termopile and valves, testing for gas and carbon monoxide leaks, cleaning the burner orifice, rotating the embers, and adjusting the sand. The new service costs $59.95 for gas logs and $69.95 for fireplaces.

If you live in an apartment or condominium or have a Florida room you want to heat, you will be glad to learn that the very realistic electric fireplaces that I have been writing about for years, have been purchased by Hahn Industries, and are now being distributed as part of the Heatilator line of Hearth Technologies, (800) 843-2848.

The Heatilator fireplaces, which can be mounted flush to the wall or in a corner, look like the real thing, yet cost only around $1,500. No expensive hook up is required, all you need is an electric plug and you're in business. Best of all, if you are a renter, when you move, just pull the electric plug and you can take your fireplace with you. Frances says that his company has more information on their website at: williamspanelbrick.com. All lower case, no spacing between words.

I can't provide someone to hug, but there is now no reason for you not have a toasty warm fire to come home to.

DECEMBER 5, 1998

Protect home from burglars during thieves' favorite holiday season

by Glenn Haege,
America's Master Handyman

There are few greater pleasures than to see little ones, eyes big as saucers, looking at a wealth of gifts underneath the Christmas tree.

Unfortunately for millions of families the holidays are ruined when all those wonderful presents, and even more precious memories, are ruined because a thief has broken in and taken or trashed the Christmas or Hanukkah presents.

Kevin Jamison, the National Accounts Manager for Ademco, one of the world's largest manufacturers and distributors of security devices, warns that "the two times of the year that see big spikes in the number of break ins are June/July and November/December. People let their guard down during vacations and holidays."

Most Christmas break ins are crimes of opportunity, not well planned operations like you see in the movies, according to Jamison. Quite often the burglar isn't a professional, just a kid, or a group of kids, looking for easy-pickings. Almost no one "cases" the joint. Usually the burglar just drives down the street and sees a house with all the lights off.

The burglar says to himself, "At this time of year they will be gone for at least a couple of hours, so I have plenty of time to look around for something to sell on the street, or possibly use for myself."

Then he sneaks into an enclosed area, like a patio, that has some bushes or a high fence around it, that will hide his activities from passersby. Usually, he gets in through a sliding glass door by jimmying it off its track or crawls through a basement window.

It doesn't matter if the perpetrator is a professional or not, if it's your house that is "smashed and trashed," it's a tragedy.

Jamison recommends several very low cost or no cost things you can do to outwit the bad guys:

■ Take your hedge clippers along with you when you put up the Christmas decorations. Trim back anything that can give protective cover to the bad guys. That includes all the overgrown bushes that are casting shadows around the patio.

■ Turn on the outside lights, especially around patios, windows and entrances. All the warm weather is over so take out the bug lights from your outside lights, clean out the canisters, and put in white lights. For just a little bit of money you can install smart lights that will automatically come on at dusk and go out at dawn.

■ Lock your doors. Too many people get swept up in the season and just walk out the house leaving the doors unlocked.

It doesn't matter if you are just going down the street for a Christmas drink or if cousin Bob is flying in to stay with the family and doesn't have a key. A minute after you walk out the door, Mr. Bad Guy may walk in and help himself to the silverware, or your favorite shotgun, or the micro-wave oven you were giving the kids

I also like putting some lights in the house on timers, so that any time you are away, the lights will go off and on in different parts of the house. They don't have to be on long, you just want a rotation of lights so that it appears that someone is moving around in the house. You can also have a radio tuned in to a talk show, so that it sounds like there is a conversation going on.

If you are going to be away for any period of time, even just a couple of days, stop newspaper delivery and enlist a friendly neighbor to pick up your mail and check to see that everything is all right. See if a neighbor will park in your driveway too, so that it looks like someone is home.

If you are a little high-tech, many other things can be done to give your house that lived-in look. With X-10 technology, you can have complete control of the lighting throughout the house. You could even turn your CD player and TV on and off at your phone command.

Learn more about X-10 home security and smart house systems by looking up the web sites of X-10 USA at X10.com, or telephoning them at (800) 675-3044. Another company is Home Automation Systems at smarthome.com. (800) 762-7846.

As we grow increasingly comfortable with technology, more and more new homes are pre-wired for fire and home security. Jamison says almost all new homes above $100,000 in value are now pre-wired for fire security, and nearly 40 percent are prewired for burglar alarms.

Burglar alarms, like any other security device, are only good if used. Quite often people have a fear of accidentally tripping their burglar alarm and waking their entire neighborhood when the thing goes off in the middle of the night.

The net result is that many folks let their guard down during one of the most break-in prone periods of the year.

My advice is to keep your guard up. Take the time to instruct everyone in the house about the burglar alarm system if you have one. If you don't, at least do the basics: Keep the doors locked and the lights on, and you won't have to worry about a grinch stealing your holiday.

Lubricate garage door to prevent winter's cold from making it sluggish

by Glenn Haege,
America's Master Handyman

Winter's coming, so don't let yourself get stuck with a sluggish garage door. Garage doors that seem to work perfectly during the summer, become stiff, groaning monsters when you have to open and close them during cold weather.

The only way to keep them moving smoothly is proper lubrication. I asked Henry Tarnow, of Tarnow Garage Doors in Farmington Hills, (800) 466-9060, for some tune-up tips. Tarnow has been in the door business since 1966, and was the first president of the Michigan Door Operator Dealer Association (MIDODA), so he knows his subject.

The first thing Tarnow mentioned, was that last year's garage door maintenance article was wrong. The expert I quoted then loves WD-40. Tarnow hates the stuff.

As is usually the case when experts disagree, there is truth on both sides. WD-40 is a better cleaning agent than lubricant. It's value is that it cuts through rust, grease, and grime, freeing up the hinges. The problem is that after the WD-40 has cut through the oil and grease, there is often no lubricant left.

Tarnow believes that you are much better off using a light lubricant, like 3 in One oil, or a good Silicone or Teflon spray.

There are two steps to lubricating the garage door – first the door, itself, then the garage door opener. We'll handle lubricating the doors first, then tackle the openers.

The two most common garage doors are the old one-piece units that pivot up and down from a pivot point and the newer sectional doors that roll up and down the tracks.

"On the old one-piece door, look where the arms connect to the pivot point on the wall and make sure that that is properly lubricated. There are two door pivots, left and right. Look at the roller at the top corner of the door, make sure there are no broken corners. Lubricate the roller and the part where the arm connects to the door, and where the spring connects to the arm" Tarnow says.

He also suggests inspecting the door when it is half open. If the arm has twisted it probably means that the bearings in the arm have worn out and it is time to buy a new door, because replacement parts are no longer available.

"If that's the case, start shopping right away," he says. "The situation will only get worse and you do not want to wait until the door falls off, or is hanging half open, or lands on your car because the arm broke."

On sectional doors Tarnow recommends that you lubricate the overhead torsion springs, all of the rollers, the hinges, everything that moves. Proper lubrication will reduce the noise and movement problems you have in cold weather.

There are two types of sectional panels used on garage doors. Most doors have pivot hinges mounted on the back of the sections. These pivot hinges should be lubricated.

"In this market we also have Taylor sectional doors. Typically these doors have springs on each side of the door. Each one of these springs has two pulleys, one above the spring and one at the top of the track. The pulleys should be lubricated. These doors have no external hinges between the sections. Each section is hinged within itself. Squirt some lubricant along the inside edges of each section. The lubricant will work a lot of rust out of the enclosed hinges and help the door move better during the winter," he says.

As far as garage door openers are concerned, Tarnow believes that homeowners should perform safety checks all year long. "I recommend that every month or two you lay a 2-by-4 under the garage door, hit the opener, and make sure that the door reverses automatically when it hits the 2-by-4.

"You should also disconnect the door from the opener and work the door by hand. If the door is properly balanced, you will be able to stop the door action midway and the door will neither fall nor rise. If it is not properly balanced and goes up or down, call a professional door installer to come in and make any necessary adjustments.

When it comes to lubrication of door opener systems, you should not lubricate the track or the tube on most garage door openers. Lubricating gunk's them up and can make action almost impossible during the cold winter months. Many of the manufacturers recommend that you do not lubricate the chain or the tracks. On the other hand, some screw drive openers do need to be lubricated, so read the owner's manual before reaching for the oil can.

If you are uncertain about what to do, or don't have the time, most good garage door installers will do tune ups. According to Tarnow, a tune up costs between $60 and $75. The service call should include the trip to your house, a half hour on the job, complete safety check, door adjustment, and lubrication.

Winter's coming. So grab this article and a can of lubricant, and do it yourself, or pick up the phone and have it done. Either way, you garage door will be ready for winter and you can brag about the result.

Special formula will keep stains from ruining your holiday party

by Glenn Haege,
America's Master Handyman

Country Christmas Party

"Oh it's Christmas in the city,
The house is shining bright,
But before the evening's over
Someone will have a big fight.

All that Christmas bounty
Can leave you crying in despair,
When someone drops the gravy
Or spills wine on your favorite chair.

Do not worry my little darlin',
The Handyman brings hope to you,
When you read this holiday article,
You'll know just what to do."

Now you know why I had to settle for being a talk show host instead of a country western singer.

All the silliness aside, emergencies happen every party season. I can't tell you how to make Uncle Gordon and Cousin Rupert best of buddies (since they hate each other), but I can tell you what to do when the Jell-O or carrot cake hits the carpet or couch.

Way before the party begins you should assemble the Handyman Emergency Stain Kit and put it some place that will give you instant access to the materials when the inevitable happens. The quicker you work on a spill or stain, the more successful you will be.

My emergency stain kit includes club soda, foam style shaving cream, and facial tissue and two new additions: Motsenbocker's LIFT OFF #1 and #2. Get the cheapest club soda, shaving cream and tissue you can find. The Motsenbocker products come in small pour and larger spray bottles. Get the spray bottles for better, quicker coverage.

The tissue, shaving cream and club soda can take care of 90 percent of the spills and stains. The Motsenbocker products are included to give you heavy artillery if necessary.

The first rule for any spill is to blot with facial tissue immediately. Never rub, blot. Don't use cloth or paper toweling. The only substitute for facial tissue is toilet paper. Trust me, you will look more sophisticated rushing around carrying a box of tissue rather than a roll of toilet paper.

Don't try to do the job with one or two tissues. Put a 1/2-inch thick wad on the wet spot. If the spill is on the carpet, lay the tissue on the spill, and let it absorb the surplus by itself. Then pick up the wet tissue and replace with a new wad. Step or press on the tissue. The pressure of your weight will wring out the carpet and padding like a sponge while the tissue instantly absorbs the moisture. Repeat the procedure until the area is quite dry.

If the spot is gone, you're home free. If a faint residue remains, pour on a small amount of club soda. It will fizz up. When the fizzing stops, use a wad of tissue to absorb the liquid.

Repeat the entire procedure if necessary.

If the spill is gravy, soup, baked beans, gooey frosting, or another grease-based concoction, pick up the excess with the tissue, then apply a little shaving cream and work in the foam with your fingers. Always use a "plucking" motion with your fingers. Never rub back and forth or around in a circle because these motions spread the stain, we want to contain and remove it.

When you have worked the shaving cream into the pile, pick everything up with the tissue. Repeat if necessary. When everything is picked up, start the club soda and tissue routine. Ninety times out of a hundred, the problem should be solved. If not, bring out the heavy artillery.

Gregg A Motsenbocker and I go way back. Motsenbocker won the inventor of the year award for his Motsenbocker's LIFT OFF products in 1996. You should be able to find them in most good hardware and home centers. If you can't, call Motsenbocker at (800) 346-1633 for the store nearest you.

What makes these products special is that they do not try to destroy the offending spill or stain, they break down the bond between the spill or stain and the surface being treated. This makes removal easy.

Motsenbocker's LIFTOFF #1 is made to remove water and protein based stains. That means you can use it on juices, barbecue sauce, beer, berries, blood, chocolate , coffee, cream cheese, egg, frosting, yogurt, scuffs and heel marks, liquor, marmalade, mud, pet stains, red vinegar, pop, soy sauce, syrups, red and white wine.

LIFTOFF #2 is designed to remove petroleum and natural oil based products. Use it on bacon grease, butter, candle wax, chicken soup, chili, cooking oil, cosmetics, crayons, eye liner and other makeup, gum, hair spray, lipstick, margarine, peanut butter, salad oil, shoe polish, and shortening.

Some of the spills and stains you may come across are combinations of water base, protein and grease stains, so don't be afraid to use a combination of LIFTOFF 1 and 2 on the same stain if necessary. Sorry, but nothing in my bag of tricks is guaranteed to remove mustard.

Of course the best cleaning agent of all, is the true spirit of Christmas. Keep your eye on the prize, your mind on the miracle, and have a blessed day.

DECEMBER 26, 1998

Millennium adds a new dimension to your resolutions for 1999

by Glenn Haege,
America's Master Handyman

For most of us, New Year's Resolutions are those things that, if we're real conscientious, we write down, start to do, then forget about by Jan. 15. If we are not conscientious types, we forget before they even get written down. I like resolutions that are actually meaningful so that I am not so likely to forget or say, "OH well."

Here are some of my New Year's Resolutions. If you don't have your list made out yet, use these for thought starters or add them to your list.

■ Plan for the Millennium. I don't mean going up on a mountaintop or walking around shouting "The end is near." I mean start planning now to have a memorable day with family and friends. Barb and I have been socializing with one very special group of friends since high school. We started making our plans for our group's Millennium celebration over a year ago. If you want to rent a hall or go some place special, you'll be surprised at how tight reservations are already. Try to have your plans cast in concrete by April 15th (tax day, now there's a scary thought).

■ Have your information system checked out for Y2K problems. I don't think that the banking system, power, or phone companies are going to crash. I don't have electric generators and am not hoarding survival rations in my back yard bomb shelter. However, I do think that there will be a lot of little Y2K glitches. It doesn't hurt to play it safe. Be sure to keep physical copies of all your important written documentation, including medical, bank and investment records.

Make sure that at least your own personal computer and information system does not have a problem. All DOS based systems are suspect. Even if you have an Apple Macintosh computer, your software could have a glitch.

At a very minimum, call the manufacturers of all your major hardware and software and ask if any Y2K problems have been discovered. If so, what can you do about them? Make sure you have crossed this off your list by June. The closer we get to January 1, 2000, the harder it will be to get through to these companies.

■ Map out 1999's home improvement projects now.

If you are planning on making any home improvements in next year, try to have the projects laid out within the next two weeks.

Keep in mind that contractors will have an even harder time getting and keeping good workers in 1999 than they did in '98. Many of the major construction projects, like the casinos, are scheduled to start this year. Because they can make around 50 percent more money on commercial than residential work, many of the skilled trades will be switching over.

Meanwhile, we not only have not trained more skilled trades workers, we haven't even been successful at giving construction trade tuition scholarships away at some community colleges. The result is that we are now 2,000 carpenters short in the Detroit Area. The same goes for plumbers, brick layers, and skilled installers of any kind. Guess who may not be showing up on your job?

So make sure you have your orders in very early and get completion dates guaranteed in writing. Then be prepared to wait. If your contractor says there is no problem, ask him why? If he has to depend on independent contractors, he too may be up the creek without a paddle.

■ Arrange financing early, too. Money matters. It also talks. Most Home Improvement projects need to be financed. January is an excellent time to arrange financing. Rates are at an all time low and the month of January is usually slow. So make your plans, get your quotes, and arrange financing before the spring rush. If you have cash in hand, your job may be able to be put on a fast track.

■ Get ideas at home improvement shows. If home improvement is on your list, make plans to visit a home improvement show. All the shows will have in-depth seminars as well as displays by the area's leading contractors, retailers and manufacturers. Mark the following dates on your calendar.

Feb 4-7: Spring Home & Garden Show at the Novi Expo Center
Feb 19-21: Macomb Home Improvement Show at the Macomb Sports & Expo Center
March 4-7: Michigan Home & Garden Show at the Pontiac Silverdome
March 18-21: Builder's Home & Detroit Flower Show at Cobo Hall
March 26-28: WXYT Home Expo at the Macomb Community College Center Campus
April 8-11: Home Improvement Show at the Novi Expo Center

Be prepared to make the most of your time at these shows. Learn all you can before you say "yes." Make lists of what you are looking for, take and bring measurements and photographs of the areas to be remodeled with you.

■ The biggest New Year's Resolution of them all: Make a heartfelt resolution to keep your resolutions.

I'd write more, but Barb tells me we have to go to the store to get more champagne and other New Year's Eve goodies. After 30 years I know where my priorities lie, so …

Happy New Year everyone!

Chapter 5

1999 Articles reprinted from The Detroit News HOMESTYLE

A powerful housewares market has hot items for specialty needs

by Glenn Haege,
America's Master Handyman

Fewer people attended the National Housewares Manufacturers Association's annual show in Chicago this week, and while snow may have kept some attendees away, I believe the real reason is the consolidation of the housewares market.

According to a the group's 1998 State of the Industry Report analyzed in the January issue of "Homeworld Business", discount and warehouse stores now account for 57.8 percent of housewares sales. Add 10 percent for specialty stores like Bed Bath and Beyond and you have accounted for 70 percent of the market, leaving slim pickings for the rest of the stores.

Despite the consolidation, '97 housewares sales were up 2.5 percent to $58.4 billion. In case you don't believe this information has any relevance to your life, that figure represents $560 of sales for every US household last year. This was more money than we spent on education.

Here are some of the products and trends I spotted at this year's show:
Steam cleaning and sanitizing is the big growth industry: Hoover, Eureka, and Bissel, all have powerful, good looking machines. But the real attention getter was an Italian import, the EuroStar Vapor Cleaning System, a machine that sanitizes at the same time it cleans. The EuroStar creates vapor at about 400 degrees Fahrenheit, much hotter than steam.

Not just for carpeting, hardwood, tile and vinyl floors, the EuroStar cleans venetian blinds and fixtures while they are still hanging, hard to clean items such as can openers, even upholstery and clothing that would usually have to be dry cleaned. The EuroStar, (800) 656-8541, retails for $399.

A nice advance in the heater category is the new Pelonis Disk Furnace III, (800) 842-1289, a five ceramic disk electric heater. Set the control for the heat you want and the heater turns on and regulates itself. If you put the heater in a big box, and set the temperature setting for 72 degrees, the Pelonis would maintain a perfect 72 degrees in-the-box temperature, regardless of the temperature outside the box. The heater retails for about $39.95.

Hearthware Home Products, (888) 287-0763, had two very interesting products. The first was a stand alone, radiant oven, called the Infrared Cooking system, that retails at $249. The radiant oven saves about 25 percent of cooking time and sears meat so rapidly it seals in all the juices.

The second product is a green coffee bean roaster. This $180 item roasts a half cup of coffee beans at about 500 degrees. The process takes fifteen minutes. According to the manufacturer, green coffee beans retain their flavor for about two years. Roasted coffee beans start losing flavor after two weeks. Ground coffee only retains its flavor for two days. What does that say for the coffee most of us wake up to every morning?

Top 10 Housewares Retailers

Store	Type	Sales (in millions)	Percent Increase
Wal-Mart	Discount	$9,175	11.9
Kmart	Discount	$4,010	2.2
Costco	Warehouse	$2,580	11.2
Target	Discount	$2,325	12,9
Sam's Club	Warehouse	$2,240	3.9
Sears	General merchandise	$1,900	5.3
Williams-Sonoma	Specialty	$775	14.0
Home Depot	Home center	$755	18.0
Bed Bath & Beyond	Specialty	$600	29.0
TruServ	Hardware	$550	1.9

Three steam collector kettles manufactured by MKI caught my eye. Each is priced at $75. They include a carousel that goes round and round; a rocket kettle with two circling rocket ships; and a locomotive with spinning wheels.

At the opposite end of the cycle, Better House Corporation, (800) 562-1311, is distributing two new plungers. The first, the Super Asco double action, spring enhanced, plunger pulls and pushes clogs out of kitchen sinks, and retails for $9. The second, the FixMi Quick Drain Buster, uses a unique pump design to clear the new, easy to clog, 1.6 gallon toilets. It retails for $19.95. Both products are available by mail order.

In the cleaning categories, the big story is the movement from general, do-everything products to specialized products that are especially tweaked to perform specific functions.

For example, Scot Laboratories, (800) 486-7268 has introduced two new products: Zap-It Microwave Cleaner with odor neutralizer and Pot Shot. Just spray Zap-It on the microwave oven surface, put in a cup of water, and turn the microwave on for two minutes. By the end of the cook cycle, the almost impossible to remove baked on crud can just be wiped away with a soft cloth.

Spritz Scot's Pot Shot on hard baked-on, burned-on stains on pans, casseroles, and crock pots, and the stain can be wiped away in just a couple of minutes.

Whink Products, (800) 247-5102, Little Squirt Upholstery Spot Remover, is safe for all colorfast fabrics and will remove stubborn spots from juices, coffee, chocolate and lipstick.

Elgin Miller, a Royal Oak company, (Ed. note: can't find a current phone number) is making a name for itself with products like Freezer Defroster, which speeds freezer defrosting, and Plastic Cleaner, which can be used on all plastics from computers to fake diamonds.

The list goes on and on. Once you use them, you will fall in love with many of these cleaners, so be prepared to make more room for cleaner storage in the coming year.

JANUARY 23, 1999

Builders show addresses the future needs of an aging population

by Glenn Haege,
America's Master Handyman

DALLAS

Do you find your home's lighting no longer does an adequate job? Did you have an accident and discover that the hallways and doors were too narrow, and the steps too steep to use a walker or wheel chair? Perhaps your hearing is not quite what it used to be, and you don't hear the phone until after the fifth or sixth ring, sometimes missing a call?

If the answer was "yes" to any of these questions the National Association of Home Builders (NAHB) hears your pain and is trying to do something about it.

Finding a solution to your problems, while making an honest buck in the process, is so important that it was the subject of nine different educational seminars at last week's 55th Annual NAHB Convention in Dallas.

The reason why Senior's Housing is such a hot topic is that the baby boomer generation is going 50. Soon, the biggest blip in American Demographics will be solidly in the senior circuit. But it isn't just the Boomers. More than half of all the people in history, who have lived past the age of 65 are alive today.

This year's convention offered a solid one-two punch to solving the senior housing dilemma. First, Judith Miley, a top seniors housing expert, told what type of things needed to be done to make housing hospitable to independent seniors in their 70s and 80s.

Then, "Builder" Magazine and Masco Corporation and their partners built a concept home on the Convention's Exhibit Floor that showed how these ideas could become an extremely attractive reality. The home was built to conform to needs expressed by older buyers in a Mature Market Study commissioned by "Builder" Magazine and Masco Corporation. A major finding from the study was that couples in their 40s, often with teenage children, wanted to move into a home and stay there into their 80s.

So how do you build a home that will accommodate these two vastly different lifestyles?

At her seminar, Miley, who is president of J. E. Marketing Communications, Inc., (352) 867-0678, and a member of the NAHB Senior Housing Council and Remodelers Council, said the answer is to build in luxury Universal Design items now that will become necessities for independent living later.

Universal Design does not just refer to seniors, it means designing living areas that are user friendly for everyone – young people, old people, healthy people, and those with disabilities.

A significant number of Americans in this country have a disability. Miley cited these statistics:
■ In 1992, 48.9 million people in the US were estimated to have a disability.
■ About 3.8 million of those with disabilities were younger than 17.

■ Seven million people will develop back pain for the first time this year. Back pain is the second most common reason people see a doctor.

If you live long enough, you will become handicapped to some degree. Your vision, hearing and mobility will be affected. So you might as prepare yourself.

It turns out, that spoiling ourselves a little in our 40s, 50s and 60s may give us what we need and keep happier, healthier, and more self -sufficient in our 70s, 80s and beyond.

Here are a few examples of Miley's luxurious necessities:
■ 60-inch wide aisles and 36-inch-wide doorways. They give a open gracious feel now, but are needed when some one uses a walker or a wheel chair.
■ Skylights, nonglare lights, and task lighting are attractive today, but will become vitally important when decreased eyesight and increased sensitivity to glare begins to take a toll.
■ Large walk-in showers stalls with hand-held showers and multiple shower heads, lever faucet handles, grab bars and bench seating. All these features can be luxurious, even romantic now, but have the ability to make a wheel-chair-bound person self-reliant later.
■ In the kitchen, varied counter top heights, pull down cabinets, and pull-out faucets with lever handles are pleasing design elements today that will become absolute necessities as age limits freedom of movement.

The Builder/Masco Life Stages Home shows how all these ideas can be put together to make one to die for house. The 3,175 square foot home was designed by Devereaux & Associates and manufactured by Fleetwood Homes, the nation's largest home builder. Many of the products featured in the home were manufactured by Masco's operating companies.

Guests enter a soaring 20-foot-high foyer capped by a Four Seasons glass cupola. Four Season skylights are a design constant throughout the house assuring easy-on-the-eyes natural light in every room.

The Master Suite has an adjoining den which can easily become a second master bedroom if one spouse requires an adjustable bed or separate rest needs.

The master bath features a commodious two person shower enclosure that divides his-and-her bathrooms. The enclosure includes two stainless steel Franklin Brass grab bars, and a chrome pressure balance Monitor II shower with scald protection and an Alsons adjustable height, chrome, hand-held shower unit. It's for the present, but practical for the future.

The spacious kitchen boasts two work areas. The main area has a Kindred stainless steel sink on an adjustable counter that moves up and down to accommodate a wheelchair-bound person. Both work areas have Delta Gourmet pull-out spray faucets and hand-rubbed quality cabinets.

I've just listed a few of the highlights in the Life Stages concept home. I'll write more about it, and about ways you can adapt your house to become more future friendly.

Snow leaves millions in home damage and could affect your health

by Glenn Haege,
America's Master Handyman

A lot of people wish they had done a better job cleaning their roof gutters and down spouts this year. Clogged gutters, leading to ice damming, were one of the major causes of millions of dollars of homeowner damage in the past month. And it may only get worse.

It doesn't take much to clog a downspout – just a few leaves and twigs can do it. Then the freezing water creates an ice dam, causing snow and water to back up the roof. After a few days the water works its way under a few shingles. Repeated freeze-and-thaw cycles cause a few shingles to curl up and lift 1/4 to 1/2 inch. Then a trickle of water that may become a torrent starts working its way into the home.

The water works its way down hill. Through the roof into the attic soaking the insulation. From the attic into the ceilings, walls, and light fixtures.

The water ruins the insulation and drywall. Ductwork fills with water. Plywood delaminates. Plaster gets soaked and, if not dried in a timely manner, begins to decompose. Any damp organic material, such as drywall and wood, becomes a breeding ground for microorganisms such as Stacybotrys, Alternaria, and Cladosporius.

How bad is it? According to Joe Smith of Complete Content Restoration (CCR), in Troy, (248) 650-6080, his company's business is already up 300 percent over last January. "We're treating weather-related calls like an emergency room situation, trying to get people out to the worst cases first," Smith says.

Another company getting lots of calls is Burton Bros., (248) 357-7000, a 77 year old firm in Southfield, that specializes in storm and fire damage.

"I have 18 years experience as a carpenter and 13 years as a supervisor, and this is the worst I've seen," says Peter Nakoneczny, a Burton Brothers supervisor who says the company has already received more than 1,000 storm-related calls.

According to his estimate, about 15 percent of the damage is to exteriors, and covers everything from shingles lifting to roof valleys collapsing, and even entire soffit systems falling off of houses.

The remaining 85 percent of the damage is interior and covers everything from drywall replacement, to cupping of hardwood floors, and even complete kitchen replacement. Nakoneczny estimates that most storm related repairs average between $5,000 and $30,000.

All of this storm damage could relate to health problems in the future. Wet insulation has to be removed and damaged drywall cut out. This often will require the removal of ceiling drywall in one or more rooms as well as all the wall drywall that had moisture damage.

Connie Morbach, of Sanit-Air, a Troy-based duct cleaning, air quality testing, and remediation firm, (888) 778-7324, says that if you have water damage in a wall or ceiling, the first thing to do is let the area drain. Then remove any wet insulation. If there is just a small amount of water damage to a plaster or wood wall or ceiling, you may let the area dry and hope for the best. If the water damage covers a large area, or the affected surface is drywall, the drywall must be cut out and replaced.

According to Morbach, a moldy smell or a family member developing a cough may be signs of potentially very dangerous Stacybotrys mold and extra care must be taken. If removal of water damaged wall or ceiling sections, or carpeting, exposes a black, tarry mold, the entire area has to be sanitized.

If you feel unsure in your diagnosis, you can get a swab test, or have a chunk of the effected material tested by Sanit-Air or other laboratory testing organization. Charges for swab tests start at $95, Morbach said.

"If the effected area is 2 feet by 3 feet or less, you may be able to do this as a do-it-yourself project. Professionals should definitely be called in for larger areas. Do not even consider doing it yourself if you have small children, the elderly, or any immune-compromised person living in the house," Morbach says.

Sanit-Air, Burton Brothers and Complete Content Restoration all do remediation work. Dr. George Regal of Healthy Homes, (248) 358-3311, has gained a national reputation for major microbial and asbestos removal.

On the other hand, if you just have a small water stain on the wall or ceiling, you can just spray the affected area with an aerosol can of Kilz by Masterchem Industries (800) 325-3552, or Cover Stain by William Zinsser (732) 469-4367. Either product will stop the stain from bleeding through the finish coat.

If the original paint was off white, I recommend Kilz because it is already off white in color. The Kilz coating might be enough to satisfy your significant other. When dry, paint over if necessary.

FEBRUARY 6, 1999

Do your homework before having cracks in the basement wall fixed

by Glenn Haege,
America's Master Handyman

What do you do when the basement wall cracks and starts bowing in? The foundation is crumbling before your very eyes. Will the house be next?

I've wanted to write an article about this subject for years, but I needed a specific job on which to center the article. Kathleen, my editor at Master Handyman Press, has a small rental house in Royal Oak. The 50-year-old house had been built next to a 150-year-old tree. After half a century of peaceful co-existence, the now 200-year-old tree's root system started to push in the basement wall. Clearly the tree had to go, but its roots also caused two big spider web cracks in the wall.

A couple of years passed. There were no leaks and no further deterioration, but the cracks did not go away. Meanwhile, Kathleen decided to sell the house, so the cracks had to be fixed. Bingo! A perfect case study for my article.

We called three contractors for quotes: Calculus Construction of Farmington Hills, (888) 746-5464; Insta-Dry Waterproofing of Southfield, (800) 356-0820; and Jackson Waterproofing of Belleville, (800) 404-8342.

Calculus Construction and Jackson Waterproofing are big guns in structural repair. They are the kind of folks the Detroit Tunnel Authority would call if the Detroit-Windsor tunnel sprung a leak. Todd Jackson teaches waterproofing for the National Association of Waterproofing Contractors. Luckily, both companies also do residential work.

Insta-Dry Waterproofing is a franchisee of Basement Systems, Inc. and does waterproofing and structural repair in Michigan and Ohio.

With three good companies and what appeared to be a simple repair, I expected their quotes to all be in line. Not so. The quotes varied from $750 to $11,000, perfect examples of how important it is for the homeowner to get multiple quotes and really do his or her homework

The Insta-Dry folks were the first out. They use a "Grip-Tite" Wall Anchor System which features anchor rods inserted through the wall then attached to rectangular steel earth anchors about eight feet from the wall exterior. An accompanying steel plate connects to each rod on the inner side of the wall.

Their representative inspected the inside and outside of the wall and discovered an old crack at the opposite end of the basement. He said that before work could start the offending tree stump had to be removed by a landscaper (we estimate a $500 cost). Since the wall had cracks at both ends of the basement, he suggested the drilling and placement of eight wall anchors at a cost of $500 per anchor, or $4000 for the job. The job would have a 25-year warranty.

Waterproofing quotes

Company	Repair	Warranty	Cost	Tree removal	Total cost
Calculus	2 steel beams	None	$750	0	$750
	2 Helix steel piers	10 years	$1,400	0	$1,400
Jackson	Steel beam, epoxy	None	$2,300	$500 est	$2,800
Insta-Dry	8 wall anchors	25 years	$4,000	$500 est	$4,500
Jackson	Waterproofing,reinforcement	Lifetime	$9,000	$500 est.	$9,500
	If Sump needed	Lifetime	$11,000	$500 est.	$11,500

Calculus came out next. Their representative looked at the new crack and the old crack and told us that, since the old crack hadn't caused a problem for 35 years, it probably wouldn't cause a problem for the next 35 years. I agreed. To stabilize the new cracks he proposed two solutions, neither of which called for stump removal. The simplest solution was to brace the wall in the cracked area with two heavy steel beams. The wall would not be as good as new, but it probably would not get any worse. The job could not be guaranteed, but the cost would be only $750.

His second alternative was to install two 10-foot to 20-foot steel piers attached to helical plates on the exterior and 20-inch steel plates on the interior surface. The Helix pier assembly is a very sophisticated wall anchoring system developed by the AB Chance Company. The cost for the job would be $1,400 and would have a 10-year warranty.

The Jackson Waterproofing representative came out and proposed an entirely different solution. Before work could begin, he said, the stump had to be removed and the entire exterior length of the basement wall had to be trenched down to the footer. The wall would then be straightened, cracks welded with epoxy, and the top interior wall reinforced with 2- by 8- inch steel bracing. Hydro-

Guard (dimpled plastic) exterior waterproofing sheathing would be applied to the entire wall and tied in to the exterior drainage system. The cost would be $9,000. If needed, a sump pump would be installed for an additional $2,000. The job would have a lifetime warranty.

The Jackson representative also suggested a low cost alternative of bracing the inner wall with a 2- by 8-inch steel beam and welding the cracks with epoxy for $2,300.

The vexing part about these waterproofing quotes was that, the more I studied them, the more I decided that they were all correct. If I were on a very tight budget, the $750 fix would be a gift from heaven. The two Helix piers for $1,400 with a 10-year guaranty is a very practical solution and was eventually selected by Kathleen.

Jackson's steel beam and epoxy solution had the advantage of a waterproof epoxy and was another very practical plan. Insta-Dry's 8 wall anchors were an excellent conservative approach.

Jackson's waterproofing and reinforcement was expensive, but, if I were going to use the basement for an office or living space, could very well be the way to go. Depending on a person's needs, any one of the quotes could be the right choice.

Great home exhibits steal the show

by Glenn Haege,
America's Master Handyman

If you didn't go to the Novi Show last weekend you missed out on some good exhibits. Many of the exhibitors we talked to aren't going to bother with any other shows this year. They all gave the same reason: Too much business.

Some exhibitors are already booked through July. The money is fine, but what you are actually talking about is 60- to 70- hour work weeks for management, skilled trades being worked to exhaustion, and some poor soul has to take care of the business that just walks in the door? Oops!

Here's my review of the show. If I were handing out awards they'd go to:

Most Beautiful Award: It goes to a fireplace vignette from The Tile Shop, (800) 433-2939, a regional tile distributor with showrooms in Farmington, (248) 442-8888, and Sterling Heights, (810) 731-9999. The vignette featured an emerald

Elegant curved cherry cabinets by KraftMaid were part of the Kurtis Kitchen & Bath display at the Novi Home Show.

green tile mantel and fireplace surround. The imported English tiles were fired in Stoke-on-Trent by the H & R Johnson Company. The wainscot was marble and the floor limestone. The effect was totally elegant.

Most Educational Award: This also goes to The Tile Shop (phone numbers above). Their cut away tile shower and tile floor displays showed the steps it takes to construct a tile shower pan, tile shower walls, or tile floors. Rod Sill, a member of The Tile Shop's marketing team said that a Do-It-Yourselfer can make a tile shower pan with only $80 in materials. Labor adds about $200 to the job. The company conducts free tile installation clinics at each of its stores every Saturday.

Most Beautiful Kitchen Display: Kurtis Kitchen & Bath, (734) 522-7600, for their large exhibit featuring many different kitchen vignettes.

The most eye-catching featured KraftMaid curved cherry cabinets that bowed out into the kitchen. If you have the space, you couldn't beat the look.

A close runner up for Most Beautiful Kitchen was the Living Spaces Exhibit, (248) 682-3600, of Sylvan Lake. This display featured very handsome green-glazed Acorn cabinets and a very attractive ceramic hood trim.

Most Interesting Floor Display: Waterford's Woods of the World, (248) 646-2422. Their wood flooring display featured four squares of Chilean Cherry, African Zebra Wood, American Tiger Maple and White Oak.

Most Interesting Appliances: The first was the new Gaggenau Steamer at the Travarro appliance display, (800) 274-2502.

The Specialties Showroom Exhibit, (248) 548-5656, had very attractive Dacor dual fuel ranges, with sealed gas burners and Pure Convection ovens.

Specialties also displayed the English Creda and Swedish Asko front loading washing machines and their companion dryers.

These very quiet, very energy efficient washers clean with less water and less wear-and-tear than traditional top loaders. The dryers dry faster than conventional models, too.

Most Interesting Food Preparation Area: The granite/acrylic composite made by Blanco of Italy, and distributed by Mathison Kitchen, Bath & Plumbing Supply (734) 455-9440.

The sink contained a built-in cutting board, colander, and disposer slot. Much too pricey to be a mere sink, it is so tough that you can place a 400-degree pan on the surface and not cause any damage.

Favorite Cleaning Item: Dan Zimmerman of Zimm's Vacuums, (734) 425-1105, was exhibiting the VacPan by Vacuflo. This ingenious little item eliminates the need for a dustpan. Just sweep the dust and debris toward the VacPan slot and whoop, it's gone, sucked into the central vacuum system.

The second reason for my mentioning Dan Zimmerman, is that he spent most of last year upgrading and expanding his labor force. The result is that not only can Dan offer installation within one week of sale, he is one of the few exhibitors who has been able to maintain a full show schedule. Zimms will be at both the Pontiac Silverdome (March 4 - 7) and the Ann Arbor Home Improvement Show (March 26 - 28).

Sy Frielich's AquaTest Laboratories, (888) 307-TEST, was featuring two residential water test show specials. One for people with wells included testing for total coliform bacteria, E-coli bacteria, nitrates, nitrites, arsenic, lead, sodium, and turbidity for only $99.50. For people on city water he had a six-test package covering lead, copper, fluoride and chloride for $100. They sounded like fairly good deals. Frielich told me that he would extend the show special for a few weeks to give my readers a chance to take advantage of them.

Last on my list, was the Marvin Window display, which showed how Marvin has taken their simulated divided lite technology and turned it into an art form. You can now have sliding glass and other windows and doors with simulated lites in a profusion of designs. Literally, any design your architect can draw, Marvin can make. Call (800) 346-5128 for a dealer near you.

But you better call fast. If you don't get your order in soon, your installer may tell you to wait until the next millennium.

FEBRUARY 20, 1999

How to choose kitchen cabinets

They're the cornerstone of any kitchen remodeling job, so serious shoppers will put quality first

by Glenn Haege,
America's Master Handyman

If you are one of the 4.5 million Americans who are going to spend $30.7 billion remodeling your kitchen in 1999, this story is for you.

The official kitchen-hunting season in Metro Detroit starts with the Spring Home Shows. These annual pageants are the best and easiest way to see all the new trends as well as a whole host of beautiful displays by manufacturers, distributors and kitchen and bath remodelers.

Updating your kitchen is a smart idea. According to the National Association of Homebuilders, dollar for dollar, remodeling the kitchen adds more value to the resale value of your home than any other remodeling job.

The most important, most expensive, and least understood parts of any kitchen remodel are the cabinets. If you have appliances you don't like, you can replace them without disturbing the rest of the kitchen. The same is true with the fixtures, even the countertops and floors. But if you don't like the cabinets, or they are starting to break down, it means the entire kitchen has to be torn apart.

Every kitchen cabinet in every kitchen display looks good. How to choose cabinets that will hold up well and stay looking good is the $64,000 question. According to Larry Wilson, director of marketing services for Merillat, the nation's largest cabinetmaker, about 50 percent of all cabinets are made by a local cabinetmaker, which means they do not have the backing of a national company. They may be just as good or even better than those made by the big boys, but there is no way for you to tell, unless you know what to look for.

My staff at Master Handyman Press and I asked manufacturers, installers and big and small kitchen and bath remodeling companies what to look for in a quality cabinet. This article is a distillation of what they said. Not every good cabinet has all the features listed here, but this list is a good way for you to weigh the pros and cons of different manufacturers' products.

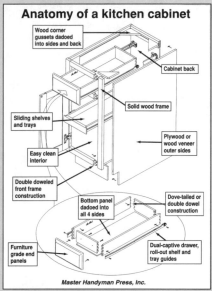

Anatomy of a kitchen cabinet

Wood corner gussets dadoed into sides and back

Cabinet back

Solid wood frame

Sliding shelves and trays

Plywood or wood veneer outer sides

Easy clean interior

Double doweled front frame construction

Bottom panel dadoed into all 4 sides

Dove-tailed or double dowel construction

Furniture grade end panels

Dual-captive drawer, roll-out shelf and tray guides

Master Handyman Press, Inc.

The Oak Sandrift finish, raised panels and crown and base moldings give a classic look to these semi-custom cabinets by KraftMaid.

Cabinets are made of four major ingredients: the cabinet itself, which is called "the box" in the trade; the shelves; the door; and the drawer. And then there are the design elements such as the finish, decorative hardware, molding, etc., that add to the cabinets' appeal.

Here's what to look for in each area:

The box

Sturdy, square, symmetrical construction of the box is important. There should be nothing fragile about a cabinet. It should be built on a square within very close tolerances. All the same size and style cabinets should be identical. There should be no variations due to sloppy workmanship.

■ Frame vs. frameless: Cabinets can be either framed or frameless. The standard American style is framed construction. This means you see a frame on all four sides of the cabinet front, and doors and drawer front panels overlap the frame. Door hinges are attached to the frame.

Frameless construction is a European influence and is found most often in Euro-style cabinetry. In frameless construction, there is no front frame. Since no frame exists, doors and drawers do not overlap. They slide directly into the cabinet. Many people like this more tailored appearance.

As a practical matter, frameless construction is considered to be a little stronger than framed cabinetry. Frameless construction also provides a bit more useable room in the cabinet because no allowance has to be made for the width of the frame when placing dishes.

continued on next page

■ Solid wood vs. veneer: There is a lot of discussion as to whether solid wood or veneer-covered engineered wood is best. There is no "best." Which you choose is up to you.

The perception is that solid wood is superior. It has all of wood's beauties, strengths and weaknesses. Solid wood is solid. However, it moves with changes in temperature and humidity. It dries out and becomes smaller, loosening joints. It absorbs humidity and swells slightly. When loose, it can squeak. It becomes brittle and splinters or cracks when dry. Solid wood doors are usually made of several pieces of wood glued together. That means that there can be variations in the finish.

Wood veneer is peeled, not sawed. A veneer surface over engineered wood is therefore more uniform than solid wood. Engineered wood doesn't expand or

Cabinets today have a wide range of options to use space efficiently and make items easy to reach. A fold-out pantry, above, is one.

contract and is engineered for a specific purpose. If the correct engineered wood is used in cabinet construction, it cannot be beat.

Purists prefer real wood. Most practical people are very happy and get better results with veneer-covered engineered wood.

The frame is no place for engineered wood. Inner edges should be profiled or rounded on the inside to eliminate scrapes and splinters. Outside profiles should be sharp 90-degree angles for uniform cabinet-to-cabinet installation.

Look for wood gussets. While every manufacturer uses gussets at the top of their base cabinets, wood gussets dadoed into the sides are strongest. Looking for wood gussets is important because with the new solid, granite and even concrete counter tops, the base cabinets are supporting a tremendous amount of weight. The stronger the gusset, the greater the stability of the cabinet.

This otherwise dead space was turned into a pocket cabinet for spices.

The back of the cabinet should be composed of at least 1/8-inch to 1/4-inch plywood dadoed into the base and sides. Walls are not perfectly flat. A good back panel is necessary for the cabinets to hang properly and look uniform. Some cabinet makers save money by not putting backs in their cabinets. They figure that you don't see the back, so why bother? The back provides a great deal of the cabinets' structural integrity. It is a good idea to back away from backless cabinets.

Outer sides, which means any exposed side, should be solid wood, plywood, or as is often the case with quality cabinets, veneer-covered plywood. Scuff and wear resistance is very important here, especially for base cabinets.

The interior should be an easy care surface that matches the exterior of the cabinet.

The shelves

Shelving should be a minimum of 1/2-inch thick, 3/4-inch is better. Weak shelving often needs a support in the middle of the back. All your heavy pots and pans, plus heirloom dishes and glassware, will be on these shelves. You don't want them to let go.

Shelving should be adjustable with very sturdy die-cast shelf rests. It should also extend the full depth of the cabinet. Roll-out shelves are a blessing. However, some designers believe that every bottom base cabinet shelf should be a roll out. They cost more, but they turn dead space into easy-to-use space. If you're over 40, they really save the back.

KraftMaid

Customizing can extend to drawer dividers for utensils and a bread board.

The drawers

Drawers are a true expression of the cabinetmaker's art. If the drawers look like they are flimsy, cheaply made and thrown together, you can bet the rest of the cabinet is, too. If the drawer is strong, square and glides in and out of the cabinet effortlessly, you are dealing with a manufacturer who is proud of his product.

The drawer box should be double doweled or dovetailed, rather than stapled and glued. The stress on drawers is down, not side to side. Therefore, drawer side thickness is not as critical as shelving thickness. Nevertheless, drawer sides should be at least 1/2-inch to 3/4-inch thick. Drawer bottoms must be dadoed into all four of the drawer's sides. Drawer bottoms and the drawer glides should be rated to hold at least 75 pounds.

The drawer with the heaviest load in your kitchen is probably the silverware drawer. According to Wilson at Merillat, the typical contents of a silverware drawer weigh 30 or 40 pounds. Very rarely, a silverware drawer may hold 50 pounds of weight. A drawer that is rated at 75 pounds gives extra security.

continued on next page

417

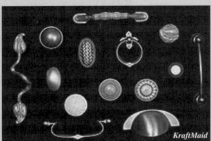

Many styles of drawer pulls and knobs can help "customize" your cabinets, adding style and complementing the rest of the kitchen's decor.

Drawer glides can be mounted on each side, or on the bottom. Some people find bottom-mounted drawer glides more attractive because they are invisible. A few manufacturers get by with a single glide mounted under the middle of the drawer. This is very antiquated technology and not acceptable.

From a practical point of view, side-mounted glides take a little bit of the useable width of the drawer. Bottom-mounted glides take a little bit of the useable height. No big deal either way. Whichever type of glide your drawers have, make certain that the glide system has a capture and hold mechanism, so you cannot accidentally pull the drawer off the glide. A loaded drawer dropping on your foot can cause serious injury. It will probably also break the drawer.

One often overlooked area is how far the drawer extends into the depth of the cabinet. You look at a drawer and automatically believe that it goes all the way to the back. That is not necessarily the case. Cheap cabinets may have vanity drawers that only extend half the depth of the cabinet. Even many good cabinets only extend 3/4 of the way.

Full-depth drawers, or at least the option of having full-depth drawers, are a sign of quality.

The doors

Doors are usually solid wood or wood veneer. They come in four basic styles: raised panel, recessed panel, frame and panes, and flat panel.

Raised panels can be square, arched, or cathedral arch. Raised panel or sunken panel doors are made from a door frame with center panels dadoed into the frame structure. Central panels are often very thin. The thicker the central panel, the firmer the door. Flat doors are solid pieces of wood or engineered wood with a vinyl or veneer outer skin. Glass mullion doors and leaded glass doors are also available.

Doors should have hidden, adjustable hinges that close automatically when the door is within 2 or 3 inches of the cabinet. This sounds like a little thing, but a slightly open door can be a safety hazard. You should also know that hinges can open 90 degrees or 180 degrees. Many just open 90 degrees, which could be a major drawback to you, or no inconvenience at all. Your best bet when cabinet shopping is to try to open the doors all the way.

Doors should also have bumpers at the bottom of the door frame so that constant closing of the door does not wear away the surface of the cabinet frame or shelving.

The finish

The color of a cabinet is a design choice, so I am not going to say much about color in this article. The number of colors available and the quality of the finish definitely impacts the overall quality of the cabinet.

When you are in a showroom or at a builders' show, every cabinet you see looks good. All the major companies invest large amounts of money into getting and applying a superior finish. KraftMaid, as an example, advertises a 14-step furniture finish that beautifies and protects their doors, drawers and cabinets.

You are probably not an expert, so how do you tell the difference between the once-over-lightly and the multi-stage finish that will keep your cabinetry looking good for a long, long, time?

According to Kim Craig, the public relations manager of KraftMaid Cabinetry, the fastest way to tell the quality of a finish is to rub your hand lightly up and down on the door panels. If you feel any roughness or differences in texture, it is a sign of a bad finish.

The finish should not only look good, it should be strong enough to protect your cabinetry from all the household chemicals they are likely to come in contact with. To mention only a few, this includes gasoline, water, alcohol, fingernail polish, acetone, household soaps, trisodium phosphate, olive oil, citric acid, wax, crayon, tea, beet juice and vinegar.

You have every right to ask the salesman if the cabinet finish is strong enough to protect against all these chemicals and still look good.

Many cabinets, doors and drawers have had a vinyl or laminate applied to their exterior surface. This is fine. However, not every company has invested the money necessary for proper vinyl and laminate application. Merillat, as an example, uses a pressure-forming process that makes the outer layer adhere so tightly that it almost becomes an integral part of the inner structure. No matter how hard you try, you should only be able to see and feel one continuous surface. That's good.

"If you are looking at cabinetry and can see or feel a seam, don't buy it," warns Wilson from Merillat. "Sooner or later that seam will begin to chip and come apart."

The interior finish of the cabinet should match the exterior. The cabinet, shelving, even inner side of the door should all be an easy-care surface. Very often, this is a vinyl finish. The surface should be impervious to moisture and staining. This type of surface eliminates the need for shelf liners forever.

Design features

Moldings are a "design choice" that says a great deal about cabinet quality. Crown and base moldings are the easiest way

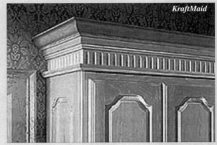

KraftMaid

Having a good selection of moldings, which gives the cabinet a "finished" look, is a sign of quality.

continued on next page

to give stock and semi-custom cabinets a "custom" look. If you don't have a broad selection of moldings available to you, the manufacturer, not you, has made the final decision. If you want the choice to be yours, shop elsewhere.

Decorative hardware is another design option that helps you customize your kitchen.

I could write an entire article on cabinet options (I probably will). There are some, like glass front drawer panels, spice boxes and stem glass holders, that are purely design choices. Others, such as roll-out trays, knife drawers with cutting boards, mixer shelves, multi-shelf pull-out pantries, and lazy susans, are such work-savers they should almost be classed as necessities.

Having a wide variety of options is one of the keys to a functional kitchen. If your manufacturer doesn't make them available, you have to do without. My advice: Look at all your options before you fall in love.

Company reputations

The most important test of cabinet quality is the reputation and dependability of the manufacturer, distributor and installer. Do they provide products in a timely manner? Do they provide replacements, if and when necessary? Can you get repairs in a timely manner? Do they stand behind their warranty?

If the cabinets you choose fill all these criteria, you can feel confident that you will have a kitchen that you will be pleased with for a long, long time.

Next week I'll discuss the pros and cons of installing kitchen cabinets yourself.

How much should a kitchen cost?

Over the past 10 years, kitchen-remodeling jobs have climbed about 20 percent, according to Kitchen & Bath Business (KBB), the industry bible. Most of the growth has been at the low end of the market, which KBB classifies as less than $7,000. High end kitchen remodeling – more than $20,000 – represents only about 2 percent of the business. So, if you don't plan to spend much money, don't be shy. You are in the majority.

The National Association of Home Builders (NAHB) defines a minor kitchen remodel as replacing cabinet doors, oven and cooktop, laminate countertops, sink, faucet, floor and repainting the walls. They classify a major kitchen remodel as redesigning the kitchen, replacing the cabinets, oven and cooktop, countertop, sink, faucet, floor, built-in microwave, custom lighting, installing a cabinet island and repainting.

According to NAHB figures, the national average cost for a minor kitchen remodel is $8,395. The national average for a major kitchen remodel averages $22,509. Installing new flooring would add to that cost.

Wayne Weintraub, vice-president of operations at Kurtis Kitchen and Bath Centers in Livonia, said that in the Metro Detroit market, an inexpensive kitchen remodel for an average size older home would range from $6,000 to $9,000 including new cabinets, cabinet tops and flooring. This figure includes installation costs.

A kitchen remodel using higher quality semi-custom cabinetry, solid countertops and better flooring would cost $15,000 to $20,000 or more, including installation, says Weintraub. Naturally, if you start putting in custom cabinetry, granite countertops, slate floors and high-end gourmet sinks and appliances, the cost could double or even triple that.

How much do people spend on remodeling?
In 1997, more than two-thirds of all kitchen remodeling projects in the United States cost $5,000 or less. Here is the breakdown.

How much do people spend on remodeling?

In 1997, more than two-thirds of all kitchen remodeling projects in the United States cost $5,000 or less. Here is the breakdown.

Price Range	Number of jobs	Percent
$5000 or less	3,053,537	69
$5,000-$6,999	608,875	14
$7,000-$9,999	346,128	8
$10,000-$14,999	247,276	6
$15,000-$19,999	95,510	2
$20,000-$49,999	80,030	2
$50,000 or more	22,183	< 1

Source: Kitchen & Bath Business

continued on next page

421

Stock, custom, or semi-custom? Here's the difference

By Glenn Haege
Special to The Detroit News

There are three types of cabinets available: stock, semi-custom, and custom. You can think of them as the Chevrolets, Buicks, and Cadillacs of the cabinet kingdom. Just like all three kinds of cars give transportation, all three classes of cabinets will do a dandy job of holding your dishes and utensils.

It's also important to remember that you can dude up a Chevy so much that it costs as much as a low-end Cadillac. You can do the same thing with cabinets. If you're on a budget, contain yourself.

■ Stock cabinets: They got their name because they were made to specific measurements and stocked by the local distributor. Because they are mass-produced to utilitarian specifications and you buy them out of the distributor's inventory, prices are at the low end of the spectrum.

■ Custom cabinets: They are made to order. Because the craftsman and his employers choose the exact species of wood, type of finish and hardware, and because the cabinets are designed and cut and made to order, pricing is two or three times as much as stock cabinets, depending on the options you choose.

■ Semi-custom cabinets: This intermediate class offers a great deal more sizes and styles than stock cabinets, but the units are not made to the specific order like their custom cousins. Because of the greater variety, pricing usually costs 10 percent to 30 percent more than stock cabinets yet is considerably lower than custom cabinetry.

Most stock and semi-custom cabinet companies also have "builder" lines. These are basic lines with limited variety and options. They also cost less. Kitchen & Bath Business, an industry magazine, estimates that 75 percent of cabinets manufactured this year will be used in remodeling projects.

Today, the distinctions between the three types of cabinets have blurred. For instance, Merillat, the nation's largest maker of "stock" cabinets, has an almost infinite variety of sizes, woods and finishes. They also will make some modifications, and they even have an extra quality Amera line that is really semi-custom cabinetry.

KraftMaid, the country's largest maker of semi-custom cabinetry, has such a large variety of woods, finishes, moldings, styles and will modify sizes to such an extent that the final product looks very much like custom cabinetry.

Custom means infinite variety. Exotic woods, copper, stainless steel, lacquer finishes and even rice-paper veneers are available. If you want it and are willing to pay for it, a manufacturer of custom cabinets will make it for you.

A decent stock cabinet should last 20 years. Custom and semi-custom cabinetry might last many times that.

Japanese cabinetmaker Sokee produces custom cabinets in striking contemporary styles and colors.

Merillat, left, is one of the largest stock cabinet makers. Kraftmaid. right, specializes in semi-custom cabinets.

In fact, most cabinets are torn out many years before the end of their service life. There are many 100-year-old houses with their original cabinets. Like an old Model T Ford, they are still hanging tough and could continue to perform their function for as long as the house is standing. Unfortunately, they do not have any of the pizzazz, or ease of use and ease of maintenance features of their newer counterparts.

Bottom line: You change cabinets because you want to, not because you have to. You buy the extra good stuff because you like style and quality, not because it will outlast stock cabinetry.

continued on next page

The panel of experts

Glenn Haege and his staff at Master Handyman Press asked the following manufacturers, installers and big and small kitchen and bath remodeling companies what to look for in a quality kitchen cabinet. Their answers formed the basis for this special report.

Chris Ehlin

Company: American Classic Kitchens & Baths, Troy, (248) 528-9190.

Profile: A small, "hands on" kitchen remodeler, Ehlin and an assistant design and build every kitchen his company does.

Sam Warwick

Company: Living Spaces, Inc., Sylvan Lake, (248) 682-3600.

Profile: Warwick owns a midsized kitchen & bath store with certified kitchen designers. He is very passionate about quality and the value of what he does. Living Spaces specializes in designing and building mid- to upper-priced kitchens and baths.

Larry Wilson

Company: Merillat Industries, a Masco Company, (800) 575-8759.

Profile: A consummate professional, Wilson is director of marketing and the person that people in the field call when they have a tough cabinet question. Merillat, America's Cabinetmaker, is the country's largest manufacturer of kitchen and bath cabinetry.

Kim Craig

Company: KraftMaid Cabinetry, Inc., a Masco Company, (800) 914-4484.

Profile: Craig, public relations manager for KraftMaid, is always well prepared when called upon for technical information. KraftMaid is the largest semi-custom cabinet maker in the U.S. and is known for its large selection of woods, finishes and options.

Howard Kuretzky, President; Wayne Weintraub, VP-Operations; Marla Burns, Store Manager.

Company: Kurtis Kitchen and Bath Centers, Livonia, (734) 522-7600.

Profile: Kurtis Kitchen believes in the team approach. When Glenn Haege asked for someone to answer tough cabinet questions, he got the entire team. They use the same philosophy in selling and installing kitchens. It has made them one of the largest sellers and installers of KraftMaid cabinetry in America.

Mark Renn

Company: H.J. Oldenkamp, distributor for Merillat and Corian, (800) 444-7280.

Profile: A retail specialist, Penn is his company's "man with the answers" to consumer questions.

Tom Grady

Company: Sierra Design & Building Co., Royal Oak, (248) 399-7062.

Profile: Grady is a modular home builder who makes room in his schedule to build three or four major kitchen remodels every year because he loves to do kitchens.

Check out cabinet manufacturers at home shows, or give them a call

You'll see many of these companies' cabinets at the upcoming building shows in Metro Detroit, including this weekend's Home Improvement Show at Macomb Expo Center in Warren; the Home & Garden Show, March 4-7, at the Pontiac Silverdome; the Builders Home & Detroit Flower Show, March 18-21 at Cobo Center in Detroit; and the Home Improvement Show, April 8-11 at Novi Expo Center, Novi.

Most manufacturers' cabinets are found in their distributors' exhibits. For instance, Merillat will be at the H.J. Oldenkamp and KSI exhibits, KraftMaid will be at the Kurtis Kitchen and Bath Exhibits.

If you want to learn more about these major cabinet companies, give them a call and ask for their local dealers, or visit them on their web sites. The companies are listed in descending order according to the amount of their yearly sales.

■ Merillat Industries, div. of Masco, (800) 575-8759, www.merillat.com, the leader in stock cabinets.
■ KraftMaid Cabinetry Inc., div. of Masco, (800) 914-4484, www.kraftmaid.com, the country's largest maker of semi-custom cabinetry.
■ Aristokraft, Inc., div. of Masterbrands, (812) 482-2527, www.aristokraft.com, a large producer of stock cabinets.
■ American Woodmark Corp., (800) 388-2483, www.irinfo.com/amwd/, deals entirely in stock cabinets.
■ Mill's Pride, (800) 441-0337, offers both stock and ready-to-assemble cabinets.
■ Triangle Pacific Corp., (214) 887-2000, www.brucecabinets.com, offers only stock cabinets.
■ Schrock Cabinet Co., (217) 543-3311, www.schrock.com, offers both stock and semi-custom cabinets.
■ RSI Home Products, Inc., (714) 449-2200, all stock cabinets.
■ Texwood Industries, div. of Masco, (800) 284-3888, all stock cabinets.
■ Cardell Kitchen and Bath Cabinets, (210) 225-0290, www.cardellcabinets.com, all stock cabinets.
■ Wood-Mode, Inc., (570) 374-2711, www.wood-mode.com, offers only custom cabinets.
■ Sokee-USA, (888) 765-3387, www.Sokee.com, small importer of Japanese custom cabinetry.

Helpful websites

Two very useful sites on the Internet for general consumer information on cabinetry:
■ KBB Kitchen and Bath Business: www.kitchen-bath.com
■ National Kitchen and Bath Association: www.nkba.org

– Glenn Haege

If you've decided to remodel the kitchen, can you do it yourself?

by Glenn Haege,
America's Master Handyman

Last week, we talked about what you should look for in quality kitchen cabinets. Now, should you remodel the kitchen yourself, or have it done?

If you are thinking about doing it yourself, you are not alone. According to Kitchen and Bath Business, the industry bible, 50 percent of all kitchen remodels are sold through home centers. Home Depot, accounts for 20 percent of the total. A large number of those jobs are being done by Do-It-Yourselfers.

To help them, many Home Depot stores schedule free classes on cabinet, plumbing, tile, and flooring installation. Many other retailers and distributors do the same thing.

There is also a lot of support from books, videos, and websites. You can call my show on the weekends and I'll walk you through the hard parts. If you don't have the tools you can rent them from places like Buttons, (248) 542-5835, or Chets Rent-All, (248) 543-0118. By doing a major kitchen remodel yourself, you can not only cut the remodeling bill in half; you earn bragging rights big time.

All that being said, Howard Kuretzky of Kurtis Kitchen and Bath says, "Sure you can do it yourself, but why?"

He says that because the kitchen is the most important room in the house. Screw that up and you have done major damage to the resale value of your biggest single investment.

Doing a major kitchen remodel is undertaking weeks of work. Translate that into evenings and weekends and you are signing up for a minimum two- or three-month commitment.

If you are the kind of person who likes to work with their hands, this can be very gratifying. However, unless you live alone, it is a shared experience.

All family members will be sentenced to two or three months with the kitchen torn apart and all the dishes, pots, pans, groceries, and appliances, stored in other parts of the house. Microwave cooking, no entertaining, the making of morning coffee becoming a major event – all these fun-filled experiences are included at no extra cost. The garage becomes your parts staging area, so plan on parking in the driveway for the next few months.

If you and your significant other love this sort of thing, you will have many a rib tickling war story with which to regale guests for years to come. If one of you had to be arm-twisted into this, you could be talking major battles, maybe even a broken marriage, before the water goes back on and the dishes are put into their beautiful new cabinets.

On the other hand, a company like Kuretzky's can stage everything at their warehouse and finish an entire kitchen in four or five days.

If you don't want the major hassle, there are still many things that you can do, and money you can save. I've included a checklist with this article.

Dreaming

This is the fun part. Read magazines, go to home shows, and look at model homes in fancy subdivisions. Think of everything you want to have in your kitchen. The sky's the limit when you concentrate on wants, not needs. The next step will bring you back to reality.

Information gathering

Now's the time to get real. What do you really need? Find out how much things cost, then make a budget and stick to it. The rule of thumb is that you can spend 10 to 15 percent of the resale value of your house. This includes all kitchen cabinets, fixtures, appliances, flooring, electrical upgrades and installation. Spend too much, and you'll never get a proper return on your investment; spend too little, and you can decrease the value of your house.

The National Kitchen and Bath Association web site, www.nkba.org is filled with useful information. Learn all you can before you do the project.

Planning the design

If you want a simple plan, there are helpful books and CD's at your computer or bookstore. You probably are not going to do as good a job as a design professional. No computer program can duplicate their years of experience. Designers are on the cutting edge. They know exciting things you can put into your kitchen that you may not even realize exist. They can also tell you if your plans and budget are realistic.

Measuring

Books and manufacturers' brochures and websites really help. KraftMaid, (800) 914-4484, has a free brochure, "Your New Kitchen," that gives a lot of information. You can do this. A professional can do it a lot better.

Purchasing

You can buy the cabinets from Home Depot, Builders Square, Kurtis Kitchen, KSI, or any of the distributors listed in the Yellow Pages without giving them the installation job. Marla Burns, Kurtis Kitchen's Livonia store manager, (734) 522-7600, says they often sell cabinets without installation and include a computer design work up and measurement as part of the package.

Tear out

This is the muscle part of the job. Many installers are so busy that they would be delighted to let you do the heavy work while they do the installation. Make the installer give you the exact day and time he will begin installation in writing. Reconfirm before you begin swinging a sledgehammer. A wife, who sees her totally gutted kitchen sitting there with nothing happening for weeks, is not a happy camper. Make certain that you tie off the water, electrical, and gas, and have made a provision for debris removal. He who tears out is responsible for hauling away.

Installation

You can do it, but do you really want to? If you are doing anything more than replacing a few cabinets, I recommend a professional. If a solid countertop is in your plan, do not even think of working that expensive Corian or Korstone by yourself unless it is prefabricated at the factory.

Finishing

The cabinets are finished, but the walls aren't. This is a great place to save.

The Bottom Line

The more you do, the more you save. But only do it if it will be enjoyable. Remember that the most important tool in your toolbox is your checkbook. The most precious commodity you have is your time. Use both wisely, then brag about it.

It's almost spring – time to tackle annual home cleaning projects

by Glenn Haege,
America's Master Handyman

Spring is just 15 days away. That means that Spring Cleaning Time is definitely here.

You can't do everything yourself. If it's time to clean carpets or air ducts, the good carpet cleaners, like Modernistic, (800) 609-1000, or Duraclean by Maryanne, (800) 372-5427, and duct cleaners, like Dalton, (800) 675-2298, Sterling Environmental, (888) 992-1200, Safety King, (800) 972-6343, and Sanit-Air, (888) 778-7324, are already very busy. Call now and hope they can work you in before the holidays.

Now, let's tackle the in depth, do-it-yourself cleaning.

Walls: The walls are covered with a winter's worth of grease, dirt, and all-around yuck. You can make painted walls a couple of shades lighter with a good cleaning. Use 2 ounces dry measure of Trisodium Phosphate (TSP) per gallon of water. If the kitchen walls are greasy, add 1/2 cup of household ammonia per gallon of the TSP solution. You can also use Dirtex instead of TSP.

Wall washing is an excellent two-person job. Each person should be equipped with a 2-1/2-gallon bucket, a long handled sponge mop, rubber gloves and goggles. One person's bucket is filled with the cleaning solution. The other person's bucket is filled with rinse water. The long handled sponge mops keep you from having to bend, stretch, or climb a ladder. Start from the bottom and work up. The first person applies a liberal amount of cleaning solution. After letting the solution work for a couple of minutes, the second person finishes the job with the rinse water. Change the rinse water at least every wall.

Cabinets & counter tops: Use a 2-ounce-per-gallon solution of Simple Green or Clear Magic to get rid of the stickies. Follow up with a thin coat of Doozy Furniture Polish by Mr. Furniture Finish Products, (888) 851-8500. It's a secret weapon used by the Pros. Hope's Counter Top Cleaner, (800) 325-4026, will bring back the luster to counter tops.

Wallpaper: Mix up a 40- or 50-to-1 solution of a general purpose cleaner like Simple Green or Clear Magic (that's about 2 ounces of cleaning solution to a bucket of water) and put it in a spray bottle. Spritz on and wipe off.

Clean delicate wallpaper and lampshades with the brush attachment to the vacuum cleaner. If very dirty, wipe them down with the Soot & Dirt Remover sponge by Bloch/New England, (800) 344-2171 or The Wonder Sponge by Gonzo Corp. (800) 221-0061. This sponge can also be used for cleaning acoustical tiles or any surface you want to clean without water.

Vinyl flooring: Use a 50-to-1 solution of Simple Green. If you have to strip wax or acrylic build-up I suggest New Beginnings Floor Cleaner and Stripper by Armstrong. To put the shine back on, apply Armstrong's Shine Keeper.

Hardwood floors: For light cleaning just spritz on liquid glass cleaner WITHOUT AMMONIA and damp mop. Do not use any product with ammonia, it can damage your expensive hardwood. For tougher work use a specialized cleaning product like Clean 'n Strip Wood Cleaner by Bruce or Enforcer Products' Hardwood Floor.

Tile & grout: Clean the tile with a general cleaner or a specialized tile cleaner like Armstrong Floor Cleaner for No Wax & Ceramic Tile Floors.

Clean grout with a specialized grout cleaner from Tile Helper, Tile Pro, Aqua Mix, or SCI (Stone Care International). Then seal the grout with a liquid penetrating grout sealer by the same company.

Grout is best cleaned on hands and knees with a cuticle brush. This is strong stuff so wear rubber gloves and goggles. Dip the brush into the cleaner and scrub the grout, then rinse with water. When clean and dry, seal with a liquid penetrating grout sealer. The sealer closes the profile of the grout and keeps it looking good longer.

Windows: To clean inside windows use a solution of 4 ounces of household ammonia and 1 teaspoon of liquid hand dishwashing detergent to a gallon of water. Apply with a sponge, then remove the solution with a squeegee. Wipe up drips from sills with an old bath towel.

If the temperature is over fifty and you have really dirty windows outside, use 2 ounces of TSP, 4 ounces of white vinegar and a gallon of water.

Where to find products: I only listed phone numbers for hard-to-find products. Most of these cleaners at Meijer, Dammans or other good hardware store or home center. You'll also find strippers and specialized cleaning products at cleaning supply stores like Scrubs, (248) 569-5995, Bed Bath & Beyond, and Home Place.

Appearances

My favorite Detroit News Homestyle garden writers will be joining me at the Pontiac Silverdome this weekend. Janet Macunovich and Nancy Szerlag will give talks and answer questions from the Garden Stage, Saturday. I'll be giving talks on the Builder's Stage and answering questions at the Master Handyman Press Booth, Saturday and Sunday. My old friends Joe Gagnon and Murray Gula will also be giving talks and answering questions both days. Come on out and say "Hello."

MARCH 13, 1999

Do your homework before you jump into buying a home spa

by Glenn Haege,
America's Master Handyman

If you judged the importance of a business by the amount of floor space they take up at spring home and garden shows, you would have to believe that hot tubs and spas are some of the most important companies in America. Unfortunately, more people walk by them than buy them.

If you're one of those folks who just sigh and walk by, this article is for you.

I bought my first spa six years ago at Tony V's Sunrooms & Spas, (810) 412-6050, and have been very happy with my investment ever since. But spas are not for everyone; my wife is completely oblivious to ours. Whenever I go away I worry that I may return to find that my bride has turned our spa into a planter.

Some people have good medical reasons for not getting into a spa. People with high blood pressure or who have a heart condition should consult their doctor. For most people, a good spa is one of the best antidotes for road rage, hectic work schedules, sore legs or backs, arthritis pain, you name it.

Many people also have practical objections to getting a spa. For one thing, they believe that although a spa looks attractive, the novelty will soon wear off and it will just sit there. Most unused spas I see were cheap to begin with or are so old they just don't work. Years ago people had to turn on a heater three or four hours before they planned on using the spa. The modern spa is on and ready to soothe you, 24 hours a day, 12 months a year.

Another common objection is that a spa can be used only a few months out of the year. I use my spa ten months a year. Many people I know use their spa every week of the year.

There is a concern that spas are expensive to operate. Everyone has a different idea about what expensive is. Kathleen, my editor at Master Handyman Press, bought a relatively large, 8-by-8-foot Cal Spa from Fireplace and Spa, (734) 425-5340, last year. She says that the unit increased her electric bill this winter by about $36 a month. Summer bills were half that. Her spa is used primarily by Kathy and her husband. If they had four youngsters getting in and out of the spa constantly, and leaving the spa cover off, the electrical cost would be considerably more. If they kept their spa at a lower temperature, or had purchased a better spa cover, the operating cost of the spa would also be lower.

There is also the fear factor. Most of us have never purchased a spa before.

So how do you know what to look for? Like windows, furnaces, or any big-ticket item, the spa is only as good as the people from whom you are getting it. Good retailer's only stock quality tubs because they make a long-term commitment to their customers, and can't afford callbacks.

Most quality spas have these features.

Construction: What you don't see is more important than what you do. The spa should be constructed from multiple layers, reinforced by wood and steel. Heavy foam insulation should cover the entire underside of the spa. Any spot the manufacturer doesn't insulate costs you money.

Motors: Powerful electric motors are needed for the pumps. The key here is not horsepower; it is gallons per minute (GPM). A good pump system will be rated at 150 to 180 GPM.

Setting options: A spa should have a wide assortment of jets and therapy configurations. This also ties in with the size of the spa. Even though only one or two people may use the spa, you need a number of different seating options.

For instance, Fireplace and Spa's Cal Spas, (734) 425-5340, have Comfort Shoulderssage, Lumbar Therapy, Longevity Neck & Body Restoration, Quadrassage, and Max Rejuvenator seats. Each seat provides a different hydromassage therapy. Anyone sitting in a spa for fifteen or twenty minutes will find himself or herself using three or four of the different seats.

Life Styles' Hot Spring Spas, (800) 591-7727, have an exclusive Moto-Massage jet that sends a warm stream of water sweeping up and down your back. Portable Spas Plus Sundance Spas, (800) 323-6776, have an Accu-Pressure Jet seat with 10 jets designed to target specific pressure points and deliver a deep tissue massage.

Filters: Filter size and method of water purification are also important. Sundance uses Ozone, most others rely primarily on chemicals but may have an ozone option. Which you choose is up to you.

Warranty: This is also important. Jim McDonald of Portable Spas Plus says that the limitations are more important than the warranty. "The first page of a warranty gives you the moon, the second page limits coverage, and the third page takes it away," he says.

Service policy: Finally, the most important person at any spa retailer is the service person. The salesman may give you an unbeatable price, but the service guy or gal is going to be most responsible for keeping you happy with your investment. The only way that happens is if senior company management has made a commitment to service and every customer should expect to receive good service.

"The amount you pay for your spa should not determine the level of service you receive," says Blaine Richel, the service manager at Fireplace and Spa. "The companies set the price, so they have to give the service."

Now that this article is over, I think I'll get into my spa. … Aha.

If you can't afford a brand new kitchen, spiff up the one you have

by Glenn Haege,
America's Master Handyman

You want a new kitchen. You need a new kitchen. In your heart, you lust after a new kitchen. The only problem is that there is a vast, impenetrable chasm between your wants and needs and your bank account.

But there's hope. Uncle Glenn is here to save the day. I can't make you rich, but I can tell you how to have a kitchen that looks so good, in just three days.

Getting ready: Like any major undertaking this job takes prior planning. I'm including two secret weapons from the Handyman's Private Tool Box. It's up to you to track them down.

Product #1: Graham Aqua Borne Ceramic Paint, (800) 255-2628. It is a totally flat paint that combines ceramic microspheres with high quality 100 percent acrylic resins. The ceramic additives make the surface so tough that dirt and stains just roll off. The paint applies easily, is ready for a second coat in just two hours, and provides a tough, washable, mar-resistant surface. This paint can't be found everywhere. Try Arno Paint in Royal Oak, Decorating Depot in Allen Park, Paint Plus in Monroe, or The Paint Can in Sylvan Lake.

Product #2: Chartpak Secret Solutions. A new dry transfer decorating system that enables you to transform old, outmoded kitchen tiles into full color, designer tile squares, and even murals.

Glenn Haege's 3-day kitchen make-over

Day One
■ Clear all dishes, pots, pans, cleaners, and furniture, out of the kitchen.
■ Remove drawers and cabinet doors, and put them in a another area.
■ Wash down walls, cabinets, drawers, and cabinet doors.
■ Remove all hardware from drawers and cabinet doors.

Day Two
■ Paint walls, cabinets, drawers and doors.

Day Three
■ Paint trim, install new hardware, and add designer touches.
■ Put back drawers and cabinet doors.

They also have matching wall and fabric borders. Call Chartpak, (800) 628-1910, and ask for Dee.

I also suggest getting new hardware. If you are in love with your present hardware, great, clean and polish it. If you want flat out beautiful (read expensive) stop by Russell Hardware, (888) 991-4991, in Birmingham, or Classic Hardware, (734) 542-9940, in Livonia.

OK, let's get to work.

Day One: Clear the kitchen. That means everything out of all the cabinets, counters, and closets, plus all the furniture. Set up a secondary workroom. Clean and vacuum the floor of this room then lay down a large paper or canvas tarp. Put kitchen drawers and cabinet doors on the tarp.

Wash down kitchen ceiling, walls, cabinets, drawers, and cabinet doors. Use Dirtex or 2 ounces dry measure of Trisodium Phosphate (TSP) and 1/2 cup of household ammonia per gallon of water.

Use long handled sponge mops and the buddy system. One person applies the cleaning solution. The second person rinses. Change the water every wall.

If you are not going to paint the cabinets, you can just wash them down with a solution of 2 ounces of Simple Green or Clear Magic per gallon of water. Remove all hardware from the cabinet doors and drawers and clean thoroughly.

If you are going to paint over varnished cabinets, lightly sand with 100-grit garnet sandpaper. You're not trying to take off the varnish, just cutting the shiny surface. Vacuum, then wash down the entire surface with Liquid Deglosser and wipe with a tack rag. Cover with an oil-base stain kill like Wm. Zinsser Cover Stain or Master Chem Kilz. Patch all dents and nail holes with Dap's Wood Fix.

Day Two: This is the day we paint walls, cabinets, drawers and cabinet doors. My book *Take the Pain Out of Painting – Interiors* is filled with many time saving tips on how to get a professional-looking, long-lasting job.

My recommended paint for this job is Graham Aqua Borne Ceramic. If you can't get that, use Kurfee's Supreme Water Borne Acrylic, (800) 626-6147, from Damman's or Harrison Paint, (810) 268-0808.

Paint surfaces in the following order: Go to the secondary work room and paint one side of the drawers and cabinet doors. Next, do the kitchen ceiling and walls. Paint the inside of the cabinets. Go back to the secondary workroom and paint the other side of the drawers and cabinet doors.

Break for lunch, you've earned it.

After lunch, finish with a second coat in the same order.

Day Three: Paint trim and install new hardware on drawers and cabinet doors.

Be creative. Use the Chartpak Secret Solutions. If you have a back splash, consider one of their kitchen murals. Apply borders. If you don't want to use store-bought, use a stencil around the entire circumference of the room.

Put back the drawers and reattach the cabinet doors. It will be a week before the paint on the shelving has cured sufficiently to return dishes, pots, pans, etc. so take the rest of the day off. Now brag about it!

MARCH 27, 1999

Support brackets may rid home's foundation of sinking feeling

by Glenn Haege,
America's Master Handyman

Could the value of your home be falling out from under you? At a time when the stock market is at an all time high, the bottom is falling out of some Michigan residents' largest investments.

According to Todd Jackson of Jackson Waterproofing, (800) 404-8342, some of the tell-tale signs that your home's foundation may be sinking are:
■ Stair-step cracks in the wall brickwork.
■ Doors and windows not opening.
■ Cracks in garage and room addition slabs.

Sinking foundations have become such a wide-spread problem that as soon as the Spring Thaw sets in, many Michigan firms will begin lifting or stabilizing residential foundations throughout southeast Michigan.

Usually, companies such as Calculus Construction, (888) 746-5464; Anchor Tech, (800) 875-2379; and Wall Anchor of Michigan, (800) 638-1983, concentrate on big commercial jobs. According to Dave Kaatz, vice-president of the Foundation Division of Calculus Construction, there has been a major increase in calls about residential foundations sinking. This phenomenon is most often associated with newer homes erected on bad soil. But last fall, he said, footings and slabs were sinking on well-established, 20-year, or even older, houses.

Most of the homes with sinking slabs and footers were built on expansive clay soil. When the moisture in the soil evaporated during last year's long, dry spell, the clay shrunk like a dry sponge and in some areas could no longer support the weight of the structure.

Todd Jackson, of Jackson Waterproofing, said that on the homes his company tested, the draught problem was solely with slabs and footers 42 inches below grade. Kaatz, said Calculus Construction inspected several homes where the problem went down to the 8-foot basement level.

Most basement problems were associated with trees. Trees give us shade and protect our homes from the elements. All they require in return is a little water and fertilizer. Unfortunately, a mature tree can remove as much as 20 to 30 percent of the moisture in the surrounding soil. This is not usually a problem, but during a draught, trees can cause increased soil dehydration.

Whatever the cause, when the slab or footer drops, the recognized way to

This illustration shows Chance Helical-Piers with Foundation Support Brackets supporting a basement.

solve the problem is to sink helical steel piers down through the clay layers to solid soil, and then stabilize or lift the slab or footer. The decision as to whether the home is stabilized or lifted is up to the homeowner. The process of lifting exerts additional strain to the foundation and can cause more cracks to walls, windows and brickwork.

This is not a cheap fix and it is not usually covered by insurance. In some instances core soil samples have to be dug and analyzed by civil engineers. Then, heavy equipment is brought in, and the ground is excavated down to below the footer or slab and helical-piers are sunk 12 to 15 feet down to load-bearing soil.

A helical-pier is a round or square steel shaft to which a heavy steel helix (spiral-shaped steel plate) has been attached. Every pier is connected to an L-shaped boot, called a foundation repair bracket, with the outer edge placed beneath the footer or slab.

Unfortunately, you don't usually get by with one or two piers. Helical-piers have to be put in place along the entire affected area. The slab or footer is then lifted to its former position, or leveled and stabilized.

Jackson said that in some instances, such as a sinking porch or very inexpensive Florida room, a chemical soil stabilization technique could be used. In this procedure chemicals are injected into the soil, changing the chemical composition of the clay so that it neither expands nor contracts.

This technique is not universally accepted. Its major benefit is that it costs only 25 to 45 percent as much as helical-pier stabilization. The major drawbacks are that the chemical procedure can only be injected into a limited area and can only be used to stabilize, not lift, the structure.

This problem is so prevalent in Texas that special sprinkling systems are sometimes installed to keep moisture in supporting soil. I don't think we have to do this in Michigan. However, during a draught, be sure to water around your house and deep-water mature tree roots. They will love it and it will give your house a lift.

Out and about

This is a great weekend to be on the move. Start off by attending my WXYT Home Show, at the Macomb Community College Central Campus, Garfield and Hall Roads, today from 8 a.m. to 6 p.m., and Sunday from 8 a.m. to 4 p.m.

Then get inspired by going to all the free showings at the art galleries on South Huron in Pontiac. Be sure to see Southfield's own Franklin Jonas, a one-man show at Galerie Blu.

The use of color in this young man's acrylic on linen Geostructures is truly amazing. Call (248) 454-7797 for directions.

APRIL 3, 1999

Patio, lawn furniture goes hi-tech by combining metals and fabrics

by Glenn Haege,
America's Master Handyman

If you haven't been shopping for lawn and patio furniture for the past few years, you'll have a few surprises. A wide variety of styles and at least a little sticker shock await you.

In the style department, lightweight woods and cheap aluminums and stackable resins await the next garage sale. In their place is a tantalizing collection of furniture that looks so good it belongs indoors.

Many high-end exterior styles are very substantial. In addition to the traditional sling backs, look for patterned cast aluminum, wrought irons and steel. Metal and teak combinations are also popular.

Fluffy seats and cushions in solid, striped, and floral designs are in. Popular new colors include cognac, anthracite, champagne, hammered pewter, sage, and holly green.

Fabrics are high tech. As an example, Homecrest Industries' Comfortext fabrics are constructed of thermal bonded, vinyl-coated polyester threads. The company also uses acrylics, acrylic blends, and olefins. All have mildew inhibitors and UV stabilizers to resist sun damage.

Big is in. Bigger chairs, bigger tables, bigger umbrellas. Bar height tables and chairs that enable you to look over deck railings and hedges are popular.

The imaginative combinations of metals and high tech-fibers can lead to amazing results. Imagine a wide wicker armchair with a big, fluffy, cushion seat. The inspiration was probably Colonial India, but the color of this particular chair is either a very intense, dark, blue or pristine white. The wicker is an all-weather weave of coated aluminum and a twisted paper fiber that has been bathed in latex to make it impervious to the elements.

The chair isn't imported from some Italian design house, and it doesn't come from California. The All-Weather Wicker chair and its companion table are made by Lloyd Flanders, of Menominee, Michigan, (800) 526-9894.

They aren't cheap, a five piece grouping of four armchairs and a 54-inch table costs $2,622 at Jimmies Rustics, (888) 560-JIMS, in Livonia , Novi , and Birmingham, .

Not everything has to be that pricey. Homecrest Industries of Wadena, MN, (800) 346-4852, makes one of the best outdoor swivel chairs in the world. Bob Wilkes, the manager of Evergreen Home and Garden Centers in Clinton (810) 791-2277; and Eastpointe, (810) 778-7400, says that you can get a top-of-the-line Homecrest – a five-piece grouping with two cushioned arm chairs, two cushioned swivel chairs, and a 60-inch round table – for slightly over $1,000. Other quality five-piece groupings start about $700.

Follow these simple cleanup steps

Once you get your new furniture, you want to keep it looking good for as long as possible. With proper care, lawn and patio furniture should be a 10-year investment. That means washing the furniture frames and cushions two or three times a year.

Harsh cleaners are not necessary. Metal finishes are now so sophisticated that a mild hand dishwashing solution is all that is necessary for cleaning, says Jim Sica of Jimmies Rustics. "After washing, rinse thoroughly, let dry and finish with a good automotive wax." Textured frames should have a clear liquid wax.

Automotive vinyl cleaner is recommended for the vinyl straps.

Bob Wilkes, manager of Evergreen Home and Garden Centers, recommends cleaning cushions by soaking them for a couple of hours in a bathtub full of water, with 1/2 cup of Dawn detergent and a cap full of household bleach. "The Dawn detergent seems to put back the oils in the fabric fibers at the same time it cleans them. The bleach kills mold and mildew spores, but can bleach out dark colors," he says.

The variety of choices is staggering. Homecrest, for example, has 125 different fabrics and 13 different frame finishes, in the full spectrum of chair and rocker styles.

Jimmies Rustics maintains such a large inventory, it has three warehouses at its main Livonia Store. One 10,000-square-foot warehouse is devoted exclusively to Brown Jordan, one of the most exclusive manufacturers of outdoor furniture.

Jim Sica of Jimmies Rustics says the big story in outdoor furniture is not its expense, but its relative affordability. "It used to be that high quality cast aluminum and teak were something that the average person could not afford. We now have very good cast aluminum being brought in from Mexico at very affordable prices and bring in genuine Indonesian teak furniture by the container load."

Whether you consider the new patio furniture styles affordable, or expensive, if you want the good stuff, you better order early. Sica expects that almost all of their cast aluminum, teak, and synthetic wicker will be sold out by June 15. "After that, the manufacturers are working on next year's inventory, so there is very little hope of re-ordering," he says.

APRIL 10, 1999

Cleaning your home's air ducts keeps internal environment healthy

by Glenn Haege,
America's Master Handyman

When I read a home maintenance article in the April issue of Better Homes and Gardens, it was enough to make me start chewing nails. The article seemed to pan the idea of cleaning ductwork siting "a recent study by the Environmental Protection Agency (EPA) (that) found little reason to recommend duct cleaning."

It sounded like a government study performed by either a Ph.D-NX (no experience), or a Ph.D NWS (no walking around sense). Although there are many fine people in the government, I have found a number of these kinds of Ph.Ds in the bureaucracy.

I'm taking the time to analyze the story because it shows how important it is to read an entire article (even this one) before jumping to conclusions.

Further reading showed the following. The EPA recommended duct cleaning on only three occasions: Where "there is substantial visible mold growth inside the ducts, when ducts are infested with vermin, or when ducts are clogged with so much dust and debris that particles large enough to see are blowing into the home from supply registers."

I have four problems with this:

1. Unless you are no bigger than a squirrel you can't get into your air ducts to inspect them.

2. If there is substantial visible mold growth inside the ducts, it is probably a job for a remediator, not a duct cleaner. Get the air tested. If dangerous mold spores are found, call a remediation specialist. There is a good chance that you and your family should get out of the house until the remediation is complete.

3. If your home is infested with vermin call in pest control experts and get out of there. After the vermin have been cleared, have the air tested and call in remediators or very experienced duct cleaners.

4. What exactly are "particles large enough to see?" In the real world, Mike Palazzolo, of Safety King, (888) 382-8776, said that he doesn't know of anyone who would call a duct cleaner unless they saw dirt. And there is always dirt.

"According to national averages, cleaning the ducts of a brand new 1,500 square foot house, yields 17 pounds of debris. That includes saw dust, chunks of drywall, pieces of workman's sandwiches, as well as the regular dirt and debris," he says.

"Older homes have much more. The accumulated dirt, dog and cat hair, etc., is often 1-inch to 1-1/2-inches thick in the cold air returns. Sometimes we see it up to 3-inches thick," he says.

By the way, Palazzolo is talking about return air ducts, something not even mentioned in the article.

There were other points of contention, but this is enough to show why I was an unhappy camper. On the plus side, magazine article listed the EPA web site for the brochure (www.epa.gov/iaq/pubs/). My staff and I spent the majority of Good Friday morning downloading EPA brochures.

The name of the EPA web site is *Sources of Information on Indoor Air Quality*. I don't agree with everything listed there, but the site is a treasure trove of useful information on Air Quality. I recommend it highly.

Should You Have the Air Ducts in Your Home Cleaned?, the brochure I have been maligning, turned out to be excellent. It is filled with 22 pages of advice on how to select a good duct cleaner, what to ask for when you get the air ducts cleaned, and includes a check list to rate the job after the work has been done. All at my favorite price, free.

If you are not on the web, you can call the Indoor Air Quality Clearinghouse and ask for a free copy of document EPA-402-K-97-002.

I strongly recommend two other brochures on the site. *The Inside Story* is a 44-page summary of home and office air pollution at home and what you can do about it. For still more information, get *Indoor Air Pollution, An Introduction for Health Professionals*. This brochure is more technical, but actually names the names of the people who did the studies. Both publications list excellent resource material.

Also available on the site were brochures on *Ventilation and Air Quality in Offices, Sick Building Syndrome, Residential Air Cleaners, Home Humidifiers, Carbon Monoxide Poisoning, Combustion Appliances, Asbestos, Biological Pollutants, Formaldehyde, and Cleaning Up After A Flood.*

If you're traveling the road to high technology, you'd better take a map

by Glenn Haege,
America's Master Handyman

I am a high tech junky. I love state of the art toys, tools, appliances and audio and video systems. As America's Master Handyman, I get to taste test many of the newest technologies.

One of the universal laws of new technology is: "Nothing is exactly like the advertising says it is, or may some day be." On Star, the General Motors' satellite locating system, is a good example.

"Clear, concise, how to get there advice" at the touch of a button. Even before seeing the commercials about the guy and gal who went to pick up their boss and got broadsided by an invisible deer, or the couple that wound up in a ditch full of rattle snakes, the system seemed like it belonged on every vehicle.

Everyone in our organization agreed that Captain Klutz, the publisher of Master Handyman Press, should be the first to benefit from the new technology. The Captain is a dear friend. If I have a question on religion, philosophy or history, he is the guy I ask. On the minus side, he can get lost on his way to the bathroom.

The Captain Klutz and On Star seemed made for each other. On the day he picked up his mini van from Hamilton Chevrolet, the system was tested while still in the parking lot.

"On Star, how do I get to Van Dyke?" (Smart but devious, the Captain actually knew where Van Dyke was.) Silken Voiced Lady Operator: "You are presently immobile at the corner of 14 Mile and Mound. Drive out of the parking lot onto 14 Mile Road. Turn right and proceed East."

Kowabunga!

The test continued while driving.

"On Star, how do I get to Royal Oak?" (The Captain lives in Royal Oak and was pretty sure how to get there.)

Very Alert Young Male Operator: "You are proceeding East on 14 Mile Road. At the next intersection, turn right and drive South approximately 3.2 miles, then turn right and enter the West bound 696 Expressway. Proceed on 696 until you see the Royal Oak turn-off."

"How do I get to The Green Lantern?"

"Get off at the Dequindre Exit and drive North for 2 miles."

Yes! Yes! Yes! The Captain had seen the future and it was his. We toasted the new minivan and On Star with a little bit of bubbly that night.

Months passed.

My version of the Three Musketeers – the Captain; Rob, my Marketing Director; and I – were on our way to Chicago for the Hardware Show. As always, the show was at McCormick Place. We've been going for years. The only problem is Mal Function Junction, a confusing merging of expressways that make it very easy to take a wrong turn. No problem, this time we were empowered with the latest technology.

"On Star, how do we get to McCormick Place?"

Very helpful, Sprightly Voiced, Male Operator: "McCormick Place. One minute please." Many minutes passed. "Sir, we don't show any McCormick Place."

If memory serves, the McCormick was built before World War II. It has grown over the years and is presently about five times the size of Cobo Hall.

"OK, how about McCormick Exhibition Center?" That's what the multi-building hotel, exhibit complex is now called.

Baffled Young Operator several minutes later: "We don't show any McCormick Exhibition Center, either."

By then we had guessed our way through the merges and turn offs and were heading for the complex via a side road. We had the address, but always had trouble finding one little street that was the best turn off.

"Don't worry kid, we're looking for such and such a street and can never find it."

Several minutes passed (we were already in the parking lot). Baffled but Helpful Young Operator: "Sorry about that sir, we always get lost in Chicago, too."

Months passed.

I was on a remote broadcast at Damman Hardware's Telegraph and Maple Road store. The Captain was supposed to meet me at the Birmingham Athletic Club. We both knew that the club was located close to the store, but had never been there.

The Captain wasn't worried, he had On Star.

The first directions he got from the always-cheerful operator were to go to Downtown Birmingham, about 4-1/2 miles East. "Nope, I don't think so." The next directions were to some place on Northwestern Highway, about 2 miles West. "That's OK, I don't need lunch anyway."

We still have faith in On Star. With the Captain's luck, he will one-day drive off the road into a ditch full of rattlesnakes or alligators. When that happens, the bright, bubbly On Star Operator will doubtless save the day and the system will have been worth every dime we paid for it. Just like in the commercial.

Until then, the Captain takes pride in the squiggly little antenna sticking out of the windshield that proves that he and his minivan are on the cutting edge of technology. Go to it Captain. A man's gotta have his toys.

The newest ideas for kitchens and baths sparkle at Florida show

by Glenn Haege,
America's Master Handyman

ORLANDO

I've been going to hardware, paint, and kitchen and bath shows for 21 years. I don't bring my wife along because I'm not there for enjoyment, I'm there to work the show. This year, all that changed.

The Masco Corporation invited me down to broadcast my weekly *Ask the Handyman* radio shows from the Kitchen/Bath Industry Show in Orlando. They graciously invited my crew and I to bring our wives.

So our group included my blushing bride of 30 years, Barbara, Kathleen, my edi-

This self-contained potting shed by Merillat has Woodward cabinets, raised work area and pegboard for hanging tools.

tor at Master Handyman Press, and Marcia, wife of Rob David, my Marketing Director,. They toured the show last Saturday. Each was uniquely qualified to see the show from a different perspective.

Barbara, majored in fine arts at school, is a heavy-duty arts and crafts enthusiast, and has a large amount of technical knowledge through being married to me. Kathleen is a Registered Dietician and has a Master's Degree in Food Service, so she qualifies as a food preparation pro. Marcia is a nationally prominent senior sales executive for a food processing company.

Here are some of the interesting things they found.

Cabinets:

The fine furniture look is in. KraftMaid Fine Cabinetry, (800) 571-1990, led the trend with a huge 3,000 square foot display. Many of their base cabinets didn't just go down to the floor, they actually had furniture feet. They added new designer colors like Platinum Luster, Buttercream, and Taupe and Frost Glazes for a faux finish look.

KraftMaid also introduced new decorative moldings, leaded glass door options, and even entertainment center cabinetry.

Kathy Stief was impressed with KraftMaid's innovative space saving ideas. "My kitchen is too small. I loved the way their designers worked to eliminate dead space. If you have 4 or 5

What many kitchens could use: a moveable island by KraftMaid. It features a 2-inch-thick butcher block top and is mounted on casters so that it can be pushed against a wall to save space, then pulled out to become a separate food preparation area.

inches between cabinets, you can install a spice rack. With a 15-inch width, you can have a pull-out pantry. They even designed a 'floating island' so that you can have an island for food preparation when you need it, but can just push it away when you don't."

My wife thought that Merillat Industries, (800) 575-8759, should have gotten an award for real world practical solutions. "Their designers showed how cabinets can give a finished look throughout the house for not a lot of money. They used Amera cabinets to create a laundry room to die for. Tile and cabinets enclosed the laundry tub and GE washer and dryer."

"In addition, they created a little potting shed, with just a couple of cabinets and peg board. They also used inexpensive cabinets to show how to finish off a garage and make a really attractive work area."

Sinks:

Marcia David was amazed by the variety of sinks. "The manufacturers displayed bathroom sinks like pieces of art," she notes.

Elegant hand-painted bath suite is imported from France by Porcher Ltd.

continued on next page

American Standard, (800) 442-1902, and The Kohler Co., (800) 4 KOHLER, featured hand painted and gold embossed sinks. The Absolute Company, (800) 359-3261, had a bowl painted like a leopard skin. Porcher Ltd., (800) 359-3261, had entire hand painted bathroom sets imported from France.

Gravity Glas, (877) 852-4437, had kiln-cast glass bowls, and Sonoma Cast Stone, (877) 939-9929, had sinks cast from concrete.

Kitchen sinks were not left out of the equation. Stone Forest, (888) 682-2987, had kitchen sinks carved out of granite, and Kallista, Inc., (888) 4-KALLISTA, had one cast from blue Terrazzo.

Casta concrete bathroom sink by sonoma Cast Stone.

Faucets:

One of the talks of the show was Kallista's $300,000 platinum, gold and diamond faucet set. Each handle was topped with a 3.3-carat diamond. If you're not into diamonds, the set can also special order it in emeralds, rubies or sapphires.

On a more practical note, Delta Faucet Company, (800) 345-DELTA, the world's largest faucet manufacturer, introduced a new finish call called Pearl Nickel, to their vastly expanded Brilliance line. Delta was the originators of the Brilliance brass finish which uses an application of NASA developed technology to create a non tarnish brass finish that never dulls and is so strong it can be scrubbed with steel wool and not be damaged.

Price Pfister, (800) 732-8238 and Moen Incorporated, (800) 321-8809, also had attractive permanent shine fixtures as well as filter faucets that provide filtered and non filtered water from the same tap.

Knobs and Pulls:

My wife loved the variety that smaller companies brought to this category. She said that "You can change the personality of an entire room for a very little bit of money just be changing the hardware."

Some of the most fun were: solid pewter and brass leaves, pine cones and twigs by Modern Objects, (203) 378-5785; frogs, turtles, butterflies and alphabet building blocks by HobKnobs, (888) 367-5662. Modern art and hammered bronze by World Accents, (800) 701-1972. Pewter and brass seashells and flowers by Out to Lunch, Inc., (847) 679-1255.

Appliances:

The big trends were increased speed and double ovens. GE, (800) 626-2000, introduced the Advantium, a new kind of oven that bakes food in about one-fourth the time of a conventional oven. With the new oven a 12-ounce sirloin steak takes 9 minutes, baked chicken takes 8 minutes and crescent rolls take 4 1/2 minutes. The cooking speed comes from fan driven air heated by three halogen bulbs.

Kitchenaid, (800) 422-1230, had a special microwave/oven combination that actually browns food.

Stoves of America, (800) 940-5356, had built in gas ovens that featured their unique Rotostar cooking system. The system consists of a gas burner/rotating fan combination that circulates heat at 1,500 rpm, delivering a combination of radiant and convection heat.

Maytag, (800) 688-9900, featured a small warming oven and regular oven combination that really looked good if you like to bake bread or use yeast based recipes.

With a total of over 3,600 exhibit booths, I have not given more than a very small glimpse of all the exciting new products at the Kitchen and Bath Show. Suffice it to say that Barbara, Kathy and Marcia all decided that they needed new kitchens by the time they left the show.

Most of these items are in the pipeline and should be available by summer or fall. If you're going to redo your kitchen or bath in the next year or two, start calling the companies and getting brochures now. There is a lot of excitement ahead of you.

MAY 1, 1999

Paint manufacturers promote a spring cover-up with free brochures

by Glenn Haege,
America's Master Handyman

I often advise folks to make their own "how to" library out of a shoebox filled with the many free brochures they can find at paint and hardware stores and home centers. Spring is an especially good time for paint brochure collecting.

To give you an idea about the wealth of free information available I went to Home Quarters, Meijer and Home Depot. I picked those three chains because you can find them almost everywhere.

I found (and brought home) 34 paint brochures at Home Quarters, 24 at Meijer and 47 at Home Depot. Here are some of the highlights:

Home Quarters

■ Pittsburgh Paints' excellent 10-brochure set for their Premium Distinction paint line. Each brochure contains color swatches, decorating ideas, how to information, and color photos showing how the ideas can be implemented. There were also brochures on faux finishing, stamping and striping.

■ Dutch Boy offered seven brochures including four swatch cards, one comprehensive brochure giving technical information on each of their lines, plus very creative Cabinet & Trim and Exterior Door & Trim guides.

■ Four interior stain guides including the excellent Minwax 30 page *Tips On Wood Finishing.*

■ Eight deck and exterior stain guides including The Flood Company's *Wood Care Guide;* three Olympic guides on Deck Stain, Water Repellant Oil Stain and Acrylic Latex Stain; and Thompson's Exterior Stain and Deck Care guides.

■ Four Concrete & Masonry brochures including 2 UGL DryLok Concrete Applications and a very good Waterproofing brochure, and 2 H & C Concrete Stain guides (one shows concrete stencils you can use to make your patio look like pavers or tiles).

Meijer

■ Eight Faux Finish brochures for McCloskey's Special Effects line of very easy-to-use finishes. Also included, but not counted, was a fabulous collection of swatch cards showing how to achieve specific faux finish effects. These brochures and cards alone are worth a trip to your nearest McCloskey dealer.

■ Pittsburgh Paints' kitchen & bath and exterior color selectors showing full color application photos.

■ Meijer's brochures on premium interior wall, porch & floor, and basement waterproofing paint.

■ Valspar Prep/Step Primer guide, super gloss enamel, exterior aluminum, and a very good accent color guide.

■ Valspar Skid Resistant Coating and Concrete Stain color and application guides.

Home Depot

It is easy to see that the powers that be at Home Depot have laid down the law that high quality, very informative print support is required of everyone selling paint in their centers.

Behr is the major brand at Home Depot. I have often complemented them on their deck care brochures. This year Behr went all out with 22 paint and stain brochures. Among the Behr brochures were:

■ Six deck preparation and stain brochures.

■ Six exterior paint and stain guides including their Premium Plus Exterior Color Palette which demonstrates how all the colors work together and has full color photos of the final results.

■ Six interior paint brochures including very extensive color palettes on Premium Plus interior, high gloss enamel, and kitchen & bath, in addition to a universal guide on the entire Premium Plus line. These brochures are like mini interior decorating books.

■ Two texture paint guides, one conventional and one for faux finishes.

■ Two concrete color guides, one on stains, one on acrylic epoxies.

■ One "how to paint like a pro" and one faux finish guide.

There was an extensive collection of Glidden instructional materials especially made for Home Depot. It included:

■ Five Glidden Evermore color guides on exterior house & trim, interior wall & trim, kitchen & bath, cabinet, trim & shutter, and masonry & stucco.

■ One Glidden exterior painting guide that is so extensive it is a mini painting book with tips, paint estimating formulas, complete color palette, and excellent four color photos. Some photos show the same house with different paint jobs.

■ One small but good Glidden interior priming guide.

■ One off-white guide which shows 39 (we counted them) different off-white colors. This must have been either the print production manager's worst nightmare or his greatest accomplishment.

■ An approximately 40 piece collection of Glidden Idea Cards. The front or each card shows a full color picture of a finished room. The back contains an outline drawing of the room showing which paint went where. Very innovative, informative, and fun!

Other paint brands offerings included:
■ Two Ralph Lauren Paint brochures.

One was a swatch card. The other was a very elaborate piece on glaze painting techniques that is so "artsy" it qualifies as a super thin tabletop book.

■ Two UGL DryLok Masonry Waterproofing and Concrete Floor Paint Guides.

■ Two Epoxi-Tech Epoxy Shield brochures on basement floor and garage floor applications.

■ One Conco-Pro *Professional Coatings Specification Manual* and swatch card.

■ Thompson Deck Care and Minwax tips on Wood Finishing and Stain Guide.

Like I said at the beginning, everything reported here was free. If you've got painting to do, go get them. Read and learn all you can before you do. Then brag about the results.

How to track them down

All the brochures I listed should still be at the stores. If you can't find them, here are the Manufacturers' phone numbers and web sites.

■ Behr, Behr Process Corp., (800) 854-0133, www.behrpaint.com
■ Conco Paints, (800) 486-7889
■ Dutch Boy, (800) 828-5669
■ Epoxi Shield, Epoxi-Tech, Inc., (888) 683-5667, www.epoxi-seal.com
■ Flood Company, (800) 321-3444, www.floodco.com
■ Glidden, the Glidden Co., (800) 634-0015, www.ici.com
■ H & C Concrete Stains, (800) 867-8246, www.concretestain.com
■ Kilz, Masterchem Industries, Inc., (800) 325-3552, www.masterchem.com
■ Krylon, (800) 832-2541, www.krylon.com
■ Ralph Lauren Paints, (800) 379-7656
■ McCloskey, (800) 345-4530, www.valspar.com
■ Minwax, (800) 462-0194, www.minwax.com
■ Olympic Stains, (800) 441-9695, www.ppgaf.com
■ Pittsburgh Paints, (800) 441-9695, www.ppgaf.com
■ UGL, United Gilsonite Laboratories, (800) 845-5227, www.ugl.com
■ Valspar Corp., (800) 345-4530, www.valspar.com

MAY 8, 1999

National drywall shortage could hurt remodeling projects

by Glenn Haege,
America's Master Handyman

Drywall is in short supply. This could spell trouble if you have a new home or major remodeling job on the horizon. And the tornado damage in Oklahoma and Kansas will only make it worse.

Drywall, or wallboard as it is called in the industry, is what builders use instead of plaster. With drywall you have walls and ceilings. Without drywall you have bare studs. No house, apartment, condominium, office building, hotel, casino, or commercial building can be completed without drywall.

Two weeks ago I had Kevin Cortney, vice-president of sales for United States Gypsum on my Ask the Handyman radio show. He confirmed that manufacturers cannot keep up with the demand.

Although manufacturers have started building new plants and improved high speed production lines, it takes three years to build a plant.

New and improved plants are also expensive. A plant capable of producing 700 million square feet of wallboard, such as the ones USG Corp. is building in Bridgeport, Ala., and Ranier, Ore., cost about $120 million. Updating an existing plant to 700-million-square-foot capacity, like USG Corp. is doing in Plaster City, CA, and East Chicago, IN, costs about $105 million each. That's a lot even for a huge international corporation.

According to the Gypsum Association, demand for wallboard increased 48 percent between 1990 and 1998 when it reached 27.8 billion square feet. As of January, the gypsum industry's capacity was 28.9 billion square feet. Production capacity will increase to 34 billion square feet within four years.

How do shortages effect us? To find out, we talked to Pat Sill, the drywall buyer at Home Depot; Troy Seamans, the yard Supervisor at Ryan Building Materials, one of the big drywall and building materials suppliers; Kevin Humphries, a manager at Utica Drywall Products, a smaller supplier; Steve Edwards, the owner of Drywall, Inc., a medium-sized drywall installer; and Joe Aiello, owner of Pine Building Co., a prominent local remodeling company.

At Home Depot, the demand for drywall is so great that they sell all they get their hands on. The trouble is, they are on allocation just like everyone else. Two weeks ago, I checked the drywall inventory at their high volume Southfield store. They only had 90 sheets of drywall. Sill would like to have five or six truckloads at that size store.

Ryan Building Materials, (248) 353-2805, is such a big buyer they do not yet have a problem. They service their long standing accounts but cash sales or sales to less than premium accounts are honored only if there is something extra. There is nothing extra.

Kevin Humphries at Utica Drywall, (248) 739-3100, says that his company has had to cut off retail and counter drywall sales. "I'm sold out. If I need 20 truckloads, they give me 10. We deliver on a daily basis to established customers. If a load comes in, it goes out immediately. We have no inventory," he said.

Steve Edwards, the owner of Drywall Inc., (248) 524-0707, is in the catbird's seat and loving it. With 25 installers, Edwards is a force in Oakland and Macomb County. His company does everything from individual homeowner's jobs to million-dollar renovations, office and apartment construction, and insurance repairs.

Although he gladly accepts work from individual homeowners, he and many of his colleagues are the living embodiment of the expression "What goes around, comes around." Builders who treated Edwards and his colleagues badly, now call pleading to get someone to do their jobs, but get no satisfaction.

Edwards runs a close-knit organization. His sons, Steve Jr. and Anthony, supervise 25 craftsmen. With all the new construction scheduled for Detroit, he believes that the biggest shortage will be in trained installers not drywall.

"When the big casinos and hotels are under construction, they will be paying two or three times the current rate. When that happens there will not be enough people to do the work," he says.

Joe Aiello of Pine Building, (248) 539-9600, is not having a problem with drywall supply. Aiello has always treated his subcontractors like part of his family. His drywall installer makes certain that plenty of drywall is allocated to Aiello's jobs.

"But you have to understand that when the casinos are under construction and the good guys can double or triple their income, they are going to follow the money. I tell folks if they are going to get modernization done, get it done now," Aiello said.

Humphries is pessimistic. He advises "put your remodeling job on hold until next year. If you don't, you will pay between 1/3 and 1/2 more for labor and materials; and a job that usually takes six months, will take 9 or 10."

What should you do? Analyze your needs carefully. If you are dealing with a builder, make certain that he has a good reputation and a long track record with his subcontractors. Also put in penalty clauses and don't be afraid of walking away from a builder who does not have a reputation for completing work on time. Do your homework.

MAY 15, 1999

Composite and vinyl decking materials cut down on maintenance

by Glenn Haege,
America's Master Handyman

Wooden decks are like wooden boats, beautiful but a definite maintenance drag after a year or two. The only people who actually like to varnish wood are boat owners, and they invented fiberglass.

If you decide to throw in the sponge, Durable Deck by Anchor Decking Systems, Inc., and distributed by Biewer Lumber in the Midwest, (800) 482-5717, can be applied over your existing decking to provide a long-lasting, skid resistant cap.

If you have to tear off the old and lay down new decking, manufacturers have developed two, increasingly good wood substitutes: extruded wood/plastic composites and vinyl decking. Both are more expensive than wood but should last 10 or 20 years and reduce maintenance.

Extruded composites

These include Trex, the granddaddy of them all, ChoiceDek, and newer entries like Smart Deck Durawood EX and TimberTech. Extruded wood composites are used for decking not understructures. All are almost impervious to insect and weather damage.

■ Trex, made by the Trex Company, (800) 289-8739, is a combination of ground-up plastic milk cartons and wood waste. It is smooth and solid. You cut and nail it like wood decking. You can also use it to build the deck rail system. It never splits or rots. The biggest disadvantages of Trex are that it looks exactly like what it is – a semi/plastic extrusion – and it is slightly moisture absorbent. It will take a solid stain, but then you are back into the maintenance thing. My advice is to let it weather light gray.

■ ChoiceDek, manufactured by AERT (Advanced Environmental Recycling Technologies, Inc.), (800) 951-5117, is a 100-percent recycled-content, wood-plastic composite decking material distributed in some parts of the country by Weyerhaeuser. Because it is made from 48-percent recycled milk bottles and 52-percent waste wood fiber from aromatic red cedar chips, the composite has a wonderful cedar smell.

ChoiceDek is dark brown when installed, but weathers to silver gray. Unlike Trex, ChoiceDek has a corrugated bottom surface. ChoiceDek also has a rough, non-slip surface.

■ Durawood EX is a wood fiber/polymer composite made from 70-percent recycled wood waste and 30-percent recycled milk jugs. It is part of the SmartDeck system made by Chicago-based Eaglebrook Products, (888) 733-2546. EX is manufactured in continuous extrusions up to 12 inches wide. The type of wood fiber used in the manufacturing process determines coloring. It can be coated.

This is part of Dillman & Upton's artificial wood dcking display showing a composite rail system anchored to gray stained Trex composite decking with Gray Durable Deck deck cap in background.

Eaglebrook also make Durawood PE a 100 percent purified plastic lumber. PE comes in various wood tones and in popular colors such as cedar, weathered redwood, light oak, gray, white, green, dark brown, black, and custom colors and comes in most lumber sizes. It cannot be painted

■ TimberTech is made from virgin, not recycled, plastics and wood fiber. Even though it is as strong as solid deck board, it is made with a hollow core and is bottomless. This makes it lighter and easy to string electrical wiring for on-deck lighting. The product has a nonskid surfaces, comes in 6-inch widths that fit tongue 'n groove. It can be stained, but weathers to a nice driftwood shade.

Vinyl decking

Vinyl decking's biggest plus and minus is the same. It looks like plastic. That said, it can make a beautiful deck. If you buy vinyl, make certain that it has been treated to resist Ultra Violet rays to keep the material from becoming brittle.

Although there may be some fading from the sun, the color you buy is the color you keep. This makes Vinyl an excellent combination of long life, good looks and easy care.

The product comes from the dock and fencing industries. Some of the names to look for are:

■ Brock Deck, built by a division of Royal Crown Ltd., (800) 365-3625, distributed in Michigan by Dexter Innovations, (248) 433-3339. Planks are 5 7/8 inches wide.

■ DreamDeck by Thermal Industries, (800) 245-1540. Planks are 5 1/2 inches wide.

■ EZ Deck by Pultronex Corporation, (800) 990-3099. Planks are 4 or 6 inches wide.

■ Kroy's Vinyl Decking by Kroy Building Products, (800) 933-5769. Planks are 8 inches wide.

The Brock Deck and EZ Deck have bottomless construction. All four have their own railing and attachment systems.

To learn more about decking alternatives, come see them and me from 8 a.m. to noon today, at Dillman and Upton, on Woodward, South of Tienken and West of Rochester Road in Rochester, (248) 651-9411. I'll be broadcasting from there and many manufacturers reps will be on hand to explain the products to you.

If Downriver is more convenient, look for us at N.A. Mans, Ford Road in Canton, (734) 981-5800, from 8 a.m. to noon next Saturday. They also have a wide selection of manufactured decking and manufacturers reps will be on hand to give technical support. Both places will also have pop and hot dogs, all at my favorite price, free!

Simple process can make almost-new furniture look 'distressed'

by Glenn Haege,
America's Master Handyman

For years I've been looking at worn out furniture and dilapidated rooms featured in Country Living, Martha Stewart Living and various cooking magazines. I always felt sort of guilty thinking that if we had all paid a quarter more per copy for the magazines, they could have afforded to get some good stuff, or at least bought a gallon or two of paint.

Then I went to the Kitchen & Bath Show last month, and I'll be darned if I didn't see the same things there.

Early this month we received an Exposure HOMES catalogue that promised to show how to "Fill your home with spirit and style." The catalogue was filled with furnishings reminiscent of what you used to find in a used furniture store.

Page 3 had a beat-up TV table with a repainted wooden pop box for $295. Page 5 featured a dining room table that looked a lot like one my grandmother threw away my freshman year in high school. Kathy, my editor at Master Handyman Press, is in the corner crying because Page 22 featured a Bouvier Nightstand reproduction on sale for $1490. She threw out two that looked like that ten years ago.

Which brings me to the subject of this article. Since what looks like old is new again, there's a good chance that things you have stored in the basement, attic, or garage, can now be dusted off and dragged back into the living room to impress the neighbors.

If you have to get "new" because you threw out all your legitimate "old," you can restock by trolling the neighborhood about 6:30 or 7:00 a.m. on trash collection days. If you've already left for work at that time, try about 10:30 p.m. the night before. It's already dark so the neighbors won't see and most of the heavy stuff is out by then.

Should you not be able to find exactly what you want, much of the catalogue stuff is made from reclaimed lumber. You can get your own reclaimed lumber supply by carefully tearing apart that old TV cabinet, cast off bench or shelving. Bang together a rough bench or bookcase and you have an authentic, new/old object d'art.

Here are a few tips on rehabbing the old, or making the almost new look old again.

That beaten-up varnished coffee table can be cleaned up with some Formby's Furniture Face Lift by the Thompson/ Formby Company, (800) 367-6297. Furniture Face Lift brings back the shine, but will do nothing to hide the raw, scuffed spots. That's exactly how it's supposed to look.

Much of what the designers are showing, has a worn away painted look called "distressed". It's surprisingly simple to do. I've attached step by step directions you can use to get this in vogue designer look.

By the time you're done, people will believe the piece has been in the family for a hundred years. So brag about it!

How to create distressed look

1) Completely strip the wood. Dab on a thick coat of Citristrip, (800) 235-3546. Let stand for a half-hour then scrape off with a plastic putty knife. Repeat if necessary.

2) Smooth down the surface by lightly hand sanding with fine 180-grit sandpaper. Hand sand all edges – a power sander would make the surfaces too smooth. Vacuum, then rub down the surface with a tack rag.

3) Seal with a stain. Use a light stain if you are going to apply a dark paint. Use a darker stain if you are going to use a light paint. Let dry.

4) Brush on a generous coat of paint and let dry thoroughly.

5) "Distress" the paint by sanding with 180-grit paper. Use the green kind made by 3M. It doesn't clog as rapidly. You can use an orbital sander, hand sand, or use a combination of the two. This is the creative part of the job. Just sand through the paint letting the stain show through in various places. Along portions of the edges you will probably want to sand even the stain away to reveal places where everything has "worn away."

Glazes give distressed look

If you want to have an old, cracked paint effect, the McCloskey Division of Valspar Corporation, (800) 767-2532, has a couple of glazes in their Special Effects line that will give you just the look you want. Apply a base coat, then a coat of Porcelain Crackle Glaze or Weathered Crackle Glaze. Finish off with a top finish coat of flat latex paint. As the finish coat dry, the cracks will appear. Applying the paint with a roller creates uniform small cracks. A brush application creates cracks in a large variety of sizes.

You'll find the McCloskey line at Shelby Paint & Decorating, (810) 739-0240, in Shelby; Arno Paint and Wallpaper, (248) 549-5440, in Royal Oak, and most Meijer stores. Most good specialty paint stores will carry a similar product. Paint 'N Paper, (248) 646-6996, in Birmingham, carries Crackle by the Old Fashioned Milk Paint Co., (978) 448-6336. Just read the directions on the can and you'll do fine.

MAY 29, 1999

Tips for the spills-and-spoilage season

by Glenn Haege,
America's Master Handyman

The Memorial Day Weekend is one of the big travel weekends of the yea. It is also the start of the spill and spoilage season.

Go on an extended road trip and spills are bound to happen. Go away from home for several days and, inevitably, something in the refrigerator spoils. There is no way to eliminate these phenomena from our lives, we can only try to outwit them.

Traveling in a car or van full of kids and/or pets, is an open invitation for all manners of spills and stains. When the pop, chocolate ice-cream Sunday, Sloppy Joe or chilly dog plops down on the seat or carpet, don't use paper toweling or try to scrub the mess up with household cleaner or soap and water. That technique just spreads the stain.

Here's what you need to keep on hand in your car to clean up messes:
- A small bottle of club soda.
- A can of foam shaving cream.
- A box of facial tissue.

When the spills occur, scoop the mess up with facial tissue immediately. When everything is picked up, pour a little club soda on the stain and wick it away with facial tissue. Technique is everything. Take a half-inch-thick wad of tissue and press down on the stain. Most of the discoloration will be absorbed. Repeat if necessary.

If you can't get everything out, squirt a little shaving foam onto the stain and gently work into the fabric. Blot up with facial tissue, then repeat the application of club soda and tissue.

As many of us get up and go gallivanting around the state we spend more and more weekends, extending to weeks, away from home. Many split our time fairly equally between the house in town and the cottage.

Sooner or later we open the refrigerator door in our house, cottage, camper or boat, and are almost knocked over by the smell. Oh boy! How could we have forgotten to do something about the liver and onions, or freeze that batch of freshly caught fish. Even worse, the power may have gone out while we were away and we are stuck with a revolting conglomeration of spoiled foods.

I won't ask for a show of hands, but almost everyone has been in that situation at one time or another. There is no perfect solution.

Pull the plug on a refrigerator full of food, go away for a couple of months and you will come home to an unsalvageable mess. The food will have spoiled and the smell will have irreversibly permeated the appliance walls making disposal the only option.

On a lesser note, just eating leftovers that have been stored a wee bit too long can give you a minor case of food poisoning and fluelike symptoms.

Alpine Industries' Refresh unit is a battery-powered ozone maker, retarding spoilage and destroying odors in the refrigerator.

Alpine Industries, (800) 989-2299, has come up with a handy little refrigerator ozone maker called the Refresh. This device is about the size and shape of a large mustard jar. It is impervious to power shutdowns and brownouts because it is powered by four D-size batteries.

Just insert the batteries and put the unit on the top shelf of the refrigerator. The Refresh unit starts making ozone immediately. Ozone is an unstable Oxygen molecule often used as a sanitizing agent. It is produced naturally whenever there is a thunderstorm.

In your refrigerator, ozone goes to work immediately killing microbes (those little critters that cause decomposition), reducing odors, retarding spoilage and maintaining freshness. Placing the container with the cap up creates enough ozone for normal use. If greater odor and spoilage control is needed, turning the container cap down increases ozone production.

Some critics believe that ozone is too active an anti-microbial to be used around people. The thick walls and sealed doors of a refrigerator make it an ideal environment for ozone sanitation.

If you get one unit for the cottage refrigerator and one for in town you'll take a lot of the worry out of leaving either place for an extended period. It's not the perfect solution, but it should give you an extra couple of days.

The Refresh unit retails for $55. It is available locally from Pure Air Plus, (800) 455-5247. Pure Air Plus also sells mail order throughout the country and ships within 24 hours.

If you're on the road this weekend, have fun and drive safely. I need all my readers and listeners.

JUNE 5, 1999

Fix your cracked concrete or asphalt driveway with specialized products

by Glenn Haege,
America's Master Handyman

We had a long tough winter but now is the perfect time to fix your concrete or asphalt drive, sidewalk or patio.

There is such a wide variety of products out there. Many were developed by two major companies: Quikrete, (800) 282-5828, and SealMaster, (800) 395-7325.

Quikrete has its major emphasis on concrete. SealMaster has its major emphasis on asphalt. Some of their products overlap. Both companies' product lines are manufactured under license by Gibraltar National, (800) 442-7258, for the Michigan Market. Gibraltar has a very good help desk and you can call them if you can't find a particular product.

Asphalt

Asphalt is weather sensitive. Pick a day when there will be no rain for 24 hours after the repair is completed.

Sealing: In the next few months, many thousands of gallons of sealer will be applied by well meaning Do-It-Yourselfers. Bob Waldvogel of Gibraltar's SealMaster Division thinks that we're putting too much on and sometimes actually harming the asphalt.

Many people apply sealer every year as a beautifying agent. They like the deep, rich black color. Over time the sealer builds up and causes reflective cracking. If you apply a good quality sealer, you only have to re-apply it every two to four years.

Chuckholes: The secret to a long-lasting patch is to have the chuckhole clean and dry before you start. Gibraltar makes two different products. Quikrete Black bag Blacktop Patch and Quikrete Green bag Commercial Grade Blacktop Patch. Black bag is good. Green bag is better. It is a lot more forgiving, can be applied in any weather and there can even be water in the hole. Pour the patching material directly from the bag into the hole. Over-fill so that there is a nice little mound. Then drive over the mound to tamp it down. You're done.

Smaller Cracks: If the width of the crack is 2 inches or more, treat it like a chuckhole. A narrower crack can be fixed using pourable crack filler. Be sure that the crack is clean and dry with no vegetation before you begin.

There are three different types of crack filler: Asphalt Emulsion, Elastromeric, and Acrylic Crack Sealant. The Asphalt Emulsion is the least expensive and does not irritate human skin.

An Elastromeric crack sealer, like Seal-Master TruGuard, costs $10 to $13 a gallon. It can cause a slight irritation if too much of it gets on your hands, but it lasts twice as long as an Asphalt Emulsion. Acrylic Crack Sealant can last slightly longer than Elastromerics and costs about $16 a gallon.

SealMaster has developed a product called Crack Stixs that gives the quality of a hot tar patch without any mess. Crack Stixs come in boxes of 1/4-, 1/2-, and 3/4-inch widths. To repair a crack, just break off a length of the proper width Crack Stixs and stuff it into the crack.

Always choose the wider Crack Stixs for a repair. If a crack is a little too wide for the 1/4-inch, and a little too narrow for the 1/2-inch Crack Stixs, push in the 1/2-inch. Then melt the Crack Stixs with a Bernz-O-Matic torch. When the Crack Stixs has melted, you're done.

If the crack is deep, fill with play sand to within 1/4-inch of the top. Tamp down the sand with an ice chopper, and then over-fill with your choice of crack sealer.

Concrete

The two most common homeowner concrete problems are spalling and cracking. Spalling is a condition in which a relatively large but shallow surface area has lost its cohesive quality and exposed the aggregate.

Spalling: Clean away all broken and loose concrete, dirt and plant remains. If a large area has to be repaired, pressure wash the surface a few days beforehand. Dirt and grease stains can be removed with Quikrete Concrete and Asphalt Cleaner or a mixture of four ounces dry measure of Trisodium Phosphate (TSP) per gallon of water.

Resurface the area with Quikrete Vinyl Concrete Patcher. This product is a blend of vinyl resin, fine sand and Portland Cement. It has very strong adhesive properties and can be troweled to a 1/16-inch featheredge.

Do not mix more than you can use in a half-hour because it becomes unworkable after that period of time.

If the area being repaired only has to be built up 1-inch or less you can do the job in one application. If you need more than one inch, it should be done in two or more applications. Allow the product to cure for a couple of days between applications.

Cracks: Fill thin cracks less than 1/2-inch in width with a ready-to-use crack sealer. Just snip the top and pour. The crack sealer acts like an expansion joint. Many crack sealers or fillers are black like traditional expansion joints. Alcoguard is considered one of the best of these. If you don't want the black lines, both Quikrete and Mr. Mac's make gray concrete crack sealers.

When the cracks are 1/2-inch or wider, water will have washed a channel under the concrete. Back fill these with play sand and tamp down with an ice chopper. Repeat the process several times. Fill the last 1-1/2-inches with a backer rod and crack sealer or Quikrete Vinyl Concrete Patcher.

Brag about it!

JUNE 12, 1999

Surprise Dad and doll up the deck just in time for Father's Day

by Glenn Haege,
America's Master Handyman

A special note to folks who can't decide what to do for Father's Day. Mom often dusts and vacuums, but let's Dad maintain the Deck. He also barbecues on it and it is his pride and joy.

If your not up to buying him one of the new Teflon coated Ties at J C Penney, what nicer way is there to show your affection than to do something special for his deck?

Decks are a lot of work. If dad hasn't done it already, you could make super big points by doing the necessary spring maintenance for him. Depending on the species of wood and the overall condition of the deck this could be a lot of work.

Make Dad a cement brick border or walk around the deck and eliminate weeds.

Cleaning

If you just have to give the deck a general cleaning, you can use organic cleaners like Simple Green, Clean Away or Clear Magic. Use 1/2 gallon of concentrate to one gallon of water. The Bio-Wash Company makes a special deck cleaner called Simple Wash. The Cabot company makes a special purpose product called Problem Solver Wood Cleaner. If Dad's deck has mildew or bird droppings, you are better off using one of the special purpose products. If the deck has a really major mildew problem, deck cleaners don't have sufficient muscle. Do not use household bleach. Chlorine is dangerous and can ruin wood. Move up to a deck brightener.

Brightening

When untreated deck wood has turned gray, or there are a lot of tannin and rust stains, the wood needs to be brightened. This is especially true for woods like Cedar and Redwood. Brightening takes off the top layer of cells, which have been killed and discolored by the ultra violet rays of the sun.

Some of the best brighteners have an Oxalic acid base. Some of the brand names to look for are Behr Wood Cleaner Brightener, Cabot Problem Solver Wood Brightener, Flood Dekswood, Superdeck Deckdoctor, Woodtec Rescue and Wolman Cedar & Redwood Deck & Fence Brightener.

A few other companies use very effective chemicals that are even easier on the environment than Oxalic acid. Bio-Wash WoodWash and Specialty Environmental Weathered Wood Restorer have a citric acid base. Wolman Deck & Fence Brightener for Pressure Treated wood uses sodium percarbonate.

Any one of the brands I listed here will do a good job. Most of them just have

Night Fire will allow you to have a campfire on the deck.

to be mixed with water and applied with a garden pressure sprayer or roller. Keep the deck wet and brush it with a deck brush for fifteen minutes. Then rinse and you're done.

Stripping & resealing

If your deck has been stained or sealed a couple of years ago, the surface may have to be completely stripped and re-sealed or stained. That's a big job. Consult with Dad before doing this. The strippers that have done the best on my test deck are Bio-Wash Stripex L and Specialty Environmental Technologies Woodpal Deck Stain & Finish Stripper. They are made especially thick and cling to vertical surfaces and problem areas.

Choosing deck stains and sealers is a highly subjective matter. Mom and Dad both have to agree so do not even think about doing this before there has been a family pow-wow.

Heatilator Night Fire

There are a lot of great things you can do to doll up the deck. Many of them Dad would never think of getting for himself. Here are two suggestions.

Imagine being able to have a campfire on the deck. In the Detroit area, the Night Fire is available at Williams Panel Brick, (800) 538-6650, for only $219. They also ship the unit nationwide for just $15. This gas campfire can use pro-

pane or be hooked up to natural gas. You have to buy the rocks or paving stones separately.

If you use propane the Night Fire can be set up in about 15 minutes. Just take it out of the box, attach the line, arrange the logs and rocks or bricks and you are done. The Night Fire not only looks cool, it will let the family get a lot more use from the deck by keeping them warm on cool nights.

Quikrete Paver Border

Decks are wonderful. Weeding and trimming around the deck is not a lot of fun. You can actually make Dad a cement brick border or walk around the deck and eliminate the weeds: this can be "way cool" because you actually make the bricks. Quikrete makes special, reusable plastic Walk Maker, Cobblestone StepMaker and Border Maker forms. You buy the forms and mix Quikrete Fiber-Reinforced Concrete and water. You can even color the concrete with cement color if you want.

This may sound as easy as making mud pies, but trust me it is a lot of work. On the other hand, imagine the pride Dad will get showing off the border and telling folks you made it for him.

Sources

Deck Care Products:
Bio-Wash (800) 858-5011
Behr (800) 854-0133
Cabot Stains (800) 877-8246
Flood (800) 321-3444
Duck's Back (800) 825-5382
William's Panel Brick (800) 538-6650
Wolman (800) 556-7737
Woodtec (800) 338-3175
Night Fire
Heatilator Night Fire (800) 843-2848
Williams Panel Brick (800) 538-6650
Paver Borders
Gibraltar National (800) 442-7258
Quikrete (800) 282-5828

JUNE 19, 1999

The brick dilemma: To Paint or not?

by Glenn Haege,
America's Master Handyman

To paint, or not to paint brick? That is the question. Whenever someone asks me, I have a one-word answer: DON'T.

Brick, of course, provides the closest thing to a permanent exterior. Even though it is five times more than vinyl siding, according to the Masonry Industry Council, (www.maconline.org), it's worth the money because of its long life and greater perceived value in the eyes of the public.

That being said, nothing lasts forever. Over time brick becomes increasingly porous and can develop problems. When that occurs, you have several options.

Cleaning and sealing

One of the best non-painting strategies is to clean and seal the brick surface every three to five years.

As regular maintenance, power washing is fastest, but scrubbing the surface down with a long-handled brush, using a solution of TSP and water is easier on the brick. Use a mixture of 2-ounces dry measure of TSP per gallon of water. If there is a mildew problem, add two cups of household bleach.

Wash, and then rinse copiously with a garden hose and let dry for 48 hours. When dry, spray on a masonry sealer like Thompson's, (800) 367-6297, PPG Olympic, (800) 441-9695, or UGL Concrete Protector, (800) 272-3235.

This sounds like a big job but you can do it with a garden sprayer. Make certain you saturate the surface. Go back and forth, up and down. The better you seal the brick the longer the job will last.

Repairing damage

Even when brick has begun to degrade, painting is not the only solution. Try to repair the surface damage before you take the drastic step of painting. Once you start to paint brick it becomes a continuous maintenance problem.

If brickwork is very dirty or the bricks have begun to deteriorate, clean and seal the surface. At this stage, I suggest power washing done by a company with a reputation for doing restoration work.

After a thorough cleaning, inspect the grout carefully. This is the time to do any needed tuck-pointing. You can either do the tuck-pointing yourself, or check with a nearby masonry supply wholesaler and get the names of a few craftsmen who specialize in this kind of work. You will probably find yourself on a long waiting list.

A minimum of 48 hours after the brick has been power washed, seal with a good masonry sealer. The same company that power washed the brick may provide this service.

The brick should now look better than it has in years and be protected for the next several years. Reseal the brick when water stops beading on the surface.

Removing paint splatters

If the problem is that the brick has been splattered by painting trim over the years, you can remove the old paint, power wash and seal the brick. If the splatters are small use Motsenbockers #4 Graffiti Remover or #5 Latex Based Paint Remover, (800) 346-1633. If splatters cover a large area use a heavy-bodied paint and varnish remover like Citristrip, (800) 782-9926.

When brickwork has been stained by chalking of the paint on old aluminum siding the stain has most likely been absorbed into the brick.

If the problem is just in a small area, use a freestanding brick like an eraser and cover the stain with brick dust. Rub the edge of the brick back and forth until the chalking has been covered.

If chalking has covered a wide area, power wash both the brick and the aluminum siding surfaces and see if the result is satisfactory. If it looks good, seal the surface and you're done.

When this doesn't work, my suggestion is to stain not paint the surface. A good cement stain like Coronado, (800) 883-4193, or H & C, (800) 867-8246, will penetrate the brick and hide a lot of imperfections. The stain can be applied with a long handled roller or with commercial grade spraying equipment. Make certain that coverage is even. Uneven coverage will leave a splotchy surface.

Painting Brick

If you just have to have that "painted brick look" you can either go high-tech or DIY. For high-tech use one of the highly specialized Coronado products or INSL-X Vinyl-Flex # 51-8000 series, (800) 225-5554.

The do-it-yourself solution is a premium exterior latex like Benjamin Moore MooreGuard, (800) 672-4686; Pittsburgh Paint's Manor Hall, (800) 441-9695; or Sherwin Williams Duration, (800) 474-3794.

Here's the procedure. Power wash the entire surface. If you have a colonial that is brick on the bottom and wood, aluminum or vinyl on top wash everything. Let dry for at least two days. If it is very humid, wait a little longer.

Cover the entire surface with a Water Base Stain Kill that is rated for exterior use like Wm. Zinsser 1-2-3, (732) 469-4367, or Masterchem Total One, (800) 325-3552.

Let the Stain Kill dry for at least four hours, then apply two coats of a premium exterior acrylic latex. If the brick is old and weathered, be prepared to use a lot of paint. The more the surface drinks in the paint, the better.

If no matter how hard you worked, the brick starts shrugging off the paint in just a few years, remember this is the look you wanted. An artist has to suffer.

Happy Father's Day!

JUNE 26, 1999

In the annual Battle of the Bugs, here's how to identify the enemy

by Glenn Haege,
America's Master Handyman

Every year I ask pest control experts to give an overall assessment of our battle against the bugs. Two weeks ago I interviewed Tom Thompson of Thompson Pest Control, (800) 934-4770.

Thompson believes in the rifle, rather than the shotgun approach to pest control. He pinpoints problems and uses as few chemicals as possible to get the job done.

In difficult situations, Thompson uses Molly, his highly trained ant and termite-sniffing beagle, to literally sniff out the enemy. Molly is one of only 30 specially trained pest control dogs in the United States. Her sophisticated nose can ferret out live carpenter ants and termites that even the most high tech equipment might miss.

Here are some of the things Thompson thinks you should know about the insects that are trying to take over your home.

Carpenter Ants

If carpenter ants aren't in your house, they are probably in that old stump or fence post in the backyard. Carpenter ants grow up to 1/2-inch in length. Worker ants travel up to 300 feet from the nest to keep the family fed. They are nocturnal. While you sleep, they are crawling around looking for food.

Carpenter ants feed on other insects, decaying fruit and the sweet nectar from aphids and other insects. They will also be delighted to make a trail to your sugar or fruit bowl or snack on cookies, butter and meat.

As long as the queen stay outside ants are not much of a problem inside the house. When a queen and her hoard migrate into the house, she will probably take up residence in some damp timber between the walls. Worker ants tunnel into the wood to make nests and significant structural damage can occur.

Spraying liquid Diazinon around the exterior of the house helps but won't stop them. Electrical wiring provides a handy highway into your home. Sprinkling insecticide granules around their nests may help, but it also places poison where other wildlife, pets and children can get at it. If you see a significant number of carpenter ants have your home checked and treated by a professional.

Carpenter Bees

Carpenter bees look like bumblebees but have less yellow and more black. They love cedar and will even laughingly burrow into pressure treated lumber. These pests can do a lot of damage to soffits and fascia boards.

462

Before attacking make sure that they are carpenter bees not yellow jackets. Yellow jackets are smaller and a whole lot meaner. If you are certain that it is a carpenter bee, spray an insecticide like Yard Guard into the hole and·plug it with 3/8-inch dowels. If you don't plug it another carpenter bee may take up residence.

If you decide that you saw a yellow jacket going into a hole in the wood, do not plug the hole. A yellow jacket queen lays lots of eggs. Plugging a yellow jacket nest can mean that you suddenly have a couple hundred very angry wasps flying around inside your house, making it inhabitable. Call a professional if you have a yellow jacket problem.

Termites

Termites look like pieces of white rice. They are tough to detect because they stay in the wall and don't come out. Here in Michigan we are primarily effected by Subterranean Termites. If you open a wall and see termites, you have a definite problem. Have the entire house checked and treated by professionals.

Mosquitoes

After all the rain we've had this spring, all we need is a few hot days and millions of mosquitoes will be on the attack. Large swampy areas have to be handled by specialists. Call the Michigan Mosquito Control Association, (517) 687-5044, for a referral. They are also on the web at www.mimosq.org.

Even if you don't have a major problem, a little standing water can breed a large mosquito population. A mosquito can go from egg through larva and pupa stages to full blown adult in just a few days.

Boy mosquitoes won't bug you. Girl mosquitoes are out for your blood. A lady mosquito can hitch a ride on a friendly wind and crash your next party from as far as five miles away.

If you don't want her to come to your barbecue, cut the grass short and trim back large leafy areas. About one hour before the party, spread a mosquito repellent like Mosquito Beater by Bonide Products Inc., (800) 552-8252, around the yard.

Mosquito Beater is sold at Home Depot, ACO, Damman and many independent hardware stores and home centers. It is a granular naphthalene-based product. To apply, spread 1/2 cup per 10 square feet. One bag treats about 5,000 square feet. The treatment should be effective for about five days. If it rains, re-treat or you will have to retreat.

If there is not much of a breeze, bring out a few fans and keep the air circulating. Aim the fans to blow under tables and keep insects from attacking your legs.

If other insects are bugging you, tell 'em the Handyman said to "Buzz off."

JULY 3, 1999

10 tips to help you and your house keep cool over the summer

by Glenn Haege,
America's Master Handyman

If your house has got the "hots" for you and you don't like it, here are my top ten tips for keeping cool.

1. Be realistic. Central air conditioning is only designed to make the inside temperature 15 degrees lower than the outside temperature. If it's 100 degrees Fahrenheit outside, the air conditioning has the power to lower the inside temperature to 85 degrees. It can't do more than that.

If you are using a room air conditioner, don't expect it to cool the entire house. It was made to cool a limited number of cubic feet. Window air conditioning units operate most effectively when you close the door of the room in which they are located.

2. Don't open the windows. Your central air conditioner has a hard enough time trying to cool the house. Don't expect it to cool the neighborhood. Remember that it is "conditioning" the air in your house. This means reducing the humidity as well as cooling the air. If you open the windows, humid air rushes in and the air conditioner has to do its job all over again.

3. Pull down the shades when the sun is beating down during the heat of the day.

4. Don't turn on unnecessary electric lights. They waste energy and create heat.

5. Keep the temperature constant unless you will be going away for a long period of time. Bouncing the temperature up and down between 75 and 85 degrees, causes the air conditioner to work twice as hard every time you lower the temperature. Pick a temperature you can live with and leave it there.

6. Turn on the fans. Colder air sinks to the floor where it makes our feet cold. Hot air rises, making heads hot and second story rooms uninhabitable. A breeze circulates the air and makes air conditioning more efficient.

7. Keep the compressor clear. The compressor is that hard-working box located outside your house. It often becomes clogged with ragweed or other air-borne contaminants. When clogged it can overheat and burn out. Spray away the fuzzies with the garden hose.

If you see ice forming on the pipes leading from the compressor into the house, the cooling plant is low on coolant. Call your air conditioning contractor immediately.

8. Remember that it is the furnaces fan not the air conditioner that distributes cooled air. The furnace fan does not want to work any harder than it must. Cold air is heavy so the fan dumps it as soon as possible.

Insulation tips

Add insulation before you buy a new air conditioner.

Most ceilings only had enough insulation installed to give them an R-19 Rating. This has compressed over the years and is far less. Installing enough insulation to bring the Insulation Rating up to an R-38 or even an R-45 is the single most cost efficient thing you can do to make your home cooler in the summer and warmer in the winter.

When you add insulation you must add ventilation, too.

It is also a good idea to increase the insulation in the walls of the house.

Air conditioning tips

Bigger is not always better. An oversized unit cools too fast and does not dehumidify air properly. Specify a coil that is a half-ton larger than the compressor. The compressor will run longer and give you a bigger bang for your air conditioning buck.

An air conditioner's Seasonal Energy Efficiency Rating (SEER Rating) should be a key factor in your decision process. In Michigan, a 10.0 SEER Rating is the bare minimum. A 12 or 13 SEER Rating is above average.

The only way an air conditioning salesman can determine the proper size air conditioner for your house is to make a thorough heat gain study. Don't let him just come to a snap judgement or give you a quote based on your old unit.

Generally rooms closest to the furnace get cooled most. Rooms farthest from the furnace (like the bedrooms on the second floor) get cooled least.

If you have some rooms that are too cold and some rooms that are too hot you can out wit the furnace. Start by closing the cold air vents in the rooms that are too cold. If that doesn't solve the problem, take off the return air vents in the cooler rooms and seal the vents with plastic wrap. This forces the furnace to draw more hot air from warm rooms replacing it with cooler air.

9. Change your furnace filters. The furnace fan is working hard circulating the cool air. Clogged filters can burn out the motor.

10. Don't expect air conditioning to do everything. Drink plenty of fluids and walk, don't run. Be very careful about going from a cool building into the hot sun. The transition can be a shock to your system.

Just thinking about this made me work up a sweat. A glass of iced tea would be nice. Remember, cold summer salads keep the kitchen cooler than boiled potatoes. So heap on the greens and pass the fat-free dressing.

JULY 10, 1999

Vacation means more than just booking a ticket: First, make a list

by Glenn Haege,
America's Master Handyman

School's out. The car companies have scheduled vacation breaks. The Highway Department has al their orange barrels in place. It must be time to get the kids and dog in the car and start gallivanting. Here are some things to do before you take off.

First, make provision for pets if your household is so blessed. Clearly, they can't all fit in the car and boarding them can be a logistical and financial nightmare. Leaving them home alone is cruel, even if a neighbor promises to check on them two or three times a day. Seriously consider employing a house sitter.

Every year thousands of homeowners come back from a week at the beach to find their home flooded by a water connection that sprang a leak. If you don't have a lawn sprinkler system or water powered back-up sump pump, the easiest way to make sure that leaks don't happen to you is to turn off the water at the meter.

If you have equipment in your home that needs water pressure to function, you can get the same security by turning off the water valves at all the major water hookups: commodes, sinks and water heater. Be sure to turn off both the hot and cold water.

If you have a dehumidifier in the basement unplug it.

While you're in the basement, turn back the thermostat on the water heater. The water tank is one of the biggest energy users in your home and this will save a bundle.

There is a temptation to turn off the central air conditioning while you're away. Bad idea. Letting your house become hot and humid is an invitation for mold, mildew and musties to move in. They are real problem guests. Turn the thermostat up to 80 degrees. That's warm enough to save on electricity, but the air conditioner will still be at work dehumidifying the house.

The trick to maintaining that lived-in look is to set lots of timers to turn on/off at different times of the day and night. Include all the rooms: kitchens, bathrooms, bedrooms, the family room. Everywhere that you would normally go, should have light and sound on at the time of day you would normally be there. Turn the radio to talk stations. Turn the volume up a little higher than you would normally have it if you were actually in the room. You want someone standing outside the house to be able to hear voices coming from inside.

Stop newspaper and mail deliveries, or alternatively, have a neighbor pick them up and stack them inside the house on a daily basis.

Speaking of neighbors, be sure to tell the neighbors that you will be away for a while. Give them the telephone number of the person you have delegated to look after the house and ask them to call him or her and the police if they see a problem developing.

Ask one of your neighbors to park in your driveway every night so that it looks like someone is home. Also tell them who'll be picking up your mail and checking on the gold fish. You don't want the poor guy reported to the police for breaking and entering.

Ask the person who is checking the inside of your house to check all the rooms, especially the kitchen to check all the rooms, especially the kitchen and baths. If the water is still on, you could be developing a leak. If you have left food in the refrigerator and freezer, they should check to make certain that the units are still functioning.

This individual should also have your itinerary and know how to contact you if a problem arises.

If you have an automatic lawn sprinkling system, ask that the sprinkler be turned off when it is raining. Better still, get a rain gauge that automatically turns off the sprinkler if there has been substantial rainfall. Call your sprinkler installer or pick up the Mini Clik II Rain Sensor from Premier Distributors, (810) 228-5400. It costs $35.95 and they say it is very easy to install.

Make certain that someone is cutting and trimming the grass.

Finally, call your local police and tell them exactly how long you will be gone and whom to contact if there is a problem.

Be sure to get a pound of Mackinaw fudge for everyone who has helped you. I know this works.

Vacation checklist
Pets: Make provisions for pets.
Water: Turn off water at meter. Turn down the temperature of the water heater
Air conditioning: Set air conditioning thermostat up to 80 degrees
Electricity: Set timers at different schedules for lights, TV, and talk radio stations. Unplug all major electric appliances except refrigerator and freezer
Deliveries: Stop newspaper and mail delivery or arrange for someone to pick them up daily. Also check for UPS.
Neighbors: Let neighbors on both sides and across the street know you will be away for awhile. Make arrangements with a neighbor to check the lawn sprinkler so that it is not watering while it is raining. Also, ask a neighbor to park a car in your driveway, and cut and trim the lawn if you don't have a lawn service.
Police: Call police and tell them you will be away.

JULY 17, 1999

Figure out whether it's better to move, or to improve your home

by Glenn Haege,
America's Master Handyman

Sure, you've been in your house long enough to have built up a substantial equity. The interest rates are historically low, but beginning to move upward. Nevertheless, moving is not always the answer. There are still a lot of things you have to consider before hanging up the "For Sale" sign.

Do a detailed analysis of what has given you the moving bug. Do you like your present house but want to move because the kitchen is out of date or need an extra bath or bedroom?

Sometimes the core reason is the need for a home office or a family room for the kids. Perhaps a mother or father has to move in with you for health reasons.

According to the National Association of Home Builders, the average single family house in America is 28 years old. The average home size has grown from 1,400 or 1,500 square feet to over 2,000. Design concepts that were not even thought about back then, are all the rage now.

Back then, one or one and a half baths was the norm. Today, you see two or three baths in most model homes and the master bath will feature a whirlpool tub and a huge preparation area.

Kitchens are bigger. They are laid out to be entertainment as well as work areas with lots of extra counter, pantry and cabinet space. Floor plans are more airy. Cathedral ceilings and ornate floor-to-ceiling window treatments are in.

If you live in a house built in the '70s or earlier, just visiting a new model can make you feel deprived. That's the dilemma. At least 50 percent of us live in out dated housing.

On the other hand, you moved to your present area because you liked it. That like may now be a full-fledged love affair. You and the family are established in the community, schools and churches. The same, relatively low, interest rates that are luring many folks into new home purchases also make it a good time to refinance and use the money to make needed home improvements.

Deciding whether to move into a new house or make your present house into the home of your dreams is a tough decision.

Here are some pointers.
■ Decide what you really want. Is it a large master bedroom, bath and kitchen? Do you need to add a mother-in-law addition so that a loved one can move in, yet still have a sense of being independent and not intrude on your privacy?
OK write it down.

■ Find out how much it would cost to update your house to make it fill your needs.

■ Find out what your home is worth today just as it is. Take what a good real estate agent says and reduce it by 15 percent to 20 percent. This should get you down to within shooting distance of the actual sale price, less sales commissions, improvements needed to bring the house up to code, and moving expenses.

■ Add the net value of the house to the amount needed to make your present house into the home of your dreams. You now have the Value Added Price of your present home.

■ Go shopping. You may find a beautifully decorated house nearby that has everything you want, and is selling for $10 or $20,000 less than the Value Added Price of your present house.

On the other hand, the new or used housing that meets your requirements, might be $50,000 more than the Value Added Price.

■ Compare the Value Added Price of your present house to what you've found shopping.

■ Have a family council. You may decide that it doesn't matter how much more it costs to renovate, you want to stay put. Every business has a certain added value put on the books for "good will." That good will has value when it comes to your house too. "Nice neighbors" or "close to the park" has to be worth $5 or $10,000.

On the other hand, you may decide economics don't really matter. You just want something "Exciting and new." That's an OK reason to move. Whatever you decide, you've done your homework.

Next week: If you decide to sell, there are things you need to be sure to do before you list your house.

Want to sell your home? First, get moving on this list of chores

by Glenn Haege,
America's Master Handyman

Deciding to sell your house is not something you should rush into. Even if you can sell your house in a day, there will still be a lot of hard work getting the house ready to sell and your family ready to move.

You will make more money and have an easier time if you put your faith in hard work and careful planning rather than luck.

Six months before you want to list your house, start going to open houses. Look at what the sellers have done to make their house more interesting and spend time with the sales agents. Make a list of the agents who go out of their way to show special features and try hard to sell the home. If they will do it for your neighbor's house, they will do it for your house too.

Now comes the hard part.

Outside
You can't sell a house if potential buyers drive by and don't walk in. Curb appeal is important.

The spring of the year you list your house pay special attention to the front yard. A couple hundred dollars in artistically arranged plants can pay for themselves 10 or 20 times over when it comes time to sell.

Side and back yards should look cared for, but are not the place for maximum effort.

If it's the fall, do an especially good clean up job. Trim everything that should be trimmed. Rake every nook and cranny. Make the yard look well cared for.

The same thing holds true for the outside of the house. Start with the roof and go all the way down to the foundation. The goal is not to make big changes, just make what you have look the best it can be.

Old worn-out shingles are a turnoff. You may not want to replace them, but you want a written quote on how much replacement cost would be. I'll get into the reason for that later.

If you haven't power washed the exterior of your house for several years (how about ever?) this may be the year. Krud Kutter House Wash by Supreme Chemical, (800) 466-7126, is a good general purpose cleaner. It will even kill moss and mildew. Alumin-Nu, (800) 899-7097, makes both aluminum and vinyl siding cleaners.

Freshen up the trim. Make certain the front door makes a statement. Polish the brass. Wash the windows. These are just little things, but very important.

Inside

The kitchen and bath are the heart and lungs of the home. Money previously invested updating these two rooms will be returned when you sell.

If your kitchen looks grungy, my Handyman article of March 20, 1999 gave step-by-step instructions on how to make a kitchen look beautiful economically. If you are on the internet, you can access this article at either www.detnews.com or my Master Handyman Help Site, www.masterhandyman.com.

Make the rest of the home look and smell squeaky clean and uncluttered. Anything you don't want to move, get rid of now.

Carpets, walls and cabinetry make big impressions.

Clean the carpets. If you have dogs, cats kill the odor with Smells Be Gone by Punati Chemical, (800) 645-2882. If the carpets really look old and ratty and you don't want to replace them, get a quote on how much new carpeting would cost.

A good washing will make dirty walls look fresh. Mix 2 ounces dry measure of Tri-sodium Phosphate (TSP) and water. Dirtex is another good wall washing product. Both products are made by the Savogran Company, (800) 225-9872.

Furniture and cabinetry should look clean and shinny. Doozy Furniture Polish, (888) 851-8500, makes getting and keeping a gloss finish easy. It is the secret weapon many furniture stores use to keep their furniture looking beautiful with no fingerprints.

Get a house inspection. It shows you care. A glowing written report that you or your real estate agent can show potential buyers is a great selling tool.

If the inspector finds big problems, don't try to hide them. Either fix them or get written quotes on necessary repairs. Your real estate agent can use the quotes you have collected to add realism to final negotiations and get you a better selling price.

You've worked hard. Sit down, relax and reflect. The house looks so good do you really want to move? If you do, selling should be easy. Put up the sign. Make the sale and brag about it!

Seller's checklist

Roof: This is the first thing buyers see. Clean off debris. Patch cracks. If shingles are bad, you may have to replace or be prepared for a substantial decrease in the selling price

Exterior: You may just have to clean the paint and touch up the trim. Take special care with the front door. Wash windows and repair any damage to the screens.

Front yard: It's too late to re-sod, but use summer fertilizer. Flowers, mulch and wood chips cost little, but give a "cared for" look.

Kitchen and baths: These are the most important rooms. Brighten hardware. Clean cabinets, countertops and appliance exteriors. Repaint cabinet doors.

Rest of interior: Make glass brilliant. Polish all furniture. Clean carpets. Wash walls. Remove clutter.

There is an art to taking care of hardwood floors

by Glenn Haege,
America's Master Handyman

Taking care of hardwood flooring is a lost art. Most of us were brought up in a sea of wall-to-wall carpeting with occasional islands of vinyl and tile. We are unprepared when old carpet is removed and we discover a hardwood treasure trove.

Recently, Kathleen, my editor at Master Handyman Press, had the hardwood floors refinished in a small house she owns. The house was about 50 years old and the floors had never been desecrated by carpet tack strips. Originally she thought that carpeting the floors of a rental house would be more practical, but looking at the battered but beautiful old floors, she couldn't bring herself to pound nails into them.

Instead, she sent an SOS to Jim Moody at Paynter Floors in Nov., (800) 471-9091. They are the folks that did the floor I have pictured on the cover of my hardwood floor care book. I consider them, along with G and G Floors, (800) 806-1798, Cameron the Sand Man, (248) 477-8108, and Dance Hardwood Floor Co., (800) 522-7701 to be among the top floor finishers in our area.

While they sometimes cost a little more because they insist on doing the job right, as a consumer, that's OK by me.

Paynter also gives each customer a hardwood information-and-care package that Moody has assembled over the years. Moody let me condense the highlights in this article.

Finish selection

Designers love light, bleached, or white/pastel-stained hardwood floors. Many homeowners become disenchanted with these finishes because the flooring often has a splotchy look caused by the differing absorption levels of various pieces of wood. Also when the wood becomes dry, dark cracks appear. These cracks are a natural phenomena and will disappear with a change in humidity but are far more obvious in bleached or white/pastel-stained wood.

Modern homeowners have their choice of oil-based urethane or water-based urethane. Although the newer waterborne finishes are easier to apply and create a very hard surface, they are as clear as a glass of water. This lack of pigmentation gives hardwood a different appearance than the slightly ambered look most people are used to. The clear finish also highlights imperfections in the wood.

Waterborne finishes are far thinner than oil-based urethane. According to Moody, this means that it takes four coats of waterborne finish to provide the protection wood receives from two coats of an oil-based product. Since time is money, a four coat finish often costs one or two dollars a square foot more than the traditional urethane finish.

Moody said that his company's finish of choice is Basic Coatings Wood Floor Finish Oil-Modified Urethane Satin.

Before refinishing

Moody recommends that homeowners do the following immediately before their hardwood floors are refinished.

Remove all furniture, pictures and wall hangings from room.

Drape plastic or sheets over openings leading to other parts of the house since sanding creates a great deal of dust.

If the room has an entrance leading out of the house, place a small box fan in the doorway. Set the fan on low and aim it to blow out of house.

After refinishing

Even though the refinishers are constantly sweeping and vacuuming, there will still be a good deal of dust on the walls and ceilings. The temptation is to grab buckets of water and frantically start washing. DON'T DO IT! After the finish is thoroughly dry, vacuum the walls and ceilings.

Furniture can be replaced 24 hours after job is completed. However Moody recommends waiting two weeks before placing rugs and other floor coverings on new finish.

Preventative maintenance

Dirt and grit are hardwood floorings worst enemies. Use dirt-trapping, walk-off mats at all exterior doors to help prevent dirt, grit and sand from getting inside the building. Keep doormats clean. Use throw rugs just inside of entrances to trap the remainder.

Hardwood chemicals oxidize in strong light causing the wood to change color. To avoid an uneven appearance, move area rugs occasionally and drape or shade large west-facing windows.

Put fabric-faced glides on the legs of all furniture. They will allow furniture to be moved easily without scuffing the floor. Clean glides regularly to keep grit from becoming imbeded in fabric. Change ball type casters to barrel type roller casters to avoid damaging wood. Gray, non-marking rubber casters are best. Avoid any type of plastic caster.

Sweep or dust mop daily and vacuum at least two or three times a week. Never use a household spray dust treatment.

Wipe up spills promptly with a dry cloth, tissue or paper toweling.

For general cleaning add 1/2 cup of white vinegar to 1 gallon of water and damp, not wet, mop. You can also use Bona Kemi Floor Cleaner. Dip clean cloth or sponge mop into water, wring nearly dry, and clean floor. Wipe dry with a 100 percent cotton towel immediately. My wife Barbara prefers to clean our hardwood floors by spraying non ammonia window cleaner on the surface and damp mopping.

Never wax a hardwood finish. Once waxed, the floor cannot be merely buffed and recoated but will have to be completely sanded down to raw wood to restore the finish.

Larry Vernier of Paynter Floors in Novi removes the old finish from a hardwood floor is an art. This is an art because if the operator pauses for just a few seconds with the drum engaged, the powerful drum sander can dig into the wood and ruin the job.

Summer is perfect for do-it-yourself caulking job

by Glenn Haege,
America's Master Handyman

Those lazy, crazy, hazy days of summer are a perfect time for the do-it-yourselfer to caulk. Sealing all the cracks and crevices around your home now will keep drafts, dust, dirt, water and insects from entering later.

We all know that we have to caulk. That paint job isn't done, the gutters aren't hung, and that exterior light isn't really installed, until all the cracks, crevices, and joints are sealed. Ditto with the plumbing repairs, the windows or countertop installation. Caulking and seam sealing are vital steps in many projects.

The good news is caulks are now better than ever. They last longer, apply easier and match the surface to which they are being applied. The bad news is that you can go to the caulk and sealant section of any hardware store or home center and find so many tubes of 'stuff' that all you'll get is confused.

Don't worry. If you are not a caulking whiz now, you will be by the end of this article.

Caulking choices

There are three basic types of caulking compounds for do-it-yourselfers: latex/acrylics, silicones, and combinations.

Latex/acrylics have a lot going for them. They are durable, easy to use, fast drying, can be coated with paint with no problem, and when the job is done soap and water clean up is all you need. Once their service life is over, latex/acrylic caulks are relatively easy to remove.

One of the leading makers of latex/acrylic caulks is United Gilsonite Laboratories, (800) 272-3235.

Silicone caulks are more finicky. Good surface preparation is a must. You cannot paint them, but pre-tinted or clear caulks are available. They have excellent flexibility, superior durability, and will stand up to extreme weather and temperature conditions. Once silicone caulks are on, they stay stuck practically forever. Getting them on is relatively easy. Getting them off is next to impossible. Clean up should be with alcohol or mineral spirits.

GE (800) 255-8886, is one of today's leading makers of silicone sealants. Dow Silicone by DAP, (800) 543-3840, was the grand daddy of all silicones. This innovative company is now leading the way with aerosol spray caulks that do not require a caulking gun

DAP and OSI, (800) 624-7767, make both latex/acrylics and silicones. Almost all manufacturers now make some form of siliconized latex/acrylic caulks which seek to combine the benefits of both.

After you decide between latex/acrylic and silicone your next decision is between a general purpose and a job specific caulk. I usually choose a job specific caulk.

Many of the manufacturers offer so many caulking choices it can get confusing. OSI gives specific product recommendations for over 40 different caulking jobs on their web site. Since they make both types of caulks, they recommend latex/acrylic when they think it is best for the particular job.

GE has web-based Surface Adhesion Tables showing which products adhere best on specific metal, plastic, masonry, wood and glass surfaces. Their Silicone II brand is the hands down winner on almost every surface.

DAP has a very innovative web do-it-yourself house that gives instructions and product recommendations at the click of a mouse.

What should be caulked?

GE recommends a "caulk walk" around the house inspecting everything that's mounted to your home or enters the house. That includes spigots, windows, vents, TV and phone cables, air-conditioning lines, siding connections and the line where the siding meets the foundation as well as along side chimneys.

On the inside of the house you should caulk windows, counters and countertops, sinks, bathtubs, tub enclosures, around pipes, miscellaneous openings and plumbing.

Surface Preparation

For Latex/Acrylic caulks clear away old caulk, wash down with a good cleaner and air dry.

For Silicone caulks, GE recommends that concrete, masonry & stone have all old sealant and dirt removed with a wire brush and all contaminants such as water repellents and surface treatments removed. Porous surfaces should be sanded. Metal, glass and plastic should be cleaned with solvents such as mineral spirits and alcohol, then wiped dry with a clean cloth or lintless paper toweling. Solvents should never be allowed to air dry without wiping.

Application

A good caulking gun and a gentle hand are key ingredients. Paying a little extra for your caulking gun will make a big difference in the quality of the job.

Cut the tip of the caulk cylinder on a 45-degree angle and load it into the gun. Then use either the push or pull method of application. In pushing you inject the bead in front of the gun. In pulling you reverse the gun and trail caulk after the gun. Pushing applies caulk more deeply into the crevices. Pulling is often the only way rough surfaces can be caulked.

Whichever method you choose, GE recommends that you apply as narrow a bead as possible because you can always apply more caulk, but removing surplus caulk can be a big problem.

When you're done, brag about it!

Sources

For more information, check out these caulk and sealant web sites:

■ Advanced Coating Systems, www.advanced-coatings.com/product.htm has information on 100 percent acrylic flashing grade caulks.
■ DAP house, www.dap.com, gives how-to and product tips for every part of the house
■ GE Silicones, www.ge.com/silicones/sealants/diy, gives step-by-step instructions on how-to projects in their home project library.
■ OSI Sealants, www.osisealants.com, has specific product recommendations for over 40 jobs.
■ UGL (United Gilsonite Laboratories), www.ugl.com/caulk, tells which products are best.
■ Adhesives & Sealants Industry Magazine, www.adhesivesmag.com, has hot links to the magazine's advertisers to help you track down elusive products.

Glenn Haege pulls Washington's chain on 1.6-gallon flush toilets

by Glenn Haege,
America's Master Handyman

Photos by Rob David

Glenn Haege has a Capitol idea and takes his case to the U.S. House of Representatives.

Tuesday, July 27, I was your man in Washington and testified before the US House of Representatives, Commerce Committee Subcommittee on Energy and Power. As an individual citizen it was a big moment in my life. Part of me wished my mom and dad could see me in the halls of power.

As a taxpayer it made me angry that I and a lot of other people, as well as powerful members of the US Congress, were wasting time and money arguing about what should be a non-issue. Rep. Joe Knollenberg (R-Michigan) was trying to get the government out of our toilets.

Several months ago Rep. Knollenberg asked if I would accept an invitation to testify before the Subcommittee in favor of House Bill, H.R. 623. I jumped at the chance.

For the past several years, Rep. Knollenberg has introduced legislation to amend a 1992 law which federally mandated the reduction of toilet water tanks to 1.6 gallons. The same legislation reduced the flow rate of faucets and showerheads to 2.5 gallons a minute.

Knollenberg's bill does not seek to reverse the legislation, merely permit citizens the right to choose between a low-flow and a regular flow appliance.

I have no financial interest in the outcome of the legislation, nor am I a spokesman for a lobbying group. The reason for my involvement is that as soon as the low-flow rate legislation took effect, I started getting phone calls from homeowners complaining about their new toilets and what they perceived to be plumbing and water pressure problems caused by low-flow shower heads and faucets.

I also studied the matter enough to be concerned about the possible long-term health risks involved with fine mist showerheads. Filling my lungs with a fine diluted chlorine mist is not my idea of a good time.

On a purely personal level I get angry that my government should have the audacity to try to strong arm me into using an ineffective toilet or a shower head that doesn't even get my body wet.

A few years ago, I asked readers and listeners to write "Get the Government out of my toilet" on a piece of toilet paper and send it to their representative. I also interviewed Rep. Knollenberg on the air and wrote a story about the legislation. This combined to make me known as a "commode activist."

A majority of the Subcommittee members present for the hearing made opening remarks in favor of the Bill. Rep. Richard Burr of North Carolina went so far as to read his statement from a roll of toilet tissue.

Knollenberg reported that 10,000 pieces of toilet paper and letters had been sent to Congress calling for changes in the current legislation. Knollenberg's bill is so popular that 82 representatives have signed on as co-sponsors.

When I walked into the Committee Room in the Rayburn House Office Building, I felt a little like David in David and Goliath. Arrayed against Jerry Kosmensky, a local builder and mayor of Orchard Lake, and myself were George Whalen, representing the Plumbing-Heating-Cooling Contractors National Association; David Goike of Masco, representing the Plumbing Manufacturers Institute; and Edward Osann, president of Potomac Resources, Inc. a lobbying group for the National Wildlife Federation, Sierra Club, and Friends of the Earth, among others.

In testimony against H.R. 623, Masco's Goike cited a report entitled, "Saving Water, Saving Dollars," "documenting a 15 percent savings of interior residential water use by the use of 1.6 gallons per flush (gpf) water closets ... and a reduction of ... as much as 30 percent of interior, residential water use, if all plumbing product provisions of EPAct

'92 are applied along with the use of new, more efficient clothes washers."

He also pointed out that if the Federal law mandating 1.6 gallon toilets were reversed, different levels of government might set their own standards causing price increases in plumbing products.

When it came time for Jerry Kosmensky to testify he told the Subcommittee that many of the people for whom he built houses had accused him of installing inferior toilets and fixtures because the toilets didn't function properly and required at least two flushes; the showers didn't shower; and the faucets released water so slowly that buyers thought their houses had water pressure problems.

I testified that I received many calls from consumers complaining that regular gravity feed 1.6 gallon toilets didn't work; that the only 1.6 gallon toilets I knew worked were equipped with rather expensive vacuum-flush systems from Masco's WC Technology or Sloan Flushmate; and that having to flush two or three times to get the job done was not my idea of saving water.

If you want more information, there is a more detailed coverage on the bill and the testimony of the various witnesses on my web site: www.masterhandyman.com.

After the Subcommittee listened to our weighty arguments Congress adjourned for their summer recess. If you want to regain your freedom of choice on toilets, shower heads and faucets, it is not too late to write "Get the government out of my toilet. Support H.R. 623," and send it to your congressman or woman. Then brag about it!

Hanging out at the hardware show gives glimpses into the future

by Glenn Haege,
America's Master Handyman

Chicago

I just returned from the 54th. Annual National Hardware Show at the McCormick Place complex August 15 - 18. Parking was a bear, but about 70,000 of us had a wonderful time checking out the 3,000 exhibits that covered what is and what will be.

The show is the hardware/how-to industry's greatest collection of new products and ideas. Rarified prognosticators see the show from a bird's eye view and discern industry trends. Working the miles of floor, I just see a bunch of neat stuff. Some is available today. Some will be available tomorrow, maybe.

That's how I've divided my Hardware Show reporting. This week I'll cover new things you can get right now. Next week, we'll report about tomorrow, with the full understanding that, for some products, tomorrow never comes.

The Swivel Dust Mop by Space Invader makes it easy to reach way under difficult-to-move objects. The flexible nylon/fiberglass composite extension bends to go in any direction.

Cleaning products

Starting small, Simple Green, (800) 228-0709, has just come out with Simple Green Antibacterial Kitchen & Bathroom Cleaner/Disinfectant. The new cleaner cleans like Simple but also kills a broad spectrum of common household bacteria including Salmonella, E. coli, Staphylococcus, and Streptococcus. The manufacturers say the new product is a safer alternative to hazardous household disinfectants. It is already being shipped to Ace Hardware stores. Look for it everywhere Simple Green is sold.

The Quickie folks introduced their model #071 Floor Cleaner. A very versatile foam-backed swivel mop that uses disposable magnetic cloths to clean hardwood floors and other hard surfaces. Used after sweeping or vacuuming, it needs no water and deep cleans surface grime.

Space Invader Cleaning Products, (800) 343-3368, have two new pivoting sponge mops that pivot in almost any direction to clean behind and around toilets, appliances and counters. Their new swiveling, telescoping dust mop will reach 87 inches in any direction to dust under and around anything.

Kitchens and baths

Decora North America, (877) 353-6410, just introduced peel and stick, black and white contact sheets. In white they transform any old cork board or solid surface area into a dry erase Memo Board. Notes made in Dry Erase marker just wipe off. Black sheets turn old corkboards into chalk boards.

If you love you kitchen but lust after labor saving Lazy Susans and pull out shelving, Knape & Vogt has got you covered. They now supply the Do-It-Yourselfer almost all modern cabinet features: Cutlery and Spice Drawer inserts, Slide Out Waste and Under-sink Baskets, Pull Out Shelving, Lazy Susans and Half-Moon shelving that makes inaccessible cabinets useable. These DIY items could save you $10,000 or $20,000 in remodeling bills. They are available by special order at Home Depot or call Superior Distributing for a catalogue, (800) 622-4462.

On a more mundane level, the Plunger Pal by Western Slope Designs, is available by mail order, (877) 206-1937. A necessity for 1.6-gallon toilet owners, this plunger sized bucket has a locking lid that keeps the yucky stuff out of sight and off the floor. All you see is the plunger handle coming out of a small plastic bucket.

Plumbing and heating
Does your house suffer from clogged drains? Starting this Sunday, August 22, Ted Funger Enterprises (877) 654-4077, will be selling the AquaPlumber water pressure drain cleaner for $29.99 on QVC cable.

If a Kerosene heater is in your Y2K plans, W.M. Barr, (800) 238-2672, has introduced Exxon Clear Lite, Odorless Synthetic Fuel. The product costs four times as much as regular kerosene but has no odor or soot.

Outdoors and in
Most of us do not have a problem with asbestos or lead-based paint. But if you do, it could be life threatening. For product information on barrier technologies that can protect your family call Fiberlock Technologies, Inc., (800) 342-3755.

On a less lethal note, if your concrete patio or porch is dull and boring, DecoArt, has listened to your prayers and brought forth Patio Paint. This faux finish product lets you create a brick,

stone or rock design on concrete or wood. The sample didn't really look like brick, but it did look like fun. Patio Paint is available mail order from Artist Brush and Color, (800) 828-0359.

For folks who like to sculpt metal in their spare time, Hobart Welders has a complete line of DIY welders and plasma cutters that have professional power but are in the $500 to $1000 range. To learn more, call (800) 626-9420.

If woodpeckers or other flying fiends are driving you crazy, Weitech's Electronic Outdoor Yard & Garden Protector has a built-in motion sensor that detects the feathered intruder and sends out a heart-stopping series of distress calls letting the critter know that it is time to get out of Dodge. For more information call (800) 343-2659.

It is time for me to get out of Dodge, too. See you next week with Tomorrow's Finds from the Hardware Show.

Aquaplumber uses water pressure to clear slow, sluggish and clogged drains in minutes. All you have to do is attach the hose connection to the faucet, then put the Aquaplumber over your drain and turn on the water.

Get a peek of the niftiest hardware products of tomorrow today

by Glenn Haege,
America's Master Handyman

Every time I visit the National Hardware, Housewares, or Home Builders shows I find myself singing my own version of Charles Strouse and Martin Charnin's show stopper "Tomorrow". My version goes like this:

"Bet your bottom dollar
these products will come your way,
Tomorrow, tomorrow,
There's always tomorrow.
It's only a day away."

Many of the most exciting products are "only a day away." Some will ship October first. Some will be in Limbo for years. I classify them all as "tomorrow products."

Mirrored acrylic bevel strips from Millennium International Development, attach to the edges of an ordinary bathroom mirror and give it the look of expensive beveled glass.

Here are some of the National Hardware Show's nifty "tomorrow products".

Bathrooms

The big toilet manufacturer, American Standard, (800) 223-0068, will release the Smart Valve 2000 and Smartparts Flapper Replacement Kits in the next 90 days. Designed to help extend the life of 3.5 gallon toilets, the new flushing system is whisper quiet, has water-saving capabilities and installs in minutes.

Should person or persons unknown forget to put the toilet seat down in your house, HydraGlide's Considerate Seat, (800) 257-7844, will do the job for them. It stays up for four minutes, then slowly closes. Considerate Seat ships October 1.

Loose toilet seats cause premature replacement. Ginsey Industries' Toilet Seat Tightening Kit solves the problem with special washers and a plastic wrench. Each kit will tighten three seats. It starts shipping October first.

Big bathroom mirrors are susceptible to water damage which blackens the bottom of the mirror. The Millennium International Development Corporation, (800) 757-2990, has developed the Mirr.Edge. The kit consists of self-stick, mirrored acrylic bevel strips that attach to the edge of the mirror. The product masks the discoloration and makes the mirror look like beveled glass. The company is trying to get distribution but my advice is to try mail order.

In three seconds, small fry can sustain third degree burns from 140 degree water. The Idea Factory, (800) 867-4673,

My Own Shower child showerhead from The Idea Factory senses dangerously hot water and decreases the flow to a trickle until water temperature is brought down to 98 degrees Fahrenheit.

is introducing My Own Shower child showerhead. It senses dangerously hot water and decreases flow to a trickle until the temperature is brought down to 98 degrees Fahrenheit. My Own Shower is shaped like a frog. It attaches to an adult shower via a hose that brings it down to child level.

Whole house

Energy-efficient houses can be so tight they develop sick house syndrome. We try to solve the problem with air infiltrators. Dr. Sea Park of A-Tech Enterprise Corp. has a new concept. His USAccuSensor Oxy-2000 is a window air conditioner-sized device that continuously tests, humidifies, and filters the air. When the Oxy-2000 senses less than an optimum Oxygen level it starts making Oxygen and releasing it into the home. Production details are not yet finalized. Stay tuned.

The combination of combustible vapors from paint thinner, gasoline or mineral spirits and a natural gas water heater can be deadly. The new Flame Guard water tank safety system from the American Water Heater Company, (423) 283-8138, has a specially designed combustion chamber and flame trap to help prevent combustible gas fires. The first to have this safety feature will be 40-gallon American PROline, Envi-ro-temp and U.S. Craftmaster water heaters. Shipping date is October 1.

Gouging a hole in linoleum or vinyl used to be a real problem. Crew Inc., (800) 490-2001, has just developed the Floor Saver Linoleum Repair Kit. It patches a quarter-sized hole in 15 minutes. John and Jim from Damman's seemed impressed. Let's hope.

Just one squirt of Dourmar Products' new Un-du Candle Wax Remover releases the bond between candle wax and any surface.

continued on next page

481

These new MiraVista shingles by Owens Corning look like cedar shakes but are really composites. They have a Class A Fire rating and can withstand winds up to 80 mph.

Dourmar Products, (888) 389-8638, has a new Un-du Candle Wax Remover that should be in the pipe line soon.

W.M. Barr & Co, (800) 782-9926, is introducing Citristrip Aerosol Paint & Varnish Remover. The product's foam spray hangs tough on vertical surfaces. It should be in hardware stores and home centers within 30 to 90 days.

Messaging Products, (888) 467-2776, has a wonderful 8-inch-long parrot refrigerator magnet that holds a 20-second voice message. Attention all moms: this is so much fun it will make the kids want to listen.

Outside

American Metal Products the Gutter Helmet people, (888) 4-HELMET, developed a new paintable, metal exterior trim that masks gutters beautifully. It should be available next Spring.

Owens Corning is introducing the MiraVista line of composite shingles made to look like slate, tile, and cedar shakes. They look real without the weight and have a 50-year warranty. First introduced in California, I'm pushing to make Michigan next. Call (800) 438-7465, if you'd like to see MiraVista in Michigan soon.

There is nothing more necessary than a garden hose. Swan, (800) 848-8707, is introducing Hoselink, a revolutionary new, non-leaking hose and hose fast-connecting system.

Want to clean and seal your deck or fence with just a water hose? The Griffin Corporation, (877) 747-NOAH, and DuPont have teamed up to introduce the Noah Deck & Fence Renewal System. Noah's handy spray top attachment lets you clean, rinse and coat the wood by just dialing the AutoJet selector.

Next Spring, Ducks Back, (800) 825-5382, will introduce Super Deck transparent concrete stain. The industry's first transparent concrete stain, it will have a faux finish look that resists chemical discoloration and tire burn.

Last on my list, GrassMasters (888) 810-5050, will introduce two very creative three-in-one products. The Work Station is a gas-powered 3000 Watt generator, a 1,750 pounds per square inch power washer, and a 4000 gallons per hour water pump. The Trail Boss changes from a sickle bar mower, to a snow plow, to a garden tiller. Both pack a lot of versatility into very little space.

All lawn and garden products should be in stores next Spring.

Detroit has banner year for home fix-ups

by Glenn Haege,
America's Master Handyman

Well it's the Labor Day Weekend. Time for all us hard working folk to take the day off, kick back and enjoy the fruit of our labors – especially those of us in the hardware/home center/construction trades/and do-it-yourself business. For all of us it has been a very good year.

To cite just one statistic, David Koenig, the editor of Building Products Digest, say the demand for Gypsum Drywall is three times that of what it was in the building boom of the 1980's. Three times!

Every piece of drywall took someone to make it, someone to put it up, someone to skim coat it, someone to paint it. Then add those very important someones who manufacture and install the hardware, electrical, doors and windows connected to that drywall and it has been a very good year indeed.

As many of us as possible will take a breather this weekend, then start banging away until Christmas. There is no shortage of jobs, just people and supplies to complete them.

Detroit has always been a great town, but now it is being recognized by more home improvement industry leaders. This can only make it better for those of us who live and work here.

Here are three things on my list of good things happening around here:

1. This past year, Home Depot decided that Metro Detroit had so much business potential its local stores will soon have their own buying office. For any of you not in the know, that is like declaring the Metro Detroit market its own country.

2. Lowe's Home Improvement Warehouse is coming to town. Lowe's is second only to Home Depot. Home Depot has greater sales and profits than any other home center chain, but Lowe's is known for super competitive prices. Put on your gloves, boys, and come out to the center of the ring. No kicking. No gouging. Fight fair.

3. To add a little more zest, Wal-Mart is planning to increase the number of stores in Metro Detroit. Not just one or two stores but all over. Meijer, too, is adding new stores and introducing an even stronger, more vigorous marketing plan for their paint and hard goods departments. Think about it – 24-hour convenience in what could well be the most competitive market in the country.

You and I have ring-side seats for what could be the fight of the new century.

You want to buy paint? I'll show you paint. You want to buy doors, or tools, or any other thing the DIY-er drools over? Just hold tight, listen to my radio show and read your weekly circulars.

Detroit consumers should benefit from all this competition with more opportunities, better selection, more competitive pricing and hopefully better service.

SEPTEMBER 11, 1999

Top off your house in style

Today's Materials Can Give You A Permanent Roof That Looks Great

by Glenn Haege,
America's Master Handyman

So ya want a new roof? What'll it be – shingle, high dimensional laminate, cedar, slate, composite, tile, concrete, steel, or aluminum?

Did you want that with a 20-, 30-, 40-, 50-year, or lifetime warranty? How about the fire and the wind rating?

It doesn't matter whether you are designing a new house or have an older home, sooner or later you have to make a roofing decision. There have never been as many choices as you have now. Many of them have just been developed in the past few years.

"The first two things people see when they are looking for a house are the landscaping and the roof," says Gary Newville of Birmingham's Hall and Hunter Realtors. "If you can add a dimensional look to the roof, go for it. People are spending so much for a house these days that they want the look of cedar or slate."

According to Owens Corning, 90 percent of the homes still have shingle roofs. But more than a third of these are the more expensive high definition two ply shingles.

Nationally, high end roofing is the second most popular upgrade in new construction today. According to Joe Aiello, president of Pine Building Company in Farmington Hills, this is because "the homeowner gets a better look with the high end dimensional shingle and it lasts twice as long as a regular roof."

Adds John Bolton of Concrete Tile Roofing, Inc., of Walled Lake, Time is very precious to these people and the last thing they want to do is waste time on upkeep, when for just a little bit more they can have a permanent roof."

Roofing materials comparison

	Cost per square	Est. cost for 2,000 SF	Benefits
Asphalt and fiberglass One-ply shingles	$15–$225	$3,750-$5625	Least expensive; easy to install; 20-year warranty
Two ply laminated shingles	$25–$350	$6,250-$8750	Deep shadow line; double the life of single ply
Deluxe Cedar	$400	$10,000*	Classic wood look; natural product
Concrete tile	$500–$1,200	$12,500-$30,000	Prestige look; no maintenance; lifetime warranty
Metal and composite Aluminum Rustic Shake	$400	$10,000	Classic look; light weight; installed over previous roof; 50-year warranty
Most composite shakes	$400	$10,000	Classic look; 50-year warranty; environmentally friendly

*Estimated $225/square for labor

All these influences fell into play when Jerry Berhorst and his wife were looking for a home. They fell in love with a cedar-roofed ranch in West Bloomfield.

"The cedar roof was one of the primary things that sold us on the home," Berhorst said. We had the roof inspected very thoroughly and were assured that it was in good condition." But less than three years later, they needed a new roof.

"We first explored getting another cedar roof because we love the look. But in doing the research I found out that to maintain our cedar roof properly would cost about $3,000 ever three years, or $1,000 a year. That was too much.

To maintain the cedar look but not have the constant maintenance, the Berhorsts chose a cedar shake design concrete tile installed by Concrete Tile Roofing, Inc. of Walled Lake, (248) 669-3409. The Tiles were made by the MonierLifetile Company, (800) 571-8453.

Ron and Joni Lipsom also went for permanent good looks for the stately home they are building on Cass Lake. "I chose tile for the roof because I like the look and wanted something that would be maintenance-free," Lipsom says.

Other new roofing materials are coming in to play. Many are not in Southern Michigan yet, but most will be here by spring or can be special-ordered.

Aluminum, the newest metal roofing material, is light weight, very adaptable and gaining popularity. Classic Product's, (800) 543-8938, offers an aluminum Rustic Shingle that looks like wooden shakes. The lightweight aluminum is put directly over the existing roof. It provides a permanent cedar shake look that will not burn and reflects heat keeping the home cooler in summer.

Owens Corning's MiraVista line, (800) GET PINK, uses slate, shale, clay, fiberglass, high-tech resins and who knows what else to create roofing that looks like slate and shake. These beautiful designs have 50-year limited warranties and a Class "A" fire rating which can be important. In one instance, a California home with a MiraVista roof was completely surrounded by cedar roofed homes that had burned to the ground.

Re-New Wood's Eco-Shake, (800) 420-8576, is a wood shake look-alike made from recycled pallet wood and leftover plastic from vinyl hose, shower curtain and bottle manufacturers. Eco-Shake can be applied over existing roofing. It is made in Oklahoma and shipped factory-direct. The product weighs 250 pounds a square and has a Class "A" fire rating.

Authentic Roof by Crowe Bldg. Products of Ontario, (905) 529-6818, is a slate look-alike product. A 100-percent recycled product, it is made from automotive rubber, polymers and scraps from the manufacture of baby diapers. It is black/gray and has a 50-year warranty.

Cembrit B7 is imported from Denmark by Northern Roof Tile Sales Co., (905) 627-4035. The product is very lightweight, looks like tile and is easy enough to install that a fairly handy do-it-yourselfer could do the roof job himself. It can be applied over existing roofing.

These new roofing products all have a classic look. Many are made from industrial waste products. All are built for the long hall with an average of 50-year limited warranties and require little or no upkeep. You may pay a little more for them, but they will probably be the last roofing you ever have to buy. Do your homework, then brag about it.

continued on next page

How do you pick a roofing contractor?

Choosing a contractor always poses a dilemma. The three-tiered approach will get you a good one every time. The three tiers are: friends & family; neighbors; and suppliers.

1. Ask your friends and family who have had a house re-roofed recently or who know people in the building trades, for a recommendation.

2. Walk the neighborhood. If you see a shingle job you like, knock on the door and ask who did the job and if they know the brand name or type of the shingles. You win two ways using this technique: You get the name of a good roofing contractor and you have found a shingle line you like.

3. Go where roofing contractors buy their supplies and ask for recommendations. Look up suppliers under Roofing Materials in your Yellow Pages. ABC and Wimsatt are all over this area, but every roofing materials dealer can give you the information you need.

You'll be surprised at how easy it is to get a list of good contractors names. People love to brag about them. Kathy, my editor at Master Handyman Press, walked three doors down her Royal Oak street and found both the roofer and the shingle she was looking for. She recommends Paul Costigan (Ed Note: we could not get a current phone number) to everyone. Her mother calls Joe Murray at TKO Home Maintenance , (810) 776-3989, for roofing, painting, and construction work on her home and commercial buildings. He's never let her down.

Make certain the contractor you choose is licensed and insured. Also check your home owner's policy to see if you require additional coverage while the work is being done. Do your homework and you will get a roofing job that will keep you smiling for years.

Sources

Here is a list of roofing manufacturers and local contractors mentioned in these stories, and their phone numbers and web site addresses:

■ Cedar Shake and Shingle Bureau, (604) 462-8961, www.cedarbureau.org

■ Classic Product's, (800) 543-8938, www.classicroof.com

■ Crowe Building Products Authentic Roof, (905) 529-6818

■ Elk (800) 944-4344, www.elkcorp.com

■ GAF (800) 678-4285, www.gaf.com

■ Metal Roofing Specialists, Inc., www.metalroofingspecialist.com

■ MonierLifetile Company, (800) 571-8453, www.monierlifetile.com

■ Northern Roof Tile Sales Co., (905) 627-4035

■ Owens Corning, (800) GET PINK, www.owenscorning.com

■ Re-New Wood's Eco-Shake, (800) 420-8576

■ Thermo Manufacturing, (800) 445-9856, www.thermomfg.com

■ Watkins Saw Mills, LTD, www.watkinsawmills.com

■ A & Z Commercial Roofing, (734) 513-7300

■ Concrete Tile Roofing, Inc., (248) 669-3409

■ Pine Building Company, (888) 500-PINE

■ TKO Home Maintenance, (810) 776-3989

Sometimes there is only one solution for a problem roof: A Contractor

There are really two types of roofs: inclined roofs, that is roofs with some kind of a pitch to them, and flat roofs. Most houses have inclined roofs. A few people have houses that are blessed with a combination of both. We usually call these problem roofs because they almost always leak.

Joel and Denise Faddol of Oak Park have two kids, a nice California style ranch house and a combination roof from hell. The inclined roof did not present a problem, but the flat roof always leaked.

The Faddols had never been able to solve their flat roof problem. They finally called Joe Aiello at Pine Building Company, (888) 500-PINE, for help, which in addition to remodeling, has a very successful roofing division specializing in shingle roofs.

Aiello saw immediately that the Faddol's problem could not be solved with shingles. They needed a top quality commercial roofer. Aiello turned to Angelo Zerbo of A & Z Commercial Roofing, (734) 513-7300. It's been three years, and the roof has not leaked since.

"There's no one roofing system that can solve every problem roof, you have to have a multi-system approach," Zerbo says. "If you have a problem roof, you have to make certain that the contractor has both the skills and the technology to solve the problem, no matter what it's cause."

In the Faddol's case, Zerbo's company had to cut an eight-inch swath of rotten roof overhang away, then cover the roof with a continuous heat-sealed membrane.

"It was wild. The job was done in December so it got dark early and it looked like they were using flame throwers on the roof," Denise Faddol says.

continued on next page

Today's asphalt and fiberglass shingles can give you the look and shadow line of cedar and shake

By Glenn Haege
Special to The Detroit News

Since most consumers still choose single-ply shingles, one of the most common questions I get on the radio or at building shows is "Which is best – a fiberglass or an asphalt shingle?"

I have two stock answers.

1. Whichever your roofing contractor recommends. He is the one doing the job. You are paying for his expertise. Let him use the shingle with which he gets the best results.

2. If you are in a high wind area, asphalt has the edge. If you are in a high fire risk area, fiberglass has the edge.

Actually the industry classifies all shingles as asphalt. The only difference between asphalt and fiberglass shingles is the scrim, the mat upon which the shingle is made. If the mat is felt paper the shingle is called asphalt. If the mat is made out of fiberglass the shingle is called fiberglass.

The rest of the shingle is composed of one or more layers of asphalt and granules and adhesive. Granules give the shingle its reflective quality, color and UV (ultra violet) ray protection. Asphalt holds the granules and provide a tough water-tight seal. Adhesive helps the shingle lay flat and withstand the winds.

One-layer shingles are called single ply. Two-layer shingles are the high end of the asphalt shingle market and are called laminates. The lamination provides the shingle with a layered color effect and an increased shadow line- a three-dimensional look. This depth and color is easily discernible from ground level and greatly increases the curb appeal of the house.

Examples of high end laminated shingles are GAF's Grand Sequoia, Country Mansion, Timberline Ultra; Elk's Prestique and Capstone; and the new Owens Corning Oakridge 40 Deep Shadow line.

Construction of a laminated shingle

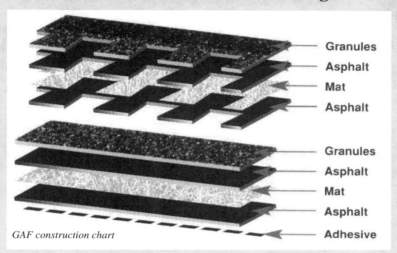

Granules
Asphalt
Mat
Asphalt

Granules
Asphalt
Mat
Asphalt
Adhesive

GAF construction chart

The costs

To get a rough idea about price, single ply shingles cost about $28 a square. Dimensional and laminated shingles cost between $75 and $140- a square. Add $125 to $250 a square for labor. Single ply shingles weigh about 240 pounds a square. Laminated shingles can weigh up to 480 pounds.

Owens Corning says high-end laminated shingles are now 35 percent of the market. To make a businesslike decision take a drive around your neighborhood. If all the new roofs have single-ply shingles,

you can have single-ply also. If quite a few homes have attractive shadow lines, investing your money in laminated shingles is a good idea.

Owens Corning says high-end laminated shingles are now 35 percent of the market. To make a businesslike decision take a drive around your neighborhood. If all the new roofs have single-ply shingles, you can have single-ply also. If quite a few homes have attractive shadow lines, investing your money in laminated shingles is a good idea.

SEPTEMBER 18, 1999

Better fixes for troublesome flat roofs are here – with more coming

by Glenn Haege,
America's Master Handyman

As a general rule flat roofs and happy building owners don't go together because of the problems with leaks. These days, flat roofs can be made leak-proof, which is important to know should you ever consider buying a house or a commercial building that has one.

Most residential flat roofs are constructed from wood decks covered by hot tar systems. The decking could also be steel, concrete, lightweight insulating concrete or even cementitious wood fiber.

Hot tar is an asphalt coating that is often protected with gravel. Michigan's many freeze and thaw cycles are very hard on this type of roof. If the asphalt dries out, it cracks and leaking occurs.

Single-membrane roofing systems were introduced to solve hot tar's problems. These systems are often called rubber or vinyl roofs. The membrane comes on rolls which are laid down over a prepared surface. The membrane is either overlapped or butted together then sealed to make the roof one continuous waterproof membrane.

Single-membrane systems like those made by Firestone, Thermo and Johns Manville, or Bobson Construction's Poly Bond, (248) 357-1240, are often very good roofing solutions. They can be the original roof, or an almost miraculous "fix" for an older hot-tar system. Properly installed by a factory-approved contractor, single-membrane systems usually have a service life of about 15 years.

Wood nailers are installed around the perimeters and all openings in the roof. If there was gravel, the surface should be covered with a 1/2- to 3/4-inch insulated recovery board. A modified fiberglass base sheet is laid down and covered with the single membrane. Finally the membrane is anchored with cold adhesive, torched or mopped into place. There is a potential for leakage wherever there are seams, where the membrane must be cut to go around something, and at the edges where the membrane is anchored. If the fasteners pull out of the wood or the wood fails for any reason the seal breaks and leakage begins.

When the single membrane system has come to the end of its service life, it is time for the new liquid system.

According to Dominic Morelli, vice-president of sales for Thermo Manufacturing, this new third wave of flat roof systems is now coming into play. Liquid systems, developed by companies like Thermo, (800) 445-9856, are applied by factory authorized installers such as A & Z Commercial Roofing, (734) 513-7300. The work is inspected and materials, or work and materials, guaranteed by the factory.

The theory behind liquid systems is that Thermolastic Acrylics and Thermolene Urethanes can seal existing waterproofing systems or provide a new impermeable roof outer surface.

Workers use squeegee and mop to apply the finish coat of Thermo Liquid System to a flat roof. Roof materials and labor can then be warranted for up to 10 years.

There is no one perfect re-roofing fix. Contractor Angelo Zerbo of A & Z Commercial Roofing tells me that he has a 5-foot high stack of specifications for the various types of flat roof systems.

If you have a house, office or commercial building with a flat roof that has come to the end of its service life it is very important that you get a knowledgeable, multi system commercial contractor or a roofing consultant to look at the roof and draw up specifications before committing to a final solution.

Some of the roofing consultant and inspection companies in our area are Detroit Roofing Inspection Service, Inc, (810) 759-2143; CTI and Associates of Brighton, (800) 468-7499; NTH Consultants Ltd. of Farmington Hills, (800) 736-6842; or the Roofing Industry Promotion Fund or Warren, (810) 759-2140. I have a more complete list on my website at www.masterhandyman.com.

A thorough inspection may call for infrared thermography or test cuts to determine the soundness of the present roof. Wherever the present roof is not sound, the existing roofing and insulation must be removed and replaced and the roof brought up to level.

Ideally, a Liquid System can save a building owner many thousands of dollars because it can save the original roof instead of replacing it. Building inspectors consider Liquid Roof Systems maintenance rather than re-roofing because they eliminate expensive, time-consuming tear-offs.

Liquid System roofs can be cleaned and resurfaced periodically further extending the warranty. Additionally, the outer surface can be highly reflective reducing the heat build-up associated with older, heat-absorbing systems.

We have seen many flat roof "sure fixes" over the past 20 years. The Liquid System concept seems promising and could be the answer to many commercial and residential flat roof problems.

If you're the owner of a flat roof, it's very important that you do your homework and get all the facts before you even think of taking out your check book.

It's worth it to check and clean out dirty duct work

by Glenn Haege,
America's Master Handyman

What's one of the dirtiest parts of your house that you haven't cleaned in years? If you guessed duct work go to the head of the class.

Mix common air-borne dust with a little bit of moisture, add heat from a newly turned-on furnace, and the duct work becomes a perfect breeding ground for *Stachybotrys, Aspergilis,* and their friends. A trade journal, "The Indoor Air Quality Update" reports that *Stachybotrys* is found in about 5 percent of American homes and is associated with neurological disorders such as memory loss and sleeplessness.

Not even new houses have clean duct work. Carpenters and other building trades have a habit of using a new home's open floor grates as dust bins. This does nothing good for new home air quality.

The majority of us have natural gas, forced air heating systems The duct work in these homes should be cleaned every seven or eight years. While electric air cleaners and extra thick media filter help filter out impurities circulated through heating ducts, they do nothing to keep the cold air return ducts sanitary.

If you want to check to see if your ducts need cleaning, Connie Morbach of Sanit-Air, (888) 778-7324, suggests that you take off the return air registers in a couple of rooms and see how much dust and debris has collected. If it looks dirty, go to the furnace room and bang on the air-return duct work. If you hear a hollow booming sound, the duct work is clear and you don't have to worry about duct cleaning for a couple of years.

But the ducts need to be cleaned if:

■ You hear rattling it means that there are chunks of concrete, drywall and nails in the ducts.

■ If it sounds like a dull thud, there is so much debris lining the ducts that it is deadening the sound.

Once you have determined that the duct work needs cleaning, who do you call? It seems like there are a million duct cleaners out there. How do you know that they have the proper equipment and training?

It's easy to recommend the big guys, Safety King, (888) DUCT PRO, Sanit-Air, Dalton Environmental, (800) 675-2298, or a big heating contractor like Bergstrom's (734) 522-1350, that also does furnace cleaning. But they can't do all the work.

Smaller concerns, like Sterling Environmental, (888) 992-1200, and A-1 Duct Cleaning, (800) 382-8256, have an advantage in that they are run by owner-operators. The guy who owns the company is often the person cleaning your ducts.

Great idea. But how do you know the person knows what they are doing?

I asked, David Felker, the owner of Sterling Environmental, what to look for in a good duct cleaning contractor.

"The four things I'd look for are reputation, state licensing, years in business and equipment," Felker says. Before you invite someone into your home to go through every room in your house and drill holes in the duct work, you want to talk to people who already had him do the work.

"Did he clean up after himself or leave the house a shambles? Did they notice a definite improvement in air quality after he was gone? Overall, did they think the company did a good job?"

"Also, has the company stood the test of time? Anyone can buy some cheap equipment and call themselves a duct cleaner," says Felker. "All too often those guys are out of business in one or two seasons. The customer has a right to expect that the company has been around for awhile and has a solid base of satisfied customers."

If you have trouble finding a good duct cleaner, the National Air Duct Cleaners Association, (202) 737-2926, has stringent membership requirements and gives certification testing. If you give them a call they will tell you the names of members near you. Do your homework and you and your family will breath a lot easier.

Duct cleaning equipment

The equipment used to clean ducts can vary from huge trucks to portable units. David Felker of Sterling Environmental and most of the "old pros" prefer the big, truck-mounted super vacs. These trucks cost $30 to $50,000, and bring tremendous duct cleaning power into the home.

Eight-inch-diameter vacuum hose is attached to both return and hot air ducts near the furnace. Truck-mounted vacuum pulls loosened debris from ducts at 12,000 cfm.

Mike Palazzolo of Safety King, has one Canadian-made super unit he calls the "Boss" that pulls 16,000 cfm (cubic feet per minute) and cost $ 72,000. A big believer in cleaning power, even Palazzolo's smallest trucks are the largest made in America and pull 12,000 cfm.

Some portable equipment can also do a good job. Both Safety King and Sanit-Air use portable equipment if the job requires it. A good indoor portable unit pulls 3,000 to 5,000 cfm so the job takes longer than with a truck-mounted unit. As with everything else, the people doing the work are more critical to quality than the equipment used.

Unfortunately, some low-cost portable units now on the market only pull about 200 cfm (about as much power as your dryer vent) and lack the power necessary to do the job properly. Be sure to ask about the cleaning equipment and the experience level of the technicians who will actually do the work, before you sign a contract.

Take proper steps to purchase the best ladder for home projects

by Glenn Haege,
America's Master Handyman

I got the call Tuesday. Captain Klutz, my colleague at Master Handyman Press was on his way to National Ladder & Scaffold in Madison Heights, (800) 535-5944, to buy not one but two ladders – one extension ladder to use while cleaning out the gutters and one 6-foot step ladder for inside work.

By the time the captain found National Ladder's big extension ladder display, I had alerted Leno Corrade, the owner, who convinced the captain he would be better off with a 12-foot aluminum straight ladder.

"Add a stabilizer to protect the gutters and keep the ladder secure and you have everything a single-story homeowner needs," Corrade says. "This is all the height required to paint or even crawl up on the roof (something the captain should never do)."

Owners of two story homes occasionally need extension ladders. When asked about them, I recommend borrowing the neighbor's. Extension ladders are relatively heavy, take up a lot of room and are only used a few times a year. The captain's new 12-foot straight ladder has a heavy duty, 250 pound rating but only weighs 20 pounds. It can be easily lifted and stored out of the way on hooks in his garage.

For inside use, Corrade recommended a new aluminum 5-way combination ladder by the R. D. Werner Co., (888) 523-3371. Also rated for a 250 pound load capacity, this versatile ladder has extension ladder rungs in the back and step ladder steps in the front. It comes in 6-, 7- and 8-foot lengths and is really five ladders in one.

When needed, the back extension ladder slides out of its retainer and the ladder becomes two single ladders. The back ladder is also fully adjustable, so it pulls up and the ladder becomes a stairway ladder which can be a lifesaver when painting or wallpapering stairway walls.

Close the ladder and it becomes an easily adjustable extension ladder. Open it and it is a stepladder. Since the back of the ladder has rungs, not braces, the ladder can also be used as a two man ladder enabling one person to hold a light fixture or fan while the other person works on the wiring. The 5-in-1 ladder is priced from about $140.

As tempting as this ladder was, the captain had his heart set on the 6-foot Fiberglass Werner makes for National Ladder. Wherever you shop for your ladder, whether it be at Home Depot or your local home center or hardware store, Fiberglass is the premium choice.

A Fiberglass ladder is usually a lifetime investment. Since Fiberglass does not conduct electricity, it is safer to use around wiring than metal. It is also essentially weather proof because Fiberglass does not rot.

Fiberglass also has a very good strength-to-weight ratio. A 6-foot step ladder weighs only 22 pounds and is classified 1A, Extra Heavy Duty, with a maximum work load of 300 pounds. The features which make National Ladder's exclusive model special are extra rear horizontal supports, heavy-duty fiberglass rail shields at each foot and an economical price. The 6-foot model costs $98.65, a bargain for a top-quality ladder.

To comparison shop, we checked Home Depot and they had a top-quality Ridged Fiberglass 6-foot ladder with full metal boots at each foot for $117. Their 6-foot Werner two man fiberglass step ladder was $144.

Anyone who has read my columns for any length of time knows that I am a believer in renting scaffolding for house painting or other major projects. "Rent" has always been the keyword in my scaffolding vocabulary. National Ladder now has a 6-foot rolling tower on sale that could change my mind.

Made by Bil-Jax, (800) 537-0540, the rolling tower is a 6-foot wide, six-foot high scaffolding unit that rolls on 5-inch casters. Since the two ends are independently adjustable, it can be used on rough terrain, even stairs. It would come in handy for washing windows, caulking, electrical, or painting. But what do you do with it the rest of the year?

This is where the six-foot size comes in handy. Roll the tower into a corner of your garage and it becomes a height adjustable, 6-foot wide by 29-inch deep workbench. The wood scaffold bed is rated for 500 pounds and can take any project that is likely to come its way.

The 6-foot multi-purpose tower costs $339. It could make a very useful addition for anyone who has an occasional need for scaffolding.

The 6-foot rolling tower is on display at all three of National Ladder and Scaffold's Madison Heights, Canton and Grand Rapids stores. Stopping could give you a leg up hanging Halloween and Christmas decorations.

How much will a ladder hold?

American National Standards Institute Rating

Type	Max. load	Rated use
IA	300 pounds.	Extra-heavy duty
I	250 pounds.	Heavy-duty Industrial
II	225 pounds.	Med.-duty commercial
III	200 pounds.	Light-duty household

The total load supported includes the weight of the person, his clothing, tools and any materials, such as a can of paint on the ladder. Test requirements have a safety factor of four. In other words a Type IA has been tested up to 1200 pounds.

For safety's sake, I recommend choosing Type I or IA Heavy-Duty Industrial and Extra Heavy-Duty rated ladders in the home. They cost only a little more, but give much greater security. Regardless of the rating, no ladder is safe if it is not used properly.

An electric generator could be a lifesaver if the power goes out

by Glenn Haege,
America's Master Handyman

Let me start this article by saying that the Handyman does not have an all terrain vehicle, assault rifle, or a six-month supply of dried food and water squirreled away in a bunker someplace.

The government and the utility companies have assured me that I do not need to worry about Y2K glitches and I believe them. I do not have an electric power back up system.

That said, I have to report that electric generators are some of the hottest products in town. Don Collins at Budget Electric, (800) 400-8941, has opened an electric generator division specializing in the sale and installation of power generators.

Discount Air Compressor & Generator in Pontiac, (248) 338-2255, which not only sells and services, but also assembles diesel, natural gas, propane and multifuel generators says their only problem has been finding enough inventory.

Who needs an electric generator?

1) If you wake up in the middle of the night worrying about what happens if the power goes out. Put in a light duty 5,000-watt system. You may never need it, but you're prepared.

2) If the power goes down at your house every time there is a big wind, get a generator and stop being inconvenienced.

3) If you have a well or an electric-powered sump pump that works a great deal, your minimum generator needs is a 7,000-watt system.

4) Anyone with a medical condition that makes the cut-off of electric power life threatening should have a 7,000 watt system. I prefer a 7,000- or 10,000-watt multi fuel system. The three fuels are gasoline, natural gas, and liquid petroleum (LP). A 500-gallon LP tank will give you 200 to 300 hours of power in case of emergency.

5) A person with a home office who does not want the loss of power to put him or her out of business. The computer room comes first, everything else is just camping. A 7,000-watt to 10,000-watt multi fuel system would be good. A 20,000-watt permanent system that automatically switches on when power goes off, or when it senses that the line is in a brown-out condition would be better.

Phil LaCoursiere of Discount Air Compressor & Generator in Pontiac, (248) 338-2255, says a person concerned about Y2K should buy their generator and have it installed immediately.

"A generator should be run for 100 hours before you need it. That way if a problem develops the generator should be replaced before there is an emergency."

How much do they cost?

You get what you pay for. A light duty generator has a lawn mower engine. More expensive generators have heavy duty OHV (Over Head Valve) engines.

Residential generators go from about $400 to $800 for a light duty 3000- to 5,000-watt portable generator, to $15,000 plus for critical duty rated 20,000- to 25,000-watt models. Home Depot has a 3,000-watt Techumsie generator for $439 and a 4,000-watt Generac for $779.

Factor in installation of the generator into your calculations. This is not a DIY project. Collins of Budget Electric says that the average installation cost for a 5,000-watt generator is $695 including transfer switch and cord assembly. Larger units cost more.

Budget Electric has a light duty 5,000-watt Generac generator and installation package available for $1,595. A higher quality 4,000-watt costs $1,995 including installation and switch box. The 4,000-watt generator has an OHV engine and a running time three times longer than the light duty 5,000-watt model.

Budget also sells a 20,000-watt Generac Guardian Power System for $11,000 including installation, with a six to eight week delivery.

Discount Air Compressor & Generator does not sell or service light duty generators. The company currently has 7,000-watt heavy duty Honda LR 70-EZ multifuel generator for $3,995 and is scheduled to receive 200 10,000-watt multifuel generators with Isuzu Mongo engines this week. Over half of the shipment has already been sold, but they should have slightly under 100 units available at $3,995.

Home Depot advertised a 6,000-watt Generac Guardian system for $4895 installed. Their installed price for 10,000-watt systems is $6495.

How much power do you need?

Unless you are willing to invest big money into electrical generation, everything not vital must be off line. A house with 10 electric lights, 2 radios, a computer and miscellaneous hardware, color TV, gas powered furnace, freezer, refrigerator, electric stove, coffee maker, water heater and a sump pump would use almost 15,000-watts of power.

Power demand should only be 75 percent of generator capacity. That way, when a well pump or sump pump goes on, you won't have any unpleasant surprises.

Use this chart to determine approximate needs. For a more complete listing of appliances and tools go to Discount Air Compressor & Generator's Website at www.gohonda.com.

Appliance	Watts
Radio	50
Color TV	300
Clothes Dryer (gas)	400
Dishwasher	400
Computer	400
Furnace Fan (1/3 hp)	1200
Refrigerator/Freezer	600
Coffee Maker	850
Microwave Oven	800
Water Heater (elec.)	300
Well Pump 1/3 hp	750
10,000 BTU Air Conditioner	1500
Toaster	1150
Electric Oven	4000
Space Heater	1200
Hot Tub	1700

OCTOBER 16, 1999

Old sliding glass doors may need replacement – and it'll cost you

by Glenn Haege,
America's Master Handyman

Nothing brings the outside in like sliding glass door walls. They were probably one of the 'Ooh' and 'Ah' features that made you choose your house. After 20 years or so, that beautiful sliding glass door can start looking fairly ratty and acting cantankerous.

The glass seal may have broken and condensation started to collect on the inside of the windows. The paint has worn away in places. When you try to loosen or tighten the door the adjustment screws, they just laugh at you. The easy slide, easy glide that existed when the door was new is gone for good.

A sliding glass door used as a primary entrance for twenty years could have been jerked open and banged shut 150,000 times or more. Mud, grime and gravel may have ground the roller mechanism to shreds.

If you want to try to repair, H & R Window Repair of Detroit, (248) 366-8282, or Alco Glass & Mirror in Berkley, (248) 547-1214, can replace windows with broken seals or repair roller mechanisms.

If replacement seems the better option, you'll find that sliding glass door walls have come a long way in the past several years. The majority of the national brands are carried by most major home centers including Dillman & Upton, (248) 651-9411, and Erb Lumber, (248) 644-3636, Home Depot, N.A. Mans, (734) 981-5800, and Siding World, (313) 891-2902.

Here are some of the stand-out features: Pella and Marvin have very good multipoint locking systems that permit sliding glass doors to lock as securely as entrance doors.

Andersen, Weather Shield, Pella, and Marvin all give the option of divided lites (the little wood pieces which divide the window). Weather Shield gives you a choice of five different hard and soft wood interior panels. Most use lites to provide ornate design options.

If you are tired of that floor-to-ceiling glass look, Kolbe & Kolbe Millwork Co., of Wausau, Wis., (800) 477-8656, has a paneled wood sliding patio door that comes in five different woods and looks as beautiful (and expensive) as the most ornate main entrance doors.

All the major manufacturers make swinging French doors that fit into the same opening as sliding glass doors.

Although every manufacturer makes its sliding glass doors in a selection of colors, you would be hard pressed to find any color other than white in stock at any of the local suppliers.

Some important but unseen features include Marvin's top mounted sliding door screen that keeps it securely on track, no matter how often it is slammed or pushed by dogs and small fry. Weather

Shield's sliding patio door's tandem door rollers have ball bearings for extra smooth operation.

If you have a standard-size sliding glass door you can get by relatively inexpensively. Standard-size double sliding glass doors are usually 6 foot, 6 foot 10 inches, or 8 foot high by 6 or 8 feet wide.

Unfortunately, many sliding glass doors are not standard size. Most manufacturers either do not customize door size, or charge a very hefty premium for the extra work involved. Manufacturers, like Andersen, that do not make custom-size units make do with fill-in trim packages. If the size difference is just a couple of inches per door, this is OK. If it is any more than that, the fill-in is very obvious.

To give some idea about pricing, Home Depot stocks a white 6 foot wide Andersen Permashield sliding glass door with basic hardware and a screen for $705 and a white Pella Pro Line Patio Door cost $874 including screen and grilles.

A slightly more elaborate Andersen door wall was $946 including screen. Brass hardware would add $119. The upper end of Home Depot's price range was represented by an Andersen Frenchwood Door priced at $1,210 including brass hardware and screen.

None of these prices included delivery. Home Depot's basic sliding glass door installation charge was $299.

To give you an idea of how these prices compare with locally produced sliding glass doors, we checked out Weathergard Window, (800) 377-8886,

of Oak Park, a vinyl replacement window manufacturer, that does a big sliding glass door replacement business. According to Dave Fishman, the general manager, their 6-foot-wide vinyl sliding glass door costs $849 including installation. An 8-foot-wide model is $949 installed. Custom-size doors cost $300 more than standard sizes.

Fishman says that Weathergard sliding glass doors have several glass options available. Doors can be made with beveled glass or brass grid borders. Interior frame options include white, tan, earth tone, light or dark oak.

Price is only one criterion. You have to do your homework and determine the insulation value (U Value) of the doors, how they match your interior and exterior decor, and if they offer secure locking systems. Timely delivery and availability of experienced, professional installers are also very important factors.

Phone numbers and web sites

Andersen, (800) 426-4261, www.andersenwindows.com

Kolbe & Kolbe Millwork, (800) 477-8656, www.kolbe-kolbe.com

Marvin, (800) 346-5128 www.marvin.com

Pella, (800) 847-3552, www.pella.com

Weather Shield, (800) 477-6908, ext. 998, www.weathershield.com

Wallside, (800) 521-7800

Weathergard, (800) 377-8886

If you gaze into a crystal ball, you see the home of your future

by Glenn Haege,
America's Master Handyman

Recently, I was mulling over a series of articles I may do about building in the new millennium. I pictured a house built in 1990 or 1995 and thought about how it would be different from one built in 2005 or 2010. The outward appearance of the houses might be the same. Almost everything else would be different.

Starting at the bottom, the 1990s basement was poured concrete or block. Basement walls were 8-feet high. Plumbing was a mixture of cast iron and copper. The basement was built to damp proof, not waterproof, specifications. Basement windows were single glazed with metal frames.

The equivalent basement in 2005 or 10 will be waterproof foam insulated concrete forms (ICF). Walls will be 10 ft. high. Basement windows will be block or larger double-glazed metal, composite or vinyl framed.

Plumbing will be PVC for drains and CPVC for the supply side. CPVC can't corrode, pit or scale and retains water purity. Heavy duty plastic drains won't rust. Both are easier to use than their metal predecessors. Most homes will have whole-house water quality systems making the water more pure than anything found in nature.

Inside the 1990s basement you usually had a forced air natural gas furnace, hot water tank, laundry tub, washer and spin dry dryer. Homes built by the more for-ward-thinking builders had laundry areas on the first floor.

In the basement of the 2010 house, everything will be up for grabs. Heating plants will be so small that they can literally be put anywhere. Most geothermal and boiler/hydronic heating systems will still be in the basement. Both these systems will eliminate the need for hot water tanks. Almost limitless amounts of hot water will be available at any time.

If you choose to have separate hot water capability, on-demand units could very well be located where they are needed with separate systems in the kitchen and bath areas. Hot water will be instantaneous, no waiting.

Hot air ductwork will be a thing of the past with more efficient hot water coils in floors and walls standard. Cold floors and drafts will not exist unless programmed into the heating system.

Top loading automatic washing machines are already being phased out. Front loading washing and drying machines will be in. For those who do not like the wear created by spin dry machines, fast microwave units should be available.

By 2010 joists, studs, rafters, all the load bearing beams may well be engineered wood, metal or some kind of a composite. The term a "stick built house" will have faded from the vocabulary. Panelized building will have taken over. Framing will be delivered on site constructed to exact specifications.

Wiring may be massive. The average house could well have power requirements double or triple those of residential building in the 1990s.

Here's where the crystal ball grows a little foggy. Lucent Technologies and AMP Building Systems are betting that most houses will be strung with low-voltage, heavy-wire cables that will make every room in the house instantly upgradable to any power or communication need.

At the same time, wireless connectors being introduced by the computer industry may make heavy wire obsolete.

Will both heavy-cable and wireless systems coexist or will one out-do the other? It's a horse race.

Rough carpentry as we think of it today may well be a thing of the past. The crew that accepts on-site delivery and is in charge of overall assembly will be highly trained professionals and paid that way.

Brain will account for a lot more than brawn. If you know a young man or woman who is very adaptable, learns rapidly, and is a hands-on, take-charge individual they could do very well in the construction trades.

Now that the shell is complete, let's go upstairs – and the stairs will be twice as wide as the basement stairs of 1995.

Living rooms will have made way for entertainment centers. That big picture you see over most couches will have been traded in for a just-as-big flat screen monitor which can be programmed to segue between fifty or so of your favorite photos. If you'd rather look at the news or a favorite television show, just give a voice command.

Expect big changes in the kitchen, too.

Kitchens will be cooking/socializing centers. You have always used them that way, by 2010 they will be built to suit your lifestyle. Food preparation will be easier. You won't have to reach for anything on the top shelf because kitchen cabinets will pull down.

■ Boiling water will be just another spout on the sink.

■ The dishwasher will be noiseless.

■ The oven will be able to roast a big turkey in a half hour. A thick steak seared on both sides should take about five minutes.

■ Cooktops will have highly decorative design patterns.

■ Counters, tables, seating, even some cabinetry will be so maneuverable that you will be able to easily adjust the kitchen floor plan to meet party arrangements.

Baths will be bigger with lounging areas. Sound, steam, sauna and whirlpool will all be included.

Lighting will be infinitely adjustable. Windows will be composites that should last as long as the house.

The walls will often be concrete-filled foam forms. Ceilings will be high.

Air quality will be tightly controlled assuring a much healthier living environment than you find today.

Roofing will be fireproof and rated for the life of the structure.

I'd like to tell you more but I don't have the space. The future is coming and I can hardly wait.

Expo gives a glimpse into what new technology is exciting builders

by Glenn Haege,
America's Master Handyman

Remember the old tire commercials with the line, "Where the rubber meets the road"? The advertiser meant that at the point of contact, where the action was most critical, their product was superior.

Last weekend, I sent my publisher to scout out the JLC LIVE Construction Business and Technology Conference & Expo in Las Vegas. The Journal of Light Construction, (800) 375-5981, www.jlconline.com, is a truly excellent magazine that focuses on the lead carpenter, building supervisor, smaller custom contractor and remodeler.

(If we are lucky JLC LIVE might come to Lansing next March. Call Sherry Daniels, JLC Exhibit Manager for more information, (800) 552-1951, ext. 146.)

My publisher and I decided that we needed to know what the guys who wear the tool belts were getting excited about. By the way, I'm writing guys because we estimate that 95 percent of the attendees were men.

Even with this preponderance of men, the show demonstrated the truth of another old advertising slogan, "You've come a long way, baby." Fifteen percent (6 of 40) of the seminar leaders were women. About eight percent of the people manning the booths were female, many of them active partners in the family business. A good number of women were "the boss" running their own construction, remodeling or design companies with nary a man in sight, except in the labor force.

While there are always women on a trade show floor, quite often they are model types who just look pretty. But the women manning the booths at the show were there for their expertise. They were field representatives, field managers, and, in the high-tech areas, often the brains of the operation that everyone went to with the tough questions.

Kitchens and baths are more important than ever.

The expo showed that, at the cutting edge of the construction business, "where the rubber meets the road," there is a definite green light for women at every level. Women are taking advantage of that green light and making great strides.

Kitchens and Baths are more important than ever, and three of the six seminars on this topic were led by women. Standing Room Only audiences learned about Creative Kitchen Solutions, How to Make Small Baths Look and Feel Bigger, Hot New Kitchen and Bath Products, Ceramics and Solid Surfaces.

Seminar leaders estimated that about 70 percent of the baby boomer generation want their kitchen and/or bath remodeled (the percentage among generation X-ers is even higher). Bath remodeling costs today quite often surpass what people used to spend on big kitchen remodeling jobs.

Other major trends were evident on the exhibit floor. Almost 10 percent of the exhibits had something to do with foam-insulated concrete forms. Another 10 percent were dedicated to computer design, estimating and quotation packages. Next on the list were tools.

Boy are these guys serious about tools. They were buying tools by the semi-trailer load. Manufacturers and distributors stood shoulder to shoulder hawking their wares. Old time tools such as ladders and custom designed tool belts as well as the latest in tool technology from BOSCH, DEWALT and Hitachi were drawing crowds.

That the small builder is very serious about getting his or her business organized was evident. QuickBooks Pro is the leading construction accounting package and the company had standing room only audiences for two day-long classes, as well as numerous seminars.

For all the laser, computer and internet technology, the show had the feel of an old time country fair. Instead of farmers competing in hog calling, wood chopping and corn chucking, attendees competed in Reciprocal Sawing, Cutting, Drywall Fitting and that all time favorite, Nail Driving. The events were sponsored by BOSCH and the prizes were, what else, tools.

Educational programs started a day before the exposition. There were full-day programs on Lead Carpenter Training, Accurate Estimating & Job Costing, and QuickBooks Pro for Contractors.

Seminar topics showed what was getting the small builder's attention. Improving Kitchen Design and Construction was highlighted. Other subjects – Managing Multiple Jobs, Common Framing Problems, Stucco that Lasts, and Solving Leakage Mysteries – showed what the small builder perceives as his biggest field problems.

It was also evident from the seminar topics that the construction trades are getting a great deal more sophisticated and independent. Firms have so much business that contractors are not so much trying to sell you, the customer, as they are trying to decide whether they want to do business with you.

Seminar topics included: "Choosing the right customers, Prequalification," "Just say No," "Dealing with Difficult Clients," "To Grow or Not to Grow," and "Hanging up the Tool Belt." Think you're having trouble getting jobs done now? In a couple years, unless the builder likes you, he may not do business with you.

If you want to learn more about the show, check out my website, www.masterhandyman.com.

'Oopsies' and squeaks often come along with owning a home

by Glenn Haege,
America's Master Handyman

If you moved in the past couple of years, you are not alone. We've been experiencing a building boom in Michigan. Peter Burton, president of the Building Industry Association of Southeast Michigan, says that 37,000 new homes have been built in the seven county Greater Detroit Area over the past two years.

Add used-home sales and you've got a lot of people moving. According to the folks at Detroit Edison about 200,000 families in the seven-county area move into a new or used house every year.

Every one of those families have to deal with the "Oopsies" and the "Squeaks."

Oopsies

The "Oopsies" include accidental overspraying by painters, mysterious spots and stains, dumps on driveways and gummy labels that won't come off counters, mirrors or woodwork. If you bout a used home you may have discovered a lot of miscellaneous soils and stains. Even if you haven't moved in the past two years, you may still have to deal with these problems.

Here are the cleaners that get rid of the "Oopsies." Most can be found at your local hardware store or home center. If you have trouble finding them, I've included the manufacturers phone numbers.

504

Cleaning and stain removal sources

Here's my special all-purpose cleaning and stain removal chart. You will use it many times over the next few years.

General heavy-duty cleaning
■ TSP/Dirtex by Savogran Company, (800) 225-9872
■ Simple Green by Sunshine Makers, (800) 228-0709
■ Krud Kutter by Supreme Chemicals, (800) 466-7126

INSIDE
Dull sinks and tile
■ Bon Ami, (800) 821-5565
■ The Works Bath & Shower Cleaner by Lime 0 Sol Co., (800) 448-5281
Dull stainless steel
■ Bar Keepers Friend by Servas Laboratories, (800) 433-5818
Mold and mildew stains
■ X-14 by Block Drug Co., (800) 365-6500
■ Mildew Stain Remover by Amazon Premium Products, (800) 832-5645
Stains and scuff marks on vinyl and linoleum
■ Go Jo Hand Cleaner by Go Jo Industries, (800) 321-9647
■ DL Hand Cleaner by Loctite Corporation, (800) 243-4874
Dull countertops
■ Hopes Counter Polish by Hopes, (800) 325-4026
■ Wood & Countertop Polishes by Parker & Bailey, (888) 727-6547
Icky/sticky stains
■ Goo Gone by Magic American, (800) 321-6330
■ De-Solv-It & Clean Away by Orange Sol, (800) 877-7771

Old dull furniture and paneling
■ Doozy Furniture Polish by Mr. Furniture Finisher, (888) 851-8500
■ Restorex Wood Cleaner by Surco Products, (800) 556-0111
Grafitti, paint and stain removers
■ Lift Off #1, 2, 3, 4, and 5. These five specialized cleaners for cleaning oil and latex paints, grease and ink stains, etc. by Motsenbocker's, (800) 346-1633, use completely new technology to make soils and stains loose their adhesive power. You can buy a five pack that includes small amounts of all of the cleaners and a very comprehensive brochure. They also sell large bottles for major projects
■ Goo Gone #2 by Guardsman, (800) 321-6330 for Latex paint removal.
Rust stains
■ CLR Rust & Stain Remover by Jelmar Industries, (800) 323-5497
■ Whink Rust Remover, (800) 247-5102

OUTSIDE
Dirty aluminum and vinyl siding and gutters
■ Nice N Easy and Power Cleaners by the Alumin-Nu Company, (800) 899-7097, are an excellent line of special purpose aluminum and vinyl cleaners.
Bug stains
■ Bug Stuff by Lilly, (800) 253-3957
Grease, oil and rust stains
■ Bix Driveway Cleaners by Bix Manufacturing, (800) 251-1098

continued on next page

Remove over-spray and paint spots and dots from hardwood floors, glass surfaces by using one of these three products. Dirtex in the spray can by Savogran Company, (800) 225-9872 is an ammoniated cleaner that cleans almost anything. Citrus based Goo Gone by Magic American, (800) 321-6330, cuts through anything sticky. Motsenbocher's Lift Off #5, (800) 346-1633, eliminates the adhesive power of latex based paint and turns it into a dust that you can wipe or sweep away.

Un-Du Adhesive Remover by Doumar Products, Inc., 888-BUY-UNDU, gets stickers off without damaging the surface.

Moans, groans, smells and squeaks

Brand new homes are not haunted, but they usually have more moans, groans and chemical smells than older homes. Almost everything used to build a house has to dry out and acclimate to the environment. As the home alternately settles and shrinks, stress develops and we hear moans and groans caused by movement of the materials.

The drying-out process takes about 18 months. The house may feel damp and muggy. Windows and water closets will sweat. There is nothing wrong with this.

There may also be various smells associated with the drying process. The technical term is "off gassing". Moisture evaporating from the materials includes chemicals. You will especially notice paint and carpeting odors. Most are not dangerous. If you have asthma or allergies you may have a sensitivity and should consult your doctor.

A musty smell in an older home indicates that there may be serious microbial problems or the house may not have sufficient air infiltration. If the musty smell is merely caused by not enough air circulation, have your heating contractor install a Skuttle Model 216, (800)

848-9786, or go to your local hardware store and get an Equalize Air by Xavier Inc, (734) 462-1033, that you can install yourself.

A pronounced moldy rotting odor means the house may have serious health problems. It should be tested by a company like Sanit-Air, (888) 778-7324, or Cote's Air Analysis, (800) 416-2323.

Squeaks are annoying. Most new or used houses have them. Here's what you need to get rid of them for ever: Goop Carpenters' Adhesive & Sealant (not the hand cleaner) by Eclectic Products, (800) 767-4667, Wooden Shims, Squeak No More floor squeak inhibitors by O'Berry Enterprises, (800) 459-8428, Squeak Enders by E & E Engineering (800) 323-0982, and an extra pair of feet.

Stopping squeaks is a two-person job. Your extra pair of feet walks on the floor while you and your squeak ending tools are in the basement. When you hear a squeak, holler "stop," apply some Goop to the nearest joist and hammer in a shim.

Have the person above walk over the floor again. If the squeak has stopped, you've won!

If the squeak is still there, use a Squeak Ender by E & E Engineering. A Squeak Ender is a very simple device that pulls the sub floor snug against the joist, eliminating squeaks.

If you don't have access to the underside of the floor, Squeak No More is the weapon of choice. The Squeak No More unit screws down through the carpet, through the Sub Floor and into the joist. Once securely tightened the floor should be squeak free.

NOVEMBER 13, 1999

Simple finishing techniques dress up the new Plunger Pal

by Glenn Haege,
America's Master Handyman

Let me start out this article by saying that I am one of Martha Stewart's greatest fans. Almost every woman over 30 that I know dotes on her every word and wishes she knew half as much about so many things. The handyman does too.

Whether it is cooking her dogs' food, making mince marmalade or decorating a home for Christmas, Martha towers above us all. She is the ultimate autocrat of homemaker knowledge; but she left us down on this one.

When 1.6 toilets became the law of the land I told the world not to fear because Martha would soon be coming out with a designer line of plungers. The need grew as powder room after powder room succumbed to the easily plugged nonfunctionality of the new water closets.

Where before, the homely, old-fashioned plunger could be hidden in the basement because it was rarely needed, suddenly it was becoming a necessity and needed a permanent place beside the commode.

Martha must have been busy baking cookies or working on her stock offering, because we heard nary a peep about the bathroom problem from the style powerhouse.

Congress felt the people's pain and one hundred congressmen led by our own Rep. Joe Knollenberg, R-Bloomfield Hills, held hearings in the hope of reversing the odious piece of plugged-up plumbing legislation. The bill is awaiting a final vote.

Still Martha did not answer the call and our plumbing problems continued to overflow the land.

Luckily, two people did hear my plaintive pleadings and came forth to answer America's need.

John Taylor of Western Slope Design, developed the Plunger Pal. This product is a little plastic pail that holds and hides the plunger when not in use. When used the bucket lid becomes a splash guard protecting the user from water

Chari Weiskrich of the Do-It-Yourself Centers in Sterling Heights, who says there are about 50 things you can do to doll up a Plunger Pal, showing one she decorated with prepasted border wallpaper.

backup. After use, the plunger is anti-septically re-stored in the handily little bucket and the pail lid locked shut.

There is a patent pending on the Plunger Pal. It is available in ivory, blue, green and plum, for just $9.95 plus $3 shipping by calling Western Slope Designs, (877) 206-1937 toll free.

The problem as I see it is that the product is a shiny plastic pail that hides the plunger but looks utilitarian.

This is where Chari Weiskrich of the DO-IT-YOURSELF CENTERS, in Sterling Heights comes in (Ed note: we were unable to find a current phone listing for Ms. Weiskrich's enterprise). Weiskrich is a very creative woman who, with her side kick, Tammy Domke, teaches do-it-yourselfers how to turn trash into treasures, easily and inexpensively reupholstering or making slip covers for chairs and couches, refinishing furniture, resurfacing Formica counter tops, or making expensive-looking window treatments with just a glue gun and a stapler. The classes only cost $30 and can literally save a do-it-yourselfer hundreds or even thousands of dollars.

I figured that if anybody could make the Plunger Pal into a decor asset, Weiskrich could. She didn't let me down. She used two of the simplest finishing techniques. The first was faux finished using a sponging technique. She used easily available border wallpaper on the second. If you wallpapered a powder room and used a border, you could just paste some matching border paper onto a Plunger Pal to turn it into a very attractive looking accessory. The plunger handles were finished to match the pail.

The lid of the Plunger Pal isn't just for show. It becomes a splash guard to protect the user from backsplash during use.

Other finishing techniques Weiskrich suggests are decoupage, using glass or fabric paints to create a dimensional look, gluing sea shells or craft stones onto the base and top, or almost anything you can imagine.

The reason why I'm writing about this is that a Plunger Pal, most especially a hand-decorated Plunger Pal, would make a mind boggling, but easy to create, gift for any new homeowner, or anyone saddled with one of the 1.6 gallon toilets.

If you are going to faux finish or paper the product lightly sand the surface, then apply a coat of a water based stain kill like KILZ 2 by Master Chem, X-Out by XIM, or Bulls Eye 123 by Wm. Zinsser.

As soon as the stain kill dries, you can apply your base coat or wallpaper. To make certain that there is extra good paper adhesion, be sure to use prepasted wallpaper paste.

Whichever technique you choose, your gift that will be long remembered. When they ask how you got the idea, tell them the Handyman told you. What Martha didn't do, America's Master Handyman did.

Super-efficient electronic air cleaners can help you breathe easier

by Glenn Haege,
America's Master Handyman

My publisher was so excited about the new Dynamic electronic air cleaner that he dragged me over to see it at the Sanit-Air Display at this Fall's WXYT Home Expo. He had made an instantaneous decision that he wanted the Dynamic installed in his home as soon as possible.

The reason for my publisher's excitement was that the new product combines the maximum efficiency of an electronic air cleaner with the disposability of a heavy media filter.

The concept behind electronic air cleaners like the Trion SE 1400 or the Honeywell F50, is first rate. Through a combination of electronic charge and filtration an electronic air cleaner can filter airborne particles up to .01 microns in size. Both Trion and Honeywell claim that, at their best, electronic air cleaners have an efficiency rating of up to 95 percent on the ASHRAE (American Society of Heating, Refrigeration and Air Conditioning Engineers) Atmospheric Dust Spot Efficiency Test.

By contrast, media air cleaners have an efficiency rating of between 20 and 40 percent. That might sound low but it is two to four times better than electrostatic filters and four or five times better than the filters most people have on their furnaces.

The reason why all this is important is that according to Environmental Protection Agency (EPA) studies, the air inside today's homes is 10 to 100 time more polluted than outside air. Forty million Americans suffer from allergies and asthma.

According to Trion Corp., a leading manufacturer of filtration and air cleaning equipment, 10.3 million of us have chronic asthma, 22.2 million suffer from hay fever and allergic rhinitis, and 12.6 million suffer from bronchitis.

Most of these maladies are caused by the two heaping teaspoons full of microscopically small pollutants the average person breaths into his lungs every day, says Roger Ferguson, regional sales manager for Environmental Dynamics Group, which makes the Dynamic Electronic Air cleaner. A vital first step to getting healthier is getting rid of the pollutants in the air we breath.

Properly functioning, a good electronic air cleaner does just that. It can filter out viruses and smoke particles up to 100 times smaller than a top-of-the-line thick media filter. It can filter out pollutants 1,000 times smaller than the typical replaceable filter most people use in their furnaces.

The problem is that electronic air cleaners are high maintenance items. Most are so filthy that they are ineffective. Electronic air cleaner manufacturers warn that the products need to be cleaned at least once every 90 days.

Even when you wash an electronic air cleaners in the dishwasher, it is a rather time-consuming process. In the real world, most people are so rushed that they do not do the proper maintenance

Roger Ferguson, of Environmental Dynamics Group installs a Dynamic Electronic Air Cleaner. The air cleaner's 1-inch width means that it can be installed in any natural gas furnace without extensive sheet metal modifications.

and their electronic air cleaner become less and less effective.

Because of the high maintenance, Jim Williams of Williams Refrigerating and Heating in Warren, (888) 268-5445, says that most reputable HVAC (Heating, Ventilating, Air Conditioning) contractors recommend the less effective media filters such as the Trion Air Bear or the Honeywell F25 Media Air Cleaner, which only require annual replacement.

These units are effective on particles as small as one micron in size. They do an excellent job filtering out pollen, skin flakes, plant spores, dust mites, much household dust and some insecticides.

Unfortunately they are ineffective against pollutants in the .5 to .01 micron-size range. These exceptionally small pollutants include most viruses, smoke, smog, many insecticides and some bacteria.

Media filters are very effective against "hunks and chunks." However, if you have asthma, allergies or any other breathing condition, you really need an electronic air cleaner, which can become

worthless within a year if not maintained properly.

That's why my publishers hopes were so high when he discovered the Dynamic Electronic Air Cleaner by Environmental Dynamics Group (EDG). It combines the efficiency of the electronic air cleaner and the ease of maintenance of a media filter.

Unlike ordinary electronic air cleaners and media filters, the Dynamic is only one inch thick so it may be installed in any forced-air furnace without extensive revisions to the duct work.

The unit is made up of three parts: a powerhead, aluminum screen exterior and a disposable fiberglass pillow with an aluminum or charcoal mesh center. The powerhead converts a 2-watt trickle of electricity into a 6,500-volt charge that runs through the aluminum screen and polarizes the pad trapping particles as they pass through.

The only maintenance required by the homeowner is to replace the central pillow every 90 days.

Connie Morbach says that Sanit-Air, (888) 778-7324, charges $360 for the Dynamic Electronic Air Cleaner including installation. A year's supply of four disposable pillows costs about $50.

Roger Ferguson, the Regional Sales Manager for EDG, (800) 916-7873, says that most Lennox Dealers and many other heating and cooling contractors are starting to carry the new product.

They can help you start breathing a lot easier.

Make sure water leaks don't ruin your home while you vacation

by Glenn Haege,
America's Master Handyman

A commercial running on my favorite radio station starts with the sound of water, then a sleepy voiced woman says, "What's that?"

An equally sleepy man says, "Oh no, one of the pipes must have burst, but I don't know where." Cue the announcer: "Call ABC Plumbing Royal Oak …"

Let me ask you one question: Who wakes up whom and asks what's wrong when nobody's home at your house? Nobody, right?

This is the holiday season. Like the song says, multitudes of us are going "over the river and through the woods" to grandmother's house. Multitudes more will be going on cruises and minivacations. Snowbirds are heading South.

When all these wonderful things happen, there is no one to ask, "What's wrong?"

How big a deal is this? Let me introduce exhibit "A." This could be your bathroom after you've been away for a couple weeks. I'm sorry you can't see this picture in color. It is a delightful collection of blues, greens, blacks, grays, yellows, browns and oranges.

Little monsters didn't spray graffiti and it is not some kind of weirdo wallpaper. This is a picture of a bathroom turned mold garden.

When the homeowner returned after two weeks he found that a water pipe had burst and flooded the area. Upon reporting the disaster his insurance adjuster wanted to have the walls washed down and repainted.

Luckily the homeowner was an independent kind of guy and said, "No." He fought the insurance company for two solid months. During this period Connie Morbach of Sanit-Air in Troy, (888) 778-7324, was brought into the fray. Among other things she took this picture. She also took mold and air samples.

Morbach warns that if this should ever happen in your home insist that air quality be checked by an independent testing company of your choice, not the insurance company's.

On this house, Morbach had her colleague, microbiologist Terry Baker, of T. Baker & Associates in Flint, grow mold cultures and identify various species. His findings included the following cast of characters: Penicillium chrysogenium, and Gliomastix murorum, as well as Bacillus, Mucor, Stachybotrys, Stapylococcus, Corynebacterium, Micrococcus, and Cladosporium spores, and Gram negative bacteria.

The only thing all those names tell me is that I wouldn't want to be down wind of the place. Stachybotrys is probably the best known. It is a slimy black mold associated with crib deaths, dermatitis, immunosuppression, and hemorrhaging among other things. Many are considered carcinogenic.

Remember the insurance company just wanted to wash and repaint the walls.

The clothes in a closet adjoining the room had a fuzzy green hue. The owner said he was going to have them all dry-cleaned. Morbach told him that the only place those clothes should go was a toxic waste dump.

The entire area had to be sealed air tight while folks in moon suits and facemask respirators came in, tore out the drywall, sanitized everything with anti-microbials and encapsulated the entire area. All waste had to be double bagged before being transported to the dump.

The reason I am writing this is to demonstrate what water damage can do to your house in just two weeks.

It doesn't have to be a burst pipe. Remember last winter? Heavy snow can cause water to invade the house through the roof, or cracks in the windows or walls. A sudden snowmelt can cause sewers to back up. A toilet can overflow. All are invitations to disaster.

According to Morbach of Sanit-Air time is critical. Severe damage can usually be averted if discovery is made and drying started within 48 hours of the occurrence.

This means that it is best to have a trusted friend or neighbor inspect your house two or three times a week. If you are on a cruise or some place where they can not get in touch with you, they should be empowered to start drying immediately.

The water has to be stopped and the area drained and dried. Large fans should be set up to assist in drying. If water has gotten between the walls, they have to be opened and drained. Water soaked drywall should be removed.

You might be tempted to turn off the water at the meter to keep your house safe. This is not a good idea if you will be away for more than a week. Your house needs water. Without it, the fur-

Connie Morbach of Sanit Air calls this her OMG photo because the first thing people who see it say is, "Oh my gawd." Severe mold growth was caused by flooding of an unattended, drywalled bathroom. The house was only left unattended for two weeks, but during that time a broken water pipe flooded the area.

nace humidifier cannot function. Desert dry air is very hard on floors and furniture. The seals in toilets and dishwashers have to be kept moist.

Before you go, set the thermostat to sixty degrees in older houses and fifty degrees Fahrenheit in newer ones (not more than ten years old). Sweet-talk a trusted friend into inspecting the basement and every room of the house a couple of times a week. Once a month they should flush the toilets and pour a glass of water into the dishwasher. Tell them not to leave until the toilet water tanks have completely refilled and they can hear that the water has stopped.

Hopefully nothing will happen and they will have had a totally boring job. You still owe them a big favor when you get home. Oh, one thing more, have a nice trip.

A last-minute checklist of chores to do around the home this weekend

(And your neighbors will be thrilled if you end up giving them a hand, too.)

by Glenn Haege,
America's Master Handyman

Can you remember a longer fall? Up until last week many people were still wearing spring jackets. When it stays nice this long two things are bound to happen. We tend to dawdle about getting those "get ready for winter" chores finished and Mother Nature pays us back big time. You can be certain that any cold we didn't have in the fall, we will get back with interest this winter.

Here's a last-minute checklist of things you can easily do this weekend.

1. Give your house it's annual Fall Walk Around. If you're a reader of this column you already know the drill. Walk around the house three times with a note pad and write down things that still need to be done.

First time around, check the chimney, roof and gutters for problem areas. Curling shingles, cracks in the flashing or valleys, and sagging gutters, have to be fixed now.

Second time you walk around the house, check windows and siding. Make certain that the downspouts are not pulling away.

Third time around, look at the way the ground slopes away from your house. Winter snow pile-up, followed by spring thaws is the prime cause of basement leaks. That bed of annual flowers you pulled out or the bush you transplanted can easily cause birdbath-style depressions, retaining water and soaking the ground around your basement walls.

The rule is that the ground should slope away from your house one inch for each of the first five feet. The gradual neutralization or reversal of that slope over the years can send tons of water cascading toward your basement walls next spring. The ground is still easily worked, so the time to fix the problem is before you have to bail out the basement. Get to it now.

2. Crawl up on the old ladder and check inside the gutters and down spouts. They probably were cleaned a month ago. But it only takes a few well-positioned leaves to clog a downspout. Remember, clogged downspouts were a prime cause for last winter's roof related water damage.

Don't procrastinate. This job only takes 15 or 20 minutes. The real hassle is getting the ladder out of the garage. Once begun, doing the work is not all that bad.

Here's a thought – while you're at it, why not be a hero?

If there are some elderly homeowners in your neighborhood, why not clear their home's gutters, too? You know that the gutters on their house probably have not been cleared. If water damage occurs they are even less likely to have the stamina to fix it.

Just walk over to their house with your ladder and knock on the door and say, "Hi Martha (John), have you had the gutters cleaned out this year?"

"Well, er, no."

"It'll only take five minutes, let me do it for you now."

Fifteen minutes later you will be feeling like a king, Martha and John will appreciate knowing they have neighbors who care, and their gutters will be clear.

3. Lubricate all doors and locks. 3 in 1 Oil is fine for door hinges. Use powdered graphite on the locks.

Don't forget to use a little 3 in 1 Oil on the long-suffering garage door. If you have a one-piece tilt door, clean and lubricate the pivots and rollers. On sectional doors, lubricate each sectional door hinge, rollers, overhead torsion springs, everything that moves.

One thing that should not be lubricated is the garage door opener's track or tube. Oiling that just gunk's it up and makes it harder to operate during the cold winter months.

Just three more things and you can go in and watch the football game.

4. If you haven't already done so, start up the lawnmower and all your other warm weather gas operated tools, and burn up the gas in their tanks. Drain and replace the oil.

Take out the spark plugs and clean them, then pour a couple drops of clean oil into the spark plug channel and screw the spark plug back in.

5. Make certain the snow blower is filled with fresh fuel and clean oil, then start 'er up. It is a lot smarter to learn if you have problems now, than waiting until our first 5-inch snow fall.

If you don't use a snow blower, today is the perfect time to coat both the top and bottom sides of snow shovels with several coats of a good silicone spray. If you have never done this before, you will be amazed at how much easier it makes shoveling. Repeat the silicone procedure after every shoveling.

6. Store away the lawn furniture. This is a great togetherness project. It doesn't take any time at all if everybody grabs a table or chair. Garage storage is always the best, but if you no longer have any room in the garage, lay three or four wooden pallets in back of the garage. Stack the furniture securely on the pallets, then cover with a couple of the large, heavy-duty blue plastic drop clothes secured by bungie cords.

You're done. You're a hero. You're ready to be a winter warrior. It's time to go in, grab an adult beverage and brag about it!

DECEMBER 11, 1999

Full-spectrum bulbs that emulate sunlight are worth the extra cost

by Glenn Haege,
America's Master Handyman

Have you ever been clothes hopping and had to take something out of the store to find out what color it really was? Or gone into an important meeting, only to discover that you had on one dark blue sock and one black? Or worse, that you were wearing midnight blue slacks with a black jacket?

The good part is that it ain't you kid, it's the lighting. Most of the lighting in our homes, schools, offices and factories is so bad that it is almost impossible to tell dark blue from black, and as far as flesh tones go, forget it.

The bad part is that most of us don't know how to do anything about the situation.

When it comes to lighting, you can go good, or you can go cheap. Light bulb manufacturers have the good, but they know that the public is price-oriented so they push the cheap.

If you want to understand light and light bulbs you have to go back to the basics. In the mid-1800's, William Thomson Kelvin was a professor at the University of Glasgow. Kelvin discovered that a block of iron would have a specific color when heated to an exact temperature. At about 3,500 degrees, the iron would have a warm, reddish glow. Above 6,000 degrees, it took on a bluish glow. At 5,000 degrees, it gave off a light that looked a lot like sun light.

A light bulb that gives off a warm, reddish glow is in the 2,000 to 3,500 Kelvin range. A light bulb with a Kelvin rating of 5,000 is considered a daylight bulb.

Another important lighting criterion is the Color Rendering Index (CRI). CRI rates the color shift an object undergoes when lighted by a specific source. Natural sunlight has a CRI of 100.

Many light bulbs have CRI's in the 30, 40 and 50 range. A very good fluorescent can be in the high 90's. Bulbs with CRI's in the mid-80's and above are considered "daylight" quality.

If an area is lit with daylight-quality bulbs, we can tell blues from blacks, flesh tones are warm and vital and we can see all the colors that our eyes were meant to see. The average cheap bulb or fluorescent tube is high on the output of blue light, but gives off very little yellow, red and green and has a low CRI. Our eyes weren't meant to function in this light so they function poorly.

Natural sunlight doesn't merely help us see better, it is considered by some to be a nutrient. Full-spectrum sun equivalent artificial light helps plants, fish and people grow, assists in the absorption of calcium, makes workers work and children learn more efficiently and lessens hyper-active behavior. In zoo tests, animal birth rates rocketed off the charts when the lighting was switched from inexpensive to full-spectrum bulbs and flourescents.

Man used to spend about 90 percent of his time out of doors. Now he spends 90 percent of the time indoors. During the winter, when we spend more time indoors and have even less light, there is now a medical phenomena called SAD – Seasonal Affective Disorder.

This disorder can usually be taken care of with a two-week vacation in the Bahamas or a couple 20-minute sessions a day with a full-spectrum light like the Verilux Happy Light.

All the major light bulb manufacturers produce full-spectrum bulbs. Duro-Test produces Vita-Lite tubes, GE produces Chroma 50, Philips produces Colortone 50, and Osram Sylvania produces Full Spectrum Fluorescent and the T12 Sunstick. Verilux introduced their Natural Spectrum Compact Fluorescent Bulb addition to their full-spectrum line at the 1999 Howsewares Show in Chicago. The trick is finding these products.

Aquarium supply and some garden stores carry them but their bulbs are usually very expensive.

Damman's carries a complete line of Real Lites Natural Lights, rated at about 6500 Kelvin at their Birmingham, West Bloomfield and Grosse Pt. Stores. The bulbs range from $5.79 for a 40-watt floodlight to $15.99 for a 48-inch fluorescent.

Home Depot carries both GE's Kitchen & Bath Fluorescent, which is rated at 3000 Kelvin, 82 CRI, and gives excellent skin and food colors, and the GE's Full Spectrum Fluorescents, rated at 5000 Kelvin, and 90 CRI. Home Depot's fluorescent prices are a real bargain at

Where to learn more

If you'd like to find out more about lighting, two good sources are on the Internet. The first is a technological paper on artificial lighting by Richard Sexton at www.thekrib.com/Lights/faq.html. The second is Harvey Moore's commercial web site at http://maxpages.com/durotest. (No www is needed.) Moore is a rep for Duro-Test, a light bulb manufacturer.

$5.97 for the 24 inch and $6.97 for the 48 inch.

The Harmony Catalogue put out by Gaiam, Inc., (800) 869-3446, has a good selection of full-spectrum bulbs, compact fluorescent spiral, and extended-long-life, full-spectrum fluorescent tubes. Prices range from $8 for a 60W full-spectrum incandescent light bulb, to $44 for a 20-watt (the equivalent to a 100-watt incandescent) compact Ott-Lite, to $56 for a set of four, 48-inch full-spectrum fluorescent tubes.

The best retail site I found on the web was www.naturallighting.com, the web site of Houston, TX based Natural Full Spectrum Lighting, (888) 900-6830. They list a broad assortment including Duro-Test's Vita-Lites and Spiralux super compact flourescents, as well as some GE's. Almost every bulb listed showed both the Kelvin temperature and the CRI ratings.

This isn't everything you should know about bulbs but it should shed a little more light on the subject.

DECEMBER 18, 1999

Last-minute gift ideas for the do-it-yourselfer? Just ask Santa Glenn

by Glenn Haege,
America's Master Handyman

If you are one week away from the big day and don't have your shopping done, do not despair. The Handyman has done it for you.

The psychology of gift giving is all-important. For some people the box or store the gift comes from is just as important as the gift itself. I shopped Restoration Hardware, Brookstone and Sharper Image at Somerset just for these folks as well as my usual digs at Home Depot and Damman Hardware.

Gifts should also be out of the ordinary so that the recipient knows you spent hours shopping. I picked out some real zany stuff for just this reason.

I went looking for gifts ranging from $1.00 to $1,000.00. $1.96 was as low as I could go. I included some practical things, but Christmas is special, so I also picked fun and extravagant stuff.

Practical

One or two 60-pound containers of Quikrete TubeSand in the trunk of a rear-wheel drive car will give it the extra weight needed for traction on icy streets. This could be a real lifesaver. A very loving gift that costs only $3.46 at HD.

Get him or her organized with a Contico Wall Tool Organizer. Made from heavy-duty plastic, it can organize a house full of hand tools. Just $1.96 at Home Depot.

Hang up to six shovels, rakes or other heavy tools with a four-foot wide, Heavy Duty Tool Hanger Rack by Suncast, $9.96 from Home Depot.

A battery-operated mini-fluorescent light by Ameritec can light up a dark clothes closet or tool area, $7.99 at Damman Hardware.

Fine print on directions and labels can be a real eyestrain. The Full Page 2X Magnifier, $10 at Brookstone, makes the tiniest print easy to read.

Should you know some one who actually uses a pocket protector, they will go "ga ga" when you give them a Hands Free Flashlight. Elastic head straps hold the light on the forehead. Just $15 from Brookstone.

Know someone who likes to use a push broom? He positively must have the 18-inch Ultimate Aluminum Dustpan, just $15 at Restoration Hardware.

The 29-piece Home Office Tool Set includes most commonly needed office tools: screw drivers, scissors, a claw hammer, stapler and glue gun. Only $19.99 at Home Depot.

If you know someone who constantly forgets his or her keys, the Smart Key Tracker, $25 from Brookstone, can save the day. Clap four times and the Key Tracker starts beeping. Little LED lights turn on so keys can even be found in the dark. Ladies with big purses will love this.

Damman Hardware has just knocked $10 off the price of the new Black & Decker 3.6 Volt Two Position Cordless Screwdriver. The new tool has the versatility needed to set screws in hard to reach places. $29.99 at Damman Hardware.

If your friend sometimes gets up late on Saturday or Sunday morning and misses my program because they are in the shower, save the day with a Water Resistant Fun Radio. $80 from Brookstone.

Fun Stuff

Your friend will never be caught in the dark with an Emergency Squeeze Powered Flashlight, just $10 at Restoration Hardware.

For someone panicked about Y2K, Free Play's very stylish, lightweight, reel-type, hand-powered radio would be the perfect gift. With this little beauty they can listen to the end of the world even after their electric generator has run out of fuel. $69.95 at Restoration Hardware.

If your friend has a boss like mine, he or she needs a set of boxing robots like the Roboxing Fighters at Sharper Image. A set of two costs $35 and can save thousands of dollars in couch time. Each robot needs 4 AA batteries. Handyman Hint: only put the batteries in one of the boxers, and you can beat the heck out of the other guy without his laying a glove on you.

Extravagant

Forget about a friend, you need this. A brass or stainless-steel Bath Caddy from Restoration Hardware. It lays across the tub and holds your soap, book, drink, and washrag. You can just sit, soak and relax without having to reach to get anything. $95 to $115.

If your friend has Tiffany tastes, let him or her set the tone for their palace with a black or white Fine Marble Address Plaque, 6 x 12 inches, a mere $100 at Restoration Hardware.

Help your friend cruise through life at up to 15 miles per hour on a fun, stand up, Deluxe Cityburg Scooter. A four-hour electric charge will take them up to 14 miles. $599 at Sharper Image.

If you know someone with an apartment or condo who wants a fireplace but thinks they can't have one, Williams Panel Brick, (800) 538-6650, Atlas Veneers and Fireplaces, (248) 524-1020, and Fireplace and Spa, (248) 353-0001, have very realistic electric fireplaces in the $1,600 range. The flames are absolutely captivating.

Heat-N-Glo has introduced a New England Style Cast Aluminum Electric Fireplace Stove. It looks better than the wood burning original yet costs only $999 at all Fireplace & Spa stores. Buy it, put it in the trunk and play Santa Claus. As soon as you plug it in your loved one will have a wonderfully warm fireplace/stove. If they move, they just pull the plug and take it with them.

Well my shopping is done. Now, where's the scotch tape?

Sources

■ Brookstone, Somerset Collection, Troy, (248) 643-7055

■ Damman Hardware, 17 locations in Metro Detroit, (248) 471-1256 (Farmington store)

■ Home Depot, many locations in Metro Detroit, (248) 423-0040 (Southfield store)

■ Restoration Hardware, Somerset Collection, Troy, (248) 614-6984

■ Sharper Image, Somerset Collection, Troy, (248) 643-4747

Keep your grandkids safe this holiday with a child-proof home

by Glenn Haege,
America's Master Handyman

When my daughter, Heather, had our first grandchild, Emily, I realized that every baby is a miraculous gift from God. If I could I would pick up that little munchkin and carry her around for the rest of my life so that she would always be safe.

I can't do that, of course. Emily has had to crawl, then walk and fall, and now gets her fair share of bumps and bruises. But as grandparents it is Barbara's and my job to make certain that our home is as child-proof as possible for the holidays. If you are a grandparent you know the feeling. It is an awesome responsibility.

If your home is not already child-proof and you will hear the pitter-patter of tiny feet at your house, making your home a safe place for the wee ones is the most important do-it-yourself project you will have this or any other year.

Luckily the internet has a host of sites with helpful information for amateur grandparents.

The Promina Health System of Metropolitan Atlanta, has a handy "Grandparent's Guide to Childproofing Your Home" at www.promina.org.

Some of the tips listed include walking around your house on your knees to see your home's dangers from a child's point-of-view. You will be surprised at the sharp corners, electrical cords and dangerous or breakable objects you will discover. Other child safety tips the Promina people recommend are:

- Store cleaning supplies and household chemicals in upper cabinets.
- Secure all medications out of reach.
- Purses are filled with pills, pins, keys and other no-no's. Keep purses out of reach.
- Install covers over electrical outlets. You can pick up electrical plug covers at most hardware stores.
- Cover sharp edges of tables, cabinets and book cases.
- Install screw-in type safety gates at stairways. Pressure gates look good but can be pushed in.
- Close off unused rooms. These rooms still should be child-proofed, but closing the doors securely will keep small-fry from exploring the rooms unattended.
- Make sure that curling irons and all small appliance cords are out of reach.
- Keep pets and children separated during short visits, or carefully watched during longer stays. Dogs and cats are magnetic attractions to little ones; but from the dog or cat's point-of-view a toddler is often a dangerous invader, not a beloved grandchild.
- Buy your own playpen, or better still, have the parents bring theirs so that baby is safe while you get a cup of coffee.

A woman who lists herself as Mrs. Fixit on the internet suggests that parents of small children who are staying overnight at a strange place should hang a towel over the top of the bathroom door before going to bed so that small-fry cannot accidentally lock themselves in the bathroom.

She also suggests that parents make certain that there are night lights on in the children's bedroom, halls and bath and advises hanging bells over door knobs so that parents are awakened if kids go exploring in the middle of the night.

I found four sites that give extensive child-proofing information:

■ www.cpsc.gov.
This site from the U.S. Consumer Product Safety Commission (CPSC) includes a free child safety brochure, *Childproofing Your Home: 12 Safety Devices to Protect Your Children,* it is produced in conjunction with the CNA Insurance Company.

This CPSC tip is a good one, grandparents: Use a cordless phone while babysitting so that it is never necessary to leave the child when answering or making a phone call.

■ www.Safebaby.net
This site has extensive information on child-proofing an entire home, and lists all the child safety hazards that can be found in every room of the house. One of the general tips listed is to never take medicine in front of a child. Children learn through imitation. If they see grandma or grandpa taking pills to make them feel good, little ones are prone to swallow any pills they may find around the house.

Two simple but awe-inspiring kitchen tips the site lists are: Only use the front burners to simmer, never boil water; and place all pans on the stove with their handles pointing toward the back of the stove.

These three tips could save many a trip to the emergency ward.

Child safety checklist

✔ Store cleaning supplies, household chemicals, medications and purses where they can not be reached.
✔ Install covers over electrical outlets.
✔ Cover sharp edges on furniture.
✔ Install screw-in safety gates at stairways.
✔ Close off unused rooms.
✔ Make sure that curling irons and electrical cords out of reach.
✔ Keep pets and children separated.
✔ Have a child safe play pen on hand.
✔ Install night lights in bedrooms, baths, and hallways.
✔ Hang a towel over the bathroom door so it can not be completely closed.
✔ Put alarm bells on doorknobs.
✔ Don't take pills in front of small children.
✔ Don't boil water on front stove burners.
✔ Place pans on stovetop with handles pointing toward the wall.

■ www.childproofers.com and www.childsafetyco.com.
These two commercial sites have good child-proofing information. They also include links to other child-safety shopping information.

For all you grand parents out there, I hope this article will help you make your home child-safe. These tips could save many trips to the emergency ward. Have a wonderful holiday! Spoil the grand kids rotten. Take lots of pictures. That's what Barb and I will be doing.

Appendix A

Most Asked for Phone Number and Web Sites

Category/Company Name	Product/Service	Phone Number	Web URL Address
*Emergency Phone Numbers			
Consumer's Energy (L)		(800) 889-1252	
Detroit Edison (L)		(800) 477-4747	
Michcon (L)		(800) 942-5571	
Michigan Public Service			
Commission (L)	Telephone Slamming	(800) 292-9555	
Air Quality			
Asbestos Removal Tech. (L, N)	Asbestos Removal	(248) 358-5577	
Broan (N)	Venting System Manufacturer	(800) 548-0790	www.broan.com
Buttons Rental (L)	Ozone Generator Rental	(248) 542-5835	
Christopher Cote's (L, N)	Air Testing	(800) 416-2323	
Healthy Homes (L, N)	Radon, etc.	(248) 358-3311	
Honeywell (N)	Enviracaire Manufacturer	(800) 328-5111	www.honeywell.com
Humidex (N)	Basement Ventilation	(888) 486-4339	
Pure Air +Plus (L, N)	Ozone Air Purfiers	(800) 455-5247	
Sanit-Air (L, N)	Air Testing	(888) 778-7324	
Skuttle (N)	Model 216	(800) 848-9786	www.skuttle.com
Starbrite (N)	Mil Du Gas Bags II	(800) 327-8583	www.starbrite.com
Sunbeam Housewares (N)	Humidifiers	(800) 597-5978	www.sunbeam.com
Trion (N)	Air Bear & Trion Air Cleaners	(800) 338-7466	www.trioninc.com
Vornado (N)	Vornado Heaters & Fans	(800) 234-0604	www.vornado.com
Xavier (N)	EQUALIZ-AIR	(734) 462-1033	members.aol.com/equalizair/Equalizair.html
Appliance Repair			
Carmack Appliance (L)	Parts & Repair	(734) 425-1790	
Servall Co. (L)	Parts Distributor	(810) 754-9951	

Category/Company Name	Product/Service	Phone Number	Web URL Address
Associations			
Automated Builders Consortium (N)	Mod. Home Builders Asso.	(847) 398-7756	www.automatedbuilder.com/abc.htm
Building Industry Assoc. of S. E. MI (L)		(248) 737-4477	www.builders.org
Cedar Shake & Shingle Bureau (N)		(604) 462-8961	
Concrete Contractors Assoc. (N)		(312) 792-0980	
Construction Assoc. of Michigan (L)		(248) 972-1000	www.cam-online.com
Great Lakes Ceramic Tile Council (L)		(248) 476-5559	
Habitat for Humanity Michigan (L)		(517) 882-2611	
Habitat for Humanity (N)		(800) 422-4828	
Insulated Concrete Forms Assoc. (N)		(847) 657-9730	www.forms.org
Masonry Institute of Michigan (L)		(734) 458-8544	
MI Manufactured Housing Assoc. (L)		(800) 422-6478	www.michhome.org
Michigan Mosquito Control Assoc. (L)		(517) 687-5044	www.mimosq.org
Michigan Pest Control Assoc. (L)		(810) 498-8480	
Michigan Roofing			
Contractors Assn. (L)	Inspections	(810) 759-2140	
Natl. Air Duct Cleaners Assoc. (N)		(202) 737-2926	www.nadca.com
Natl. Assoc. of Home Builders (N)		(800) 368-5242	www.nahb.com
Natl. Assoc. of Home Inspectors (N)		(800) 448-3942	www.nahi.org
Natl. Assoc. of Real Estate Brokers (N)		(202) 785-4477	www.nareb.com
Natl. Assoc. of Realtors (N)		(312) 329-8200	www.realtor.com
Natl. Assoc. of the Remodeling Ind. (N)		(800) 440-6274	
Natl. Burglar & Fire Alarm Assn. (N)		(301) 907-3202	www.alarm.org
Natl. Waterproofing Council (N)		(800) 245-6292	www.waterproofers.org
Structural Insulated Panel Assoc. (N)	SIP Manufacturers Assoc.	(253) 858-7472	www.sips.org
The Vinyl Institute (N)		(800) 969-8469	www.vinylinfo.org

Basement Problems

Affordable Dry Basement (L)	Waterproofing	(800) 310-5700	
B-Dry (L, N)	Waterproofing	(800) 875-2379	www.bdry.com
Calculus Construction (L, N)	Structural Restoration	(888) 746-5464	
Insta-Dry Waterproofing (L)	Waterproofing	(800) 356-0820	
Jackson Water Proofing (L, N)	Structural Restoration	(800) 404-8342	
Mr. Sponge (L, N)	Waterproofing	(800) 491-4686	
SAS (L)	Waterproofing	(800) 894-5115	
Sure-Seal (N)	Waterproofing (Injection)	(708) 430-2522	

Brick & Concrete

J. C. Cornillie (L)	Supplier	(810) 293-1500	
Williams Panel Brick (L, N)	Thin Brick	(800) 538-6650	www.williamspanelbrick.com

Building Specialists

A & Z Commercial Roofing (L)	Roofing Problems	(734) 513-7300	
Benchmark (L)	Insulated Concrete Walls	(248) 853-9400	www.benchmarkwalls.com
Coy Construction (L)	Basement Remodeling/Decks	(248) 363-1050	
Fairway Construction (L.)	Additions & Dormers	(800) 354-9310	www.fairwayconstruction.com
Four Seasons (L, N)	Sun Room Manufacturer	(800) 368-7732	www.four-seasons-sunrooms.com
Mr. Enclosure (L)	Sun Room Manufacturer	(877) 786-1131	www.mrenclosure.com
Pine Building (L)	Additions & Dormers	(888) 500-7463	www.pinebuilding.com
Temo (L, N)	Sun Room Manufacturer	(800) 344-8366	www.temosunrooms.com

Building Supply & Hardware

3 M (N)	Construction Products	(800) 480-1704	www.3M.com
Chicago Metallic (N)	Embossed Metal Ceilings	(800) 560-5758	www.interfinish.com
Dalton Ltd. (N)	Airport Grade Pli-STIX	(800) 851-5606	
Dillman & Upton (L)	Lumber/Paint/Hardware	(248) 651-9411	
Dryvit (N)	Interior Wall Manufacturer	(800) 556-7752	www.dryvit.com

Category/Company Name	Product/Service	Phone Number	Web URL Address
Erb Lumber (L)	Lumber/Paint/Hardware	(248) 644-3636	
Louisiana-Pacific (N)	Wood & Vinyl Siding Mfg.	(800) 648-6893	www.lpcorp.com
N.A. Mans (L)	Lumber/Paint/Hardware	(734) 981-5800	
Siding World (L)	Roofing/Siding/Windows	(313) 891-2902	
USG Corp. (N)	Durock Cement Board Mfg.	(800) 874-4968	www.usg.com

Cleaners/Polishers

Category/Company Name	Product/Service	Phone Number	Web URL Address
Alumin-Nu (N)	Nice N Easy	(800) 899-7097	www.aluminnu.com
Bix (N)	Driveway Cleaner	(800) 251-1098	www.bixmfg.com
Block Drug (N)	X-14	(800) 365-6500	www.blockdrug.com
Bon Ami (N)	Bon Ami	(800) 821-5565	www.bonami.com
Dourmar Products (N)	Candle Wax Remover	(888) 289-8638	
Flitz International	Metal Polish/Fiberglass Cleaner	(800) 558-8611	
Go Jo Industries (N)	Go Jo Hand Cleaner	(800) 321-9647	www.handcare.gojo.com
Hopes (N)	Counter Top Polish	(800) 325-4026	www.hopecompany.com
Lilly Industries (N)	Bug Stuff/Goof Off	(800) 253-3957	www.lillyindustries.com
Lime 0 Sol Co. (N)	The Works Bath & Shower Cleaner	(800) 448-5281	
Loctite (N)	DL Hand Cleaner	(800) 243-4874	www.loctite.com
Magic American (N)	Goo Gone	(800) 321-6330	www.magicamerican.com
Mr. Furniture Finisher (L, N,)	Doozy Furniture Polish	(888) 851-8500	www.doozy.com
Orange-Sol (N)	De-Solv-It & Clean Away	(800) 877-7771	www.orange-sol.com
Oxisolv, Inc. (N)	Rust Remover	(800) 594-9028	
Parker & Bailey (N)	Wood & Countertop Polishes	(888) 727-6547	www.parkerbailey.com
ProSoCo (N)	Shure Klean	(800) 255-4255	www.prosoco.com
Savogran Co. (N)	TSP/Dirtex	(800) 225-9872	www.savogran.com
SerVaas Labs (N)	Bar Keepers Friend	(800) 433-5818	www.barkeepersfriend.com
Space Invader Cleaning Products (N)	Pivoting Sponge Mop	(800) 343-3368	

Stone Care (N)	Stone Care	(800) 839-1654	www.stonecare.com/sci
Sunshine Makers (N)	Simple Green	(800) 228-0709	www.simplegreen.com
Supreme Chemicals (N)	Krud Kutter	(800) 466-7126	www.krudkutter.com
Surco Products (N)	Restorex Wood Cleaner	(800) 556-0111	www.surco.com

Coatings

Artist Brush & Color (N)	Concrete Patio Paint	(800) 828-0359	
Benjamin Moore (N)	Paint Manufacturer	(800) 672-4686	www.benjaminmoore.com
Bio-Wash (N)	Supernatural Protective Wood Finish	(800) 858-5011	www.biowash.com
Carver Tripp (Parks) (N)	Safe & Simple	(800) 225-8543	www.parkscorp.com
Coronado Paints (N)	Cement Stain Manufacturer	(800) 883-4193	www.coronadopaint.com
Cuprinol Stains (N)	Exterior Wood Stain Mfg.	(800) 424-5837	
Dutch Boy Paints (N)	Paint Manufacturer	(800) 828-5669	
Envirochem (N)	Sta-Clean Mildicide Additive	(800) 247-9011	
Epoxi-Tech (N)	Epoxy Concrete Paint	(888) 683-5667	www.epoxi-seal.com
Flecto (N)	Watco Oil Finishes	(800) 635-3286	www.flecto.com
Graham (N)	Aqua Borne Ceramic Paint	(800) 255-2628	www.grahampaint.com
H & C (N)	Cement Stain	(800) 867-8246	www.concretestain.com
INSL-X (N)	Paints & Stains	(800) 225-5554	
Kurfees Coatings (N)	Fresh Air Paint	(800) 626-6147	
Lilly Industries (N)	Super Mildex Additive	(800) 253-3957	www.lillyindustries.com
Masterchem (N)	Paint Manufacturer	(800) 733-4413	www.masterchem.com
Mr. Long Arm (N)	Paint Roller & Brush Extension Pole	(800) 334-8388	
Painters Supply (L)	Paint Distributor	(734) 946-8119	
Pittsburgh Paints (N)	Paints & Stains Mfg.	(800) 441-9695	www.ppgaf.com
Pontiac Paint (L)	Paint Retailer	(248) 332-4643	www.pontiacpaint.com
Rohm & Haas (N)	Paint Quality Institute	(215) 641-7038	www.paintquality.com
Shelby Paint (L)	Paint Retail	(810) 739-0240	www.shelbypaint.com

Category/Company Name	Product/Service	Phone Number	Web URL Address
Sherwin-Williams (N)	Paint Manufacturer	(800) 474-3794	www.sherwinwilliams.com
Spraytex (N)	Spraytex	(800) 234-5979	www.spraytex.com
UGL (N)	Dry Lok	(800) 272-3235	
Waterlox (N)	Transparent Urethane	(800) 321-0377	www.waterlox.com
William Zinsser (N)	Perma-White Paint	(732) 469-4367	www.zinsser.com
Coatings - Stain Kills			
Masterchem (N)	Kilz And Kilz II	(800) 325-3552	www.masterchem.com
William Zinsser (N)	B-I-N Primer Sealer	(732) 469-4367	www.zinsser.com
X-I-M Products (N)	X-I-M Stain Kills	(800) 262-8469	www.ximbonder.com
Concrete Lifting (Mud Jacking)			
A1 (L)	Concrete Leveling	(800) 538-3514	
Calculus Construction (L)	Concrete Leveling	(888) 746-5464	
Concrete Restoration Services (L)	Concrete Leveling	(810) 997-4001	
Kent Concrete Raising (L)	Concrete Leveling	(313) 532-8803	
Original Concrete Raising (L)	Concrete Leveling	(810) 774-5855	
Concrete/Asphalt			
Ardex (N)	Concrete Resurfacer	(888) 512-7339	www.ardex.com
Concrete Technologies (N)	Resurfacing & Stamping	(888) 727-6001	
Gibraltar National (L, N)	Quikrete Products	(800) 442-7258	www.gibraltarnational.com
Macklanburg-Duncan (N)	Mr. Mac's Concrete Products	(800) 654-8454	www.mdteam.com
Michigan Paving Concepts (L)	Concrete Forms for Driveways	(248) 673-7001	
Quikrete National (L, N)	Cement & Concrete Patch	(800) 282-5828	www.quikrete.com
SealMaster (L, N)	Asphalt Sealer	(800) 395-7325	www.sealmaster.net
Stampcrete (L)	Concrete Stamping	(800) 233-3298	www.stampcrete.com/contact.html
Ytong USA (N)	Autoclaved Aerated Concrete	(800) 986-6435	www.ytong-usa.com

Construction Materials

AAB Building Systems (N)	Insulated Block Walls	(800) 293-3210	www.bluemaxxaab.com
Acoustical Distributors (L)	Ceiling Panels	(810) 465-2010	www.acousticaldistributors.com
Aqua Glass (N)	Shower & Bath Components	(901) 632-9011	
Century Superior (L)	Wood Basements	(248) 350-9510	
Delta Faucets (N)	Faucets & Fixtures	(800) 345-3358	www.deltafaucet.com
Franklin Brass (N)	Fixtures	(800) 829-0089	www.franklinbrass.com
Hanson Marketing (L, N)	Tyvek, Barker Ceramalite	(800) 552-4877	
Red Devil (N)	One Time Filler	(800) 423-3845	www.reddevil.com
Reddi Wall (L, N)	Foam Block Wall Systems	(810) 752-9161	www.reddi-wall.com
Sashco Sealants (N)	Lexell Crystal Clear Caulk	(800) 289-7290	www.sashco.com
Superior Walls (N)	Structural Insulated Panels	(800) 452-9255	www.superiorwalls.com
Tapco (N)	Cove Master	(800) 521-8486	www.tapco-intl.com
Team Industries (N)	Structural Insulated Panels	(800) 356-5548	www.teamindustries.com

Consumer Protection

Consumer Affairs Dept. of Detroit (L)	Consumer Complaints	(313) 224-3508	www.ci.detroit.mi.us
Joe Gagnon (L)	Appliances	(734) 425-1790	
MI Construction Protection Agency (L)	Lien Law & License Checks	(800) 543-6669	www.mcpanet.com
Mich. Dept. of Commerce (L)	License Checks	(900) 555-8374	

Deck Construction Materials

Advanced Environmental (N)	ChoiceDek	(800) 951-5117	www.choicedek.com
Biewer Lumber (L, N)	Durable Deck	(800) 482-5717	www.biewerlumber.com
Crane Plastics (N)	TimberTech	(800) 307-7780	www.timbertech.com
Dec-K-ing (N)	Vinyl Sheet Deck Covering	(800) 804-6288	www.dec-k-ing.com
Dexter Innovations (L)	Brock Deck	(248) 414-3900	www.dexterinnovations.com
Hickson (N)	Wolmanized Chemical	(800) 264-4222	www.hickson.com
Kroy (N)	Vinyl Fence & Decking	(800) 933-5769	www.kroybp.com

Category/Company Name	Product/Service	Phone Number	Web URL Address
Osmose Wood Preserving (N)	Osmose Chemical	(800) 241-0240	www.osmose.com
Pultronex (N)	E-Z Deck	(800) 990-3099	www.ezdeck.com
Royal Crown (N)	Brock Deck	(800) 365-3625	www.royalcrownltd.com
Thermal Industries (N)	DreamDeck	(800) 245-1540	www.thermalindustries.com
Trex Company (N)	Trex	(800) 289-8739	www.trex.com
US Plastic Lumber (N)	SmartDeck Manufacturer	(888) 733-2546	www.smartdeck.com
Deck Finishes, Maintenance			
Akzo Nobel (N)	Sikkens Decroative Coatings	(800) 833-7288	www.nam.sikkens.com
Behr Process (N)	Wood Cleaner Brightener	(800) 854-0133	www.behrpaint.com
Bio-Wash (N)	Simple Wash/Natural Deck Oil	(800) 858-5011	www.biowash.com
C.J. Link (L)	Distributor	(810) 773-1200	
Cabot Stains (N)	Problem Solver	(800) 877-8246	www.cabotstain.com
Duckback (N)	Superdeck	(800) 825-5382	www.superdeck.com
Flood Company (N)	Seasonite/Dekswood	(800) 321-3444	www.floodco.com
Griffin (N)	Noah Renewal System	(877) 747-6624	
Howard Davison Lumber (N)	Timberseal	(800) 543-0469	
Performance Coatings (N)	Penofin	(800) 736-6346	www.PENOFIN.com
PPG Industries (N)	Olympic Wood Sealer	(800) 441-9695	www.olympic.com
Wolman Products (N)	Wolman Toner & Sealers	(800) 556-7737	www.wolman.com
Woodtec (N)	Timber-Seal	(800) 338-3175	www.timber-seal.com
Doors			
Atlas (N)	Commercial Overhead Doors	(800) 959-9559	www.atlasdoor.com
Home & Door (L)	Garage & Entry Doors	(248) 547-8900	
Raynor (N)	Garage Doors	(800) 545-0455	www.raynor.com
Stanley (N)	Garage Doors	(800) 521-5262	
Tarnow (L)	Garage & Entry Doors	(800) 466-9060	www.tarnowdoor.com

Duct Cleaners

A.1 Duct Cleaning (L)	Duct Cleaning	(800) 382-8256	
Dalton Environmental (L)	Duct Cleaning	(800) 675-2298	
Dusty Ducts (L)	Duct Cleaning	(313) 381-7801	
Fresh Air Solutions, Inc. (L)	Duct Cleaning	(800) 341-4076	www.tdi.net/freshair/
Safety King (L)	Duct Cleaning	(888) 382-8776	www.ductpro.com
Sanit-Air (L)	Duct Cleaning	(888) 778-7324	
Sterling Environmental (L)	Duct Cleaning	(888) 992-1200	
Vent Corp. (L)	Duct Cleaning	(248) 473-9300	

Electric Heaters

Duracraft (N)	Heater Manufacturer	(800) 554-4558	www.honeywell.com
Pelonis (N)	Ceramic Heater Manufacturer	(800) 842-1289	www.pelonis.com

Electrical

Budget Electric (L)	Surge Suppressors & Residential Install	(800) 400-8941	www.hometown.aol.com/budgetelectric
Discount Air Compressor & Generator (L, N)	Multi fuel Electric Generators	(248) 338-2255	www.gohonda.com
Ditek (N)	Surge Suppressors	(800) 753-2345	www.ditekcorp.com
Haig Electric (L)	Lighting Retailer	(810) 791-2380	
House of Lights (L)	Lighting Retailer	(888) 843-5483	
Illuminations (L)	Lighting Retailer	(248) 332-7500	www.illumlighting.com
Weingartz (L)	Electric Generators	(810) 731-7240	www.weingartz.com

Electronics

C. Crane (N)	Audio Equipment	(800) 522-8863	www.ccrane.com
X10 (N)	Home Automation Products	(800) 762-7846	www.smarthome.com
X10 USA (N)	Home Automation Products	(800) 675-3044	www.x10.com/homepage.htm

Category/Company Name	Product/Service	Phone Number	Web URL Address
Finishing Products			
3 M (N)	Synthetic Steel Wool Pads	(800) 364-3577	www.3M.com
Deft (N)	Danish Oil	(800) 544-3338	www.deftfinishes.com
Guaranteed Furniture Services (L)	Antique Furniture Restor.	(248) 545-1130	
Meguiar's (N)	Swirl Remover	(800) 347-5700	www.meguiars.com
Thompson & Formby (N)	Furniture Face Lift	(800) 367-6297	www.thompsonsonline.com
Wood Kote (N)	Jel'd Wood Stain	(800) 843-7666	www.woodkote.com
Fireplace Products			
Fireplace Manufacturing (N)	FMI Fireplace	(800) 888-2050	
Fuego Flame(N)	Fireplace Manufacturer	(800) 445-1867	www.fuegoflame.com
HearthStone (N)	Fireplace Manufacturer	(800) 827-8683	www.hearthstonestoves.com
Heat-N-Glo (N)	Fireplace Manufacturer	(800) 669-4328	www.heatnglo.com
Heatilator (N)	Fireplace Manufacturer	(800) 843-2848	www.heatilator.com
Hunter (N)	Fireplace Manufacturer	(800) 634-0233	www.huntertechnology.com
Jøtul (N)	Cast Iron Stoves & Fireplaces	(207) 797-5912	www.hearth.com/jotul/jotul.html
Majestic (N)	Fireplace Manufacturer	(800) 842-2058	www.majesticproducts.com
Top Hat Chimney (L)	Chimney Sweep, Repair & Video Inspection	(888) 793-3741	
Wolf Steel (N)	Napoleon Fireplace Mfg.	(800) 461-5581	www.napoleon.on.ca
Fireplace Retailer			
Atlas (L)	Retailer/Installer	(248) 524-1020	
Emmett Energy (L)	Retailer/Installer	(810) 752-2075	
Fireplace & Spa (L)	Retailer/Installer	(248) 353-0001	
Michigan Fireplace & Barbecue (L)	Retailer/Installer	(248) 689-2296	
Williams Panel Brick (L, N)	Retailer/Installer/Service	(800) 538-6650	www.williamspanelbrick.com

Floor Finishers

Cameron the Sand Man (L)	Install & Restoration	(248) 477-8108
Dande (L)		(800) 522-7701	www.dandefloors.com
G & G Floors (L)		(800) 806-1798
Paynter Floors (L)		(800) 471-9091
Rex Boyce Floor Service (L)		(248) 642-8244

Floor Finishes

Basic Coatings (N)	Street Shoe Wood Finish	(800) 247-5471	www.basiccoatings.com
BonaKemi (N)	Pacific Strong	(800) 872-5515	www.bonakemi.com
Fabulon (N)	Crystal II	(800) 364-1359
Hartco (N)	Pattern Plus	(800) 442-7826
Minwax (N)	Duraseal	(800) 462-0194	www.minwax.com
Valspar (N)	Gym Seal	(800) 767-2532	www.valspar.com

Floor Finishing DIY

Buttons Rent-It (L)	Rental Equipment	(248) 542-5835
Chets Rental (L)	Rental Equipment	(248) 543-0118
Crandall Worthington (L)	Rental Equipment	(248) 398-8118
Flecto (N)	Square Buff Sander	(800) 635-3286	www.flecto.com

Flooring

Beaver (L)	Ceramic Tile Distributors	(248) 476-2333	www.beavertile.com
Bio-Wash (N)	Foam Off Adhesive Remover	(800) 663-9274	www.biowash.com
Bondex International (N)	Bondex Flooring	(800) 231-6781	www.rpm.com
Bruce (N)	Bruce Hardwood Flooring Mfg.	(800) 722-4647	www.brucehardwoodfloors.com
Crew Inc. (N)	Linoleum Repair Kit	(800) 490-2001
Duraclean (L)	Carpet Cleaning	(800) 372-5427	www.mrzar.com
Erickson's Flooring (L, N)	Wood Flooring Distributor	(800) 225-9663
Fairway Tile & Carpet (L)	Envira Cushion	(248) 588-4431

535

Category/Company Name	Product/Service	Phone Number	Web URL Address
Hartco (N)	Pattern Plus	(800) 442-7826	www.homasote.com
Homasote (N)	Comfort Base	(800) 257-9491	www.homasote.com
Modernistic (L)	Carpet Cleaning	(800) 609-1000	www.modernistic.com
O'Berry (N)	Squeak No More Tool	(800) 459-8428	www.oberry-enterprises.com
Pergo (N)	Laminated Flooring	(800) 337-3746	www.pergo.com
Smith & Fong (N)	Bamboo Flooring	(650) 872-1185	www.plyboo.com
Furniture Refinishing			
Furniture Medic (L)		(888) 624-3914	
Guaranteed Furniture Services (L)	Antique Furniture Restoration	(248) 545-1130	
Heating & Cooling			
Bryant (N)	Manufacturer	(800) 428-4326	www.bryant.com
Carrier (N)	Manufacturer	(800) 227-7437	www.carrier.com
Detroit Edison (L)	Geothermal Heating	(800) 833-2786	www.detroitedison.com
Detroit Safety Furnace (L)	SpacePak Distributor	(800) 682-1538	
Heat Link USA (N)	Hydronic Radiant Floor Heating	(800) 968-8905	www.heatlink.com
Heil/Intl. Products (N)	Heil Products	(615) 270-4179	
Lennox (N)	Manufacturer	(972) 497-5000	www.davelennox.com
Mestek (N)	SpacePak Manufacturer	(413) 568-9571	www.mestek.com
Rheem/Ruud (N)	Manufacturer	(800) 621-5622	www.rheem.com
Trane (N)	Manufacturer	(888) 872-6335	www.trane.com
Vanguard (N)	Hydronic Radiant Floor Heating	(800) 775-5039	www.vanguardpipe.com
WaterFurnace (N)	Geothermal Heating	(800) 222-5667	www.waterfurnace.com
York (N)	Manufacturer	(877) 874-7378	www.york.com
Heating & Cooling Contractors			
Bergstrom (L)	General	(734) 522-1350	www.bluedotservices.com
Flame Furnace Co. (L)	General	(888) 234-2340	

Hartford & Ratliff (L, N)	Water Heating Specialist	(800) 466-3110	
Lizut (L)	General	(248) 858-2525	
Vincent's (L)	Comfort Zone Control TLC	(888) 985-7103	www.vhpinc.com
Williams (L)	General	(888) 268-5445	

Heating Products

Bionaire (N)	Humidifiers	(800) 253-2764	
Duro Dyne (N)	Zone Heat Control Manufacturer	(800) 966-6446	www.durodyne.com
Environmental Air Controls (N)	Enviracaire Ev-1	(800) 332-1110	www.honeywell.com
Holmes Products (N)	Humidifiers	(800) 546-5637	www.holmesproducts.com
Honeywell (N)	Magistat & PC 8900	(800) 328-5111	www.honeywell.com
Hunter (N)	Thermostat Manufacturer	(901) 743-1360	www.hunterfan.com

Home Security

Ademco (L)	Security Device Manufacturer	(800) 645-7568	www.ademco.com
ADT (N)	Security & Fire Protection	(800) 238-9490	www.adt.com
Home Automation (N)	DIY Kits	(800) 229-7256	www.homeauto.com
Kwikset Locks (N)	Motion Activated Deadbolt Lock	(800) 327-5625	www.kwikset.com
Mag Security (N)	Door Reinforcers	(800) 624-9942	www.magsecurity.com
Weiser Lock (N)	Powerbolt Remote	(800) 677-5625	www.weiserlock.com
X10 (N)	DIY Kits	(800) 762-7846	www.smarthome.com
X10 USA Inc. (N)	DIY Kits	(800) 675-3044	www.x10.com/homepage.htm

Insulation

Ace & Sons (L)	Cellulose	(248) 642-4311	
Astro-Foil (N)	Polyethylene Bubble	(888) 946-7325	www.insul.net
CertainTeed (L, N)	Fiberglass	(800) 233-8990	www.certainteed.com
Dow (N)	Styrofoam	(800) 441-4369	www.dow.com
Flexible Products (N)	Great Stuff Polyurethane	(800) 800-3626	www.flexibleproducts.com
Icynece (N)	Foam	(800) 946-7325	www.icynene.com

Category/Company Name	Product/Service	Phone Number	Web URL Address
Johns Manville (N)	Roofing & Insulation	(800) 654-3102	
Macomb (L)	Fiberglass	(810) 949-1400	
Owens-Corning (N)	Foam & Fiberglass	(800) 438-7465	www.owenscorning.com
Kitchen Cabinets			
Cabinet Clinic (L)	Refacing	(734) 421-8151	www.cabinetclinic.com
CabinetClad (L)	Refacing	(248) 541-5252	
Kitchen Tune Up (L)	Refurbishing	(248) 738-5075	www.kitchentuneup.com
KraftMaid (N)	Cabinet Manufacturer	(800) 571-1990	www.kraftmaid.com
Kurtis (L)	Design & Construction	(734) 522-7600	www.kurtiskitchen.com
Merillat (N)	Cabinet Manufacturer	(800) 575-8759	www.merillat.com
Kitchens & Baths			
DuPont (N)	Corian Surfaces	(800) 426-7426	www.corian.com
Formica (N)	Plastic Laminate Surfaces	(800) 524-0159	www.formica.com
H.J. Oldenkamp (L)	Formica Distributors	(800) 444-7280	
Hydromaid (N)	Garbage Disposer Manufacturer	(888) 824-9376	www.hydromaid.com
In-Sink-Erator (N)	Garbage Disposer Manufacturer	(800) 558-5712	www.insinkerator.com
Nu-Way Supply (L)	Parts & Fixtures	(810) 731-4000	www.nuwaysupply.com
Re-Bath Company (N)	Bathtub Liners	(800) 426-4573	www.rebath.com
Resources Conservation (N)	Scald Safe Adapter	(800) 243-2862	
StarMark Cabinetry (N)	Cabinet Manufacturer	(800) 594-9444	www.starmarkcabinetry.com
Super Jet (N)	Bath Brite/Grout Brite	(888) 217-3509	www.superjetco.com
Superior Distributing (N)	Pull Out Shelving	(800) 622-4462	
Talon Industries (L, N)	Korstone Solid Surface Counters	(877) 567-7866	
Universal Plumbing (L)	Parts & Fixtures	(248) 542-3888	
Virginia Tile (L)	Ceramic Tile Distributors	(800) 837-8453	
Western Slope Designs (N)	Plunger Pal	(877) 206-1937	

Ladders & Scaffolding

Bil-Jax (N)	Rolling Scaffold	(800) 537-0540
National Ladder & Scaffold (L)	Retailer & Rental	(800) 535-5944
R.D. Werner Co. (N)	Ladder Manufacturer	(888) 523-3371

Lawn & Garden

Evergreen (L)	Fireplace & Patio Furniture	(810) 791-2277	www.evergreenhomeandgarden.com
GrassMasters (N)	Work Station/Trail Boss	(888) 810-5050	
Jimmies Rustics (L)	Barbecues & Patio Furniture	(248) 644-1919	
Rock Shoppe (L)	Patio Stones, Statues & Waterfalls	(734) 455-5560	
Security Products (N)	Moss & Mildew Remover	(888) 241-9547	
Swan (N)	Hoselink	(800) 848-8707	
Thermo Fire Distr. (L)	Ducane Barbecue	(800) 878-7400	
Weitech Electronic (N)	Outdoor Protector	(800) 343-2659	

Modular Homes

Active Homes (L)	Manufacturer	(800) 228-4834	www.activehomes.com
Sierra Associates (L)	Builder	(248) 399-7062	

One of a Kind

Alumin-Nu (N)	Pond Restorer & Bacterial Cleaners	(800) 899-7097	www.aluminnu.com
E & E (N)	Squeak Ender	(800) 323-0982	www.eandeconsumerproducts.com
Environmental Water Services (L)	Water Filters & Systems	(800) 371-7873	
Fiberlock Technologies (N)	Barrier Coating	(800) 342-3755	
Gibraltar National (L, N)	Gibraltar Ice Melters	(800) 442-7258	www.gibraltarnational.com
Hobart Welders (N)	DIY Welders & Plasma Cutters	(800) 626-9420	
Home Builders Workshop (N)	Education	(800) 462-0899	
Marsh Power Tools (L)	Tool Retailer & Repair	(800) 433-8665	www.marshpowertools.com
Millennium Int. Develop. (N)	Mirr.Edge	(800) 757-2990	
Monroe Infrared (L)	Thermal Imaging	(800) 221-0163	www.infrared-center.com

Category/Company Name	Product/Service	Phone Number	Web URL Address
New Life Copper & Brass (N)	Brass Roof Shiners	(800) 894-7862	
Premier Distributors (L)	MiniClick II Rain Sensor	(810) 228-5400	
Punati Chemical (N)	Smells Be Gone	(800) 645-2882	
StreetPrint (N)	Asphalt Stamping	(800) 688-5652	www.streetprint.com
Universal Weather Strip (L)	Weather Stripping Sup.	(800) 776-0277	
W.M. Barr Co. (N)	Odorless Synthetic Fuel Heater Mfg.	(800) 238-2672	
Wash On Wheels Mich. (L)	Brick & Siding Cleaning	(810) 979-7890	
Yankee Carpenter (L)	Unfinished & Custom Finished Furniture	(248) 338-0441	www.yankeecarpenter.com
Zimms Vacuums (L)	Central Vac Systems	(800) 664-1105	www.zimmsvac.com
Painting Supplies			
Bio-Wash (N)	Waste Paint Hardener	(800) 663-9274	www.biowash.com
Detroit Quality Brush (N)	Rag Roller	(800) 722-3037	
Lilly Industries (N)	Super Mildex - Additive	(800) 253-3957	www.lillyindustries.com
Wagner Spray (N)	Paint Sprayers	(800) 328-8251	www.wagnerspraytech.com
Pavers			
Advanced Coatings (L, N)	Proseal 2000 Sealer	(810) 465-7842	
Decra-Loc USA (N)	Manufacturer	(800) 447-5898	
Fendt (L)	Manufacturer	(888) 706-9975	www.fendtbuilderssupply.com
Lafarge (N)	Manufacturer	(800) 876-6257	www.lafargepavers.com
Outdoor Supply Co. (L)	Landscaping & Stone Distr.	(800) 507-1166	
Stone City Products (L)	Landscaping & Stone Distr.	(810) 731-4500	
Unilock (N)	Manufacturer	(800) 864-5625	www.unilock.com
Pest Control			
Bonide Products (N)	Mosquito Beater	(800) 552-8252	www.bonideproducts.com
Environmental (L)	Varmit Control	(248) 626-7199	

Name	Description	Phone	Website
Four Star (L)	Varmit Control	(800) 870-7096	
Maple Lane (L)	Varmit Control	(800) 870-7096	
Thompson (L)	Molley, The Ant Sniffing Dog	(800) 934-4770	

Plumbing

Name	Description	Phone	Website
Advance (L)	Distributor	(800) 560-7474	
Alsons (N)	Shower Fixtures	(800) 421-0001	www.alsons.com
American Standard (N)	Smart Valve	(800) 223-0068	
American Water Heater (N)	Flame Guard	(423) 283-8138	
Controlled Energy (N)	Aquastar Tankless Water Heaters	(800) 642-3111	www.cechot.com
Delta Faucet (N)	Faucet Manufacturer	(800) 345-3358	
Nu-Way Supply (L)	Parts & Fixtures	(810) 731-4000	www.nuwaysupply.com
Pred (N)	Ultra Seal Wax Ring Mfg.	(800) 323-6188	
Sloan Flushmate (N)	Toilet Power Flush Insert	(800) 875-9116	www.flushmate.com
State Industries (N)	Water Heaters	(800) 365-0024	www.stateind.com
Ted Funger Enterprises (N)	Aqua Plumber	(905) 336-4077	
The Idea Factory (N)	Child Safety Shower Head	(800) 867-4673	
Universal Plumbing (L)	Sump Vac	(248) 542-3888	
W/C Technology (N)	Power Flush Insert	(888) 732-9282	www.pf2wctc.com
Zoeller (N)	Water Powered Sump Pump	(800) 928-7867	www.zoeller.com

Repair

Name	Description	Phone	Website
Abatron (N)	Load Bearing Epoxy Wood Repair	(800) 445-1754	www.abatron.com
Case Handyman (L)	Home Repair Specialist	(248) 799-0129	www.CaseHandyman.com
Elmer's (N)	Elmer's Carp. Wood Glue	(800) 848-9400	www.elmers.com
Loctite (N)	Adhesives	(800) 243-4874	www.loctite.com
Nuporce Products (N)	Porcelain Crack Repair	(800) 994-9970	

Roofing

Name	Description	Phone	Website
A & Z Commercial (L)	Thermo Flat Roof Installer	(734) 513-7300	

Category/Company Name	Product/Service	Phone Number	Web URL Address
American Metal (N)	Gutter Helmet	(888) 443-5638	www.americanmetalproducts.com
CertainTeed (N)	Roofing & Ventilation	(800) 233-8990	www.certainteed.com
Cetco (N)	Urethane	(888) 826-8846	www.cetco.com
Chicago Metallic (N)	Shingle Shield	(800) 323-7164	www.chicago-metallic.com
Classic Products (N)	Aluminum Manufacturer	(800) 543-8938	
Concrete Tile (L)	Tile Roofing	(248) 669-3409	
Crowe Building (N)	Composite Roof Manufacturer	(905) 529-6818	
Elk (N)	Roofing	(800) 944-4344	
GAF (N)	Cobra Ridge Vent	(800) 688-6654	www.gaf.com
GAF (N)	Shingle Manufacturer	(800) 678-4285	www.gaf.com
Globe (N)	Combo Vents	(800) 456-5649	www.globebuilding.com
Joy (L)	Gutter Helmet Installer	(800) 378-1924	
Leafguard (N)	Gutter Protector	(800) 532-3482	
MonierLifetile (N)	Roof Tile Manufacturer	(800) 571-8453	
Northern Roof Tile (N)	Cembrit B7 Distributor	(905) 627-4035	
Oregon Research (N)	Roof Guard Roofing Patch	(800) 345-0809	
Owens Corning (N)	Shingle Manufacturer	(800) 438-7465	www.owenscorning.com
Paragon Technologies (L)	Consultants	(810) 726-8440	
Rainhandler (L)	Gutterless Gutters	(800) 942-3004	www.rainhandler.com
Re-New Wood (N)	Composite Roof Manufacturer	(800) 420-8576	
Roofing Industrial (L)	Inspections	(810) 759-2140	
Security Products (N)	Moss & Mildew Remover	(888) 241-9547	
Thermo Manufacturing (N)	Flat Roofing Product Mfg.	(800) 882-7007	
TKO Home Maintenance (L)	Roofing, Painting & Remodeling	(810) 776-3989	
Weathertech (L)	Consultants	(248) 649-6710	

Sealers

Mr. Furniture Finisher (L, N)	Doozy Furniture Polish	(888) 851-8500	www.doozy.com
TR Industries (N)	Gel Gloss	(800) 553-6866	
Unelko (N)	Invisible Shield/Rain X	(800) 528-3149	
Westley's Blue Coral (N)	Clear Magic	(800) 545-0982	www.bluecoral.com

Stain Removers

Amazon Products (N)	Mildew Stain Away	(800) 832-5645	www.enviro-magic.com
Jelmar Industries (N)	CLR Rust & Stain Remover	(800) 323-5497	
Motsenbocker's (N)	Lift Off # 1,2,3,4, & 5	(800) 346-1633	www.liftoffinc.com
Whink (N)	Rust Remover	(800) 247-5102	www.whink.com

Sun Rooms

Four Seasons (L)	Manufacturer	(800) 368-7732	www.four-seasons-sunrooms.com
Mr. Enclosure (L)	Manufacturer/Installer	(877) 786-1131	www.mrenclosure.com
Temo (L, N)	Manufacturer	(800) 344-8366	www.temosunrooms.com

Surface Prep

Bio-Wash (N)	Interior Paint & Varnish Stripper	(800) 858-5011	www.biowash.com
Cul-Mac Industries (N)	Wash Before You Paint	(800) 626-5089	www.cul-mac.com
Custom Tapes (N)	Pro Mesh	(800) 621-7994	
DAP (N)	Dow Silicone Sealants	(800) 543-3840	
DCP-Lohja (N)	Easy Mask Tape	(800) 634-1303	www.easymask.com
Dumond Chemicals (N)	Peel Away Paint Stripper	(800) 245-1191	www.peelaway.com
FibaTape (N)	Drywall Repair	(800) 762-6694	www.fibatape.com
GE (N)	Silicone Sealants	(800) 255-8886	
General Liquids Corp. (N)	Liquid Sandpaper	(410) 484-7222	
Ice Blast Midwest (L)	Exterior Ice Blasting	(419) 249-7440	
Magna Industries (N)	Sand & Kleen	(800) 969-3334	
OSI Sealants (N)	Sealants & Patch	(800) 624-7767	www.osisealants.com

Category/Company Name	Product/Service	Phone Number	Web URL Address
Oxisolv, Inc. (N)	Rust Remover	(800) 594-9028	
Strip It (N)	Paint & Rust Removal (Plastic Pellets)	(810) 792-7705	
Tile Helper (N)	Old Hard Adhesive Remover	(708) 453-6900	
United Gilsonite (N)	Latex & Acrylic Sealants	(800) 272-3235	
Universal Ice Blast (N)	Ext. Ice Blast Cleaning	(888) 419-1743	www.iceblast.com
W.M. Barr (N)	Citristrip	(800) 235-3546	www.kleanstrip.com
Wash on Wheels (L)	Pressure Washing	(810) 979-7890	
Windows			
Alco Glass & Mirror (L)	Complete Window Repair	(248) 547-1214	
American Weather-Seal (N)	Wood & Vinyl Manufacturer	(800) 468-4996	www.amerarch.com
Andersen Windows (N)	Manufacturer	(800) 426-4261	www.andersenwindows.com
Bi-Glass Systems (N)	Bi-Glass Conversion	(800) 729-0742	www.bi-glass.com
Cadillac Window (L)	Distributor/Installer	(248) 352-5404	
Caradco (N)	Windows & Zap Pack Mfg.	(800) 238-1866	www.caradco.com
Champion (L, N)	Manufacturer/Installer	(800) 946-9930	www.championwindow.com
D.J. Enterprises (L)	Mich. Solatube Dealer	(248) 969-5968	
H & R Window Repair (L)	Complete Window Repair	(248) 366-8282	
Hallmark Builders (L)	Traco Reseller	(810) 775-7500	
Hoosier Manufacturing (N)	St. James Composite Windows	(800) 344-4849	
J & E (L)	Traco Reseller	(248) 473-6999	
Kimball & Russell (L)	Andersen/Renewal Distr.	(800) 686-2300	
Kolbe & Kolbe Millwork (N)	Wood Manufacturer	(800) 477-8656	www.kolbe-kolbe.com
Magic Windows (L)	Traco Reseller	(734) 762-9090	
Marvin (N)	Wood Window & Tilt Pack	(800) 346-5128	www.marvin.com
National Fenestration Rating (N)	Window Ratings	(301) 589-6372	www.nfrc.org
Pella (N)	Windows & Door Mfg.	(800) 847-3552	www.pella.com

Solatube (N)	Skylight Manufacturer	(800) 773-7652	www.solatube.com
Solatube North America (N)	Solatube Skylight Mfg.	(800) 966-7652	
Sun Pipe (N)	Pipe Skylight Manufacturer	(800) 844-4786	www.sunpipe.com
Sun Tunnel (N)	Tube Skylight Manufacturer	(800) 369-3664	www.suntunnel.com
Traco Windows (L, N)	Distributor	(888) 292-7600	www.traco.com
Velux USA (N)	Skylight Manufacturer	(800) 888-3589	www.velux.com
Wallside Windows (L)	Vinyl Window Mfg. & Instl.	(800) 521-7800	
Weather Shield (N)	Manufacturer	(800) 477-6808	www.weathershield.com
Weathergard (L)	Vinyl Window Mfg. & Instl.	(800) 377-8886	
Windows, Interior Storm			
3 M (N)	Scotchtint UV Film	(800) 364-3577	www.3M.com
A.1 Technologies Inc. (N)	Interior Storm	(800) 533-2805	
AIN Plastics (N)	Interior Storm	(800) 926-2600	www.tincna.com
Diversified Energy Control (L)	Int. Storms-Retail & DIY	(800) 380-0332	www.d-e-c.qpg.com
Window Saver (N)	Int. Storm Window Kits	(800) 321-9276	www.windowsaver.com

545

Appendix B

Special Reports

Are the shingles curling? Have a couple gotten loose or blown away? Are they fifteen or more years old? Has the weight of the ice and snow loosened the gutters?

As soon as you see loose shingles, or cracks in the valleys, go into the attic and see if a roof leak has started, but is not yet visible on the ceiling or walls. Water from roof leaks often drains down the underside of the roof decking for a distance before dropping to the floor. If you inspect thoroughly now, you might be able to stop the leak before it causes major damage.

FIRST DECISION: WHO'S GOING TO DO THE REPAIR?
After you discover damage the first decision is who is going to do the repairs. Are you going to do the repair or have it done by a professional? Know your limitations. Ladders are accident traps to the unwary. Roofs are one of the most dangerous places a homeowner can be. If you don't belong on a roof, don't go. The important thing is to make the decision right away. Don't procrastinate because you are intelligently concerned about climbing the ladder.

If your roof has severe damage, or is covered with wood, tile or slate shingles, or if you just don't belong climbing around roofs any more, I recommend that the roof be inspected and the repairs made by a professional. The best place to call for this is often the organization that originally installed your roof. If you can't get any response, go see the people at a roofing supply company or lumber yard. Explain the problem you have to the folks at the counter and ask for a couple recommendations of people they would recommend for the job.

If the repairs are minor, consider paying for an inspection and quote or ask if the repair can be done immediately so that the roofer does not have to make a call back. Insist that who ever comes out to your home to look at the roof be licensed and bring proof of insurance with him. If the repair is so large that it can not be made on the same day as the inspection, see if the area of the roof can be tarped immediately to protect your house from further water damage.

SHINGLE FIRST AID
In the case of asphalt or fiberglass shingles, many home owners can repair the problems themselves. Curled or broken shingles, and cracked valleys can be repaired or replaced relatively easily. But they have to be repaired right away, before the damage spreads and water leakage causes water damage to the walls and ceilings. Remember, roof problems never get better. Unrepaired they can easily cause hundreds or thousands of dollars to your home's interior.

If you are going to repair the roof yourself, here are some tips. Traditional roofing cement will not adhere to damp shingles. If the roof is not totally dry, be sure to use one of the newer roofing "wet stick" mastics like Snowroof by the Oregon Research and Development Corporation, or Dewitts, that can be used on damp surfaces.

Curled shingles can be flattened by putting a dab of roofing cement under each edge and pressing down. Cracked shingles, or shingles that become loose with just a light pull, should be replaced.

Small cracks in the valleys, the joint where two roof pitches meet, or around the flashing, can often be repaired with dabs of roofing cement troweled into the crack and smoothed. An even better patch is made by using the mastic in conjunction with roof repair tapes by FibaTape 800-762-6694, or Asphalt Products Corporation. Make certain the entire joint is covered. Flashing edges should have a continuous seal of roofing cement. Any area that is growing thin, or pulling way from the surface, should be resealed with roofing cement.

Major valley cracks can often be repaired by covering the entire valley with a roof cement and membrane.

Since you are already on the roof, scoot over to the chimney and sanitary vents and make certain that the flashing is in good repair. Check the chimney for crumbling mortar while you are up there. If the mortar is not in good repair it should be repaired immediately. You can do a little tuck-pointing yourself. Major repairs should be done by a professional.

MOLD, MOSS, MILDEW, BLACK STREAKS ON ROOF

Black streaks on shingles is usually mold. Green is moss and algae. These parasites can cause serious damage to shingles and promote deterioration of the deck boards. The problem is associated with too much shade and dampness, usually caused by trees.

If the problem is not too severe, you can often eliminate it with dry laundry detergent. Do not do this in the direct sunlight or the water will evaporate too fast. Take a garden hose up on the roof and wet down the shingles in the affected area. Take a box of dry laundry detergent (I like the kind with bleach added) and sift it all over the wet shingles, so that it looks like a layer of dust.

Wait 15 or 20 minutes, then sprinkle a little more water on the roof. Scrub the area back and forth, sideways, up and down with a brush. Get into all the crack and cervices. Keep working down in the direction of the gutter.

After brushing completely rinse away all the dirt and debris with the garden hose.

If you have actual moss growing on the roof, slide an ice chopper under the moss and scrape away as much as possible before washing.

The second way to clear the area is with Copper Sulfate Crystals. This is a very effective attack, but since Copper Sulfate Crystals cost about $6.00 for two pounds, it can get expensive. If you have a major problem, or have to clear a large area, it is definitely the way to go.

Scrape off as much of the moss as possible with a long handled ice chopper. Then mix 10 oz. of Copper Sulfate Crystals to a gallon of hot water. Pour the hot blue Copper Sulfate solution all over the affected area. Scrub it in with a scrub brush, then garden hose it off.

To keep the problem from reoccurring, attach zinc strips above the affected area. There are several different makers of this type of product. One is called Shingle Shield by Chicago Metallic 800-323-7164 and is available at all major roofing wholesalers, lumber yards and full service hardware stores. Shingle shield strips are attached under the shingles and are effective through a process called galvanic action. When it rains, trace amounts of zinc flow down onto the shingles and keeps moss from growing.

Remember zinc strips will keep the moss problem from reoccurring. They do nothing to solve a pre-existing condition. So get rid of the moss first, then install the zinc strips. They will be effective for 50 years.

EXTENDING THE LIFE OF OLD SHINGLES
If your shingles are just old, but in fair condition, and your budget is not quite ready for the cost of a re-roofing, consider coating the shingles with a waterproof shingle repair coat like Roof Guardian by ORD (Oregon Research and Development Corporation). Call 800-345-0809 for information and the dealer nearest you. This type of fix costs about half the cost of re shingling and adds about 7 years to the life of your shingles. It is definitely noticeable and I would not recommend it if you are in the process of selling your house.

REROOFING
If there is only one layer of shingles on a roof, you can safely add a second, in some municipalities even a third, layer of shingles before a complete tear off is required. Roofing can not be quoted over the phone. A thorough inspection is required.

SHINGLES

Shingles used to be graded by weight. This is no longer the case. Never-the-less, better shingles, have longer warranties and weigh more than inexpensive shingles. Standard shingles have 20, 25 and 30 year warranties. The most expensive shingles may have life-time warranties. Typically only the warranties on the most expensive shingles are transferable. Where permitted, there is usually a cost involved for warranty transfer.

The price of shingles is quoted per square. A square is the amount of shingles necessary to shingle a 10' X 10' area (100 square feet). Usually a 20% factor is added to the actual square footage for scrap, cutting and ridge caps.

ORGANIC OR FIBERGLASS?

The shingle of today is either an organic, or a fiberglass shingle. The terms fiberglass or organic is determined by whether the foundation layer, or scrim, is composed of felt or fiberglass. Present day felt is often a recycled material composed of newsprint, corrugated and other fiber materials. Organic shingles are naturally thicker, heavier and acclimatize better to frequent changes in heat and cold cycles and weather conditions. Fiberglass shingles are lighter weight, more fireproof and slightly less expensive. Organic shingles have a Class "C" Fire Rating. Fiberglass shingles have a Class "A" Fire Rating. Most lumberyards and discount centers only carry fiberglass shingles.

Typically a fiberglass shingle will cost four to five dollars less per square than an organic shingle with a similar warranty.

COMPARISONS

Prices are rough estimates of the going rate as of April 1, 1995. Prices may easily go up 20 to 30% within the next 90 days due to scarcity of materials.

Warranty	Type	Cost/Square	Avg. Weight/Square
20 year	Fiberglass	$ 20.00	210 lbs.
	Organic	$ 25.00	215 lbs.
25 year	Fiberglass	$ 25.00	240 lbs.
	Organic	$ 29.00	245 lbs.
30 year	Fiberglass	$ 31.00	250 lbs.
Dimensional			
30-Life	Fiberglas or Organic	$ 33.00-$60.00	300 lbs. plus

Many roofers consider a 20 year Warranty Organic shingle to be the equivalent of a 25 year Fiberglass. A 25 year Warranty Organic is often assumed to be the equivalent of a 30 year Fiberglass.

The value of a Warranty is debatable. Most structural defects show up within the first two or three years. Americans sell their homes and move every seven years on average. Most Warranties are not transferable. Statistically, therefore, most warranties are invalid for a minimum of two thirds of the warranty period. Improper attic ventilation destroys shingles and will also invalidate the warranty.

LABOR

Roofers often figure estimates using a price per square that includes labor and materials. This price varies with the size and difficulty of the job. A current ball park average for reroofing on an existing layer of shingles is $ 75.00 per square. If the tear off of an existing roof is required the price increases to about $ 150.00 a square. The labor for Heavier and Dimensional shingles is higher because their is greater labor involved in carrying, cutting and placing the shingles.

WHERE SHOULD YOU SHOP?

The average large discounter or lumber yard will often have prices that are two to five dollars per square less than the roofing specialist. However, the big boxes are usually one man bands. They carry a limited selection of shingles by a single manufacturer. If another manufacturer offers a lower price tomorrow, you can bet your last quarter they will switch. In the event you need a bundle of replacement shingles after the switch, you will be out of luck.

Currently the shingle of choice at the big boxes is Owens Corning. This is an excellent fiberglass shingle. Some discounters carry a relatively good selection of Owens Corning in 20, 25, 30 year warranty and even dimensional shingles in a limited range of colors.

Roofing Wholesalers, on the other hand, are specialists. They have displays and literature. They have the time and talent to give you helpful hints and do a little more hand holding than the average mass merchant.

Just as important, many wholesalers track which color of a specific shingle was shipped to a particular building site. So if you are considering a major shingle purchase, such as IKO Renaissance ® XL dimensional shingles in a green slate color, they can tell you where you can drive by and see an entire house roofed in your selection.

HOW TO SHOP FOR SHINGLES?

The best way to get your house re-roofed is to shop for the shingles you want first. Then, ask the shingle wholesaler for recommendations on roofing companies. The wholesaler will usually be glad to give you the names of several roofers in your area he believes will do a good job with his shingles. Call them all out for a quote. Tell them that they were recommended by the wholesaler. Ask for references of other roofing jobs they have done, preferably with the same style of shingles you want. Don't be content to just call the references. Drive by and make sure you like the workmanship.

IS YOUR ROOF PROPERLY VENTILATED?

Improper roof ventilation will cut shingle life in half and can void the manufacturer's warranty. The roof needs both intake and exhaust venting. Old fashioned gable vents are of little use as air intakes, and should be closed off and replaced with under eve soffit vents when the roof is re shingled.

If your house does not have sufficient overhang for traditional soffit vents, the problem can be taken care of by installing Combo Vents which have a metal top flange that creates the space necessary for venting, while providing a firm foundation for gutter installation. You can get information on Combo Vents from your roofing supplier, or by requesting information from the Globe Building Materials, Inc., 2230 Indianapolis, Whiting, IN 46394, phone: 800-950-4562.

Exhaust vents can be either standard roof top ventilators, or ridge vents. If you choose the roof top ventilators, you need one ventilator per 150 square feet of attic floor. Ridge vents are a great deal more inconspicuous than roof top vents. They come in several different configurations, ranging from a rigid plastic "fabric" that folds over the ridge to preformed polypropylene. The maker is GAF Materials Corporation, 888-LEAK-SOS.

WHAT ELSE DO YOU NEED?

In high ice and snow environments, like the North East, Northern, and Great Lakes Regions, snow and ice shield should be installed under shingles and tar paper covering the final three feet of roof line extending to the drip edge. I also recommend snow and ice shield on top of all flashing around the chimney and vents.

Depending upon the condition of their condition, the decking, soffit and gutters may need to be replaced. The condition of the decking will not be known until the old shingles are torn off. However, you should know about projected decking, soffit and gutter replacement costs before the contract is let. Gutters come in both vinyl and aluminum. The biggest benefit of aluminum is that it is possible to get seamless gutters. Frankly, vinyl gutters used to be inferior. However, the new Snap Seal vinyl gutter has more tensile strength and much greater weight bearing ability than either aluminum or the old fashioned vinyl gutters. Snap Seal gutters are available through most full service roofing suppliers.

WHAT SHOULD BE SPECIFIED IN THE CONTRACT?

The estimate and contract should include the exact dimensions of your roof; the specific make, name, identification number, warranty and color of shingles you are buying; the make and names of soffit vents, roof vents, or number and name of roof ventilators; the name and style of roofing underlayment; snow and ice guard; manufacturer and style of gutters, if they are being replaced; and cost of deck or soffit replacement if needed. The contract should also include a completion date and penalty clause if work is not finished on time; schedule of payments, never pay more than a third down; and cost and timeliness of trash clean up and removal. This is especially important if the old shingles need to be torn off.

WORKMAN'S COMP. & LIABILITY INSURANCE

Roofing is a very dangerous occupation. Many homeowners have lost their homes because a worker was injured on site and the contractor was not insured. If injury or property damage is caused on the job, you, the homeowner may be liable for hundreds of thousands of dollars in workmen's compensation or liability claims. It is very important that you receive certificates of insurance directly from the roofer's workmen's compensation and liability companies before work begins. Do not accept a photo copy of an existing certificate of insurance. The coverage may have been terminated. Also check with your homeowner's insurance agent to see if you should have extra protection during the job.

MAJOR MANUFACTURERS

You can use this list to call and learn the wholesale distributor nearest you.

Atlas Roofing Corp.; phone: 770-937-9304.

Certain Teed Corp.; phone: 800-345-1145.

GAF Building Materials Corp.; phone: 888-LEAK-SOS.

Georgia-Pacific Corp., Building Products Division; phone: 800-BUILD GP.

Globe Building Materials, Inc.; phone: 800-950-4562.

IKO Industries, Ltd.; phone: 800-441-7296.

Owens-Corning Fiberglass Corp.; 800-GET PINK.

Tamko Asphalt Products Inc.; phone: 800-437-1818.

WHOLESALERS (GREATER DETROIT)

ABC Dearborn: 6550 Chase Road, 313-846-0600.
    Pontiac: 125 E. Columbia, 248-334-3072.
    Southfield: 21000 W. 8 Mile, 248-353-6343.
    Warren: 7101 E. 8 Mile, 810-757-3500.

Jenson Aluminum Products, Walled Lake: 4278 Haggerty Road, 248-363-4144.

Lee Wholesale Supply Inc., New Hudson: 55965 Grand River, 800-220-8525.
    Mt. Clemens: 46705 Erb Drive, 810-949-1981.

Wimsatt Building Materials, Wayne:
    36340 Van Born, 734-722-3460.
    Waterford: 1131 Sylvertis, 248-673-7435.
    Sterling Heights: 33663 Mound, 810-978-8740.

RSI Wholesale of Detroit, Inc., Ferndale: 1700 Nine Mile Road, 248-398-5005.

HOW TO CHOOSE A
GOOD CONTRACTOR©
by Glenn Haege,
America's Master Handyman

1. Start by asking friends and relatives for specific recommendations on somebody who is good at doing exactly what you want done.

2. Go to the suppliers of the business you want to hire. If you need a carpenter or a builder, go to lumber yards and building supply centers. If you need a plumber, go to a couple of wholesale plumbing supply stores. Roofer? Roofing wholesalers. Painters? Paint and hardware stores.

Ask the store manager or owner, or the commercial contractor desk representative, which contractors they would recommend for your particular project. They will be delighted to tell you. Each store will give you two or three references.

3. While you're at the store, as we recommended in the article, become knowledgeable about the products you will be buying. Here are a few of the questions you should be asking:

> What's the pricing?
> What's the difference between low and high quality?
> How long are the manufacturer's guaranties?
> How often does the type of product you will be having installed have to be replaced?
> How often is warranty work called for?
> Which manufacturers are the fastest to solve a problem if one develops?
> How broad is the product line?

Get specific model names, numbers and product brochures.

4. Write up a good description of what you want done.
For instance:

You don't just want to add a room, you want to add an 15' x 20', paneled (or drywalled) room to the South West Corner of the House. The room will be used for a bedroom (office, family room).

You want it to have three double hung, 36" x 48" windows and one 60" x 48" picture window. The picture window will be located in the center of the South wall, one double hung window will be on the West wall, and two double hung windows will be on East wall. It is important that the windows be Andersen vinyl clad wood windows. You want quotes on both double and triple pane insulated windows (or what ever).

A large, built in closet, approximately 6' x 8' should be located on the West wall. The closet should have (describe shelving) and be lit by (describe preferred lighting).

A half bath with commode and sink (specify brands and model numbers for both) should be located in the North East side of the room.

It is very important that there be an extra wide (give dimensions) exterior door with deadbolt lock and window (give brand and model number if possible). The interior entrance, on the North side of the room should be a conventional (describe door).

The flooring should be (vinyl (give brand and type), hardwood (site finished (give type of finish desired), or prefinished (give name and model number of preferred type of wood), carpet (give preferred name, color and stock number)).

The room should be lit with two conventional ceiling lighting fixtures (specify brand, model # and power of bulb). You need the room to be wired with sufficient power to run a fax, computer, heavy duty laser printer, video monitor, television set and VCR, plus two lamps, simultaneously. You want a whole house surge protector installed as part of the modernization.

How should the room be heated and cooled? Can it be tied into the existing service, or must new be provided?

Who is going to be responsible for the finish painting, window and flooring trim?

The three exterior walls should be insulated R-40 or better with (give the brand name).

The exterior walls of the room should be covered with brick and vinyl siding to match the house (give specifics). The soffit, trim and shingles should match existing (give specifics).

Now, sit down and draw a simple layout of the room you have just described.

Discuss your write up and layout with the rest of the family.

Now is the time to get input. Don't expect ideas or agreement to come out all at once. Your spouse may come up with a great suggestion three days after the discussion. Ideas have to incubate. This is not a test, nor an exercise in one person getting their way. The important thing is to have agreement inside the family unit before talking to sales people and contractors.

Is this what you really want?

Remember, this description is not the final plan. The description and layout is merely to give you and the family the opportunity to think the matter through, discuss, adapt, and have developed your thinking enough to be able to give the sales person, or contractor, a good idea about what you want. What you desire may be unrealistic or unaffordable. The builder should know the best products to use and may have some great ideas that will make the job even better for you. Use his or her expertise. One thing is certain, however, you can not get, what the contractor does not know you want or need.

5. Call all the contractors and set appointments in your home to discuss the job. No phone quotes. Tell them that you will be wanting to get information about the company history, officers, licensing, etc. at the appointment.

6. At the appointment tell them you will want the quote in writing and that you will not sign anything on the first appointment. If they try to force an immediate order, the industry calls it a "one call close", *get rid of them!!!!!*

7. Walk with the company representative while he or she inspects the area where you want the work done. Describe everything in detail.

8. Work with the sales person and get my Contractor Reference Form filled out completely. There are many questions on that form you will be ashamed to ask. Ask them anyway. You need to know which other people in the organization have Builders Licenses, so you can get background checks on them. You need to know if the modernization company has two or three different names available to them.

You need to know if anyone in the organization has Builder's Trust Fund Violations, criminal records associated with the building business, or bad credit. Some unscrupulous business people make a practice out of going out of business every few years and leaving their customers in the lurch. You need to know if the money you pay down is going into a trust fund as required by Michigan Law, or into the company's regular checking account where it can be spent or garnisheed to pay any bill. You need all this information before you give them a dime of your money.

9. The salesman may say that he does not have all the information you are requesting. Let him take the form back to the company. There is a good chance that if the firm does not have a record they can be proud of, they will take themselves out of the competition. That's what you want. Do not accept the form back until it is fully filled out and signed by the representative or authorized representative of the company. Remember, if they won't give you the information you need, they are probably hiding something and you can't risk your house by doing business with them.

10. Get the quote in writing. You want the exact products they are going to use specified. "Industry standard" or other innocuous terms mean nothing. Do not accept them in the quote or it will cost you money. Get the guarantees spelled out. What do they cover? How long? A life-time guarantee from a year-old firm means nothing.

11. Check out the contractor's "bragging rights" (references). Ask for names and phone number of at least 5 to 10 people who have gotten the same type of job. Get names from this year, last year, three years ago. Just being given new names, or old names, can be a warning sign that something is wrong with the company.

Call all the references, then go look at some of the jobs. Satisfied customers are always pleased to recommend a good contractor.

While you are with the referral, make small talk about the entire remodeling experience. Were the workers courteous? Was the production manager there a good deal of the time? If there were problems, were they solved in an expeditious manner? Did workers clean up daily? Who was responsible for the final clean up? Was trash taken away immediately? How long did the entire job take? Could the quality have been improved?

12. If a "greasy salesman", and I use the term deliberately (most modernization salesmen are highly professional, the bad apples are real slime balls), tries to weasel out of giving references by saying something like: "references don't mean anything because I wouldn't tell you the names of anyone that wasn't satisfied," or gives references that are about jobs nothing like your jobs, don't even think about that company. You would get nothing but problems.

13. If the job will be done in Michigan, call the Department of Commerce-BOPR, License Verification Unit, 1-900-555-8374, to ask if the builder is licensed, and whether or not there are any complaints against the builder. While you are on the phone, see if any of the other officers, sales people, or production people are licensed builders and whether they have any complaints listed against them.

14. Call Murray Gula, Michigan Construction Protection Agency, 800-543-6669, and ask for his free homeowner program construction lien information kit.

15. After you have gotten your price quotes and checked all the references, one contractor will be head and shoulders above the rest. Give him or her the job.

16. You should require that the written contract specify an exact description of the work to be done and of the brands and products to be used. It must also state that you will receive copies of all guarantees or warranties of products that have been used in your job.

17. Get in writing that you will receive release from lien forms from every supplier, sub contractor, and worker on the site.

18. Get a guaranteed completion date. There should be a mutually agreed upon penalty for failure to meet that date, plus a bonus for early completion.

19. Don't make unnecessary changes. If you do decide to make a change, put it in writing. Remember, any change you make will cost you money and slow down the job.

20. Payment terms should be no more than 30% down. Staged payments are okay. However, there should be at least 10% to be paid upon completion.

21. When you get a good job done, praise the contractor highly. Recommend him or her to friends, neighbors and relatives.

22.Always remember your check book is the most important tool in your tool box. Use it wisely and you will be a very satisfied customer.

Good luck on your remodeling project.

Glenn Haege

Contractor Reference Form

```
Name of Company:_____
Your Name: _____
Address: _____
Title: _____
City:_____ State: _____ ZIP: _____
Phone #: _____
Your Home Phone #: _____
President of Company: _____
Your Beeper #: _____
Is this company a _____ sole proprietorship,
       _____ partnership, _____ corporation?
If a corporation, in what State is the
       corporation incorporated?_____
Please list other company officers:
Vice President: _____
Secretary: _____
Treasurer: _____
Qualifying Officer: _____
```

Does the organization have a Builders License?
What is the Company's Builder's
        License #: _____
What is the Qualifying Officer's Builders
        License #: _____
Is the Qualifying Officer a QO for any other Company?
If so, what are the company names and Building License
Numbers?
Company Name: _____
Builders License #: _____
Company Name: _____
Builders License #: _____
Company Name: _____
Builders License #: _____
Company Name: _____
Builders License #: _____
Do any other officers, or employees have Building
Licenses? If so, what are their names and Building
License Numbers?
Name: _____
Builders License #: _____
Name: _____
Builders License #: _____
Name: _____
Builders License #: _____
Name: _____
Builders License #: _____
Name: _____
Builders License #: _____

Does this company, or any other company associated
with the officers, or qualifying officer of this
company, or the production manager, sales manager, or
their assistants, have complaints against them listed
with the Department of Commerce Builders Trust Fund?
If so, please describe in detail:
_____
_____
_____
_____
_____

Use another page if more space is needed.

Have you, or any of the officers, qualifying officer, sales or production managers, or their assistants, ever been found guilty of violating the Builders Trust Fund, the Builders Code, or Fraud? _____If so, please describe in detail:

_____

_____

_____

_____

_____.

Use another page if more space is needed.

Has this company, its officers and/or managers, its qualifying officer, or you, gone out of business, gone bankrupt, or been associated with a building company that did go bankrupt or become insolvent during the past seven years? _____If so, please describe in detail:

_____

_____

_____

_____.

Does the company maintain a Trust Fund Account for the deposit of customer checks? _____
If so, please give the
Name of the Account: _____
Bank: _____,
Branch: _____,
Bank Account #: _____.

Does the company maintain a Company Checking Account? _____ If so, please give the
Name of the Account: _____
Bank: _____,
Branch: _____,
Bank Account #: _____.

Does the company maintain a Company Savings Account? _____ If so, please give the
Name of the Account: _____
Bank: _____,
Branch: _____,
Bank Account #: _____.

Please give the names of three companies with which the company has established credit, the credit managers name and telephone number.

Company Name: _____ ,
Credit Manager Name: _____ ,
Telephone Number: _____

Company Name: _____ ,
Credit Manager Name: _____ ,
Telephone Number: _____

Company Name: _____ ,
Credit Manager Name: _____ ,
Telephone Number: _____

Does the company have experience in this type of work?
_____

How long has the company been in business?
_____

Please give the names, addresses and telephone numbers of six people who have had this type of work performed by your company within the past five years?

Within the past twelve months:

Name: _____ ,
Address: _____ ,
City: _____ ,
State & Zip Code: _____ ,
Phone Number: _____ .

Name: _____ ,
Address: _____ ,
City: _____ ,
State & Zip Code: _____ ,
Phone Number: _____ .

Within the past two years:

Name: _____ ,
Address: _____ ,
City: _____ ,
State & Zip Code: _____ ,
Phone Number: _____ .

Name: _____ ,
Address: _____ ,
City: _____ ,
State & Zip Code: _____ ,
Phone Number: _____ .

Job performed three years or more ago:

Name: _____ ,
Address: _____ ,
City: _____ ,
State & Zip Code: _____ ,
Phone Number: _____ .

Name: _____ ,
Address: _____ ,
City: _____ ,
State & Zip Code: _____ ,
Phone Number: _____ .

Date: _____
Information Provided by: _____ .
(Signature)

Listing of Information Needed in Remodeling Contract

The consumer should always have the following information in a remodeling contract:
1. Complete name of modernization company.
2. Name of head of company, the Qualifying Officer (the person who holds the builders license number for the company), and the name of the production manager.
3. Address of company.
4. Statement that the company will obtain all necessary building permits and blue prints, and what the costs shall be for these items.

5. Listing of Company's Workmen's Compensation and Casualty Insurance Company names and policy numbers and statement that you will receive certificates of insurance from the insurance companies or their agents before work begins.

6. Builder's License # of both the company and the qualifying officer.

7. Exact description of the work to be done, including all dimensions.

8. Drawing of work to be done showing location of all doors, windows, stairways, or special features. In the event of a simple modernization, such as furnace replacement, this item can be eliminated.

9. Listing of all special materials or equipment to be used in the modernization. This listing to include Manufacturer's name, trade and model name, model number, and exact dimensions.

For example, if a door is being installed, list who makes it, what the name and model number of this particular door is, the exact dimensions of the door. If it is an exterior door, it would also require the name, description, and model number of the lock set.

Clean up and trash pick up is part of the job. Make certain that the contract lists who will be responsible for what, when.

This may sound like a lot of work, it is. The question is, would you rather do the work and be sure of what you are getting, or not do the work up front and run the risk of not getting what you are paying for?

10. Statement that you will receive release of lien forms from all sub contractors, employees and materials suppliers before you are required to pay their bills. In other words, if cement work is done, you pay for the cement work after the cement company has been paid by the builder. You have made sure the builder has the money to do this by giving him a down payment.

11. Statement that you will receive copies of all product or equipment guarantees or warranties used on the job after the job is paid in full.

12. Statement that all work shall be done in compliance with, or exceeding applicable State, City, and County Building Codes, and that all work will be inspected and approved by the appropriate inspectors.

13. Guaranteed start and completion dates. The completion date is most important. A penalty clause should be included, specifying money to be paid to you if the work is not completed by the completion date. Likewise a bonus extra payment should be specified that will be paid the builder if the work is done before completion date.

14. Itemization of how additional costs shall be determined if unforeseen, but necessary, work is needed once work has begun.

15. Payment terms. Never pay more than 30% down. Payments should always be linked to task completions and the receipt of Release of Lein Forms signed by the pertinent subcontractors and building materials suppliers. Always hold back at least 10% until job has been finished, all cleanup has been completed, all trash taken to dump.

How do I keep cement floors or drives from getting stained?

I have a new cement floor. How do I seal it so that oil stains do not set into the cement floor? I want to keep the natural cement color.

Materials Needed: Acrylic Cement Sealer by Sett, Protek or Diamond Clear, or any of hundreds of Acrylic Cement Sealers.

Equipment Needed: 9" Roller with 3/8" to 1/2" nap Roller Cover and Extension Handle.

Time Required: 1 1/2 Days.

Acrylic Sealers are far more expensive than regular sealers, but they are definitely worth the money for interior work or any drive, walk, patio or other cement surface you want to keep especially nice. They film build and two coats will give years of extra protection.

Let your cement floor cure for sixty days before you put on a sealer. All the trapped water should be dried out of the product before sealing. Freezing weather conditions can cause fine cracking over the entire cement surface.

Follow the contractors directions for curing. If you must park on the cement surface during the curing period, cut up some heavy boxes and park on them so that oil or other fluid leaks do not stain the cement during this crucial period.

It is important that this work be done in a well ventilated area. Outside, no problem. Inside, if you are doing the cement floor in a garage, or a basement floor, keep a good flow of air with a fan and wear a dual canister respirator.

Directions:

1. After a 60 day wait, the cement will probably be dirty. Wash it with a solution of 2 oz. dry measure of TSP to a gallon of water, or a 5 to 1 solution of a good organic cleaner like Simple Green™ or Clear Magic™. If there is already some staining, you will have to remove the stain with BIX™ or other driveway stain remover a day or two before you complete the project.

2. Let dry 2 days. It is important that the cement be perfectly dry.

3. Roll on one coat of Acrylic Cement Sealer. Let dry according to label directions. Some dry very fast, some take longer.

4. Apply a second coat of Acrylic Cement Sealer. Let dry according to label directions before use.

How to remove the stains and protect an older cement floor.

I have a 10 year old cement garage floor. I want to clear the oil and gas stains off the cement and then seal it.

Materials Needed: 20° Muratic Acid, TSP, Acrylic Cement Sealer.

Equipment: Deck Brush, Roller with Extension Handle.

Time Required: 2 days.

Proper ventilation is very important. Garage door should be open. Wear a dual canister respirator, goggles, rubber boots and gloves, wool or cotton, long sleeved shirt and slacks. No polyester or other man-made fabrics: they offer no protection.

1. Pour a solution of one part 20° Muratic Acid to three parts of water directly on the oil and rust stains.

2. Let stand one hour.

3. Scrub with a deck brush. Add more of the Muratic Acid and Water Solution as needed.

4. Let stand 4 hours.

5. Repeat steps 1-4. If the formerly stained area is now noticeably lighter than the rest of the cement surface, brush the entire area with the Muratic Acid/Water Solution.

6. Wash the floor with a solution of 2 oz. dry measure of TSP per gallon of water.

7. Rinse with a garden hose.

8. Let dry for 24 hours.

9. Roll on two coats of Acrylic Cement Sealer. Follow the directions on the can.

Should I use Acrylic Sealers Out of Doors?

You can, but I wouldn't. Acrylic Sealers are at least three times as expensive as water based sealers. I would use a good concrete sealer such as Mr. Mac's Concrete & Masonry Sealer, Olympic Water Guard, Protek Weatherguard or Thompson's Concrete & Masonry Protector. There are literally hundreds of them on the market. They are all competitively priced.

The trade-off is that if you use a water based sealer, you will get weathering and natural staining over a period of time. That's OK with me. It might not be with you. Concrete & Masonry products help keep the water out of the cement and protect it from destroying itself during the freeze-thaw cycles. They do not prevent staining. If you decide you have to keep exterior cement in "like new" condition, buy a dull, not a glossy finish Acrylic Cement Sealer.

Directions for regular cleaning and sealing of exterior concrete.

Materials Needed: Cement Water Sealer

Equipment Needed: Long Handled Garage Broom, Garden Hose, Garden Sprayer or Roller with Long Napped Cover and Extension Handle.

Time Required: 2 Days.

This procedure will help you keep your sidewalk "healthy" for a long time. The sealer works to keep the water out of the cement and protects it from destroying itself during freeze-thaw cycles.

1. Sweep off any loose dirt.

2. Wash down the area with a garden hose.

3. Let dry for 24 hours. If it rains, wait another day.

4. Apply one heavy coat of a good Cement or Concrete Water Sealer such as Thompson's Water Seal, or Olympic Water Guard. If you plan ahead, you can buy these products on sale and save a lot of money. You can spray this product on with a garden sprayer or apply it with a roller. Be sure you put on a good thick coat.

5. Wait 24 hours.

6. Apply another coat. You only have to apply two coats the first time you do this. For continuous maintenance, apply one coat ever 12 to 18 months depending on wear and weather conditions.

Older Cement Walks or Patios
If you have an older cement sidewalk or patio that is good condition structurally, but needs some extra TLC to make it look beautiful, try this technique:

Materials Needed: Old Cement Cleaner by the Sure-Clean Corporation, Acrylic Cement Sealer.

Equipment Needed: Deck Brush, 9" Roller with long Napped Cover and Long Extension Handle.

Time Required: 3-4 Days.

1. Clean sidewalk or patio thoroughly according to the direction on the Old Cement Cleaner Can. If there are any stains, use Surcelan Stain Removers.

2. Rinse off liberally with garden hose.

3. Wait 24 hours.

4. Apply two coats of Acrylic Cement Sealer. Follow the directions on can.

Product Information

Concrete Sealers and Crack Fillers/Sealers are readily available at most hardware stores, home centers and lumber yards. The largest retailer of concrete, paver, and brick products in Southern Michigan is J. C. Cornillie Co., 30751 Little Mack, Roseville, 1-810-293-1500.

Concrete Sealers- Most have compete lines

Armorall All Weather Waterproofing Sealer	1-800-398-3892
W. M. Barr & Co.	1-800-235-3546
Classic Clear Waterproofing by Dutch Boy	1-800-828-5669
Mr. Mac's Concrete Resurfacer	1-800-654-8454
Mr. Mac's Concrete Primer	1-800-654-8454
Soulliere Decorative Stone Inc.	1-810-739-0020
The Quikrete Companies	1-800-282-5828
United Gilsonite Laboratories	1-800-272-3235
Waterlox Chemical & Coatings Corp..	1-800-321-0377
Thompson's Concrete & Masonry Protector	1-800-367-6297
Thompson's Water Seal Ultra	1-800-367-6297

Crack Fillers

Elmers Adhesives	1-800-848-9400
Mr. Mac's Latex Crack Filler	1-800-654-8454
Mr. Mac's Joint Filler	1-800-654-8454
The Quikrete Companies	1-800-282-5828

Mud Jacking/Concrete Leveling

Ace Concrete Pumping & Equipment	1-313-389-2913
Metro Concrete Raising Inc.	1-810-779-2220
	1-810-774-5855
Eckelberry Concrete Raising	1-800-515-1543
Metro Concrete Lifting	1-734-699-4122
Level One	1-313-292-1910
Quality Concrete Lifting	1-734-425-7349

1995 DECK CLEANER TEST REPORT©
© 1995 Glenn Haege & Kathleen Stief, MHP

Decks and deck care are big business. It is estimated that there are thirty million decks in the US and than a million more will be built this year. According to my sources there will be $40 million spent on deck washes this year. Another $180 million will spent on clear wood sealers. That's a lot of money. A great many claims will be made, not all of them true. The challenge is to find out what really works.

My editor and I started using a 600 square foot test deck last year. The idea behind the deck was to try various kinds of deck cleaning and sealing products side by side, under identical, real world conditions.

The deck was extremely grayed, pressure treated (Wolmanized) wood. It had green mildew and black mold stains, birds used it regularly for dive bombing practice, and it had not received any care other than an occasional sweeping or spray off with a garden hose for at least 8 years. The deck is approximately 40' x 13.5', making it possible for us to establish four 10' x 13.5' test deck sections plus railing. We figured the addition of the railing made each section the equivalent of 150 sq. ft.

Our test deck is a good place to use products side by side, see how they tackle the same kind of problems they might have to face in your back yard. It is not a place where products can be scientifically tested under precisely controlled conditions. Results are subjective, not scientific measurements. You might look at the same results and come up with different conclusions.

Gray Deck Treatments
Graying of wood is an indication of disintegration from exposure to the sun's Ultra Violet rays. Before you can stain a deck you have to get rid of the top decomposing layer of wood cells.

The majority of deck cleaners on the market are chlorine bleach based products. The chemical concentration in most is far stronger than you could get in bottle at the grocery store. If they list the chemicals on the package, the label will say that they contain chlorine, or use the chemical terms, Sodium Hypochlorite or Calcium Hypochlorite. Included among these products are Armorall® EZ Deck® Wash Wood Restorer, Thompson's® Deck Wash, and Olympic® Deck Cleaner. Some manufacturers buffer the chlorine to make it less aggressive.

Over the years I have recommended a strong chlorine bleach and TSP Solution for whitening gray decks and returning them to their rightful places in society. While this cleaning solution was as effective as the far more expensive prepared products, I was still not completely happy with the results.

Oxalic acid based cleaners are considered necessary to remove the gray from redwood and cedar, they are also effective on pressure treated wood. Instead of bleaching, they remove the top layer of damaged cells, leaving a new undamaged layer of cells exposed. Dekswood® Exterior Wood Cleaner & Brightener by The Flood Company is a leading Oxalic Acid based product.

A third type of cleaner uses Disodium Peroxydicarbonate or Sodium Carbonate Peroxhydrate. These very strong cleaners are biodegradable, do not contain acid or chlorine bleach, and do not harm most plants. Wolman® Deck Brightener and Cuprinol Revive® Easy Deck Cleaner are examples.

Naturally, it is impossible for me to test every deck cleaner on the market. Most are Chlorine based, so it would be like taste testing different brands of 2% milk. I decided to compare my own TSP and bleach recipe to the leading industry chlorine based product, Armorall EZ Deck Wash. Then see how the results fared against Flood Dekswood, a leading Oxalic Acid exterior wood cleaner and brightener, and Wolman Deck Brightener, the Disodium Peroxydicarbonate product, especially designed for pressure treated wood.

We found that attempting to bring back badly grayed wood, most of the cleaners, including my own recipe, took twice as much solution as called for in the directions, and needed power washing for acceptable results.

The powerwasher used was a Coleman Powermate®, that could produce up to 1200 psi (pounds per square inch). We started tearing up the deck when over 1000 psi was used. Best results were between 800 and 1000 psi.

Keep in mind that the test deck is very old and very gray. Your's might be in better condition. A deck made from pressure treated wood should be able to withstand 1200 to 1500 psi. Very soft woods like cedar and redwood should require 800 to 1000 psi.

Here's a product by product breakdown.

My Own Formula: TSP & Bleach

My formula is 4 oz. dry measure of TSP (Trisodium Phosphate), 1 gal. household chlorine bleach, 2 gal. water. This formula should have been enough for 300 sq. ft.. We needed all of the solution for 150 sq. ft. Applying with the solution with a garden sprayer, waiting, agitating with a push broom, and rinsing, had little effect on the test deck. Only a slight lightening of the gray was observed.

To be effective, a pressure washer had to be used to rinse off the solution. The final result was complete removal, but the remaining wood was not truly a natural color. It had a silver tinge.

The best thing about my own formula was the cost. Costing out TSP at $2.39 for 16 oz., bleach at $1.24 per gallon, and throwing in a dime for the water, my recipe cost only $1.94 for the cleaning. This was by far the least expensive product in the test.

ARMOR ALL® E-Z Deck Wash® Wood Restorer

One gallon of this pre-mixed product is supposed to be enough for 250-300 sq. ft. Direction states "E-Z Deck Wash® restores the natural look to weathered, discolored wood within minutes - no mixing, no scrubbing." "Just apply full strength by pump-up garden sprayer, brush, roller or mop. Wait 5-10 minutes - No scrubbing needed. Rinse off treated surface and surrounding area with large volume of water to neutralize the renewing and cleansing action."

The Armor All was much stronger than my solution. Although the bleach is "buffered", overspray onto previously treated wood, instantly "silvered" the area. We pumped. We waited. Even though the bleach was very strong, we got no satisfactory results until we added brushing and a power washer to the mix.

As previously stated, we used an entire gallon on the 150 sq. ft. The price was $4.99 for the cleaning.

FLOOD DEKSWOOD®
EXTERIOR WOOD CLEANER & BRIGHTENER

The Dekswood label direction call for the mixture to be mixed one quart product to four quarts water. Coverage is 100 to 200 sq. ft. per gallon. This is the only product that was able to clean the entire 150 sq. ft. with the recommended amount of cleaning solution. Power washing is recommended on siding.

The overall result was very good. Power washing was called for before we got the desired result. The cost of the product was $3.99 plus 5¢ for water, or $4.04 for the cleaning.

Wolman® Pressure Treated Wood Deck Brightener

This product called for 12 tablespoons of powder per gallon of water. Coverage is one gallon per 100 to 150 sq. ft. Directions also state that a second application may be needed if the wood is very grayed. We needed a second application. Power washing was required before satisfactory results were achieved. Power washing is recommended in their professional application manual.

As we said, it took two gallons to clear the gray, but the results were excellent. The cost of the product was $7.60 for the amount of product used, plus 10¢ for the water used in the mix. This gives a total cleaning price of $7.70 for the cleaning.

Although the cost for cleaning the pressure treated deck was the highest with Wolman Deck Brightener, the results were the best with this dedicated product. So much better, that we used a second application of Deck Brightener on the entire deck, to prepare a uniform surface for application of deck sealers and toners.

Deck Sealing

After grading the different deck brighteners, we applied four different deck sealers, one to every 135 sq. ft. (plus rails and spindles) section.

For this portion of the test we used Wolman Rain Coat Water Repellent - Cedar, Cetol Dek Base -Cedar, Cabot Stains Clear Solution, and Penofin Penetrating Oil Finish. All finishes were applied according to manufacturers directions. This meant that the Wolman and Cabot deck sections each received one coat, the Cetol Dek Base and Penofin sections received two coats. The deck was then allowed to weather naturally for one year.

Annual Deck Cleaning

At the end of 12 months (May 1995), each of the four deck sections was divided into five parallel strips. Each was cleaned with the following five cleaners: Simple Green, Simple Deck, Flood Dekswood, TSP and All Laundry Detergent.

No bleach based cleaners were used because most of these products have warning on the labels that they can injure finished wood surfaces. The Wolman deck cleaner was not used for the same reason. The laundry detergent was used because there is a rumor going around that laundry detergent without a bleach additive is an effective cleaner for decks.

Products were mixed as follows: Simple Green: 1 gallon of product to 1 gallon of water. Simple Deck: 1 gallon of product to 1 gallon of water. Floor Dekswood: 1 quart of product to 4 quarts of water. TSP: 4 oz. TSP to one gallon of water. Laundry detergent, was sprinkled dry on wet deck surface, then brushed according to word of mouth directions.

All products were applied, allowed to stand, brushed and rinsed, in strict compliance with manufacturers directions, if any. None of the surfaces needed, or were, powerwashed. Water was used straight from the hose.

TSP was the most effective against bird droppings, but all cleaners, with the exception of the laundry detergent, did an acceptable job overall. Remember, our grading has to be subjective. The TSP seemed to do a better job on the Cetol Dek Base. The Flood Dekswood seemed to take away some of the luster of the Cetol Dek Base. The Simple Deck seemed to do a little better job on the surface treated with Wolman Rain Coat. All were effective on the surfaces treated with Penofin and Olympic Clear Solution. TSP maintained its three to one price advantage over the specialized deck cleaners.

Water Heater Report & Work Sheet
What's New in Water Heaters?
© 1995 Glenn Haege & Kathleen Stief, MHP

In prehistoric times water heaters were armor plated cast iron affairs. Many of these monsters lasted twenty years or more. Their only weakness was rust. As the gauge of the metal grew thinner, rust became a greater problem.

To solve that problem the average hot water heater of today is a steel cylinder with a thin glass lining. Technically, since the water only comes into contact with the glass lining, the water heaters should last forever. Rust is still the primary cause of failure. Now, however, the rust is often caused by water creeping through imperfections in the glass lining or at the welds that join the glass to the steel tank, in addition to rusting from the outside, in. It doesn't matter which way the rusting is going, inside out, or outside in, rust is rust and will lead to eventual water tank failure.

The higher priced water tanks are built to combat this in three ways.

1. Better electric water heaters have a plastic inner tank. The water never gets to the metal tank so it does not rust it. Plastic tanks are possible with electric water heaters because water is heated by heating elements and the inner tank never comes into contact with direct flame.

2. State Water Heaters' State and Reliance brand's top of the line models have a patented turbo coil that swirls the incoming water at the bottom of the tank, keeping sediment in suspension. This feature means that you may never have to drain sediment from the bottom of the tank.

3. Rheem/Ruud's top of the line Marathon Water heater has a front mounted flue, a miniature boiler, which heats the water outside the tank and permits the actual water tank to be of nonmetallic construction that will never rust or corrode. Priced at around $900.00 retail, this is one of the most expensive water heaters made. The high initial price is offset by the fact that it has a lifetime limited warranty. So if you live in an area with exceptionally hard water, really object to having your water heater changed every ten or fifteen years, or just want to have the snazziest water heater on the block, it may be the way to go.

There are other water heating alternatives that have even more bells and whistles on them.

First of all, you can be brazen and go tankless. This will not get you arrested if you choose an on demand water heater like the AquaStar hot water system. This system produces hot water as you use it. The higher your need for hot water, the more expensive the system. Tankless systems start at about $600.00.

The smallest system, Model 80VP, only creates enough water for a home with one shower that uses a restricted flow shower head, and really has to strain to fill a washing machine or automatic dishwasher.

The top of the line, Model 170VP, kicks out 165,000 BTUs and can handle most situations. I would recommend restricted shower heads if you are ever going to be using two showers at time using water from a tankless system.

If you live in a state like Hawaii or Arizona, you can use solar power. A solar power system often uses a non heated water tank as a collector and something like an AquaStar On Demand water heating system as a backup. Prices for these systems are quite expensive because you have the receptor tank, the solar heater and the back up system.

Finally, if you are shopping for a heating system and a hot water tank at the same time, you can go star wars and get the Lennox® CompleteHeat™ combination heating system. Water is heated in a heating module. The hot water is used for both hot water supply and forced air heating module. According to the manufacturer it provides an almost limitless hot water supply. The heat exchanger is backed by a 15 year limited warranty.

With all these choices, which is best for you? It all depends upon the hardness of the water in your area and the amount of water you need to use. See our inserts on average water usage and costs to help you choose.

How much hot water do you use?

What you buy should be dependant on what you need. Before you go hot water shopping, it would be a good idea to decide how big a hot water heater you actually require. Use this chart to calculate the amount of hot water you use. It will give you an indication of the amount of hot water you need at your disposal.

Water Usage				
Appliance	Gallons Per Minute-Min.	Gallons Per Minute-Max.	Time Used	Total Gallons
Bath Sink	1.5	2.5		
2 Bath Sinks	3	5		
Shower	2	3.5		
2 Showers	5	7		
Bath Tub	2	3		
Washing Machine	4	6		
Dishwasher	2	3		
Kitchen Sink	2.5	3		
			Total Usage	

This information will let you estimate the amount of water you use. If you like your water temperature luke warm, you probably use 50% hot water, 50% cold. If you like it hot, you could use up to 70% hot water.

The average shower takes 7 minutes. A restricted shower head could keep the water usage down to 2.7 gallons a minute. An unrestricted head can allow 3.5 gallons or more. If two of you are taking hot water showers and have the washing machine going at the same time, you will be using 13 gallons a minute. In four minutes, you would use 52 gallons of water. At 70% hot water that would amount to 36 1/2 gallons of hot water. At that rate it won't take you long to find yourself taking a cold shower.

How Much Should
A Hot Water Heater Cost?

The chart below will give you a good approximation of the cost of a standard electric Vs a standard gas water heater. We compare a 50-gallon electric water heater to a 40 gallon gas water heater, and an 80 gallon electric to a 50 gallon gas water heater because the slower recovery rate of an electric water heater makes a large tank essential to provide the same amount of usable hot water.

GAS & ELECTRIC WATER HEATERS
Cost Comparison

STANDARD					
Type	Size	Price	Installation	Total	Avg. Life
Electric	50 Gal	$250	$125	$375	15-20 years
	80 Gal	$425	$150	$575	15-20 years
Gas	40 Gal.	$200	$125	$325	10-15 years
	50 Gal.	$305	$125	$430	10-15 years

Prices for comparison only. They may be higher or lower depending on competitive situation where you live.

Keep in mind that there are many occasions when electric hot water heat may be preferable to natural gas. If you have to use bottled (propane) gas, the outcome may be very different.

IMPORTANT

Never use gas water heater with propane. The heat of a propane flame is 10% hotter than natural gas and require a different orifice. Natural gas heaters are not built to burn bottled gas safely.

A Propane fitted water heater will usually be about 10% more expensive than a similar natural gas water heater.

Where & What Should You Buy?

Comparison Shopping Gas Water Heaters

	Mass Merch	Standard	Mid	High	Ultra
40 Gal. Tank Price	$129	$200	$375	$450	$800-$900
Limited Warranty	Self Insured[1]	5 year	8 year	10 year	15-lifetime
High Recovery Burner[2]	NA	$50 more	included	included	included
1st. hour available hot water supply	73 Gal	73 Gal	81 Gal	81 Gal	81-unlimited
Tank	Glass lined Steel	same	same	same	varies
Burner type	cast iron or aluminized steel	same	cast iron	cast iron or stainless steel	varies
Insulation	1 in. R 8	1 in. R 8	1-2 in, R 8-16	1-2 in, R 8-16	2 in, R 16
Major difference from Standard	same	same	Warranty	Warranty plus insulation	Warranty plus construction
Expected service life	10 - 15 years	10 - 15 years	10 - 15 years	10 - 15 years	May be considerable

Water Heater Manufacturers

AquaStar™ Tankless Systems
Controlled Energy Corp.
Phone: 800-642-3111

Rheem/Ruud Manufacturing
Phone: 800-621-5622

State Industries/ Reliance Water Heater Co.
Phone: 800-365-0024

ScaldSafe™ Adapter Kits
Phone: 800-243-2862

---

[1]See above.

[2]A high recovery burner may increase the heating of water by 50% or more. In practice it applies greater heat to the tank for a shorter length of time, so it probably does not shorten service life. All in all, if you like a lot of hot water it is a good investment. With some brands you have to go at least to the Mid Range Water Heater to get the extra heating capacity.

Don't Let Central Air Conditioning
Give You the Sweats.

There is no reason to fear the freon fracas
if you want Central Air

by America's Master Handyman, Glenn Haege
© 1995 Glenn Haege & Kathleen Stief, MHP

Where will it all end? If you read the newspapers, the air conditioning climate is enough to give you the shivers or break into a cold sweat. The government is yanking freon out of our autos and window units.[1] The Clean Air Act has mandated that all your little local air conditioning guys had to be certified by the Environmental Protection Agency by last November.[2] ANSI, the American National Standard Institute has rejected the energy efficiency standards for air conditioning units because no one even bothered to ask the builders if they could meet the standards.[3]

In desperation, one air conditioning manufacturer is seriously thinking of using Ammonia as its air conditioning agent (if you ever shoveled out a cow barn in August that would really scare you), and *Popular Science* reports that an Arizona home owner has solved the air conditioning problem by adding a 23 foot cooling tower to his home.[4]

What's a homeowner to do? Should you replace your aging air conditioning unit? Will it be repairable, or will the long arm of Washington dictate that you have to switch to fans or 23 foot cooling towers?

America's Master Handyman tells you to keep the faith and fear not. There is a great deal of confusion in the marketplace because automotive Freon, R 12, has been replaced with R 134. This ruling, however, has no effect on the central air conditioner in your home. Central air conditioning coolant is Freon R 22 not R 12. R 22 based equipment is not scheduled to go out of use until the year 2025. They will continue making R 22 based equipment until 2010. This means that the air conditioning unit you buy today can be serviced for the next thirty years. I don't know if the anti Freon fad will have faded away by 2010, I do know that thirty years from now, air conditioning will be a great deal different from what it is today.

It is pretty hard not to get nervous. In the American mind, air conditioning has become absolutely essential. The percent of single family homes equipped with central air was already 77% in 1992, according to Sue Chang in the June 27th. issue of Heating & Refrigeration News. It is probably even higher now. Never-the-less, the cool calculation is not a world wide phenomenon. Just one border to the North, our Canadian cousins live differently. The percentage is almost reversed, over 70% of the country's residences are not air conditioned. And I doubt that anyone even counts the percentage of people who live in air conditioned homes one border to the South where the need is far greater.

Here in the United States, according to the Wall Street Journal, many Houstonians have already risen in rebellion saying that they actually prefer hot, damp air.[5] While comrade, Yeltsin, is complaining that exposure to air conditioning is making his people sick.[6]

With all this happening is it any wonder that the average homeowner gets the sweats when he, or she, decides it's time to install or renew the air conditioning?

The most important thing to check out about your central air conditioning is not the chlorofloro carbons, or even the SEER (Seasonal Energy Efficiency Rating) rating. You don't have to worry about buying the newest of the new. While I would want to find out all about the new air conditioning technologies, I would not want to be the first boy on the block to buy into them. I work too hard for my money to pay for the privilege of being a guinea pig

Unlike room air conditioners, where the manufacturer takes center stage, the most important part of the central air conditioning package is the person who installs and stands behind the air conditioner. The air conditioning contractor is the person who is going to make you, and keep you, a happy homeowner. The only deviation from this rule of thumb is when, for some reason you are a likely candidate for Geothermal heating and cooling installation, or if your home has special problems and can not accept traditional air conditioning. Even in these cases the knowledge and experience of the air conditioning contractor makes him or her the most important person. It's just that since there are a lot fewer of them you have to go to a lot more trouble even finding them.

---

[1]Air Conditioning, Heating & Refrigeration News, April 25, 994.
[2]ibid., May 23, 1994.
[3]ibid., September 12, 1994.
[4]Popular Science, April 93.
[5]Wall Street Journal, August 30, 1994.
[6]New York Times, International Pages, July 21, 1994.

Air Conditioning
Contractor Questions

Get answers to all these questions before you choose a contractor:

How long has the contractor been in business under the current business name?

What air conditioning brand or brands does he/she sell and service?

How long has he/she sold each of the lines?

Is the organization the authorized Sales & Service contractor?

Is the Warranty through the manufacturer or the contractor?

What did he/she carry before?

How long did he/she have that line?

Why did he/she switch?

How many units does he/she sell a year?

How many units does he/she service per year?

How many people on the service staff?

What's the name of the service manager?

How many trucks?

Do they provide evening, weekend and 24 hour emergency service?

What is the price differential for non standard times?

Are they fully licensed?

In what name is the license?

Is he/she the owner?

What is your position with the firm?

Are you licensed?

If so, what license?

Name on license:_____ Number:_____

Are you an air conditioning installer?

Have you ever been?

Are you a service technician?

Have you ever been?

If not the owner, did you ever have ownership in a heating/air-condition company, or other type of modernization company?

If yes, what was the company names and your reasons for leaving?

How much money down do they want? (Never more than 30%)

Will the company give a guaranteed completion date in writing? When?

What is the penalty they pay you if they do not complete the job on time?

Do they have workmen's compensation insurance?

Do they have casualty insurance?

(If you sign a contract, you want proofs of workmen's compensation and casualty insurance mailed to you by the insurance companies before you allow work to start.)

Information Your Air Conditioning Contractor
Must Know Before He/She Can Give A Proper Quote

How many windows do you have? On what sides of the house are they? Do they get a great deal of exposure to the sun? Are they single pane, double pane, glass block? Are they low E glass?

How much sun goes through the windows? From which directions?

How thick are the walls? Are they insulated or uninsulated? What are their dimensions? How thick are they? What direction does each face? What are they made of?

What about the ceiling? How big is it? How high is it? Is it insulated? What's the R factor of the insulation? How much space is there above the ceiling? Do you have an attic? Is the space above the ceiling occupied?

What about the floor? Is it on ground level or above a basement?

What climate correction factors have to be added to the calculations?

How many people reside in the house? How much heat do they produce? Are they active, or inactive? At home all, most, much or little of the time?

How much heat do your appliances produce?

What about your lifestyle? Will you be in the house during the peak cooling season? Will you be at home during the day or do you really just want air conditioning for the evenings?

After the contractor or his/her representative has inspected the house and gotten the information he/she needs to answer all of these questions, very precise formulas can be used to determine the exact size and power of the air conditioning unit you require. If you can't count on the contractor to get the size right, how can you realistically expect a professional job?

Remember, an air conditioner is engineered to make the temperature 15° F cooler inside than outside. That means that on a day when the outside temperature is 95° F, the interior temperature should be 80° F. If you require more than that, be sure that the specific need is written into your contract.

Central Air Conditioning Manufacturers

Bryant Heating & Cooling Systems
    BDP Company
    A Division of Carrier Corp.
    7310 W. Morris   Mail: P.O. Box 70
    Indianapolis, IN 46231
    800-428-4326

Carrier Corporation
    7310 W. Morris   Mail: P.O. Box 70
    Indianapolis, IN 46231
    800-227-7437

Heil
    Inter City Products Corp.
    650 Heil - Quaker Ave. P.O. Box 128
    Lewisburg, TN 37091
    931-270-4306

Lennox Industries
    972-497-5000

Rheem and Ruud Air Conditioners
    800-548-7433

Space-Pak
    413-568-9571

Trane Company
    888-872-6335

York International
    877-874-7378

Subject Index

586

More clear, concise How-To Advice From America's Master Handyman

Fix It Fast & Easy! In over 17 years on the air Glenn Haege has answered over 60,000 listeners questions. His answers to over 100 of the most asked "How To" questions are included in this book.

166 pages $14.95

Upgrading Your House, Fix It Fast & Easy! 2 In depth information on all major remodeling jobs: kitchens, baths, dormers, basements, heating, cooling, plumbing, electrical, windows, roofing, siding, and more

416 pages $19.95

Take the Pain out of Painting – Interiors Everything you need to know to have a professional looking paint job, plus a 40 page section on faux finishing and the industry's only comprehensive stain kill guide.

264 pages $14.97

Take the Pain out of Painting – Exteriors In depth explanations on painting every exterior surface from wood and aluminum siding to shingles, concrete block and log homes; plus when to paint, when to stain and how to prepare the surface for a great looking, long lasting job.

224 pages $12.95

Ask your favorite book seller for these titles or order direct:
By Phone: Call (888) 426-3981
By Fax: (248) 589-8554
By e-mail: Go to www.masterhandyman.com and click on Book Store
By Mail: Use the handy form on the other side of this page and mail
to:
Master Handyman Press, Inc.
P.O. Box 1498
Royal Oak, MI 48068-1498

Master Handyman Press, Inc.
Quick Order Form

Please send me the following books by Glenn Haege:

Haege's Homestyle Articles, 1995-99, 624 pages $24.95, $ _____

Fix It Fast & Easy!, 166 pages $14.95, $ _____

Upgrading Your House, Fix It Fast & Easy! 2, 416 pages
$19.95, $ _____

Take the Pain out of Painting – Interiors, 264 pages $14.97, $ _____

Take the Pain out of Painting – Exteriors, 224 pages $12.95, $ _____

Send to:

Name: _____

Address _____

City: _____ State: _____ Zip: _____

Telephone: _____

E-mail address: _____

Sales tax:
Please add 6% Sales tax for all books shipped to Michigan Addresses.

Shipping:
US: $4 for the first book and $2 for each additional.
International: $9 for the first book and $5 for each additional.

Payment:
Check, Money Order or Credit card:
Visa, MasterCard, Amex, Discover

Card number: _____

Name on card: _____ Expiration Date: ___/___

Authorization signature: _____